Queer Cinema in America

Queer Cinema in America

An Encyclopedia of LGBTQ Films, Characters, and Stories

Aubrey Malone

BLOOMSBURY ACADEMIC
NEW YORK • LONDON • OXFORD • NEW DELHI • SYDNEY

BLOOMSBURY ACADEMIC
Bloomsbury Publishing Inc
1385 Broadway, New York, NY 10018, USA
50 Bedford Square, London, WC1B 3DP, UK
29 Earlsfort Terrace, Dublin 2, Ireland

BLOOMSBURY, BLOOMSBURY ACADEMIC and the Diana logo
are trademarks of Bloomsbury Publishing Plc

First published in the United States of America by ABC-CLIO 2020
Paperback edition published by Bloomsbury Academic 2024

Copyright © Bloomsbury Publishing Inc, 2024

Cover photo: *My Own Private Idaho* (1991), River Phoenix.
(Moviestore Collection Ltd/Alamy Stock Photo)

All rights reserved. No part of this publication may be reproduced or
transmitted in any form or by any means, electronic or mechanical,
including photocopying, recording, or any information storage or retrieval
system, without prior permission in writing from the publishers.

Bloomsbury Publishing Inc does not have any control over, or responsibility for,
any third-party websites referred to or in this book. All internet addresses given
in this book were correct at the time of going to press. The author and publisher
regret any inconvenience caused if addresses have changed or sites have
ceased to exist, but can accept no responsibility for any such changes.

Library of Congress Cataloging-in-Publication Data
Names: Malone, Aubrey, author.
Title: Queer cinema in America : an encyclopedia of LGBTQ films,
characters, and stories / Aubrey Malone.
Description: Santa Barbara, California : Greenwood, [2020] |
Includes bibliographical references and index.
Identifiers: LCCN 2019020185 (print) | LCCN 2019980358 (ebook) |
ISBN 9781440867156 (hardback) | ISBN 9781440867163 (ebook)
Subjects: LCSH: Homosexuality in motion pictures—Encyclopedias. | Gays in motion
pictures—Encyclopedias. | Motion pictures—United States—History.
Classification: LCC PN1995.9.H55 M25 2020 (print) | LCC PN1995.9.H55 (ebook) |
DDC 791.43/65303—dc23
LC record available at https://lccn.loc.gov/2019020185
LC ebook record available at https://lccn.loc.gov/2019980358

ISBN: HB: 978-1-4408-6715-6
PB: 979-8-7651-3096-4
ePDF: 978-1-4408-6716-3
eBook: 979-8-2161-3474-9

To find out more about our authors and books visit www.bloomsbury.com
and sign up for our newsletters.

Contents

Alphabetical List of Entries   vii

Guide to Related Topics   ix

Preface   xi

Introduction   xiii

Chronology of Milestone Events   xxxi

A–Z Entries   1

Glossary   297

Select Bibliography   299

Index   305

Alphabetical List of Entries

Adventures of Priscilla, Queen of the Desert, The
Advise & Consent
AIDS
All about Eve
Arzner, Dorothy

Bankhead, Tallulah
Basic Instinct
Before Stonewall
Bogarde, Dirk
Bound
Bowie, David
Boys Don't Cry
Boys in the Band, The
Brando, Marlon
Brokeback Mountain
Burr, Raymond

Cabaret
Capote
Carol
Celluloid Closet, The
Children's Hour, The
Clift, Montgomery
Crisp, Quentin
Cross-Dressing
Cruising
Crying Game, The

Cukor, George
Curtis, Tony
Dallas Buyers Club
Danish Girl, The
Davies, Terence
Dean, James
Deathtrap
Desert Hearts
Dietrich, Marlene
Disobedience
Divine
Dog Day Afternoon
Early Frost, An
Edward II
Everett, Rupert
Far from Heaven
Fox, The
Garbo, Greta
Glen or Glenda?
Go Fish
God's Own Country
Haynes, Todd
Hedwig and the Angry Inch
Hours and Times, The
Hudson, Rock
Hunger, The
Hunter, Tab

Jarman, Derek
Killing of Sister George, The
Kiss of the Spider Woman
Kissing
Ladies or Gentlemen
Laughton, Charles
Liberace
L.I.E.
Living End, The
Longtime Companion
Looking for Langston
Lumet, Sidney
Midnight Cowboy
Milk
Milk, Harvey
Mineo, Sal
Monster
Moonlight
Mulholland Drive
Murder
My Own Private Idaho
Myra Breckinridge
Oscars, The
Paris Is Burning
Parting Glances
Perkins, Anthony
Personal Best
Philadelphia
Prick Up Your Ears

Queen Christina
Rebecca
Rebel without a Cause
Reflections in a Golden Eye
Rocky Horror Picture Show, The
Rope
Servant, The
Silkwood
Smoking
Some Like It Hot
Staircase
Strangers on a Train
Suddenly, Last Summer
Suicide
Sunday Bloody Sunday
Swoon
Tea and Sympathy
Thelma and Louise
Times of Harvey Milk, The
Torch Song Trilogy
Transamerica
Van Sant, Gus
Victim
Victor/Victoria
Vidal, Gore
Warhol, Andy
Waters, John
Wilde, Oscar
Williams, Tennessee

Guide to Related Topics

Actors
Bankhead, Tallulah
Bogarde, Dirk
Bowie, David
Brando, Marlon
Clift, Montgomery
Crisp, Quentin
Curtis, Tony
Divine
Everett, Rupert
Garbo, Greta
Hudson, Rock
Hunter, Tab
Laughton, Charles
Liberace
Mineo, Sal
Perkins, Anthony

Directors
Arzner, Dorothy
Cukor, George
Davies, Terence
Haynes, Todd
Jarman, Derek
Lumet, Sidney
Warhol, Andy
Waters, John

Films
Adventures of Priscilla, Queen of the Desert, The
Advise & Consent
All about Eve
Basic Instinct
Before Stonewall
Bound
Boys Don't Cry
Boys in the Band, The
Brokeback Mountain
Cabaret
Capote
Carol
Celluloid Closet, The
Children's Hour, The
Cruising
Crying Game, The
Dallas Buyers Club
Danish Girl, The
Deathtrap
Desert Hearts
Disobedience
Dog Day Afternoon
Early Frost, An
Edward II

Far from Heaven
Fox, The
Glen or Glenda?
Go Fish
God's Own Country
Hedwig and the Angry Inch
Hours and Times, The
Hunger, The
Killing of Sister George, The
Kiss of the Spider Woman
Ladies or Gentlemen
L.I.E.
Living End, The
Longtime Companion
Looking for Langston
Midnight Cowboy
Milk
Monster
Moonlight
Mulholland Drive
My Own Private Idaho
Myra Breckinridge
Paris Is Burning
Parting Glances
Personal Best
Philadelphia
Prick Up Your Ears
Queen Christina

Rebecca
Rebel without a Cause
Reflections in a Golden Eye
Rocky Horror Picture Show, The
Rope
Servant, The
Silkwood
Some Like It Hot
Staircase
Strangers on a Train
Suddenly, Last Summer
Sunday Bloody Sunday
Swoon
Tea and Sympathy
Thelma and Louise
Times of Harvey Milk, The
Torch Song Trilogy
Transamerica
Victim
Victor/Victoria

Themes
AIDS
Cross-Dressing
Kissing
Murder
Oscars, The
Smoking
Suicide

Preface

The book you're holding in your hands is an alphabetical guide to LGBTQ films from the early days of cinema to the present day. The oldest film I've featured is *Queen Christina* (1933). The most recent is *Disobedience* (2018). As befits its title, the primary focus is on American films. British and European ones are included if they were important enough to qualify for global status or if they were major hits (or controversial talking points) in the United States.

The encyclopedia is also a guide to the people who appeared in the films, and to who directed them, who were involved in their preparation, their casting, and their path from the pages of a novel or play to the screen. Finally, it deals with how they were received by the public and the critics and, in some notable cases, became the recipients of awards in such places as Sundance, Cannes, and at the annual Oscar ceremonies.

Though LGBTQ themes are predominant in my evaluation of such films and characters, that isn't to say other themes aren't important in such films as well. I've tried to keep a balance in my analyses from this point of view, without skewing the emphasis too much either way. Sometimes the LGBTQ character or characters are central to a film's plotlines. Sometimes they're peripheral, but they're always important. Many of the films under scrutiny changed the way society viewed sexual orientations; sometimes they even influenced the laws regarding sexual orientation.

The entries are listed alphabetically. The characters referred to in the book's title are featured in some entries and the films in others. In the "Guide to Related Topics" section, I've outlined instances where various themes, events, and organizations are mentioned in the course of it. Students of film, or the casual reader, may gravitate from entry to entry if they're interested in a particular person or film. One may ideally lead to the other. The book's chronology contains thumbnail references to seminal events in LGBGQ history as they relate to the world of film.

Some of the entries are longer than others. The reason for this is usually because of the importance of the film—or person—being written about with regard to the theme of the book. If an entry is short, it's no reflection on the person or film being written about; it's merely an indication that they haven't featured as significantly in LGBTQ history as they might have, or that their influence has waned with time.

With regard to my vocabulary, I've alternated the terms "gay" and "queer" to suit the times I'm writing about, or in some instances because the term in question was used by a speaker I'm quoting. There was a time when "queer" was offensive to the LGBTQ world. Since 1990, when the critic B. Ruby Rich originated the term "New Queer Cinema" to refer to the independent ("indie") LGBTQ films being made around this time, that all changed. The term had been in use in academic writing before this. Now it became appropriated under the cinematic umbrella, where it's remained.

The intention of the book is to reach out to anyone who's felt underrepresented or misrepresented with their sexual identity or who's experienced abuse as a result of it. It's hoped that readers will identify with the characters in the films and learn something from their fight for acceptance in a sometimes harsh environment.

The films generally celebrate sexual inclusiveness. When they don't, that creates its own drama. In some entries, I've included a sidebar dealing with a person or film that has some relation, either thematic or biographical, to the person or film being discussed in the main corpus of the entry.

At the end of many entries, under "Related Films," I've listed a number of films that have a connection to the main person or film being featured. Any reader who's enjoyed reading the entry, or who's been influenced to see the film being written about as a result of reading it, may wish to also see these other films, or at least some of them. I've also listed a number of books that relate to the film or film star being discussed. The books may also relate to the film's director. It's hoped that will throw further light on their role in the film, or spur the reader on to learning more about the world they've brought to life on celluloid.

The films under scrutiny cover a wide spectrum. There are dramas, comedies, biopics, musicals, documentaries, period pieces, thrillers, remakes, sequels, TV, films, art house films, films from the school of realism, and some that are directed in a more surreal manner. I wish to emphasize the fact that the book isn't a history of LGBTQ films or LGBTQ lives. It isn't structured chronologically, which means that films made long ago sit astride contemporary offerings. By reading about these films, and/or seeing them, the reader will hopefully empathize with the plight of the characters in them and with how they dealt with their problems. Or, in some cases, failed to.

People growing up today may not be aware of the depth of the challenge faced by their forebears to have their voices heard by a society that defined sexuality in polarized forms that brooked no diversity. In the entries dealing with events like the Stonewall Riots, where gay people finally reacted against oppression, or people like Harvey Milk, who did so much for gay rights in his political life before he was assassinated, such challenges are highlighted.

At the beginning of the last century, LGBTQ characters were frequently satirized. In later years they suffered from invisibility and censorship. It's been a long and winding road toward acceptance. This hasn't been without its tripwires, and sometimes it has seemed like a case of "One step forward, two steps backward," but in general the perception of LGBTQ lives has changed for the better, which has led to a more sympathetic appraisal of LGBTQ characters on celluloid through their struggles for acceptance. This book attempts to be a record of such struggles in all their vicissitudes.

Introduction

The history of LGBTQ films mirror the history of LGBTQ lives in the sense that, almost from the beginning, they were fraught with difficulty. Censorship restrictions and, later on, the Production Code of 1934, placed enormous restrictions on their content. From the first time a director called, "Lights, camera, action!" he was aware of what he could show and what he had to hide, or pretend didn't exist. If he was clever enough he could telegraph a message, or the sexual nature of a character, in a subtle manner.

There was a certain amount of liberation in the "Roaring" Twenties. Rudolph Valentino was allowed to evince an androgynous quality on screen while being viewed primarily as a love god for women. This despite the fact that in some circles he was seen as having a unique sexuality offscreen, a perception buttressed by the fact that he was rumored to have married two lesbians, one of whom was said to have locked him out of the bedroom on his wedding night.

Regardless, queer actors didn't come out in those days. With some notable exceptions, like William Haines, LGBTQ people kept their heads firmly down in the early days of cinema. Directors like Dorothy Arzner and, slightly later, George Cukor, had prolific careers, but they were well aware they were expected to lead double lives, especially after the introduction of the aforementioned Production Code.

This self-censorship stratagem from within the industry was instituted to supposedly clean it up. It came about as a result of pressure from the government and groups like the Catholic Legion of Decency. The legion was worried about the supposedly pernicious effects of the exposition of sex on society. Gay people became one of its especial targets. From now on, "good taste" was seen as *de rigueur*. A film released without a code was usually rejected by theater chains. Even if it was accepted by them, it could be boycotted by audiences. In some states, priests and nuns stood in the lobbies of cinemas watching people who came in and even taking down their names. They ran the risk of being shamed from pulpits as a result.

Mae West was a prime target of the PCA. She used to joke that she would be offended if a film of hers didn't endure the rancor of the censorship authorities. She was amiable toward the LGBTQ community but failed to understand it in depth. Even so, she was a pioneer in this regard. Though she fell afoul of the censorship boards on many occasions, she still managed to carve out a career. They could force her to trim her scripts, but they couldn't censor her expressions, which spoke volumes.

When World War I broke out in 1939, the virtues of machismo took center stage. The search for anything smacking of moral turpitude continued in the forties and fifties with Senator Joseph McCarthy's aggressive interrogations of his quarries during the HUAC (House Un-American Activities Committee) hearings. His primary target was communism but his "Spanish Inquisition" style interrogations infiltrated into the LGBTQ world as well.

The America of Dwight Eisenhower in the fifties was one of white picket fences and mom's apple pie. Nuclear families led binary lives. The father went out to work and the mother stayed home and cooked. In the evening, Dad might play baseball with Junior in the back garden. When he reached a certain age, he too would get a job and a wife—a female one. Anything else was unthinkable.

The Mattachine Society was set up in 1950 to try to achieve equality for gay men, but it was almost like Freemasonry in its clandestine nature. Gay people met in secret and stayed in the closet. When a gay actor appeared at a function, even if he was living with another gay man at the time, he did so with a woman on his arm.

Major stars like Montgomery Clift and James Dean were thought to be bisexual, but such ruminations were expressed—if at all—behind closed doors. To the moviegoing public they were, like Valentino, figures to be drooled over in the aisles by women, not men. To suggest that Marlon Brando, another fifties icon, had had gay experiences (as he did) would have been anathema. Even when gay actors died, their sexuality wasn't mentioned. In obituaries they were described as "confirmed bachelors" survived by sisters or nieces or other relatives rather than significant other male partners.

The same restrictions applied to women. Lizabeth Scott had her femme fatale career cut short by *Confidential* magazine in the mid fifties when it ran a piece on her lesbian predilections. She sued but lost the case. Her actions, which were understandable, merely gave more publicity to the article and swelled the magazine's coffers. The magazine, however, closed down soon afterward.

Women with lesbian tendencies were usually regarded as venal in the early years of cinema, like the Mrs. Danvers of Judith Anderson in *Rebecca* (1940), the Eve of Anne Baxter in *All about Eve* (1950), or Lauren Bacall in *Young Man with a Horn,* also 1950. Kirk Douglas tosses up between "bad" girl Bacall and "good" girl Doris Day as a troubled trumpet player in this film. "You're a sick girl, Amy," he rasps at her in one scene. "You'd better see a doctor."

In *Caged*, made the same year, there was an implication that other "bad" girls—in this case, prisoners—would gravitate toward one another rather than toward the "healing" male. "If you stay in here too long," one of them says to another, "you don't think of guys at all. You get out of the habit." The jailers also succumb to such so-called unnatural predilections, like the one played by Hope Emerson, who refers suggestively to the new jailbirds as "fresh meat." The dictates of the time wouldn't allow her to be any more specific, though she's allowed to be cruel.

Rock Hudson was almost outed by *Confidential* magazine in 1955, but they did a feature on Rory Calhoun instead in the end. A subsequent feature appeared on Hudson's gay friend, George Nader. Nader was sacrificed on the burnt altar that

Introduction

spared Hudson, the bigger star, his outing being a ragtag trade-off for the continued closeting of Hollywood's favored hunk. Hudson left money in his will to Nader and his partner Mark Miller. This was presumably done from guilt. Hudson played a clever game by staying in the closet despite being generally known to be gay. Other stars such as Tab Hunter, Anthony Perkins, and Raymond Burr had the same policy. People who came out, including Sal Mineo and Nader, seemed to be doomed to minor careers or none at all.

George Cukor hosted all-male pool parties. He didn't confirm or deny being gay, leaving people to draw their own conclusions. Anyone close to him in the industry could only draw one. Charles Walters and Vincente Minnelli didn't come out verbally either, though their actions spoke volumes. Most people knew James Whale, another talented director, was queer. He was too open about it and paid the price. He was discarded by the industry, leaving one to wonder how many wonderful films he could have made if he was only more discreet—or Hollywood more understanding.

In front of the camera, gay people continued to be portrayed as traumatized, guilty, evil, suicidal, and/or murderous. They played walk-on parts where they were light relief to the main action or an ominous undertow to it. Audiences either laughed or shrieked when they appeared.

The stereotyping of gay figures was even apparent in horror films like *Psycho* (1960) where the villain was a cross-dressing, mother-obsessed, identity-confused psychopath. He was also played by a man who was gay in real life. There was an invisible line uniting horror films and gay themes all the way back to the thirties where a lesbian subtext was suggested in films like *Dracula's Daughter*. In many ways, this genre provided the only avenue by which one could feature such themes. One had to wait for something like *The Rocky Horror Picture Show* (1975) for a revisionist approach. In this genre definer everything was knocked out of the ball park. Whatever templates were in evidence here were tolerable because they were eroticized in Jim Sharman's comic hybrid.

Tokenism was the order of the day for LGBTQ people at this time. In *A Taste of Honey* (1961), for instance, Murray Melvin plays Geoffrey, a shy art student who moves in with Jo (Rita Tushingham) after she becomes pregnant by a sailor who went off to sea. It was directed by Tony Richardson, a bisexual man who was at one time married to Vanessa Redgrave. This British film, while capably directed, failed to explore his sexuality in any depth. "You're unique, Geoffrey," Jo tells him, as if he's the only gay man in the world. He attempts to kiss her in one scene.

The critic Stephen Bourne found this offensive, "a pathetic attempt at demonstrating heterosexuality," which was disturbing for a gay audience because it revealed the fear he had of his orientation (Bourne, 1996: 149). Surprisingly, it was left to Britain to usher in a new age with its film *Victim*, which was also released in 1961. The word "homosexuality" was uttered for the first time on screen here. Ironically, it was spoken by a closeted gay man, Dirk Bogarde.

Cicely Courtneidge played a lesbian in another British film, Bryan Forbes's *The L-Shaped Room* in 1962. Forbes telegraphs her sexuality in a cleverly muted manner. She's reminiscing about a dead friend she loved to her costar, Leslie Caron, in one scene. Forbes has his camera pan to a photograph of this friend; it's only then one realizes the friend was a woman.

Barbara Stanwyck played a lesbian in *Walk on the Wild Side* in the same year. This was an American film. In some ways, America trailed Britain in its sensitivity toward sexual inclusiveness. Many American lesbians, even in the sixties, were treated less sensitively than their British counterparts. Here Stanwyck is an unsavory character, a brothel madam. Interestingly enough, she's also married to a man, though her husband is disabled. For one viewer, this confirmed "a commonly held belief that lesbians are frigid, and that their relationships with women are safely spiritual rather than basely carnal" (Darren, 2000: 216–7).

There was some solace for LGBTQ people in the sixties. Many of the old taboos surrounding being gay were removed with the reworking of the ratings under a more enlightened censorship system. But in some ways the cure was worse than the disease. LGBTQ people weren't as hated as before, but the hatred was replaced by pity rather than acceptance in too many cases. The new compassion from Hollywood meant LGBTQ people had to commit suicide in films like *Advise & Consent* and *The Children's Hour*, both made in 1962, to be fully "forgiven" for their aberrations.

In *The Fox* (1968), one of the queer characters (Sandy Dennis) is killed by a falling tree. In *Caprice* (1967), Ray Walston is pushed off a balcony. *The Detective* (1968) shows both murder of and suicide by gay people. At the end of this film the gay murderer played by William Windom—he kills his own kind, like the Mafia—leaves a suicide note saying, "I was more ashamed of being a homosexual than a murderer," a classic case of internalized homophobia.

The original script of *Bonnie and Clyde* had Warren Beatty as gay, but it was felt this wouldn't work with audiences so they made him impotent instead. That was expected to garner more sympathy for him. It seems to have worked. It called up memories of Paul Newman in *Cat on a Hot Tin Roof* (1958). Newman spent much of his time on crutches in the film and also struggled with impotence. The viewer was led to believe this was his only problem. What Tennessee Williams wrote in the play was that he was traumatized by the suicide of his gay friend from college. Newman thought he killed himself from loneliness.

It wasn't only lesbians and gays who were victims of homophobia but bisexuals too. In *The Detective*, a psychiatrist tells a patient that a bisexual is "a homosexual without conviction." The demonization of queer people reached its nadir in the 1969 release *The Gay Deceivers*, which concerned two straight men who dodged the Vietnam draft by pretending to be lovers. A generation of men who'd signed up for this war quietly without announcing their sexuality for fear of censure but who were anxious to serve their country were outraged.

But hope was around the corner. Desperation forced the gay world into the actions taken by its most visible members in New York in 1969 when they finally cried "Time's up."

Stonewall was a watershed moment for the LGBTQ community, a liberation almost as great as the one that happened in the fifties when the "love that dared not speak its name" was finally acknowledged if not approved. Now they could go a step further and seek equality with the heterosexual world rather than just being tolerated as a minority group within its matrix.

Or could they? Hollywood was hardly going to let go of its treasured prejudices that easily. In the seventies, many jaded stereotypes were trotted out again in self-piteous sagas like *The Boys in the Band* (1970) and the highly offensive *Myra Breckinridge* (1970). John Waters came along and threw the conventions of the time out the window with films like *Pink Flamingos* (1972). Waters didn't feature that many queer people in his films. When he did, they were often stereotypes or farcical figures. There were negative depictions of gay people in films like *Play It as It Lays* (1972), *Cleopatra Jones* (1973), *Theatre of Blood* (1973), *Freebie and the Bean* (1974), and *The Eiger Sanction*. Al Pacino was endearing as a man robbing a bank to pay for his transgender wife's forthcoming sex change operation in *Dog Day Afternoon* in 1975, but he was also married to a woman in the film, which diluted its impact.

An era of enlightenment seemed to be in the offing, but there were many stumbling blocks and double standards. When gay sex appeared on screen, it was often in violent form, as in John Boorman's *Deliverance* (1972) when Ned Beatty is raped by a backwoods man.

Quentin Crisp personified both elements. He burst upon the scene with *The Naked Civil Servant* (1979) with his hennaed hair and lipstick, becoming an overnight success after forty years. He was gentle and harmless and had suffered a lot by being beaten in England, his home country, but he saw being gay as a mental illness, and thought LGBTQ people could never find love. If this was the message coming from inside, what was to be expected from everywhere else?

In the old days, and even some of the new ones, there existed a notion that one could be "cured" of being gay by having sex with a member of the opposite sex. This happens to Bob Moore in Otto Preminger's *Tell Me That You Love Me, Junie Moon* (1970) after Moore makes love to a black female prostitute. In the same year a surgeon in Robert Altman's *MASH* is relieved of suspicions that he's queer when he has a sexual encounter with a female nurse.

Richard Chamberlain, playing the bisexual composer Peter Ilyich Tchaikovsky in Ken Russell's *The Music Lovers* (1970), thinks marriage to the nymphomaniac Nina (Glenda Jackson) will cure him of being gay, but he ends up having a relationship with a man called Chiluvsky (Christopher Gable) unbeknownst to her. Like many queer people in films, he has a violent death, perishing from cholera in a vomit-filled tub of boiling water. This kind of drama was nothing new to Russell. Some would say his career thrived on it.

The lesbian hitchhikers whom Jack Nicholson and Karen Black take into their car in *Five Easy Pieces* (1971) have nothing to do with the plot. They're inserted as light relief, a stereotypical couple that seem to fit the image heterosexual people might have of lesbians. One is assertive, the other quiet. The assertive one rants on about the ecological evils of the world. She isn't portrayed as either sympathetic or idealistic; more like an irascible eccentric who could have no place in "normal" society. They're headed for Alaska, somewhere Nicholson and Black are entitled to feel will be safely out of their way.

In the same year, another pair of hitchhikers were picked up by Barry Norman in Richard Sarafian's *Vanishing Point*. They were obviously gay. Tom Hanks remarked in the film version of Vito Russo's *Celluloid Closet* that they were therefore to be laughed at, even when they told Norman they were going to rob him. What does Norman do? He kicks them out of the car. And then smiles smugly. The implication is that a gay man could never have the ability to rob anyone.

In *X, Y and Zee* (1972), Elizabeth Taylor sleeps with Susannah York, but only to save her marriage to Michael Caine. There was usually such a qualification for scenes like that at this time. The seventies also saw more suicides (*Play It as It Lays*) and more murders (*Cleopatra Jones*). Other films were less grim but equally patronizing. Woody Allen tried to "intellectualize" the gay experience when he had a character ask in *Love and Death* (1975), "I wonder if Socrates and Plato ever took a house on Crete during the summer?" In Clint Eastwood's *The Eiger Sanction*, one of the characters has a dog called by a gay slur name.

La Cage aux Folles was regarded as one of the funniest films of 1978, but LGBTQ audiences had mixed reactions to it. Were they meant to be laughing *with* transgender people or *at* them? Viewed negatively, the film harked back to the "limp-wristed sissy" stereotype that was common in the early days of cinema. It centered on a pair of drag queens who ran a nightclub and gave new meaning to the term "over the top." *The Birdcage* (1996) tried to copy it some years later in an American context. The same questions applied to this unashamed piece of plagiarism.

Richard Gere became something of a gay icon after *American Gigolo* in 1980, but this was a seriously homophobic film. He played a gigolo. Subsidiary characters included a gay killer, a gay wife-beater, and a lesbian pimp. Another 1980 film, *The Last Married Couple in America*, had George Segal and Natalie Wood watching all their friends' marriages break up around them. In fact the only happy couple in the neighborhood is a queer one. Was this refreshing or merely tokenistic? It was difficult to say.

Personal Best was promoted as a lesbian-friendly film in 1982, but it returned to the status quo when a man appeared on the scene. One was still back in the ideological terrain of *The Fox*. Another 1982 release, *Making Love*, was directed by Arthur Hiller. It had Kate Jackson having to face the fact that her husband, played by Michael Ontkean, tells her he's in love with another man (Harry Hamlin). It was based on a story by A. Scott Berg. He said he got the idea after six of his male friends came out after getting married to women. He made large claims for the film, saying, "This is the next big social movement—men leaving their wives for other men. What the black movement was in the sixties, and the feminist movement in the seventies, the gay movement will be in the eighties" (Porter, 2010: 454).

Barry Sandler wrote the screenplay. His ambition in doing so, he said, was to rescue gay men from stereotyped roles. "The image of gay people on screen," he said, "has been one of perverts and killers or freaks or grotesques or screaming queens or interior decorator" (Hadleigh, 1993: 14). Sadly, the film didn't perform as he'd hoped. In fact it had a negative impact on Hamlin. He was accused of being queer in real life as well, despite the fact that at the time he was living with one of the most beautiful women in the world, Ursula Andress. The allegations affected his career too. "A man can play an ax murderer," he blasted, "and still be considered sexy, but if you play a homosexual, suddenly you're not in contention anymore—even for an ax murderer" (Porter, 2010: 454).

Bigger stars than Hamlin had turned down the role. Harrison Ford passed on it. So did Michael Douglas and Richard Gere. No doubt they were now feeling relieved. Perhaps the problem with *Making Love* was that it was too soft. Even the title seemed to carry such softness in it. "Making love" sounded less offensive than having sex; in some ways it was a euphemism for it.

John Sayles's *Lianna* (1983) provided a more formidable treatment of a similar theme. It featured a woman who left her husband for another woman. This was new. Sayles didn't sugarcoat her predicament, focusing on the custody problems surrounding her children, something that would also be taken up years later in Todd Haynes's *Carol* (2015).

The problem with the film is that Lianna embraces her sexuality not so much because she's that way inclined but because she wants to escape her philandering husband. Sayles's implication is that if men weren't so terrible, women wouldn't turn to each other. The lovers may not die at the end, as they might have a few decades before, but Rex Reed still found this a thoroughly depressing film. "Don't lesbians have any fun?" he asked (Russo, 1987: 280).

Two years later a lesbian pair did have fun, in Donna Deitch's *Desert Hearts*. This was less of a polemical film and less stilted too. There was no husband clogging up the relationship; it just happened. It was refreshing to see that the increasing sensitivity toward LGBTQ issues was being exhibited toward women as well as men. In a male-dominated industry like the film world, this was always going to take longer to achieve.

But a new enemy was around the corner: AIDS. It had been a problem from the beginning of the decade, but few people wanted to talk about it. Described as the gay "cancer," it was as taboo a subject as cancer itself in years gone by. People whispered about it, and about who had it, but it wasn't until Rock Hudson contracted it that it became front-page news. It forced him out of the closet more than any gossip magazine could, and when he died from it, suddenly it was okay for Hollywood to make films about it. It had got "the Rock's" imprimatur.

The anger of Stonewall had a new target now. At that time the rage was about fomenting victimization and invisibility; now it was about something more absolute: dying. Ronald Reagan regarded being gay as an aberration. He put his head in the sand. When information about the disease was forced out by activists, he grudgingly acknowledged there was a crisis after all. The experience of AIDS—having it or knowing someone who had—gave rise not only to a spate of films about the disease but a change in the way being gay was seen by queer people.

The black experience of being gay was dealt with by Marlon Riggs in his 1989 feature, *Tongues Untied*. This documentary-style film lifted the lid on gay black sexuality at a time when such a subject was taboo. "The most poignant part of the film," wrote Andy Klein, "revolves around black gays who, steeped in a subculture that is predominantly white, fixate on white men as romantic objects and avoid each other out of a culturally determined lack of self-esteem" (Klein,

Hollywood Reporter, July 16, 1991). It was well received, but there was still a lot of homophobia about. In February 1992, when it was aired on TV, Republican presidential candidate Pat Buchanan took offense, accusing the sitting president of the time, George Bush, of wasting taxpayers' money on an insult to traditional religion and morality.

Cheryl Dunye became Hollywood's first black lesbian director in 1992 with *The Watermelon Woman*. This was a satire that dealt with a woman trying to make a film about a black actress from the 1930s who was pigeonholed into "mammy" roles. This too received critical acclaim, winning the Teddy Award at the Berlin International Film Festival.

There was a tonal shift in many queer-themed films made around this time. *My Own Private Idaho, Edward II*, and *Poison* all came out in 1991. *Swoon* was released a year later. People like Todd Haynes, Gregg Araki, Tom Kalin, and Gus Van Sant challenged the old order with their shape-shifting narratives and dark moods. As Peter Biskind remarked, their films were more interested in shocking straight audiences than reassuring them with the "We're just like you" characters who populated films like *Parting Glances*, which had seemed so daring just a few years before (Biskind, 2007: 117).

The mood had shifted from fear to anger, but the same downbeat tone was in evidence. New Queer Cinema wasn't user-friendly. It didn't produce feel-good films. Many of them were grim parables, and many had art house overtones. The influence of the French *nouvelle vague* movement was evident in some of them. The sex scenes in them tended to be rough, and often mechanical. New Queer directors weren't seen as just coming out of the closet but bashing it into the ground.

Not everyone practiced such bluntness. Many "retro" films were still being made at this time, replete with all the old prejudices and oversights. Another 1991 film, Jon Avnet's *Fried Green Tomatoes at the Whistle Stop Café,* almost totally obliterated the lesbian content of Fannie Flagg's novel, making the two central characters (Mary Stuart Masterson and Mary Louise Parker) best friends rather than lovers. It was a well-made film but was regarded as being too safe, slinking away from anything to do with the bedroom in a cowardly about-turn.

Nicole Conn's *Claire of the Moon* (1992) was more explicitly lesbian, featuring a lengthy lead-up to a love scene at a writer's retreat. There was perhaps too much of a Freudian influence in the sexual analyses to which these characters—one of whom is assuredly gay and the other uncertain—subjected themselves, but at least the treatment wasn't patronizing. It delivered what it promised at the end after a coy lead-up. Its assertive mood was indicative of a newfound confidence in transgender people, the kind of confidence expressed by the cross-dressing Vaughn Cromwell in Jamaa Fanaka's *Street Wars* (1992) when, in response to a gay slur, he says to the person who delivered it: "I happen to be a proud homo sex child. That makes me a woman by desire and a man by nature. Which do you want to deal with?"

Three of Hearts (1993), meanwhile, desexualized the lesbian character and affirmed the supremacy of the male in the ménage à trois. It featured more lazy stereotypes in its rules of attraction when Kelly Brook employs a male escort (William Baldwin) to seduce and then dump her lover (Sherilyn Fenn). The implication, as in *Lianna*, is that only when women become badly treated by men will they choose other women as sexual partners.

When *Philadelphia* came out in 1993, the LGBTQ world felt that they'd received visibility from a major studio at last, not only for its treatment of being gay but also the fact that AIDS was its central theme. Tom Hanks was seen as the new millennium's answer to stalwart stars of a previous era in films like Gary Cooper and James Stewart, having being cast as the tragic victim. He was Mr. Ordinary, John Doe from Main Street, America. If he could be gay, and if he could get AIDS, anyone could. His casting gave the film a universal appeal.

People flooded into the multiplexes to see it, but from an LGBTQ point of view it was too saccharine. If it really meant to break down the walls of misinformation about the disease, why did it not show more physical contact between Hanks and his partner, Antonio Banderas? Both of them were also straight, as was the film's director, Jonathan Demme. This was something else that concerned LGBTQ audiences. If they weren't, they felt, perhaps it wouldn't have been made at all. The film was denounced as being dated in many ways. It was seen as being in the tradition of Frank Capra, a director who made "feel-good" films with upbeat messages. "Capracorn" was a term often applied to such films.

A more ambitious edge was displayed in films like *Interview with the Vampire*, which was made by the Irish director Neil Jordan in 1994. Like most of Jordan's films, it was highly stylized. The connection between vampires and being gay had gone back to the beginnings of films, the sucking of blood seen as a symbolic exchange of bodily fluids, a form of sex. Tom Cruise and Brad Pitt, Hollywood's two squeaky-clean poster boys, costarred. Both of them were equally nervous that their heterosexual status would be questioned. Jordan may have had other ideas. He eroticized Anne Rice's novel. When Cruise "puts the bite" on Pitt, it's an "epiphanous, operatic moment" (Ferguson, 2004: 224).

Cruise's performance was camp, but tentatively so. As one writer remarked, it was "the brand of camp favored by up market female impersonators and downmarket male game show hosts—the kind that draws attention away from homosexuality, not towards it" (Burston, 1995: 149–50). He hedged his bets, which made *Interview with the Vampire* into a straight film that tried to play it both ways.

Cruise played down the gay subtext of the film. In fact he went to court when it was suggested he may have had queer experiences in the past (Davies, 2008: 148). The reason he did so, he said, wasn't because he was homophobic but because he felt the insinuation would make it more difficult for him to play heterosexual roles in the future. Cruise was harking back to the experience of Harry Hamlin in *Making Love* with this fear.

Simon Callow thought his attitude was nonsensical: "You might as well say that the point at which Tom Cruise got divorced and became a single man meant he could never in the future be convincing as a married man on film. Or that an actor who wears a wig is not convincing because we all know he is bald. I'm not interested in whether Tom Cruise is gay or not. But that he should say that if he were thought to be gay he could no longer be taken seriously playing heterosexual parts, it doesn't work like that. Otherwise, I wouldn't keep playing all these heterosexual parts I keep getting offered" (Davies, 149).

Callow played a gay character himself that year in *Four Weddings and a Funeral*. He gave a touching performance, the relationship with his partner being portrayed in a restrained manner. They weren't shown in bed together until well on in the film. The idea was that his character would be developed before sex was brought into the equation but when it was it would be explicit.

It seemed to be good thinking. The singer Boy George once said, "There's this illusion that homosexuals have sex and heterosexuals fall in love" (Hadleigh, 1993: 16). Arthur Hiller could have been accused of this with *Making Love*, a title that telegraphed the softness mentioned earlier. Callow's character was seen as one of the most affectionate ones in the film. The fact that his partner died in it also created sympathy for him. Sir Ian McKellen, another British gay man, wrote to him after seeing it. He said he preferred it to *Philadelphia* "with its welter of chaste histrionics" (Davies, 2008: 10).

Ellen DeGeneres came out as a lesbian in 1997, thereby ending much speculation about her sexuality. She was in a relationship with Anne Heche at the time. Talk show host Conan O'Brien made fun of her dilatory disclosure to the media when he said, "Ellen and Anne are talking about having a baby. They're worried, though, because if it's anything like Ellen it's going to take much more than nine months to come out" (Hadleigh, 1999: 250). Their relationship ended in 2000. Some years later, DeGeneres moved in with Portia de Rossi. They were married in 2008, the year same-sex marriage became legal in California.

The early years of the new millennium had some surprising LGBTQ hits, like the eccentric rock opera *Hedwig and the Angry Inch,* the unfathomable *Mulholland Drive*, and the subdued, engaging *L.I.E.* from independent director Michael Cuesta. The following year brought *The Hours, The Rules of Attraction*, and Todd Haynes's stylized *Far from Heaven*. *Dorian Blues* was a major talking point in 2004, a year that also saw the release of *A Home at the End of the World* and *My Summer of Love*.

The issue of straight actors playing gay roles raised its head again when *Brokeback Mountain* was released in 2005. Simon Callow pointed out that no gay person was involved with the project. "Perhaps someone in makeup slipped through," he remarked sardonically. He saw it as a film about a friendship that turned sexual rather than one about being gay per se (Davies, 2008: 10).

It performed well at the Oscars, as *Philadelphia* had. This was also the case with *Capote* (2005). Philip Seymour Hoffman won the coveted statuette for playing the queer writer Truman Capote. Ironically, he beat Heath Ledger to the award for *Brokeback Mountain*. Hoffman was straight, just as Ledger was. The LGBTQ world waited for the day when Oscars would be handed out to openly queer filmmakers working with openly queer actors. Perhaps a more interesting 2005 release than *Capote* was *Transamerica*. It explored the theme of being transgender through an old-fashioned storyline.

Many versatile films were made in 2006. *The Gymnast* was a visually stunning work that told the story of a woman leaving a loveless marriage to seek a new identity for herself with a female lover. *A Girl Like Me: The Gwen Araujo Story* brought one back to the world of *Boys Don't Cry* in documenting the fate of a transgender woman who was brutally murdered by four men in 2002.

Further off the Straight and Narrow explored the manner in which TV sitcoms and reality shows featuring LGBTQ issues have become more sophisticated over the years. *Dirty Laundry* brought a transgender theme into a black context in the Deep South. *Coffee Date* dealt with society's unwillingness to accept the fact that a straight man could have a close relationship with a queer without being queer himself. *Another Gay Movie* was anything but that. The title was ironic as the plot was really more like a heterosexual one: four teenagers strive to lose their virginity before they go to college.

Audiences were returned to a traditional theme the following year with *Save Me*, which again posited the notion that being gay could be "cured." The central character here is forced into a Christian-run ministry to bring this about. Another 2007 release, *Red without Blue*, chronicled the relationship between two identical twin brothers after one of them decides to transition. *Naked Boys Singing* was a musical that was reminiscent of *A Chorus Line* in its exploration of being gay through music and dance. In a lighter vein, *I Now Pronounce You Chuck and Larry* had two straight New York firefighters pretending to be a queer couple so that one of them, a widower, could avail of insurance benefits. *Gay Zombie* reminded one yet again of the connection between being gay and vampirism in films. Here it was played mostly for laughs.

For the Bible Tells Me So, like *Save Me*, navigated the vexed relationship between being gay and religion, intertwining the stories of five Christian families with gay or lesbian children who face homophobia from a fundamentalist church. *Butch Jamie* was like a female version of *Tootsie* with its theme of a lesbian actress who becomes mistaken for a man at an audition. *Two Minutes Later* had a film noir feel with its *Maltese Falcon*–style plot.

In 2008, Gus Van Sant's *Milk*, a biopic of assassinated politician Harvey Milk with Sean Penn, garnered most of the headlines. But there were many other queer-friendly films made that year. Chief among these was *Prodigal Sons*, a film with a unique set of circumstances. It told the story of a transgender woman returning to her hometown to try to reconcile with her estranged adopted brother who's possibly the grandson of Orson Welles and Rita Hayworth.

There were also some important documentaries made that year. *Sex Positive* concerned a man called Richard Berkowitz, an AIDS activist from the 1980s. *Bi the Way* looked at the changing sexual landscape of the United States through a series of interviews with people exploring their various proclivities outside binary grooves. *Be Like Others* featured a number of Iranian men undergoing sex reassignment surgery. The theme acquired added resonance when one considered the fact that Iran was a country where being trans or gay is regarded as a crime punishable by death. *Pedro* was a docudrama about Pedro Zamora, the first HIV-positive gay man to appear on a reality TV show. During the course of it he forced audiences to confront the gravity of AIDS. The film was cowritten by Dustin Lance Black, who also wrote the screenplay for *Milk*.

Colin Firth appeared in *A Single Man* in 2009. It had a unique format, the whole film taking place in a day. He played a 1960s professor who feels he's unable to cope with the recent death of his long-term partner, so he contemplates suicide. In another director's hands this could have been depressing, but director Tom Ford lifted it onto a cathartic level. *Redwoods* was a softer offering from the same year, documenting the manner in which a gay man in a crumbling relationship has his life turned around by the arrival of a drifter to his California home. It was accused of being saccharine by some viewers.

Of more moment was *Outrage*, Kirby Dick's denunciation of closeted politicians who lobbied for antigay legislation in the United States. Like Dick's earlier *This Film Is Not Yet Rated* (2006), his satire of Hollywood's ratings system, it was an uncompromising indictment of hypocrisy within the corridors of power.

The survival of lesbian love through infidelity, war, marriage, and societal taboos was the theme of *Hannah Free*, which starred Sharon Gless as a lesbian woman fighting for the love of her childhood friend (Maureen Gallagher) over many years, despite all the above obstacles.

In a similar vein, *Edie and Thea* moved from the 1960s to the present to tell the inspirational story of a lesbian couple who endured both personal and political problems in their relationship. The film was based on the life of Edie Windsor, a woman who sued the IRS after her (wealthy) partner died and she was served with an inheritance tax bill of $360,000. She campaigned for the right to be treated like any other widow and won her case, thereby creating a precedent for all the women who came after her in similar circumstances. It was directed by Susan Muska and Greta Olafsdottir, who also helmed *The Brandon Teena Story*.

Ticked Off Trannies with Knives (2010), a film about the revenge wreaked by a group of transsexual women after they're savagely attacked, was looked on as a cross between the kinds of films made by John Waters and Quentin Tarantino, a kind of *Kill Bill* meets *Pink Flamingos*. It was never meant to be taken seriously, appealing mainly to the type of audiences who enjoyed low-budget cult farces.

Of more substance was *Stonewall Uprising*, also made in 2010. This was a documentary about the Stonewall Riots of 1969. It didn't have any live footage of the riots, only photographs of them, but there were many interviews of people involved in them, including, perhaps surprisingly, a police officer. A third 2010 release, *The Sons of Tennessee Williams*, was also of interest to LGBTQ viewers as it investigated the phenomenon of gay drag balls in New Orleans in the late 1950s. These were held in Mardi Gras clubs scattered throughout the city. They set the tone for later ones in New York, the world so entrancingly captured in Jennie Livingston's *Paris Is Burning* (1990).

There were many other films made that year that held interest for LGBTQ viewers, among them *Periods of Rain, A Marine Story, Role/Play, Leading Ladies, You Should Meet My Son, The Kids Are All Right, Kaboom, Dirty Girl, Bloomington, Beginners,* and *BearCity*. Two documentaries that stood out were *Beautiful Darling*, which concerned the life of Andy Warhol stalwart Candy Darling, and *Howl*, named after Allen Ginsberg's most famous poem and dealing with the man himself. The standout film of the year from an LGBTQ perspective was Darren Aronofsky's *Black Swan*. This won an Oscar for Natalie Portman, who gave an electrifying performance as the troubled ballerina in Aronofsky's chilling demimonde.

The following year held equal riches. Its most interesting documentary was *Wish Me Away*, which concerned Chely Wright, the first commercial country-and-western singer to come out as gay, a brave move in such a conservative heartland as Nashville. *Vito* was a study of the life and times of Vito Russo, author of *The Celluloid Closet* and someone often seen as the founding father of the Gay Liberation Movement; *Hit So Hard* dealt with the life of Patty Schemel, the openly gay drummer of Courtney Love's rock band, Hole, while *Sexing the Transmen* was an investigation of the changes transgender men experience after their transition, both physical and psychological. It didn't pull its punches.

Other films of interest made that year included *You and I, Weekend, I Want to Get Married, Heart Breaks Open, Gun Hill Road, The Green, Going Down in La La Land, What You Looking At?, A Wedding Most Strange, Circumstance, Break My Fall, Blinders, August, (A)Sexual, Abrupt Decision, We Once Were Wide*, and *Walk a Mile in My Pradas*. These were refreshing treatments of themes and characters once deemed taboo in the dark days of homophobic cinema. The floodgates had been opened and all sorts of genres were creeping through. New voices were heard, both in the mainstream and independent channels, with big budgets and small. Clint Eastwood lifted the lid on years of speculation concerning J. Edgar Hoover's sexuality when he had Leonardo DiCaprio play him in *J. Edgar*, an uncompromising profile of the bullish FBI boss.

In *Cloudburst*, Brenda Fricker and Olympia Dukakis were two octogenarian lesbians who've lived together for thirty-one years. The plot takes off when they escape from a nursing home to get married in Canada. This was a sweet and funny film that celebrated both old age and sexual diversity. *Becoming Chaz* explored the transition of Cher's son. *Tomboy* was another 2011 release. It was unusual in the sense that it explored gender dysphoria from a young person's point of view—in this case a ten-year-old girl presenting herself as a boy in the new neighborhood her family has just moved into.

Sal was a film about the last day in the life of the openly gay actor from *Rebel without a Cause*, Sal Mineo. He was stabbed to death outside his apartment in 1976 in circumstances that are still clouded in mystery. Director James Franco deliberately played down the drama of the piece, a curious decision. He said this was because Mineo wasn't to know it was his last day. That was fine in theory but audiences did know this, so the sense of realism was arguably misplaced. The film ran the risk of being called boring despite its best intentions.

The most entertaining LGBTQ title of the year was *Codependent Lesbian Space Alien Seeks Same*. Many would-be comic sci-fi ventures failed to hit the target in the past, but this one was so eccentric it was well received both by critics and public alike. Having invaded Earth, the eponymous alien makes overtures toward a bashful greeting card store employee without telling her she isn't human. The film was directed in the delightfully trashy manner one associates with Ed Wood. It was nominated at the Gotham Independent Film Festival for Best Film *Not* Playing at a Theater Near You. That didn't matter. It was a niche affair; it never expected to threaten the blockbusters at the multiplexes.

The following year had a unique assortment of themes in its LGBTQ releases. As the years went on, such themes became become more sympathetic toward people of divergent sexuality. *Question One* was a study of the 2009 Maine state referendum on same-sex marriage. This was the first state to legalize it, but some months later it reversed its decision. The film gives both sides of the story with commendable impartiality, but its U-turn was still a bitter pill to have to swallow.

Private Romeo was a contemporary take on Shakespeare's *Romeo & Juliet* with the interesting addition of a gay element in Romeo's past. It was a dangerous move to tamper with literature's iconic Adonis, but somehow it seemed to get away with it. *The Perfect Family* unpicked cultural mores with a potentially sensational storyline. Kathleen Turner played a conventional mother who's been nominated for the award of Catholic Woman of the Year. Before she receives it she learns that her (pregnant) daughter is about to marry her girlfriend and her son is leaving his wife. The two shocks mean she has to redefine exactly what "perfect" means. It would certainly not be the definition of people like Dwight Eisenhower or J. Edgar Hoover. But America was changing. All the old verities were being whittled away, slowly but surely, to make way for a new and more inclusive culture.

Pariah went in another direction, examining the parameters of same-sex relationships among African American women. *United in Anger* was a documentary about the AIDS activist organization ACT UP. *How to Survive a Plague* was like a companion piece to this. It focused on the alliance of ACT UP with another organization, TAG (Treatment Action Group), to try and halt the spread of AIDS, or at least treat it more successfully. These were compelling in their way, but films were always more involving to audiences when their concerns became more personal than propagandist. *Any Day Now* was a moving film about a 1970s gay couple who took on the legal system in a bid to retain custody of an intellectually disabled teenager they adopted. The fact that one of its stars (Alan Cumming) was gay in real life helped its credibility.

Call Me Kuchu was a documentary about an openly gay politician in Uganda called David Kato. Not many people knew about him, but that all changed after the film was released. He was murdered as he fought to defeat a bill that was going to make being gay a crime punishable by death in that country, which made him into a kind of African Harvey Milk, another slain martyr for his cause.

The One was a more escapist divertissement, a comedy about a man who falls in love with a male friend from his past on the eve of his marriage to a woman. Once again, binary stereotypes of the heteronormal alpha male were being challenged, even if the focus was frothy. Other releases of the year included *Jobriath A.D., Jack and Diane, I Want Your Love, I Do, Gayby, Keep the Lights On, Jamie and Jessie Are Not Together, Tennessee Queer, The Skinny*, and *Scenes from a Gay Marriage*. Some of these films were more thought-provoking than others, but they all had their heart in the right place.

Dallas Buyers Club (2013) won an Oscar for Matthew McConaughey as a straight man battling AIDS. He was praised highly for his performance, but LGBTQ viewers were bothered by the supporting role played by Jared Leto as a transgender woman McConaughey befriends. Why, they asked, was a straight cis-man chosen for this role rather than a transgender woman? The general perception was that Leto played her as a drag queen. The fact that he too won an Oscar seemed to add insult to injury.

Another film that seemed to add insult to injury in 2013 was the sexually explicit *Interior. Leather Bar*. This was a short film—it was only an hour in length—that was conceptual in nature, inserting a putative forty minutes that William Friedkin excised from his 1980 film *Cruising*. The insertion wasn't Friedkin's but that of the film's codirectors, James Franco and Travis Mathews. Many people scratched their heads in confusion as they left the cinema. The general feeling was, why revisit a film that wasn't liked in the first place, and which enraged GLAAD and all its supporters at the time it was being shot?

More entertaining by far was *Bambi*, a documentary about Algerian trans woman Marie-Pierre Pruvot, while *52 Tuesdays* was a coming-of-age tale of a teenage girl trying to deal with a transgender mother who was transitioning to become a man. Other releases of the year that attracted LGBTQ notice were *We Are Animals*, *Truth*, *Test*, *Concussion*, *Bridegroom*, *Breaking the Rules*, *Ashley*, and *Blue Is the Warmest Color*. The final title attracted the most column inches from reviewers.

I am Divine (2014) was a profile of 300-pound drag queen Divine, a.k.a. Harris Glenn Milstead, whom John Waters made famous–or, depending on one's point of view, made John Waters famous. Milstead died young, but in his relatively brief career, he managed to shock and endear in almost equal measure. *The Case Against 8* was a study of the ultimately unsuccessful four-year court case to overturn California's decision to legalize same-sex marriage in 2008. It was an emotional roller coaster for constituents, having fought so hard for something and then undergoing the threat of it being whisked away again. But thankfully that didn't happen. Other 2014 releases included the cult film *The Duke of Burgundy* and *Boy Meets Girl*.

Carol was highly regarded in 2015. It was directed by Todd Haynes, one of the leading lights of New Queer Cinema. He'd already made *Far from Heaven*, a film about a man (Dennis Quaid) in total denial about his orientation in 1950s America. This explored similar terrain from the distaff side, charting the budding lesbian romance of two women (Cate Blanchett and Rooney Mara) against the backdrop of Blanchett's dead marriage to a man, Rooney's sexual confusion, and a plethora of child custody headaches. It was up to the standard one had come to expect from Haynes, a sumptuously shot parable that was justifiably rewarded at the Oscar ceremonies that year, weighing in with a number of nominations.

The Pass was a more offbeat release from 2015. It dealt with two soccer players who shared a kiss one night that changed their lives forever. It moved forward in time in an interesting manner, which made one forget its stage-like feel, being shot mainly in a hotel room. Parts of it made for uneasy viewing, but once again it dealt intelligently with the theme of sexual denial.

Other films from that year were equally versatile. Queen Latifah earned many positive reviews for essaying the role of Bessie Smith, the lesbian blues singer from the 1920s and 1930s, in *Bessie*. Lily Tomlin had her first lead role in almost thirty years in *Grandma*, playing a lesbian poet mourning the death of her partner and trying to bond with her granddaughter on a road trip. *Vita and Virginia* explored the relationship between Vita Sackville-West and Virginia Woolf, something that was previously touched on in films like *Orlando* and *The Hours*.

The Danish Girl was perhaps the most high-profile film of the year. It was criticized by LGBTQ viewers for the same reason as *Dallas Buyers Club*, in that it cast a cisgender actor, Eddie Redmayne, in the role of Lili Elbe, a woman who pioneered sex reassignment therapy in the 1930s. Alicia Vikander won an Oscar for playing Redmayne's wife but Redmayne was bypassed for one. In other words, the straight woman in a supporting part was honored but not the transgender one in the starring role. To the casual viewer, this could have sent out a signal that Vikander was the eponymous Danish Girl, not Redmayne. This was an added cause for concern to the gay community considering what Elbe went through to achieve her transition.

I Am Michael (2016) was based on a true story. It had a gay man struggling against his orientation to embrace a Christian ethos. This is a theme that occurs frequently in LGBTQ cinema, and it generally suggests suffering on the part of the characters in question, and intolerance from the ecclesiastical and/or governmental forces trying to change their nature. What made this treatment of the theme most interesting was that Michael seemed to be in denial about his orientation right up to the final reel as he prepares himself for marriage . . . to a woman. *Holding the Man*, also made in 2016, was based on an award-winning play by Tommy Murphy. It earned many plaudits for its evocation of a queer relationship that began in high school and lasted a lifetime.

Beach Rats (2017) told the story of a gay teenager coming of age in Coney Island. Another 2017 film, *Battle of the Sexes*, had Emma Stone as former tennis ace Billy Jean King squaring off against Bobby Riggs (Steve Carell) in a grudge match after Riggs made a gibe against the poor standard of women's tennis vis-a-vis the men's game. (He'd earlier played a similar match against a former legend, Margaret Court.) He was fifty-five and King only twenty-nine at the time of their encounter, but he still felt he could beat her. He was wrong about that. She won the match and proved a point about the game, if not about male chauvinism. The film is set against the backdrop of her lesbian relationship with her hairdresser Marilyn Barnett (Andrea Riseborough).

More recent LGBTQ releases cover the same broad spectrum as those of former years. *The Miseducation of Cameron Post* (2018) dealt with a teenage girl forced to attend a gay conversion therapy center by her conservative guardians. *Boy Erased* explored a similar theme, featuring the queer son of a Baptist pastor who's faced with the choice of undergoing conversion therapy or exile. In *A Kid Like Jake*, a loving mother and father try to come to terms with the fact that their four-year-old child is transgender. It's interesting that the transgender theme seems to feature younger and younger demographics with each passing year. This is no doubt indicative of the growing awareness of society about the fact that people are conscious of their sexuality much earlier than was realized in former decades.

Every Act of Life was a biopic of the playwright Terrence McNally, a man who devoted his life to LGBTQ causes when he wasn't writing innovative plays and musicals. With *The Happy Prince*, Oscar Wilde devotee Rupert Everett finally got the chance to make a film about a previously ignored part of Wilde's life—what happened to him after he came out of jail. It was an elegiac portrait of the beleaguered playwright who suffered so much for "the love that dared not speak its name."

Why aren't more gay-themed films being made today? Richard Barrios speculated that it's not so much homophobia as financial concerns. With the exception of films like *Victor/Victoria, Philadelphia,* and *The Birdcage,* he noted, not enough people went to see them (Barrios, 2003: 315). *Philadelphia* and *Brokeback Mountain* were exceptions in this regard. Was that because they were directed by straight men?

Philadelphia was also sexually coy. Even high-profile films with gay themes—*The Boys in the Band, Making Love, Torch Song Trilogy, Longtime Companion,* etc.—all lost money. Oscar-winning LGBTQ films usually gain more prestige than dollars. *The Crying Game* was a hit but it wasn't, strictly speaking, a "gay" film. It was a political mystery story featuring a beautiful woman who was transgender, something that wasn't known to her boyfriend until a scene that caused the biggest surprise of the year, if not the biggest one of a decade.

Straight actors continue to play queer roles, right up to *Moonlight,* which controversially won the Best Film award for 2016 at the Oscar ceremonies after the wrong name was read out by Faye Dunaway.

It seemed almost like a Freudian slip, a grimly appropriate footnote to a century of mistreatment.

Further Reading

Barrios, Richard. 2003. *Screened Out*: *Playing Gay from Edison to Stonewall.* New York and London: Routledge.

Biskind, Peter. 2007. *Down and Dirty Pictures: Miramax, Sundance and the Rise of Independent Film.* London: Bloomsbury.

Bourne, Stephen. 1996. *Brief Encounters*: *Lesbians and Gays in British Cinema 1930–1971.* London: Cassell.

Burston, Paul. 1995. *What Are You Looking At?* London: Cassell.

Darren, Allison. 2000. *Lesbian Film Guide.* London and New York: Cassell.

Davies, Steven Paul. 2008. *Out at the Movies*: *A History of Gay Cinema.* Herts, UK: Kamera Books.

Ferguson, Michael. 2004. *Idol Worship*: *A Shameless Celebration of Male Beauty in the Movies.* Sarasota, FL: Starbooks Press.

Hadleigh, Boze. 1993. *The Lavender Screen.* New York: Citadel Press.

Hadleigh, Boze, ed. 1999. *Hollywood Bitch.* London: Robson.

Parish, James Robert. 1993. *Gays and Lesbians in Mainstream Cinema.* Jefferson, NC: McFarland.

Porter, Darwin, and Danforth Prince. 2010. *50 Years of Queer Cinema.* New York: Blood Moon Productions.

Russo, Vito. 1987. *The Celluloid Closet*: *Homosexuality in the Movies.* New York: Harper & Row.

Chronology of Milestone Events

1922
Will Hays becomes president of the Motion Picture Production Distributors of America (MPPDA).

1923
William Haines becomes Hollywood's first openly gay actor. Louis B. Mayer goes into denial about it, telling fans he's in love with Pola Negri.

1926
Rudolph Valentino dies, causing a national outpouring of grief in the United States. Some fans even commit suicide in their distress. This was despite rumors that Valentino may have been gay, and married to two lesbians.

1927
The first gay kiss takes place in an American film, *Wings*.

1930
The MPPDA announces the introduction of the Production Code, which aims to "clean up" films. Part of this aim is the removal of any imputation of gay people from films. William Haines's career goes into free fall. People questioning their sexual orientation are driven further into the closet.

1931
Germany releases *Mädchen in Uniform*, a film that has being lesbian as a central theme. It's the first time an LGBTQ film has appeared in the mainstream.

1934
Establishment of the Production Code Association (PCA). This means that films released after July 1 will require certificates of approval. Instituted by Will Hays, it becomes known as the Hays Code. It builds on the aims of 1930, with a mission statement of ridding films of "moral turpitude." Many pre-Code films that have LGBTQ elements are withdrawn from circulation.

1939
Being gay becomes loathsome to a nation at war, and apparently obsessed with its macho credentials. A raft of films are made that ramp up the national morale by espousing such alpha male values.

1940

The purge of gay people in films continues. Gay themes and characters have to be coded by visual and/or verbal cues. A gay element is permitted if a character is evil, like Peter Lorre of *The Maltese Falcon* (1941), or if they're pitiable.

1947

The so-called lavender scare of Senator Joseph McCarthy suggests queer people are unfit for public office, as they could be "patsies" for communist influences. A fictitious link between communism and being gay finds its way into various Cold War movies.

1948

Alfred Hitchcock releases *Rope*, a homophobic film based loosely on the Leopold/Loeb murders, which draws a connection between gay people and psychosis. Farley Granger stars.

Alfred Kinsey's book *Sexual Behavior in the American Male* discloses the fact that 37 percent of adult American men have had gay experiences. Three seminal gay novels are published: Gore Vidal's *The City and the Pillar*, Truman Capote's *Other Voices, Other Rooms*, and James Baldwin's *Giovanni's Room*. Vidal and Capote will go on to become Hollywood screenwriters.

1951

Hitchcock releases *Strangers on a Train*, another film with a gay subtext. Robert Walker engages in a dual murder pact with, again, Farley Granger, though Granger is an unwilling accomplice.

1955

Confidential, a magazine that specializes in digging up scandals on stars, threatens to "out" Rock Hudson. Hudson is spared after a rumor of hush money being paid to the editor of the magazine. Instead they run a story on Rory Calhoun, a minor actor.

1961

The Motion Picture Production Code Association issues an amendment to its ban on gay people on screen. LGBTQ themes will now be permissible if handled with "care, discretion, and restraint."

The Dirk Bogarde film *Victim* gives a sympathetic depiction of being gay. Bogarde, a closeted gay man in real life, plays a barrister who's being blackmailed. Up until now, gay figures were often caricatures. Bogarde is also married in the film, which opens people's eyes to the area of bisexuality.

1966

The Production Code is relaxed, advocating more tolerance in the treatment of sexual themes rather than an outright ban on them.

1967

In Britain the Sexual Offences Act is changed. Lesbian and gay acts between consenting adults in private are decriminalized. It's believed *Victim* played a part in the framing of the new legislation.

1968

The Production Code is abolished, giving way to a new body called the Code and Ratings Administration. *The Killing of Sister George*, a UK film with a lesbian relationship at its core, will play in theaters, though with an X certificate, which denies it newspaper publicity. The film flops as a result.

Valerie Solanas, the founder of SCUM (Society for Cutting Up Men), shoots Andy Warhol and then gives herself up to a traffic policeman in Times Square.

1969

On June 27, police arrive at the Stonewall Inn in Greenwich Village, New York, to make their routine gay arrests. In contrast to the usual compliance of those arrested, they're met with an uncharacteristic level of resistance. Transgender people and people of color refuse to be taken into custody. The police have the tables turned on them. They're trapped in the bar, which is subsequently set on fire. Three days of protest follow. The "Stonewall Riots," as they come to be called, spearhead more positive attitudes toward LGBTQ people.

1970

William Friedkin directs *The Boys in the Band*, which features an all-gay cast. The normalization of being gay is unprecedented, though it's disappointing that so many of the characters have such poor self-images.

Midnight Cowboy wins the Best Picture award. It's the first time an X-rated film has done so. The central relationship it portrays, between Dustin Hoffman and Jon Voight, is more covertly gay than overtly so, but the theme is still prominent. The film's director, John Schlesinger, is a closeted gay man at this point of his life. He picks up an Oscar for the film.

1971

Schlesinger continues his pioneering ways by having a mainstream star, Peter Finch, engage in a relationship with a bisexual man, Murray Head, in his film *Sunday Bloody Sunday*. The film also features a kiss between them, which shocks many viewers. Finch becomes the first man to receive an Oscar nomination for a gay role.

1973

The Gay Activist Alliance and the National Gay Task Force lobby the film world for stronger portrayals of gay people. Hollywood promises to do its best to bring this about.

1979

The Gay and Lesbian Alliance Against Defamation (GLAAD) protests against the Al Pacino movie *Cruising*, which shows gay people in a very violent light. Pacino insists it isn't a homophobic movie, but the protests continue after its release in 1980.

1980

AIDS, known at the time as the "gay plague" or the "gay cancer," starts to make itself manifest, though its spread is kept quiet by the powers that be, especially

Ronald Reagan, president of the United States, who fails to acknowledge the existence of the disease as thousands die from it.

1981
The Celluloid Closet, a book documenting the history of LGBTQ issues from the Production Code era to the present, is published. It becomes a veritable bible on the theme for many years to come and is referenced in most books on the subject in some shape or form.

1982
Making Love becomes the first mainstream American film to address being gay in a significant and substantive manner. The theme is ahead of its time: a gay doctor (Michael Ontkean) falls in love with one of his patients, Harry Hamlin, who's married to a woman, Kate Jackson.

1985
The documentary *Before Stonewall*, which deals with gay life in America preceding the Stonewall riots, is released. It features archival footage and revelatory interviews. It also deals with discrimination in the armed forces, in politics, in the media, and in everyday life. The film covers four decades from the twenties to the sixties.

On July 25, Rock Hudson's publicist confirms that the star was diagnosed with AIDS a year earlier. On October 2, Hudson passes away. He's the first major actor to die of the disease. Many people in the film business knew of his sexuality, but it was hushed up. There's anger at him for not coming out. On the credit side, it's hoped politicians might now be spurred into action to do something to halt the spread of the disease, which has reached epidemic proportions.

On November 11, perhaps emboldened by Hudson's death, NBC airs the TV film *An Early Frost*, featuring Aidan Quinn as a gay attorney suffering from AIDS.

1988
William Hurt wins a Best Actor Oscar for *Kiss of the Spider Woman*. He's the first actor to win an Oscar playing an openly gay character—and in drag.

British actor Ian McKellen comes out, which puts pressure on some of his gay contemporaries (Dirk Bogarde, John Gielgud, Nigel Hawthorne) to do likewise. But they remain silent.

1990
Paris Is Burning, a celebration of New York's "Ball" culture in the 1980s, becomes a sensational hit and introduces terms like "vogueing" (a combination of dancing and catwalk movements) to the general public, as well as opening their eyes to ethnic and sexual diversity among the disenfranchised.

1991
The Silence of the Lambs wins four Oscars and inflames anger as it features a repellent gay killer who wants to turn into a woman. He imagines he can achieve this by "skinning" young women and making suits from their flesh.

Ian McKellen is knighted. Derek Jarman, the British gay director, accuses him of endorsing the values of a homophobic government by accepting the knighthood.

The New York organization OutPost, formed to "out" gay celebrities, puts Jodie Foster on an "Absolutely Queer" flier.

1991

Callie Khouri's *Thelma and Louise* reappraises the buddy-buddy genre for women, giving viewers a *Butch Cassidy and the Sundance Kid* from the distaff side as Susan Sarandon and Geena Davis leave their unfulfilling suburban lives and go on the road, creating mayhem as they reach liberation through their newfound bohemianism. A lesbian subtext is muted.

The gay organization ACT UP sends out a thousand letters to Academy members asking them to speak about AIDS during their Oscar acceptance speeches and to wear "Silence = Death" buttons on their lapels. Only Susan Sarandon and Bruce Davison, who'd been nominated for directing the film *Longtime Companion*, agree to wear the buttons.

1992

Gay rights activists protest against the Paul Verhoeven film *Basic Instinct* for featuring a gay killer, Sharon Stone. Memories of *The Silence of the Lambs* are still raw.

Film scholar B. Ruby Rich coins the term "New Queer Cinema" to refer to the crop of innovative LGBTQ films currently being made that are more radical, subversive, sexually explicit, and antithetical in theme and tone to conventional notions of so-called heteronormal behavior.

1993

And the Band Played On, a TV movie based on Randy Shilts's book of the same name, documents the shocking catalog of lives that have been lost to AIDS since the early 1980s, and the efforts of medical researchers to halt its spread against the intransigence of many sociopolitical forces—and not a little infighting among themselves.

Brandon Teena, a transgender man from Nebraska, is raped and murdered when his secret is discovered.

Tom Hanks wins a Best Actor Oscar for *Philadelphia*, playing a lawyer who contracts AIDS and is sacked from his job as a result. He takes his firm to court for unfair dismissal. The film represents a seismic change in Hollywood's growing acknowledgment of the need to publicize these issues. It's the first gay-themed film to be a blockbuster. It goes on to earn over $70 million during its first run.

1994

Release of the documentary *Stonewall 25: Global Voices of Pride and Protest*, which celebrates the 25th anniversary of the Stonewall riots. It features contributions from Ian McKellen, Kate Bernstein, and Chita Rivera.

1996

Nigel Finch directs *Stonewall: The Fight for the Right to Love*, another film set around the time of the Stonewall riots, with an inference that the death of Judy Garland provided an important spur to them.

1997

Ellen DeGeneres comes out as a lesbian.

1999

John Scagliotti follows his 1985 documentary *Before Stonewall* with a sequel, *After Stonewall*. It examines the changes that have taken place in the gay rights movement since the 1969 riots. Containing interviews with people like Larry Kramer and Rita Mae Brown and narration by Melissa Etheridge, it becomes a partner piece for its precursor.

Hilary Swank wins an Oscar for playing Brandon Teena in *Boys Don't Cry*.

2001

Publication of William Mann's book *Behind the Screen: How Gays and Lesbians Shaped Hollywood*. It's an important guide to the LGBTQ experience in the studio era and a long-overdue accompaniment to *The Celluloid Closet*.

Lily Tomlin comes out, ending decades of debate about her sexual orientation.

2002

The lesbian serial killer Aileen Wuornos is executed. She was sentenced to death in 1992 and spent over a decade on death row.

2003

Charlize Theron wins an Oscar for playing Wuornos in *Monster*.

2005

Brokeback Mountain wins a string of Oscars. Jake Gyllenhaal and Heath Ledger play gay cowboys in the film, which resonates in the public consciousness for the manner in which director Ang Lee reinvents the Western genre.

2007

Ellen DeGeneres hosts the Oscar ceremonies. It's the first time an openly lesbian person has been chosen for this task.

André Schäfer directs *Here's Looking at You, Boy*, a documentary on LGBTQ films. Featuring interviews with the likes of John Waters, Gus Van Sant, Rainer Maria Fassbinder, and a host of others, as well as voluminous clips from seminal movies, it's hailed as a worthy successor to Vito Russo's *The Cellulloid Closet*.

2008

Sean Penn plays Harvey Milk, California's first openly gay elected official, who was assassinated in 1978, in Gus Van Sant's biopic, *Milk*.

2010

Harvey Milk Day is organized by the Milk Foundation in honor of the much-loved politician.

2015

The Oscar ceremonies are hosted by the openly gay Neil Patrick Harris, which builds on the Ellen DeGeneres precedent of 2007.

Same-sex marriage is legalized in the United States.

A

The Adventures of Priscilla, Queen of the Desert (1994)

Director/Screenwriter Stephen Elliott pulled out all the stops in this camp classic featuring Terence Stamp as Bernadette, a heavily mascaraed transsexual woman traveling across the Australian Outback in a ramshackle bus with drag queens Tick/Mitzi (Hugo Weaving) and Adam/Felicia (Guy Pearce). The fourth queen is Priscilla—the bus. It's bringing them to a resort in Alice Springs for a four-week engagement where they plan to resurrect their old cabaret act.

Each of them has dreams. Felicia wants to climb to the top of Kings Canyon in a Jean Paul Gaultier frock and high heels; Mitzi wants to be a better father. Bernadette is looking for love. Elliott amiably captures the manner in which they realize these dreams against a background of sniping, driving, and grooving along to fairly nonstop music.

The film contains a thundering rendition of "I Will Survive" by Gloria Gaynor and other numbers by Village People, Patti Page, Lena Horne, etc. And, of course, Abba, which calls up memories of another popular Australian film, *Muriel's Wedding*.

Cabin fever festers as they get their adventurous odyssey under way. Bernadette, who objects strongly to being called Ralph, has her sulks. These often dictate the prevalent mood on the bus. She also sets the tone of the conversations—or nonconversations.

The fact that she's in mourning over the death of a lover who was asphyxiated by peroxide is the main reason for her tantrums—and her drinking. Viewers wait for the volcano to erupt. One viewer of the film saw Bernadette as a transgender version of Blanche DuBois, the fragile character of Tennessee Williams's *A Streetcar Named Desire* (1951) who's brutalized by Marlon Brando's Stanley Kowalski. John Anderson wrote: "Stamp refines resolve and regret into the kind of fractured faded class that Vivien Leigh gave Blanche DuBois" (*Newsday*, February 14, 1994). The other two play off her with perfectly pitched comic timing. Sometimes they even steal the limelight.

The scene where Felicia walks into the bar of a rural mining town in her full drag regalia is generally seen as one of the funniest in the film. This is not a place where a drag queen would be expected to turn up under any circumstances.

Elliott emphasizes the right of his tempestuous trio to be themselves in a world that frowns on their differences from the norm. The scene where Mitzi pretends to go straight is another humorous attack on the world of narrow-minded people, a world the three central characters combat in their way. It's a world light-years away from their spangles and feathers, but they manage to find a place in it in their own eccentric ways. There's a soft center to all three of them, despite their near-constant bickering. Perhaps this is the reason for it: to protect themselves from hurt in a world that has already hurt them so much.

The film is a comedy rather than a tract about different lives. Elliott plays down the hostility they endure from the straight world. He's more interested in what happens between them as they go about their daily business. Or when the bus is painted—lavender, needless to say—or when it breaks down. (The man who fixes it turns out to be a fan and ends up traveling with them.)

Priscilla was shot out of sequence. Elliott couldn't afford to keep repainting the bus, so he did the next best thing: he painted the two sides of it different colors and shot whatever color he needed for each given scene. The film winged its way to an uncertain conclusion under such tenuous contours. Like most road movies, it's a journey of the heart as well. Here Elliott spares us any unnecessary schmaltz. He also spares us sex, which is somewhat ironic in a film about one's right to sexual self-determination.

Is it a frock opera? A comedy? A musical? A plea for understanding? It's all these things and more. It won an Oscar for costume design, which was appropriate for a film that had a poster carrying the legend, "Finally a comedy that will change the way you think, the way you feel, and most importantly, the way you dress." It was a commercial and critical success and was also enjoyed by non-LGBTQ audiences, no doubt in part because it contained no gay sex or even the suggestion of it.

The following year Beeban Kidron tried to jump on Elliott's bandwagon (or bus) with the uncomfortably similar *To Wong Foo, Thanks for Everything, Julie Newmar*. The title was imaginative, but there the originality ended. Kidron tried to ape Elliott both in style and in tone, but critics emphasized his failure on both counts. *To Wong Foo* was another road movie featuring an array of drag queens (this time played by Patrick Swayze, Wesley Snipes, and John Leguizamo) en route to a beauty pageant, but the unashamed plagiarism meant most of the comic moments were contrived. The film did some business among those who'd hoped for a development on *The Adventures of Priscilla*, but it was difficult to avoid seeing it in every derivative frame.

One critic dismissed it as a bland exercise that could comfortably play in Middle American shopping malls without threatening anyone (*Variety*, September 5, 1995). Today, *To Wong Foo* is seen as *The Adventures of Priscilla* for a straight audience.

Related Films
La Cage aux Folles (1978); *Muriel's Wedding* (1994); *Welcome to Woop Woop* (1997); *Transamerica* (2005).

Further Reading
Newsday, February 14, 1994.
Porter, Darwin, and Danforth Prince. 2010. *50 Years of Queer Cinema*. New York: Blood Moon Productions.
Salin-Pascual, Rafael J. 2009. *Cinema and Sexual Diversity*. www.lulu.com
Stamp, Terence. 2017. *The Ocean Fell into the Drop*. London: Repeater Books.
Variety, September 5, 1995.

Advise & Consent (1962)

Adapted from Allen Drury's novel of the same name, this Otto Preminger feature explores the wheeling and dealing surrounding the appointment of a secretary of state in Washington, DC. The U.S. president is dying of cancer and requests the Senate to approve Robert Leffingwell (Henry Fonda) for the position.

Don Murray is another senator, Brigham ("Brig") Anderson. He disapproves of Leffingwell because he once belonged to a communist group. When he refuses to endorse him, he's blackmailed about something in his own past: a queer experience he had when he was in the army.

Because of this aspect of the plot, Preminger knew he was going to have trouble with the censors. Equally, they knew they were going to have trouble with him. In 1953 he announced his intention to release his film *The Moon Is Blue*, which contained lines such as, "Men are usually bored with virginity," without a seal from the Motion Picture Association of America (MPAA). When one wasn't forthcoming, he did precisely that.

Because Joe Breen, who made the decisions at the MPAA, feared history repeating itself, he allowed him some leverage. In past years it would have been unheard of to feature such material in a mainstream release, but Breen knew who he was dealing with—*The Moon Is Blue* had fared well commercially even without the code—so he rowed back on his demands. Breen said he was revisiting the code to allow "prudent treatment" of sexual aberration. "In keeping with the culture, mores and values of our time, homosexuality and other sexual aberrations may now be treated with care, discretion and restraint" (Bryant, 1997: 38). It was difficult for Breen to write these words.

Anderson's experience had been with a man called Ray (John Granger). It's been years since he saw him, but now Ray starts phoning his home. His wife takes the calls. She wants to know what they're about.

Anderson has to do something about the situation fast. He flies to New York and locates Ray's pimp. He directs him to a queer bar where he thinks Ray will most likely be.

This was inflammatory in itself. The very existence of such places was hardly recognized in the Hollywood of 1962. The fact that Preminger decided to feature one is to his credit, even if the way he did so was highly melodramatic. The bar in question looks more like an opium den than anything else.

It's called Club 602. In the background, Frank Sinatra croons the line "Come to me and be what I need you to be" in a vague allusion toward sexual diversity. Spotlights in this den of iniquity expose men in makeup, some of them black. "In 1962," one critic observed, "movies were still portraying segregation in public places, but Preminger's nightmare land is an equal-opportunity place for losers" (Barrios, 2003: 312).

Preminger could have set the scene in ancient Greece or in Sodom and Gomorrah. The ambience is deliberately repellent. Here, as Parker Tyler noted, one can feel superior to the gay man, can "fluff him off as one of the *declassés*, the 'unfortunates' of social prejudice" (Tyler, 1973: 67).

Anderson runs out of the bar. Ray follows him. He tries to excuse his blackmailing of him, telling him he needs the money. They argue on the street, and a scuffle ensues. Anderson flees away from him in a taxi and then gets a flight back to Washington. But he can't handle what's happened, or the scandal he's sure it's going to cause. He sees his career as finished, so his life is too. When he gets to Washington, he slashes his throat.

Why is he so shocked by what he saw in the bar? He has gay tendencies himself even if he's been sublimating them, or has "outgrown" them in his marriage. His disgust seems like a kind of homophobia—from a gay man. He's behaving like someone who doesn't know what gay men do, who's shell-shocked by seeing so many of them together in one room. They're not being unduly intimate with one another. It's really his own sexuality he's disgusted by; he sees himself in them.

Was the scene exploitative or a brave move by Preminger? Perhaps both. He overplayed it, but maybe that was the price 1962 audiences had to pay for it. Nuance would come later. For now, seeing the handsome Murray having an alternative sexual orientation was enough to be going on with. If it was tokenistic and had melodramatic overtones, so be it. The surprise, as Dr. Johnson once said of a dog standing on its hind legs, wasn't that it was done badly but that it was done at all.

Gay characters weren't prominent in films at this time, but the blackmail aspect of the plot—no more than in the British release, *Victim* (1961)—made it into a storyline rather than an issue. Hollywood seemed more comfortable with that. It meant it didn't have to have "the conversation" about being gay. It was safely contained within the plot.

These two films pointed to an important statistic: a huge number of blackmail victims were gay men. Exposure could lead to the loss of their jobs and their social standing. In the case of Murray and Dirk Bogarde from *Victim*, it would most likely lead to the end of their marriages too. Blackmailers also knew they could tap into a queer person's poor self-image at this time.

"To rob blackmail of its potency," Quentin Crisp opined, "it would be necessary to remove the homosexual's feeling of shame. This no power on earth can do" (Bailey, 2001: 126). In other words, blackmailers of queer people had an important ally in their crime: the person they were blackmailing.

The film makes an interesting partner piece to *The Best Man*, another Henry Fonda film made two years later. This also has the whiff of a gay scandal lurking around the corridors of power.

Related Films
Victim (1961); *The Best Man* (1964).

Further Reading
Bailey, Paul, ed. 2001. *The Stately Homo: A Celebration of the Life of Quentin Crisp*. London: Black Swan.
Barrios, Richard. 2003. *Screened Out: Playing Gay in Hollywood from Edison to Stonewall*. New York and London: Routledge.
Bryant, Wayne M. 1997. *Bisexual Characters in Film: From Anais to Zee*. New York and London: Harrington Park Press.
Drury, Allen. 1977. *Advise and Consent*. West Chesterfield, MA: Franklin Library.

Frischauer, Willi. 1974. *Behind the Scenes of Otto Preminger.* New York: William Morrow & Co.
Pratley, Gerard. 1971. *The Cinema of Otto Preminger.* New York: A&S Barnes.
Tyler, Parker. 1973. *Screening the Sexes: Homosexuality in the Movies.* Garden City, NY: Anchor Books.

AIDS

Queer people—and a minor number of heterosexual people—were dying of AIDS starting in the early 1980s, but it wasn't until Rock Hudson contracted it in 1985 that the media started talking about it.

Hudson's death gave AIDS a celebrity face. Before that it was as taboo a subject as being gay itself. Now that someone beloved by the masses had passed away from it, it rose in prominence.

Then the silence turned to paranoia. After Hudson died, almost overnight AIDS went from the disease nobody had to the one everyone might get. People worried that it could be contracted from shaking hands with someone or kissing them, never mind having sex.

Rabid homophobes saw being gay as the disease and AIDS as the cure. Almost overnight, people started to shy away from queer actors, or those suspected of being so. Contracts were canceled and parts lost. Even cursory physical contact became something to be dreaded.

Some of the paranoia made its way onto cinema screens. In *Down and Out in Beverly Hills* (1986), Bette Midler's character is shocked to see her husband giving mouth-to-mouth resuscitation to a homeless man who's tried to commit suicide in their swimming pool, terrified that he'll pick up the virus from him. "Don't touch him!" she cries in a panic. If there was any chance closeted stars such as Anthony Perkins or Liberace would come out of the closet, AIDS put paid to that notion, pushing them further back inside it because of the fear factor surrounding it. And, by extension, being queer. (Both of these men would die of the disease in time.)

It was inevitable that Hollywood would make films about it at some stage. When it did, they came in all shapes and sizes: the good, the bad, and the ugly. One of them—generally regarded as a good one—had started filming before Hudson died. It was an NBC film with Aidan Quinn called *An Early Frost* (1985). He played a lawyer who contracts it. The treatment was tasteful and sensitive.

Buddies (1985) focused on the relationship between an AIDS patient and the volunteer assigned to treat him by the local outreach group. The patient is a queer activist who sees the volunteer as someone who minds him more from duty than care, but as the film goes on they develop a close relationship.

Robert Epstein and Jeffrey Friedman codirected *Common Threads: Stories from the Quilt* in 1989. This was a no-holds-barred documentary chronicling the early days of the disease told from the perspective of various people suffering from it. It unreservedly blames the government for its inaction. The film chronicles the diverse fates of an Olympic athlete, a drug addict, a naval commander, a

And the Band Played On (1993)

Roger Spottiswoode directed this 141-minute TV movie based on Randy Shilts's 620-page history of AIDS. The script had numerous rewrites and went through two directors (Joel Schumacher and Richard Pierce) before Spottiswoode came on board. It chronicled government inaction around the disease, and subsequent red tape. According to the film, 300,000 cases of AIDS had been reported in the United States by 1993. Nearly two-thirds of those afflicted had died. And yet people were saying there was no crisis.

Spottiswoode focused on the internecine squabbles that went on between blood banks and officials in the early days of AIDS research, as well as the way the people who could have done so much more to halt the spread of the disease dragged their heels for no good reason.

He asked Richard Gere to take part in the film. Film stars didn't usually appear on TV when they were in the prime of their career, but he made an exception for this. Once he was on board, others—including Steve Martin, Alan Alda, Anjelica Huston, and Lily Tomlin—followed suit.

Spottiswoode, like Shilts, traced the origins of the virus. (Did an airline employee carry it from Africa?) He spent years trying to get his film onto the screen, and then when he did he found it wasn't approved of by either Shilts or the gay groups who previewed it. The film was taken away from him in the cutting room, so we have no way of knowing if the people who reworked it made it better or worse. Spottiswoode insisted they sanitized it. One sensed an element of bitterness in his attitude, perhaps caused by the shabby manner in which he felt he was treated after putting his heart and soul into the project over so many years. Spottiswoode wasn't even allowed to show his version at the Cannes Film Festival.

And the Band Played On was earnest and thorough, but it's perhaps more of interest as an informative tract than a human one. The various stories it conscientiously examines tend to overbulk the project with facts and figures. Spottiswoode might have been better employed to treat fewer cases in more detail.

---

gay activist, and an 11-year-old hemophiliac as Epstein and Friedman weave the "common threads" together using the Names Project AIDS Memorial Quilt as the metaphorical link.

Brad Davis, who starred in Alan Parker's blitzkrieg film *Midnight Express* (1978), died of AIDS in 1991 at the age of 41, thus cutting short a career that had many highlights and looked set to have even better ones if fate hadn't dealt him such a cruel hand. Before he died, he issued a broadside against Hollywood that shocked many with its bitterness. "I work in an industry," he blasted, "which professes to care very much about the fight against AIDS, giving umpteen benefits and charity affairs, but in actual fact if an actor is even rumored to be HIV-positive he gets no support on an individual basis—he does not work" (Murray, 1994: 188). Davis wasn't queer, as his widow was at pains to point out. He was often thought to be so because of his health situation, combined with the fact that he'd played a gay man in Rainer Maria Fassbinder's *Querelle* in 1982.

In *The Living End* (1992), Gregg Araki's black comedy about AIDS, two characters suffering from the disease speculate about the possibility of going to the White House and injecting the president with the virus so to speed up measures to help cure it. In *Peter's Friends* (1992), a group of university friends get together on New Year's Eve after a ten-year hiatus and catch up on the way their lives have gone in the interim. The film ends with one of them, Stephen Fry, dropping the bombshell that he has AIDS before the night is out.

Philadelphia (1993) was the first major movie to be made about AIDS. Tom Hanks played a lawyer who takes his employers to court for unjustly sacking him. His bosses claim he was sacked for incompetence, but he suspects the fact that he's suffering from the disease has been behind it. He employs an attorney, Joe Miller (Denzel Washington), to plead his case. Miller is homophobic. "These people make me sick," he barks. Nonetheless, he believes his client has been wronged. Jonathan Demme directed.

Hanks said he made the film not for any agitprop reasons but simply because he thought it was "a great part with a great director" (Trakin, 1995: 173). He threw himself into it with dedication, losing thirty pounds for the role and talking to a number of AIDS victims to try to understand their plight better.

That said, there were problems with it. Hanks and his lover (Antonio Banderas) are never seen kissing, for instance, and Washington's "conversion," accelerated by watching Hanks do a "dance of death" mime to Maria Callas's "La Mama Morta" from the opera *Andrea Chénier*, seems too contrived. Could an intolerant person become gay-friendly this easily?

AIDS: Words From One to Another came out in 1994. Two years later, *It's My Party* was released. Penelope Cruz played a HIV-positive nun who was pregnant in Pedro Almodovar's *All about My Mother* in 2002. In 2005, we had *3 Needles*. *Rent* (2005) dealt with bohemians in New York struggling with AIDS. *Life Support* (2007) was a TV movie starring Queen Latifah as a drug user who became an AIDS activist in the black community after she was diagnosed as being HIV-positive.

We Were Here (2010) was a documentary on the impact of AIDS in San Francisco during the first years of the pandemic. Matthew McConaughey gave an Oscar-winning performance in *Dallas Buyers Club* (2013) as an AIDS patient trying to get others the medication they need after he's diagnosed. *The Normal Heart* (2014) dealt with a gay activist raising awareness of AIDS in the 1990s. The same theme featured in *120 Beats Per Minute* (2017), which centered on the advocacy group ACT UP in Paris demanding action by the government and pharmaceutical companies in the early nineties.

Related Films
Killer in the Village (1983); *AIDS* (1985); *The AIDS Show: Activists Involved with Death and Survival* (1986); *Parting Glances* (1986); *A Death in the Family* (1987); *Living with AIDS* (1989); *They Are Lost to Vision Altogether* (1989); *Absolutely Positive* (1990); *Longtime Companion* (1990); *Voices from the Front* (1990); *Our Sons* (1991); *Savage Nights* (1992); *Living Proof: HIV and the Pursuit of Happiness* (1993); *Boys on the Side* (1995); *The Cure* (1995); *A Mother's Prayer* (1995); *In the Gloaming* (1997); *Our Brothers, Our Sons* (2001); *The Hours* (2002); *Beat the Drum* (2003); *Girl Positive* (2007); *Life Support* (2007).

Further Reading
Creekmur, Corey K., and Alexander Doty. 1995. *Out in Culture*. London: Cassell.
Gever, Martha, Pratibha Parmar, and John Greyson. 1993. *Queer Looks*. New York: HarperCollins.

Murray, Raymond. 1994. *Images in the Dark: An Encyclopedia of Gay and Lesbian Film and Video*. Philadelphia: TLA Publications.

Shilts, Randy. 2011. *And the Band Played On: Politics, People and the AIDS Epidemic*. London: Souvenir Books.

Trakin, Roy, 1995. *Journey to Stardom*. London: Virgin.

All about Eve (1950)

Bette Davis was a gay icon long before *All about Eve* was made but the film solidified that status for her. In fact it became its emblematic testimony, at least after *What Ever Happened to Baby Jane* (1962). In Margo Channing—a character who was most likely modeled on the bisexual woman Tallulah Bankhead—she received the ideal opportunity to unleash her acidic bile.

A full-frontal attack on the dog-eat-dog world of show business delivered in an array of razor-sharp exchanges, this high-octane movie that bisected the century seemed to signal a more open attack on entrenched norms in its latter half. Coming hot on the heels of *Sunset Boulevard* (1950), it served as a corollary to that equally pulverizing requiem for Tinseltown's not-so-tender mercies.

The film is called *All about Eve*, but in some ways this is a misnomer as viewers learn very little about Eve (Anne Baxter) beyond what she does. Her actions—attempting to destroy Channing's love life and career—define her.

Is she a lesbian? Her sexual orientation is kept under wraps for most of the movie, but in the last scene director Joseph L. Mankiewicz, who advised Baxter to play Eve *like* a lesbian, "comes out" with this true intent. In this scene she returns from an awards ceremony to find an admirer, Phoebe (Barbara Bates), in her living room. At first she's startled. She picks up the phone to ring the police, but when Phoebe explains that she's the president of Eve's fan club, she puts it down. The pair then begin to talk, Phoebe eagerly asking questions about all aspects of Eve's life. Eve lights up a cigarette and stars to show an interest in Phoebe beyond that of an actress to a fan. She says to Phoebe, "It's after one. You won't get home till all hours," with a "hint of expectation" in her voice (White, 1999: 213). Phoebe trills enticingly, "I don't care if I never get home."

Before the film ends, Phoebe has already placed herself in Eve's shoes, admiring herself in front of her mirror as she dons her evening cape and holds one of her acting awards aloft. She bows; the wheel has come full circle; the backstabber is about to be stabbed in the back.

How could Eve fall for the same kind of trap she'd just laid for Margo, having somebody line themselves up to betray her? It's the one moment in the film where she steps out of character and lets her defenses down.

What Eve did to Margo is probably going to be done to her by Phoebe. She's going to ruin her career, if not her sex life, by appropriating it for herself. This is her punishment for being so self-aggrandizing. Once again an "evil lesbian" will get her comeuppance on screen as Mankiewicz plays into the common tradition. But at least she doesn't die at the end, the fate of so many of her predecessors.

One of Channing's most famous lines in the film is, "I hate men." Another one is, "Fasten your seat belts, it's going to be a bumpy night." Maybe Eve could have said that to Phoebe in the last scene as well—if she were allowed.

Mankiewicz, who would also direct another camp classic, *Suddenly, Last Summer* (1959), was straight himself but said, "Male behavior is so elementary that *All about Adam* could be done as a short" (Staggs, 2001: 242). He also said, "Men react as they're taught to react, in a 'manly' way. Women are, by comparison, as if assembled by the wind" (Colombo, 1980: 152). Statements like these, for author Sam Staggs, made Mankiewicz resemble "a heterosexual trapped in a gay sensibility." Bemused by the number of heterosexual cast members present and correct here, Staggs asked, "When did so many Hollywood straights ever create such a gay entertainment?" (Staggs, 2001: 242).

Eve doesn't fall into the pattern of other film lesbians from this decade. Unlike them, she isn't mannish in her ways. Her femininity was more dangerous to Hollywood on that account. She was attractive to men and therefore more dangerous to homophobic people. Here was a lesbian who might "corrupt" female members of the audience who were latent lesbians. And who might corrupt Margo.

The film, Robert Corber wrote, "underwrites a homophobic construction of female homosocial desire." Margo's attraction to other women makes her "vulnerable to the manipulations of the predatory lesbian, Eve" (Corber, 2011: 132).

Margo's lesbian tendencies are sometimes coded, like in the scene where she wears only one earring at an airport, having mislaid the other one in her dressing room. But her language, and its husky delivery, is straight out of Bankhead, making one hardly surprised that so many drag queens have portrayed Channing in their lives.

Davis played many roles on film that Bankhead had done on stage, such as *Dark Victory* (1939) and *The Little Foxes* (1941), but she met her only once. It was at a party given by Jack Warner. Most of the guests had left when Bankhead approached her. "Dahling," she crowed, "you've played all the parts I've played, and I was so much better." Davis replied, "I agree with you, Miss Bankhead." She knew she was spoiling for a fight and refused to accede to that (Staggs, 2001: 218–9).

When Bankhead was asked if she'd seen *All about Eve*, she snorted, "Every morning when I brush my teeth." After seeing the actual film, she said of Davis, "If I ever get hold of that hag I'll tear every hair out of her mustache" (Jarski, 2000: 151). Bankhead's resemblance to Davis, as one writer put it, "queered" her character. It also reinforced the lesbian subtext of her relationship with Eve (Corber, 2011: 39).

Besides Davis, there were many other interesting women in the cast—Thelma Ritter's pragmatic Birdie, Celeste Holm, and, of course, Marilyn Monroe in an early cameo. They also enjoyed George Sanders. As the waspish critic Addison DeWitt, he resembled a latter-day Oscar Wilde. At one point DeWitt is referred to as "that venomous fishwife." He tells Eve they share contempt for humanity. Sanders would eventually commit suicide. So would Monroe and Bates. The film, as a result, was labeled a "triple suicide" movie.

Clifton Webb, a well-known Hollywood queen, was originally thought of for DeWitt. Sanders carried the effeteness of the gossipmonger equally adeptly. Both he and Eve act as the villains of the piece: they like each other because they see themselves as mirror images of their mutual disregard for others. DeWitt speaks of his "inability to love or be loved," a common code for the celluloid gay "introvert," while Eve is the cold lesbian figure who'll make it to the top any which way. "Eisenhower isn't half the man you are," DeWitt informed her in a line subsequently excised from the script (Barrios, 2003: 225).

Related Films
Sunset Boulevard (1950); *Stardust: The Bette Davis Story* (2006); *Queer Icon: The Cult of Bette Davis* (2010).

Further Reading
Barrios, Richard. 2003. *Screened Out: Playing Gay in Hollywood from Edison to Stonewall*. New York and London: Routledge.
Colombo, John Robert, ed. 1980. *Wit and Wisdom of the Moviemakers*. London: Hamlyn.
Corber, Robert J. 2011. *Cold War Femme: Lesbianism, National Identity and Hollywood Cinema*. Durham, NC, and London: Duke University Press.
Darren, Alison, 2000. *Lesbian Film Guide*. London and New York: Cassell.
Jarski, Rosemarie, ed. 2000. *Hollywood Wit: Classic Hollywood Quips and Quotes*. London: Prion.
Staggs, Sam. 2001. *All about* All about Eve. New York: St. Martin's Griffin.
White, Patricia. 1999. *Uninvited: Classical Hollywood Cinema and Lesbian Representability*. Bloomington: Indiana University Press.

Dorothy Arzner (1897–1979)

Arzner is an unusual figure for New Queer Film theorists in the sense that, while her demeanor could be read as "lesbian," her films, with few exceptions, seemed to ally themselves to a more conventional heterosexual zeitgeist. One might even describe them as sentimental.

Was this because she wanted to take attention away from her orientation? To deflect suspicions of it? By flying under the radar in a male-dominated industry, she managed to carve out a prolific career and still avoid being outed—and possibly thrown on the celluloid scrapheap as a result.

She wore garçon-style outfits in the French style, "garçon" being French for "boy." This was construed either as a lesbian statement or an attempt to de-sexualize herself. It could have been an example of what today we would call "power dressing." The same could be said of her tendency to wear her hair close cropped.

The press was complimentary about her dress and discreet about her sexuality. Here's an example: "Miss Arzner wears tailored clothes, low-heeled shoes. Her bob is mannish, her hair dark and frosted with silver. She's unmarried, probably because no man has been able to overcome the fascination of her work" (Mann, 2001: 74).

Her first assignment was as a script girl for Alla Nazimova, with whom she was alleged to have had an affair. She made *Fashions for Women* in 1927, starring

Esther Ralston. Ralston said she resented some of the sexual scenes Arzner asked her to do: "The photographing of my backside and the display of my legs just wasn't me" (Mann, 69). Two years later she directed *The Wild Party*, starring the "It girl" Clara Bow.

Her contract at Paramount expired in 1932 and wasn't renewed. The forthcoming Depression hinted. So did the dreaded Production Code. This severely curtailed her freedom of expression as it banned anything smacking of sex. Despite the success of her last film, *Merrily We Go to Hell*, she wasn't in a strong enough position to battle such negative forces. She took her punishment and moved to RKO.

Katharine Hepburn starred in Arzner's *Christopher Strong* in 1933. Way ahead of its time, it had Hepburn as a female pilot embroiled in an affair with a married politician. She dresses like a man—like Arzner—in the film and espouses pre-feminist ideas. Her decision to commit suicide at the end, as William J. Mann observed, is as much due to her decision not to compromise her career as it is not to compromise her love (Mann, 71).

Hepburn didn't get on with Arzner. Judith Mayne wrote in her biography of her that she complained to David O. Selznick, the producer of the film, that Hepburn was trying to interfere with her direction of it (Mayne, 1994: 60). When Arzner received a Director's Guild tribute in 1975, Hepburn wrote her a telegram that read, "Isn't it wonderful you've had such a great career when you had no right to have a career at all?" Such a comment sounded homophobic, but Hepburn didn't mean it that way. She was merely being cheeky in her congratulations. James Robert Parish wrote that the intended compliment came out the wrong way because of Hepburn's penchant for biting candor (Parish, 2003: 138).

In 1940 she directed *Dance, Girl, Dance*, a Maureen O'Hara/Lucille Ball offering that had a controversial scene featuring O'Hara lambasting a primarily male audience for undressing her with their eyes. She refers to "The Look" in her tirade. It's a landmark scene in a film that didn't have too much else to distinguish it. "I know you'd like me to take off my clothes," she rasps at the men in attendance, "so you can look your fifty cents' worth. Fifty cents for the privilege of staring at a girl your wives won't let you. What's it for? So you can go home when the show's over and strut before your wives and play at being the stronger sex for a minute? I'm sure they see through you like we do."

If this speech contains the substance of Arzner's feelings about the sexual objectification of women in Hollywood, she never expressed such ideas herself, adopting a more laid-back attitude to men throughout her life. In an interview she did long after she retired, she railed against the fact that most of the good-quality roles in films went to men, the women being relegated to "darned sappy" ones (*New York Times*, August 20, 1976). But by and large she kept her opinions to herself.

In *The Celluloid Closet*, Vito Russo quotes Robert Aldrich talking about his fellow director James Whale. Whale refused to stay in the closet and lost his career as a result. He knew he was a talented director, but once he presented himself as openly gay his cinematic goose was effectively cooked. After his career meltdown, he grew depressed. In 1961 he was found dead at the bottom of his swimming pool. To this day, nobody knows if it was an accident or not. Arzner, according to Aldrich, didn't suffer like Whale did because she played the Hollywood game. She became "one of the boys" (Russo, 1987: 50). Judith Mayne, in her biography of Arzner, took issue with Aldrich's language here. Calling her "one of the boys," she argued, equated lesbians with women in drag. It imputed that they looked at other women the way heterosexual men looked at women (Mayne, 1994: 64).

Arzner lived with Marion Morgan, a dancer and choreographer—she did the choreography for many of Arzner's films—for over forty years. Morgan was sixteen years older than her. She'd also been married, and had a child. Their relationship publicized Arzner's orientation and Morgan's bisexuality, and yet nobody disapproved of it in the film industry, at least publicly. There was less suggestiveness in two women living together than two men. Morgan's marriage also acted like a cover, even though it was over.

Arzner left few clues as to the exact nature of their relationship. One can only presume it was a loving one from the affectionate postcards that were exchanged between herself and Morgan when Morgan went on vacation, which she did often. There's little else to go on. In any photographs taken of the two of them together, they look like a pair involved in an intimate relationship.

Related Films
Fashions for Women (1927); *The Wild Party* (1929); *Anybody's Woman* (1930); *Honor Among Lovers* (1931); *Merrily We Go to Hell* (1932); *Christopher Strong* (1933); *Nana* (1934); *Dance, Girl Dance* (1941); *First Comes Courage* (1943).

Further Reading
Acker, Ally. 1991. *Reel Women: Pioneers of the Cinema, 1896 to the Present.* London: B. T. Batsford.
Beauchamp, Cari. 1997. *Without Lying Down: Frances Marion and the Powerful Women of Early Hollywood.* Berkeley, Los Angeles, and London: University of California Press.
Cook, Pam. 1975. *The Work of Dorothy Arzner: Towards a Feminist Cinema.* London: British Film Institute.
Mann, William J. 2001. *Behind the Screen: How Gays and Lesbians Shaped Hollywood, 1910–1969.* New York: Viking.
Mayne, Judith. 1994. *Directed by Dorothy Arzner.* Bloomington and Indianapolis: Indiana University Press.
New York Times, August 20, 1976.
Parish, James Robert. 2003. *Hollywood Divas: The Good, the Bad and the Fabulous.* New York: Contemporary Books.
Rosen, Marjorie. 1973. *Popcorn Venus: Women, Movies and the American Dream.* New York: Avon Books.
Russo, Vito. 1987. *The Celluloid Closet: Homosexuality in the Movies.* New York: Harper & Row.
Smith, Sharon. 1975. *Women Who Make Movies.* New York: Hopkinson and Blake.

B

Tallulah Bankhead (1902–68)

"There are only three people in England who are front-page news," Lord Beaverbrook said once. "The Prince of Wales, George Bernard Shaw, and Tallulah Bankhead" (Braun, 2002: 55). Named after a waterfall, Bankhead lived her life like a force of nature as well, dropping wit like a female Oscar Wilde. "Have you ever been mistaken for a man?" a reporter with a falsetto voice asked her once. "No," she replied. "Have you?" (Murray, 1994: 159).

Bankhead's mother died giving birth to her, so she was raised by her grandmother. She won a beauty contest as a teenager, and the prize was a role in a motion picture. She started her career in silent movies, but when the talkies came in she graduated easily to them thanks to her droll and smoky voice. She didn't like Hollywood, however, preferring to live in New York and act on Broadway instead of on the screen.

She returned to Hollywood in 1943 to make a guest appearance in *Stage Door Canteen*, a propaganda movie for the soldiers of World War II. Alfred Hitchcock's *Lifeboat* followed soon after that. She got on famously with Hitchcock, who enjoyed her after-dinner stories.

A social butterfly, Bankhead lived her life largely in the public eye, which means many of her witticisms have been preserved for posterity. "I have three phobias," she confessed, "which, could I mute them, would make my life as slick as a sonnet but as dull as ditch water. I hate to go to bed, I hate to be alone" (Winokur, 1992: 110). She also said, "I'm bored to the point of suicide when I'm not in love" (Brian, 1980: 16).

She married once but it didn't last. Her wandering eye saw to that. She echoed Mae West's "I used to be Snow White but I drifted" with her, "My heart is as pure as the driven slush" (Roth, 1995: 51). Claiming to be "ambisextrous," she was never quite sure what gender her bed partners were going to be (Braun, 2002: 58). There were rumors of her being intimate with Patsy Kelly, an openly lesbian actress, as well as Barbara Stanwyck and Greta Garbo.

She told Joan Crawford one day, to Crawford's horror, "I've had an affair with your husband. You'll be next." Crawford had just married Douglas Fairbanks Jr. at the time. "I'm so sorry, Miss Bankhead," she muttered apologetically, "but I just love men" (Brian, 1980: 68). Bankhead said to Ginger Rogers, "Any husband of yours is a husband of mine." Rogers wasn't amused by the remark (Hadleigh, 1999: 137).

Asked where her lesbian leanings came from, she offered this "explanation": "Father warned me about men but he never said anything about women" (Jarski,

2000: 286). Her attraction to women became accentuated when she drank or took drugs. When she stayed away from these, she usually confined herself to the opposite sex.

"She was a strikingly beautiful young woman," wrote her biographer Denis Brian, "with the manners of a southern belle, the language of a drill sergeant, the daring of a trapeze artist and the talent to become the greatest actress of her time. But for Tallulah life was the thing, not the play" (Brian, 1980: front matter).

Such a life, lived from the ground up, took its toll on that beauty relatively early on, but she laughed this off too. "The less I behave like Whistler's mother," she lamented, "the more I look like her the next morning" (Brian, 7).

Bankhead never balked at other people's reaction to her behavior. Maybe she even invited negative responses. Neither did she balk at being seen as having a masculine image. A radio program that she presented on NBC in 1950 always ended with her musical director saying, "Thank you, Miss Bankhead, sir!" This didn't bother her in the slightest (Corber, 2011: 46).

She died of pneumonia complicated by emphysema just a month short of her sixty-seventh birthday, leaving behind a fortune of $2 million. Her last words were reputed to be, "Codeine! Bourbon!" (Parish, 2003: 12). Shortly before her death, she said, "The only thing I regret about my past is the length of it. If I had to live my live over again I'd make all the same mistakes—only sooner" (Jarski, 2000: 144).

Related Films
Stage Door Canteen (1943); *Lifeboat* (1944); *A Royal Scandal* (1945); *Main Street to Broadway* (1953); *Fanatic* (1965).

Further Reading
Braun, Eric. 2002. *Frightening the Horses: Gay Icons of the Cinema.* London: Reynolds & Hearn.

Brian, Denis. 1980. *Tallulah, Darling: A Biography of Tallulah Bankhead.* New York: Macmillan.

Corber, Robert J. 2011. *Cold War Femme: Lesbianism, National Identity and Hollywood Cinema.* Durham, NC, and London: Duke University Press.

Hadleigh, Boze, ed. 1999. *Hollywood Bitch.* London: Robson.

Hadleigh, Boze, ed. 2000. *In or Out: Gay and Straight Celebrities Talk about Themselves and Each Other.* New York: Barricade.

Jarski, Rosemarie, ed. 2000. *Hollywood Wit.* London: Prion.

Jarski, Rosemarie, ed. 2007. *Grumpy Old Wit.* London: Ebury.

McLellan, Diana. 2001. *The Girls: Sappho Goes to Hollywood.* London: Robson.

Murray, Raymond. 1994. *Images in the Dark: An Encyclopedia of Gay and Lesbian Film and Video.* Philadelphia: TLA Publications.

Parish, James Robert. 2003. *Hollywood Divas: The Good, the Bad and the Fabulous.* Chicago: Contemporary Books.

Roth, K. Madsen. 1995. *Hollywood Wits.* New York: Avon Books.

Summers, Claude J., ed. 2005. *The Queer Encyclopedia of Film & Television.* San Francisco: Cleis Publishing.

Winokur, Jon, ed. 1992. *True Confessions: The World's Most Famous People Reveal Their Intimate Secrets.* London: Victor Gollancz.

Basic Instinct (1992)

Sharon Stone didn't do much for LGBTQ morale when she played a bisexual killer in this kitschy sizzler which was scripted by Joe Eszterhas. It was helmed by Paul Verhoeven, who would soon make the critically panned *Showgirls* (1995). The part required her to reject her lesbian lover Roxy (Leilani Sarelle) when she decides to bed lascivious, ex-alcoholic cop Nick (Michael Douglas)—at least until he's outlived his usefulness as fodder for her books. She's an author by trade.

Outraged members of GLAAD picketed the production almost from day one, all too well aware of the incendiary nature of the material. Verhoeven and Eszterhas protested that their intentions were honorable. Stone, for her part, uncrossed her legs, cut her ice, and cooed, content in the realization that after all these years knocking on the door of fame, she'd arrived. The pneumatic psychopath that was Catherine Tramell was finally going to help her make the crossover from the anodyne performer she'd been up to this to a serious actress employed for her ability rather than her looks.

The protest groups carried banners saying, "Catherine did it!" to spoil the surprise for those standing in line to see what advertisers were touting as the whodunit of the year. But not even these could drive them away.

The word was out that almost every scene was a firecracker and nothing was going to dent that. As the saying goes, there's no such thing as bad publicity. For every member of GLAAD who went to the press with grievances, Verhoeven and Eszterhas focused instead on the extra tickets they knew they could sell on account of that.

GLAAD activists railed about the fact that the story reinforced negative stereotypes about lesbians because of their association with murder here. The idea of putting a queer disclaimer on the movie was considered, but Douglas didn't think this was a good idea. If they went down that road, he believed, every film with a killer, queer or straight, would have had to have had a disclaimer. Verhoeven said it was about evil in general rather than evil gay people. Everyone was quoting scripture for their purpose. Eszterhas was asked to rewrite the script, but he refused.

The film presented a world where lesbian and bisexual women hated straight men enough to want to kill them. For GLAAD representatives, this was unalloyed homophobia. Stone disagreed: "My character is sociopathic and motivated by power. Gender choice is a secondary and irrelevant issue for her" (Thompson, 1994: 122).

Stone was more bothered by some intricate details in the sex scenes between herself and Douglas. Verhoeven wanted her to react to Douglas's lovemaking extremely eagerly, but she told him this wasn't the way women behaved in real life. Stone's mother had a different kind of problem with the movie. According to Stone, she said the most shocking thing about it was that people were more concerned about whether or not she was a bisexual lesbian than the fact that she was a serial killer (Thompson, 169).

Rich Jennings, the executive director of GLAAD, initially thought Verhoeven was going to be sympathetic to the bisexual theme, but he soon learned he was

Basic Instinct 2: Risk Addiction (2006)

Hollywood's philosophy has always been: never break a winning formula. And so it came to pass that in 2006 viewers were treated to this potentially appetizing sequel.

Michael Douglas failed to reappear, David Thewlis filling in for him. This wasn't surprising as the original film made Sharon Stone rich and famous. Douglas received much less publicity from it.

Something similar happened with *Speed*, the film that made Sandra Bullock's name in 1994. Keanu Reeves didn't appear in the sequel. At least that came about three years later. The people behind *Basic Instinct* waited a whole fourteen years, which is never a good idea for a sequel. Time is of the essence for this type of film. One has to catch the ball on the bounce.

Viewers arguably get the films they deserve just like they get the politicians they deserve. This was made because there was a market for it rather than any other reason. Flawed and all as the original was, at least it had drama. *Basic Instinct 2* lacked this quality. It also had a questionable director in Michael Caton-Jones. (Paul Verhoeven followed Douglas in his refusal to have anything to do with the film.)

It was set in London. This was seen as a mistake because the target audience was primarily American. Stone's latest lover is played by Stan Collymore, a soccer player in real life. The fact that he wasn't a professional actor was something else that worked against the film's credibility. David Morrissey played her psychiatrist. He wasn't well-known either. It was a second-string cast all around.

The Village Voice praised the original for being a distillation of a late eighties/early nineties zeitgeist: "The end of second wave feminism, the peaking of AIDS anxieties, the dawning of the Clinton years." The sequel, it alleged, wasn't even "accidentally relevant" (Eszterhas, 2000: 103).

The franchise ended with this offering. It was time for Catherine to put the ice cubes back.

Further Reading

Eszterhas, Joe, 2000. *Hollywood Animal*. London: Arrow.

---

going flat out for sensationalistic trash. Afterward the GLAAD protestors took to the streets with placards proclaiming Douglas to be racist, sexist, and antigay. Some of them paint-bombed the set (Thompson, 117).

Stone came in for just as much abuse, which surprised her. "I was a model before I worked as an actress," she explained, "and the gay community is an active part of the fashion business. Many of my dating experiences included me, my date, and a gay couple. I was sensitive to issues that would concern gay people, so the flap over *Basic Instinct* was beyond comprehension. My perception of the lesbian relationship in the film was that it was a pure, loving one. At the same time, Catherine was clearly not a lesbian. She was a party girl" (Thompson, 117). The sentiments expressed here seem to overlook the toxic nature of the plot. Stone went on to suggest that she had semi-lesbian experiences herself. "I've never had sex with a woman," she said, "but I've been on dates with a woman" (Hadleigh, 1999: 136).

GLAAD sent letters to film critics claiming that no major Hollywood studio had ever produced a film featuring a lesbian or bisexual protagonist with positive and redeeming qualities. They said the film was lesbophobic because the bisexual at its core was a psychotic killer. Douglas organized a fund-raiser for AIDS organizations on the set, but this was regarded as a defensive move by GLAAD that avoided the issue in a cosmetic, politically correct gesture. "Somebody has to be the bad guy." Douglas protested, "and it can't always be the Italians." (The Italians were frequent villains in films, especially Mafia ones.) Tammy Price, the president of the LA branch of the National Organization for Women, claimed lesbians used their orientations to both provoke and titillate men in equal measure (Thompson, 121).

Tramell, meanwhile, thrilled audiences—and Nick—with her seduce-and-destroy credo, kissing the same way she killed. Verhoeven, as ever, was going for the Friday night drive-in audience who would chew on their popcorn and roar at the screen and/or sit terrified in their seats.

Nick's refusal to acknowledge the fact that being lesbian exists as a legitimate sexual orientation comes out in the Freudian slip he's guilty of when he tells Catherine he's going to confront Leilani "man-to-man" to drive her away from her.

Not everyone despised Stone's portrayal of her character. Judith Halberstam expressed the view that at least she was assertive: "I'd rather see lesbians depicted as outlaws and destroyers than cozy, feminine, domestic, tame lovers" (Davies, 2008: 127). B. Ruby Rich, a well-known commentator on New Queer Cinema, wrote: "I crossed the picket line on opening night. I loved the movie and wondered why, with half a dozen films in the multiplex showing men murdering women, I was expected to boycott the only one in which a woman killed men instead" (Rich, 2013: 105).

Katharine Hepburn thought it was a new low for women in films when one had to wonder what an actress had between her ears than between her legs (Jarski, 2000: 207). It was a moot point. *Basic Instinct* did little for the dignity of women, either straight or queer. For Douglas, who'd also appeared in other films that seemed to devalue women, like *Fatal Attraction*, it was more of the same.

In one scene he tells Catherine she's the epitome of what a sexual conquest should be: a woman to die for. Judging by the film's final moments, she's going to make him do just that.

Related Films
In the Eyes of a Stranger (1992); *Single White Female* (1992); *Personal Justice* (1996).

Further Reading
Davies, Steven Paul. 2008. *Out At the Movies: A History of Gay Cinema*. Herts, UK: Kamera Books.
Eliot, Marc. 2013. *Michael Douglas: A Biography*. New York: Three Rivers Press.
Eszterhas, Joe. 2005. *Hollywood Animal*. London: Arrow.
Hadleigh, Boze, ed. 1999. *Hollywood Bitch*. London: Robson.
Jarski, Rosemarie, ed. 2000. *Hollywood Wit*. London: Prion.
Osborne, Richard. 1992. *Basic Instinct*. London and New York: BCA Publications.
Rich, B. Ruby. 2013. *New Queer Cinema: The Director's Cut*. Durham, NC, and London: Duke University Press.
Thompson, Douglas. 1994. *Sharon Stone: Basic Ambition*. London: Little Brown.
Whatling, Clare. 1997. *Screen Dreams: Fantasizing Lesbians in Film*. Manchester, UK, and New York: Manchester University Press.

Before Stonewall (1984)

On June 28, 1969, a cavalcade of drag queens and other gay people finally called time out on their repressed identities as they fought the might of the law. That was the night a Molotov cocktail was thrown at a police car. Other violent acts ensued, leading to three days of rioting in and around the Stonewall Inn, a queer-friendly bar in Greenwich Village. It had traditionally been a familiar port of call for policemen looking for easy arrests. They wouldn't anymore.

Pre-Stonewall, being gay meant being a fifth wheel, a second-class citizen, or a third sex. It meant social stigmas, job discrimination, and possible imprisonment. Post-Stonewall, as codirectors Greta Schiller and Robert Rosenberg make clear in this documentary, it meant the clarion cry of "Out of the closets and into the streets" was heard far and wide. The rioting became world news. It galvanized anger that had been mounting for decades over promises made and broken, over town councils sitting on their hands every time the subject of being gay came up.

Narrated by Rita Mae Brown and released to coincide with the twenty-fifth anniversary of the riots, the film features a wide cross-section of people talking about their experiences. They relate how they had to hide their sexuality throughout their lives for any number of reasons. Some of them didn't even know what they were hiding, being profoundly ignorant of what being gay meant when they were young. They sneaked looks at medical books in bookshops and libraries to try to understand what made them "different."

For these people, denial was the most preferred option, according to the documentary. Declaring oneself gay was a tripwire they didn't feel ready to negotiate. "We didn't even have the *word* 'gay,'" says Harry Hay, cofounder of the Mattachine Society, one of the earliest gay rights organizations in the United States. "All we had was 'temperamental.'"

Gay encounters occurred on the fringes of society in those days. People met near rivers and woods, anywhere hidden away from the public gaze. Unless one lived in a gay-friendly city, intimacy wasn't forthcoming. The "lucky" gays lived in San Francisco on the Barbary Coast or in New Orleans's French Quarter. Or if they were black, in Harlem, which had a larger demographic of black to white.

Subtitled "The Making of a Gay and Lesbian Community," the film traces the development of gay culture from the days of the Depression when, as one speaker says, "You broke the law and lived as best you could."

Oases of comfort were treasured by the disenfranchised. There were gay parties where people drank bathtub gin. Occasionally a voice that threatened the establishment was heard. The black singer Gladys Bentley was one such. She married her girlfriend, an action that was way ahead of its time.

Some lesbian women interviewed in the documentary talk about how they woke up to their sexuality. Reading was one way. Radclyffe Hall's *The Well of Loneliness* created seismic waves when it was published. So did Édouard Bourdet's play *The Captive*, and Oscar Wilde's *Salomé* when it was staged with an all-lesbian cast. In 1930 Magnus Hirschfeld wrote, "Beneath the duality of sex there is a oneness. Every male is potentially a female and every female is potentially a male." These were revolutionary words when they were first spoken. Today we probably regard them as commonplace.

The film touches on the manner in which the rise of Nazism virtually obliterated being gay in Germany in the 1930s. Under Hitler, queer men and lesbian women were targeted by the Nazis and generally became Holocaust victims. From 1933 onward, gay organizations were banned, as were books about being gay. Queer men within the Nazi party itself were executed. The Gestapo put pressure on queer men to conform to the Aryan norm or die. Between 1933 and 1945, an estimated 100,000 queer men were arrested and either imprisoned or sent to concentration camps. Their death rate there was as high as 60 percent, according to statistics from the film. It wasn't until 2002 that the German government apologized to the queer community.

America felt the ripples too. When World War II was declared, many gay men joined the army to "prove" that they were real men. Some of them were distinctly unsuited to it, as the film elucidates. One man couldn't even throw a ball, never mind operate a rifle or a tank. He relates an embarrassing incident of dropping a hand grenade on his foot one day during maneuvers. There were many lesbians in the forces as well. They performed necessary functions and were "tolerated" because of this. But they could never declare themselves as being so. It would take many more decades before such a luxury was afforded them.

The documentary also mentions the impact the biologist Alfred Kinsey had on LGBTQ lives. Kinsey founded the Institute for Sex Research at Indiana University in 1947. He wrote *Sexual Behavior in the Human Male* in 1948 and *Sexual Behavior in the Human Female* five years later. He conducted an extensive survey of sexuality among American men and women and drew some highly revelatory conclusions from his research, his investigations providing evidence that there were over twenty million gay people in the States. Such a statistic changed the perception of being gay profoundly. No longer could such people be seen as a tiny majority, which was the thinking up to this. The HUAC witch hunts conducted by Senator Joseph McCarthy in the 1950s made gay people feel like pariahs. The Soviet Union was alleged to be using them as spies. A connection was drawn between being gay and communism. This made their plight even more pernicious.

People trying to secure government positions were beaten before they began. The documentary makes this clear in a number of anecdotes from people who suffered in such a manner. Those who were already in such positions were frequently outed and dismissed, with no possibility of alternative employment. They were the "lavender" people, the enemies of those who married Stepford wives and raised Stepford children in suburbia.

"Lavender" was a pejorative term at this time, indicating effeminacy in men. It didn't denote queerness then but rather straight men who exhibited female traits. It later became a collective term. Today it's used to denote the hidden lives of LGBTQ people in these restrictive times. There are "lavender" films and "lavender" books testifying to the double life such people had to live to avoid being named and shamed.

Three-bedroom houses sprung up. The biggest worry of the straight people moving into them was how they were going to fit four children into three bedrooms. When the Mattachine Society had its first meetings, it did so with the doors locked and the blinds drawn. At this time it was frowned upon to even discuss being gay. "You didn't think of your rights," one speaker states. "You just slid by."

The first gay magazine published in the United States was called *One*. It was sold under counters, mailed surreptitiously between states to nervous subscribers. In 1956 the Daughters of Bilitis Society was founded for lesbians in San Francisco. A magazine for lesbians called *The Ladder* started up as well. This was also circulated secretly. The Bilitis Society was the first lesbian civil and political rights organization in the country. "We knew we were outside the pale," says lesbian activist Audre Lorde. "We were dykes, the gay girl version of the beatniks."

Another woman tells of not being invited to family gatherings, of her mother tearing up an invitation her brother sent her to attend his wedding. She didn't want a "queer" to be at it. "You tried to look like a boy," the woman says, "so you wouldn't get beaten up."

It wasn't only civilians who engaged in "gay bashing" but the police as well. They arrested gay people on flimsy pretexts, afterward printing their names on public documents, which meant they lost whatever jobs they had. Some policemen engaged in blackmail and extortion at the Black Cat Bar in San Francisco, resulting in the famous "Gayola" trial, but it went nowhere. The accused went unpunished.

In the sixties, Martin Luther King had a dream. His call of "We Shall Overcome" resonated with gay people; they also needed to "overcome" a repressive social hierarchy. This subsequently became allied to the rise of women's liberation. All three civil rights movements worked in unison with one another.

The world was waking up to a new dawn. The right to love oneself was talked about, regardless of one's sexuality. Gay people began to realize their problems weren't in themselves but in the society that spawned them. They started to crack the shield of invisibility that had surrounded them up to now.

The "flower children" of the hippie cult arrived in the late sixties. San Francisco became the city of love. It also became a favored city of gay people because it had a large queer population and was queer-friendly. All of this led to the throwing of the Molotov cocktail on June 28, 1969. It was a date, and an action, that would go down in history. The gay icon Judy Garland had died a week before and people were hurting. Their nerves were frazzled, so when another rout by the police began, everything boiled over.

"If you were there," one man says in the film, "you knew this was it. This was what we'd been waiting for." Rocks and bottles were flung and trash cans set on fire. A feeling of released anger percolated across the country like a sprung trap.

Gay liberation was born.

Related Films

Army of Lovers (1979); *Stonewall* (1995); *Hope Along the Wind: The Life of Harry Hay* (2001); *After Stonewall* (2005); *American Experience: Stonewall Uprising* (2010).

Further Reading

Bausum, Ann. 2015. *Stonewall: Breaking Out in the Fight for Gay Rights*. New York: Viking Books.

Carter, David. 2010. *Stonewall: The Riots That Sparked the Gay Revolution*. New York: St. Martin's Griffin.

Hall, Radclyffe. 1928. *The Well of Loneliness*. New York: Avon Books.

Poehlmann, Tristan. 2016. *The Stonewall Riots: The Fight for LGBT Rights*. New York: Essential Library.

Dirk Bogarde (1921–99)

Dirk Bogarde was a man who played cat and mouse with those who sought to divine his sexuality for four decades. He gave more of it out than many openly queer people, and yet he died, at least theoretically, a heterosexual. (Some would say a heterosexual virgin.)

He described himself as the "male Loretta Young." Maybe the "British Rock Hudson" would have been a more apt sobriquet. It was only after he died that his forty-year relationship with his partner, Tony Forwood, became public knowledge. He referred to Forwood only by his surname in all his books, which seems to have been his way of distancing himself from him. It's surprising that he never came out, even in old age when it couldn't have done any damage to his career. This was his decision and people respected it because he'd done a lot for gay people through his brave film choices over the years. Some people may choose to call him cowardly for not coming out publicly, but Bogarde did come out through the personality he exhibited in his films, not in suggestive smirks or adolescent scripts like Hudson but in more significant ways.

The famous "raised eyebrow" was almost a sign in itself. So was the walk, the delicate gesturing, the haunted sensitivity he espoused in so many of his roles. He played a queer character in *Victim* (1961), a probable queer character in *The Servant* (1963), an old man obsessed with a pretty young boy in *Death in Venice* (1971). These are the obvious clues. In almost every other performance he gave there were more subtle ones. And yet he never said, in any of his multiple books or interviews, "Yes, I am queer." A program called "The Private Dirk Bogarde," which aired on BBC in 2001, was anything but that. The old rascal carried his secrets to the grave. Keith Howes wrote, "He managed to preserve the niceties of the Idol of the Odeons while being one of the screen's most finessed decadents" (Griffiths, 2006: 66).

Bogarde appeared as an outlaw in Roy Ward Baker's Mexican Western *The Singer Not the Song* in 1964. The film was weighed down by Baker's leaden-footed direction and also by the comatose performances of Bogarde and John Mills, who did a poor Irish accent as the priest trying to reform him. It's memorable today chiefly as a sartorial phenomenon. Bogarde is kitted out in black leather from head to toe. His suit is so tight-fitting it looks as if he's been poured into it and somebody forgot to say "When." The impression created is of a body made of so much tar. Stephen Bourne saw this as Bogarde's first overtly queer

Death in Venice (1971)

Bogarde's standout performance for LGBTQ viewers occurred in Luchino Visconti's mesmeric adaptation of Thomas Mann's novella about an artist—here he's a composer—searching for beauty and finding it in an angelic young boy, Tadzio (Bjorn Andresen). As Aschenbach, a man close to death in turn-of-the-century Venice, Bogarde gives the performance of his life. It's an achingly sad threnody to impossible love delivered with just the right mix of poetry and pain by Visconti.

The moment Von Aschenbach spots Tadzio in his sailor suit he's smitten. Tadzio is only fourteen but he seems to have a sexual awareness beyond his age. A relationship between them would be impossible. Von Aschenbach knows this, but he can still dream. He admires Tadzio from afar. When they finally meet, the young boy seems to gaze knowingly at him. "You must never smile like that to anyone," Von Aschenbach tells him. "I love you."

It is, of course, an impossible love. Time is also running out for Von Aschenbach. Venice is in the grip of a cholera epidemic, but he refuses to leave the city because of the boy. Then he contracts it. As he lies dying on a beach chair in the last scene, he watches Tadzio swimming in the ocean. He appears to be waving at him. He makes an effort to get up from the chair, but he's too frail. He falls backward. A wave from the waves is the extent of his response from the young Narcissus. The old man dies unfulfilled.

Death in Venice was criticized for being too self-indulgent, but this was unfair. Its sense of lethargy was intoxicating. Visconti films Venice beautifully; it becomes like another character in the film. One feels in the middle of a visual symphony. Von Aschenbach's love for Tadzio has a kind of Greek poetry about it. In seeking the boy's love, he seeks his own youth as well—but in the end both slip away as the life ebbs out of him.

role. "With one hand on his hip," he wrote, "a swishy walk, a white shirt, leather trousers and riding a white horse, he's as camp as Christmas" (Bourne, 1996: 152).

His most interesting film from an LGBTQ point of view was *Victim*. Here he played a married man who's queer. He's being blackmailed, which means he either has to pay a lot of money to a gang of thugs or risk his career and marriage. At his time in Britain, approximately 90 percent of blackmail cases involved queer men.

Most people commended Bogarde for his courage in taking on the role. He saw the situation differently. For him, breaking out of his heartthrob status was liberation. He was bored rigid with the "Doctor" films he was making at the time, which were like a straitjacket for him artistically. *Victim* "might not have been Shaw, Ibsen or Strindberg," he said, but it probed a social problem clearly and intelligently. The "countless letters of gratitude" he received from closet queers in its aftermath endorsed the advisability of taking it on for him (Bourne, 157). It was the first film in which a man said, "I love you," to another man. Bogarde chose the line. He said, "There's no point in half-measures. We either make a film about queers or we don't" (Russo, 1987: 126).

At the time the film was made, "sexperts" believed marriage could "normalize" queer men. Bogarde knocks that theory on the head when he roars at his wife, "I wanted him!" Going up the aisle with her was a mask, at best, a sublimation of his deeper nature.

Some people embraced *Victim* as endorsing a way of being they'd embraced for as long as they knew what it meant to have sexual desires. Others found it disgusting and walked out.

Magazines advertising it spoke of its exposure of a "twilight world." There were actually two: blackmail as well as being gay.

In 1966 Bogarde appeared in the spy spoof *Modesty Blaise*, camping things up like never before. In 1974 he went in another direction for Liliana Cavani's *The Night Porter*, playing a former SAS officer engaged in some kinky S&M games with Charlotte Rampling. He was always trying new things. That's why he never went stale. When the good parts weren't coming, he wrote books. He proved to be as capable a writer as he was an actor.

Queer director Stephen Frears—he made *My Beautiful Launderette* (1985) and *Prick Up Your Ears* (1987)—was even a fan. "I remember how sexy Dirk Bogarde was," he enthused. "I mean, he was the sexiest girl (sic) in British cinema" (Bourne, 1996: 161).

Related Films
Victim (1961); *The Servant* (1963); *The Singer Not the Song* (1964); *Modesty Blaise* (1966); *Death in Venice* (1971); *The Night Porter* (1974).

Further Reading
Bourne, Stephen. 1996. *Brief Encounters: Lesbians and Gays in British Cinema* 1930–1971. London: Cassell.
Coldstream, John, ed. 2009. *Ever, Dirk: The Bogarde Letters*. London: Phoenix.
Griffiths, Robin, ed. 2006. *British Queer Cinema*. London and New York: Routledge.
Morley, Sheridan. 1996. *Dirk Bogarde: Rank Outsider*. London: Bloomsbury.
Russo, Vito. 1987. *The Celluloid Closet: Homosexuality in the Movies*. New York: Harper & Row.

Bound (1996)

Think *Goodfellas* meets the Coen brothers by way of Andy Warhol's *Trash*. This gives one some idea what to expect from this cyberpunk porthole into lesbian sex as practiced by two get-rich-quick women dicing with death among the sheets as they take on the Mafia—and one another—in a black comedy that really rocks from Lana and Lilly Wachowski, formerly the Wachowski brothers. Lana transitioned in 2008. She was the first major Hollywood director to come out as transgender. Lilly did so in 2016. Both of them relish their privacy today. Lana said she had suicidal feelings in her youth as a result of sexual confusion.

Bound was their directorial debut. It grabs one by the throat from frame one and doesn't let go. It chronicles the twin fates of two characters whose orientation isn't the focus of the film but merely an incidental part of it.

Corky (Gina Gershon) is ready for some romance. She's just out of prison after serving a five-year stretch for what is euphemistically called "the redistribution of wealth." As she decorates an apartment for a criminal friend, she puts her eye on an attractive woman living next door, Violet (Jennifer Tilly).

When we see her first she's in a closet. The symbolism is obvious. When she comes out of it she brings Violet out too.

They share an early kiss and meet again later that night. Violet says she's sorry she was so intimate. "Don't apologize," Corky tells her. "I can't stand women who apologies for wanting sex." "I'm not apologizing for what I did," Violet says. "I'm apologizing for what I *didn't* do."

Violet is in a relationship with a mobster called Caesar (Joe Pantoliano) when the film begins. He's sidelined after she gets physical with Corky. When Caesar is given the task of holding $2 million for his boss, the pair of them hatch a plan to relieve him of it.

The first sex scene between Violet and Corky was shot in a single take to prevent any unwarranted interference from the censors. Their loving is as uncompromising as their ability to throw (and take) punches when the Mob cottons on to their plan. There's also the possibility that Violet is just dallying with Corky before going back to her man. This would place her in the irksome tradition of screen lesbians heretofore.

Corky is the masculine member of the relationship with her tightly cropped hair and her sweaty vest, but Violet isn't the traditional femme. It's she who really seduces Corky. She's also more active in their physical encounters. Both of them are straight in real life, but one would never guess this from their behavior here. Part of the credit for this must go to Susie Bright, a sex expert the Wachowskis employed to oversee the scenes. She didn't encourage them to hold back.

The noir lesbian had been in films from the inception of the industry, especially in movies made before the Production Code of 1934 issued restrictions on moral content. In these she was often cast as a gangster's moll. In the post-Code era, she was cleaned up but still visible. Here she's neo-noir radical chic.

The Wachowskis said their ambition in making the film was to expand the noir tradition, making a film that would push the boundaries and still be entertaining: "We tried to play with people's expectations and the clichés of the genre, including the sexual dynamics implied by those clichés. If people walked out of the cinema talking about the roles of men and women, that would be cool. But we'd settle for, 'That movie kicked butt! Let's go see it again' " (*Bound* Pressbook, AMPAS files).

The mood is playful, but with a whiff of cordite to keep us all guessing. What might happen? Will they die? Will they kill? Will they get to keep the money? Or rat on one another when push comes to shove? One imagines the young Quentin Tarantino asking these questions as he dreamed of doing something similar one day.

Gershon—who played a different kind of lesbian in *Showgirls*—became something of a gay icon after this sleeper became a cult success. Refreshingly free of the clichés of so many similarly themed films with similar ambitions but infinitely less bite, it's "street" to the core.

This pair are something more than "lipstick lesbians." Though appearing to play things for laughs, they leave us in no doubt that they mean business when they do business.

This generally involves dismissing the male of the species. "That wasn't sex," Corky tells Violet when she hears her making love to her boyfriend through a thin apartment wall. "That was work." When a perplexed Caesar asks her what she's done to Violet, she says, "Everything you couldn't."

Related Films
Thelma and Louise (1991); *Showgirls* (1995); *Benzina* (2001); *V for Vendetta* (2006).

Further Reading
Keegan, Cael M., ed. 2018. *Lana and Lilly Wachowski*. Champaign: University of Illinois Press.
Pennington, Jody W. 2007. *The History of Sex in American Film*. Westport, CT, and London: Praeger.
Rich, B. Ruby. 1998. *Chick Flicks*. Durham, NC, and London: Duke University Press.
Tasker, Yvonne. 1998. *Working Girl: Gender and Sexuality in Popular Culture*. London and New York: Routledge.

David Bowie (1947–2017)

Like a glamorized version of Frank N. Furter from *The Rocky Horror Picture Show* (1975), the man who was born David Jones—not to be confused with the other David Jones from The Monkees—gave new meaning to the term "chameleon." He reinvented himself continually during his life.

From the sci-fi bisexuality of Ziggy Stardust to the Thin White Duke of 1975, Bowie was the quintessential experimenter—with music, with dress, with hairstyles, with himself. The fact that he managed to carve out a film career in between the albums is another testament to his versatility.

In 1970 the British gay magazine *Jeremy* published an interview with him, but he didn't identify himself as being queer until two years later. In the interim he'd appeared on the cover of his third album, *The Man Who Sold the World*, reclining on a chaise longue in a silk dress.

Was it all a pose? Was he merely marketing, as some imagined, just rock 'n' roll with lipstick? Was his bisexuality even a pose? One never knew for sure with the Great Artificer. He delighted in shedding skins as soon as he'd grown them. The secret was to keep changing. It was hard to hit a moving target.

Most of the questions about him concerned his sexuality. He married the model Angela ("Angie") Barnett in 1970 and had a child, Duncan, by her but even then one couldn't be certain he'd gone straight. He said he'd met her when they were both "laying the same man" (Murray, 1994: 170). He allegedly proposed to her with the words, "Can you handle the fact that I don't love you?" (Hadleigh, 2005: 112). They divorced in 1980. Duncan went on to become a film director.

Bowie played a visitor from outer space in *The Man Who Fell to Earth* (1975). Outer space would figure strongly in his song lyrics. He also had an extraterrestrial look about him with those strange eyes and the esoteric wardrobe. In *Just a Gigolo* (1980), he was an escort to a host of society women in post-World War II Germany. The film had a glittering cast—Kim Novak, Marlene Dietrich, David Hemmings—but fell below most people's expectations. Dietrich hadn't made a film in eighteen years before it. Bowie didn't even get to meet her: "It turned out that, instead of acting with her, he was acting with a chair" (Trynka, 2011: 285).

He gave one of his most praised performances in *The Hunger* (1983), playing a 250-year-old vampire and looking every day of it. Susan Sarandon is the doctor he goes to after he starts to panic about the rapidity at which he's aging. She ends up sleeping with his wife (Catherine Deneuve) and sharing bodily fluids with her. Bowie gets his revenge on her before the film ends.

After this he seemed to make roughly a film a year, each as different from the other as it was possible to be. He was always looking for some new image, some new alter ego. He undertook a villainous role in *Into the Night* (1985) and a conventional one in *Absolute Beginners* (1986). He was a goblin king in *Labyrinth* (1986). In Martin Scorsese's *The Last Temptation of Christ* (1988), he played Pontius Pilate.

Camp since the age of seven, Bowie shocked the first person to whom he revealed his bisexuality: "The guy didn't know what I meant. He gave me this horrified look" (Miles, 1980: 37–8). Some people thought his alleged orientation was a ruse to get girls. A lot of them tried to "convert" him. They'd say things like, "Come on, David, it isn't all that bad. I'll show you." Or, better yet, "*We'll* show you." He always played dumb in situations like this (*Playboy*, September 1976).

Bowie never seemed to be able to make up his mind about his sexual orientation. Angie wrote about their life together in her book *Backstage Passes*, published in 1993. Steam rose from the pages. The best anecdote had her opening a door one morning to find her husband in bed with Mick Jagger. What did she do? She cooked breakfast for them, of course.

In 1992 he decided he wasn't queer after all and married the supermodel Iman. Theirs was a loving relationship of true sexual equality. By now he'd been divorced from Angie for over a decade. The split was acrimonious.

His film career went on in fits and starts. He never thought of himself as a great actor, but his name filled theaters. Some of his fans would probably have gone to see him reading the telephone directory.

He was Andy Warhol in *Basquiat* in 1996. *Everybody Loves Sunshine* (1999) was his next outing. He played himself in *Zoolander* (2000). After that there was a gap until *The Prestige* (2006) and *August* (2008). He took many roles purely to advance his profile as a "generalist" (Trynka, 2011: 286). His crossover from the world of rock missed the target sometimes, but he didn't mind. He was, after all, David Bowie; he couldn't stop experimenting.

He died of liver cancer two days shy of his sixty-ninth birthday. He'd been diagnosed with it eighteen months before. He knew how ill he was, but he worked until the end. He always said he'd die with his boots on.

Angie was on the United Kingdom's *Celebrity Big Brother* show when she got the news of his passing. She said she was upset, but she chose to stay in the house for the rest of the show, which seemed to contradict that. She hadn't seen him for forty years.

His last album, *Blackstar*, was released just two days before he died. One of the songs was called *Lazarus*. The video of it suggests he's coming back from the grave like the biblical character. Well, why not? He'd done everything else—including precisely this in *The Hunger*.

Don't rule it out.

Related Films
The Man Who Fell to Earth (1976); *Just a Gigolo* (1980); *The Hunger* (1983); *Absolute Beginners* (1986); *Becoming Bowie* (2014).

Further Reading
Bowie, Angie. 1993. *Backstage Passes*. New York: Jove Books.
Buckley, David. 2005. *Strange Fascination: The David Bowie Story*. London: Virgin.
Duncan, Paul. 2017. *David Bowie: The Man Who Fell to Earth*. Cologne, Germany: Taschen.
Hadleigh, Boze, ed. 2005. *Celebrity Diss and Tell*. Kansas City: Andrews McMeel.
Jones, Dylan. 2017. *David Bowie: A Life*. London: Preface.
Miles, ed. 1980. *Bowie in His Own Words*. London: Omnibus.
Murray, Raymond. 1994. *Images in the Dark: An Encyclopedia of Gay and Lesbian Film and Video*. Philadelphia: TLA Publications.
Playboy, September 1976.
Trynka, Paul. 2011. *Starman: David Bowie—The Definitive Biography*. London: Sphere.

Boys Don't Cry (1998)

Hilary Swank gave a resounding performance here as Brandon Teena, a transgender man who was born Teena Brandon but who felt trapped in a woman's body. His sexuality wasn't accepted in the conservative area of Nebraska where he lived. He ended up being raped and murdered in 1993. The film was directed by Kimberly Peirce.

Brandon stuffs a sock in his jeans in an early scene to make the shape of a penis. His cousin Lonny (Matt McGrath) is shocked. He shrieks: "That's the most horrifying thing I've ever seen in my life. It's a deformity."

His efforts to conceal his physique are elaborate. He binds his breasts, puts a sock in his crotch area. Later on he replaces this with a prosthetic penis. He wants to have sex reassignment surgery but can't afford it. He tries to buy a box of tampons at a store without being seen. He struggles to hide periods and cleavage.

He decides to go to Falls City to carve out a new identity for himself. He lives like a man there and is popular with the other men he drinks with. He's popular with the women too, being more caring and sensitive than the average men they meet.

In Falls City one night, Brandon is threatened with violence in a bar. He's rescued by an ex-convict called John (Peter Sarsgaard). Through him he meets John's former girlfriend, Lana (Chloe Sevigny). She lives with her alcoholic mother (Jeannetta Arnette). Both Lana and her mother are treated as second-class citizens by John and his friend Tom (Brendan Sexton III). Lana's friend Candace (Alicia Goranson) is also subjugated by John and Tom.

Brandon falls in love with Lana. When he tells Lonny he intends to marry her, his outraged cousin exclaims, "Before or after you tell her you're a girl?"

Brandon makes love to Lana. At one stage of their lovemaking, an outline of Brandon's breasts becomes visible to her. She looks surprised but she says nothing.

Brandon Teena (1972–93)

Brandon was born Teena Brandon in Lincoln, Nebraska, in 1972. He was sexually assaulted by his uncle as a child. He identified himself as male during his adolescence, but his mother couldn't accept this, continuing to refer to him as her daughter. He ran into trouble at school by dressing as a boy and disagreeing with the school's strong disapproval of being trans. He tried to enlist in the army when he was eighteen but was rejected after listing his sex as male. Later that year he bound his breasts and started dating girls. He was expelled from school three days before graduation.

He began a serious relationship with a girl in 1991 and planned setting up house with her, but his mother intervened and stopped this. She had Brandon submitted for a psychiatric examination. It concluded that he was suffering from a crisis of identity and needed therapy. During one therapy session he revealed that he'd been raped.

In 1993 he moved to Falls City. Here, as in the film, he became friends with the locals and also a girl called Lisa Lambert. He then began dating another girl called Lana Tisdel (played by Chloe Sevigny in *Boys Don't Cry*). He also began socializing with two ex-convicts, John Lotter and Tom Nissen. At the end of the year he was imprisoned for forging checks. It was now that Lana discovered he was trans. When news of his biological gender reached Lotter and Nissen, they raped him, but it didn't result in an arrest.

On December 31, 1993, Lotter and Nissen drove to Lisa Lambert's house. Lotter shot Brandon and Lambert and also a man who was visiting Lambert's sister, Phillip DeVine. Both of them were arrested for murder. Lotter was convicted and Nissen sentenced for being an accessory. Since then, Lotter has strenuously denied he committed the murders, but his denials have been consistently ignored.

Because Brandon didn't have sex reassignment surgery, he's sometimes described as a lesbian. His mother believed he was one but now accepts that he was, to all intents and purposes, a man. She didn't like the film and neither did Tisdel. Tisdel sued the makers of the film for having her continue to date Brandon after learning he was biologically female. The case was settled out of court for an undisclosed sum. Teena's mother sued Richardson County for failing to prevent her son's death and was awarded $80,000 in damages.

When Candace discovers a tampon under Brandon's mattress, and a court summons with the name Teena Brandon on it, the penny drops. She digs further and finds literature about gender change. John gets this information out of her one night after plying her with drink. When he sees the documentation, he's shocked.

Brandon is detained in custody and Lana comes to visit him. He's in the woman's section so there's no point in lying anymore. He's worried about how she'll take the news, but his fears are unfounded. Lana isn't as judgmental as most of the other people in Falls City. When he documents his confused sexual history to her, she says, "I don't care if you're half monkey or half ape." It doesn't matter to her if Brandon is male or female. Whatever the biological gender, he's fulfilled her sexually more than any man she's ever known.

When Brandon is released from prison, Tom and John confront him. When they get physical, Lana screams, "Get your hands off him!" The "him" is interesting. It's an endorsement of his new identity. But Tom and John are getting violent now. They strip him to find out what's "down there." After seeing he has a vagina, they rape him. They then take him back to their place, telling him they'll silence him forever if he reveals what happened. He reports the rape, but no real interest is shown. The policeman on duty says, "Why do you go hanging out with the guys, being you're a guy yourself?"

Realizing he has no further recourse in law, Brandon knows he has to hide from John and Tom. Candace shelters him, but John and Tom find them. When they do, they shoot both of them. Candace was based on a girl called Lisa Lambert, who was killed alongside Brandon in real life.

Swank lived as a man for a month in preparation for the role. Her commitment bore dividends. She also looked the part. At her audition, she even fooled the doorman at the studio. It was a good omen.

Swank won an Oscar for her performance. Sevigny was nominated. "We've come a long way, Mom," Swank said to her mother in her acceptance speech. "I guess it was worth living out of the car." She was referring to the fact that, nine years previously, she'd driven from Seattle to Hollywood with her mother with just seventy-five dollars between them. With the bounty accruing from her Oscar win, she could probably afford that amount now to have her car parked (Piazza and Kinn, 2008: 303).

A year before *Boys Don't Cry*, Susan Muska and Greta Olafsdottir made a documentary called *The Brandon Teena Story*, which dealt with the last few weeks of his life. It sheds more light on Teena's life than the film in some ways, especially in scenes such as when he reports his rape to the police. It also informs us that a third person, Phillip DeVine, was murdered alongside Brandon and Lisa Lambert in the final shootout.

Related Films
The Brandon Teena Story (1997); *Soldier's Girl* (2003); *A Girl Like Me: The Gwen Araujo Story* (2006).

Further Reading
Aaron, Michele, ed. 2004. *New Queer Cinema*. New Brunswick, NJ: Rutgers University Press.
Clum, John M. 2002. *He's All Man: Learning Masculinity, Gayness, and Love from American Movies*. New York: Palgrave.
Epstein, Julia, and Kristina Straub. 1991. *Body Guards: The Cultural Politics of Gender Ambiguity*. New York: Routledge.
Piazza, Jim, and Gail Kinn, 2008. *The Academy Awards: The Complete Unofficial History*. New York: Black Dog & Leventhal.
Rich, B. Ruby. 2013. *New Queer Cinema*. Durham, NC, and London: Duke University Press.
Stryker, Susan. 2008. *Transgender History*. Berkeley, CA: Seal Press.

The Boys in the Band (1970)

William Friedkin's controversial version of Mart Crowley's Broadway hit features eight queer men who convene for a birthday party in Manhattan. Matters become complicated when a heterosexual guest from the host's past turns up leading to an orgy of bickering that's unrelenting both in its range and tone.

With lines such as, "Show me a happy homosexual and I'll show you a gay corpse," the script was said to have drawn far too much attention to itself for its own good, thereby rowing back on its chances of presenting a cast that might have grown on audiences gradually, but anyone who enjoys post-Wildean one-liners will have been entertained. It's just a pity Friedkin didn't attempt to get inside the skins of the people behind the wit, or to explore just how much of it came from a kind of whistling in the graveyard. There's poignancy at the heart of the film that doesn't quite come out, but taken for what it is it's still a watershed in queer cinema.

This is the first mainstream Hollywood film in which all of the main characters but one are queer, and there's even a question mark about him. It's a pity that they suffer from such negative self-images.

Lonely, guilty, repressed, the gathering with which one is confronted here is like a support group for losers. We have a man who lives in terror of growing old, an introverted prostitute, a screaming queen, a self-loathing Catholic, a promiscuous fashion photographer. As the night goes on and tongues loosen, all of the Freudian hang-ups of the motley crew are unleashed in more detail.

Michael (Kenneth Nelson) is the Catholic. His unfaithful lover, Donald (Frederick Combs), prepares the party with him. It's the thirty-second birthday of Harold (Leonard Frey).

Emory (Cliff Gorman) is the drag queen. Bernard (Reuben Greene) is a black man who works in a bookshop. Hank (Laurence Luckinbill) is a teacher. Larry (Keith Prentice) is his lover. Cowboy (Robert La Tourneaux) is Emory's birthday gift for Harold. Alan (Peter White) is the heterosexual.

Alan is the last to arrive. When he does, he promptly gets into an argument with Emory. When Harold appears, the sniping is upgraded. Before the night is over, Michael insists everyone play a truth game that involves people saying who they love most in the world. It's in the course of this that his bisexuality emerges. Harold pounces on it, which ratchets ups the tension even further. A mutual declaration of love between Larry and Hank makes everyone uncomfortable. The game of truth, as ever, has thrown up some unexpected revelations.

When *The Boys in the Band* was staged on Broadway, the Stonewall Riots—which crystalized all the grievances of the gay rights movement and gave them a look and a voice—hadn't happened. By the time Friedkin made his film, they had. In that interim, much of its potency had dissipated. Stonewall largely made it irrelevant to the burgeoning new culture of self-determination. It became, in Edward Guthmann's words, "the gay equivalent of a minstrel show" (*San Francisco Chronicle*, January 15, 1999).

Sometimes the self-pity has a defiant edge, as in Harold's, "What I am is a thirty-two-year-old pockmarked Jew fairy, and if it takes me a while to pull myself together, and if I smoke a little grass before I get up the nerve to show my face to the world, it's nobody's business but my own." There are also some funny quips like, "What's more boring than a queen doing a Joan Crawford imitation? A queen doing a Bette Davis one!"

"If we could just not hate ourselves so much," Michael says in a moment of near catharsis. "If we could just learn not to hate ourselves so very much." If they did, the film would have been more entertaining. When self-loathing reaches a certain level, it becomes a kind of indulgence, a masochistic pleasure. The tragedy of this group isn't so much that they're queer as that they've fallen in love with their misery. Most of them also slot themselves into stereotypes created for them by heterosexuals.

In their defense, it should be said that they're products of their time. Crowley emphasized the fact that for people growing up in the fifties, as they did, it was well-nigh impossible to feel good about being queer. Love them or hate them, at least he gave them visibility. If there was one queer person in eight films in 1970, it would have been talked about. Here we had eight in one film. It explored the problem of trying to survive in a world where one's very existence was denied.

Crowley's characters might have been losers, Vito Russo remarked, but they paved the way for winners (Russo, 1987: 175). That has to be said too.

"This film isn't about homosexuality," Friedkin insisted. "It's about human problems. I hope there are happy homosexuals. They just don't happen to be in my film" (Russo, 178). He would make similar declarations about *Cruising*, a project with more obvious homophobic overtones, in 1980. Both films raised the question: Why didn't he go in search of such "happy homosexuals" if they existed, and put them into his work? Being gay is the elephant in the room in *The Boys in the Band*. Suggesting anything else is an abrogation of responsibility. The characters are there for a reason. They seem to represent the way Friedkin feels about queer people—that they're inordinately self-piteous. Otherwise why not pick people from a different script?

Thankfully, more recent depictions of LGBTQ characters have been more positive, though there are still exceptions, like the self-loathing lesbian schoolteacher played by Dame Judi Dench in *Notes on a Scandal* (2006).

Related Films
Fortune and Men's Eyes (1971); *Some of My Best Friends Are . . .* (1971); *That Certain Summer* (1972); *Time Piece* (1994).

Further Reading
Crowley, Mart. 2010. *The Boys in the Band*. New York: Samuel French.
Doty, Alexander. 1993. *Making Things Perfectly Queer: Interpreting Mass Culture*. Minneapolis: University of Minnesota Press.
Russo, Vito. 1987. *The Celluloid Closet*. New York: Harper & Row.
San Francisco Chronicle, January 15, 1999.
Stewart, Steve. 1994. *Gay Hollywood Film and Video Guide: 75 Years of Gay and Lesbian Images in the Movies*. Laguna Hills, CA: Companion Publications.

Marlon Brando (1925–2005)

The most consummate actor of his era didn't disavow his ambivalent sexuality. He was never in the closet about it. He just chose not to talk about it unless someone brought it up.

According to Darwin Porter's book *Brando Unzipped* (2006), he slept with nearly every man he met. Porter tends to heave an overactive imagination in that regard, but Brando did have his share of male lovers. Some of these were probably for experimental purposes, as his libido was primarily channeled toward the opposite sex. He was dubbed "a walking hormone factory" in the fifties when so many women seemed to desire him.

Porter alleges he had flings with Burt Lancaster, Tyrone Power, Montgomery Clift, James Dean, Cary Grant, and John Gielgud. That's just the actors. There was also Gore Vidal, Bob Dylan, and Leonard Bernstein. He even provides a visual in his book of Brando allegedly performing fellatio on his best friend, Wally Cox. He claims the photograph was entered into the official court record of his divorce from Anna Kashfi (Porter, 2006: 404). Porter says Brando's appetite for women was partly activated by his queer side. He quotes him as saying, "I have guilt about sleeping with men and, almost to atone for it, I go in the opposite direction. The more the merrier. That way, I manage to convince myself I'm a bona fide heterosexual—until the queer side of me comes out again" (Porter, 98–9).

In *Somebody*, Stefan Kanfer quotes Robert Lewis, cofounder of the Actors Studio, as saying Brando had an affair with the playwright Clifford Odets but then rejected him. "Marlon could be there for you one day," Lewis is quoted as saying, "and then he'd be gone the next . . . Perhaps he decided Clifford was never going to write that Broadway play for him" (Kanfer, 2008: 40). Kanfer further alleges an affair between Brando and Laurence Olivier. He has Olivier's wife, Vivien Leigh, claiming Brando slept with her too. "I must say this for Marlon," Leigh is quoted saying to Elia Kazan. "When it comes to couples, he's an equal opportunity seducer. On many a night he rose from Larry's bed and joined me in mine" (Kanfer, 99). Kanfer even had Brando's sometime fiancée Joanne Mariani-Berenger—they didn't marry—telling Tennessee Williams at dinner one night that Brando and the director Christian Marquand had been lovers. Brando didn't deny it (Kanfer, 137). He had a deep friendship with Marquand, so deep that he named his son after him.

Williams became infatuated with Brando when they were working together on *A Streetcar Named Desire*. So had some young stars who worked with him at the Actor's Studio around this time. Brando, according to his biographer Peter Manso, slept with some of them as "a favor" (Manso, 1994: 430).

"Deep down I feel ambiguous," Brando admitted, "and I'm not saying that to spite the seven out of ten women who consider me—wrongly perhaps—a sex symbol. According to me, sex is something that lacks precision. Let's say sex is sexless" (Manso, 164).

When he was making *Sayonara*, he was interviewed by Truman Capote in a hotel room in Kyoto in January 1957. They both got drunk and Capote enticed him into saying much more than he intended to about his life.

Joshua Logan, the director of *Sayonara*, had tried to steer him away from Capote. "Don't let yourself be left alone with him," he warned. "He's after you." Brando didn't listen. He felt comfortable with him and admired his writing. He didn't know then that Capote had a 96 percent recall of conversations he had, even under the influence of copious amounts of alcohol (Manso, 429).

During the course of the interview, Capote mentioned to Brando that a queer actor they both knew boasted to Capote that he'd gone to bed with the actor. His name was Sandy Campbell. Brando didn't deny it. He told Capote he went to bed with lots of other men too but didn't consider himself to be gay. They were all very attracted to him, he said, and he wanted to expand his sexual horizons to see what sex with them would be like. It was no big deal. In some ways it was like having a meal or going to the bathroom, something he forgot about five minutes afterward (*New Yorker*, March 1957).

Brando played a queer army man in *Reflections in a Golden Eye*, the John Huston film based on Carson McCullers's gothic novel. He put so much of himself into the role, one has to suspect part of that self was gay—or else he was an even greater actor than the world generally takes him for. The way he walked, and talked, all these seemed the actions of a gay man. It was almost as if he chose the film as the way he would finally "come out." He also explored this side of himself in *The Missouri Breaks* (1976), though with psychotic overtones. Here he plots the destruction of cattle rustlers in a Mother Hubbard costume with a bonnet on his head.

Elia Kazan said Brando was the only actor he ever knew who contained the essence of machismo and femininity within one body. Kazan directed him in some of his best films, including *On the Waterfront* (1954). In a famous scene from that film, his costar, Eva Marie Saint, drops her glove accidentally and Brando picks it up. Kazan let the camera run. Brando played out the rest of the scene wearing the glove. The fact that he liked doing so showed he was very comfortable with his feminine side.

Some of the scenes in *Reflections in a Golden Eye* reduced audiences to laughter. Perhaps it was a nervous laughter, the laughter of people afraid of their own natures. The way he hyped up the effeminacy of his character made some people think he made him into a caricature, but there was enough depth in the performance to give it resonance. The scene where he beats a horse after it throws him, and then breaks down crying, was a triumph of acting. It's one of his greatest moments on screen, as good as the one he did by his wife's coffin in *Last Tango in Paris*.

Maria Schneider, Brando's costar in *Last Tango in Paris*, was a bisexual. She said she didn't enjoy the sex scenes with him in the movie, pointing out that he was beautiful only from the neck up (Manso, 1994: 742). She said they had one major thing in common: they were both bisexual (Manso, 763).

Ingmar Bergman always believed *Last Tango* was a film about two queer men. "There is so much hatred of women in this film," he insisted, "but if you see it as being about a man who loves a boy, you can understand it." Bergman believed the director, Bernardo Bertolucci, hadn't the "nerve" to cast a boy in it. When he put this theory to Brando, Brando replied, "Well, he got pretty close to that because Maria is gay" (Manso, 744).

His sensitivity was such, he often said if he was in a room with a hundred people and only ninety-nine of them liked him, he would want to get out of the room. He was sensitive with regard to physical things too. It was part of what made him such a wonderful actor. There was a gentleness in the way he touched people, both men and women, or even himself. Sondra Lee, an actress who knew him from his early days in theater, said, "He was one of the first men I knew who loved soft fabric. Under his sweater he usually wore a silk shirt" (Manso, 213).

His secretary, Alice Marchak, had the sheets for his bed ordered from France. One can safely look on all these traits as "feminine" characteristics. He probably inherited them from his mother, a woman who also instigated in him a love for acting—which, again, allowed him to explore his sensitivities in all their metrosexual vicissitudes.

Related Films
Reflections in a Golden Eye (1967); *The Missouri Breaks* (1976); *Brando: TCM Documentary* (2007); *Listen to Me Marlon* (2015).

Further Reading
Kanfer, Stefan. 2008. *Somebody: The Reckless Life and Remarkable Career of Marlon Brando*. London: Faber & Faber.

Manso, Peter. 1994. *Brando: The Biography*. New York: Hyperion.

Marchak, Alice, and Linda Hunter. 2000. *The Super Secs*. Lincoln, NE: iUniverse.

New Yorker, March 1957.

Peardon, Nancy K. 2013. *Marlon Brando: A Memoir*. Los Angeles: Falcon Press.

Porter, Darwin. 2006. *Brando Unzipped*. New York: Blood Moon Productions.

Vergin, Roger C. 1997. *Brando with His Guard Down*. West Chester, PA: Cabot Riley Press.

Brokeback Mountain (2005)

Ennis Del Mar (Heath Ledger) and Jack Twist (Jake Gyllenhaal) mind sheep on the slopes of a mountain in Wyoming in the 1960s.

Jack wants to be a rodeo rider. Ennis is a ranch hand. One evening Jack invites Ennis into his tent. They have sex. "I ain't no queer," Ennis says afterward. "Neither am I," Jack assures him. They fall in love but can't express this publicly for fear of public approbation.

When Jack goes back to the mountain looking for work the year after he's been there with Ennis, he's refused by Joe Aguirre (Randy Quaid). Aguirre has seen them together and deduced that they have, as he puts it, "stemmed the rose."

Both get married to keep their respectability intact, but meet for "fishing trips" where their primary sexual orientations are expressed. Ang Lee charts their relationship over two decades as the "thing" between them grows.

Ennis marries Alma (Michelle Williams), who's poor like himself. Jack enters a marriage of convenience with Lureen (Anne Hathaway), who comes from a wealthy family. Neither woman knows what to make of the so-called fishing trips where little or no fishing seems to get done. Then one day Alma sees Ennis kissing Jack when he meets up with him after a long absence. The marriage is effectively over from this point.

The film was based on a thirty-one-page novella by Pulitzer Prize–winning author Annie Proulx. Lee exploits Proulx's minimalistic dialogue to amplify the introversion of the two men. This makes their involvement with one another more potent. They don't speak much. When they do, it's often with their hats pulled down over their faces.

They live like a traditional husband and wife. One day when Jack arrives at the campfire, he's in a bad mood. He says to Ennis, "I'm with sheep all day and come here and there's nothing but beans." It's a statement a conventional cowboy like John Wayne or James Stewart might have made to the "little lady" back on the homestead. Lee preserves the staples of the Western genre to make his departure from it more effective.

He uses the stereotype of the "strong, silent" cowpoke to good effect here. If Cooper was a man of few words in most of his Westerns, there was no agenda to it; it was just the way he was. Here the silence roars with unfulfillment, the claustrophobic tensions of the men clashing with the wide-open spaces that surround them.

Even in the so-called enlightened 1960s, this was a forbidden love. "Sometimes I miss you so much," Jack tells Ennis, "I can hardly stand it." Ennis replies, "I wish I knew how to quit you." Because their circumstances are impossible, separation seems the lesser of two evils. Either that or the mutual denial of the way they feel about one another.

From early on, one senses their relationship isn't going to end well, and it doesn't. The marriages break up when their involvement with one another is discovered. Then Jack is murdered in a hate crime, though Lureen pretends he died in an accident so people won't gossip.

He's asked to be cremated, so Lureen arranges this. Afterward, Ennis visits his home to ask for his ashes. He wants to scatter them over Brokeback Mountain, but he meets with resistance from Jack's father, who seems to know about their relationship. His mother, a kinder person by far, allows him to go up to Jack's room. Here he sees two shirts in a closet. They enfold one another from behind, reprising the manner in which they embraced at a campfire when they first became close.

Jack's mother allows Ennis to keep the shirts, thereby ratifying their relationship in a manner his father isn't willing to do. The film ends with Ennis thinking of what might have been.

The queering of the Western didn't begin with *Brokeback Mountain*. This strain harks back to supposedly hypermasculine films like *Red River* (1948), *Warlock* (1959), *Butch Cassidy and the Sundance Kid* (1969), and a host of others. They created the cultural landscape for Lee's pastoral tale of two ranch hands who fumble their way toward an unlikely intimacy.

Brokeback Mountain was a film that was waiting almost a century to be made. All of the Westerns going back to the 1930s where men gazed into the middle distance on cattle drives paved the way for it. In former years it wasn't possible for such scenarios to suggest male bonding. Relationships had to be triangulated to legitimize them. To that extent it's a watershed. It's a landmark film not only for what it is but for the retrospective light it sheds on the queer subtexts of its forbears. Lee reinvented the Western for New Queer Cinema, using the iconography of a century of frontier values to both underline and undermine their heteronormative parameters. Marlboro Man masculinity is no more here. As one writer put it, the film "corralled the cultural *zeitgeist*" (Handley, 2011: 229).

No matter how revisionist *Brokeback Mountain* is in terms of its sexual charge, it preserved the hard-bitten dialogue of the stolid heroes of yesteryear. "If you can't fix it," Ennis tells Jack about their unique predicament, "you gotta stand it." His Western forefathers might have used a similarly fatalistic attitude to refer to an imminent Indian attack or a duel on Main Street with a villain in a black hat.

The film also has something to say to us about dignity, as in the scene where Ennis tries to reclaim Jack's ashes. "The last thing in the world I'd been thinking about when I wrote the story," Proulx claimed, "was gay rights. But here is this poor wretched Ennis at the end and he has zero rights. He doesn't even have the right to express his sorrow in public" (*Screen International*, December 21, 2005).

Proulx is to be commended for creating a set of circumstances that were widely outside her orbit of experience. "Put yourself in my place," she said. "An elderly white straight female trying to write about two 19-year-old gay cowboys in 1963" (*USA Today*, March 2, 2006). It was something of a reach.

A New Wave "bromance," *Brokeback Mountain* wins one's respect not just because of its breaking down of genre walls but because it does so in a muted manner. Both men are awkward with one another, which is why it was probably better the parts were played by "straight" actors. B. Ruby Rich said, "I don't believe they would ever have allowed an openly queer director to make this movie, nor do I believe that actors of this caliber would have signed on. It took these guys with impeccable heterosexual credentials to make this kind of breakthrough" (San Filippo, 2013: 162).

It's beautifully directed by Lee. Larry McMurtry, who cowrote the screenplay with his long-term writing partner Diana Ossana, advised him about the "nonverbal" culture of cowboy films, which helped his work (*From Script to Screen: Brokeback Mountain* DVD: Special Features). Both actors gave resounding performances, Ledger being nominated for an Oscar. Despite being Australian, he did a very credible U.S. accent. "When he talks," Hathaway said, "it's as if the words are pushing themselves out of his mouth" (*Sharing the Story: The Making of Brokeback Mountain*. DVD: Special Features). She didn't mean this as a criticism. It suited his personality, and the awkward situation in which he finds himself in the film. Williams was also nominated for an Oscar. She conveyed the heartache of learning her husband was gay brilliantly. "In Alice's world," Williams said, "the word 'gay' didn't exist" (*Sharing the Story*).

There's only one sex scene in the film, and both Jack and Ennis keep their clothes on during it. Even so, we're still a long way from John Wayne riding the prairie and "doing what a man's gotta do."

Related Films
The Dude Wrangler (1930); *Red River* (1948); *Lonesome Cowboys* (1968); *Butch Cassidy and the Sundance Kid* (1969); *Midnight Cowboy* (1969).

Further Reading
Handley, William R., ed. 2011. *The Brokeback Book: From Story to Cultural Phenomenon*. Lincoln and London: University of Nebraska Press.

Proulx, Annie. 2005. *Close Range: Brokeback Mountain and Other Stories*. New York: Harper Perennial.

San Filippo, Maria. 2013. *The B Word: Bisexuality in Contemporary Film and Television*. Bloomington and Indianapolis: Indiana University Press.

Screen International, December 21, 2005.

Tinkcom, Matthew. 2017. *Queer Theory and Brokeback Mountain*. New York and London: Bloomsbury.

Tompkins, Jane. 1992. *West of Everything: The Inner Life of Westerns*. New York: Oxford University Press.

USA Today, March 2, 2006.

Raymond Burr (1917–93)

Though Burr is mostly remembered today for *Perry Mason*, which ran on television from 1957 to 1966, and the later *Ironside* (1967–75), where he played the wheelchair-bound detective, most of his film roles had him as "heavy," both literally and figuratively. As was the case with most stars, any rumors of being gay could have ended his career prematurely.

Like Rock Hudson, he engaged in a brief marriage to offset such rumors. He added two more fictional ones to his biography for good measure, and a son who died. He told people his first wife was a woman called Annette Sutherland. She died, he claimed, when the plane on which she was traveling during World War II was shot down by the Germans. It was, he said, the same plane on which the actor Leslie Howard died on route from Lisbon to London (*TV Radio Mirror*, October 1957). No record of such a woman has ever been found on the plane's passenger list.

His "second" marriage—which was really his first—was in 1948 to actress Isabella Ward (1919–2004). She never heard him talking about Sutherland. "I was Ray's first wife," she insisted. "If there had been one before me he would have told me" (*TV Radio Mirror*, 1968). It broke down within months but wasn't officially annulled until a few years later. Ward never remarried. Neither did Burr, though he said he did. His third wife, at least according to his very active imagination, was one Laura Andrina Morgan. This marriage supposedly took place in 1953 and ended when she died of cancer two years later.

Burr said he had a son by Sutherland and that he died of leukemia at the age of ten in 1953. Ward disputed this as well. "I never met him," she stated, "because there was no son" (*TV Radio Mirror*, 1968). Burr claimed he took the boy around the world as a deathbed treat. This is as unlikely as his many other fictions. He was busy with his career at this time and would hardly have had time for such globetrotting.

He also alleged that he was romantically involved with the actress Natalie Wood around this period. He was friendly with Wood but not in that way. Her studio, he claimed, guillotined their relationship.

All these circumstances were geared toward building a backstory for himself and deflecting unwanted attention from his queer endeavors. He also garnered sympathy for himself as a result of all the tragedies. The Natalie Wood story is particularly fantastic. It suited Wood's studio to have her seen at events with Burr. She was deeply involved with Robert Wagner at this time, and it was felt that such an involvement could lessen the fan base of both stars.

Audiences liked actors to be "available" to them, at least in theory, and the seriousness of the Wood/Wagner liaison threatened that illusion.

Burr's screen list of villains is prolific, beginning with *San Quentin* (1947) and extending through films such as *Desperate* (1947), *Pitfall* (1948), *Raw Deal* (1948), and many others. Even when he made comedies such as *Love Happy* (1949), he was the token thug. The performance he was most happy with, however, was that of the prosecuting counsel in George Stevens's *A Place in the Sun* (1951). He revered Stevens and was also highly impressed with the rest of that film's cast—Montgomery Clift, Elizabeth Taylor, and Shelley Winters. He was proud to be among them. He was also proud to work for Alfred Hitchcock in *Rear Window* (1954), probably his best-known role. Again he was the villain, a white-haired one this time. Two years later he gained more positive notices for his role as a reporter in *Godzilla, King of the Monsters*.

Burr's stories about his life were sometimes more interesting than the plots of his films. He seemed to be addicted to telling lies, not all of which concerned his sexuality. He told reporters he traveled around the world five times, for instance, and at one time lived in China with his parents. The closest he ever came to China, according to Burr's biographer Michael Seth Starr, was "a whiff of fine porcelain" (Starr, 2008: 40).

Sometimes, however, the mask slipped, like on the set of his film *Maru Maru* in 1952. This was an adventure story with Errol Flynn and Ruth Roman. Burr played a shady promoter in it. During the shoot, he flirted with costar Paul Picerni. One night when they were playing cribbage, Picerni saw a look in Burr's eyes that made him think he was "on the make." Picerni said he felt "like a dame." "He was gay and he was making a move on me" (Starr, 52–3).

Burr met Robert Benevides, the love of his life, on the set of *Perry Mason* in the midfifties; they became a couple in 1960. Benevides was a small-time actor who was thirteen years Burr's junior. He gave up acting in 1963 to become a production consultant on the series. They kept their relationship discreet, but most people in the film industry knew Burr was queer by now. If he was a leading actor he might have been outed. Being a supporting one meant he could fly under the radar. Or, as the title of Starr's biography of him phrased it, "hide in plain sight."

The only time his gayness threatened his career was in 1961 when he spent a night with a barman called Ray Reynolds. Reynolds moonlighted as a drag queen, "Libby" Reynolds. He sold the story of their night together to *Confidential* magazine, but a totally different version of the events he related was what appeared in the magazine's pages. The story was titled "TV's Perry Mason Gets Fooled: The Case of the Miss Who was a Mister-y" (*Confidential*, April 1961). In the printed article, Burr came across as someone who thought Reynolds was a woman. Reynolds vehemently denied this. "They changed the story," he rasped, "prettying it up" as "a drag queen thing" to save Burr's heterosexual reputation (Starr, 2008: 125). The magazine was possibly paid more to kill the story than it paid Reynolds to run it.

Hedda Hopper wrote to Burr shortly afterward to say she'd received a compromising letter about him in the mail but that she wasn't going to divulge its contents to the media (Summers, 2005: 57). Her protectiveness may have owed something to the fact that her son William was in the cast of *Perry Mason* (Mann, 2001: 313).

In 1963, Burr and Benevides bought a Fijian Island called Naitauba where they raised and sold orchids through their company Sea God Nurseries. They also ran a cattle ranch there and built houses and schools to help the island's 150 residents have better lives. Burr showed his benevolent nature now. He had a big heart and wanted to share the money he'd made in films with those less fortunate than himself. He also fostered children here. He loved children; it was one of the regrets of his life that he couldn't have a child himself. This was perhaps the reason he "invented" one.

Away from the media spotlight in Naitiuba, he could be his real self with Benevides. More often than not he played the "wife" to his partner. "If you went to their house," a spokesman stated, "Raymond would be wearing a frilly pink apron and doing the ironing." He fussed around like the woman of the house, referring to Benevides as his husband. He also knitted sweaters for him in front of the fire (*Sunday Mail*, November 30, 2003).

Burr and Benevides moved their orchid business to California in 1980, donating many of their flowers to the California State Polytechnic University of Pomona. Afterward they ventured into grape growing and wine production. By now Benevides was producing the many *Perry Mason* movies that Burr made at the tail end of his career to capitalize on the nostalgic fervor the series still held for those viewers who'd been nurtured on it during the fifties and sixties. He completed his last *Perry Mason* film in August 1993. By now he was suffering from cancer. He died of the disease the following month.

In his will he left everything to Benevides, omitting all family members, including his sister, Geraldine, whom he was close to. "I give all my jewelry," he wrote, "my clothing, books, works of art, household furnishings and furniture, automobiles and other items of a personal nature, together with any insurance on such property, to Robert Benevides." Burr's biographer wrote, "Just what sin Geraldine committed to be written out of his will remains anyone's guess" (Starr, 2008: 217).

Geraldine didn't bear any grudges toward her brother, having as much affection for him as he had for her, but in February 1994 the will was contested by a nephew and niece of his. Both of them claimed he'd been manipulated by Benevides into bequeathing everything to him.

The case was eventually thrown out. Benevides had the last word on his deceased (and very generous) lover: "Anybody who thinks that anybody could ever have influenced Raymond Burr to do anything is crazy" (*London Daily Mail*, February 18, 1994).

Further Reading

Confidential, April 1961.

Hughes, Dorothy B. 1978. *Erle Stanley Gardner: The Case of the Real Perry Mason*. New York: William Morrow.

London Daily Mail, February 18, 1994.

Mann, William J. 2001. *Behind the Screen: How Gays and Lesbians Shaped Hollywood, 1919–1969*. New York: Viking.

Starr, Michael Seth. 2008. *Hiding in Plain Sight: The Secret Life of Raymond Burr*. New York: Applause Theater and Cinema Books.

Summers, Claude J., ed. 2005. *The Queer Encyclopedia of Film and Television.* San Francisco: Cleis Press.
Sunday Mail, November 30, 2003.
TV Radio Mirror, October 1957.
TV Radio Mirror, 1968.

Cabaret (1972)

This film was Bob Fosse's musical version of Christopher Isherwood's short story collection, *The Berlin Stories*. It had previously been filmed as *I Am a Camera* in 1955 by Henry Cornelius using a screenplay from John van Druten, who adapted his own play of the same name to write it. It wasn't too well received, particularly by *Time* magazine, the film critic there dismissing it with the devastating pun, "Me no Leica" (Freedland, 1988: 161).

Cornelius's feature looked almost quaint in comparison with the razzle-dazzle atmosphere Fosse created here. Liza Minnelli was also more vibrant as the new Sally Bowles, despite the fabulous performance Julie Harris gave in the original film. Here Bowles's dizzy joie de vivre acquired a surreal tinge under Fosse's manic direction. He catapults his heroine and her sometime lover Michael York into a pre–World War II Germany with an electrified magnetism.

York plays Brian Roberts, an ambitious author who's traveled to Berlin to look for work as an English tutor while completing a doctorate in philosophy. Bowles has gone there with acting aspirations but has instead become a dancer in the Kit Kat Club. It's presided over by the leering, lascivious master of ceremonies played by Joel Grey, reprising the role he played in the Broadway production of the film. He appears in white makeup, rouged lips, and plastered-back hair. He took his look from the androgynous café performers of the 1930s.

Before long, Bowles is living with Roberts in the Schneider rooming house. She's attracted to him. She tries to arouse his interest in her, but he rebuffs her advance. This she accepts philosophically. "Sex always screws up a relationship if you let it," she drones, "so we won't let it."

She feels he's bisexual but she isn't sure. She wants to find out. "Listen," she teases, "we're practically living together. If you only like boys I wouldn't dream of pestering you." Pretty soon she learns he doesn't "only" like boys as they begin an affair.

She doesn't "only" like Roberts either. After a while she starts dating the aristocrat Maximilian Von Heune (Helmut Griem). Then Roberts begins romancing Von Heune.

"Screw Max," Roberts says to her one day when he's been annoying him. "I do," Sally replies, drawing the further response from Roberts, "So do I!" This became the film's most quoted interchange.

Sally oscillates between the two men and then becomes pregnant by one of them. She announces the news with typical ebullience in the silence of a library. She tells Roberts she isn't sure who the father is, but he says he still wants the baby. Notwithstanding this, she refuses his offer, not being ready to be a mother yet. She decides to have an abortion, paying for it with her beloved fur coat.

The film relishes its sense of "divine decadence" (Carrick, 1993: 75). In one scene during a show at the Kit Kat Club, a woman whips another one who's chained to a bed frame. At the other end of the stage a man in a hat watches them while smoking a cigar. Beside him is a nude woman playing a violin.

Like Bowles's life, it moves at a frantic pace, rarely pausing for breath in its two-hour running time. Fosse captures Berlin on the cusp of the Holocaust. Nobody at the Kit Kat Club seems to want to know about this, content to belt out riotous dance tunes such as "Money, Money, Money" (an incomparable duet between Minnelli and Grey) as a group of Nazis beat a man unconscious outside. Their violence is intercut with a parody of Tyrol folk dancers wearing lederhosen.

Fosse telegraphs the military fervor gradually, having a Nazi sing a song called "Tomorrow Belongs to Me" in a manner that begins innocently and then works up to a nationalistic frenzy. The three lovers seem oblivious to Hitler's rise, which makes it even more ominous. Sally fiddles as Berlin prepares to burn. Grey ushers in the forthcoming inferno with his Luciferean leers.

Minnelli had a wild time making the film, immersing herself in the debauchery of German *beerkielers*. "It was so glamorous in Berlin then," she gushed. "The writers were in Paris but the fun seekers were in Berlin" (Mair, 1996: 120).

Her main problem was trying to find the best wardrobe for her character. She considered going for a Marlene Dietrich look but then thought: Why repeat something that's already been done? In the end she opted for a pixie image: bowler hat, halter top, bow tie, belts, garters, black net stockings.

For research purposes she toured other cities besides Berlin. "In Hamburg we went to the dens of sin on the Reepersbahn," she recalled, "where they still had semblances of cabarets going. There were lesbian fights in mud puddles on stage and pornographic shows in which the audiences were invited to participate" (Mair, 121). Fosse wasn't able to dredge up as many drag queens as he wanted for the film, so some of them were played by women. He forbade them to shave under their arms until shooting was completed.

This is Liza Minnelli's talismanic performance just as much as *The Wizard of Oz* was her mother's. Famous posters of her feature her doing her nightclub routine in *that* hat, *that* bandanna, *that* getup. The way she sang "Come to the Cabaret," the film's title song, had as much of an impact on her career as the rendition of "Over the Rainbow" had for Judy Garland in the earlier film.

York can't compete with her effervescent richness. Like hers, his sexuality is confused. It increases the allure of the film that it isn't explained or explored fully. Sex, like politics, hangs on the fringe of everything. Fosse commits himself fully only to the dancing and the music—his *forte*.

Roberts was indeterminately queer in *I Am a Camera*. Isherwood was a detached figure in this version of the story, a fact telegraphed by the film's original title. "I am a camera with the shutter open," Isherwood wrote in *Goodbye to Berlin*, the story on which *Cabaret* is based. "Recording, not thinking. Recording the man shaving at the window opposite the woman in the kimono washing her hair"

(Isherwood, 1978: 11). Minnelli and Grey occupy opposite ends of the spectrum, throwing themselves into the action like people possessed.

Cabaret swept the boards at the Oscar ceremonies, winning almost everything except Best Film. It would probably have gotten that too if it wasn't facing *The Godfather*. Minnelli won Best Actress, Grey got Best Supporting Actor, and Fosse was named Best Director. The film also won awards for Cinematography, Sound, and Editing.

"Come to the cabaret," she sang, and they did. The film cost just $4 million to make but earned $18 million in North America alone. It made Minnelli an international star and became the role for which she would be most remembered.

Related Films
I Am a Camera (1955); *The Damned* (1969); *All that Jazz* (1979); *City of Lost Souls* (1983); *Escape to Life: The Erika and Klaus Mann Story* (2000).

Further Reading
Carrick, Peter. 1993. *Liza Minnelli*. London: Robert Hale.
Freedland, Michael. 1988. *Liza with a Z: A Biography of Liza Minnelli*. London: Robert Hale.
Grubb, Kevin Boyd. 1989. *Razzle Dazzle: The Life and Work of Bob Fosse*. New York: St. Martin's Press.
Isherwood, Christopher. 1978. *Goodbye to Berlin*. London: Vintage.
Leigh, Wendy. 1993. *Liza Minnelli: Born a Star*. London: Hodder & Stoughton.
Mair, George. 1996. *Under the Rainbow: The Real Liza Minnelli*. Secaucus, NJ: Birch Lane Press.
Parish, James Robert, with Jack Ano. 1975. *Liza: Her Cinderella Nightmare*. London: W. H. Allen.

Capote (2005)

Instead of giving us a cradle-to-grave trawl through Truman Capote's life, director Bennett Miller chooses to focus here on his involvement in the circumstances surrounding *In Cold Blood*, his best-known work. It was also the book that evinced his ability to merge fact and fiction seamlessly into one narrative. The film shows us his ruthlessly ambitious qualities, and the manner in which he's willing to subjugate the people at the center of that book—the innocent as well as the guilty—to his own self-aggrandizement. Miller takes Gerald Clarke's biography of Capote as his template.

In Cold Blood, as most people know, is a fly-on-the-wall account of the senseless murder of a rural family in Kansas in 1959. Two small-time criminals, Perry Smith and Richard Hickock, broke into a farmhouse imagining they would net $10,000 from their night's work. Instead it descended into a bloodbath. After their arrest and lengthy court proceedings, they were sentenced to death for the slaughter of four members of the Clutter family.

Always the opportunist, Capote is aware from early on that the book he's working on is a potential gold mine. He's inspired to write it from an article from the *New York Times* of November 1959. The heading, "Wealthy Farmer, 3 of Family

Slain," catches his eye. He decides to visit Holcomb, the town where it happened. His childhood friend, Harper Lee, who'd just published *To Kill a Mockingbird*, agrees to go with him. She's played by Catherine Keener.

Philip Seymour Hoffman played Capote. He was delighted with the fact that Miller was using Clarke's book as the basis for the film. He said he wouldn't have been interested in a straight-up biopic, though he liked the idea of playing a real person because it gave him the chance to research him (*Capote*: Special Features).

He studied videotapes to learn how to best do his voice, his walk, the way he rolled his eyes or smoked a cigarette, even the way he stroked his hair. The voice was more important than anything else. Hoffman had this down cold. He sounded so much like Capote he could have *been* him. He imitated the "pansy" voice, as Karl Bissinger described it, to perfection (Plimpton, 1998: 90). He also got the trademark lisp, giving it an "artificial sophistication" when he was speaking formally or reading from his books (*Capote* DVD: Special Features).

When Capote first arrived in Kansas he was disliked by the locals. They thought he looked down on them as "a bunch of hicks" (Plimpton, 1998: 170). Afterward he won them over by his charm. "Now I'm practically the mayor of the town!" he crowed (*Capote* DVD: Special Features).

Hickock and Smith were still on the loose when Capote started writing his book. It was an evolving story, which made it more exciting for the journalist in him. When they were arrested, it became exciting for him in a different way. He didn't know why they killed four people for no apparent reason. They weren't even sure themselves.

Smith said he had nothing against the Clutter family. Capote believed his life was such a disaster zone, he would have killed anyone that night. "They never did anything to me," Smith admitted, "the way other people have all my life. Maybe they were just the ones that had to pay for it" (Plimpton, 1998: 203).

Both Smith and Hickock had lived reckless lives. Smith's mother abandoned him when he was a child, and his father was absent more often than not as well. Two of his sisters committed suicide. Hickock had been in and out of jail for bouncing checks. The pair of them were actually cell mates for a time.

Capote succeeded in getting both men to trust him. Smith was quiet at first, but when he began to talk he told him everything about himself. Both of them knew about the book he was writing. He read parts of it to them. Hickock wanted to change the style of it so it could help him escape the death penalty. Smith kept asking him why he was writing it. When Capote said he wanted it to be a work of art, Smith said, "What an irony. That's all I ever wanted to do my whole life, and now what's happened? An incredible situation where I kill four people and you're going to produce a work of art" (Plimpton, 205).

Capote felt the book would have had more of a "wow" factor if the two men were executed. He milked Smith for the recollections of his past and then jettisoned him when he was no further use to him from a literary point of view. No more than Marlon Brando, whom Capote aurally raped for an interview when Brando was in the early stages of his career, Capote took no prisoners when it came to the collating of material for his work. He spared no blushes either. If an interviewee was willing to kiss and tell, whatever the circumstances (he got Brando drunk; Smith was facing down the gallows), Capote was only too delighted to transcribe the material in whatever way he saw fit. Literature was the burnt altar upon which he sacrificed the sensitivities of his quarries.

One writer went so far as to say that Smith and Hickock were executed "for the personal convenience of Truman Capote" (Plimpton, 215). It was a joke but it held a grain of truth. Capote was very hurt by the comment, aired on the *Tonight Show Starring Johnny Carson.*

"There was nothing I could have done to save them," he says to Lee after they're executed. "Maybe not," she replies, "but the fact is, you didn't want to." He knows she's right about this, so he doesn't dispute it.

Capote was a complex man. He had childlike tantrums. Sometimes he was mistaken for being a woman, so effeminate was his voice. This didn't bother him (Plimpton, 173). Beneath the timid appearance lurked a rock-hard stubbornness.

Hoffman won an Oscar for his performance. He promised he would "bark like a dog" if he won, but in the end all he did was say to his mother, "Be proud, Mom, because I'm proud of you and we're here tonight and it's so good" (Piazza and Kinn, 2008: 332).

He died from a drug overdose in 2014 but left a legacy of work that's mind-boggling. *Capote* is arguably his finest hour. It has all the nuances that separate merely good performances from great ones. His secret was not letting his tics take over the mood that's called for in any particular scene, making them subservient to such moods so that audiences weren't aware of an impersonation taking place. They were too immersed in the action.

After *Capote* was released, writer/director Douglas McGrath made *Infamous*, which traded on much of the same material. Toby Jones gave an adequate performance as Capote, but he was no Hoffman. Neither was Sandra Bullock in the same league as Catherine Keener in the role of Lee. There are some efforts made in the film to suggest a sexual charge between Capote and Smith. McGrath trades on George Plimpton's biography of Capote rather than Gerald Clarke's, but the subject matter—the Clutter murders and their aftermath—is the same, making this like an unnecessary footnote to Miller's pulsating movie.

Related Films
In Cold Blood (1967); *Other Voices, Other Rooms* (1997); *Capote* DVD: Special Features (2005); *Infamous* (2006).

Further Reading
Capote, Truman. 2000. *In Cold Blood*. London: Penguin.
Clarke, Gerald. 2006. *Capote: A Biography*. London: Abacus.
Grobel, Lawrence. 1985. *Conversations with Truman Capote*. Plume.
Hunter, J. T. 2016. *In Colder Blood*. Toronto: RJ Parker Publishing.
Piazza, Jim, and Gail Kinn. 2008. *The Academy Awards: The Complete Unofficial History*. New York: Black Dog & Leventhal.
Plimpton, George. 1998. *Truman Capote*. New York: Picador.
Whale, Chase, ed. 2016. *Philip Seymour Hoffman. Brilliant. Troubled. Tragic.* London: Plexus.

Carol (2015)

It's Christmastime. A sales assistant in a Santa hat stands behind a counter in Frankenberg's department store in Manhattan. An older woman in a fur coat approaches her. They engage in conversation about a proposed Christmas gift for the woman's daughter. The assistant suggests a train set. The woman thinks it's a good idea. Before she goes away she says to her, "I like the hat." With these four words their relationship has already begun. It's love at first sight.

Patricia Highsmith wrote *Carol* in 1952. It was then called *The Price of Salt*. She'd already written *Strangers on a Train*, another novel with a queer subtext that Alfred Hitchcock adapted for film. She wrote both novels under a pseudonym, Claire Morgan. The subject matter was too hot to handle for a woman using her real name at the time.

Being lesbian wasn't usually dealt with by high-class writers like Highsmith in the fifties, only lower-grade ones who specialized in pulp fiction. Highsmith's prose was, as one writer put it, "as exotic as a leopard in a third Avenue deli" (Highsmith, 2010: v). She received a lot of fan mail from closet lesbians who found in her work a liberating sense of joy. She also received many letters from closeted gay men. These meant just as much to her, if not more.

The Price of Salt was before its time. "My young protagonist," wrote Highsmith, "may appear a shrinking violet but those were the days when gay bars were a dark door somewhere in Manhattan" (Highsmith, 2010: 311). If people wanted to go to one, they usually got off the subway a stop before or after where it was to avoid drawing attention to themselves.

Carol is sometimes referred to as the first lesbian novel that had a happy ending. Lesbians in literature before this often ended their lives suicidally or had broken hearts mended by men who conveniently arrived on the scene when the inconvenient "other" woman departed.

The story of *Carol* was based on fact. As a young woman, Highsmith worked in the toy section of a department store in New York. One day a society matron came in looking for a gift for her child. Highsmith was immediately smitten with her. "I felt odd and swimmy in the head," she recalled, "near to fainting yet at the same time uplifted, as if I'd seen a vision" (Highsmith, 2010: 309).

In the film version, Rooney Mara plays Therese Belivet. She's an aspiring young photographer who's engaged to be married to her boyfriend. She doesn't really love him but could easily drift into marriage with him like so many others of her time. Cate Blanchett is Carol Aird, a suburban housewife in her thirties who's in the throes of a messy divorce. Todd Haynes directs.

Haynes had directed Blanchett once before, in the kaleidoscopic portrait of Bob Dylan, *I'm Not There* (2007). She played a female version of the rocker. Haynes joked of *Carol*, "I wanted to see how she'd look playing a woman for a change." Rooney was interested in it because it was the only one of Highsmith's novels that wasn't about the criminal mind: "It was about the amorous mind" (*Carol* DVD: Special Features).

When Carol and Therese begin their relationship, it angers Carol's husband, Harge (Kyle Chandler). He's hostile to her when Carol invites her out to their luxurious house in New Jersey. He refuses to accept it on moral grounds. If she doesn't end it, he says, he'll see that she loses custody of their daughter, Rindy. Another man would have been acceptable to him but not another woman. That's the ultimate indignity, even though their marriage is over.

To take her mind off her problems, Carol invites Therese on a road trip with her. It's during this that they become lovers. A private investigator, however, has been employed by Harge to spy on them. The information he receives has huge repercussions for Carol's divorce, and it also affects her psychologically. She eventually has to see a psychiatrist.

Therese, meanwhile, concentrates on her photographic career. It looks like her romance is over. Carol then admits to her divorce lawyers that she's been intimate with Therese. She lets Harge have Rindy. Later on, Carol meets Therese in a hotel lounge. She tells her she loves her and wants to live with her. Therese doesn't know what she wants.

In the final scene, Therese decides Carol is the woman for her. She goes to a hotel where Carol has said she can meet her if she wishes. When she gets there, she sees her among a group of people. She looks over at her. After a few moments, Carol looks back. She smiles. It mirrors the opening scene. Carol hasn't changed—she always knew what she wanted—but Therese has. The film is really about her journey. All Carol's struggles have been about her situation. Therese's have been about herself.

Carol doesn't need to do or say anything beyond this brief acknowledgment of Therese. She doesn't even need to stand up. Another director might have created melodrama here, but Haynes doesn't. He refuses to employ the melodramatic style of *Brief Encounter*, preferring to play things down. Carol's expression says: "I knew you would come to me." Highsmith wrote in her book, "Perhaps Carol knew at this moment, because Carol had known such things before." She gives an "eager greeting" to Therese (Highsmith, 2010: 306–7). In the film, she just glances casually at her. This was better. Therese's being there is enough. Together they've beaten the odds.

Haynes directs in his usual sumptuous style, the lavish sets combining with Ed Lachman's stunning cinematography to create the kind of lush atmosphere he wants. Dialogue is kept at a minimum. The faces of the two women make language redundant. The film plays out like a visual symphony, using an evocative score from Carter Burwell. The attention to detail is exquisite.

The emotion between Therese and Carol takes a while to come to a boil. When it does, Haynes handles it with the delicacy one has come to expect from this fine director. *Carol* is a cool, leisurely paced mood piece that echoes the sexual terrain of *Far from Heaven* (2002), Haynes's other gay parable set in the fifties, if not its tension. To replace that, here there are two stars at the top of their game: a tutor and a tyro, uniting body and mind in an elegant film that achieves its effects delicately.

From a thematic point of view, the film evokes two television films, *A Question of Love* from 1978, which had Gena Rowlands leaving her husband for another woman, and *An Unexpected Love* (2002) where Leslie Hope undertook a similar odyssey from marriage with a man to a lesbian relationship with a woman.

Haynes works hard to make it look easy. For *Far from Heaven* he used the works of Douglas Sirk to get the look right. Here he preferred old photographs of the period to procure the grainy texture he sought. A muted color palette gave the film its visual sensibility. Lachman used rain-soaked windows and nighttime condensation to frame the "emotional context" (*Carol* DVD: Special Features).

Carol won the GLAAD Media Award for Outstanding Film of the Year in 2015. In March 2016, the British Film Institute (BFI) voted it the best LGBTQ film of all time. This was something of an overstatement but an indication nonetheless of the high critical esteem in which it was held.

Related Films
Desert Hearts (1985); *Lianna* (1985); *Far from Heaven* (2002); *Carol* DVD (2014).

Further Reading
Aldrich, Ann. 2006. *We Walk Alone*. New York: The Feminist Press.
Highsmith, Patricia. 2010. *Carol*. London: Bloomsbury.
Rich, B. Ruby. 1998. *Chick Flicks*. Durham, NC, and London: Duke University.
Schenker, Joan. 2009. *The Talented Miss Highsmith: The Secret Life and Serious Art of Patricia Highsmith*. New York: St. Martin's Press.

The Celluloid Closet (1995)

Codirected by Robert Epstein and Jeffrey Friedman, this film version of Vito Russo's landmark book of the same name covers the same ground he did but, for obvious reasons, in an infinitely less detailed manner. Narrated by Lili Tomlin and containing clips from over one hundred movies, it has interviews with people like Tony Curtis, Susan Sarandon, Tom Hanks, and Shirley MacLaine. Epstein and Friedman had previously collaborated on *Common Threads: Stories from the Quilt* (1989) and *The Times of Harvey Milk*, which won a Best Documentary award in 1984. Russo died of AIDS in 1990, so he didn't live to see the film.

It goes back to 1895 to show us two men dancing together in Thomas Edison's *Gay Brothers*.

In the beginning, the narrator states, queer people were no more than comic characters. This was evident in films like *Algie the Miner* (1912). In *Behind the Screen* (1916), Charlie Chaplin kissed a girl who was dressed like a man. He knew she wasn't one, but a man looking at him didn't. As a result, the man swished around in an effeminate manner to make fun of Chaplin.

The queer as an effeminate man was the film world's first stereotype. It was evident in films like *Broadway Melody* (1929) and *The Gay Divorcee* (1934). In *Myrt and Marge* (also 1934), a woman hands a dress to an effeminate male dress designer. She says, "Put that in the trunk—and don't wear it!" The designer snorts back, "Selfish!"

Tomlin says the sissy, as it was defined then, made men feel more manly and women feel more womanly by "occupying the space in between." Harvey Fierstein says this never bothered him. "I like the sissy," he claims, advocating

The Celluloid Closet (Book)

Vito Russo's astounding study of the portrayal of LGBTQ characters in films was first published in 1981. It's gone into numerous reprints since then. This is hardly surprising as it's been referenced in the lion's share of books that have come out on this subject since, being an encyclopedic guide to the injustices, oversights, stereotypes, bigotry, and convoluted history of the subject since the inception of the film industry.

Drawing on a huge range of sources and investing them all with his laser-like pen (often dipped in acid), Russo here produced the definitive work on his theme, name-checking over three hundred films from eighty years of filmmaking as he draws an arc from an era where the mere mention of anything smacking of sexual deviancy was strictly taboo to the present.

Russo begins when being gay is a "dirty secret" (Russo, 1987: xii). Such days were still in existence when he was writing the book. If anyone was in any doubt about this, the fact that so many people refused to be interviewed by him would enlighten them to the fact. Most of these were actors. Directors and producers proved more willing. They had a lower profile.

For many years, *The Celluloid Closet* was the "bible" of LGBTQ movie scholars. It was the definitive text they deferred to when searching for an insight into a film, or an explanation of it, or an ironic enlightened commentary on what it said—or failed to say. In more recent times, New Queer theorists have found issue with some of Russo's points, but even when they disagree with him they're referencing him. This in itself is an indication of the long shadow he casts.

In her book *From Reverence to Rape*, Molly Haskell says that society's lie about women is that they're inferior to men. The lie about lesbians and gay men, Russo writes, "is that we do not exist." Gay people, he felt, collaborated in that veil of invisibility (Russo, 1987: xii).

The Celluloid Closet removed such a veil forever.

visibility for queers at any cost, "because negativity is better than nothing. And besides, I *am* a sissy."

At the other end of the scale there were men-like women. Cue Marlene Dietrich in *Morocco* (1930) where she kisses a woman on the lips while dressed in a top hat and tails. The scene had nothing to do with the plot, which had her chasing Gary Cooper across a desert, but it lingered in many people's minds much longer than anything Dietrich did with Cooper. For Susie Bright, the romance with Cooper went "right out the window" after Dietrich's cheeky kiss.

The year after *Morocco* was made, the Catholic church and the Legion of Decency decided it was time to clamp down on the dangerous signals Hollywood was putting out regarding divergent sexuality. It employed a postmaster from Indiana as the chief guardian of virtue. His name was Will Hays. Along with Joseph Breen, who worked for the Motion Picture Association of America for two decades, he saw to it that anything even vaguely representing being gay was airbrushed out of films.

Directors had to be clever to sneak queer themes in under the wire. One of the ways they chose to do this was in vampire films like *Dracula's Daughter* (1936), which had a strong lesbian subtext. The clip shown from this film in *The Celluloid Closet* makes it abundantly clear what's going on between the vampire and her protégé, but it was still passed by Hays and Breen. "These guys weren't rocket scientists," says screenwriter Jay Presson Allen. "They missed a lot of stuff." In 1941, they also missed the fact that the character played by Peter Lorre in *The Maltese Falcon* was most probably gay. Or did they let it go because he played a villain? He's described as "queer" in the book. In the film he wears perfume.

A blind eye was also turned to a lesbian element in the prison drama *Caged* in 1950. This was probably because the women in question were behind bars and therefore not a danger to society. In the extract from the film that's shown in the documentary, the warden says to an inmate she fancies, "Let's you and me get acquainted, honey. Sit down on this chair. It's kind of roomy."

The documentary examines the queer element in films such as *Tea and Sympathy* (1953), *Rebel without a Cause* (1955), and *Ben-Hur* (1959). Cowboy films like *Red River* (1948) and "cowgirl" ones like *Johnny Guitar* are also discussed. A scene in *Gentlemen Prefer Blondes* (1953) where a very sexy Jane Russell walks through a gym full of muscular men who fail to show the slightest interest in her is very entertaining. "Is there anyone here for love?" she pines. "Doesn't anyone want to play?" Apparently not.

Narrating from a script by Armistead Maupin, Tomlin comments on the negative depiction of the lesbian character played by Barbara Stanwyck in *Walk on the Wild Side* (1962). Stanwyck was a bordello madam in the film. In the scene featured, she fears losing Capucine, one of her staff, to a male friend. To prevent this happening, she tells Capucine she needs to advise him of the fact that she's been "rolling around in the mud" for years.

The fact that many queer people had to die in films is made patently clear in the documentary as it looks at works such as *The Detective* (1968), *The Children's Hour* (1962), and *The Fox* (1968). If a woman slept with a man in a film, Arthur Laurents remarks, she was sent out in a storm as a punishment. If she slept with another woman, she had to hang herself.

A new era appears to dawn in the last part of the documentary as films like *The Boys in the Band* (1970) reach the screens. But there are still negative aspects to the depictions of queer people here. There are worse ones in *Staircase* (1969), *The Vanishing Point* (1971), and *Freebie and the Bean* (1974). In the last film, a killer transgender person gets "five million holes" pumped into him in the finale, the slaughter seeming to represent not only the death of a person but a condition as well.

A more positive sign is apparent in *Making Love* (1982). A precredit message explains that the film is about gay love rather than gay hate, or gay *self*-hate, as in previous years. The cast members were warned that it could destroy their careers, but they still agreed to appear in it. It wasn't a masterpiece, but it was a step in the right direction, making way for films like *Thelma and Louise* years later. Susan Sarandon is quoted as saying she was happy to be able to star in this, which is more about female empowerment than being lesbian. She says she saw it as a kind of partner piece to *Butch Cassidy and the Sundance Kid* (1969). The two women die at the end, but at least it's their decision. Before they die, they kiss. Wouldn't it have been nice, she suggests, if Paul Newman and Robert Redford kissed in *Butch Cassidy* before they went to their death?

The documentary ends with a discussion of one of the most high-profile queer films of the nineties, *Philadelphia* (1994). Jay Oxenbay gives it only a qualified recommendation. It was a well-made film, she allows, but the hero still dies at the end. Would it not have been better if he lived?

Related Films
Before Stonewall (1984); *Dry Kisses Only* (1990); *Ladies or Gentlemen* (2000).

Further Reading
Hays, Matthew. 2007. *The View from Here: Conversations with Gay and Lesbian Filmmakers.* Vancouver, BC: Arsenal Pulp Press.
Mann, William J. 2001. *Behind the Screen: How Gays and Lesbians Shaped Hollywood.* New York: Viking.
Russo, Vito. 1987. *The Celluloid Closet.* New York: Harper & Row.

The Children's Hour (1961)

The Children's Hour was based on Lillian Hellman's play of the same name. William Wyler, directing, had originally made it as *These Three* in 1936. It concerned two female teachers in a prestigious school, Martha Dobie and Karen Wright. In the play, Martha is in love with Karen, but it isn't reciprocated. A meddlesome child spreads a rumor about them, which exposes their relationship. In the end, Martha shoots herself when her romantic overtures toward Karen are rebuffed.

In the film version the teachers, played by Miriam Hopkins and Merle Oberon, weren't lesbians, just friends. Martha is in love with Karen's fiancé. Wyler wasn't allowed to use the word "lesbian." In fact he wasn't even allowed to mention the fact that it was based on Hellman's play. As a result, the conversations between Martha and Karen were cryptic to the point of being meaningless. Being lesbian was the sin that dared not speak its name.

In *These Three*, Hopkins played Martha and Oberon was Karen. Both of them vied for the affections of the handsome Dr. Cardin (Joel McCrea). Karen became engaged to him but Martha was accused of having an affair with him, an untrue rumor that brought the school—and the women's friendship—to ruin.

Sam Goldwyn produced *These Three*. He paid $50,000 for the rights to it but was informed that this was probably a waste of money. At that time the Production Code Administration (PCA), which oversaw films for sensitive moral content, was very powerful. As a result, he was informed the PCA's strictures would probably make much of the women's dialogue unusable. Goldwyn thought for a moment and then shot back chirpily, "So what's the problem? Make them Americans!" (Leff and Simmons, 2001: 73).

Wyler had to make the same compromises with the censors that another director who fell afoul of the PCA, Vincente Minnelli, had made five years before with his film *Tea and Sympathy*.

To get the film made he had to pretend his main character wasn't queer but effeminate, even though the whole film was about his sexuality. Directors played a kind of "double bluff" with the Production Code in those days, creating scenarios on celluloid that said one thing and meant another. A nod was as good as a wink to a blind horse.

The lesbian references were made more obvious in *The Children's Hour* than they were in *These Three* even though the word itself wasn't used. Even after a quarter of a century, Wyler still had to tread gently on this taboo subject, but the rumor spread by the meddlesome pupil to her grandmother is about the two women embracing. This was a step closer to Hellman's text.

Miriam Hopkins was relegated to the subsidiary role of the grandmother in this version, the main ones being played by Audrey Hepburn (Karen) and Shirley MacLaine (Martha). Both of them were mothers at the time and therefore thought as "safe" by casting agents. The prevailing attitude of the time was that a mother couldn't do anything sexually licentious to another mother. James Garner played Joe, Karen's boyfriend.

Martha and Karen are still teachers at a boarding school in this version. They're good friends but don't see themselves as being anything more than that. Then one day they're spotted embracing by the pupil, and she tells her grandmother. One thing leads to another and before long they're deemed to be involved in a sexual relationship together. It's a lie but it has the force of truth. Tongues wag. Eventually, pupils start to be withdrawn from the school.

As the parents arrive at the school to remove their children, they don't even tell Karen or Martha why they're doing so. When one parent finally does, Wyler shoots the scene mutely and from a distance so audiences won't be, as it were, contaminated by the dialogue. Joe is later sacked from his job at a local hospital merely because he's connected to Karen.

The lie has an element of truth in it. It makes Martha examine her feelings for Karen more deeply. When she does, she realizes there is indeed a sexual element there. In a sense, the child could be said to intuit something about her sexual orientation that she hasn't been aware of.

"There's something in you," Martha tells Karen in the play, "and you don't know it's there. It's been there since I first knew you." "It" was a frequent term for being lesbian in films just as it was for sex a generation before. It was the all-encompassing abstraction that was well-known in Hollywood. Wyler chose not to feature this speech in the film. MacLaine wanted him to, as did Hepburn, but if he did, he would have had a bigger headache with the church and the PCA than he already had. MacLaine believed he "chickened out" (Corber, 2011: 63).

Wyler, as one writer remarked, reinforced "the Cold War discourse of female homosexuality" because of Karen's failure to openly admit her sexual proclivities. As the final credits roll, it still remains indeterminate (Corber, 70).

"Good-bye," she says at Martha's coffin. "I'll love you until I die." This footage was an interesting concession from the Hays Office, the film industry's self-regulating censorship body that oversaw films for immoral content just as the PCA did. It was probably allowed because Arthur Krim, the then president of United Artists, threatened to release the film without a code. Hays, presumably, was mollified sufficiently by the fact that the dead Martha couldn't reciprocate Karen's love, at least in this life.

Even though Wyler made the film tamely, he put certain things into it that are sexual codes. When Martha locks herself into her room as she prepares to hang herself, Karen tries to break the door down by using a candlestick, a phallic symbol. This is meant to indicate a world of male supremacy where two women trying to live together haven't succeeded. The fact that Karen walks away from Garner in the final moments seems to suggest this isn't inviolable, as does her touching valediction to Martha at her coffin. Yes, Martha had to die to satisfy the moral guardians of the time, but even in death she had importance because she "lives," if you like, in Karen's memory.

The Children's Hour left many questions hanging in the air, but despite its sense of incompletion it was explicit enough for audiences to fill in the blanks the censors wouldn't. It also opened the door to other directors as enterprising as Wyler to feature lesbian themes in their films in the succeeding years. *The Fox* fudged its core message, but there were other films lining up to present viewers with different approaches to the lesbian experience—Shelley Winters in *The Balcony* in 1963 and Jean Seberg in *Lilith* the year after that, as well as Candice Bergen in *The Group*.

The film ends conveniently with Martha's suicide, a familiar "solution" to lesbian desire at this time. It differs from earlier explorations of the theme in that Karen mourns her dead lover more than previous screen lovers might, thereby endorsing the "forbidden love" to an extent.

At the end of the day, *The Children's Hour* was much ado about very little. Without being salacious, could Wyler not have intimated something more visual about the two women's physical relationship? A courthouse scene where a judge berated them for having "sinful sexual knowledge" of one another was deleted for fear of the censors. Wyler became as much a victim of Hollywood's sexual politics as women like Karen Wright and Martha Dobie were of the greater world's intolerance.

Everyone knew he had to make compromises to get the film onto the screen, but in many ways it was as tame as *These Three* because the characters' orientations weren't explicit. As a result, Martha's suicide seems an overreaction on her part, making the climax melodramatic. Martha has to die for her sin at the end because, as far as heterosexuals were concerned in 1961, "the only good lesbian was a dead one" (Darren, 2000: 45).

Wyler said *The Children's Hour* was more about the power of gossip than sex. This didn't make sense as the poster for it said the women were "different." "Different" was a code for "lesbian." Showing the two of them close together, it said, "Did nature play an ugly trick and endow them with emotions contrary to those of normal young women?"

The film took Hepburn's career into a new direction, even if she didn't exploit this to its full potential in future years. MacLaine had already played some edgy roles, so her casting was less of a surprise. *The Children's Hour* probably went as far as it could, something that's underlined by the fact that in the late 1970s, almost two decades after it was made, a senator called John Briggs proposed a bill in California that would have barred queer teachers from working in that state's schools. It was defeated, but only just.

Related Films
These Three (1936); *The Fox* (1968); *In & Out* (1977).

Further Reading
Benshoff, Harry M. 2006. *Queer Images: A History of Gay and Lesbian Film in America.* Oxford, UK: Rowman & Littlefield.
Corber, Robert J. 2011. *Cold War Femme: Lesbianism, National Identity and Hollywood Cinema.* Durham, NC, and London: Duke University Press.
Hellman, Lillian. 1972. *The Collected Plays.* Boston: Little Brown & Co.
Leff, Leonard J., and Jerrold J. Simmons. 2001. *The Dame in the Kimono: Hollywood, Censorship and the Production Code.* Lexington: University Press of Kentucky.
Spoto, Donald. 2007. *Enchantment: The Life of Audrey Hepburn.* London: Arrow.
White, Patricia. 1999. *Uninvited: Classical Hollywood Cinema and Lesbian Representability.* Bloomington: Indiana University Press.

Montgomery Clift (1920–66)

Clift was essentially a woman's star, as Mary Burton noted. "Women flocked to see him in droves," she said, "but he had difficulty attracting male audiences. Men found him too soft, too effeminate" (Burton, 1983: 97). The kind of men he appealed to were often dephallicized ones. Both Marilyn Monroe and Elizabeth Taylor said they felt protective toward him; he was like the brother they never had.

"The male Garbo" was another epithet ascribed to him. His biographer Patricia Bosworth said he walked with an androgynous swagger in his films. This seemed to say to women, "You think you're beautiful? Well I'm beautiful too" (Bosworth, 1978: 213). Several scenes from *Freud*, John Huston's biopic of the famous psychologist, had to be reshot because Clift's walk in them seemed to be too effeminate.

The romantic scenes in his films were characterized more by affection than intense desire. Lee Remick, who appeared opposite him in *Wild River* (1960), thought he was incapable of acting as the dominant party in such scenes: "In every love scene, his head would end up on my shoulder" (LaGuardia, 1977: 207).

Such scenes were narratively problematized. In *The Heiress* (1949), his attraction to Olivia de Havilland is more to her purse than her body. In *A Place in the Sun* (1951), he can't devote himself totally to Elizabeth Taylor because Shelley Winters is in the way and had to be killed off. In *I Confess* (1953), he can't consummate his love for Anne Baxter because he's a priest. Such plotlines suited him because of the troubled persona he exuded so well on screen. Jane Fonda compared him to a wound (McCann, 1991: 47).

With his wide eyes and his air of remote fragility, Clift spoke to queer men and lonely women. He was never going to be an alpha male in the Clark Gable/John Wayne mold. He hunched his shoulders and wore a hunted, haunted look. The weight of the world seemed to be on them. Allied to that was his incredible charisma. The camera loved him just as much as it did Tyrone Power, another photogenic actor who was rumored to have queer tendencies. These two stars were

Red River (1948)

One of Clift's most suggestive queer scenes features in this early film of his from Howard Hawks. In it he compares his six-shooter with that of John Ireland.

Ireland says to Clift, "That's a good-lookin' gun you were about to use back there. Can I see it?" Clift shows it to him and he fondles it. "Nice, awful nice," he remarks. "Maybe you'd like to see mine." Clift takes him up on his offer.

Ireland plays a character called—appropriately—Cherry. "There are two things more beautiful than a good gun," he tells Clift, "a Swiss watch or a woman from anywhere. You ever had a Swiss watch?" Later on, Ireland says he went on the cattle drive that's at the center of the plot because he took a liking to Clift's gun. Another character observes that Clift and Ireland are having "a peculiar kind of fun, sizing each other up for the future."

Clift coded his orientation to viewers in a manner that protected him from full disclosure. This also meant he escaped the rigors of the Motion Picture Production Code Association. The MPPCA seemed oblivious to phallic imagery like this but blew a fuse at the first sign of anything more overtly sexual.

Clift's primary relationship in the film is to John Wayne, a more rough-and-tumble cowboy than he was. Clift wore his cowboy suit almost as effeminately as Dirk Bogarde would his in *The Singer Not the Song* (1960). Wayne was often partnered with "pretty" young costars, like Ricky Nelson in *Rio Bravo* (1958) as he was with Clift here. Joanne Dru roars at them in one scene when they're arguing, "Why don't you two recognize that you really love each other?"

Steven Cohan wrote, "Through the performativity and bisexuality that coalesced in his star persona to signify his mercurial boyishness, Clift crosses the boundaries structuring the virility of a 'he-man' star like John Wayne, causing a disturbance in the traditional ground of gender representation" (Cohan, 1997: 263).

The last scene in the film, significantly, has him looking at Wayne—not Dru.

---

probably the only two in Hollywood who were gazed at just as much by men as women when they were in romantic clinches.

Clift disappeared from the screen between 1953 and 1957. He spent most of these years drinking. Then he had a horrible accident outside Elizabeth Taylor's house when he drove his car into a tree on the way home from a party. He was drunk at the time. She heard the collision, which happened on the winding driveway from her home. She tried to get him to talk when she reached the car but he couldn't. He was choking on two teeth that had come loose and gone down his throat. She put her hand into his mouth and pulled them out, probably saving his life in the process. It was something he wouldn't forget. In an industry where most people betrayed you in some way sooner or later, she was one of the few stalwart friends he had.

In the years after the accident, which both disfigured and partially paralyzed his face, the now even more fragile Clift became addicted to both booze and painkillers. Tennessee Williams said he sometimes saw him washing down codeine with bottles of brandy.

Other friends and colleagues had to watch him turn from pinup of yesteryear to a stumbling, stuttering wreck. At the premiere of *Judgment at Nuremberg*, he arrived drunk out of his mind and proceeded to jump on Spencer Tracy's back. He crawled between the aisles of the cinema and hollered out inanities at anyone he recognized. On other occasions he threw himself off sofas and tables for fun when he drank too much, even in the middle of conversations. Sometimes he was so drunk in bars he would slump from his chair onto the ground. His friends would leave him asleep in a ball until it was time to go home.

One of his favorite stunts was dangling from the windows of high-rise apartments. Sometimes he tried it bat-style, hanging by his legs. A fall would have meant instant death, but he never seemed concerned about that. Sometimes he pretended to have leaped out of the window, only to reappear moments later sporting a broad grin. On one occasion he even hung out of the porthole of a ship.

On a shopping spree with Truman Capote in 1963, he bought sixteen sweaters in an exclusive store, dumped them all in the gutter outside, and then went back in and paid the bill. This was after just one drink.

Clift had a dominant mother and an absent father. His best friends, ironically, were women; people like Taylor, who stuck by him through thick and thin, and Marilyn Monroe, who claimed he was the only person in Hollywood who was more troubled than she was. The men he knew (Frank Sinatra, Clark Gable, John Huston) were generally intolerant. On the set of *The Misfits*, Gable continually referred to him by a gay slur.

Clift's biographers have been as slow to uncover any of his male lovers as Clift himself was to identify them during his lifetime. One who spoke said, "Our affair was for me the most beautiful experience of my life. When we were alone it was like Monty and I were shut away from reality for a couple of hours. Alone we could be emotional and passionate but outside we had to hide our feelings . . . One of the things that was starting to torture Monty back in 1940 was the fact that he had to hide his sexual feelings. He despised deception and felt the intolerable strain of living a lie" (Waugh, 2000: 95).

He blamed his mother for being gay. He asked his doctor once if it was possible that he'd started life as a female embryo (Leonard, 1997: 170). "He wanted to love women," said Deborah Kerr, who starred with him in *From Here to Eternity* (1953), "but he was attracted to men and he crucified himself for it" (Leonard, 155). When he was sober he fought his urges, but when he was drunk he succumbed to them. Every morning he was sober. Almost every night he was drunk.

When he wasn't shooting a film, he cruised the bars near his apartment looking to pick up men or be picked up by them. Anything was better than tossing and turning in his bed trying to sleep. As time went on, the sleeping pills to which he'd become addicted after his accident didn't work anymore.

Sometimes he went for "rough trade" in the bars. When these men saw who he was, they couldn't believe their eyes (Leonard, 273). He was rarely attracted to men who approached him, preferring "the meaner types, the sort who just looked, dangerously, from across the room, although he was terrified one of them might be a journalist in disguise. Yet part of him flirted with disaster. Like a nun, he needed to be flagellated for his sins" (Leonard, 160).

He was about to come out of the closet, at least on celluloid, when he died. He'd been slated to play the repressed queer character in John Huston's adaptation of Carson McCullers's *Reflections in a Golden Eye* in 1966, despite Huston's terrible treatment of him in *Freud*. He was looking forward to working with Elizabeth Taylor. She was going to be playing his wife in the film.

On the night of July 22, 1966, Clift's partner, Lorenzo Jones, noticed that *The Misfits* was on television. He asked him if he wanted to see it. "Absolutely not," Clift rasped. Was this his way of renouncing the past? Was it too painful for him to have to think of Marilyn Monroe, who'd died so recently from a drug overdose with a telephone in her hand? Whatever the reason, he went up to his room, locked the door, and took down a book to read. He was found dead the next morning, naked as the dead Monroe had been, with a book beside him instead of a telephone. He was only forty-five years old (Leonard, 292).

Related Films
Red River (1948); *The Heiress* (1949); *A Place in the Sun* (1951); *I Confess* (1953); *Suddenly, Last Summer* (1959); *Wild River* (1960); *Judgment at Nuremberg* (1961); *The Misfits* (1961); *Montgomery Clift: The Prince* (1988).

Further Reading
Bosworth, Patricia. 1978. *Montgomery Clift: A Biography*. New York: Harcourt Brace.
Bradshaw, Jon. 1985. *Dreams That Money Can Buy: The Tragic Life of Libby Holman*. New York: William Morrow & Co.
Burton, Mary. 1983. *Stars of the Forties and Fifties*. Sydney: Endeavor Books.
Cohan, Steven. 1997. *Masked Men: Masculinity and the Movies in the Fifties*. Bloomington and Indianapolis: Indiana University Press.
LaGuardia, Robert. 1977. *Monty: A Biography of Montgomery Clift*. New York: Arbor House.
Leonard, Maurice. 1997. *Montgomery Clift*. London: Hodder & Stoughton.
McCann, Graham. 1991. *Rebel Males: Clift, Brando and Dean*. London: Hamish Hamilton.
Waugh, Thomas, ed. 2000. *The Fruit Machine: Twenty Years of Writings on Queer Cinema*. Durham, NC, and London: Duke University Press.

Quentin Crisp (1908–99)

Crisp was born Denis Charles Pratt on Christmas Day, 1908. He was the youngest of four children born to a solicitor and a nursery governess. "As soon as I stepped out of my mother's womb," he famously pronounced, "I realized I had made a mistake" (Bailey, 2001: 123).

He's an unusual gay icon in the sense that he never embraced being gay. In fact he reviled it. He delighted in playing the role of the limp-wristed queen, the kind of figure the New Queer Movement actively seeks to excoriate.

Crisp saw being gay as a disfigurement, a crippling liability. "I regarded all heterosexuals, however low," he wrote once, "as superior to any homosexual, however noble" (Bailey, 125). The sentiments he espoused throughout his life, similar in tone to this, flew in the face of everything the Stonewall age fought so hard to achieve. "The problem which confronts homosexuals," he argued, "is that they set out to win the love of a real man but in this they're doomed to failure

Orlando (1992)

Tilda Swinton lives for four hundred years in this, first as a man and then as a woman. The man is from the Elizabethan era, the woman from the twentieth century. An adaptation of Virginia Woolf's 1928 novel by writer/director Sally Potter, it's a strangely beguiling film that's redolent with wit and splendor.

Crisp plays an octogenarian Queen Elizabeth. She says to Orlando in one scene, "Do not fade, do not wither, do not grow old." Her words act as a spell, keeping him young. It enables him to live through different eras with all the experiences, romantic and otherwise, that this entails.

When Orlando falls for Sasha (Charlotte Valandrey) and kisses her, it's not strictly speaking a lesbian kiss because Orlando is a man. The book states that as a woman Orlando loved both sexes equally. The pictures of her that appeared in it were actually photographs of Woolf's bisexual lover Vita Sackville-West. Vita's son described the book as "the longest and most charming love letter in literature" (Bryant, 1997: 58).

Orlando searches for his/her identity for four hundred years. Along the way, we get various history lessons as Potter's picaresque comedy sees her journey through Britain's Colonialist period to the present. It's all gloriously filmed and costumed. Swinton takes to its eccentric riches with equanimity.

Crisp had no problem being cast as a drag queen. How could he? He'd been one all of his life. He envied Swinton her facility with androgyny. "Had surgery existed in my youth," he told her, "I would have had the op and opened a knitting shop in Carlisle" (Andrews, 2003: 124).

Further Reading

Andrews, Robert, ed. 2003. *The New Penguin Dictionary of Modern Quotations*. London: Penguin.
Bryant, Anita, 1997. *Bisexual Characters in Film from Anais to Zee*. New York and London: Harrington Park Press.

---

because a man who goes with other men is not what one could call a 'real' man" (MacHale, 1999: 102).

Crisp had a difficult youth. He was bullied and beaten from his early years in Britain because he exhibited his campness so demonstrably. Later on his painted face and hennaed hair made him even more noticeable. "I never came out of the closet," he declared, "because I was never in it" (Hadleigh, 1999: 134).

Exempted from war duty because of his orientation, he became a nude model for a government-funded art school for a time. Hence the title of his 1968 autobiography, *The Naked Civil Servant*. He also had a brief career as a street hustler. He went into this, he claimed, not for the money but love. After six months of brutal sex with self-loathing married men, however, he gave it up as a bad job.

He said he dressed in drag from the age of nine, but he saw himself more as an effeminate gay man rather than transgender. He risked violence by highlighting such effeminacy. He went to New York in 1977 and felt at home there immediately. It was his first time outside England. The cosmopolitan nature of the city enabled him to fully relax in his extravagant guise.

It was here he developed his Wildean persona. He performed many one-man shows. In these he gave full vent to his wit. After they were over he invited questions from the audience. His answers often gave rise to howls of laughter. "Should

I tell my mother I'm gay?' asked one audience member. Crisp replied, "Never tell your mother anything!" (Jarski, 2010: 138). In time he became an *eminence grice* on the New York social scene. The apparel that had once gotten him beaten up was now more like a badge of honor.

Little enough is known of his love life. He was said to have had a partner called Barn Door who spent most of his time eating and sleeping. Another one was a Czech man from a mental institution who smelt of cod liver oil. One never knew how many of his anecdotes were fact or fiction. As was the way with most writers, they were probably a combination of both.

The Naked Civil Servant was made into a TV film with John Hurt in 1979. It won Hurt a British Academy Award. The two men became friends afterward, but Hurt was advised by many of his friends not to do the part. "I must confess," he told a journalist, "that it wasn't an immediate decision. There's been lots of unfortunate events when people have played homosexuals. But there's nothing like playing a hero, and he's a hero" (Howes, 1993: 536).

The film chronicled Crisp's troubled years growing up in a repressive England. It features the abuse he received from neighbors, police, gay bashers, the draft board, and even his father. "Do you intend to spend your entire life admiring yourself?" he asks him at one stage. Crisp can't see what the problem might be in that.

"An exhibitionist has no friends," an acquaintance tells him in another scene. He learns the truth of this to his cost but remains resolutely himself throughout all his travails. "Every moment has been agony," he says at the end, "but I couldn't have done otherwise."

The following year, *An Evening with Quentin Crisp* came out. This was, in Crisp's own words, "a straight talk with a bent speaker." Introduced by John Hurt, it had Crisp declaiming on everything from hygiene ("Don't clean. After four years the dirt doesn't get any worse.") to living with style even when one is in indigent circumstances. ("Don't bother keeping up with the Joneses. It's cheaper to drag them down to your level.")

Another documentary, *Resident Alien*, was released in 1991. Originally a play, it was a dramatic monologue cobbled together from his diaries. In this case, "alien" means nonconformist rather than extraterrestrial. Crisp sits in his New York apartment declaiming on all the subjects dear to his heart in his inimitably droll tones. The drag queen Holly Woodlawn does a cameo, as does the talk show host Sally Jesse Raphael. Crisp himself appeared in cameos in films such as *Philadelphia* (1994), *To Wong Foo Thanks for Everything, Julie Newmar* (1994), and *The Celluloid Closet* (1995).

His one-liners have preserved his memory. The war between the sexes, he pronounced, was the only one in which one repeatedly slept with the enemy. Sex was a poor substitute for masturbation and "the last refuge of the miserable" (Bailey, 2001: 144). Anal sex was "like undergoing a colostomy operation without any anesthetic" (Bailey, 223).

He was before his time but gay liberation, ironically, made him feel like an anachronism. By wearing bright clothes and growing his hair long, he felt, he said, like "the oldest teenager in the business" (Bailey, 138). He thought he'd made liberation possible for queer people by challenging codes of behavior, belief, and dress, but now, sadly, he was being disowned by them.

In his dark times he thought of suicide but rapidly ruled it out. "I can't," he explained, "throw myself under a car or leap from the top of a skyscraper . . . It's very difficult. You see, I'm a nancy" (Bailey, 42).

He died in 1999, suffering a heart attack while on tour with *An Evening with Quentin Crisp*. "If there's a heaven for homosexuals," he speculated, "which doesn't seem very likely, it will be poorly lit and full of people they can feel pretty confident they'll never have to meet again" (Lloyd and Mitchinson, 2008: 147). He never lost his bitterness with queer people even at the end, but it was, as ever, tinged with that razor-sharp wit.

Related Films
Entertaining Mr. Sloane (1970); *The Naked Civil Servant* (1979); *An Evening with Quentin Crisp* (1980); *Resident Alien* (1990); *Orlando* (1993); *Philadelphia* (1993); *Stonewall 25: Global Voices of Pride and Protest* (1994); *The Celluloid Closet* (1995).

Further Reading
Bailey, Paul. 2001. *The Stately Homo: A Celebration of the Life of Quentin Crisp*. London: Black Swan.
Crisp, Quentin. 1985. *Manners from Heaven: A Divine Guide to Good Behavior*. New York: Flamingo.
Crisp, Quentin. 1986. *How to Have a Lifestyle*. London: Cecil Woolf.
Crisp, Quentin. 1996. *The Naked Civil Servant*. New York: Flamingo.
Crisp, Quentin. 1996. *Resident Alien: The New York Diaries*. New York: HarperCollins.
Hadleigh, Boze, ed. 1999. *Hollywood Bitch*. London: Robson.
Howes, Keith, 1993. *Broadcasting It*. London: Cassell.
Jarski, Rosemarie, ed. 2010. *The Funniest Things You Never Said 2*. London: Ebury Press.
Lloyd, John, and John Mitchinson, eds. 2008. *Advanced Banter*. London: Faber & Faber.
MacHale, Des, ed. 1999. *Wit: The Last Laugh*. London: Prion.

Cross-Dressing

Early references to being gay or trans on screen were often coded in scenes of cross-dressing, but it doesn't usually impute an LGBTQ element, especially in its more mainstream manifestations like *Some Like It Hot* (1959), *Tootsie* (1982), and *Mrs. Doubtfire* (1993).

One of the earliest screen cross-dressers was Fatty Arbuckle, who dressed up as a black woman in *That Minstrel Man* (1915). Charlie Chaplin's delicate features and his sweet smile made him very credible as a female impersonator in *A Woman* (1915). Mary Pickford disguised herself as a boy to learn about slum life in *The Hoodlum* (1919). Ben Turpin satirized the purportedly queer Rudolph Valentino by portraying him as a "houri" in *The Shriek of Araby* (1923).

Buster Keaton rarely donned female garb in silent movies, but he did so twice in the talkies, in *The Dough Boys* (1930) and *Sidewalks of New York* (1931). Eddie Cantor, like the Tony Curtis and Jack Lemmon of *Some Like It Hot*, went female in *Palmy Days* (1931) to hide from a gang he's robbed. He ends up in the ladies' changing room of a large bakery. Joe E. Brown, Lemmon's love interest in *Some Like It Hot*, did the same thing in *Shut My Big Mouth* (1942).

Brown also played a female role in the 1935 movie of Shakespeare's *A Midsummer Night's Dream*. His costar was an unlikely James Cagney, also in drag. It was a long way from the gangster career he was about to forge. This was in contrast to the traditional practice where women dressed up as men to play Shakespeare. Mickey Rooney played a scene as Shakespeare's Juliet from *Romeo and Juliet* in *The Adventures of Huckleberry Finn* (1937).

The Marlene Dietrich of *Morocco* (1930) and *Blonde Venus* (1932) and the Greta Garbo of *Queen Christina* (1933) led to the cult of mannish lesbians. Women put on men's clothes and some of their characteristics, even if they had to subjugate themselves in the last reel.

There were others besides Garbo and Dietrich. In 1934 Dolly Haas dressed in drag for the British feature *Girls Will Be Boys*. Katharine Hepburn donned male attire both in *Christopher Strong* (1933) and *Sylvia Scarlett* (1935). She was booed at the premiere of the former film. In the latter, Brian Aherne looks at her and admits—comically in retrospect—to "a queer feeling when I look at you." The fact that the film's director—George Cukor—was queer gave added frisson to such moments.

Time magazine thought Hepburn looked better as a man than a woman in *Sylvia Scarlett* (*Time*, January 13, 1936). Rebecca Bell-Metereau added: "She offered a contrast to the figures played by stars like Bette Davis and Joan Crawford who, although they rarely wore women's clothes, managed to take on a number of negative masculine attributes to become figurative castrators and literal murderers, or else dependent, love-starved neurotics" (Bell-Metereau, 1993: 114).

Rumors about the Garbo and Dietrich's orientation—and possibly Hepburn's—circulated around Hollywood for years, though it's unlikely Hepburn was lesbian.

One of the more interesting films of the pre-Code era was *Blood Money* (1933). It had Sandra Shaw playing a brothel madam. In one scene she dresses up in a tuxedo with a white shirt, a dickie bow, and a fedora hat. As she asks her lover George Raft for a cigarette, she's every inch the Dietrich clone.

Stars like Shaw knew what they were doing. Many others didn't. There was a funny moment in *Bringing Up Baby* (1938) where Cary Grant, wearing a frilly woman's negligee, jumps up in the air saying, "I've just gone gay all of a sudden!" His use of the word was prescient. At the time it didn't have the connotations it does today.

Queer speculation surrounded Grant when he set up house with his friend Randolph Scott for a year and openly attended premieres and other social functions with him. Grant, like Rock Hudson after him, seemed to give hints of his orientation in many films, or at least an effeminate streak. He went into full drag in Hawks's *I Was a Male War Bride* (1949), playing an army officer in France accompanying his WAC bride (Ann Sheridan) back to the United States.

Just as the character Hollywood referred to as a "gay pansy" was transformed into the "asexual sissy" in the forties, so were mannish women turned into equally asexual tomboys at that time. Once sex was taken out of the equation, both genders were entitled to behave as uncharacteristically as they liked. Androgyny became an allowable display as long as it didn't lead to the boudoir. Men dressing up as women became largely comical, if not camp, whereas women dressing as men was a kind of power statement.

Many stars cross-dressed in the forties: W. C. Fields in *My Little Chickadee* (1940), Will Hay in *The Black Sheep of Whitehall* (1941), Bob Hope and Bing Crosby in *The Road to Morocco* (1942). Hope continued such routines in the years to come in films like *The Princess and the Pirate* (1944) and *The Lemon Drop Kid* (1951). Merle Oberon played the novelist George Sand (who always dressed like a man) in Charles Vidor's *A Song to Remember* (1945), a biopic of the composer Frederic Chopin. (Sand was his lover.)

Joan Crawford became a gay icon after becoming one of the most suggestive cross-dressers ever to appear in a Western in Nicholas Ray's *Johnny Guitar* in 1954. At the time it was made it was regarded as a straight Western, but revisionists unearthed a queer subtext in Crawford's relationship with Mercedes McCambridge in the film. This feature becomes clear if we contrast it with Doris Day's *Calamity Jane* (1953). Day masculinized herself for this Western, but only in the bland manner one associates with her. She was a tomboy pure and simple. Crawford and McCambridge had different kinds of fires burning inside them.

Gloria Swanson did a brilliant takeoff of Charlie Chaplin in *Sunset Boulevard* in 1950. Most cinephiles are aware of this. Not too many people know that she first dressed up as Chaplin in Allan Dwan's *Manhandled* as far back as 1924. Swanson also liked to impersonate Cecil B. de Mille, right down to the riding breeches.

Edward D. Wood Jr.'s (Ed Wood) docudrama *Glen or Glenda?* (1953) is regarded as one of the most unusual films of all time, an unintentionally hilarious tract about cross-dressing and transitioning that has cult status today. Wood was open about his fetishes. Other stars stayed in the closet or emerged from it tentatively. Danny Kaye was alleged to be queer, but he never came out. He went into drag with Bing Crosby for the song "Sisters" in *White Christmas* (1954) but offered no other indications of his orientations.

The cross-dressing in Billy Wilder's *Some Like It Hot* is more playful than sexual. The film's placement in the past takes the edge off its drag element because this allies with its "period" setting, as Billy Wilder pointed out (Bell-Metereau, 1993: 40). It was more ominous in Alfred Hitchcock's *Psycho* (1960), being mixed in with issues of identity confusion and Freudian derangement.

Cross-dressing in sixties films was largely too safe, which was disappointing after *Some Like It Hot* and *Psycho*. Paul Gilbert dressed up as a cigar-smoking bordello madam in *Sylvia* in 1965. The following year, Jean-Paul Belmondo did a drag striptease in the comic thriller *Up to His Ears*. The Irish actor Milo O'Shea dressed up as a woman for Joseph Strick's quirky adaptation of James Joyce's *Ulysses* (1967) when Strick tried to visualize one of the fantasies of Joyce's alter ego, Leopold Bloom. Rod Steiger played a murderous cross-dresser in *No Way to Treat a Lady* (1968). Helmet Berger did a drag impersonation of Marlene Dietrich—a man imitating a woman imitating a man—in Luchino Visconti's *The Damned* (1969).

George Sanders played an aging San Francisco drag queen who becomes the toast of Moscow's literary set in John Huston's Cold War spy thriller *The Kremlin Letter* in 1970, but the film everyone was talking about that year was Michael Sarne's *Myra Breckinridge*. This had Huston on the other side of the camera. The story of a film critic who has sex reassignment surgery and then embarks on a war against the entire male population of the movie world, it was a monument to bad taste.

In one scene, Sarne tried to intercut an ejaculatory moment with archival footage of Shirley Temple. This was refused under threat of legal action, as was an effort to replace her with Loretta Young. In the end, Sarne settled for Laurel and Hardy. The comedy pair had done drag in *Get 'Em Young* (1926). In *Twice Two* (1932), they played their own wives.

Sarne abused their memory to index an orgasmic scene, thereby alienating any sections of his audience he hadn't yet outraged by the many other outrageous elements in the film. Audiences had been more empathetic to the sight of Beryl Reid and Susannah York dressing up as Laurel and Hardy for a scene in Robert Aldrich's *The Killing of Sister George* (1968). Reid and York, playing lesbian lovers, visit an actual gay bar in London for a fancy dress party as the comic duo.

Anne Heywood was a lesbian in Mark Rydell's *The Fox* in 1968, but she gave a more interesting performance in *I Want What I Want* (1971). Here she played the part of an alienated young man, Roy, who dresses as a woman, Wendy, and later decides to have surgery to become one. Roy is forced out of her family home by her intolerant father after being found in women's clothing. When her sister asks her if she thinks she can be cured of her problem, she replies, "I *am* cured."

Perhaps the most famous cross-dresser in films was Harris Glenn Milstead, better known to moviegoers as Divine, especially moviegoers who saw him in a bevy of John Waters films, becoming increasingly more outrageous in each. With his shaved forehead, fake wig, 300-pound girth and the kind of makeup that made one think "serial killer," Divine's most notorious moment came when he ate dog poo in *Pink Flamingos* (1972).

Jeff Bridges received an Oscar nomination for his cross-dressing turn as Clint Eastwood's thieving sidekick in Michael Cimino's amiable melodrama *Thunderbolt and Lightfoot* in 1974. Christopher Morley was equally effective as a policeman pretending to be a woman to nab racketeer boss Jack Kruschen in *Freebie and the Bean* (1974).

Tim Curry took cross-dressing to new levels in his career-high performance as the sci-fi bisexual in Jim Sharman's cult favorite, *The Rocky Horror Picture Show*. Like *Glen or Glenda?*, this is a film that stands outside any genre because it fuses so many of them so innovatively. Nobody has done anything to equal it since, nor looks likely to.

A less well-known film, *The Tenant* (1977) cast Roman Polanski as a timid office clerk who rents out a seedy apartment. The previous occupant attempted suicide. Becoming convinced that the other tenants want to take her place, he becomes fascinated by her, going so far as to visit her in the hospital where she's heavily bandaged as she recovers from her wounds. Polanski puts on her clothes and makeup every night to confuse the neighbors who annoy him by looking at him from across the courtyard.

Eventually he seems to merge into her, like the two characters in Ingmar Bergman's *Persona* (1966). In a final act of identity submergence, he throws himself out of the building. The fall doesn't kill him, so he goes back to his room and throws himself out of the window again, fatally this time. Some viewers saw the film as horror; others as comedy. With Polanski one was never sure. Neither was one sure of what was real in it or what imagined. The same applied to his earlier *Repulsion* (1965).

Marlon Brando donned a Mother Hubbard costume to play a psychopathic Irish/American bounty hunter in Arthur Penn's *The Missouri Breaks* (1976), a quixotic departure even by his standards. Diane Keaton set off a fashion trend by her garçon gear in *Annie Hall* (1977).

La Cage aux Folles (1978) was a laugh-a-minute farce featuring two queer owners of a Saint Tropez cross-dressing club meeting the straight parents of the daughter their heterosexual son is planning to marry. In *Private Benjamin* (1980), Goldie Hawn joined the military to show people that anything a man can do, a woman could do better. In *Dressed to Kill* (1980), Brian de Palma's plagiarization of Alfred Hitchcock's *Psycho*, one had the prospect of Michael Caine as a cross-dressing psychiatrist who slashes Angie Dickinson to pieces in an elevator.

In *Victor/Victoria* (1982), Julie Andrews made a gallant effort to extend her fan base beyond the *Mary Poppins/Sound of Music* demographic with an interesting performance as a female gender impersonator opposite the queer character played by Robert Preston. It fed into a lot of stereotypes, but these were forgivable because of the feel-good factor it exuded.

In *Tootsie* (also 1982), Dustin Hoffman played an unemployed actor who decked himself out like a woman because he believed he'd have a better chance of getting a job that way. It worked, but then he fell in love with the costar of the daytime TV soap in which he appears, played by Jessica Lange. "Don't you find it confusing being a woman in the eighties?" Lange asked him at one point. He certainly does, because he isn't one. The film was successful, but not in all quarters. Andy Warhol huffed, "Dustin plays it really straight in *Tootsie*. It's not like a drag queen. It's like having an aunt that you didn't know was a man" (Wrenn, 1997: 178).

In *Yentl* (1983), Barbra Streisand wasn't quite as convincing as Hoffman in her gender bending when she dressed up like a boy to receive a better religious education in an adaptation of a story by Isaac Bashevis Singer. To complicate things further, she sings in it. Singer wasn't happy with this and neither were audiences.

Paris Is Burning (1990) lifted the lid on New York's subculture of drag queens and transsexuals and introduced a new word to the language—"vogueing." This was a cross between catwalking and dancing. Jennie Livingston's documentary was eye-opening in many different ways and broke down barriers of class, sex, creed, and color.

Rosa von Praunheim made a biopic of the famous East German cross-dresser Charlotte von Mahlsdorf in 1992. Von Mahlsdorf was a woman who defied Nazism and started the German gay liberation movement. *The Ballad of Little Joe* (1993), based on a real story, had Josephine Monaghan dressing up as a cowboy to avoid being treated as a menial by the sexist mores of the Wild West in the 1860s.

Mrs. Doubtfire (1993) was Robin Williams's hilarious turn as a Scottish nanny. He dresses up in order to see more of his kids during a bitter divorce battle with his wife. He threw himself into the part and created great comedy and also some pathos. Both of these elements were also present in *The Adventures of Priscilla, Queen of the Desert* (1994), which took the road movie genre into a whole new direction as it explored the various fates of two drag queens and a transsexual woman on board a bus in the Australian Outback. *The Birdcage* (1996), also starring Williams, would have been funnier if it didn't lift so much of its material from *La Cage aux Folles*. *To Wong Foo, Thanks for Everything, Julie Newmar* (1995) was guilty of the same plagiarism, this time *The Adventures of Priscilla, Queen of the Desert* being the source.

Martin Lawrence played an undercover FBI man in drag in *Big Momma's House* in 2000. Matt Le Blanc and Eddie Izzard were two army men infiltrating a German factory dressed as women in *All the Queen's Men* (2001). *The Hot Chick* (2003) had Rob Schneider as a girl who turns into a man and then wants to change back. Tyler Perry appeared briefly in drag toward the end of *Meet the Browns* (2004). Glenn Close disguised herself as a man to find work in nineteenth-century Ireland in *Albert Nobbs* (2011), a throwback to the *Tootsie* plotline.

In all of these manifestations over the decades we can see similar plotlines being jigged and rejigged to make them seem different from their forbears. Some succeeded better than others, but there's one immutable factor in them all: men dressing as women will always raise more laughs than women dressing as men.

Further Reading

Bell-Metereau, Rebecca. 1993. *Hollywood Androgyny*. New York: Columbia University Press.

Dickens, Homer. 1984. *What a Drag: Men as Women and Women as Men in the Movies*. New York: Quill.

Hollander, Anne. 1978. *Seeing Through Clothes*. New York: Viking Press.

Horak, Laura. 2016. *Girls Will Be Boys: Cross-Dressed Women, Lesbians, and American Cinema, 1908–1934*. New Brunswick, NJ, and London: Rutgers University Press.

Newton, Esther. 1979. *Mother Camp: Female Impersonators in America*. Chicago: University of Chicago Press.

Time, January 1936.

Wrenn, Mike, ed. 1997. *Andy Warhol in His Own Words*. London: Omnibus.

Cruising (1980)

This movie was directed by William Friedkin, who'd already made *The Boys in the Band* ten years before. It was a hit on Broadway and was regarded as daring for featuring a large number of queer men in its cast. Today, however, it's seen as dated, with a very strongly negative gay presentation of characters. *Cruising* would earn Friedkin similarly negative reactions.

Based on a novel by Gerald Walker, it dealt with a policeman on the trail of someone killing a spate of queer men in New York. As the murder hunt progresses, the policeman realizes he himself is queer. Then he too starts killing gay men. The motives of both men are fuzzy in the book and even fuzzier in the film. Many of the queer characters in the book are stereotypes filled with the self-loathing that used to characterize gays in pulp fiction. Friedkin doesn't do much to liberate them from that status.

Al Pacino played the policeman, Steve Burns. He'd been endearing as a queer man in *Dog Day Afternoon* (1975), so hopes were high in the gay community that he would bring a mite more understanding to Burns here than Walker did. Sadly, the film ended up manifesting most of the clichés about the gay underworld that dogged the novel.

Cruising was one of the few films in Hollywood's history that was hated before it was even made. Word of mouth let people know how negatively it portrayed being queer quite apart from making the killer gay. On July 26, 1979, the National Gay Task Force filed a demand with the mayor's office that the city revoke the permit to start shooting it. The NGTF feared it would cause a "potentially inflammatory and explosive reaction" from gay people. It organized a march on July 27, 1979, in which over one thousand people blocked traffic in Sheridan Square, Greenwich Village, for half an hour. Demonstrators shouted at the extras and confronted the crew members, throwing bottles and cans at them (Sova, 2001: 86–7).

Pacino tried to keep himself out of the firing line. His star had fallen dramatically with the gay community since his amiable turn as Sonny Wortzik in *Dog Day Afternoon*. This portrayal didn't seem to have any justification for it at all. It wasn't only a muddled attack on queer people but an even more muddled mystery film as well.

"It isn't a film about gay life," Friedkin said. "It's a murder mystery with an aspect of the gay world as background" (Yule, 1991: 216). Queer men bridled at this comment because of the number of scenes in the film depicting the seediness of the gay bars where Burns sets himself up as bait. Friedkin segues from here to many scenes of leather-clad sadomasochism. Burns infiltrates this seedy underbelly with something more than normal job dedication. Its aura of danger exerts a perverse fascination for him as he immerses himself in its dark allure.

When he finally catches the killer (Richard Cox), the viewer is entitled to feel that's that. Nasty and all as *Cruising* has been, it's over. His job is done. Except it isn't, because now another murder takes place. It can't have been committed by Cox because he's behind bars. So who did it? Could it have been Pacino himself, as was the case in the book? Is he secretly gay? Yes, he's married, but he doesn't seem committed to it. "Don't let me lose you," he says to his wife, Nancy (Karen Allen). You feel he could be as happy with the queer people he's been spending most of his time with lately as with her.

Friedkin's film was justifiably accused of being homophobic. "Homophobia" is a term that usually means hatred of queer people, but here its literal meaning, "phobia," coming from the Latin word for "fear," is particularly apt. Alonso Duralde called *Cruising* "the most controversial gay film ever made" (Duralde, 2005: 58).

It was also exploitative. While purporting to portray a storyline about a killer of queer people, it leaves us with the teasing ending that the policeman investigating these murders is himself gay, and himself the killer. This isn't spelled out but it's implied. Once again the queer is the bad guy, for no ostensible reason. Burns doesn't appear psychotic during the film, so this possibility comes from nowhere. Has he been killing queer people because he hates the queerness within himself? Maybe a better film could have been made on this theme.

Everything here conspired to present queer life as menacing, even the cacophonous rock music that punctuates the score. Toward the end, Allen dons Pacino's jacket and shades as if she's morphing into him just as he's morphed into the queer killer. Friedkin's attempt at turning everyone into everyone else looks like another copout to absolve himself from having made an antigay movie. He tries every trick in the book to abnegate the film he's just made—which is perhaps its greatest offense. It's almost easier to take more openly offensive homophobia than this "willing to wound and yet afraid to strike" approach.

Many people scratched their heads leaving the cinema, locked somewhere between anger and bewilderment about the events they'd just seen. Friedkin later released a statement saying he wasn't sure who the final killer was, or even if he was queer. This looked like a pathetic attempt to justify the unjustifiable. He obviously meant us to think it was Pacino. Why was he going back on that now? Did he not have the courage of his convictions? Or was he afraid of a queer backlash?

The film, he insisted, "wasn't intended to be an indictment of the homosexual world. It's set in one small segment of that world, which is not meant to be representative of the whole" (Russo, 1987: 238). This was the old argument directors used against various minority groups in the past when they realized they were in trouble. It didn't mean anything. A blind man could have seen that his depiction of this world was decadent and defamatory.

The scenes of violence are straight out of any low-rent slasher film. As the villain, Cox is a two-dimensional character one might find in a nickel-and-dime schlock shocker written by some fifth-rate Mickey Spillane clone anxious to make a name for himself as the new Stephen King. Friedkin makes no attempt to humanize him. When Pacino appears to be taking over from him in the final scene, we feel we're looking at another sick killer who's going to tie people up before he whips them with chains and then chops them to pieces. Is he telling us he's the killer in the last scene or merely confused about his sexuality? Has Burns become queer as a result of his immersion in queer culture, like a kind of litmus paper transmogrification? Or does he merely *think* he's queer? We're not told, and there's no good reason why we aren't.

The film left a bad aftertaste in people's mouths. Queer men were becoming fed up of seeing themselves being repeatedly relegated to criminal status in gratuitous fashion in films like *The Detective* (1970), *Freebie and the Bean* (1974), and *The Eiger Sanction* (1975).

Cruising was made shortly after the "White Night" riots, which expressed the queer community's reaction to the soft sentence given to Dan White, the killer of Harvey Milk. As a result, it caused more outrage among the community than it would otherwise have done. This isn't to condone its excesses or its prejudices, merely to place them in context. It's an unashamedly exploitative porthole into a murky world that is in no way representative of the way most queer men live their lives. To that extent, it should be condemned in the strongest possible terms. But if we wish to cut Friedkin some slack, we can give him the benefit of the doubt. We can credit him with being misguided in his intentions rather than blatantly antigay.

One of the queer activists' slogans said, "This film will kill people" (Yule, 1991: 219). A few months after it was released, a minister's son shot two queer men outside a bar that had been featured in it. Such an action rendered all the debates about it moribund.

Related Films
Dog Day Afternoon (1975); *Windows* (1980); *Basic Instinct* (1992); *Interior. Leather Bar* (2013).

Further Reading
Duralde, Alonso, 2005. *101 Must-See Movies for Men*. New York: Advocate.
Grobel, Lawrence. 2007. *Al Pacino: The Authorized Biography*. London: Simon & Schuster.
Russo, Vito. 1987. *The Celluloid Closet: Homosexuality in the Movies*. New York: Harper & Row.
Sova, Dawn. 2001. *Forbidden Films: Censorship History of 125 Motion Pictures*. New York: Checkmark Books.
Yule, Andrew. 1991. *Al Pacino: A Life on the Wire*. London: Warner.

The Crying Game (1992)

Part romance and part political thriller, this hard-to-pin-down movie was directed by Neil Jordan. Stephen Rea plays an IRA terrorist, Fergus, who captures a British soldier, Jody (Forest Whitaker) and becomes friends with him before falling for his lover, Dil (Jaye Davidson). Davidson, in the film's major surprise, turns out to be a transgender woman.

As Jody waits to be executed, he tells Fergus to look up Dil when it's all over. Fergus says he will. Soon afterward, Fergus is ordered to shoot Jody, but he can't do it. Jody runs away from him. He seems to be headed for freedom, but then he runs into a truck and is killed. Fergus is distraught because they've become friends while he's been guarding him.

Fergus now goes to London to see Dil. She sings in a nightclub. Fergus is immediately smitten with her. As they get to know one another, he doesn't mention anything about having known Jody.

Their relationship is one of the strangest in film history. Dil can't tell Fergus she's transgender and he can't tell her he's responsible for the death of her lover. Jordan plays beguilingly with his central dynamic while taking the story in many other directions as well—like the fact that Fergus might be a closeted queer man. In an early scene, Jody asks Fergus to hold his penis while he urinates.

The love affair between Fergus and Dil moves in fits and starts. It's conducted in a fog of subterfuge and ambivalence. Sex, gender, and politics are all motifs in the film. Jordan refuses to give us closure on any of them.

One of Fergus's IRA contacts, Jude (Miranda Richardson), now arrives on the scene. She offers Fergus a high-risk mission, the shooting of a British judge to test his loyalty to "the cause."

The assassination of the judge is botched. Dil then shoots Jude, but Fergus takes the rap for this. When Dil visits Fergus in prison, he promises to wait for him. That will be in 2,335 days. As the film ends, we hear Lyle Lovett singing "Stand by Your Man." It's difficult not to smile, especially at lines like "Sometimes it's hard to be a woman." For Dil it certainly is—in all senses.

The Crying Game posed as many questions about the confused parabolas of politics as it did about the tangled identities of sexuality. "Would you rather," asked Julie Wheeler, "find out your boyfriend is an IRA killer or your girlfriend is a man?" (*New Statesman Society*, October 30, 1992).

It was made relatively cheaply and expected to have only modest success, but its central surprise meant it went viral for audiences, making it one of the sleeper hits of the year. Harvey Weinstein of Miramax had been leery about taking it on at the outset. According to Jordan, he said he'd do so only if Jordan agreed to cast a girl as the cross-dresser. He thought audiences would find it "revolting" otherwise. Finding an actor to play Dil proved difficult. It was Derek Jarman's boyfriend who recommended Davidson.

Jordan won an Oscar for Best Screenplay, which isn't too surprising considering he was a prize-winning short story writer and novelist before he became a film director. (He continues to pursue both activities to this day.) Having said that, the script is stripped to the bone here, and it's all the better for that. *The Crying Game* is a visual treat as well as a verbal one, and indeed an aural one as well. This is evidenced by the number of songs Jordan features in the course of it. Boy George sings one of them. He's gay, which queers the film further.

The scene most people talked about was the one where Dil strips for Fergus and shows her male member. Fergus throws up. The shock felt by him is one thing; the fact that such a scene was featured in a mainstream movie is almost as surprising. Formerly, the penis was usually shown only in art house films or pornography.

Dil's exposure of her penis was Jordan's "money shot," to quote B. Ruby Rich. The fact that Fergus vomits when he sees it skews the scene, making such a "voyeuristic ambush" that one journalist went so far as to describe the film as "a heterosexual horror movie" (Rich, 2013: 272). Paul Burston remarked in a book he wrote about queer cinema, "Show me a man who didn't twig straight away that the soldier's girl was a man in drag and I'll show you a homosexual who doesn't get out enough." Burston doesn't credit Dil with being transgender (Burston, 1995: 149).

The film asks more questions than it answers. Why, for instance, does Jody tell Fergus to look up Dil when he knows Dil's secret will shock him? Was it a kind of political revenge? Or had he suspected that Fergus was queer from their time together? The fact that Fergus held Jody's penis while he urinated was a practical necessity—Jody's hands were held behind his back at the time—but Jordan is possibly suggesting something else here.

Fergus dresses Dil in Jody's cricket gear, which seems like another admission of his queer feelings for Jody. He then cuts his hair. (This could also be a way of atoning for the guilt he feels at being responsible for Jody's death.)

The dialogue is rife with irony. "I kinda liked you as a girl," Fergus tells Dil. Ignoring the purported insult, Dil shoots back, "Well, that's a start." The script also has a lot of fun with the mixture of politics and sex in the film, as when Fergus tells Jude he's leaving the IRA. "I'm out," he says, leaving the interpretation to mean he's out of the closet, having fallen in love with Dil. "You're never out," Jody snaps back. In another scene he says to Dil, "You're something else," a phrase that means, "You're amazing." (He isn't aware of Dil's secret at this point.) Dil replies, "You never said a truer word." When Dil's sexuality is finally revealed to him, he says dumbly, "You're not a girl." She trills, "Details, baby!" recalling Joe E. Brown's end line from *Some Like It Hot*, "Nobody's perfect."

Ambiguity is central to *The Crying Game* on a number of levels: Fergus's name (he's sometimes called Jimmy), Jody's nationality (Is he African or English?), and, of course, Dil's sexuality. Dil queers Fergus by donning Jody's cricket gear. By morphing into him, he allows Fergus to make vicarious love to the man whose death he's been responsible for. When Fergus tells Dil he was assigned to kill Jody, Dil takes out a gun and aims it at him. It becomes a phallic symbol, a fake penis he waves in his face to punish him for rejecting his actual one. The main issue of the film is whether they can continue their relationship when both of their secrets (Dil's gender; Fergus's republicanism) are exposed. Fergus proves they can when he takes the rap for Dil after Dil shoots Jody.

Davidson was nominated for a Best Supporting Actor Oscar for it, which caused tension with Weinstein as it gave the secret of her character's identity away. He decided the only way to reduce the risk of everyone talking about this was to get Davidson out of the way. He whisked him off to Egypt to stop the press from interviewing him. But Davidson got bored and came back after a day. Because the country was Muslim, he complained, he couldn't find anywhere to get a drink (Biskind, 2007: 147–8).

Related Films
In a Year with 13 Moons (1978); *Angel* (1982); *Breakfast on Pluto* (2005).

Further Reading
Barton, Ruth. 2004. *Irish National Cinema*. London: Routledge.
Biskind, Peter. 2007. *Down and Dirty Pictures: Miramax, Sundance and the Rise of Independent Film*. London: Bloomsbury.
Burston, Paul. 1995. *What Are You Looking At? Queer Sex, Style and Cinema*. London: Cassell.
Carty, Ciaran. 1995. *Confessions of a Sewer Rat*. Dublin: New Island Books.
McGurk, Dr. Paul David. 2016. *Neil Jordan: The Films: A Quiet Man in Babylon*. Champaign: University of Illinois Press.
New Statesman Society, October 30, 1992.
Perren, Alisa. 2012. *Indie Inc.: Miramax and the Transformation of Hollywood in the 1990s*. Austin: University of Texas Press.
Rich, B. Ruby. 2013. *New Queer Cinema: The Director's Cut*. Durham, NC, and London: Duke University Press.

George Cukor (1899–1983)

Joseph L. Mankiewicz described Cukor as "the first great female director of Hollywood" (McGilligan, 1991: 114). He was trusted by women because they knew he wouldn't abuse them. In an era when they were so often molested by wolf-like men, this was a blessing that was never taken for granted.

Asked by Louis B. Mayer if he was "a homosexual," he replied firmly, "Dedicated." He didn't fear a backlash from the industry because his films were successful (McGilligan, 157). He didn't deny his sexual orientation, but neither did he flaunt it. Most times he flew under the radar. Apart from his famous Sunday parties where like-minded colleagues cavorted openly, the most common description of him in the trade papers was "confirmed bachelor." Most people knew what that signified.

Cukor used to become annoyed when people referred to him as "the woman's director." He thought this implied he couldn't direct men equally well. The point was that he could, but working at a time when directors weren't as empathetic to women's concerns as they are today—at least hopefully—being gay seemed to act as an extra weapon in that department. He also had more respect for actresses than actors. "An actress has to be more than an ordinary woman," he maintained, "and an actor somehow has to be less of a man" (Lessard, 2008: 11).

His contract had a "moral turpitude" clause in it, however, so he had to be careful not to sail too close to the wind. His efforts to have this removed failed, though his studio, MGM, had enough respect for him to hush up an incident where he was mugged by sailors one night as a young man when he was cruising the gay bars.

The titles of his films testify to his fondness for directing works concerning women—*Girls about Town* (1931), *A Bill of Divorcement* (1932), *Little Women* (1933), *Sylvia Scarlett* (1935). The last film had Katharine Hepburn dressed as a boy engaging in jewel theft in cockney England. Cukor liked playing with Hepburn's androgyny. She had a natural facility for it. "I only remember Katie wearing a skirt once in her life," he recalled, "It was to a funeral" (Hadleigh, 1999: 74).

Despite his prolific output, he was most noted for a film he *didn't* make than all the ones he did. David O. Selznick commissioned him to direct *Gone with the Wind* in 1939, but Clark Gable expressed dissatisfaction about him to Selznick. One explanation for this was a story going around Hollywood that, some years earlier, a friend of Cukor's called William Haines—Hollywood's first openly gay actor—had seduced Gable. Gable regretted the incident, and regretted even more the fact that Cukor knew about it. The atmosphere between them even in preproduction was tense.

It spilled over onto Vivien Leigh, Gable's costar. When *Gone with the Wind* began shooting, Leigh was bothered by Gable's bad breath, especially in their kissing scenes. Of more concern to her was the fact that he refused to put on a Southern accent for the role. Gable felt Cukor was "throwing" the film to Leigh by favoring her too much in the close-ups. He also thought Cukor was too effeminate to handle such an epic. "I can't go on with the picture!" he exploded at one point. "I won't be directed by a fairy. I have to work with a real man!" (Davis, 1993: 126).

Cukor ended up being sacked. He was replaced by Gable's friend Victor Fleming. Fleming's style of direction was much less nuanced than Cukor's. "Ham it up," he advised Leigh (whom he nicknamed "Fiddle-dee-dee" to make her feel small) when she asked him how she should play a certain scene. Another day he told Walter Plunkett, the costume designer, "For God's sake, let's get a good look at the girl's boobs." Plunkett was forced to have Leigh's breasts taped and thrust upward to give her a bodice-ripper look. Leigh was furious but could do nothing. Secretly, though, both she and Olivia de Havilland, who was also in the film, continued to visit Cukor on weekends for acting tips (Edwards, 1997: 98–103).

After being sacked from it, Cukor went on to direct *The Women*. It was given to him as a consolation. Based on Clare Boothe Luce's Broadway play, it featured an all-female cast. The screenplay was cowritten by Anita Loos and Jane Murfin. Stars such as Joan Crawford, Paulette Goddard, Rosalind Russell, and Joan Fontaine were all happy to be directed by Cukor even if the finished product didn't live up to its potential.

When Cukor worked with Greta Garbo on her last film, *Two-Faced Woman*, in 1941, the Great Queer Director teamed up with the Great Lesbian Icon for the second time. (He'd already made *Camille* with her.) Sadly, it was an anticlimactic experience, a misguided attempt to Americanize Garbo as a result of World War I reducing her European appeal.

The film had her as a woman trying to expose her husband's infidelity by posing as her promiscuous twin sister, an absurd premise that became even more absurd when the Legion of Decency insisted her costar, Melvyn Douglas, became aware of her duplicity. This meant audiences wouldn't think he was being tempted by her. It's small wonder Garbo retired after being forced to take part in such a far-fetched farce. "I have made enough faces," she droned. It was ironic that "the women's director" ended the career of the most alluring screen woman of them all.

Notwithstanding that, he went on to make a string of hits like *The Philadelphia Story* (1940), *Gaslight* (1944), *A Double Life* (1947), *Adam's Rib* (1949), and *A Star Is Born* (1954). His career peaked with *My Fair Lady*, which won eight Academy Awards in 1964. Cukor continued to make "women's films" right up to 1981. His directorial swan song was *Rich and Famous*, a "gal pal" film starring Jacqueline Bisset and Candice Bergen. Both of them adored him. People talk about "the Lubitsch touch," but "the Cukor touch" was just as enticing. He made gold from base metal for much of his career, turning ordinary films into extraordinary ones with his exquisite approach.

He remained sexually active into old age but kept this discreet. He was flattered when young men expressed an interest in him, but he was savvy enough to suspect some of that was a result of who he was (McGilligan, 1991: 119). When he was making *Rich and Famous*, the writer/director James Toback called to his house one day on a matter of business. He was a little early and Cukor wasn't expecting him. He emerged from his bedroom in a bathrobe. A young man followed him. A "flustered" Cukor introduced him to Toback as his nephew. He was in his eighties at the time. At eighty-three, he was discovered in "suggestive circumstances" with a young man in the dressing room of his swimming pool (McGilligan, 333).

Related Films
Girls about Town (1931); *A Bill of Divorcement* (1932); *Dinner at Eight* (1933); *Little Women* (1933); *David Copperfield* (1935); *Sylvia Scarlett* (1935); *Camille* (1936); *Romeo and Juliet* (1936); *The Women* (1939); *The Philadelphia Story* (1941); *Gaslight* (1944); *Adam's Rib* (1949); *A Star Is Born* (1954); *My Fair Lady* (1964); *Rich and Famous* (1981); *On Cukor* (2000).

Further Reading
Davis, Donald L. 1993. *The Glamour Factory: Inside Hollywood's Big Studio System.* Dallas: Southern Methodist University Press.
Edwards, Anne. 1977. *Vivien Leigh: A Biography.* New York: Simon & Schuster.
Hadleigh, Boze, ed. 1999. *Hollywood Bitch.* London: Robson.
Lambert, Gavin. 1972. *On Cukor.* New York: Putnam's.
Lessard, John, ed. 2008. *To Quote a Queer.* Philadelphia: Quirk.
McGilligan, Patrick. 1991. *George Cukor: A Double Life.* New York: St Martin's Press.

Tony Curtis (1925–2010)

Like Bette Davis, Elvis Presley, and a host of other stars, Curtis was a gay icon but wasn't gay himself. He said Presley copied his hairdo. "Without my hair," he declared, "there would never have been rock 'n' roll. Elvis Presley didn't invent rock 'n' roll. My hair did" (*Empire*, April 1994). Presley adapted his quiff, sculpting it into "a perfect pompadour which curled into a greasy ducktail at the back of his neck" (Nash, 2010: 193).

Curtis entered the navy in 1943 as an impossibly handsome eighteen-year-old. His features were so delicate he might have been a girl. The fact that he was heterosexual must, in Michael Ferguson's words, "have been awfully tough on fellow seamen wrestling with their homosexuality or their ability to cross their eyes just a tad and turn his pretty face into a girl's . . . jet black hair, bedroom eyes, a full lower lip begging for lipstick and a smooth sensual face with skin so radiant and unblemished it looks like a Hollywood publicity photo shot through gauze" (Ferguson, 2004: 88). Asked once what the secret of his sex appeal was, he replied simply, "Lanolin" (*BBC News*, Entertainment and Arts, August 10, 2011). This was the substance he put in his hair to make it shiny.

His parents were Hungarian immigrants. He started his film career as a swashbuckler in Arabian Nights films like *The Prince Who Was a Thief* (1951), causing young ladies (and even some young men) to salivate in the aisles, despite a Bronx accent—he grew up in its slum district—that mangled lines like the oft-misquoted "Yonder lies the valley of the sun." His studio, Universal, tried to marry him off to his costar Piper Laurie, but he wasn't interested, too busy bedding any other starlets who crossed his path.

He became friends with Rock Hudson, another Universal acquisition. He knew he was queer, but it didn't bother him as it might have some people. "He had a good time with girls," Curtis declared, "but he liked the other team better" (Curtis with Golenbock, 2008: 113).

He sympathized with the double life Hudson had to live to preserve his career. Having been tagged with being queer when he first arrived in Hollywood, he knew how it felt. When he was growing up, there was also a rumor he worked in a New York club as "a ravishing dark-haired beauty"—a woman by night and a mild-mannered Jew by day (*Empire*, April 1994).

Curtis's androgynous appeal was used to good effect in Billy Wilder's *Some Like It Hot* (1959). Here, with Jack Lemmon, he donned female attire to elude a bunch of gangsters when they have the misfortune to be witnesses to the Saint Valentine's Day massacre. Fearing a personal massacre of themselves, they go on the run. Eventually they become part of an all-girl band, Sweet Sue and Her Society Syncopators, presided over by a whiskey-sipping bubblehead, Marilyn Monroe.

Stanley Kubrick directed Curtis in *Spartacus* in 1960. On the surface this was a standard-issue gladiatorial epic, but to the queer community today it's chiefly remembered for a scene where the Roman politician Marcus Crassus (Laurence Olivier) has a bath with his poet slave, Antonius (Curtis). While in the bath, Crassus engages in a discussion with Antonius about whether he prefers oysters (for which read "women") or snails (for which read "men"). He then says, "Do you consider the eating of oysters to be moral and the eating of snails immoral?" When Antonius replies in the negative, a relived Crassus delivers his "liberal" message that for him it's a matter of taste rather than morals. The scene ends with him telling Antonius he himself is partial to both oysters *and* snails. In other words he was bisexual.

The censors immediately decoded Olivier's language, fully aware he was transmitting his bisexuality to Curtis. They suggested the scene might be allowed to stay in if snails and oysters were changed to artichokes and truffles, a ludicrous idea that, thankfully for the film, didn't materialize. But the scene still ended up on the cutting-room floor. The Production Code Administration jumped all over it, as did the Legion of Decency. "It was killed because of the Legion," wrote Murray Schumach (Sova, 2001: 278).

Geoffrey Shurlock, the administrator of the Motion Picture Association of America (MPAA), had the power to grant or refuse the film a code. The dialogue in the scene, he maintained, "clearly suggests that Crassus is sexually attracted to women and men. This flavor should be completely removed. Any suggestion that Crassus finds a sexual attraction in Antoninus will have to be avoided." He added, "Specifically note Crassus putting his hand on the boy, and his reaction to that gesture" (Bryant, 1997: 37).

Shurlock strenuously objected to the manner in which Antoninus speedily departs the bathtub after the exchange of dialogue with Crassus, insisting that the reason for his "frantic escape" would have to be "something other than the fact that he's repelled by Crassus' suggestive approach to him" (Baxter, 1997: 139).

Curtis was well aware the scene was rife with sexual symbolism. He also knew there was no way the censors of the time would allow it to pass. For Curtis it was too blunt. "Take me out to dinner first," he joked to Olivier off set. "Don't throw me in the tub and drop the soap." He was asked if it bothered him being in a bath with a man such as Olivier, who was rumored to be bisexual. "Not much," he replied. "It was better than being in one with Fatty Arbuckle" (*Empire*, December 2001). Despite the speculation surrounding Olivier, Curtis believed he preferred oysters to snails in real life (Spoto, 1993: 277–8).

The scene was deleted from the 1960 print of the film to placate the Legion of Decency, but it was restored in a 1990 version. Olivier had died by that time and the soundtrack to the footage had been lost, so his lines had to be redubbed by another actor, Anthony Hocking. Curtis was still alive so he was able to speak his ones himself.

Curtis felt *Spartacus* was essentially a love story involving three men—Spartacus, Crassus, and Antoninus—but the public wouldn't have been interested in that: "We deliberately avoid the physical love between men. We never really discuss those scenes. If we do, they're always salacious and lewd and never really capture the real sense of what we are as people" (*Metro Weekly*, August 22, 2002). "The studio," he said, "couldn't handle the fact that the three men were in love with each other so they loaded the picture with Spartacus and his wife" (*Empire*, December 2001).

Curtis's career in the sixties was stop-go, the promise he showed in films like *Sweet Smell of Success* (1957) and *The Defiant Ones* (1958)—his only Oscar nomination—hardly equaled by the number of fluffy comedies in which he became mired afterward. Curtis completists should check out *Black Mama, White Mama* (1973), Eddie Romero's camp version of *The Defiant Ones* where two lesbians who are chained together escape from a Filipino prison camp.

It wasn't until 1968, with *The Boston Strangler*, that he made a genuine attempt to give a deep performance, but the film was too dark and few people went to see it. In the seventies and eighties it was, by and large, more of the same. In 1977 he went into drag for a scene in *Casanova & Co*. He expressed an interest in appearing in *The Adventures of Priscilla, Queen of the Desert* in 1994, but it didn't come to anything, the role going to Terence Stamp instead. Three years later he made a spoof of action heroes called *The Continuing Adventures of Reptile Man and his Faithful Sidekick Tadpole*. The film wasn't as imaginative as the title suggested, but Curtis was excited about its drag queen possibilities, claiming, "I'm gonna have a 20 foot long tongue that I attack my enemies with" (*London Independent*, May 25, 1995).

He lived to the ripe old age of eighty-five, painting and rescuing abused horses with his fourth wife, Jill. He'd come through addictions to alcohol and drugs, the failure of three marriages as well as a heart attack and the suicide of one of his sons. He also became an author of some note, and a very warm and witty interviewee, which the present author can testify to. He may not have quite invented rock 'n' roll, but he made a generation swoon with that quiff and those baby-blue eyes. He once made a film called *The Great Imposter*. "The Great Survivor" is a sobriquet that would probably have described him more accurately.

Related Films
The Prince Who Was a Thief (1951); *Houdini* (1953); *Trapeze* (1956); *Sweet Smell of Success* (1957); *The Defiant Ones* (1958); *The Vikings* (1958); *Some Like It Hot* (1959); *Spartacus* (1960); *Sextette* (1978); *Insignificance* (1985); *The Continuing Adventures of Reptile Man and His Sidekick Tadpole* (1989); *The Celluloid Closet* (1995); *The Jill and Tony Curtis Story* (2004).

Further Reading

Baxter, John. 1997. *Stanley Kubrick: A Biography*. London: HarperCollins.

BBC News. *Entertainment and Arts*, August 10, 2011.

Bryant, Wayne M. 1997. *Bisexual Characters in Film: From Anais to Zee*. New York and London: Harrington Park Press.

Curtis, Allegra. 2011. *Ich Und Mein Vater*. Munich: Langen Muller.

Curtis, Tony, with Barry Paris. 1994. *The Autobiography*. London: Heinemann.

Curtis, Tony, with Peter Golenbock. 2008. *American Prince*. London: Virgin.

Empire, April, 1994.

Empire, December, 2001.

Ferguson, Michael. 2004. *Idol Worship: A Shameless Celebration of Male Beauty in the Movies*. Sarasota, FL: STARbooks Press.

London Independent, May 25, 1995.

Metro Weekly, August 22, 2002.

Nash, Alanna. 2010. *Baby, Let's Play House*. London: Plexus.

Sova, Dawn B. 2001. *Forbidden Films*. New York: Checkmark Books.

Spoto, Donald. 1993. *Laurence Olivier: A Life*. New York: HarperCollins.

Dallas Buyers Club (2013)

Illness does strange things to a body—and a mind.

At the beginning of most diseases, everyone is flying blind, doctors and patients alike. There's a gap in the market for a maverick to crawl through. In this fact-based film, Ron Woodroof (Matthew McConaughey) becomes that maverick.

He's an electrician whose main interests are rodeo riding and womanizing. When he's diagnosed with AIDS, he's given just thirty days to live. He can't understand how he's contracted the disease because he's heterosexual. He worries about the fact that his doctor might imagine he's more attracted to men than women. At times he seems more afraid of being called gay than he is of dying.

He loses both his job and his home as a result of his illness. In a desperate bout of straw-clutching, he heads to Mexico to see if there's anything he can do to halt his decline. Here he meets a doctor who's been struck off by the establishment. Dr. Vass (Griffin Dunne) is an intelligent man who monitors all his patients individually, unlike the lazy groupthink gurus from Woodroof's local hospital in Dallas.

He puts Woodroof on a drug called AZT, which hasn't been approved by the FDA. He buys as much of it from him as he can bring back to the United States. A problem with customs is negotiated by this suddenly resourceful con man donning a clerical collar to plead his case more fervently. When he says the drugs are for his personal use, he's believed. This is somewhat surprising as there are enough pills in the trunk of his car to fell an elephant.

Back in the United States, the former horseman turned snake oil salesman begins his operation in earnest. "Welcome to the Dallas Buyers Club," he drawls, selling his stock to all comers. Like him, his customers have been given little hope, so they have nothing to lose by experimenting with it. "Screw the FDA," he says "I'm gonna be DOA."

Denis O'Hare plays Dr. Sevard, a man who refuses to divert even 1 percent from standard operational procedure as he consigns his patients to their happy hunting grounds. His colleague Dr. Eve (Jennifer Garner) has a better attitude to Woodroof and they become friends. A more unlikely relationship begins with a transgender woman, Rayon (Jared Leto). She's also been given the dreaded AIDS diagnosis. In addition she's a heroin addict. Substance abuse is all she has in common with Woodroof at first.

They start to bond as time goes on. She sees his human side and he begins to look on her as a person rather than a sexual orientation. In a moving scene in a shopping mall, he forces a homophobe to shake hands with her when it's the last thing he wants to do. Rayon is touched. She doesn't say anything and she doesn't need to. Her face says it all. This is the moment where their friendship is firmly forged, where he sheds his sexual prejudices. "God sure was dressin' the wrong doll," he says in a grudging acknowledgment of Rayon's forthcoming reassignment.

The imminent prospect of "The Reaper" makes it imperative that Woodroof becomes a crusader for the other AIDS patients availing of his concoctions. He draws himself more and more into their circle and away from the people he used to belong to: the rodeo-riding, hooker-using set who have nothing to offer him now except sneering.

As his unique cocktails of AZT begin to show positive results, the authorities become threatened by him. Then they make moves to close down his business—not because they fear his methods will fail but rather *succeed*. They confiscate his supplies, which results in him taking out a restraining order against them. This is surely a historical precedent. It's almost like suing the government.

He visits Sevard and gloats, "You gave me thirty days to live and I'm still here a year later."

That one year becomes seven. Woodroof survives somehow, dispensing his medication to himself and countless others as the medical establishment gapes in bewilderment.

His health finally begins to falter as his disease catches up with him and he becomes debilitated. Then Rayon passes away. There are no tearful farewells, just the brutal fact of death. Woodroof is away when she dies. When he hears the news, he's numb with grief. He blames the hospital. Then he himself dies. He's lasted 2,527 days longer than he was supposed to. Nobody can quite believe it. His longevity has been a medical phenomenon. Neither does he become forgotten. His legacy is to those suffering from the disease in the next generation. He's been a torchbearer for hundreds, a man whose suffering was transmuted into pioneering developments.

Both McConaughey and Leto ate the heart and soul out of their parts and both were rewarded with Oscars for their troubles. For McConaughey it was an overdue commendation. He'd begun his career on a high with *A Time to Kill* in 1996 but lost his way in many of the substandard films he made in the ensuing years. Here, though, he gives it everything, refusing to look for pity and getting it on the double as a result, thanks to his cheeky charm and irrepressible stubbornness. Rayon's amiability is equally well transmitted in a totally committed performance from Leto. "If you called Jared at the weekend," Garner praised, "it would have been Rayon on the phone" (*Dallas Buyers Club*, Extras). Praise doesn't come higher than that.

Director Jean-Marc Vallée refused to trade in schmaltz, not even when Woodroof grieved Rayon's passing. Choosing humor over emotionalism, he presented a tableau that was guaranteed to win over all but the hardest heart.

McConaughey lost forty-seven pounds for the role, going the opposite direction to the Robert de Niro of *Raging Bull* to earn his statuette. In some of the scenes he looks near skeletal. He didn't starve himself; he just ate less. And he didn't give up wine. "The surprise," he said, "was how the energy I lost from the neck down transferred to the neck up. I became almost hyper. I needed three hours less sleep a night" (Daniels, 2014: 206). To make himself look pale he simply stayed out of the sun.

Woodroof's family was thoroughly supportive of McConaughey, even going so far as to give him Woodroof's diaries to pore through to aid him in the interpretation of the character. He got to know everything about a person who had a problem with finishing everything he started—until he got sick: "That was the first time when he had a purpose in his life, ironically, because he was having to fight for his life" (Daniels, 207).

His family didn't try to pretend he was a nice guy. He had a gruff manner that continued into his illness: 'He was a son-of-a-bitch but we loved him." Neither did they believe he was crusading for a cause by selling the pills he amassed. No, he was doing it because he modeled himself on the gangster Scarface: he wanted money (Daniels, 209–11).

McConaughey received a standing ovation when the film was screened at the 2013 Toronto International Film Festival. From an initial budget of $5 million it grossed over $32 million by early 2014. Audiences around the world were captivated by Woodruff's struggle, by the fact that he took on the big guns and won. His work continued long after his death. As an endnote informs us, a modified form of his AZT cocktails saved millions of lives.

Great inventions sometimes happen by accident. In Ron Woodroof's case, that accident was motivated by desperation. "I've got one life," he tells Dr. Eve. "I want it to mean sumthin'."

It did, and it continues to do so. The medical world, upon his urging, was forced to look at "the gay disease" in a new light and think outside the box.

Related Films
Midnight Cowboy (1969); *Common Threads: Stories from the Quilt* (1989); *Living Proof: HIV and the Pursuit of Happiness* (1993); *Flawless* (1999); *3 Needles* (2005); *Dallas Buyers Club: Extras* (2014).

Further Reading
Daniels, Neil. 2014. *Matthew McConaughey: The Biography*. London: John Blake.
Shilts, Randy. 2011. *And the Band Played On: Politics, People and the AIDS Epidemic*. London: Souvenir Books.
Twisted Classics. 2018. *Jared Leto: Red Hot Career Guide*. CreateSpace.

The Danish Girl (2015)

On a fairly average night for the Wegeners, landscape painter Einar (Eddie Redmayne) and Gerda (Alicia Vikander), his artist wife of six years, sit chatting in their chic 1920s Copenhagen apartment. Einar's career has been going very well of late; Gerda's not quite so well. On the night in question, she wants to paint a portrait of her friend Ulla (Amber Heard), but Ulla fails to show up. She asks Einar if he will do her a favor and put on the clothes Ulla was going to wear for the portrait. Einar is happy to oblige.

Lili Elbe (1882–1931)

Elbe is sometimes credited as being the first transgender woman in history. (She wasn't; Christine Jorgensen predated her.) She was born Einar Magnus Andreas Wegener in Vejle, Denmark. She met Gerda, who was then Gerda Gottlieb, at the Royal Danish Academy of Fine Arts in Copenhagen. They were married in 1904.

Both of them worked as illustrators, Elbe specializing in landscape painting while Gerda mainly illustrated books and fashion magazines. They traveled between Italy and France in the years after their marriage, eventually settling in Paris in 1912. Here Elbe lived openly as a woman, Gerda taking on the role of her lesbian partner to facilitate her. Sometimes she introduced Elbe as her sister.

The subterfuge continued throughout the 1920s. The marriage was then annulled by the king of Denmark. Elbe was allowed to have her new name on her passport. This was liberal for the time. Denmark was always forward-thinking in such matters. Gerda continued to use Elbe as her model. She produced many fine paintings in this way. Elbe never saw herself as an artist in the same league, but as David Ebershoff remarked, she was one in the sense that she created herself (Ebershoff, 316).

She went to Germany for her first reassignment surgery in 1930. She had four operations in the next eighteen months. The first one removed her testicles, the second implanted an ovary. The third operation removed the penis and scrotum. The fourth one was an attempt to transplant a uterus into her in order to allow her to become a mother. By now her body had had enough and it rejected this.

Elbe first came out publicly as a transgender woman in a series of interviews she did with a Danish journalist. Other newspapers then picked up on the story. In her interviews she talked about Einar as a person outside herself. Sometimes she described him as a brother or other family member. She never thought of him when she was Lili, she emphasized, whereas when she was Einar she thought of little else but Lili.

She died at the age of forty-eight, shortly after her last operation. She never expected to live long and didn't fear death, even collaborating with a journalist on one of her obituaries. After she died, Niels Hoyer published her diaries in his book *Man into Woman*. David Ebershoff's novel is largely based on these. Today she's revered as a pioneer and role model for transgender people.

Ebershoff thinks there's a little bit of Lili in all of us. He believes everyone has looked in the mirror at least once, and thought, "The world cannot see me as I truly am" (Ebershoff, 326). His book won the Lambda Award for transgender fiction and became the basis for Tom Hooper's film. A biography of Elbe is forthcoming from Nikolaj Pors.

As soon as he puts on Ulla's stockings, he feels a tremor of excitement. This isn't just a fetish; it's almost orgasmic. As David Ebershoff wrote in the book on which the film is based, "He felt warm and submerged, as if dipping into a summer sea . . . There was a distant voice in his head: the soft cry of a scared little girl" (Ebershoff, 2015, 11–12).

Einar is exultant; Gerda amused. She feels Einar's willingness to comply with her request will result in a better portrait. Einar puts on Ulla's dress. He feels another person inside him, a person who's been waiting to appear her whole life. Gerda graciously accepts this new addition to their "family."

They call her Lili Elbe, a fictitious cousin who's allegedly visiting them. The night of the missing Ulla becomes a prelude to a succession of nights where Gerda and Einar, now masquerading as Lili for the artistic set of Copenhagen with which the Wegeners socialize, become a pair of giggling women instead of husband and wife. For Einar, these are the first brushstrokes of her new identity. Gerda, for her part, turns from bemusement to confusion. Who is this new person in their marriage? How long will she be there?

Though biologically a boy, Einar always knew her true nature was female. The night Gerda asked her to pose for her was her lightbulb moment, her liberation from a false life. "Marriage produces a third person," she tells Gerda. That person is Lili. Lili feels she's lost nothing in forsaking Einar. For her he was an anomaly, a nonperson.

Lili tells Gerda she wishes to have sex reassignment surgery. Gerda is supportive, despite the fact that it will mean losing her husband, a husband who loved her and with whom she had a fulfilling sexual relationship. That's over now. Einar is dead.

The medical establishment of 1926 Copenhagen isn't quite so supportive. Doctors tell Einar he's mentally ill, that he's gay. Einar replies that this is a misdiagnosis, that "he" is actually a woman. All through "his" life another person has been living inside him: Lili Elbe.

Lili's crisis takes her to the Dresden Municipal Women's Clinic for a number of traumatic surgeries. Gerda supports her throughout all of these.

The film is directed by Tom Hooper. He captures the events with a dreamy melancholy. He isn't just making a film about a woman trapped in a man's body. He's also crafting a love story. For Gerda, that love means letting go of everything she's known. Her journey, in many ways, is as heroic as Einar's.

Redmayne made the film trailing clouds of Oscar glory from *The Theory of Everything* where he played the profoundly disabled physicist Stephen Hawking. This was an equally challenging role for him. His delicate features were ideal for playing a character described as "pretty" in Ebershoff's novel (Ebershoff, 7). He solicited the help of transgender advisers to get inside the skin of Lili, going first to Lana Wachowski, the transgender director of *The Matrix*. He then went to movement director Alexandra Reynolds. Here he learned how to sit, pose, and walk in high heels (Herbert, 2015: 2016–7).

As the film went on, Redmayne became significantly more coy. His eyes turned downward; his movements became more graceful. There's a scene in which he strips before a mirror and tries to hide his penis between his legs. Redmayne captures Lili's dysmorphia perfectly in that one gesture.

Whatever he does, Vikander does better. "Alicia is a force of nature," Redmayne commended. "She raised my game" (*Danish Girl* DVD: Bonus Features). It was fitting that it was she rather than he who won the Oscar. She's just as much "The Danish Girl" as Lili.

The film isn't perfect. The artistic rivalry between Einar and Gerda should perhaps have been emphasized more. Hooper's emphasis is obviously on Lili's life-changing (and, tragically, life-ending) surgeries, but the film begs a fundamental question: How is it that a cross-dressing moment provided the trigger for such a fundamental transmogrification? This is to posit a direct connection between cross-dressing and being transgender, which seems like a trivialization of it. A clothes change is one thing, an identity shift something else entirely.

Critics were divided on the film. Some of them rhapsodized about its painterly sense; others castigated it for being too genteel and precious. The agonies of the straight Gerda at the expense of the transgender Lili also brought unfortunate echoes to some about the manner in which Ron Woodroof's plight was highlighted at the expense of the gay AIDS sufferers in *Dallas Buyers Club*.

The film was released at an interesting time for transgender people. In the United Kingdom, the boxing promoter Frank Maloney had undergone sex reassignment surgery to become a woman called Kellie. In the United States, Olympic sportsman Bruce Jenner became Caitlin Jenner. On television, a series called *Transparent* had a father inform his children one day that he wasn't going to be Mort any more but rather Maura. In Selfridge's department store, a range of unisex clothing called Agender opened up. The British edition of *Vogue* magazine carried a feature headed, "Man, woman, neither, both" (Herbert, 2015: 218). Hooper—and Ebershoff—tapped into that seismic shift of consciousness to create the movie that everyone was talking about in 2014.

Related Films
The Christine Jorgenson Story (1970); *Metamorphosis: Man into Woman* (1990); *Laurence Anyways* (2012); *52 Tuesdays* (2013); *Tangerine* (2015).

Further Reading
Ebershoff, David. 2015. *The Danish Girl*. London: Weidenfeld & Nicolson.
Herbert, Emily. 2015. *Eddie Redmayne: The Biography*. London: John Blake.
Straayer, Chris. 1996. *Deviant Eyes, Deviant Bodies: Sexual Re-Orientation in Film and Video*. New York: Columbia University Press.

Terence Davies (1945–)

The youngest of ten children born into a poor Catholic family in Liverpool, Davies reached adulthood when the Beatles, who also hailed from that city, were at the height of their fame. The "swinging sixties," however, isn't Davies's theme or time. Most of his films are set in the fifties and concentrate on the traumatic years of his adolescence.

His father had a schizoid personality, gravitating from tenderness to brutality without any logic. He beat his wife and abused his children both physically and mentally. "When I was a kid," Davies recalled, "I'd run into a room and if he didn't want anyone around, he'd just kick me from one end of the house to the other. You don't make that mistake very often" (*Guardian*, October 6, 2000). He died when Davies was six but left an indelible mark on him. This is evidenced by his work. He was put sleeping in his bed after he died. Understandably, it gave him nightmares.

Davies left school at sixteen to become a shipping clerk. After that he spent twelve years as an accountant. He hated every moment of this, describing it as "slow death" (Levy, 2015: 122). His first work of note was *The Terence Davies Trilogy, 1974–83*. This comprises three short black-and-white films dealing with the life of a character called Robert Tucker. He's played by four different actors in all, two of them in *Children* where Tucker is portrayed both as a boy, by Philip Mawdsley, and as a twenty-four-year-old man by Robin Hooper. Terry O'Sullivan and Wilfred Brambell play him in the other two parts of the trilogy. In *Children* (1976), Robert is bullied at school, partly because of his orientation. He's also riddled with guilt, which results in frequent trips to confession. One of these takes place shortly after he knocks on the door of a gay club. Davies is very interested in the connection between religion and sex. He juxtaposes a further confession scene with one where Tucker is performing fellatio on another man. Using flashbacks and flash-forwards, he chronicles his life in a series of uncompromising vignettes. In the second part of the trilogy, *Madonna and Child* (1980), Tucker (O'Sullivan) is an adult but still suffering the same torments. In the final part, *Death and Transfiguration* (1983), Brambell plays him as a gravely ill old man in a hospital ward.

Davies's first full feature, *Distant Voices, Still Lives* (1988), was highly praised at the Cannes and Toronto Film Festivals. The first half deals with his early years at home with his parents and older sister. Life is basically gloomy. A release of sorts is provided by music and the cinema, both of which save him from descending into a pit of depression. He loves listening to the music of Judy Garland, Gene Kelly, and Doris Day. He sits in bars where members of his family and extended family mix Jewish and Irish songs with those of Hollywood movies in a manner that lifts all their spirits.

The second half of *Distant Voices, Still Lives* isn't as effective as the first. It takes place after Davies's father has died. The sepia tones give way to a spectral white. His atmospheric chiaroscuros convey claustrophobia and postwar *anomie*. Nonetheless, he was proud of the film overall. It featured a world he wouldn't have seen on screen when he was growing up. "I can't think," he said, "of any film that really captured what it felt like to be working class because working-class people didn't make movies" (Williams, 1996: 66).

The Long Day Closes was released in 1992. Generally regarded as his masterpiece, this achingly beautiful film echoed *Distant Voices* in many ways but also represented a departure from it because of his more mature style of direction. It starred Leigh McCormack as Bud, Davies's alter ego. He's an impressionable ten-year-old running—again—from his downbeat environment into the magical world of the cinema. His burgeoning orientation is captured in a muted manner in a scene where he becomes entranced looking at a muscular builder who's taken off his shirt. He winks at Bud as if he knows he's gay. Bud feels ashamed, not fully understanding what's happening. Speaking of the scene, Davies said, "It's not that he recognizes the fact that he's gay. It's recognizing that there's something wrong, and that's all. Because, at eleven, how can you know anything more?" (Everett, 2004: 218).

The film also explores the close bond he forges with his mother. As was the case with *Distant Voices*, it's infused with music, all the way from Nat King Cole to the Judy Garland of *Meet Me in Saint Louis* and the Debbie Reynolds of *Tammy*. Sensitive set pieces are movingly threaded together with care and precision, evoking bittersweet feelings of yearning and loss at the same time. In one scene, he lets the camera linger on a faded carpet for over a minute as the sun glides across it. At the end, Bud passes through a door into a pitch-black void. With a backing soundtrack of Orson Welles's *The Magnificent Ambersons* and David Lean's *Great Expectations*, we become painfully aware such comfort zones are disappearing from Bud's life. The closing image is of a moon vanishing behind the clouds, another index of change, like the door into the void. As with the carpet, Davies lets his camera linger on the scene, this time for a full three minutes.

His next undertaking was *The Neon Bible*, based on the debut novel of John Kennedy Toole, an author who became famous as a result of the posthumous publication of *The Confederacy of Dunces*. He committed suicide in 1969 after it was rejected by a number of publishers. Set in the Deep South in the 1940s, it deals with an impressionable lad who's close to his mother and distant from his father. This is familiar Davies territory apart from the location.

He adapted Edith Wharton's *The House of Mirth* in 2000. Afterward he took a long break from directing. When he came back to the screen, it was with his first nonfiction film, *Of Time and the City*. This explores his sexuality and is also a love note to Liverpool. It features much archival footage of the city whose mother lode Davies has strip-mined in almost everything he's done. "If Liverpool didn't exist," he says at one point, "it would have to be invented." He examines its transmogrification from the cobble-streeted enclave of the forties to the sixties mecca it became, largely thanks to the Beatles. His story runs in tandem with theirs as he fights the restrictiveness of church and state (and even monarchy) to carve out his niche. Like his previous features, it has nostalgia tooth in jowl with righteous indignation. The narrative mixes poetry and music with narration and snatches of old music hall songs.

Next for Davies was *The Deep Blue Sea* (2011). Based on a play by Terence Rattigan, it deals with a sexually repressed woman (Rachel Weisz) who's attracted to a World War II veteran. The play was a semiautobiographical work by Rattigan. Davies used the plot to index his love of women's films of the forties—*Brief Encounter; Letter from an Unknown Woman; Now, Voyager;* etc. In 2015 he made *Sunset Song*, which had been in gestation since 2008. It had the daughter of a farmer coming of age in the early 1900s. *A Quiet Passion* (2018) is his most recent film. It's based on the life of Emily Dickinson.

A man who thinks long and hard about what he does, Davies has produced an incredible body of work. His range is limited but within it he's able to be both moody and evocative. He adopts a formal, ponderous style with long takes to exert a deeply hypnotic effect. "I'm very black and white," he told an interviewer once. "I either feel great passion or nothing at all" (Levy, 2015: 123). Somewhere between these extremes he explores the raw beauty of art, rejection, and evanescence.

Some people accuse him of making the one film all his life. If that's true, it's a very good one, soaked in his exhilarations and demons. Unlike most other directors, he mainly works alone. Few people have captured the almost primal pain of adolescence like he has, in a city he both loves and hates. A stylist of the highest order, he often invites comparisons with people like John Boorman and Mike Leigh, but even a cursory examination of his films show that he's much bleaker than either of them. Philip Larkin once said that depression to him was what daffodils were to Wordsworth. Perhaps the same could be said of Davies.

He has often suggested that he regrets being gay, mainly because of the stigma that surrounded it growing up. Much of this was propelled by the church. "It offered me no succor," he said of that time. "I felt that if I prayed and was really good, God would make me like everybody else. Those years when I prayed until my knees bled were awful. I finally realized the priests were just men in frocks. I dropped the church when I was 22. It left a deep emotional hole in me, a sense of chaos" (Levy, 149). Davies is now an atheist.

Related Films
The Terence Davies Trilogy, 1974–83 (1984); *Distant Voices, Still Lives* (1988); *The Long Day Closes* (1992); *The Neon Bible* (1995); *The House of Mirth* (2000); *Of Time and the City* (2008); *The Deep Blue Sea* (2011); *Sunset Song* (2015); *A Quiet Passion* (2018).

Further Reading
Everett, Wendy. 2004. *Terence Davies*. Manchester and New York: Manchester University Press.
Friedman, Lester, ed. 1993. *Fires Were Started: British Cinema and Thatcherism*. Minneapolis: University of Minnesota Press.
Griffiths, Robin, ed. 2006. *British Queer Cinema*. London and New York: Routledge.
Guardian, October 6, 2000.
Koresky, Michael. 2014. *Terence Davies*. Champaign: University of Illinois Press.
Levy, Emanuel. 2015. *Gay Directors, Gay Films?* New York: Columbia University Press.
Rosenstone, Robert A., ed. 1995. *Revisioning History: Film and the Construction of a New Past*. Princeton, NJ: Princeton University Press.
Williams, C. 1996. *Cinema: The Beginnings and the Future*. London: University of Westminster Press.

James Dean (1931–55)

On September 30, 1955, an aspiring actor by the name of James Byron Dean broke his neck on a highway in Cholame after a bust-up in his treasured Porsche Spyder. The world mourned him, but for the gentle man with the soulful eyes and the carved features, shuffling off the mortal coil was the best career move he ever made. It meant he carried through on his philosophy of "Live fast, die young and make a good-looking corpse" (Ultra Violet, 1988: 6).

His face on the cover of any movie magazine, as is the case with people like Elvis Presley and Marilyn Monroe, still guarantees its sales will rocket. More than anyone else working in film, he encapsulated the angst at the core of the love-hungry fifties.

He did it first as Cal Trask in Elia Kazan's masterly adaptation of John Steinbeck's *East of Eden* and again in the role for which he will be forever immortalized, *Rebel without a Cause*. It's easy to overlook the film's hackneyed polemical edge and view it instead as a rite-of-passage for a trio of self-indulgent souls.

In *Giant*, his last movie, the increasingly confident and increasingly diva-like Dean warred openly with the director George Stevens, as indeed he did with Rock Hudson, the ostensible star of the movie. Hudson saw him as a selfish, egomaniacal introvert. Stevens prohibited him from driving his Porsche until the movie wrapped, a dictate that was vindicated by events that were to follow, though one could argue that the reason Dean went a little crazy on September 30 was as a result of being forcibly removed from his car for so long. It's a point worth noting, but one could just as easily argue that it was only a matter of time before the impetuous firebrand zoomed off into the sunset for keeps.

Whatever the circumstances surrounding his death—and there's still a lot of speculation about who was responsible for it—his image remains frozen forever for his salivating fans in those three roles, whose significance have in some ways been blown out of all proportion to their worth. But then hype has always been allowable for those sensitive souls who entered Hollywood heaven before fat on the soul set in, or that long odyssey to obscurity that seems to be de rigueur for incandescent talents that burn too brightly to last.

Had he lived, he would probably have eventually succumbed to playing more mediocre roles during the fallow periods every actor goes through. Dying as he did at his peak, he remains a kind of Lycidas figure mown down in his prime.

After he died, many of his fans refused to accept the fact that he was gone. In this he resembled Rudolph Valentino. They believed that he was sequestered somewhere remote, living a Garboesque existence far from the prying eyes of the public, but one day planning a comeback.

Even those who did accept that their idol was dead continued to make pilgrimages to his shrine to lay wreaths, and maybe commune with his spirit. They saw in him the epitome of all their twisted hopes and crazy dreams, a man straining at the leash to impress girlfriends, parents, friends—and himself.

The term "crisis of identity" didn't mean too much to people before Dean. Neither did the term "teenager." He was said to be America's first one. Sitting astride a motorcycle in a leather jacket, or fulminating against the status quo, he became a young man who, along with his heroes Marlon Brando and Montgomery Clift, gave a voice to the vulnerable.

He set the seeds for a generation that would no longer accept the bromides of their forbears, or a worldview that predicated mindless conformity at its kernel. He redefined masculinity far from the tunnel vision of locker room jocks.

One witnesses the Method writ largely in his solipsistic tics, and also the innocent buoyancy of a man who wants to break down the walls of the temple, an urbanized Samson let loose in a world that refused to bend to his dreams. Whether it destroys him, or he it, doesn't really matter. What matters is that he fights the good fight according to his own cerebral rules.

So where did all his hysteria come from? His mother died when he was nine. He spent the rest of his short life trying to find a substitute for her on the altar of his art, with a handful of women he couldn't hold on to, like Pier Angeli. Or was it they who couldn't hold on to him? Gloria Grahame claimed Hollywood built up the relationship between Dean and Angeli to try and "heterosexualize" him for audiences (Hadleigh, 2005: 101).

They are not long, the days of wine and roses. For Dean they were indeed short, but he crammed two lifetimes into the twenty-four years in which he inhabited the earth. He hit a sociological nerve that extended across the social divide and entered the hearts of young people everywhere. The way he moved, that casual shuffle of the hips, was before its time. People say he got it from Brando, but Dean claimed he did what he did long before he was aware of that actor.

Not long before his fatality on the highway, he said death was the only thing left to respect: "Everything else can be questioned but death is truth. In it lies the only nobility for man, and beyond it the only hope" (Humphreys, 1990: 139).

Dean's sexuality was androgynous. His biographer Randall Riese quotes him as saying he didn't want to go through life with one hand tied behind his back (Riese, 1991: 239). This was an indication that he was bisexual. Some biographers claim he went to bed with men for career reasons. His motorcycle friend John Gilmore said he did so for experimental purposes (Gilmore, 1998: 119–20). Liza Minnelli's sometime husband Peter Allen put a different slant on things when he said, "He preferred men who could dominate him" (Hadleigh, 1994: 156). He was alleged to have avoided being drafted into the army by filing as a gay man (Bryant, 1997: 52).

Sal Mineo claimed Nick Adams told him he had an affair with him during the making of *Rebel without a Cause*. They roomed together on the set of the film. For Mineo, that was a sign: "There's always the roomie thing in Hollywood—Brando and Wally Cox, Brando and Tony Curtis, Cary Grant and Randolph Scott" (Hadleigh, 1994: 149). Elizabeth Taylor publicly referred to him as being gay at a GLAAD Media Awards ceremony on March 25, 2011. Taylor was always a loyal friend to gay men and supported the fight against AIDS all her life with money and time. "There's no gay agenda," she believed. "It's a human agenda" (Porter, 2007: 33). On the set of *Giant*, she tried to keep the peace between Dean and Rock Hudson—a bisexual man and a gay one—when they failed to get along. "If I said hello or good morning he snarled at me," Hudson said of Dean (Humphreys, 1990: 113). He regarded him as too self-important for his good.

Dean was primarily heterosexual. He had many relationships with beautiful women like Ursula Andress and the aforementioned Pier Angeli. His heart was broken when Angeli married Vic Damone. The marriage was a failure and Angeli ended up committing suicide. She never got over Dean and he never got over her.

He was alleged to have been Clifton Webb's toyboy for a time. Nobody is quite sure if Webb was gay or just effeminate. (The great love of his life was his mother. He attended public events with her until she was in her eighties.) Dean was also rumored to have had sexual involvements with Martin Landau and Arthur Kennedy. His longest-lasting gay relationship was with the minor actor William Bast, his UCLA roommate.

Two years after he died, Robert Altman made a documentary about him, *The James Dean Story*. This didn't have much to say about the troubled genius that one didn't already know, despite the use of rare archival material. Ray Connolly's *James Dean—The First American Teenager* (1975) was more engaging, featuring interviews from people including Natalie Wood and Dennis Hopper, his *Rebel without a Cause* costars. The following year NBC-TV aired *James Dean*, a Robert

Butler biopic that explored his relationship with Bast, played here by Michael Brandon. Stephen McHattie was Dean. Both of them were portrayed as being bisexual, but this was conveyed mostly by verbal innuendo.

Dean is studying acting in the film. In one scene he approaches Bast with a script his tutor has asked him to prepare for a forthcoming class. "It's about this guy who had a thing with his best friend," he explains, "and ever since it's been tearing him apart." He adds, "I don't mean kid's stuff. Everybody does that." The implication is obvious. This is a full-blown affair.

Bast goes to a gay bar to do his friend's research for him. It isn't explained why Dean doesn't go himself. Is he afraid of his orientation? "You've got to make sacrifices for your art," he tells Bast, but it looks as if Bast is the one who's making the sacrifice—especially if he's not gay himself.

Robert Altman paid a tribute to Dean in 1982 with a film called *Come Back to the Five and Dime, Jimmy Dean, Jimmy Dean*. Set in a Texas town in 1975, it featured five female members of his fan club congregating at their local five-and-dime store for a twenty-year reunion. It's as much about them as Dean, and the changes time has wrought on their lives since they last met. Sandy Dennis played a character who claims Dean seduced her on the last night of filming *Rebel without a Cause*. She says she became pregnant as a result, eventually giving birth to a child she called, what else, Jimmy Dean. Her story isn't convincing but it helps her state of mind to worship at the altar of the dead legend. Why wouldn't it? She's carrying a piece of him within her.

Karen Black played a transsexual woman in the film. Rebecca Bell-Metereau believed its central irony was the fact that "the women have built their lives and their dreams around men, how to attract them, how to keep them, how to bring them back, while the only man has spent his life learning how to be a woman" (Bell-Metereau, 1993: 197). Black is straight in real life. "If I were out in the desert and I had no one to do it with, I'd still want to do it with boys" (*Film Yearbook*, 1985).

James Franco played Dean in the 2001 drama *James Dean*. (By now one was wondering when somebody would come up with a more original title for such ventures.) This focused more on his acting than his personal life, though some effort is made to document his fraught relationship with his father (Michael Moriarty). This was a conflict that also found its way into two of his three completed movies, *East of Eden* and *Rebel without a Cause*. Like Butler's film, *James Dean* was made for TV. Franco was convincing in the role, but it would have been more interesting to see it being played by bigger stars like Johnny Depp, Brad Pitt, or Leonardo DiCaprio, all of whom were considered for it before Franco signed along the dotted line.

Related Films
East of Eden (1955); *Rebel without a Cause* (1955); *Giant* (1956); *The James Dean Story* (1957); *James Dean* (1976); *Come Back to the Five and Dime, Jimmy Dean, Jimmy Dean* (1982); *James Dean* (2001); *James Dean: Outside the Lines* (2002); *Joshua Tree, 1951: A Portrait of James Dean* (2012); *Life* (2015).

Further Reading
Alexander, Paul. 1994. *Boulevard of Broken Dreams: The Life, Times and Legacy of James Dean*. New York: Viking.

Bast, William. 1956. *James Dean: A Biography*. New York: Ballantine.
Bell-Metereau, Rebecca. 1993. *Hollywood Androgyny*. New York: Columbia University Press.
Bryant, Wayne M. 1997. *Bisexual Characters in Film from Anais to Zee*. New York: Birch Lane Press.
Dalton, David. 2017. *James Dean: The Mutant King*. Chicago: Chicago Review Press.
DeAngelis, Michael. 2001. *Gay Fandom and Crossover Stardom: James Dean, Mel Gibson and Keanu Reeves*. Durham, NC: Duke University Pres.
Film Yearbook, 1985.
Gilmore, John. 1997. *Live Fast, Die Young: My Life with James Dean*. New York: Thunder's Mouth Press.
Hadleigh, Boze, ed. 1994. *Hollywood Babble On: Stars Gossip about Other Stars*. New York: Birch Lane Press.
Hadleigh, Boze, 2005. *Celebrity Diss and Tell*. Kansas City: Andrews McMeel.
Humphreys, Joseph, ed. 1990. *Jimmy Dean on Jimmy Dean*. London: Plexus.
Hyams, Joe, and Jay Hyams. 1992. *James Dean: Little Boy Lost*. New York: Time Warner.
Porter, Darwin, and Danforth Prince. 2007. *Blood Moon's Guide to Gay and Lesbian Film: Second Edition*. New York: Blood Moon Productions.
Riese, Randall. 1991. *The Unabridged James Dean: His Life and Legacy from A to Z*. New York: McGraw-Hill Contemporary.
Ultra Violet. 1988. *Famous for Fifteen Minutes: My Life with Andy Warhol*. New York and London: Harcourt Brace.
Variety, November 6, 1968.

Deathtrap (1980)

Ira Levin's play had been running on Broadway since 1978 when Sidney Lumet decided to make it into a movie. He employed Jay Presson Allen as his screenwriter. She preserved most of Levin's script but made every effort to make it more cinematic. The country house setting with its ornate furnishings provided the ideal backdrop for the far-fetched scenario to unfold. The wild rainstorms raging outside added an extra dimension of "hoary old horror story" to the mix.

Michael Caine plays Sidney Bruhl, a playwright who's just had another flop. A protégé of his, Clifford Anderson (Christopher Reeve), has written a play and is about to show it to Bruhl for his approval. Bruhl senses it's going to be a hit. What, he says to his wife, Myra (Dyan Cannon), if he killed Anderson and claimed the glory for himself? She's not sure if he's joking. Neither is the audience.

Could a person "kill" for a good script? That's the basic question the film poses. The phrase has entered the language today as a metaphorical way of saying someone likes something a lot. Here it acquires a literal manifestation.

Caine was coming off a string of duds himself when he made the film, which gave him the motivation to drain every ounce of drama from it (*Newsday*, March 19, 1982). His performance is over the top, but the pyrotechnics of the plot make this allowable. The film's central surprise is the fact that he's in a gay relationship with Reeve. Cannon also goes over the top and so does Irene Worth, playing a Dutch seer who lives next door.

Lumet was interested in the fact that a writer could also be a murderer. He always felt there was a thin line separating creativity from destruction: "There's a life force that makes one person turn out a hell of a painting and somebody else stab his cousin" (*New York Times Magazine*, June 6, 1982).

Reeve wasn't regarded as one of the great actors of his era, but Lumet saw something in him he liked. "What seemed such a nice, simple, artless performance in *Superman*," he gushed, "was the finest kind of acting. Reeve's timing—and humor—had to be just about perfect to make the character come off" (Shipman, 1988: 73).

Caine knew exactly what he wanted to do in a scene before it started shooting, but Reeve liked to work his way into it. "Sidney often came up to me at the last minute and gave me a new idea," he said. It mightn't have been a major change but "something fresh to put on my plate" (*American Film*, December 8, 1982). He described him as "part camp counselor, part psychiatrist and part technical director" (Shipman, 1988: 134). Dyan Cannon liked Lumet too. What made her secure with him was the freedom he gave her: "He always made me feel like I could make a fool of myself and it would be all right" (Emery, 1999: 371).

The film has as many twists as a corkscrew. Some of these are more contrived than others, but if one suspends disbelief, as perforce one must for a film like this, they have a weird kind of logic attached to them. Alone they don't work, but as a thread they gel.

The film creates its own rationale. One writer compared it to a snake eating its tail (*Monthly Film Bulletin*, September 1982). The implausibilities of the plot aren't a problem because there are so many of them. When something is played as ham-fisted as this, the sky's the limit. The demented wife, the crumbling literary career, the gay boyfriend, and the psychic are all put into the melting pot and stirred mischievously by Lumet. He teases us at every turn, rolling back his Russian dolls until we find the "real" one, the one that explains all the others.

The film's piece de resistance arrives when we learn that Caine and Reeve are in cahoots with one another to frighten Cannon—who has a bad heart—to death in a *Sleuth*-style pact. The scene that received the most attention, however, was the one where they kissed one another on the lips. There hadn't been many gay kisses on screen from A-list stars at this time, apart from Peter Finch in John Schlesinger's *Sunday Bloody Sunday* (1971). To gear themselves up for it, they both drank brandy. When Lumet shouted "Action!" Caine said to Reeve, "Whatever you do, don't open your mouth" (Caine, 2010: 210).

The kiss was remembered longer than the movie. "I can tell you that Christopher Reeve isn't homosexual," Caine joked. "When we kissed, he didn't close his eyes" (*Spectator*, September 14, 1983). A hostile preview audience in Denver booed it, and this was reported in *Time* magazine, which spoiled the surprise for many people. If it wasn't for this, Reeve believed the film would have fared much better commercially. But he was proud of his performance in it. He'd played it, he said, "without apology" (Reeve, 1999: 212). When it was screened on television, the kiss was cut out.

Some years later, Caine was in a café and sorely needed to urinate. The men's room was occupied but the ladies' was free, so he used that. As he was coming out, a woman entered. "It's okay," he said. "I'm a lesbian." She looked him up and down and said, "No you're not. I saw you kiss Superman in *Deathtrap*" (Caine, 2010: 210–11).

Related Films
Sleuth (1972, 2007); *Dressed to Kill* (1980); *Baba—It* (1991).

Further Reading
American Film, December 8, 1982.
Bray, Christopher. 2005. *Michael Caine: A Class Act*. London: Faber & Faber.
Caine, Michael. 2010. *The Elephant to Hollywood: The Autobiography*. London: Hodder & Stoughton.
Emery, Robert J. 1999. *The Directors—Take One: In Their Own Words*. TV Books: New York.
Lumet, Sidney. 1996. *Making Movies*. London: Bloomsbury.
Monthly Film Bulletin, September 1982.
New York Times Magazine, June 6, 1982.
Newsday, March 19, 1982.
Rapf, Joanna, E. 2006. *Sidney Lumet Interviews*. Jackson: University Press of Mississippi.
Reeve, Christopher. 1999. *Still Me*. London: Arrow.
Shipman, David, ed. 1988. *Movie Talk: Who Said What about Whom in the Movies*. London: Bloomsbury.
Spectator, September 14, 1983.

Desert Hearts (1985)

Adapted by Jane Rule from her novel *Desert of the Heart* and directed with both style and restraint by Donna Deitch, this is a refreshingly unsensational tale of a lesbian love affair.

Set in the summer of 1959, it has English lecturer Vivian Bell (Helen Shaver) going to Reno for a "quickie" divorce from a marriage that has, as she says, "drowned in still waters." She stays at a ranch outside Reno where she meets Cay Rivers (Patricia Charbonneau), a sculptor who moonlights at the local casino. The ranch is run by Cay's possessive mother, Frances (Audra Lindley). Her father died some years before.

Vivian hasn't acknowledged her lesbian tendencies as the film begins. When she gets to Reno, the only thing on her mind is her divorce. She imagines the break will give her some "downtime" to prepare for the new academic year.

Cay is very well aware of her sexuality. She brings out Vivian's inner lesbian and changes her image as well, getting her to replace her "sensible" pantsuit for the folksier cowboy gear she dons as their relationship takes off.

Cay stays out all night with Vivian one night and Frances becomes enraged, telling her to leave the ranch. Vivian moves to a hotel room in Reno. When Cay tracks her down, Vivian tells her she doesn't see any future in their relationship. A kiss they've shared is dismissed by her as "a moment's indiscretion, a fleeting lapse of judgment."

Vivian leaves the room to get a drink. When she comes back, Cay is lying naked on the bed. "Oh God," she says. She tells her to leave but Cay refuses. Instead she suggests that Vivian put a Do Not Disturb sign on the door. When this is done they make love.

One expects to see disapproval of their relationship from the locals, but it doesn't transpire, which seems anachronistic for the time. This is a minor fault in a film that had a huge effect on the LGBTQ world when it was released. It succeeded almost without appearing to try. Maybe that was its secret. There's a subtle artistry at work. Deitch evokes time and place realistically, using music from Elvis Presley, Patsy Cline, Johnnie Ray, and Jim Reeves to amplify the nostalgic mood.

The sex scene caused many ripples. It was, after all, the era of Ronald Reagan; it still raises a few eyebrows even today. Both women said they felt very comfortable during it. Charbonneau said it was easier for her to make love to a woman on screen than it would have been for her with a man (Redding and Brownworth, 1997: 227).

The scene is explicit but not prurient. Everything is shown but nothing is exaggerated or exploited. There are no cutaways at the "vital" moments, and no music to embellish the proceedings. In fact it's almost like a documentary in style. It's targeted toward lesbian women rather than straight men, a welcome development from Deitch. In the past, women did most things for men, including scenes like this. With this film, they reclaim their identity for themselves. The fact that Deitch is a lesbian in real life means that one is getting the real thing here, not the kind of "lipstick lesbianism" some directors favor.

Desert Hearts is praiseworthy for its unfussiness. It doesn't make any large claims for itself, doesn't look for abstruse insights into what it means to be gay in a world where one is unaccepted and/or reviled. It's a simple love story told tastefully, even casually.

If it had a man and a woman at its center rather than two women, it would have been one of the most conventional films ever to come out of Hollywood. As Mandy Merck noted, it would have been "Boy meets girl, boy loses girl due to parental disapproval, boy finally gets girl back" (Gever, Parmar, and Greyson, 1993: 379). Merck pointed out that the film was steeped in the heterosexual tradition of the active pursuit of the reluctant woman by her lover. The difference is that the lover is another woman this time. Deitch doesn't employ the clichéd masculine/feminine dialectic in their relationship, instead opting for the dichotomies of class ("cheeky casino girl pursues shy professor"), geography, ("candid Westerner courts aloof Easterner"), sexual history ("experienced lesbian brings out previously faithful wife"), and appearance ("passionate brunette warms up cool blond, who honors a long cinematic tradition by finally letting her hair down") (Gever, Parmar, and Greyson, 379).

Deitch departed from Rule's novel in a number of ways to make the film. There was no parental disapproval in the novel, nor was there a brunette/blond contrast. Neither was there a geographical one, both lovers living in the West, nor an academic one, both being college educated. With these simple antinomies, Deitch created instant drama and instant conflict. More important, *Desert Hearts* didn't end with suicide, or one or both of the lovers being "cured" by a male infiltration into the proceedings.

Deitch made a cameo appearance as a gambler. In this capacity she tells Cay, "You have to play to win." It sounds like a truism, but it's relevant in the circumstances. All too often in the past screen lesbians didn't, and they paid the price.

Deitch said she saw the film as a kind of remake of *The Misfits*, which is surprising as the only plot device it shares in common with that film is the fact that one of its characters heads to Reno to process a divorce. To get it up and running she sold shares in it for $1,000 a go to people she knew. This meant many of them had a slice of the profits if it was a success.

It took her over two years to get it to the screen, but the wait was worth it. One of those crossover sleepers that manage the not-to-be-sneezed-at feat of enrapturing straight viewers as well as gay ones, it never went for the soft option in a scene, keeping its eye on naturalism all the while and reaping the harvest of that authenticity with interest.

Related Films
The Misfits (1961); *Personal Best* (1982); *Lianna* (1983); *Fiction and Other Truths: A Film about Jane Rule* (1995).

Further Reading
Gever, Martha, Pratibha Parmar, and John Greyson, eds. 1993. *Queer Looks: Perspectives on Lesbian and Gay Film and Video*. New York and London: Routledge.
Redding, Judith M., and Victoria A. Brownworth. 1997. *Film Fatales: Independent Women Directors*. Seattle: Seal Press.
Rule, Jane, and Jackie Kay. 2010. *Desert of the Heart*. London: Virago.

Marlene Dietrich (1901–92)

When she lived in Berlin in the 1920s, Dietrich had been intimate with women like Claire Waldoff and Ginette Spanier. After she arrived in the United States, she declared boldly, "In Europe it doesn't matter if you're a man or a woman. We make love with anyone we find attractive" (Spoto, 1992: 83).

She was already famous in Germany by the late 1920s. When Josef von Sternberg put her into *The Blue Angel* in 1930, she blew everyone else off the screen as Lola, the sensuous cabaret chanteuse who sings "Falling in Love Again" in that smoky voice and destroys Emil Jannings, the middle-aged professor who becomes enraptured by her.

At the German premiere of the film, Dietrich walked onto the stage with a bunch of violets pinned to the crotch of her dress. These were well-known symbols of being lesbian. She burst upon the Hollywood scene with von Sternberg's *Morocco* in 1930, wearing the kind of men's clothing that defined her: a tuxedo and tall hat. Two years later she replaced such a wardrobe with a naval uniform for *Blonde Venus*. This wasn't quite as alluring, but she was still sending out an androgynous message.

One of her most talked-about female relationships was with the Spanish immigrant Mercedes de Acosta, a feminist playwright who was also lesbian. Dietrich

Morocco (1930)

The most famous scene Dietrich ever appeared in had nothing to do with the plot. In fact if viewers took their eyes off the screen for a few moments to tie their shoelace, or whatever, they could well have missed it. It occurs in the Josef von Sternberg feature *Morocco*, her first American film. Dietrich played Amy Jolly, a cabaret singer who gives up her career to follow foreign legionnaire Gary Cooper into the desert.

Clad in a black tailcoat, white blouse, and top hat tilted slightly to the side, it has her going over to a woman sitting at a table after singing a song. She plucks a flower from the woman's hair, lifts it to her face, and smells it. Then she leans down to her. She takes the woman's chin in her hands and kisses her on the lips. The woman is embarrassed, but Dietrich merely smiles. The people who have been listening to her singing applaud.

Dietrich then tosses the flower away, whereupon Cooper picks it up and puts it behind his ear. With this gesture he has become the woman to her man. Von Sternberg admitted he was seeking a lesbian "accent" in the scene. The motif was inspired by his seeing Dietrich wearing full evening dress at Berlin social events. The outfit had already been part of the androgyny image that had been popular in Paris and Berlin in the twenties. Von Sternberg believed women dominated men and Dietrich was the ideal vehicle to carry this message to audiences.

Sternberg played into Dietrich's appeal to liberal audiences with this publicity slogan for *Morocco*: "Dietrich—the woman all women want to see." He didn't say, "The film all women want to see" or "The woman all men want to see." Cooper wasn't even mentioned. Everyone knew who was the star of the show.

Some viewers of the film saw her behavior in the flower scene as being motivated by a desire to whet Cooper's appetite for her. If this is so, it would be the first time a woman used her attraction to another woman to make a man jealous. Even if it's true, the point has been made: the male of the species isn't the only game in town.

---

sent her many missives as introductory salvos. Afterward they started to go swimming together. Before long the relationship became physical.

"You are the first person to whom I have felt drawn," she told her. De Acosta replied, "You have exceptional skin texture that makes me think of moonlight." They carried on an open relationship throughout the 1930s, Dietrich even doing de Acosta's laundry for her in the German "hausfrau" tradition (Spoto, 127–8).

De Acosta was said to have landed two of Hollywood's biggest trophies in Dietrich and Greta Garbo. And possibly even a third, Gertrude Stein. If one was in with her, Truman Capote trilled, "You could get to anyone from Cardinal Spellman to the Duchess of Windsor" (Vickers, 1994: 12).

De Acosta was entranced with Dietrich, bombarding her with love letters and flowers. "It is a week today," she wrote in one letter, "since your naughty hand opened a white rose. Last night was even more wonderful. Each time I see you it grows more wonderful and exciting—you with your exquisite white pansy face. Before you go to bed will you ring me so that I can just hear your voice" (Madsen, 1995: 71).

Dietrich and Garbo walked about the place in men's attire, thereby flouting the dress code that had pertained in Hollywood's hallowed corridors since movies began. The "Good Time Charlenes," as they were called, were pictured together on the cover of *Vanity Fair* in 1932 under the headline "Both Members of the Same Club." Everyone knew what club that was—the sewing circle of lesbian lovers (Madsen, 14–15).

The three women threatened both the sexual and sartorial mores of the United States. Dietrich's cross-dressing was reprised on screen by the moody Garbo (*Queen Christina*, 1933) and Katharine Hepburn (*Sylvia Scarlett*, 1935) in succeeding years, but nobody could do it like she did. She was the first and the best, her influence apparent right up to the Liza Minnelli of *Cabaret* (1972). Minnelli adapted her image only slightly. This is what the boys in the back room would have—and the girls.

Both Garbo and Dietrich carried their penchant for trousers from Europe. The practice wasn't widespread for women in America at the time. Where they differed was that, apart from her role in *Queen Christina*, Garbo was happy to confine her sartorial preferences to the house. Dietrich, on the contrary, flaunted them anywhere she pleased. She got into trouble at film premieres and photo shoots for doing so. She insisted it wasn't a sexual gesture but merely a fashion statement. Put simply, suits "suited" her. What worried Hollywood particularly—and America generally—was the ripple effect of her wardrobe choices. This was captured in headlines such as "Chicago Girls Copy Marlene" from a 1930s newspaper (*Chicago Daily Tribune*, February 26, 1933).

Trouser wearing had overtones of sexual rebellion and undertones of everything from being lesbian to homewrecking. The exaggerated femininity of Mae West was more to Hollywood's taste than Dietrich's pantaloon revolution, but she didn't care. "I used to dress up in boys clothes when I was a little girl," she huffed, "I have always liked the freedom of men's garments" (*Screen Book*, November 1934).

After Dietrich and Sternberg parted, the type of films she appeared in changed. She made romantic melodramas like *Song of Songs* (1933) and comedies like Ernst Lubitsch's *Desire* (1936). In 1939, she ventured into the world of Westerns with *Destry Rides Again* opposite James Stewart. Others in the same genre followed: *The Spoilers* (1942) with John Wayne and *Rancho Notorious* (1952) with Mel Ferrer.

Confidential magazine tried to out her as a lesbian in the midfifties. "Women are better in bed," she proclaimed, "but you can't *live* with a woman." She dismissed most of the men who starred in her films as having peanuts for brains (Madsen, 1995: 71).

One of her greatest performances was in Billy Wilder's *Witness for the Prosecution* in 1957. She played a double role in an attempt to save her husband (Tyrone Power) from the death penalty when he's arrested for murder. She ends up shooting him when he blithely announces he's leaving her for a younger woman after being acquitted. Orson Welles's classic noir film *Touch of Evil* followed this in 1958. In 1961, she joined an all-star cast to play a small but significant role in *Judgment at Nuremberg*. This was really her swan song. She had other minor roles in films like *Paris When It Sizzles* (1964) and *Just a Gigolo* (1987), but her career in the sixties and seventies was mainly in cabaret. Notoriously reclusive, she surprised everyone by agreeing to be interviewed for a documentary about her life in

1984. It was simply called *Marlene*. The interviewer was her *Judgment at Nuremberg* costar Maximilian Schell.

Dietrich's talismanic status in Hollywood was exemplified by no less a luminary than Luchino Visconti when he had Helmut Berger do a drag impersonation of her in *The Damned* (1969), his chronicle of Hitler's rise to power. Dietrich was one of Der Fuehrer's favorite actresses. It was even suggested he wanted her as his mistress at one point. Such a prospect caused her to leave Germany speedily; she despised Nazism and everything it represented.

Kenneth Tynan once said that Dietrich had "sex but no gender," a phrase she liked (Shipman, 1988: 58). Some women might have been insulted to be referred to in such a manner, but she was flattered. The term "gender bender" might have been invented with her in mind.

Related Films
The Blue Angel (1930); *Morocco* (1930); *Blonde Venus* (1932); *The Scarlet Empress* (1934); *Destry Rides Again* (1939); *Pittsburgh* (1942); *Stagefright* (1950); *Witness for the Prosecution* (1957); *Touch of Evil* (1958); *Judgment at Nuremberg* (1961); *Just a Gigolo* (1978); *Marlene* (1984); *The Meeting of Two Queens* (1991).

Further Reading
Acosta, Mercedes De. 1960. *Here Lies the Heart*. New York: Reynal.
Bach, Steven. 1992. *Marlene Dietrich: Life and Legend*. London: HarperCollins.
Chicago Daily Tribune, February 26, 1933.
Dietrich, Marlene. 1989. *Marlene*. New York: Grove Press.
Madsen, Axel. 1995. *The Sewing Circle: Hollywood's Greatest Secret, Female Stars Who Loved Other Women*. New York: Birch Lane.
McLellan, Diane. 2001. *The Girls: Sappho Goes to Hollywood*. London: Robson.
Morley, Sheridan. 1976. *Marlene Dietrich*. London: Elm Tree Books.
Riva, Maria. 2017. *Marlene Dietrich: The Life*. London: Pegasus.
Screen Book, November 1934.
Shipman, David, ed. 1988. *Movie Talk: Who Said What about Whom in the Movies*. London: Bloomsbury.
Spoto, Donald. 1992. *Dietrich*. London: Bantam.
Vickers, Hugo, 1994. *Loving Garbo*. New York: Random House.

Disobedience (2018)

A strongly Orthodox rabbi, Rav Krushka (Anton Lesser), stands on the altar of his North London synagogue speaking about "the beasts of the flesh." Then he collapses and dies. His estranged daughter, Ronit (Rachel Weisz), a photographer now living in New York, is informed of the news by her childhood friend Esti (Rachel McAdams), with whom she had an affair as a teenager. Esti is now a teacher. She's married to Ronit's cousin Dovid Kuperman (Alessandro Nivola), who's set to take over as head rabbi now that Rav has died.

Ronit left London under a cloud, Rav banishing her after hearing about her fling with Esti. Since then she's confined herself (at least mostly) to the male of the species. At the beginning of the film she's seen having sex with a man, but she doesn't seem to be enjoying it. Is she still thinking of Esti all these years later?

Ronit receives a chilly welcome from the Jewish community she was banished from when she comes home for the leveya (funeral) and shivah (period of mourning). She stays with Dovid and Esti. Both of them are awkward with her and for the same reason—they fear she still has feelings for Esti and Esti for her. When she asks Dovid if he's happily married, he says he is but he sounds defensive. We suspect the marriage is a sham.

Ronit is shocked to learn her father has left all his money to the synagogue in his will. Her name has also been erased from his death notice, which says he had no family. Dovid tells her this is just "lazy journalism," but one feels there's more to it. The tightly knit Orthodox Jewish community doesn't take kindly to independent minds like hers.

It isn't long before Ronit and Esti rekindle their romance. When they're spotted kissing in public, Esti is reprimanded by her headmistress at the school in which she works. Ronit is asked why she isn't married. In the closed Jewish world in which both of them live, freedom to express oneself outside the old verities is frowned upon.

The passion between Ronit and Esti becomes more intense as the "beasts of the flesh" rise up within them, but each seems to know it's an impossible situation in which they find themselves. As Ronit prepares to go back to New York, Esti goes missing. She's at the airport about to board her flight when Dovid rings her to tell her this. She leaves the airport and goes in search of her with Dovid. When they come back to the house, she's there.

Esti has discovered she's pregnant. She's been trying to have a baby with Dovid for years, but now she doesn't want it.

She tells Dovid she plans to leave him. "I want you to give me my freedom," she says. He tells her that if she goes with Ronit she'll leave her when other lovers come into her life. He thinks everything would have been fine in their marriage if Ronit hadn't turned up, but Esti tells him, "I wanted it to happen." The way she says it reminds one of Dirk Bogarde's "I wanted him!" to his wife in *Victim* (1961). It was, after all, Esti who informed Ronit about Rav's death, which led to her homecoming. If she hadn't, it's doubtful anyone else would have.

Esti tells Dovid she's going to take her baby with her when she leaves him. She says she wants it to grow up without any restrictions on its freedom. "I was born into this community," she tells him, "I had no choice." She doesn't want her child to be confined in the same way.

At the proposed inauguration of Dovid as head rabbi, Ronit asks Esti if she would like to live with her in New York. She says it in a casual way, without too much conviction. Then Dovid begins to speak, dispensing with his prepared speech. In his valediction to Rav, he talks about the restrictions on freedom that the Hasidic religion imposes. Esti's frustration has obviously got through to him. He refuses the rabbinical post he's been offered.

In the end, Esti decides to stay with him. There's an emotional farewell with Ronit, who gets herself ready to go to the airport again. En route she diverts to her father's grave, taking a photograph of it. This acts as a symbolic reconciliation with him, albeit a posthumous one. Earlier on she's lamented the fact that she'd never taken his portrait. "Good-bye, Dad" she says as the film ends.

Weisz produced it as well as taking the lead role. The plot is thin, but it's effectively directed by the Chilean filmmaker Sebastián Lelio, who adapted it from Naomi Alderman's acclaimed novel of the same name. He also cowrote the screenplay with Rebecca Lenkiewicz. He'd already explored the area of free-spirited love in heterosexual vein in *Gloria* (2013). More recently, he directed *A Fantastic Woman* (2017). This concerned a transgender woman (Daniela Vega) trying to come to terms with the death of her boyfriend.

Disobedience has lots of lingering silences and poignant stares. Every moment it seems like something dramatic is going to happen, but it rarely does. At times one feels there's less to the film than meets the eye. But the performances of both Rachels, and also a strong one from Nivola, carry its critique of patriarchal fundamentalism engagingly.

It's impressively shot too, the bleakness of the London winter underscoring the cold world it depicts. Everyone seems to be dressed in black, and repressing their emotions. The issue of freedom is a major motif in the film, the kind of freedom Ronit obviously takes for granted in her New York life, though we see little evidence of this. Neither does Weisz show anything of the "good-time girl" about her, as she did in Alderton's novel. Perhaps McAdams could have conveyed this better if their roles were reversed. Weisz is more suitable to a role that calls for yearning rather than being a party animal. The funereal plotline obviously didn't lend itself to high jinks but some of this could have been shown in the brief section of the film dealing with the New York life of the so-called Prodigal Daughter.

There's just one sex scene, which is both erotic and explicit. It created a sensation at the Toronto Film Festival when the film was screened there. At one point, Ronit spits some saliva very slowly onto Esti's tongue from a few inches away. It's the most daring moment in the film. It was Lelio's idea and Weisz was happy to do it. Having admired *Gloria*, she felt she could trust him with such a potentially "out there" moment. McAdams said the makeup department tested out various flavors of lube the night before and settled on a lychee-flavored one (*IndieWire*, April 25, 2018).

Speaking in general about the scene, Weisz reflected, "As a woman, you're often the object of the man's desire or he's an object of yours. I felt there was something different about the female gaze" (*Daily Mail*, April 25, 2018). McAdams described it as the most "raw and vulnerable" sex scene she'd ever done. She didn't see it as a "gay versus straight" dichotomy, apart from the unfair oppression of sexuality that was behind it. It was just "humans being humans" (*IndieWire*, April 25, 2018). She thought it had more energy than any sex scene she'd ever done with a man in films (*Pink News*, May 27, 2018). In other scenes they kiss, sometimes using their tongues. It's perhaps not unusual to see two A-list stars doing this; once it would have been. They keep most of their clothes on.

Disobedience is a slow-burning fuse. What it does it does well, but it doesn't do enough. One basically ends up knowing very little about either Ronit or Esti beyond their immediate predicament. Dovid's "conversion" to the liberal ethos is also too instant to convince. His commitment to his faith is deep; there's no way he would renounce it this suddenly. Sidney Lumet handled such a theme more realistically in *A Stranger among Us* (1992), where Melanie Griffith failed to wean Eric Thal away from his Hasidic ways. Ronit's paternal catharsis is also too pat. Can alienation be patched up in five seconds by a snapping of a camera lens? It's unlikely.

The two women's penchant for wearing wigs is mysterious in the film. For Esti the *sheitel* is a formal custom, but why does Ronit practice it? Lelio hints at the kind of identity confusion we've seen in other lesbian films like *Persona* and *Single White Female*, but he doesn't develop it here, which is a pity.

There's very little levity in the film. By the end, when Esti decides to stay with Dovid, it seems a reluctant decision. We feel she really wants to be with Ronit, which calls up reminiscences with David Lean's *Brief Encounter* (1945).

Related Films
A Stranger among Us (1992); *Blue Is the Warmest Color* (2013); *Gloria* (2013); *A Fantastic Woman* (2017).

Further Reading
Alderman, Naomi. 2007. *Disobedience*. London: Penguin.
Beck, Evelyn Torton. 1991. *Nice Jewish Girls*. Boston: Beacon Press.
Brettschneider, Marla. 2017. *Jewish Feminism and Intersectionality*. New York: State University of New York Press.
Daily Mail, April 25, 2018.
IndieWire, April 25, 2018.
Pink News, May 27, 2018.
Rose, Andy. 1991. *Twice Blessed: On Being Lesbian or Gay or Jewish*. Boston: Beacon Press.
Schneer, David, ed. 2002. *Queer Jews*. New York: Routledge.

Divine (1945–88)

The real name of this underground sensation—who was in so many John Waters films one almost had to mention it when he wasn't—was Glenn Milstead. The "Divine" was in honor of three of his heroines: Sarah Bernhardt, Bette Midler, and Greta Garbo. At three hundred pounds, the drag queen was almost as heavy as the three of them put together. He wore dresses cut to within an inch of their lives to accentuate his many curves.

Waters grew up on the same street as Milstead and became both his friend and mentor as his career went in the outrageous direction it did. They first worked together on *Eat Your Makeup* in 1968. *Roman Candles* was released the same year. It wasn't much more than a piece of juvenilia from Waters, but with its mix of sex, drugs, and religion, it prepared one for his future oeuvre. There was also, sensationally, a press conference with Lee Harvey Oswald's mother. Divine went on to appear in Waters's curious short film *The Diane Linkletter Story* in 1970. He played the tragic teenager of its title.

Waters made *Mondo Trasho* in 1970. Here Divine plays a cross-dressing hit-and-run driver who runs over a woman (Mary Vivian Pearce) in his 1959 Cadillac.

The Diane Linkletter Story (1970)

This was one of the earliest collaborations between Divine and John Waters, an 8mm "mockumentary" that Waters shot the day after the young woman of the film's title—the daughter of Canadian TV personality Art Linkletter—jumped to her death from a high-rise apartment at the age of twenty-five after a bad drug trip and/or a bout of depression. Waters's film is a speculative excursion into what her last moments might have been like. Divine plays the tragic Diane. Waters suggests excessive parental control exerted an influence on her demise. The parents were played by Waters stalwarts David Lochary and Mary Vivian Pearce.

Waters shot the fifteen-minute film in a few hours and played it even before her funeral took place. This was regarded as disgusting behavior by many. For Waters the disgusting thing about Diane's life was the way her parents raised her. Her father insisted she had LSD in her system when she died; toxicology reports stated otherwise. Arguments raged on both sides. For Diane's parents it was the sixties counterculture that was responsible for her death. For Waters it was her parents' ignorance of what that counterculture represented. After she died, Linkletter ramped up his war on drugs, even getting a consultation with Richard Nixon in the White House after he became a spokesman on the subject.

As the film begins we see Diane's parents sitting on a sofa talking about her. They're worried that she's late getting home. Where can she be? When she eventually arrives in, they berate her. She tells them to lay off her. They express dissatisfaction with her boyfriend, Jim. She eventually divulges the fact that she's on LSD, which makes the excited pair even more hysterical. Diane runs to her room and pines for Jim. After a few minutes she jumps out the window.

Waters said he really shot the film just to test his camera, but that doesn't explain why he screened it or made it public. Did he push his penchant for bad taste too far here? It's debatable. A young girl died. Movies aren't life. Whatever mistakes Linkletter's parents made, had he the right to hold these up to the world in their first days of grief over her death? Even this early he seemed to have crossed a line.

The film was the first to bring Waters to a wide audience. It serves as an appetizer for treats to come. Alongside the carnage there are scenes of dismemberment, sightings of the Virgin Mary, some very bad rock 'n' roll songs, and homages to films like *The Wizard of Oz* and Tod Browning's cult horror flick, *Freaks*.

Waters followed *Mondo Trasho* with *Multiple Maniacs* (1971), a dark comedy that had Divine presiding over a freak show called *The Cavalcade of Perversions*. Its highlight is a scene where he's raped by a fifteen-foot lobster. There's also some cannibalism for good measure, and a junkie shooting up on a church altar. The film, Waters claimed, flushed religion out of his system for keeps. One imagines it didn't need much flushing.

People going to a John Waters movie generally take a deep breath before entering the theater, but nothing could have prepared audiences for the eschatological outrageousness of *Pink Flamingos* (1972). Watching people eating feces—and one another—or having sex with chickens, or incestuous fellatio, isn't exactly family entertainment. Nonetheless, the film built up a cult following, thanks mainly to the iconoclastic performance of Divine. In the course of it, he does everything in his power to become one of the filthiest people alive, despite opposition for the "honor" coming from a couple who send him a turd in the mail and burn down his trailer. Here, as a character called Sleaze Queen Babs Johnson, he lives with his 250-pound mother, Edie (Edith Massey), her hippie son, Crackers (Danny Mills), and the equally eccentric Cotton (Mary Vivian Pearce), as well as the eponymous flamingos.

It's a film in which anything can happen and usually does. Waters warms his hands at the stomach-churning fire with ill-disguised glee. David Lochary and Mink Stole round off the cast as Raymond and Connie, the couple who burn down the trailer. They also kidnap women, have them impregnated by their servant, Channing (Channing Wilroy), and then sell the babies to lesbian couples. Not many films could make *The Rocky Horror Picture Show* look tame, but this one does. It's in fairly permanent danger of giving bad taste a good name. A singing rectum acts as a wholesome addendum to the proceedings. At the end, Divine invites reporters from various supermarkets to watch her as she kills her enemies. She tars and feathers them first. Then she eats some dog poo.

It cost $10,000 to make but earned more than a hundred times that amount over the years. It made Divine into a household name—at least if one came from a particular kind of household. His weight was a large part of his appeal. He believed he ate his way into a career.

After *Pink Flamingos*, he continued to push the boundaries. In *Female Trouble* (1974), he had the dubious pleasure of having sex with himself, thanks to the magic of special effects. This film was Waters's perverse corollary to *Mildred Pierce*, documenting the teenage angst that must perforce accrue when one doesn't get that coveted pair of cha-cha heels from one's parents on Christmas morning. There's murder as well as other assorted delights from the self-styled Sultan of Sleaze and his 300-pound partner in crime in this groundbreaking farce.

Divine's character was called Dawn Davenport. A high school dropout, she becomes impregnated by a drunk driver—also Divine—who picks her up hitching. She then meets two beauticians who tell her, "Crime makes you beautiful." Thus begins her robbing career.

When the time comes to have her baby she delivers it herself . . . and then chomps through the umbilical cord. It's a girl. She later strangles her and gets herself sentenced to the electric chair. Equating the death penalty with winning an Oscar, she remains buoyant to the end, enjoying the attentions of reporters. Before she goes to her eternal reward, she says to a fellow death row inmate, "Tell everyone they have my permission to sell their memories of me to the media."

Divine embarked on a singing career in the late seventies, playing to sellout crowds. In the eighties he was a frequent guest on talk shows and cable TV programs. Waters was always looking for projects on which they could work together again, being well aware how unique his screen persona was: "I mean, you expected her to pull out a knife" (Hays, 2007: 167).

Divine also collaborated with Waters on his 1981 feature *Polyester*. This was released in Odorama meaning audiences could scratch cards that contained scents of the events being depicted on screen. Only someone like Waters could have dreamed that up. Divine played a housewife who leaves her husband for Tab Hunter. Hunter is Golden Boy Todd Tomorrow. It was an unusual role for the former MOR pinup. He assured Waters before he took the part that he wouldn't have any problems kissing a 300-pound drag queen, despite what Divine put into his mouth at the end of *Pink Flamingos*. The salary he was offered was minimal by his standards and the film was nonunion, so it didn't have much to recommend it from a pragmatic point of view. Hunter took it on because of Waters. He'd loved all his films so far. When he committed to it, Waters ran down the street screaming in delight: "Tab Hunter's going to do my movie!" (Hunter with Muller, 2005: 310).

The film was a satire of conventional romances. Hunter and Divine were ideally suited for it, neither of them having a problem with sending themselves up. For Hunter, who'd been closeted up to now, it was also an opportunity to exorcise his gay demons by playing a love scene with a man. It was his way of coming out, though not fully, because Divine looked like a woman—sort of.

Polyester "legitimized" Waters and opened Hunter up to a brand-new fan base, though the rudimentary working conditions meant he drew flak from the SAG. Waters had to pay a small fine as a result. The film was a rave at Cannes. Hunter stayed away, fearing recrimination from his old fans, but later regretted his cowardice.

The closest Milstead ever came to a straight role was as a Sydney Greenstreet–type figure in *Trouble in Mind* (1985). He also made *Lust in the Dust* that year, again with Hunter. It was a camp Western spoof in which he was gang-raped by bandits.

The pairing between Waters and Divine reached its peak in one of Waters's most well-known films, *Hairspray*, in 1988. Here Divine played the dual roles of mom Edna Turnblad and Arvin Hodgepile. By now he was grossly overweight at 375 pounds. "All my life," he joked, "I wanted to look like Elizabeth Taylor. Now Elizabeth Taylor looks like me" (Jacobson, 2003: 241).

He was on a publicity tour for *Hairspray* when he died of a heart attack in his sleep, aged just forty-three. Waters remarked wryly that he'd only had a week to enjoy the mainstream success he'd been searching for all through his life (Hays, 2007: 358).

Today one looks at his films and sees a mostly outrageous specimen, but behind his repulsive celluloid actions he was a pussycat. Like many actors, he was shy, seeking to conquer this with his Felliniesque persona. As well as being irresistibly daring on screen, he also had a wonderful sense of humor. Asked once if he was gay, he replied, "Are you kidding? I've got a wife and two kids back in Omaha!" (Murray, 1994: 121).

Further Reading

Bernard, Jay. 1993. *Not Simply Divine: Beneath the Make-Up, above the Heels and behind the Scenes with a Cult Superstar*. New York: Simon & Schuster.

Hays, Matthew. 2007. *The View from Here: Conversations with Gay and Lesbian Filmmakers*. Vancouver, BC: Arsenal Pulp Press.

Hunter, Tab, with Eddie Muller. 2005. *Tab Hunter Confidential: The Making of a Movie Star*. Chapel Hill, NC: Algonquin Books.

Jacobson, Laurie. 2003. *Dishing Hollywood: The Real Scoop on Tinseltown's Most Notorious Scandals*. Nashville, TN: Cumberland.

Milstead, Frances, Kevin Heffernan, and Steve Yeager. 2001. *My Son Divine*. Los Angeles: Alyson Books.

Murray, Raymond. 1994. *Images in the Dark: An Encyclopedia of Gay and Lesbian Film and Video*. Philadelphia: TLA Publications.

Dog Day Afternoon (1975)

This Sidney Lumet film was inspired by an article in *Life* magazine about a heist that took place in Brooklyn in August 1972. It was orchestrated by a man named Sonny Wortzik. He robbed a bank because he needed the money to pay for his transgender wife, Leon, to have sex reassignment surgery. Susan Peretz played Angie, another of his wives, from whom he had become divorced.

He bungled the robbery spectacularly. Things became even more manic when he held the manager and staff hostage inside the building as the police laid siege to it in the sweltering heat. When a crowd gathered and Wortzik didn't look like he was going to do anyone any harm, he became something of a folk hero to the crowd. The heist became a circus, what one writer called "a Marshall McLuhan media nightmare run riot" (Yule, 1992: 131).

Al Pacino played Sonny. John Cazale was Sal, his accomplice. Chris Sarandon took the role of Leon, a character based on a man called Ernie Aron, who transitioned into Liz Eden. At his audition, Sarandon told the *New York Daily News* he tried to capture the femininity of his character, the Blanche DuBois side. This was an interpretation Lumet didn't agree with. "Next time," he admonished, "think of Blanche as a hard hat" (Wiley and Bona, 1987: 512).

Pacino showed courage in playing a gay man at this time. He was one of the first mainstream actors to do so. It wasn't a decision he took lightly. He'd received Oscar nominations for three of his last four performances, so his career was on the up-and-up. A role like Wortzik could have jeopardized that, which was why he thought long and hard about taking on the part, changing his mind a few times before he finally committed to it. "We weren't just talking about a major star playing a homosexual," Lumet emphasized, "but also portraying that whole insane framework" (Yule, 1992: 133). In the wrong hands, he thought, it could easily have turned into the stuff of farce. "Since none of us ever knows how an audience is going to react," he stated, "I usually ignore them. However, on *Dog Day Afternoon* I was terrified as Al because the subject matter was so sensationalized" (Yule, 133).

Right from the bat, Lumet was impressed with Pacino's understanding of his character. He didn't see him as a bank robber; rather a confused lover trying to do a favor for his friend. Once that was established, everything else followed.

Sonny starts to become a hero when he orders pizzas for the staff of the bank, or when he chants "Attica! Attica!" at the crowd. (This was a reference to the suppression of a prison revolt there in 1971. It resulted in the killing of forty-two prisoners when police opened fire.) They join in, aligning themselves to his cause.

Sonny may be immature but this is nothing in comparison with the dysfunctional people in his life: the lost-in-his-world Sal, who doesn't know Wyoming isn't a country, the mother who never wanted him to grow up, the estranged heterosexual wife who's lost in a haze of obesity, the transgender wife who alternates between suicide bids and surgical dreams. In such a context, the deluded bank robber comes across almost like the "normal" one of the quintet.

For Lumet the most moving scene in the film was where Sonny dictates his will toward the end. He does so before going out on the street to what he thinks will be certain death. Lumet was particularly taken with the line, "And to Ernie, who I love as no man ever loved another man, I leave . . ." He went so far as to say that the whole goal of the film was to make that line work. By now all the hard hats had melted. Sonny was ours.

In his book *Hollywood from Vietnam to Reagan*, Robin Wood argued that the separation of Sonny and Leon—their only connection is on the phone—"spares the spectator the potential embarrassment of imagining anything they might do in bed together." Wood went on to say that this was consistent with the film's general desexualization of Sonny (Wood, 1986: 235). This is an overreaction. The film was never intended as a gay polemic, so it shouldn't be seen as shirking its responsibilities in such a manner. Having said that, Leon doesn't come across as a very sympathetic character in the film, especially when he has his conversation with Sonny recorded by the police to exculpate himself from involvement in the robbery. This is scant recompense for Sonny putting his life on the line for him to pay for his operation. For these and other reasons, we're left in little doubt that Lumet's loyalties lie with Sonny rather than Leon, right up to the film's final frames.

Holly Woodlawn, a transgender Puerto Rican woman who appeared in many Andy Warhol films, was set to play Leon originally, but the producers went for the tamer option of Sarandon. A disgruntled critic wrote, "They didn't want any real homosexuality in the script" (Howes, 1993: 196).

Neither Lumet nor Pacino expected it to go viral but it did, exploding into the public consciousness like a meteorite. When Sonny screams "Attica," or when the pizza boy chirps, "I'm a star!" one is far beyond bank robberies or sex change operations. Pacino's friend Charles Laughton—not to be confused with the other Charles Laughton—said it was like pulling a pin out of a hand grenade (Grobel, 2006: 31–2).

Some viewers saw the film as exploitative, including Eden. John Wojtowicz, the man on whom the character of Sonny was based, said it was "only 30 percent true" and that it was in essence "a piece of garbage" (Wiley and Bona, 1987: 512). He was sentenced to twenty years for the robbery but was paroled in 1978.

Related Films
Bonnie and Clyde (1967); *Serpico* (1973); *Flawless* (1999).

Further Reading
Blake, Richard A. 2005. *Street Smart: The New York of Lumet, Allen, Scorsese and Lee*. Lexington: University Press of Kentucky.

Bowles, Stephen E. 1979. *Sidney Lumet: A Guide to References and Sources*. Boston: G. K. Hall & Co.

Boyer, Jay. 1993. *Sidney Lumet*. New York: Twayne.

Cunningham, Frank R. 1991. *Sidney Lumet: Film and Literary Vision.* Lexington: University Press of Kentucky.

Desser, David, and Lester D. Friedman. *American-Jewish Filmmakers: Traditions and Trends.* Urbana and Chicago: University of Illinois Press.

Grobel, Lawrence. 2006. *Al Pacino: The Authorized Biography.* London: Simon & Schuster.

Horrigan, Patrick E. 1999. *Widescreen Dreams: Growing Up Gay at the Movies.* Madison: University of Wisconsin Press.

Howes, Keith, 1993. *Broadcasting It.* London: Cassell.

Wiley, Mason, and Damien Bona. 1987. *Inside Oscar: The Unofficial History of the Academy Awards.* New York: Ballantine Books.

Wood, Robin. 1986. *Hollywood from Vietnam to Reagan.* New York: Columbia University Press.

Yule, Andrew. 1992. *Al Pacino: A Life on the Wire.* London: Warner.

An Early Frost (1985)

This TV movie had to be rewritten thirteen times before NBC executives were satisfied with it. A kind of prelude to *Philadelphia*, it had Aidan Quinn playing a gay man stricken down with AIDS. The role was first offered to Jeff Daniels, who'd played Richard Thomas's gay lover in Lanford Wilson's *Fifth of July*, but he'd turned it down.

Quinn was Michael Pierson, a successful Chicago attorney. After suffering a bout of coughing one day at work, he's rushed to hospital. Here he receives the devastating news that he's HIV-positive. He later learns that his live-in lover, Peter (D. W. Moffett), has been unfaithful to him. This makes him conclude that his infidelity caused him to contract the disease. Enraged, he orders him to get out.

He now faces the ordeal of making the journey back to his conservative family in Philadelphia to break the news to them. It's going to be a two-punch revelation because they don't even know he's gay, never mind having the life-threatening disease.

For some people the film had a "disease of the week" flavor about it. This was because it spent a lot of time inserting factual data about AIDS into the narrative. This didn't always flow as naturally from the plot as it should have, but it was a forgivable sin. By now AIDS had claimed over 5,000 lives in the United States, but ignorance about it was still rife. Most people believed it was specific to being gay. Only gradually did they become aware it also afflicted heterosexuals and drug users, not to mention hemophiliacs. The misinformation circulating about it also meant people were in the dark about how it could be transmitted. Many people thought they could contract it simply by touching someone who had it. *An Early Frost* was important in dispelling many of the myths surrounding it. An articulate film that avoided both treacle and patronization, it dealt intelligently with a raft of big themes (secrets, lies, mortality) and equally big emotions (fear, anger, compassion).

Quinn visited hospitals and therapy groups to meet real-life AIDS victims before the cameras started rolling. He brought a lot of sensitivity to his character. More taciturn than Peter, he's slow to open up to his family about his predicament. "When are you going to tell your parents?" Peter taunts. "When are they going to have the honor of finding out who you are—after you're dead?"

For NBC, the film was a gamble on a number of fronts. The material was inflammatory, and Quinn wasn't as big a star as they needed to sell it. They were disappointed Daniels passed on it. They'd wanted Paul Newman to direct it, but he passed too. In the end, John Erman helmed it. Gregory Peck and Elizabeth Taylor were sought for Michael's parents, but they were unavailable. Ben Gazzara and Gena Rowlands came on board instead.

Gazzara played Nick, the owner of a lumber company. Rowlands was Kate, a former concert pianist. When Michael visits them, his sister, Susan (Sydney Walsh), is also there. She has a child and is pregnant with another one.

One night when Michael starts to feel unwell during a card game, he tells his parents the grim news. Kate is sympathetic but Nick proves a tougher nut to crack. He refuses to speak to Michael for a day after he hears the news. When he breaks his silence, it's to say, "I never thought the day would come when you'd be in front of me and I wouldn't know who you are." Nick explodes when Michael tries to kiss Kate good-night in one scene. Susan is worse, keeping him at arm's length in case he infects her child.

The title of the film comes from a comment his grandmother (Sylvia Sidney) makes about her roses. "I hope an early frost doesn't come along and nip them in the bud," she says. It's left to her to bring some sanity to the situation as paranoia about the spread of his disease grows. Sydney's husband died of cancer some years before, which gives her a reference point for it. Cancer was a kind of forerunner of AIDS. "People thought if they breathed the same air as him they'd develop a tumor," she says of her husband.

The film was shot in just twenty days. When it was screened on November 11, 1985, many advertisers refused to buy airtime. NBC lost $500,000 in advertising revenue that night, but the film still secured a third of the night's viewing figures. Thirty-four million people watched it. Many viewers turned over from the popular *Monday Night Football* to immerse themselves in it. It was nominated for fourteen Emmy Awards.

An Early Frost was respected, but people were still leery about it. Maybe it was before its time. Of the fourteen Emmys it was nominated for, it only won four: for cinematography, sound mixing, editing, and screenplay. Erman felt cheated when the results were announced. Both he and the cast all went out and got drunk to drown their sorrows.

It might have picked up a bigger audience—and more Emmys—if NBC hadn't been so tentative in its approach to it. Instead of allowing it the oxygen to breathe, it fed into the very paranoia it sought to extirpate by its caveats. This created an immediate artificiality bordering on absurdity. One commentator wrote, "Gay lovers as just roommates is an image mid-America can swallow less painlessly than queers as affectionate husbands" (Howes, 1993: 215).

NBC wanted to portray Peter as a villainous character rather than a flawed one. Erman refused to give in here, seeing him as a victim almost as much as Michael, especially in the film's later stages when his remorse grows and he tries to improve Nick's attitude to being gay in general and to Michael in particular.

When Michael suffers convulsions one night, he has to go to the local hospital for treatment. Here he becomes friendly with another AIDS patient, the flamboyant Victor (John Glover). Victor also has problems with his family's disapproval of him, but he hasn't let them get to him. He prepares for his impending death with wit and courage in what turns out to be one of the film's most affecting performances. He dictates his will to Michael but dies before Michael has a chance to give the typed version of it to him.

In the end, Michael has to learn to love himself before others can love him fully. "I'm not going to apologize for what I am," he tells Nick, "because it's taken me too long to accept it." It's only when he attempts suicide that Nick rallies round, finally realizing that his love for his son overrides whatever negative attitudes he may hold about his sexual orientation.

The film didn't go as far as it might have but it was still a torchbearer, especially considering how constrained it was in what it was trying to do. Erman went on to direct *Our Sons* six years later. This was another drama about a man dying of AIDS, with the added trauma of having to inform his estranged mother.

Rock Hudson came out of the closet when *An Early Frost* started shooting. He died just a month after it was broadcast.

Related Films
Consenting Adult (1985); *As Is* (1986); *Longtime Companion* (1990); *Our Sons* (1991); *Philadelphia* (1993); *Queer Son* (1993).

Further Reading
Gazzara, Ben. 2004. *In the Moment: My Life as an Actor*. New York: Carroll & Graf.
Howes, Keith. 1993. *Broadcasting It*. London: Cassell.
O'Connor, Aine. 1996. *Leading Hollywood*. Dublin: Wolfhound Press.

Edward II (1991)

This film about a gay king was based on a play by a gay playwright and directed by Britain's most inventive gay director. Derek Jarman's postmodern radicalization of Christopher Marlowe's Elizabethan tragedy tells of the sexual relationship between King Edward (Steven Waddington) and a male courtier, Piers Gaveston (Andrew Tiernan). Edward's preference for Gaveston over his wife, Isabella (Tilda Swinton), sparks a conflict with his barons that eventually leads to civil war.

Marlowe's drama is believed to be the first explicitly gay play written in English. Jarman turned it into a homoerotic history lesson that still has a message to impart five centuries after it was written. Laying on the anachronisms with a trowel, he dressed his cast in contemporary apparel to make the film into an attack on homophobia as well as the tale of a monarch who refused to play by the rules.

It begins with Edward being held captive in a dungeon. How he comes to be there is explained in a series of flashbacks. Isabella is understandably irritated by the fact that he's departed the marital bed, but the manner in which she plots his downfall as a result of her rejection is extreme. Palace guard Mortimer (Nigel Terry) joins with her to bring this about. The pair of them double for Margaret Thatcher and John Major, two British prime ministers Jarman saw as resembling them in their narrow-mindedness at the time he made the film. The banishment of being gay from the royal chambers, Jarman's biographer wrote, is indicative of a "monotonous monoculture" (Peake, 1999: 425).

Jarman's undisguised anger makes an already dramatic play veer toward melodrama, but such are his visual dynamics one can forgive him for the agitprop overload. He was in the throes of AIDS when he made the film, and this too added to its impact. Because of the uncertain nature of his health, the producers forced him to delegate a replacement director should he become too ill to work. He chose his friend Ken Butler, who deputized for him on the days when he didn't feel well enough to go to the set.

When he was well, though, he gave it everything. A minimalist set design contrasted with the flamboyant costumes to create an intentionally dissonant mood. Blank walls acted as a baroque backdrop to an eclectic mix of sound effects and music. What he's saying is that not too much had changed between 1594 and Thatcherite Britain. The term "queerbashing" may not have been in existence in the sixteenth century, but the practice of it was.

After Isabella employs Mortimer to help her in her demonic ambition, they become lovers. He first turns his attention to the liquidation of Gaveston. Early on we witness a scene of him being spat at by priests in a narrow corridor. Later on he's battered by police with shields. Then he's choked to death.

His murder provokes anger from a group of protestors. These are from Act Up and OutRage, two gay rights organizations in existence when Jarman made the film. He himself was a member of both. A later scene has Edward and Gaveston doing a *pas-de-deux* in their pajamas as Annie Lennox (of Eurythmics fame) sings Cole Porter's "Every Time We Say Goodbye." (Lennox would go on to record this track on her AIDS fund-raising album, *Red Hot & Blue*.) In the background is a sign with "Gay Desire Is Not a Crime" written on it. Elsewhere a man in a bed reads a book about the Gulf War.

Jarman enjoys himself throwing chronological caution to the wind in his scattergun directing style. Nobles sit around conference tables in sharp suits; Mortimer becomes a special operations military officer. One never knows what's going to happen next. Notwithstanding all this, he stays surprisingly close to Marlowe's text. When he changes it, it's for a good reason, as when he adapts Isabella's line about Edward, "Is it not strange that he is so bewitched?" to "Is it not queer that he is so bewitched?"

Marlowe purists thought he ruined the play. Jarman believed he improved it (Jarman, 1991: 471). As for the amount of sex in the film, he blithely announced that he wasn't making an Elizabethan play but rather an Elizabethan "lay" (Jarman, 16).

There's no historical proof that Edward was gay. He married Isabella when she was a mere twelve years of age and fathered four children by her. He also had an illegitimate one. Gaveston had two illegitimate children. Edward was portrayed as a screamingly camp figure by Patrick McGoohan in Mel Gibson's *Braveheart* (1995). This is an interpretation Jarman waters down. His main brief is to launch broadsides against church and state rather than harp unduly on Edward's sexual preferences.

The Hollywood trade magazine *BoxOffice* dismissed the film as more of an ideological statement than anything else (*BoxOffice*, April 1992). *Variety* accused it of provoking straight viewers with its ferocity (*Variety*, September 16, 1991). Jarman himself admitted it was "heterophobic" (*Los Angeles Weekly*, April 10, 1992). Whatever its strengths or weaknesses, it remains his most accessible work.

It's also his most nuanced one. There's no obvious hero/villain dialectic at play. Isabella and Mortimer are venal, to be sure, but Jarman resists the temptation to make either Edward or Gaveston into heroes.

For a lot of the time, Gaveston is actually distasteful in his behavior. "You don't have to like somebody," Jarman pointed out, "to accept their right to have a love affair" (Chedgzoy, 1995: 213). Tiernan plays him as a character who's cocksure of himself and at times even manipulative of Edward. "Andrew isn't playing Gaveston in a way that will endear me to *Gay Times*," Jarman remarked during the shoot (Jarman, 1991: 20). Even so, his devotion to Edward is never in question. An exchange between Edward and his executioner demonstrates this adequately. When the executioner asks, "Why do you love him who the world hates so?" he replies, "Because he loves me more than all the world."

History records that Edward died after having a poker thrust up his anus, an unsubtle reference to his gay orientation. Jarman sets the scene for this but suggests that the executioner may have changed his mind at the last minute. In the film he's played by Jarman's real-life partner, Kevin Collins; a clever touch. The finale has Edward's she-male son jigging around on top of a cage in which Isabella and Mortimer are confined. He's wearing a pair of high-heeled shoes as Tchaikovsky's "Dance of the Sugar Plum Fairy" plays in the background. Revenge is sweet: "The queer future is safe in his hands" (Peake, 1999: 469).

Jarman dedicated the film to the repeal of all antigay laws. At the time he made it, Section 28 had just been introduced by Margaret Thatcher. This made it illegal for local councils to promote being gay in any manner. Thatcher advised schools to treat it as an abnormality. This meant any books smacking of LGBTQ themes were summarily removed from school libraries. It also meant gay paintings were removed from art galleries, and gay movies from theaters. Jarman was understandably outraged.

Edward II is one of his most passionate films. It's to his credit that he was able to alchemize the excruciating pain he was in for much of the shooting time into such a dynamic socio-sexual polemic. His most expensive undertaking to date, it was funded by the BBC at a cost of £750,000. It fared well in the United States and won prestigious awards at film festivals in Venice and Berlin, but Jarman struggled to get a theatrical release for it in Britain.

Feminists accused him of misogyny because of his depiction of Isabella. She becomes positively vampiric in one scene where she kills Edward's brother by biting into his neck and sucking his blood. Jarman defended himself on this charge by saying it was Marlowe who created the character, not him. "They don't seem to understand that I'm saddled with a 400-year-old unconstructed collaborator," he argued (Rich, 2013: 51). Swinton was also responsible for some of Isabella's intransigence (Rich, 51).

Elsewhere he was accused of "wishful martyrdom" in his approach to the material (*Evening Standard*, October 17, 1991). This was closer to the bone. Because he believed he wasn't going to live long, he felt he had to make a more demonstrative statement than he might otherwise have done. Was it too demonstrative? Posterity seems to have vindicated him on this charge. To take a character from history who was only putatively gay and relocate him in the twentieth century where he most definitely *is* was an audacious stroke. Jarman pulled it off with his customary virtuosity.

Related Films
The Deadly Affair (1966); *Caligula* (1980); *Braveheart* (1995).

Further Reading
BoxOffice, April 1982.
Chedgzoy, Kate. 1995. *Shakespeare's Queer Children*. Manchester: Manchester University Press.
Evening Standard, October 17, 1991.
Jarman, Derek. 1991. *Queer Edward II*. London: British Film Institute.
Los Angeles Weekly, April 10, 1992.
Mannel, Barbara. 2012. *Queer Cinema: Schoolgirl Vampires and Gay Cowboys*. London and New York: Wallflower Press.
Peake, Tony. 1999. *Derek Jarman*. London: Little Brown & Co.
Pullen, Christopher. 2017. *Straight Girls and Queer Guys: The Hetero Media Gaze in Film and Television*. Edinburgh: Edinburgh University Press.
Rich, B. Ruby. 2013. *New Queer Cinema: The Director's Cut*. Durham, NC, and London: Duke University Press.
Variety, September 16, 1991.

Rupert Everett (1959–)

With a face—and accent—ideal for playing upper-crust English gentlemen, Everett was always going to be first choice for period dramas. Neither would that sculpted visage have been out of place in a steamy Renaissance tragedy. What makes his career interesting is the number of times he eluded these pigeonholes to take on an impressive number of contemporary guises.

He oscillated between schools in his adolescence, confused about who he was and what he wanted to do with his life. "Homosexuality bloomed like a poisonous flower," he wrote in his autobiography, "a deadly nightshade that came out after dark for secret assignations in the shadow of the bell tower, or the trees beneath which lay yesterday's monks in the monastic graveyard" (Everett, 2006: 36). Here he was speaking about the Benedictine college he attended as a youth. He later dropped out of this cocoon and made his way to London. He found there was "a cherished, half criminal stamp" on being gay there (Everett, 53).

Soon afterward he moved to Paris. While there he experienced a free-spiritedness that was missing in his home country. He was at a party one night and recalled, "There was some queen singing in a soprano voice and someone else playing a piano with candles on it. When I saw all this I thought, 'I've finally arrived in my milieu'" (Murray, 1994: 196).

A theatrical career now beckoned. In 1981 he appeared in *Another Country*, Julian Mitchell's play about a boy denied entry to his school's elite set because of a gay affair in his past. Three years later he repeated the role on screen opposite Colin Firth. The film contained erotic lines like, "There's a hollow at the base of his throat that makes me want to pour honey all over him and lick it off."

In *The Right Hand Man* (1987), he was involved in a three-way relationship with Hugo Weaving and Catherine McClements. This kind of role suited his bisexual nature. Offscreen he was as comfortable with women as men, being friendly with people like Cher, Bianca Jagger, Paula Yates, and Kate Moss. *The Comfort of Strangers* (1991) had him playing a married man with repressed longings for Christopher Walken, a character who sublimates his sexuality into fascism.

Everett didn't come out publicly until 1992, the year in which he played a gay activist who falls in love with the lesbian Patricia Arquette in *Inside Monkey Zetterland*. In 1994 he played a man dying of AIDS in *Remembrance of Things Past*. The film meant so much to him he refused to take a fee for it.

All of these roles advanced his profile, but he knew he needed a hit. That came with *My Best Friend's Wedding* (1997), a film in which he initially had only a small role. He played it so well, however, that it was fleshed out. He played a gay friend of Julia Roberts. Roberts panics when she hears her former lover (Dermot Mulroney) is about to be married (to Cameron Diaz). Both of them had agreed to marry one another if they hadn't married anyone else by the age of twenty-eight. Within weeks of that date, Diaz announces she's going to be Mulroney's betrothed. Determined to scupper the proceedings, Roberts offers to be a maid of honor at the wedding. Her motive is simple: she wants to get close to her enemy. Offering advice along the way is Everett. Roberts was by far the bigger star, but he was the one everyone talked about as they left the theater. He was the empathetic guy every woman wanted as their "best friend."

Suddenly he was bankable. His reward was a role in John Schlesinger's *The Next Best Thing* in 2000. Yesterday Julia Roberts; today Madonna. Suddenly it was all coming up roses for him. He was also gay in this role, but with a complication: one night he sleeps with Madonna and impregnates her. When their son is born, they set up house together to give the boy some stability in his life. When Madonna falls for another man, Benjamin Bratt, Everett sues for custody. It was an interesting plot, though lightweight in its presentation. It was hardly vintage Schlesinger but once again it copper-fastened Everett's bisexual credentials.

He didn't like the original script, believing it to be threadbare, so he persuaded the film's producer, Tom Rosenberg, to allow him rewrite it. His new character, he promised, was going to be "a real gay man with a real gay life, not some token queen with his weird whipped cream parallels. He would not be a decorator" (Everett, 2006: 301). He wanted the film to be "a slice of life, and to take place in LA where stories like *The Next Best Thing* were already happening" (Everett, 301). He put a lot of work into the revamped script but failed to receive a screenwriting credit for it. The film, sadly, tanked at the box office.

The foregoing account of Everett's life might suggest his roles had mandatory gay or bisexual elements. That wasn't always the case. *Dance with a Stranger* (1985) had him as an aristocrat racing driver who's shot by Ruth Ellis (Miranda Richardson), the last woman to hang in Britain. In *Hearts of Fire* (1987), he realized his life's dream of acting opposite a musical hero of his, Bob Dylan. The experience proved to be fun, but Dylan was distant and the film a dud.

Another hero of Everett's was Oscar Wilde. He was excellent as Arthur Goring in Oliver Parker's adaptation of Wilde's *An Ideal Husband* in 1999. In 2002 he played Algernon Moncrieff in *The Importance of Being Earnest*, also directed by Parker. In the same year he appeared in *Unconditional Love*, playing a valet searching for the murderer of his rock star lover. Unfortunately, this was a cringeworthy affair and went straight to cable.

Everett has always believed intolerance in the film industry has excluded him from many straight roles he would like to have played. Gay actors, he believes, can go only "a certain distance" with Hollywood producers. He believes his sexuality cost him a part in *About a Boy* (2002) and also one in *Basic Instinct 2* (2005). An MGM executive, he claims, once branded him a "pervert" who would never be accepted by the American public (Summers, 2005: 116).

He wrote his autobiography, *Red Carpets and Other Banana Skins*, in 2006. This is usually a sign that an actor's career is about to end, or has already ended, but this wasn't the case with Everett. He simply enjoyed writing. He also has two novels to his credit: *Hello Darling, Are You Working?* from 1994 and *The Hairdressers of St. Tropez* the following year. They were both spirited page-turners.

He's kept himself busy on screen as well, averaging a film every year or two. As well as playing Prince Charming in *Shrek the Third* (2007), he appeared in *Wild Target* (2010), *Hysteria* (2011), *Justin and the Knights of Valor* (2013), *A Royal Night Out* (2015), and *Miss Peregrine's Home for Peculiar Children* (2016). In 2018, he realized his dream of both directing and acting when he made *The Happy Prince*, a study of Oscar Wilde during a neglected period of his life: the time after he was released from prison. It proved to be a moving story of a broken man.

Everett has made good on his promise to try to rid films of the Screaming Queen stereotype of gay men and also to show that they can be as effective in serious roles as in comedic ones, something not generally acknowledged (Everett, 2006: 405). On the debit side, apropos his point about being denied roles because of his bisexuality, he told an *Observer* journalist in 2009 that he believed gay actors should stay closeted for the sake of their careers. "You cannot be a twenty-five-year-old homosexual trying to make it in the film business," he claimed. "It doesn't work. You're going to hit a brick wall at some point. At the first sign of failure they'll cut you right off. I would not advise any actor to come out" (*Observer*, November 28, 2009).

Further Reading

Everett, Rupert. 2006. *Red Carpets and Other Banana Skins*. London: Abacus.

Murray, Raymond. 1994. *Images in the Dark: An Encyclopedia of Gay and Lesbian Film and Video*. Philadelphia: TLA Publications.

Observer, November 28, 2009.

Summers, Claude J., ed. 2005. *The Queer Encyclopedia of Film and Television*. San Francisco: Cleis Press.

Far from Heaven (2002)

From the moment the camera pans across the streets of Hartford to the poignant strains of Elmer Bernstein's sweeping musical score, this is the world of Douglas Sirk. Todd Haynes may have called his film *Far from Heaven*, but it's really *All That Heaven Allows* revisited. The clue is in the title.

Haynes would be the first to admit he didn't so much imitate Sirk as rob him blind. Such mimesis may not be as obvious as the shot-by-shot reconstruction of *Psycho* by Gus Van Sant in 1998, but it's nonetheless there, not only in the structure of the film but its texture as well.

Haynes's most commercially successful film has Julianne Moore as Cathy Whitaker, a woman whose pristine life in leafy 1950s Connecticut is about to come apart at the seams. Beneath the patina of perfection—beautiful house, well-mannered children, handsome husband—Cathy knows something is wrong. Frank (Dennis Quaid) has been spending an inordinate amount of time at the office. He's also been losing his temper for little or no reason. He's distant from her and from the children. Is he working too hard? Is this what's behind it?

One night when he's working late, Cathy brings his dinner to him in his office. There, to her horror, she sees him in the arms of another man. The man abruptly departs the scene. Cathy is speechless. She drops the dinner on the floor and runs out.

Frank is equally distraught. Resisting his "problem" with every fiber of his being, he becomes near hysterical as he tries to come to terms with it. Both of them know it can never be revealed to any of their friends or neighbors. That would be the end of their social life—and Frank's job.

He goes to his doctor to see if there's any way he can deal with it. "I can't let this thing destroy my life," he says. "I know it's a sickness because it makes me feel despicable." The word "homosexual" isn't mentioned. The doctor just speaks about "this sort of behavior." He tells Frank there isn't much chance of being "cured." Conversion rates, he learns, run at between 5 percent and 30 percent. He's offered what the doctor calls a "talking cure." Or, if he doesn't want that, some hormonal rebalancing procedures. Or electroshock aversion therapy. He opts for the talking cure.

Cathy, meanwhile, takes comfort in the attention given to her by her black gardener (Dennis Haysbert), but she now has two reasons to be concerned. Bad and all as it is to have a gay husband, it's even worse to have black friend outside marriage. Or a black friend, period.

Raymond is a widower with a young daughter. He's infinitely more cultured than Cathy's friends, but they regard him as a nothing. When Cathy meets him at an art gallery, she sees his cultured side displayed with great clarity. He and his daughter are the only two black people there. Her friends think art is wasted on a black man. Even it if wasn't, they wouldn't want to see him in such a place.

Cathy is one of the few people in the town who isn't racist. She sees the person behind the color. As her neighbor puts it, she's "kind to negroes." This is said in the kind of tone that makes it sound like an aberration.

Haynes etches in the racism theme as a corollary to his homophobia one. Being black, like being gay, is to occupy a minority that's barely tolerated in this tightly knit community where nobody walks on the grass or runs a street sign or throws candy wrappers on the sidewalk—and black people stay at the back of the bus. They remain quiet, like Cathy's servant, Sybil, played by Viola Davis. This character recalls the Juanita Moore of another Douglas Sirk film, *Imitation of Life*.

Cathy breaks the invisible wall between black and white by consorting with Raymond, but when news of their budding relationship reaches her friends and neighbors, eyebrows are raised. Not as many as would be if Frank's orientation were to become public, but enough to make her stand out, to make the "perfect" people of Hartford gawp in horror at her new friend.

The fact that Raymond is a gardener recalls the relationship between Jane Wyman and the gardener played by Rock Hudson in *All That Heaven Allows*. How Haynes must have smiled to himself at the fact that Hudson was gay in real life. His only "sin" in *All That Heaven Allows* was dating an older woman—Wyman. Like Raymond, she was also widowed.

At a party one night, it's claimed that there are "no negroes" in Hartford. The presumption is that there are no gay people there either. Nothing out of the ordinary must be allowed to intrude on the solipsistic suburban bubble. Nothing must be allowed to disturb its effete ambience, which recalls the novels of authors like John Cheever and John Updike.

A conversation between Cathy and her friend Eleanor (Patricia Clarkson) conveys the Hartford attitude to being gay in very precise terms. Eleanor tells Cathy she prefers the males she socializes with to be "all men." She speaks of an art dealer who's reputed to be "a bit flowery" for her taste. When Cathy—who's too innocent to get the innuendo of this remark—asks her what she means, she says, "Oh, you know, a touch light on his feet." By now the penny is beginning to drop, even for Cathy. Even so, Eleanor becomes more blunt. "He's one of *those*," she declares. If Cathy is indeed "kind to negroes," will she be kind to "one of those" too?

This is a wonderful film that captures the period—and the *zeitgeist*—to perfection. Moore has rarely been better. Haynes, in fact, developed the script with her in mind. To quote Geoffrey O'Brien: "She plays her part as someone who reads the lines she's been given as if she senses the falseness but can't come up with an alternative" (*Salon*, November 8, 2002).

The mise-en-scenes, like the performances, are spot-on. The Edward Hopper–style sets are Disney-like in their Technicolor auras, replete as they are with "spotless arrays of Oldsmobiles and Plymouths" (*Salon*, November 8, 2002). Haynes, in effect, is making a 1990s film wrapped in a 1950s blanket. This is to highlight both the similarities and differences of both decades. He said he wanted the decor to look artificial to mirror the artificiality of the cast members. Mark Friedberg, his production designer, revealed: "Todd wanted us to build a set that looked like a set." This was in marked contrast to his usual modus operandi: "Most of what you do in my job is try to make sets that don't look like you built them" (*Far from Heaven* DVD: Special Features).

Haynes worked in muted tones that purloined Sirk's visual aesthetic. "Today's use of color is totally reductive," he contended. This led him toward a bleached quality that best conveyed the artifice of his milieu. It took a lot of work to lift the film above the pervading blandness of most of the ones he watched to prepare himself for it. These, he said, were set in the past but didn't look like it: "Happy scenes are warm, sad scenes are cool. If it's set in the past, sometimes an entire movie will be shot through with honey-colored gels. What's beautiful about Sirk is that every frame is a complementary palette. Every single scene, whether it's happy or sad, plays with an interaction of warm and cool colors" (*Artforum*, November 2002).

Far from Heaven has a sad ending. Cathy falls in love with Raymond but social pressure means they have to part. Frank, surprisingly, has a happier resolution, accepting himself for what he is and starting a relationship with another man. The last scene has Cathy waving good-bye to Raymond as he leaves town and then driving home alone. There was originally going to be a voiceover for the scene, but Haynes decided to cut it out. Here he departed from the Sirkian style for the first time, downplaying the melodrama for a flat finale.

Related Films
All That Heaven Allows (1955); *Imitation of Life* (1959); *Fixing Frank* (2001); *Suburbicon* (2017).

Further Reading
Artforum, November 2002.
Byars, Jackie. 1991. *All That Heaven Allows: Re-Reading Gender in 1950s Melodrama*. London: Routledge.
Davis, Glyn. 2011. *Far from Heaven*. Edinburgh: Edinburgh University Press.
Doane, Mary Ann. 1987. *The Desire to Desire: The Woman's Film of the 1940s*. Bloomington: Indiana University Press.
Morrison, James. 2007. *The Cinema of Todd Haynes: All That Heaven Allows*. London: Wallflower Press.
Salon, November 8, 2002.

The Fox (1968)

Books are generally more explicit than films regarding LGBTQ themes, or at least they used to be, but D. H. Lawrence merely hinted at the lesbianism in the novella upon which this is based, whereas Mark Rydell, directing, doesn't pull his punches. Having said that, the film is guilty of many of the prejudices and myopias of most lesbian movies of yesteryear. It broke a few taboos but underlined other ones, which made it a mixed blessing.

Rydell here substitutes Lawrence's British setting with the Canadian outback. In so doing, he loses much of the intensity that made the novel live. Lawrence only intimated the bisexuality of his characters. Its flagrant manifestation in the film robs it of much of its potency.

Jill (Sandy Dennis) and Ellen (Anne Heywood) seem to be happy in their relationship until Paul (Keir Dullea) comes along to deal with a fox that's being raiding their chicken coop. He's like a symbolic fox himself. It isn't long before he infiltrates their coop as well, surprisingly favoring Ellen over Jill, who wears her femininity more on her sleeve.

Jill is too innocent to recognize the dangers Paul poses to her relationship with Ellen, encouraging him to stay with them when he first comes into their life. After he proposes marriage to Ellen, he suggests she should sleep in a separate room to Jill. The implication is obvious. They have to be pure from now on, not Sapphic.

When Paul and Ellen become lovers, they begin plans to marry. Jill then prevails upon Ellen to abandon such plans—a fatal error. One can't break up a heterosexual relationship in 1968 and expect to get away with it.

This may appear to be a "modern" film but its basic message—that being lesbian can be cured by an affair with a man—is quintessentially old-fashioned. So is the script, which has Dullea saying to Dennis at one point, "You've never had a man. I think that's your problem. Isn't that what you need?"

Lawrence's nuanced novella is sadly reduced to a string of contrived vignettes. Most irritating of all is the scene where Ellen masturbates. This adds nothing either to our understanding of her or the film, being inserted merely for its shock value.

What irritates one most about the plot is the implication that Heywood is a closet heterosexual, or at least more bisexual than gay. This makes her being lesbian more palatable to 1968 audiences, but it means the film doesn't have the courage of its convictions, being neither one thing nor another. Lawrence would probably have turned in his grave at the compromises that were made to break Dennis and Heywood up. This is "gaysploitation" on a grand scale.

Dennis, becomes, literally, the "fall" guy, being killed by a toppling tree at the end. This plot device neatly removes her from the action. It means the New and Improved Heywood can continue her romantic commingling with a member of the "right" gender. The tree is an unsubtle phallic symbol. Paul has metaphorically "killed" Jill. And, by extension, affected the cure—by death—of Ellen.

Ellen doesn't even get to run to Jill after she's crushed by the tree. Paul takes care of everything. He's the coper now, the go-to guy. Jill, the "damaged goods" element of the proceedings, has been removed from the action for keeps. She's more lesbian than Ellen and for that reason has to be liquidated. Her death removes the "bad" side of Ellen so Paul can bring out the "good" (i.e., heterosexual) side. He's the first homophobic fox one has seen in film.

The Fox is reminiscent of *The Children's Hour* in the sense that it kills off an inconvenient lesbian when a man happens along. At least Dennis isn't responsible for her own death like in the other film, a minor consolation. It's a thankless part for her, a fact testified to by Pauline Kael, who hadn't much respect for her as an actress anyway. "She has made an acting style," she sniffed, "out of post-nasal drip" (Roth, 1995: 183).

Both films had problematic titles to add to their other weaknesses. Lucille Ball believed *The Fox* to be a nature film. One day she'd started to show a video of it to her children when she had to rush to the television set to press Stop. Many people thought *The Children's Hour* was a Disney feature because of its title.

If the film is a revamped version of *The Children's Hour*, at least it doesn't end with the same elegiac sense of longing. Ellen doesn't grieve for Jill as Karen did for Martha in William Wyler's film. What's preserved, however, is the restlessness of the heterosexual couple. If James Garner and Audrey Hepburn didn't look like they were going to be happy together in *The Children's Hour*, neither do Paul and Ellen here. In the book Paul is deflated about the fact that he didn't leave Ellen and Jill to their own devices; in the film he has to deal with Ellen's final confusion about whether she's cut out for life with a man or a woman.

The last shot is the grinning head of the dead fox, which may be taken as another symbol for Dullea's predatory nature. It's a bowdlerization of what Lawrence was trying to get at, a cheap distillation of his theme by overstatement. Everything has worked out tidily for Middle America in seeing off the bad seed of Jill.

Dennis was gay in real life as well. Her friends warned her that playing a lesbian on screen could harm her career. They also advised her to get married before she made the film. "Either get married and do the role," they said, "or stay single and don't do it." She considered their words carefully but opted to go against them on both counts in the end. Her reasoning was simple. She was a seasoned actress; she'd won an Oscar. She felt that acted as a kind of safety valve (Hadleigh, 1994: 258).

Asked what she thought of the film, she said she believed it was okay for Heywood to have an affair with Dullea but she should have come back to Dennis afterward. The idea of having the tree fall on her between her legs was, to her, too obvious a signal for Rydell's antilesbian message (Hadleigh, 260).

Related Films
The Children's Hour (1961); *Personal Best* (1982); *The Rainbow* (1989).

Further Reading
Hadleigh, Boze. 1994. *Hollywood Lesbians.* New York: Barricade Books.
Lawrence, D. H. 2013. *The Fox.* CreateSpace.
Roth, K. Madsen. 1995. *Hollywood Wits.* New York: Avon Books.
Sova, Dawn B. 2001. *Forbidden Films.* New York: Checkmark Books.

G

Greta Garbo (1905–90)

Though Garbo arrived in Hollywood in 1925, rumors about her lesbian orientation didn't surface until five years later. They reached their zenith after she made *Queen Christina* in 1933.

Like the Swedish monarch, who famously promised, "I will die a bachelor," Garbo predicted likewise and honored such a promise. She had a highly publicized romance with John Gilbert, her costar in that film, and numerous other men as well, but she always seemed remote. This meant that her premature retirement from the screen, if not from men, didn't come as too much of a surprise to those who knew her well.

Her relationships with women appeared to be more intimate than those with men during the seminal years of her career. Chief among these was her friendship with the playwright Mercedes de Acosta, whose lesbianism was well documented. It was followed by liaisons with the Broadway actress Lilyan Tashman—she married the gay actor Edmund Lowe in 1925—and French Canadian vaudeville performer Fifi D'Orsay. Salka Viertel, one of the screenwriters of *Queen Christina*, was another intimate friend, and so were Louise Brooks and Marlene Dietrich.

Garbo's appeal extended both to gay and bisexual men. Kenneth Tynan wrote of her, "What, when drunk, one sees in other women, one sees in Garbo sober" (Shipman, 1988: 79). Cecil Beaton once even proposed marriage to her, despite being gay himself. She refused his offer, hardly surprisingly.

Garbo was stereotyped, like many stars of her time. Axel Madsen summed up the situation: "People wanted Maurice Chevalier and Jeanette MacDonald to sing, the Marx Brothers to be funny, Johnny Weissmuller to swing from the trees and Garbo to play an emotionally wounded woman whose past will not let her be at peace, a woman who, despite great hurts, marches on until fate makes her meet her man" (Madsen, 1995: 6).

The jury is still out on whether she was lesbian or not because she covered her tracks so well. Most of the evidence that she was rests on the passion she brought to *Queen Christina*, a woman who renounced her throne rather than be forced into marriage. According to Patricia White, the film "mobilized everything about Garbo's already highly codified persona that connoted gender inversion" (Mann, 2001: 79). Margie Adams agreed. After she saw it for the first time, she said, "I knew right down to my molecular structure that the shimmering beauty with such a jawline up there on the screen was a dyke just like me" (*Outlook* 4: Fall 1990).

Garbo wears men's clothing in the film. She resembles a pirate with her loose pants and suede boots to the knee. She kisses her lady-in-waiting on the lips in one scene. Actions like this seemed to telegraph evidence of her "sewing circle" nature, and so did her general philosophy of relationships between men and women. Darwin Porter quoted her as saying, "I think marriage is an altogether shocking thing. How is it possible to think of a man and woman sleeping in the same room?" (Porter and Prince, 2007: 203). She famously said she always wanted to be alone, and this too can be taken as a code for being lesbian.

Garbo appeared in many films both before and after *Queen Christina*. In *Anna Christie* (1930), she uttered her most famous line, "Gimme a viskey, ginger ale on the side, and don't be stingy, baby." The billboards advertised it with the slogan "Garbo Talks!" as all her films before this had been silent ones. She received an Oscar nomination for her performance here, and also one for *Romance* in the same year. Love eluded her in *Romance*, as it did in most of her films: *Susan Lenox* (1931), *Grand Hotel* (1932), *Anna Karenina* (1935), *Camille* (1936), etc.

She retired early from the screen, to the great disappointment of her fans. Her reason was simple: she felt she'd made too many faces. Most of them were sad ones, it has to be said, but all the more alluring because of that. Joan Crawford testified to her erotic appeal when she confessed after she appeared with her in *Grand Hotel*: "For her and her alone I could have been a lesbian!" (Hadleigh, 1994: 144).

Related Films
Anna Christie (1930); *Romance* (1930); *Grand Hotel* (1932); *Queen Christina* (1933); *Anna Karenina* (1935); *Camille* (1936); *Meeting of the Queens* (1991).

Further Reading
Bret, David. 2012. *Greta Garbo: Divine Star*. London: Robson.

Bromman, Sven. 1992. *Conversations with Greta Garbo*. New York: Viking.

Hadleigh, Boze, ed. 1994. *Hollywood Babble On*. New York: Birch Lane Press.

Madsen, Axel. 1995. *The Sewing Circle: Hollywood's Greatest Secret—Female Stars Who Loved Other Women*. New York: Birch Lane Press.

Mann, William, J. 2001. *Behind the Screen: How Gays and Lesbians Shaped Hollywood 1910–1969*. New York: Viking.

Outlook 4: Fall 1990.

Palmborg, Rilla. 1931. *The Private Life of Greta Garbo*. Garden City, NY: Doubleday, Doran & Co.

Paris, Barry. 1995. *Garbo: A Biography*. London: Sidgwick & Jackson.

Porter, Darwin, and Danforth Prince. 2007. *Blood Moon's Guide to Gay and Lesbian Film, Second Edition*. Blood Moon Productions.

Shipman, David, ed. 1988. *Movie Talk: Who Said What about Whom in the Movies*. London: Bloomsbury.

Vickers, Hugo. 1994. *Loving Garbo*. New York: Random House.

Vickers, Hugo. 1995. *The Story of Greta Garbo, Cecil Beaton and Mercedes de Acosta*. London: Pimlico.

Glen or Glenda? (1953)

Also known as *I Led Two Lives, I Changed My Life*, and *He or She*, this is an insanely quirky exploration of the trials of being a cross-dresser. They're experienced by an actor listed as Daniel Davis—this was a pseudonym—who struggles with being a transsexual. Ed Wood Jr. directed it with a straight face, but nobody fell for that. Wood stalwart Bela Lugosi also turned up in this treasurable docu-fantasy at segregated intervals, saying things like, "Beware of the big green dragon that sits on your doorstep. He eats little boys." Is he a scientist? A theologian? A Transylvanian version of Elmer Gantry? Or is he just nuts?

Acting in the film as well as directing it, Wood plays Davis, aka Glen, a cross-dresser who agonizes about whether to reveal this to his fiancée, Barbara (Dolores Fuller). He also agonizes about whether he prefers Barbara to her angora sweater. As Glenda he allows his cross-dressing full rein.

The film opens with the suicide of a man wearing women's clothes. An inspector investigating the suicide, played by Lyle Talbot, consults a psychiatrist, Dr. Alton (Timothy Farrell), to try to understand cross-dressing a little better. Alton then tells him about Glen.

When Glen reveals his problem to Barbara, she becomes hysterical. Glen then starts to have nightmares, which he shares with Lugosi. Interspersed with the predicaments of Glen and Glenda are a series of tirades from Lugosi on a number of disconnected (and often cryptic) topics. He sits in a laboratory armchair as he delivers them in his East European accent to the background of jazz music. Other characters like priests and children pop up occasionally as well to complete the eclectic mix. This is the ultimate "let's throw in a few surprises" movie, conducted with mock-solemnity by Wood and his ever-faithful crew. Its comic secret is the pretense of solemnity. Or is it a pretense? One never knew for sure with this man. Was he trying to be weird or was he just weird, period?

Glen's obsession with cross-dressing goes back to the time he borrowed his sister's dress as a young boy when he was going to a Halloween party. "Then one day it wasn't Halloween anymore," he tells us. But he was still dressing up. And he still is now—with a blond wig, false breasts, earrings, a tight-fitting skirt, and a white sweater.

Wood points out that Glen isn't gay but merely a cross-dresser. This isn't quite as shocking in the film's moral axis. Both cross-dressers and trans people can be cured, one learns, through gender realignment surgery and/or psychoanalysis. The association of such "perversions" with evil remains a given within such an axis. The outrageous conflation of horror with camp comedy saves the film from coming across as judgmental.

The only conventional element in it is the happy-ever-after ending when Barbara finally learns to accept Glen for who he is. Dr. Alton tells them that with therapy there's every chance that his effeminacy will transfer itself to Barbara. This gladdens her so much she gives him her sweater to wear. Wood doesn't reveal whether he wears it to their wedding or not.

One should be glad a film like this has survived from the fifties, when nothing even vaguely resembling it was being made. Wood operated outside the mainstream, which meant he wasn't subject to the constraints of the Motion Picture Association of America. An X-certificate was imposed on it in the hope by the time's guardians of morality that it would swiftly disappear as a result, or be placed out of reach for the masses. Thankfully it hasn't, despite—or because of—its corny nature. The best "bad" film about being gay that has ever been made enjoys a currency to the present day, either despite or because of its wildly hammy inchoateness, and dialogue of near-Sequoian woodenness.

It has also acquired cult status, which has transferred itself to many mainstream figures like Johnny Depp. Depp has always been fascinated by Wood, and indeed Lugosi. In fact he went so far as to buy Lugosi's house some years ago. He played Wood in *Ed Wood*, Tim Burton's homage to the director, in 1994. "Get me transvestites!" he screams out in one scene. "I need transvestites!" He looks very good in angora in the film. Martin Landau won an Oscar for playing Lugosi in it.

Wood himself was also a cross-dresser. He reputedly landed on the beaches of Normandy as a soldier in World War II wearing a bra and panties under his uniform. He wasn't gay, however. Today he's affectionately known as The Worst Director of All Time, courtesy of films like *Plan 9 from Outer Space*, if not *Glen or Glenda?*. This was a sci-fi romp featuring a group of camp aliens who try to take over the world by resurrecting the dead—as you would.

Related Films
Plan 9 from Outer Space (1959); *Ed Wood* (1994); *The Haunted World of Edward D. Wood Jr.* (1995).

Further Reading
Bojarski, Richard. 1982. *The Films of Bela Lugosi.* New York: Citadel Press.
Grey, Rudolph. 1995. *Nightmare of Ecstasy: The Life and Art of Edward D. Wood.* London: Faber & Faber.
Holland, Steve. 2014. *Let Me Die in Drag! The Crime Fiction of Edward D. Wood Jr.* Kindle: Bear Alley Books.
Kaffenberger, William M., and Gary D. Rhodes. 2015. *Bela Lugosi in Person.* Albany, GA: Bear Manor Media.
Lennig, Arthur. 2010. *The Immortal Count: The Life and Films of Bela Lugosi.* Lexington: University Press of Kentucky.
Meikle, Denis. 2011. *Johnny Depp.* London: Titan Books.
Pontolillo, James. 2017. *The Unknown War of Edward D. Wood Jr., 1942–1946.* CreateSpace.
Rausch, Andrew J., and Charles E. Pratt Jr. 2015. *The Cinematic Adventures of Ed Wood.* Albany, GA: Bear Manor Media.
Rhodes, Gary D., and Tom Weaver. 2016. *Ed Wood and the Lost Lugosi Screenplays.* Albany, GA: Bear Manor Media.
Robb, Brian J. 2006. *Johnny Depp: A Modern Rebel.* London: Plexus.
Svehla, Gary J., and Susan Svehla. 2014. *Bela Lugosi: Actors Series.* Hailsham, UK: Hemlock Books.
Wood, Ed, Jr. 1999. *Death of a Transvestite.* Boston: Da Capo Press.

Go Fish (1994)

This indie sleeper set in Chicago was a huge crossover hit for Rose Troche after being shown to rapturous audiences at the Sundance Film Festival. Made on a shoestring and using mainly nonprofessional actors, it had a kooky authenticity that captivated, and a freeform style of direction.

Guinevere Turner, who was Troche's girlfriend in 1994, cowrote and coproduced it with Troche. She also played the lead role. She's Max, a "tomgirl" who dresses in baggy shorts and a baseball cap turned back to front. She describes herself bemusedly as a "carefree single lesbo looking for love." She's been celibate for almost a year when the film begins. Her college professor housemate, Kia (T. Wendy McMillan), secretly sets her up with Ely (V. S. Brodie), a bashful veterinary assistant she's known casually for some time.

Max isn't over the moon about the prospect of a relationship developing between herself and Ely. She tells Kia she thinks she's ugly. Also, she has "a severe case of hippieitis." And she dresses like her mother did in the seventies. As if all this isn't bad enough, she seems to have an obsession with collecting every known brand of tea on the planet.

The two women also differ in their views. After going to a film about a self-hating gay person one night, they have an argument about it afterward that reminds one of the kind of scenario that might unfold in a Woody Allen script. After Ely cuts her hair and gives herself a more masculine image, Max thaws out toward her. The pair of them even manage a kiss—in midconversation.

As Max becomes more interested in Ely, Ely seems to draw back. She starts talking about another girlfriend she has in Seattle. Kia tells her not to worry about this, that it's only a protective shield Ely puts up because she has a phobia about commitment.

The film romps along in a kinetic manner. The cast also includes Kia's lover, Evy (Migdalia Melendez), who's just escaped from a ten-year marriage to a controlling man. This results in her being evicted from her home. Also featured is Daria (Anastasia Sharp), a sex-addicted waitress who becomes castigated by the other women for sleeping with a man. This is the most disconcerting scene in the film and it leaves it open to a charge of heterophobia.

Not too much happens in it, but it bounces along at a breezy pace and draws one in with its laid-back charm. Shot in black and white—for economical reasons rather than any supposedly arty ones, Troche stressed—it has a documentary feel about it, a strong "life going on" vibe. There's a lot of talking in it, which reminds one, if one didn't need reminding, that women are generally much better at this activity than men. They also seem to be savvier about where relationships are going—or not going.

Stylistically, it's experimental in a kind of improvisatory manner. Every few scenes have the women lying on the floor as they titter and giggle about their various involvements and desires. Troche shoots these scenes from a bird's-eye view. They look unscripted, as if they're happening without her guidance. It's a simple device but a surprisingly effective one.

The film's secret was that it didn't try too hard to impress, letting the drama come out of the situations rather than being imposed on them. It's amorphous but so is life, especially the lives of these women, who let events happen to them rather than having any overarching plans. They're open to any possibilities, and that's reflected in Troche's style of direction. They jabber interminably, like four people with verbal diarrhea. If this becomes frustrating at times, it's never boring.

Turner is a talented writer, and this comes to the film's rescue whenever the plot (for what there is of it) springs a leak. The lasting impression *Go Fish* leaves is one of upbeat abandon. Even when the women "talk dirty" about sex, it isn't in the kind of way one has witnessed men do so in locker room scenes of other films. It's more fun than anything else hearing them exchange views on honeypots and whatnot.

The film climaxes—no pun intended—in a sex scene between Max and Ely. This is explicit but not exploitative. It begins—like everything else in the film—in an unusual way, with a bout of nail clipping. (Troche must be the first director in film history to use this activity as an aphrodisiac.) The two women have intended to go out, but they have a much better time sitting (or rather lying) in. Troche films them from every angle she can think of, mixing eroticism with joviality just as she has all the way through. One forms the impression that she likes her cast a lot and that the feeling is mutual. This encourages them to give the best of themselves.

Producer Ted Hope from the company Good Machine was amazed *Go Fish* took off as it did at Sundance. "Here was a movie," he said, "that was never going to have much of an audience—people in a room talking about their problems. And yet every distributor wanted it. It changed the whole tenor of the festival" (Biskind, 2007: 155). It took three years to get itself made, the delays being mostly due to financial problems. At times the cast even had to dig into their own pockets for the money to keep it going. Some of them had day jobs, so Troche had to shoot at weekends to facilitate them. For a while it looked like it was going to be abandoned, but then Tom Kalin and Christine Vachon came on board as executive producers and it was up and running again. John Pierson, a familiar friend to directors in need, also helped.

All of the problems took their toll on the relationship between Turner and Troche. By the time the film was completed, they weren't a couple any more. Troche looked set to have a sensational career as a director on the strength of it, but this didn't materialize. Instead she moved sideways into producing. For a time she considered becoming an actress, even an actress in straight roles. People like Tom Hanks and William Hurt received Oscars for playing characters with sexual orientations that weren't their own, she reasoned, so maybe she could too. If she did end up playing a straight role, she imagined the press asking her questions like, "What was it like to kiss a man?" (*Newsweek*, June 26, 1994).

Go Fish is a favorite at film festivals even today, its grainy quality and chatty fluency striking a chord with a whole new generation. Its message is straightforward, but it still needs to be emphasized. Max sums it up in her diary: "Don't fear too many things, it's dangerous. Don't say too much, you'll ruin everything. Don't worry yourself into a corner. The girl you're gonna meet doesn't look like anyone you know and when you meet her your toes might tingle or you might suppress a yawn. It's hard to say. Don't box yourself in. Don't leave yourself wide open. Don't think about it every second but don't let yourself forget: the girl is out there."

Related Films
She's Gotta Have It (1986); *Lavender Limelight* (1997); *Preaching to the Perverted* (1997); *Bedrooms and Hallways* (1998); *The Safety of Objects* (2001).

Further Reading
Benshoff, Harry M., and Sean Griffin. 2006. *Queer Images: A History of Gay and Lesbian Film in America.* Lanham, MD: Rowman & Littlefield.
Biskind, Peter. 2007. *Down and Dirty Pictures: Miramax, Sundance and the Rise of Independent Film.* London: Bloomsbury.
Darren, Alison. 2000. *Lesbian Film Guide.* London and New York: Cassell.
Newsweek, June 26, 1994.

God's Own Country (2017)

The roughness of the Yorkshire terrain mirrors the hardness in the heart of Johnny Saxby (Josh O'Connor) in this uncompromising tale of a young man who has to confront uncomfortable truths in himself when a foreign farmhand enters his life.

Johnny is emotionally bankrupt. When he first appears he's throwing up into a toilet after a night out drinking. Since his mother deserted him years ago, he's been living with his grandmother Deirdre (Gemma Jones) and his father, Martin (Ian Hart), on their West Riding Farm. Martin has recently suffered a stroke, so he isn't able to farm as he once used to. At the beginning of the film, he gives out to Johnny for not being with him when a calf died during a breech birth.

He advertises for help during the lambing season. It arrives in the form of Gheorghe (Alec Secareanu), a Romanian migrant worker. Johnny isn't too pleased to see him. Discernibly lacking in social skills, he makes little effort to welcome him to the farm. His life at this point is split between excessive drinking and sex with the men he runs into in the pub.

Gheorghe proves to be excellent at his work, treating it as a labor of love in contrast to Johnny's reluctantly dutiful attitude. He's also liked by Martin and Deirdre, creating a three-way tension between them. But then everything changes.

When Martin suggests Johnny and Gheorghe share a caravan to be near some ewes that have wandered away from the farm, the stage is set for them to become intimate. Johnny taunts Gheorghe one morning, calling him a gypsy. Gheorghe reacts angrily, wrestling Johnny to the ground. The next day they wrestle again, but this time it's sexual. One is reminded of Alan Bates and Oliver Reed in Ken Russell's *Women in Love* (1969). Afterward Johnny asks Gheorghe to share his room back at the farm. Gheorghe refuses, thinking it wouldn't work.

Martin now suffers a second stroke and is taken to the hospital. Depressed over this, and over Gheorghe's apparent rejection of him, Johnny starts drinking more heavily than ever. He also has sex with another man. When Gheorghe learns of this, he's disgusted and leaves the farm altogether. Johnny now realizes how poorly he's been treating him. When his father comes out of the hospital, he goes in search of him. He finds him on a farm in Scotland and they reconcile.

Hardly surprisingly, the film was compared to a British *Brokeback Mountain* by a number of critics. Francis Lee, its writer/director, even shared Ang Lee's surname. He grew up in Yorkshire and knew the world he depicted very well. Even though the film was his debut, he helmed it with the assurance of a much more seasoned director. He chronicles the burgeoning relationship between the two men expertly. If Johnny's attitude to sex up to now recalls the behavior of farmyard animals, one has to remember he's been bereft of tenderness since his mother left. His grandmother doesn't talk to him and his father isn't able to. Sex has been his only way of communicating with the outside world, so it's perhaps expectable that he treats it more as a bodily function than anything else.

Gheorghe gives Johnny the kind of affection he's been deprived of since he reached puberty. Lee documents this in sub-Lawrentian vein. Gheorghe is too good to be true at times, but he's the catalyst Johnny needs to slough off his Heathcliffe-style personality. He obviously has a long way to go before he develops enough maturity to sustain any kind of relationship, but the manner in which he mellows toward Gheorghe is a step in the right direction.

This is filmmaking at its most rough-hewn. Lee immerses us in the unforgiving fields of Yorkshire with the cold passion of the dawn. Cinematographer James Richards echoes such purity with downbeat evocativeness. The script is as lean as a whippet, the performances of the cast underpinning "the silence of the lambs" with monosyllabic minimalism. Everything is so buttoned down, when a mere chink of light enters Johnny's heart it becomes like a major event.

The title of the film refers to the way Yorkshire people namecheck this area of England. One is entitled to think *The Devil's Own Country* might suit it better. It carries an unremitting air of impoverishment until Johnny's reformation lifts it onto another level.

Though the sex is blunt and sometimes brutal, the love story at the film's core is traditional in structure, going from conflict to tenderness as in so many heterosexual films of yore. Johnny parts from Gheorghe and only then realizes what he's thrown up. He has to swallow his pride to relocate the part of him that went missing when his mother left. By the end, one is left thinking Gheorghe might be her replacement for him, the iron in his soul melted by Gheorghe's silent power.

One also thinks of the Brontes as Lee pans his camera over the windswept fields—though those sensitive siblings would probably turn in their graves if they witnessed the explicit sex scenes on view here. A more contemporary reference point might be Pawel Pawlikowski's *My Summer of Love* (2004). But it's unfair really to compare *God's Own Country* with anything. It remains intensely itself with its sullen *longueurs*, its refusal to sanitize its subject matter. As Gheorghe opens Johnny's eyes to the beauty of the landscape in its closing stages, it becomes a work that's firmly removed from the plethora of cotton-candy vehicles that fast-track sentimental reawakenings with a contrivance Lee could never countenance.

Related Films
Women in Love (1969); *My Summer of Love* (2004); *Brokeback Mountain* (2005).

Further Reading
Bronte, Emily. 2006. *Wuthering Heights*. London: Usborne Publishing.
Lawrence, D. H. 1980. *Women in Love*. London: Penguin.
Proulx, Annie. 2005. *Close Range*. New York: Harper Perennial.

H

Todd Haynes (1961–)

The son of a cosmetics importer, Haynes grew up in Encino, California. Attracted to film from an early age, he produced a short, *The Suicide*, while still in high school. He studied art and semiotics in university. After graduating, he directed his first film, *Assassins*, in 1985. It dealt with the relationship between Arthur Rimbaud and fellow poet Paul Verlaine in nineteenth-century France. That year he also made the more controversial *Superstar: The Karen Carpenter Story*, using Barbie dolls as a narrative device. They were ideal for his depiction of the music industry as a juggernaut that swallowed the vulnerable singer in its shoddy entrails, insisting on a standard body image everyone had to conform to if they wanted to be successful. His intentions were honorable, but Karen's brother, Richard, objected to her portrayal in the film and sued him. The upshot was that the film, sadly, was withdrawn from circulation. Only rare copies exist today.

Haynes had more success with *Poison* (1991), a trilogy of differing styles and themes that nonetheless had a unique unity. The first segment, *Hero*, dealt with a community's reaction to a missing boy who's killed his father. Haynes chose a 1950s style of direction to tell the story, which alternated between eroticism and banality. The second segment, *Horror*, was a science-fiction film about a deranged scientist (Larry Maxwell) who distills the mysteries of the sex drive and pours them into a teacup. After he drinks the potion, he turns into a leper who possesses the ability to kill people by kissing them. Haynes adopted a noirish B-movie style for this segment, parodying the genre by an excessive use of shadows and oblique angles. The final segment, *Homo*, was the story of unrequited love between two prisoners. This is probably the strangest part of the trilogy, combining elements of both physical and psychological cruelty. Essential viewing for devotees of New Queer Cinema, each episode of *Poison*, in its way, showed Haynes flexing his muscles for gems to come.

In 1993 he made *Dottie Gets Spanked*, a thirty-minute film set in the 1950s that dealt with an introverted six-year-old boy who becomes obsessed with a TV sitcom star, Dottie Frank (Julie Halston). Even this early, viewers of the director's work were learning to expect the unexpected.

His first major work was *Safe* (1995), a film that's difficult to pin down on any number of levels, carrying elements of everything from social satire to a post-apocalyptic sense. It was regarded as one of the most astounding films of the year, with good reason. Centering on a woman called Carol (Julianne Moore), it starts by showing us how her immune system breaks down to such a degree that she even finds it difficult to breathe in her refined Californian environment.

She's stopped enjoying sex. She doesn't sweat when she exercises. She hyperventilates for no discernible reason. The dust thrown up from a truck on the motorway makes her choke until she becomes near hysterical.

Is the problem within herself, or is Haynes making some kind of symbolic statement about a more general sickness in the world at large? One is never really sure. Some people have seen the film as a metaphor for AIDS, a theme close to Haynes's heart. Others see Carol as suffering from the disease of modernity, from what T. S. Eliot termed a dissociation of sensibility. Or is it a Sartrean sense of everything being excessive—*de trop*? If this is the case, it's more of an existential malaise, Carol's body revolting against the tension of her mind.

At times humorous and at other times creepily dystopian, this is a compelling critique not only of a world that's sick at the core but also polluted by Scientology-type gurus who inhabit the arid compound where Carol goes to be cured when her bewildered husband (Xander Berkeley) can see no other option. It cemented Haynes's reputation as a director working at the top end of film and Moore, as usual, gave the film everything she had. She became an actress highly desired by Haynes—and indeed other directors—as a result of her performance.

Velvet Goldmine (1998), Haynes's sprawling homage to glam rock, was more cacophonous and less muted. Again it showed his experimental nature, which is always to be admired in a director, but he failed to rein it in here, which meant that the film's diffuse elements lacked focus. Beginning with Oscar Wilde being delivered to his parents' doorstep on a spaceship, it segues into a tale of David Bowie–style rocker Brian Slade (Jonathan Rhys Meyers) faking his assassination on stage in a gambit that backfires so badly it results in him having to go into seclusion for years to escape the anger of his fans.

Ewan McGregor plays another gender-bending rocker, the American performer Curt Wild. He's just as outrageous as Slade in his penchant for stripping on stage and giving audiences two-finger salutes. When the pair of them appear together, they simulate fellatio. In another scene, a pair of Barbie dolls—echoing the Haynes of *Superstar*—lie down together with the heads of both men implanted on them.

Christian Bale plays Arthur Stuart, a journalist trying to locate his hero Slade on the tenth anniversary of his disappearance. Slade taps into the androgyny of the eighties with pronouncements such as, "I like boys, I like girls, it's all the same," and, "Everybody knows most people are bisexual." Bumper sticker pronouncements like "All that glitters is gay" are equally trendy. Toni Collette is Slade's frustrated wife, delivering post-Wildean pronouncements to him such as, "You live in terror of not being misunderstood." Haynes did his best to capture the period, but the film had too many threads and failed to unite them. As a valentine to an era it did what it intended, but as an exploratory rockumentary it bit off more than it could chew.

He was more secure in *Far from Heaven* (2002), which again united him with Julianne Moore. She played 1950s housewife Cathy Whitaker, who, like the Carol of *Safe*, has her affluent world disrupted by a strange development, in this case the repressed sexuality of her husband, Frank (Dennis Quaid).

Haynes directed the film with formal precision, capturing the hermetically sealed world in which Frank and Cathy go about their diurnal chores before the perceived evil of being gay enters their Garden of Eden. When it does, we're in the kind of movie Douglas Sirk would have been making were he alive today: a pastel-colored drama where everyone dresses to the nines and conducts themselves with exemplary good cheer while hiding the devil's own secrets inside their hearts. The most exciting thing Cathy does in her week seems to be to get her "permanent" in the hair salon, but then one day her house of cards comes tumbling down, bringing everything she knows with it, including her husband, who gives new meaning to the term "denial" when he realizes he's attracted to other men.

Haynes continued his versatile career with a film about a character just as chameleon as himself, Bob Dylan. In *I'm Not There* (2007), he used a kaleidoscopic directorial technique to try to capture the many facets of the elusive rock star who once described himself as a trapeze artist rather than a singer (Williams, 1993: 27). The music world has never thrown up such a complex figure as Dylan and looks unlikely to do so any time in the future. To capture such diversity, Haynes used six different actors to portray him, including a black boy (Marcus Carl Franklin) and even a woman (Cate Blanchett).

Other stars attempting to get inside his skin included Richard Gere, Christian Bale, and Heath Ledger. It was an audacious approach to a biopic but in retrospect a strangely logical one. This is Dylan in all his phases, from protest singer to gospel poet to literary outlaw. Each of the people playing him, in their way, peel away at that inscrutable persona. Dylan himself gave his blessing to the film, which was in itself a surprise considering he's usually so intransigent when it comes to projects like this.

In 2011 Haynes directed an ambitious TV miniseries, *Mildred Pierce*, featuring Kate Winslet in the role that won an Oscar for Joan Crawford in 1945. It was as carefully crafted as all his other work and explored layers of James M. Cain's novel that Michael Curtiz's movie, because of the constraints of his time, wasn't able to. Then came *Carol* (2015), which, like *Far from Heaven*, had Haynes exploring a tale of forbidden gay love, this time from the distaff side.

It begins with a 1950s divorcee (Cate Blanchett again) meeting a younger woman (Rooney Mara) in a New York department store and finding herself instantly attracted to her. The attraction is mutual, and thus begins a relationship that takes a while to come to the boil. When it does, it has severe repercussions for Blanchett's divorce, her affiliation with another woman being seen as making her into an unfit parent for the child she's had with her husband. Based on Patricia Highsmith's novel *The Price of Salt*, the mood was less tense than it was in *Far from Heaven*, both Blanchett and Rooney evincing a coolness that was in marked contrast to the emotional devastation of Julianne Moore and Dennis Quaid in the earlier film. Notwithstanding that, they still suffer from the coerciveness of their time, a fact Haynes documents with his customary meticulousness.

His most recent film, *Wonderstruck* (2018), plays with time, dovetailing the stories of two deaf children who run away from home, one in 1927 and the other in 1977. The first is a young girl seeking her mother; the second a boy in search of his father. The film was shot both in monochrome and color to signify the different eras. Once again, Haynes chose Julianne Moore as his star. She's always produced her best work for him and vice versa. It seems to be a partnership made not "far from heaven" but actually inside it.

Further Reading
Biskind, Peter. 2007. *Down and Dirty Pictures. Miramax, Sundance and the Rise of Independent Film*. London: Bloomsbury.
Levy, Emanuel. 2015. *Gay Directors, Gay Films?* New York: Columbia University Press.
Leyda, Julia. 2016. *Todd Haynes Interviews*. Jackson: University Press of Mississippi.
White, Rob. 2013. *Todd Haynes*. Champaign: University of Illinois Press.
Williams, Chris, ed. 1993. *Bob Dylan: In His Own Words*. London: Omnibus.

Hedwig and the Angry Inch (2001)

This story from writer/director John Cameron Mitchell features Mitchell as Hansel, a lonely young man who lives with his mother in East Germany. He's gay but has never been on a date. At twenty-six, he still sleeps with his mother.

When he meets an American GI called Luther (Maurice Dean Wint), he falls headlong for him. Luther falls for Hansel too, but thinks he's a woman. When he learns the truth, he encourages him to have sex reassignment surgery. Having the surgery would help him get out of Germany, he says, a place Hansel hates. As Luther's wife he could travel to America with him. "To walk away," he says, "you gotta leave something behind." In this case, a penis.

Hansel has the operation but it goes wrong. After the surgery is performed, he's left with the eponymous angry inch where, as he puts it, "the penis used to be and the vagina never was." To make matters worse, Hansel—who now goes by the name of Hedwig—is having her time of the month. As well as the vestigial part of the male anatomy, she has a distressing amount of bleeding to contend with. "Now all I've got is a Barbie doll crotch," she groans.

Luther later deserts her for a young boy. To cheer herself up, she buys a Farrah Fawcett–style wig. She then meets rocker Tommy Speck (Michael Pitt) and begins a singing career with him. They become a sensation on the music circuit with some "bad boy" rap numbers. "We are freaks," they roar. "We do what we choose."

It takes Tommy a while to make a physical move on Hedwig. When he does, he's surprised to see what she has under her skirt. "What's that?" he asks confusedly. "It's what I have to work with," she replies.

Tommy now distances himself from Hedwig. Embarking on a solo career, he steals Hedwig's songs and becomes famous as a character called Tommy Gnosis. Hedwig tries to win him back but fails. Her destiny, she feels, is to fail at everything. But she refuses to give in. Her spirit keeps her going.

Hedwig relates her story to us through songs rather than speech. These are sung at half-empty seafood diners to audiences who seem to be only vaguely listening to them. Hedwig both looks and sounds like David Bowie during these gigs. In the background is the bearded Yitzhak (Miriam Shor), Hedwig's gender-ambiguous sideman, played by a woman. Yitzhak does very little in the film except gaze desiringly at Hedwig's wig.

Combining elements of documentary and animation with straight drama and musical comedy, this adrenaline-charged hybrid has something for everybody. Hedwig's chameleon stage persona fits into the fractured format to create a film that, while difficult to describe genre-wise, entertains and moves in equal measure. It's a postpunk, neoglam rock opera that redefines androgyny for our time in its subtly sensitive depiction of a character who goes through so many hoops to discover who she is that she almost meets herself coming back.

The songs are catchy and the script is clever. "Do you accept Jesus Christ as your personal lord and savior?" Tommy asks Hedwig in one scene. "No," Hedwig replies, "but I love his work." In another scene Tommy asks Hedwig, "Do you think love lasts forever?" "No," he says, looking out at a woman across the way who's rehearsing the Whitney Houston number "I Will Always Love You" interminably, "but that song does." The wit may be dry but there's a fire in the film's structure that makes it compulsive viewing.

Style-wise, there's a persistent metaphor running through it that joins the "split" city of Berlin and the split identity of Hedwig. She's compared to the fallen Berlin wall at one point by the vigilant Yitzhak, who says she's in a divide between "East and West, slavery and freedom, man and woman, top and bottom."

Directed with an eccentric passion by Mitchell, who directed the Broadway production as well as starring in it, like here, it's acquired a cult following over the years that's reminiscent of *The Rocky Horror Picture Show* in the sense that people dress up as its characters and sing along to its songs while watching it. It's impossible to dislike it, or to dislike Hedwig, who's still looking for her other half at the end, though not in a frustrated way. Her life has been so crazy, maybe she would have it no other way. Whether in East Berlin or in a Kansas trailer park, confusion is all she truly understands.

Related Films
The Christine Jorgenson Story (1970); *The Rocky Horror Picture Show* (1975); *Tommy* (1975); *In a Year of 13 Moons* (1978); *Together and Apart* (1986); *Whether You Like It or Not*: *The Story of Hedwig* (2003); *Breakfast on Pluto* (2005).

Further Reading
Hays, Matthew. 2007. *The View from Here: Conversations with Gay and Lesbian Filmmakers*. Vancouver, BC: Arsenal Pulp Press.

Mitchell, John Cameron, and Stephen Trask. 2014. *Hedwig and the Angry Inch*. New York: Overlook Press.

Salin-Pascual, Rafael J. 2009. *Cinema and Sexual Diversity*. www.lulu.com

The Hours and Times (1991)

Brian Epstein had three things working against him the first time he went to see the Beatles perform in Liverpool's Cavern Club in November 1961. Firstly he was Jewish, secondly he was dressed in a pin-striped suit (in contrast to their leather) . . . and thirdly he was gay. The fact that he managed to overcome these

Brian Epstein (1934–67)

Epstein's father owned a thriving electrical supplies shop, so he was born with a silver spoon in his mouth. He had one brother, Clive, and a mother who doted on him. He grew up quiet and introverted. The realization that he was gay at a time when this was a criminal offense in Britain increased his sense of isolation.

He joined the Royal Army Service Corps after leaving school. One night he came back to the barracks in a pin-striped suit and bowler hat instead of his regular uniform. He was accused of impersonating an officer and confined to barracks. Because of his sexuality, he was referred to a psychiatrist for analysis and subsequently discharged. Afterward he spent some time pursuing an acting career in London.

His father's shop had a music sheet sales section. It was later extended into a business selling records. Epstein liked music and was placed in charge of this. People often came into the shop asking for a record called "My Bonnie," sung by the Beatles. He'd never heard of either it or them, but the orders piqued his curiosity. The following month he went to see them in the Cavern, a converted vegetable store that had rats in the toilets. He loved their sound but not their greasy hair or leather outfits.

When he agreed to manage them, he insisted they have an image makeover, with special emphasis on their wardrobe. Once voted the Best Dressed Man in Britain, Epstein knew all about sartorial splendor. Often dubbed "the fifth Beatle," he made what could have been a forgotten Liverpudlian quartet into one of the most famous groups in musical history. One of the first things he did was sack Pete Best, a mediocre drummer who was popular with the ladies who frequented the Cavern. Ringo Starr replaced him; the rest is history.

Epstein would have been the first to admit he wasn't the greatest manger in the world. He made many deals with a handshake rather than a cast-iron arrangement. These were simpler times and he had little idea what he was getting himself into. A British/American business he set up to capitalize on the Fab Four's international reputation, Seltaeb—Beatles spelt backward—led to a multimillion-dollar lawsuit for misappropriated funds, which he lost. But he had great foresight and in little time took John, Paul, George, and Ringo from nothing to everything.

Many people have speculated on his motivation. Some people claim he was sexually attracted to them and that this was behind it. It may have been a factor. Epstein had many male lovers, but most of his relationships failed to last. At the end of his short life, he cut a lonely figure. By this time the group was getting ready to stop touring and devote itself more to recordings. This made him feel irrelevant to them in many ways. He had other groups to manage besides them, but none of them were anywhere near their league.

Epstein was also fond of drink, and increasingly dependent on sleeping pills and other substances to bring him up, or down, in his jet-set lifestyle. He sometimes spoke of suicide, but on the night he died—no more than was the case with Marilyn Monroe, another lost soul in the showbiz stratosphere—it was probably due to an accidental cocktail rather than anything intentional.

obstacles and turn them into one of the biggest bands in the world was a testament both to his obstinacy and his deep belief in their genius.

He spent twelve days with John Lennon on holiday in Barcelona in 1963. That becomes four in this film of their time together, which was written, produced, and directed by Christopher Munch. There's no evidence to suggest Lennon had any gay tendencies (Coleman, 1990: 147). Epstein was, however, attracted to him, which was probably why he invited him on the trip in the first place. He wasn't the type of man to make unwanted advances on anyone, but he may have been hoping

Lennon had gay tendencies, despite having just got married. Epstein's houseman, Lonnie Trimble, once said that Epstein told him he and Lennon had been lovers, but such a claim is uncorroborated (Geller, 2000: 107). In Albert Goldman's biography of Lennon, he has him telling his friend Pete Shotton that he allowed Epstein to masturbate him one night because he felt sorry for him (Goldman, 1988: 140).

This short black-and-white film—it runs for only an hour—doesn't attempt to answer these questions. Instead it plays around with them. It's a fictional journey that boasts strong performances from Ian Hart (Lennon) and David Angus (Epstein) in roles that don't require them to do much except talk. Stephanie Pack is also effective as Marianne, a sexy stewardess they meet on the flight. Lennon flirts with her and afterward gives her his hotel phone number.

In an early scene, Lennon tells Epstein he isn't attracted to the idea of gay sex because he feels it would be painful. He isn't homophobic but neither does he seem to be interested in experimenting with that side of himself. Epstein is obviously frustrated by this.

Lennon then receives a phone call from his wife. She says she misses him. She's just after giving birth to their son. Epstein is his godfather. Epstein was never in favor of any of the Beatles having girlfriends or getting married because of his fear of their losing their fan base as a result (Geller, 2000: 75). Lennon's marriage upset him particularly. It's the elephant in the room during their conversations together in the film.

Later in the evening they visit a gay bar. There they meet a Spanish businessman called Quinones (Robin McDonald). He's gay, but married. They invite him back to their hotel and have a few drinks with him there. After he leaves, Epstein gets into bad form, telling Lennon he was rude to Quinones. Depressed over his own situation with Lennon, Epstein later asks the hotel boy, Miguel (Sergio Moreno), for oral sex, but then says he was only joking.

Lennon has a bath the following day. When Epstein comes into the bathroom, he asks him to scrub his back. They then start kissing. Epstein takes off his clothes and gets into the bath. Lennon kisses him some more, but then he stops. He steps out of the bath and leaves the bathroom. Once again, Epstein is frustrated, especially since Lennon initiated the overture in his eyes. It's as if something has been started that can't be finished, as if Lennon is teasing him, or perhaps afraid to fully confront this side of himself.

Epstein's frustration becomes heightened when Lennon invites Marianne up to their room. He's resented his flirting with her on the plane, and he does so again here. He leaves the room, prompting Marianne to ask Lennon what's upsetting him. She blames him for leading Epstein on, which causes them to argue.

Because the material is thin, Munch tries to make it interesting by his camerawork. He adopts a self-conscious style of direction that some viewers might find pretentious. There are many shots of Epstein gazing yearningly at Lennon. Each scene is separated from the other after it by a blank white screen, like chapters of a book.

One of the most interesting scenes in the film has Epstein telling Lennon about a time when he was blackmailed by a man he had sex with, which led to a court case. Afterward his mother made him see a psychiatrist. Unfortunately, like many of the other subjects raised in the film, this isn't examined in any depth, being introduced merely to be dropped. It was difficult for Munch to do much more than skirt around issues like this within his constricted time frame, but one wonders why he didn't make the film longer. This would have solved the "now you see me, now you don't" sense it conjures up.

Munch wrote it in a few weeks and shot it in eight days, just double the time of the actual trip. It won the Special Jury Recognition Award at the 1992 Sundance Film Festival and was nominated for the Grand Jury Prize. For Beatles completists it's a necessary addition to any library, but for anyone seeking a more exploratory examination of what happened between the erudite Jew and the streetwise singer during the four days in question it's an opportunity missed.

Toward the end of the film, Lennon and Epstein promise one another that they'll meet again in Barcelona in ten years' time regardless of what happens in their lives in the interim. This, needless to say, never happened as Epstein died of a drink and drugs overdose in 1967. The Beatles disbanded in 1970 and Lennon was assassinated in 1980.

Lennon and Epstein also plan to go to a bullfight. Epstein was fascinated by the *corrida*, by its edge of danger. He was also preoccupied with the idea of death generally (Geller, 2000: 86–7). He often spoke of suicide. His jet-set lifestyle with the Beatles increased his tendency toward depression, as it did his substance abuse.

Munch doesn't have time to go into any of this, but what he does he does well. He focuses on his cast's faces a lot. This was particularly effective with Hart, who does a brilliant Liverpool accent. He was so highly regarded in the role he was asked to play Lennon again in *Backbeat* in 1994.

As to whether anything actually happened between Lennon and Epstein in Barcelona, *Browbeat* magazine quotes Lennon as saying, "It was almost a love affair but not quite. It was never consummated but it was a pretty intense relationship" (*Browbeat*, April 29, 2013). Lennon was very comfortable with his feminine side, telling his wife, Yoko Ono, one day, "Do you know why I like you? Because you look like a bloke in drag. You're like a mate" (*Browbeat*, April 29, 2013). But it's unlikely he went any further sexually with Epstein in Barcelona than is shown in *The Hours and Times*.

Related Films
Imagine—John Lennon (1988); *Backbeat* (1994); *The Brian Epstein Story* (1998); *Brian Epstein: Inside the Fifth Beatle* (2001); *Nowhere Boy* (2009).

Further Reading
Aviv, Caryn, and David Schneer. 2000. *Queer Jews*. New York and London: Routledge.
Browbeat, April 29, 2013.
Coleman, Ray. 1990. *Brian Epstein: The Man Who Made the Beatles*. London: Penguin.
Davies, Hunter. 2007. *The Beatles, Football and Me*. London: Headline.
Epstein, Brian. 1988. *A Cellarful of Noise*. London: Faber & Faber.
Geller, Debbie, 2000. *The Brian Epstein Story*. London: Faber & Faber.
Goldman, Albert. 1988. *The Lives of John Lennon*. Chicago: Chicago University Press.
Tiwary, Vivek J. 2016. *The Fifth Beatle: The Brian Epstein Story*. Milwaukie, OR: Dark Horse Publishing.

Rock Hudson (1926–85)

Hudson's image as the gold standard of prototypical masculinity was shattered when he announced he had AIDS in 1985. For years his studio had protected him from the prying eyes of reporters who sought to "out" him. Many people in the industry knew full well he was gay, and also that he would never come out willingly.

The scandal sheet called *Confidential* was particularly interested in hauling him out of the closet in the 1950s. Every month when it hit the shelves, Hudson's gay friend George Nader asserted, "Our stomachs began to turn. Which one of us would be in it? The amazing thing is that Rock, as big as he became, was never nailed. It made me speculate he had an angel on his shoulder or that he'd made a pact with the devil" (Kashner and Macnair, 2002: 149).

Most male stars hid serious romances with women for fear of losing their female audience. Hudson had to go the other direction and *manufacture* one in the midfifties when gay-baiters threatened to expose his double life.

Confidential also had plans to expose him at this time but its editor, Robert Harrison, held back on it. To protect his image, Hudson married Phyllis Gates, the

---

Rock Hudson's Home Movies (1992)

It sounded good in theory. Cobble together a bunch of scenes from Hudson's movies and unveil the "real" person to audiences. However, anyone expecting revelatory insights into the star will be disappointed by this documentary from gay director Mark Rappaport.

In essence, all we're proffered from the scattergun montage is a loaded revisionism that oversells itself. Rappaport takes it upon himself to reappraise footage from the most innocuous Hudson films with a supposedly enlightened rearview lens. In doing so he comes up with a veritable cornucopia of "clues" to Hudson's orientation as posited by the footage in question. It's a bit like the breadcrumbs left by Hansel and Gretel in the forest in the famous fairy tale.

"It's not like it wasn't up there on the screen if you watched carefully," one is informed early on regarding the sexual innuendoes. This is only partly true. It's like a Rorschach test where people can see what they wish to see, hindsight always being 20/20. From the purview of history, vignettes appear like diegetic signals when all they might be are vignettes. As Freud remarked—not in a phallic context—"Sometimes a cigar is just a cigar."

The suggestive overtones of the Doris Day films are fine. These were probably negotiated with a nudge and a wink by Hudson, if not Day. It's even possible there's a gay code (as Rappaport suggests) in *Man's Favorite Sport* (1964) where Hudson plays a fishing expert who doesn't like the smell of fish. But when he quotes Jennifer Jones asking him to go downtown and find some "gay young playmate" in *A Farewell to Arms*, he becomes anachronistic. That film was made in 1957, long before "gay" meant what it does today.

Rappaport missed the best example of all that he could have given for his thesis: *A Very Special Favor* (1965). Here Hudson pretends to be gay to get the attention of a psychiatrist he fancies, played by Leslie Caron.

John Nicolella made a more authentic biopic of Hudson for TV in 1990. Based on a book written by Phyllis Gates about their marriage as well as court records brought by Marc Christian, it documents the rise and fall of the inscrutable hunk in a more sober and credible manner than anything Rappaport's eccentric musings can throw up. It was called simply *Rock Hudson*.

secretary of his agent, Henry Willson. Willson was gay too. In fact he'd been one of Hudson's former lovers.

Gates, in her innocence, imagined Hudson loved her. She was naive enough never to suspect he was gay throughout their marriage even though there were many warning signs. After their wedding, for instance, he refused to wear a ring, claiming it would be awkward having to keep removing it for movie roles. After they exchanged vows, she wanted to call her mother to tell her the news—they'd held a secret ceremony to avoid a media storm—but Willson went, "Oh no, you've gotta call Hedda [Hopper] and Louella [Parsons] first. They'll still have time to make the home editions." She could hardly have asked for a clearer indication of the reason for the marriage (Gates and Thomas, 1987: 87).

Hudson dominated Gates right through their married life, playing the media game with the "sob sisters" who voyeuristically photographed them in their so-called married bliss. After a time she began to see the light, but once again the controlling Hudson stopped her doing what any woman in her circumstances would, instead forcing her to keep silent about her miserable marriage. "If Hedda or Louella or Sheilah [Graham] come up to you at a party," he warned, "be polite but don't say anything. Talk about the weather or clothes or anything. But don't give them anything they can quote" (Gates and Thomas, 104).

Hudson himself fed such columnists the sound bites they craved, gushing, "Now that I have Phyllis to share life with, I'll never have to experience that bottomless pit of loneliness again. It's a very comfortable feeling." Such "comfort" was fortified by the fact that he had everything his way. He even demanded she leave her agenting job as soon as they married, pitting his own sin on the reasons for his control over her: "I wouldn't let her do anything outside [the home] even if she wanted to. When I got married it was my idea to have a home and a wife [in that] home" (Gates and Thomas, 152).

The ink was hardly dry on their marriage certificate when he was contemplating an exit strategy. After subjecting Gates to repeated absences—and some violence—he headed for the divorce courts. Now the fanzines had a new reason to feature him on their front pages. Instead of stories asking "Will Rock Ever Find Miss Right?" there were now features asking, "Can His Marriage Be Saved?" The reality was that there never was one in the first place.

Despite the apparent confidence Hudson showed both in his acting and his comments to the press, he had to have been tortured psychologically for long stretches of time. Because of this, maybe one should excuse him to some extent for his multiple hypocrisies. His entire life was built on a lie; that can't be easy for anyone to navigate.

Paul Lynde once stated, "Hudson was emotionally constipated. He hated having to play hetero on screen; he hated having to pretend offscreen and he hated anyone saying he was gay. We acted together but we could never have socialized. I let it all hang out; he left it all hanging in" (Hadleigh, 1994: 152–3).

No more than Dirk Bogarde, another closeted gay man, Hudson gave many signals to his true sexuality in many of his films. He mainly did this in a mischievous way in the syrupy comedies he made with Doris Day. In *Pillow Talk* (1959), for instance, he worries that he might be a "mama's boy." In *Lover Come Back*

(1961), he played an effeminate character, and did so again in *A Very Special Favor* four years later.

He seemed happy to play into the effete stereotype that characterized the first appearances of gay characters on screen in the thirties. "There are some men," he says to Day in *Pillow Talk*, "who are just very devoted to their mothers. You know the type who likes to share cooking recipes, to exchange vicious bits gossip." Day's peaches-and-cream personality offered him a safe haven in films like this. His antimarriage stance mightn't have gone down so well with a sultrier costar.

In other films he made at this time, there were more ominous signs. In *Written on the Wind* (1956) he tells Dorothy Malone that he cares for her more like a brother than a lover. "Don't waste your time waiting for me," he advises. In *Send Me No Flowers* (1964) he shares a bed with Tony Randall.

AIDS made a man of Hudson, forcing him to connect with his deeper nature. He may have been dragged kicking and screaming out of the closet, but he demonstrated his better nature toward the end of his life when he said he hoped his pain would help others.

It did. Having a high-profile star like he was developing a disease most people were still ignorant about, gave Hollywood—and the outside world—the impetus to do something about stemming its spread. Hudson was the first really famous actor to get AIDS. The fact that he did so opened the world's eyes not only to his duplicity but to its gravity. From that point of view, he didn't die in vain. Over eight thousand people were suffering from the disease by the time he contracted it. The Reagan administration remained deafeningly silent about it. In fact, Reagan didn't use the actual word "AIDS" until he called a press conference about it in 1987. The virus had been discovered in the United States six years before.

Hudson's last lover was Marc Christian, who sued his estate after he died for several millions for the health risk he exposed him to in not telling him he had AIDS.

If he were living today, when so many strides have been taken in AIDS research to prolong people's lives with the disease, he might have been able to make a *Philadelphia*-style movie about himself instead of all those silly Doris Day comedies. But that was then and this is now. The bottom line is that no matter how much *Confidential* wanted to expose him, there was always somebody willing to wave a checkbook in their direction to protect their Golden Boy. They had too much to lose by having his career cut off at the knees.

Related Films
Pillow Talk (1959); *Lover Come Back* (1962); *Send Me No Flowers* (1964); *A Very Special Favor* (1965).

Further Reading
Bret, David. 2008. *Doris Day: Reluctant Star*. London: JR Books.
Cohan, Steven. 1997. *Masked Men: Masculinity and the Movies in the Fifties*. Bloomington and Indianapolis: Indiana University Press.
Gates, Phyllis, and Bob Thomas. 1988. *My Husband, Rock Hudson*. London: Headline.
Griffin, Mark. 2018. *All That Heaven Allows: A Biography of Rock Hudson*. New York: Harper.
Hadleigh, Boze, ed. 1994. *Hollywood Babble On*. New York: Birch Lane.

Kashner, Sam, and Jennifer Macnair. 2002. *The Bad and the Beautiful: Hollywood in the Fifties*. London: Little Brown.

Scott, Henry E. 2010. *Shocking True Story: The Rise and Fall of* Confidential, *America's Most Scandalous Scandal Magazine*. New York: Pantheon Books.

The Hunger (1983)

For years—250, to be exact—Miriam Blaylock (Catherine Deneuve) has been living off the blood of pickups. With her husband, John (David Bowie), she's been cruising the discotheques of Manhattan for new supplies. It's all been going swimmingly but now, sadly, that's about to change. John, sadly, is starting to feel the pressure of time's winged chariot hurrying near.

Could Botox help? A little more exercise? A better diet? Unfortunately not. When one is 250, different laws apply. The fact is that his spouse is thinking of replacing him with someone younger. A toyboy of a mere two hundred years, perhaps? Or a toygirl?

Desperate to stop the clock, John makes his way to the office of gerontologist Dr. Sarah Roberts (Susan Sarandon) in the hope that she'll have some ideas. But when he gets there, she's busy. Which ages him even more.

Back home he sinks his teeth into yet another victim, Alice Cavender (Beth Ehlers), as a stopgap. But Alice's blood isn't enough to halt his decline and he dies. Miriam places him in a coffin in the attic along with all the other lovers she's had over the centuries who haven't been able to stay the course with her.

Sarah now calls to the house looking for John. Miriam tells her he's gone to Switzerland for treatment. Later on she calls again, some mysterious force drawing her to Miriam.

The attraction seems to be mutual. They flirt. Sapphic love beckons. Miriam plays Delibes's *Lakmé* for Dr. Sarah on the piano. "Are you making a pass at me?" she says to Miriam, sounding like Dustin Hoffman when he asked Anne Bancroft in *The Graduate*, "Are you trying to seduce me, Mrs. Robinson?"

And of course she is. She succeeds too. It isn't long before they disrobe. There's kissing and breast-sucking. Miriam even manages to give Dr. Sarah a blood transfusion while making love to her, an activity all budding vampiresses might do well to master.

Back at Sarah's lab, her coworker-cum-lover Tom (Cliff DeYoung) becomes concerned about her. A blood test shows evidence of a foreign component inside her. She goes back to Miriam to find out what's going on.

"You belong to me," Miriam tells her. "We belong to each other." Dr. Sarah is confused. Miriam offers her eternal youth. Dr. Sarah is now even more confused. She thinks about what happened to John. He got that offer too. One should never trust vampires.

Things become even more ludicrous from now on. Tom comes to Miriam's house looking for Sarah. Sarah, who's consumed with love for Miriam—or is it just infatuation?—kills him. Afterward, laden down with remorse, she stabs herself with an ankh in an attempt at suicide. Miriam, imagining she's dead, brings her body up to the attic to store with all the other corpses residing there. But a surprise awaits her as they rise up, undead, and wreak their revenge on her.

Sarah ends up as the last woman standing. She becomes the new Miriam, carrying on the torch for sexy vampiresses.

The Hunger was the directorial debut of Tony Scott, the brother of Ridley. Ridley would go on to direct Sarandon in her most well-known film, *Thelma & Louise*. Tony's background was in TV commercials. This explains the arresting visual quality of the film. It was frowned upon by the intelligentsia, but its psychedelic vibe and kinky lesbian scene made it take off. "It changed my fan base," Sarandon said, if not Deneuve's: "She's French" (*The Hunger* DVD: Bonus Features).

Alison Darren noted: "In 1983 it was still a very rare sight to see two attractive women kissing each other as if they meant it" (Darren, 2000: 105). The script required Sarandon to be intoxicated to "explain" why she would have been seduced by Deneuve. She didn't think this was necessary: "You don't have to be drunk to go to bed with Catherine Deneuve" (Darren, 105).

The film might have disappeared without a trace were it not for this scene. Harry Benshoff had problems with the manner in which the conflation of lesbian and horror was "once again cemented into the public zeitgeist" (Benshoff, 1997: 244). This was a legitimate concern, but it slotted itself commodiously into the dictates of the plot rather than being imposed upon it in a sexploitative manner. Andrea Weiss pointed out that the two women were "well on their way" in the love-making stakes before it emerged that one of them was a vampire (Weiss, 1992: 98). Deneuve herself said, "I'm not an obvious sex symbol. I create a certain reserve which is more attractive" (Hadleigh, 1993: 208). It was a pity to hear Scott trivializing the relationship between the two women as "not real lesbianism" but "more of a schoolgirl crush" (Hadleigh, 1993: 209).

A bigger problem was the ending. This went against the grain of all vampire films by having the victim outlive the vampire. "New World ingenuity," one critic wrote, trumped "Old World epicureanism" (San Filippo, 2013: 118). Neither was it credible. It seemed clunky and contrived. Scott's attempt to justify it by saying the film wasn't so much a vampire movie as the psychological study of a relationship was unconvincing (Hadleigh, 209–10).

Rarely has a more elegant vampire graced the screen than Deneuve here. She made the film slot itself somewhere between designer kitsch and underground baroque. Quentin Crisp put it well when he said her main sin was flagrantly defying the Trade Descriptions Act, offering her victims everlasting life when merely giving them a lifetime of just three or four hundred years, "at the end of which niggardly span they start to age at the rate of several days in an hour." For him the most incredible thing about the film wasn't the fact that people lived for centuries on other people's blood but that a doctor would make a house call without demanding money up front! (Kettlehack, 1984: 92).

The film was slammed by critics for being "artsy, esoteric and self-indulgent." Scott accepted it was all of these things, but he still liked it (*The Hunger* DVD: Bonus Features). Unfortunately, his affection wasn't shared by the industry executives who employed him. He wasn't offered anything else for four years. This was a pity as *The Hunger* had a lot going for it with its stylized horror. Bowie also gave one of his best performances here. (This, to some people, may not be saying much.)

Deneuve didn't need to do much except look dreamy. She was, after all, Catherine Deneuve. To quote Quentin Crisp once again: "The one thing I would not wish upon my worst enemy is eternal life, but if anything could compensate for having this appalling burden laid upon him, it would be the delight of being bitten by Miss Deneuve" (Kettlehack, 94). As for Sarandon, her cynics thought she made the film just for another excuse to take her clothes off.

Related Films
Dracula's Daughter (1936); *The Picture of Dorian Gray* (1945); *Blood and Roses* (1960); *Belle de Jour* (1967); *The Vampire Lovers* (1970); *Countess Dracula* (1971); *Daughters of Darkness* (1971); *Velvet Vampire* (1971); *Vampyres* (1976); *Cat People* (1982); *Prince of Darkness* (1987); *Because the Dawn* (1988); *The Kiss* (1988); *The Addiction* (1995); *We Are the Night* (2010); *Only Lovers Left Alive* (2013).

Further Reading
Benshoff, Harry M. 1997. *Monsters in the Closet: Homosexuality and the Horror Film.* Manchester and New York: Manchester University Press.
Darren, Alison. 2000. *Lesbian Film Guide.* London: Cassell.
Hadleigh, Boze, 1993. *The Lavender Screen.* New York: Citadel.
Kettlehack, Guy, ed. 1984. *The Wit and Wisdom of Quentin Crisp.* New York: Harper & Row.
San Filippo, Maria. 2013. *The B Word: Bisexuality in Contemporary Film and Television.* Bloomington and Indianapolis: Indiana University Press.
Streiber, Whitley. 1983. *The Hunger.* London: Corgi.
Weiss, Andrea. 1992. *Vampires and Violets: Lesbians in Film.* New York: Penguin.

Tab Hunter (1931–2018)

Born Arthur Kelm, Hunter was the son of a German mother and a father who acknowledged his birth by tossing a nickel candy bar on his wife's bed and then walking out of the hospital, leaving her to carry the baby home to their Manhattan tenement in a borrowed blanket. He had another wife before her whom she didn't know about, and two children by her. Hunter discovered this only late in his life and never managed to track them down. His mother didn't want to know.

His father soon departed the family fold, which gave the young Arthur a special bond to her. Some might say such close bonds between mother and son sow the seeds for being gay. Arthur was fourteen before he became aware of this. It was something he did his best to hide from the outside world until he wrote a tell-all autobiography at the grand old age of seventy-four.

"Better to get it from the horse's mouth," he wrote in the book, "and not from some horse's ass" (Hunter with Muller, 2005: 353). This was good thinking, but raised the question of why he waited so long. Before the "horse" spoke, there were five decades of "horse's asses" speculating about the fact that the sand-and-surf icon might have been gay.

At sixteen he ran away from school to join the U.S. Coast Guard. He lasted a year here before it was discovered he was underage. When the discovery was made, he was sent home to complete his schooling. After graduating, he became a figure skater of some note and also competed in show-jumping trials. He would love—and keep—horses all his life.

Soon after arriving in Hollywood, he was taken up by the gay agent Henry Willson, the man who was partly responsible for Rock Hudson's rise to the top. A kind of Harvey Weinstein for men, this "lecherous Svengali" extracted favors from his clients for deals he struck, but Hunter carefully avoided his clutches (Hunter with Muller, 49).

In 1950 he was at a gay party in Los Angeles when it was raided by the police. He was carted off to the county jail and charged with lewd behavior before an attorney he'd never seen before showed up and got the charge reduced to disturbing the peace. He was fined fifty dollars, given a thirty-day suspended sentence, and put on a year's probation. The incident didn't reach the papers, but it was a red flag for him that he needed to be more cautious about his sexuality if he wanted to have a career, particularly on the West Coast. In Manhattan, he remarked, "an assembly of gay men in an East Side Apartment was considered the upper crust of theater culture" but a group of them hanging out in a Hollywood suburb "might as well have been a Communist cell meeting as far as the LAPD was concerned" (Hunter with Muller, 51).

His first audition consisted of taking off his shirt. The screen test came later. "Acting skill," he pronounced, "was secondary to chiseled features and a fine physique" (*Irish Times*, July 14, 2018). His breakthrough movie was *Battle Cry* in 1955, based on Leon Uris's semifictional account of his experiences during World War II. It established his pinup credentials. The following Valentine's Day, he received no less than 62,000 cards from his fans.

Confidential magazine, the gossip journal edited by Robert Harrison, did its best to out him in 1955. Hunter believed it cashed in on the wave of exposé journalism ushered in by the HUAC investigations into political subversion and organized crime: *Confidential*, he alleged, tarred gay men with the same acid-dipped brush with which it used to vilify communists (Hunter with Muller, 117). He turned a blind eye to it when he saw it on the newsstands, as he did to the spin-off magazines it spawned: *Whisper, Uncensored, Top Secret, Lowdown, On the QT, Hush Hush*, and *Private Lives*. Like Anthony Perkins and other gay men he knew, he kept his head down when he read these stories and got on with his life. Outside the cocoon of such literary trash cans, he said, there was a "gentleman's agreement" in Hollywood regarding being gay, a "live and let live" attitude if one didn't flaunt it too much (Hunter with Muller, 117).

Confidential reported Hunter's 1950 arrest in its piece, alongside one on Rory Calhoun, citing a criminal element in his past. Hunter always thought Henry Willson served him up on a plate to the magazine to spare his bigger star, Rock Hudson, who was about to be exposed by it. Calhoun became Hudson's sacrificial lamb, being the more minor star.

Hunter appeared in *The Burning Hills* the following year with Natalie Wood. Casting a male hunk and a love goddess in a Western was a ploy to create a new fan base for both of them, and for the Western genre. It succeeded in both ambitions and also did wonders for Hunter's heterosexual image. Having a pretty girl like Wood hanging on his arm at social functions was worth any number of column inches in the fanzines.

They became good friends and were reputed to be a romantic item, but this notion was as false as the rumor that Wood was romantically attached to Raymond Burr, another gay man whose heterosexual image she protected at this time by being seen out with him at functions by the paparazzi. Burr was thirty-eight and Wood only seventeen, so Hunter was infinitely preferable to the PR people as a date for her. The people she was really interested in at this time were James Dean, her *Rebel without a Cause* costar, and Nicholas Ray, that film's director. Elvis Presley even dated her briefly, before she committed herself to Robert Wagner.

Hunter was also photographed with stars like Dorothy Malone and Debbie Reynolds in the studio's bid to keep up the sham of his heterosexuality to sell his "beach party" films. While supposedly engaged to the actress Lori Nelson, he was actually in a relationship with a man called Ronnie Robertson. This was hushed up, as was his long-term relationship with Perkins, though many people on the inside track were well aware of it. Of his so-called affair with Natalie Wood, they wrote bitchily, "Natalie Wood but Tab Wouldn't" (*Sunday Independent*, July 15, 2018). He also had something of a singing career going by now. His rendition of "Young Love" was a hit with the bobby soxers and even knocked Elvis Presley off the charts.

Hunter reunited with Wood for *The Girl He Left Behind* (1956), a service comedy. A third film starring both of them was mooted, but he wasn't interested. By now the illusion had sprung a leak and he wanted a change in direction.

Sometimes his studio set him up on double dates with Perkins and two girls to deflect suspicion about their involvement with one another. This frustrated him as much as all the other fabricated attempts to hide his true nature. Inside himself he felt fractured, conflicted and uneasy—not to mention plagued with Catholic guilt, "If it was with a man I was sinning," he said of his impossible situation. "If it was with a woman I was lying" (Hunter with Muller, 156).

He was frequently seen in public with Perkins, even appearing with him on TV game shows such as *Juke Box Jury* and *Peter Potter's Platter Parade*. At such times he was less nervous about tongues wagging than Perkins. Perkins eventually took to wearing a baseball cap and sunglasses to disguise himself, something Hunter felt attracted more attention to them as a couple than less.

Their relationship declined after Perkins told Hunter he was going to appear in Robert Mulligan's baseball film *Fear Strikes Out* in 1957. Hunter had his heart set on landing the role, and Perkins knew this. When Hunter visited him on the set, Perkins became edgy with him, which made him not want to visit him again. In later years, Perkins embraced his heterosexual side by marrying and fathering children, something Hunter accepted if not quite understood.

The tide finally turned against *Confidential* magazine in 1957 when Hunter and a number of other stars who'd been the victims of its prurient gaze joined up to confront it for its multiple inaccuracies. The Irish star Maureen O'Hara turned out to be the chief witness for the prosecution. Along with Hunter, Dorothy Dandridge, and others, her testimony resulted in the magazine folding its tent and shutting up shop. Shortly afterward, Robert Harrison's former colleague Howard Rushmore shot both himself and his wife in a New York taxi, the incident bearing all the hallmarks of a *Confidential* smear—except this time it was for real, fact mirroring fiction. The chickens had come home to roost.

In 1958, Hunter appeared in *Lafayette Escadrille*, a film about the French flying legion of World War I. His costar was a French actress called Etchika Choureau. Louella Parsons said her name sounded like a sneeze. He became romantically involved with her nonetheless, and even proposed marriage to her at one point, not knowing for sure whether he wanted her to say yes. When she did, he thought he might finally be able to kill off the gay rumors.

They tied the knot, but it was merely a cosmetic exercise. They playacted for the cameras, but both of them knew it was all wrong, "a crazily fabricated dream of what might have been our story," as Hunter put it (Hunter with Muller, 179).

One of his favorite films was Sidney Lumet's *That Kind of Woman* (1959). In it he played a GI on a furlough who spends a night on a train with Sophia Loren, the kept woman of millionaire George Sanders, and falls hopelessly in love with her. He tells her he wants to marry her, but she's unsure. Leaving Sanders for him would mean throwing up a life of material comfort for one of financial uncertainty. She also feels he's emotionally immature.

Anthony Perkins had recently worked with Loren in *Desire Under the Elms* and been intimidated by her. Hunter conferred with him about the challenge of appearing opposite her but felt up to it. They got on well together, but Loren's hydraulic sexuality was too much for the wide-eyed soldier boy. He also had the problem of all those gay slurs to contend with.

Lumet took a chance on him, but it didn't work. The film played for only three weeks before being pulled from circulation. As the critic in *Time* wrote, "That kind of woman should never be mated with that kind of man" (*Time*, September 21, 1959). Lumet agreed. "If you put Sophia in the arms of someone who's not responsive to women," he railed, "there's going to be problems" (Hunter with Muller, 211). Hunter was peeved. Why had he hired him, he argued, if he felt that way about him? "Sidney had specifically asked for me," he grumbled. When the film flopped, he became the fall guy. If it had been a success, "Nobody would have been questioning whether I belonged in Sophia Loren's arms or not" (Hunter with Muller, 211).

Stung by the failure of *That Kind of Woman*, Hunter ran back to his singing, something he drifted in and out of for the rest of his life with mixed results. Like a child star who failed to make it as an adult, his "teen idol" credentials expired as his twenties gained on him. At twenty-seven it was impossible to play the teenager anymore, even with makeup. His studio did its utmost to halt the passage of time, but heading into his late twenties he thought he was too long in the tooth to be spouting lines like, "Gee, Dad, can I borrow the big car tonight?" (Hunter with Muller, 146).

By now his star was on the wane. He bought himself out of his Warner Bros. contract that year, but little else lay on the celluloid horizon for him. He turned to television with *The Tab Hunter Show* and other short-lived delights.

He campaigned for the lead in *West Side Story* in 1961, but Richard Beymer was selected for this. Hunter settled for a more lightweight role opposite his friend Debbie Reynolds in *The Pleasure of His Company* instead. His other sixties films were equally forgettable: *The Golden Arrow* (1962), *Operation Bikini* (1963), *Ride the Wild Surf* (1964), *War Gods of the Deep* (1965), *Birds Do It* (1966), *The Fickle Finger of Fate* (1967). He did some stage work in these years as well as summer stock and dinner theater. Toward the end of the decade he made a number of spaghetti Westerns in France after moving there to live.

Hunter begged John Schlesinger to give him the Joe Buck role in *Midnight Cowboy* in 1971, but again he ran into a brick wall here. Schlesinger told him he would have been perfect for it if he were ten years younger. The barb hurt. By now he'd started reading articles in magazines entitled, "Whatever happened to Tab Hunter?" (Hunter with Muller, 286).

There were three stages of stardom, he now surmised. The first was, "Get me Tab Hunter," the second was, "Get me a Tab Hunter type," and the third was, "Who the hell is Tab Hunter?" (Hunter with Muller, 299). He negotiated this grim trajectory faster than most shooting stars who get their fifteen minutes under the klieg lights and then a one-way ticket to Palookaville.

He didn't make many films of note in the seventies, appearing in a costarring capacity in John Huston's *The Life and Times of Judge Roy Bean* in 1972 and as a deranged killer in an early Curtis Hanson feature, *Sweet Kill*, the following year. There were also minor roles in such films as *Won Ton Ton, the Dog Who Saved Hollywood* (1976) and *Katie: Portrait of a Centerfold* (1978), but he was really clutching at straws now.

He revived his career in the most unlikely way imaginable by starring opposite John Waters's 300-pound drag queen, Divine, in *Polyester* (1981). Divine leaves her husband for "Golden Boy Todd Tomorrow" here. Waters was delighted to have the former superstar in his movie. Hunter was more leery about the idea, but the film became a cult hit and made him into a gay icon, something he never wanted to be and still didn't welcome now (Hunter with Muller, 5). Even so, it put his name back in lights again. This was something other films he made at time failed to do, like *Grease 2* (1982), which tanked, and the United Artists release *Pandemonium* (also 1982), a *Friday the 13th* spoof in which he played a cross-dressing serial killer.

The writing was now most definitely on the wall. "I woke up one morning," he told a reporter in 1981, "and couldn't get arrested" (*Irish Times*, July 14, 2018). Two years later he moved in with his lover, Allan Glaser, a much younger man whom he loved dearly. They went to the altar shortly after same-sex marriage became legal in California.

Hunter reunited with Divine for the spoof Western *Lust in the Dust* in 1984, but this didn't have Waters behind the camera. Paul (*Eating Raoul*) Bartel didn't have Waters's ingenuity or his inventiveness, and the film collapsed under a welter of clichés and ineptitudes. It didn't help its racy sense that Divine refused to promote it in drag, instead insisting on being interviewed in a sharp Tommy Nutter suit and insisting that he wasn't a cross-dresser but rather a legitimate actor who specialized in portraying women.

Even so, the film continued Hunter's rejuvenated celebrity, something he exploited with Glaser by setting up a company with him called Glaser/Hunter Productions. They considered a number of possible projects on which they could work to build on the momentum Waters created by rediscovering the man who used to be Tab Hunter and was now Golden Boy Todd Tomorrow.

Though he waited until he was in his seventies to come out, Hunter had a balanced attitude to his sexuality, being neither proud nor ashamed of being gay. He didn't understand gay pride: "To me, it's like saying you're 'proud' to be hetero," he said, "Why do you need to wear a badge? You simply are what you are." Neither did he believe in pretending he was straight in his private life: "I behaved the same way all the time. With me, what you saw was what you got—and what you didn't see was none of your business" (Hunter with Muller, 126–7). Wise words from a wise man. What a pity he couldn't convert them into more hits.

Related Film
Tab Hunter Confidential (2015).

Further Reading
Ehrenstein, David. 1998. *Open Secret: Gay Hollywood 1928–1998*. New York: William Morrow & Co.

Holfer, Robert. 2014. *The Man Who Invented Rock Hudson: The Pretty Boys and Dirty Deals of Henry Willson*. Minneapolis: University of Minnesota Press.

Hunter, Tab, with Eddie Muller. 2005. *Tab Hunter Confidential: The Making of a Movie Star*. Chapel Hill, NC: Algonquin Books.

Irish Times, July 14, 2018.

Sunday Independent, July 15, 2018.

Time, September 21, 1959.

J

Derek Jarman (1942–94)

Jarman is generally credited as being the founding father of New Queer Cinema. He began his career as an art director on Ken Russell's *The Devils* in 1971. He said he found the film industry to be "violently heterosexual" at that time (Rich, 2013: 50). Most of the gay people in the cast and crew were closeted, and so was he: "It was so strange. I was out of the closet outside the studio but in the closet inside. I wasn't going to create havoc for Ken by coming to work as a radical" (Rich, 50).

He was shy about being gay even at thirty. On trips to Amsterdam, which he made frequently, whenever he went into an adult bookshop he made for the heterosexual section first, wandering over to the gay one only afterward, as if by accident. He asked his friend Malcolm Leigh once, "When people see me in the street, do you think they can tell I'm gay?" (Peake, 1999: 185).

Sex for Jarman was often violent, both on screen and off it. He liked its sense of violation, the fact that he was performing it as "a sort of revenge." Much of this revenge was against an era that had made him feel guilty for being gay: "How do you get to love yourself if everything you've been told about you is negative?" (Peake, 282–3).

Jarman sometimes had fantasies of historical figures looming over his bed when he was having sex. People like Alexander the Great, Edward II, and Caravaggio would come into his mind. He even made himself believe he was making love to these people in such instances. Many of them would figure in some of his best-known films (Peake, 219).

His first feature was *Sebastiane* in 1976. All of the dialogue was in Latin. An erotic depiction of the saint's life, its cast of nude young men engaging in various forms of S&M relegated it to art house audiences. Its fusion of sex and religion—two themes very close to Jarman's heart—set the tone for much of his future work.

It was followed two years later by *Jubilee*, an anachronistic punk fantasy set to music. The style prefigured another Jarman film, *Edward II*. He enjoyed playing with time. Here Queen Elizabeth I morphs into the present queen.

He adapted Shakespeare's *The Tempest* in 1979, giving it an avant-garde flavor by setting it in a gothic mansion and adding music to it. (Elizabeth Welch even sings "Stormy Weather" at one point.) He took a break from filming afterward, returning with *The Angelic Conversation* in 1985. That was another avant-garde interpretation of the Bard, this time concentrating on his sonnets.

Caravaggio (1986) is regarded by many as Jarman's masterpiece. A valentine to the Italian renaissance painter, it has Nigel Terry playing him as a passionate bisexual. Sean Bean is one of his lovers. Tilda Swinton, who would become one of Jarman's favorite actresses in time, plays the mistress who comes between them. It took him seven years to get the film up and running but only five weeks to shoot. He shot it in a disused warehouse.

He became HIV-positive in 1987 but continued to work through his illness, directing *The Last of England*, a portrayal of the country's post-Thatcher quagmire, in 1988. *Highlights* (1989) was a musical extravaganza featuring eight songs from a Pet Shop Boys concert. Jarman played around with the camerawork to give it a surreal overlay. In the same year he made *War Requiem*, a film that allied the poetry of Wilfred Owen—who was killed at the end of World War I—with his own health problems. It was Laurence Olivier's celluloid swan song. He played a war veteran. Tilda Swinton was a battlefield nurse. Despite such a gilt-edged cast, it remained Jarman's least favorite film.

The Garden (1990) was an experimental film about queer culture and AIDS. He made it after moving to a cottage in Dungeness, a headland off the coast of Kent comprising mainly a shingle beach in the form of a cuspate foreland. He'd gone there to give himself a conducive environment in which to battle his disease and also to busy himself with his second major passion: gardening.

Edward II, his most commercially successful film, was released in 1991. A mischievously iconoclastic study of Britain's only openly gay king, Jarman used Christopher Marlowe's sixteenth-century play of the same name as a template to unleash all his fury at the intolerance of church and state. It was highly experimental, mixing genres and time frames with the manic energy of a man who felt time was running out for him. He expected it to be his last film. His health weakened many days on set, but he rallied to make *Wittgenstein*, a spirited biopic of the gay philosopher, in 1992. Like many of his films, it was funded by Channel 4. He shot it in less than two weeks.

When Jarman made *Blue* in 1993, his sight was practically gone. To give people a sense of what it might feel like to be blind, he framed the film on a blue screen. In it he meditated on his past, his art, and the ravages of AIDS. John Quentin, Nigel Terry, and Tilda Swinton read from his diaries. In one of them he described himself as being "like a naked bulb in a ruined room." He knew full well he could never win his battle against the disease that was ravaging him, but he still found beauty in his thoughts and memories. A Brian Eno music score plays evocatively in the background. *Blue* is a mellow, elegiac film with many intimations of mortality. It's free of the rage of Jarman's previous work. He lets people know he's content to go gentle into the good night, surrendering himself to the womb of death like a soporific balm. The die was cast by now, but he still found time to oversee *Glitterbug* (1994), a collection of his videos put to music. He died that same year aged just fifty-two. By now he was famous all over the world for his iconoclastic zeal. Time hasn't dented his appeal one whit.

Related Films
The Last Paintings of Derek Jarman (1995); *A Night with Derek* (1995); *Life as Art* (2004); *Red Duckies* (2006); *Derek* (2008); *Delphinium: A Childhood Portrait of Derek Jarman* (2009).

Further Reading

James, Dominic. 2015. *Visions of Queer Martyrdom from John Henry Newman to Derek Jarman.* Chicago: University of Chicago Press.

Jarman, Derek. 1991. *At Your Own Risk.* London: Thames & Hudson.

Lippard, Chris, ed. 1996. *By Angels Driven: The Films of Derek Jarman.* Trowbridge: Flicks Books.

Loughlin, Gerard. 2004. *Alien Sex: The Body and Desire in Cinema and Theology.* Oxford: Blackwell Publishing.

O'Pray, Michael. 1996. *Derek Jarman: Dreams of England.* London: British Film Institute.

Peake, Tony. 1999. *Derek Jarman.* London: Little Brown & Co.

Rich, B. Ruby. 2013. *New Queer Cinema: The Director's Cut.* Durham, NC, and London: Duke University Press.

Richardson, Niall. 2009. *The Queer Cinema of Derek Jarman.* London: I. B. Tauris.

The Killing of Sister George (1968)

The aggressive June Buckridge (Beryl Reid) is the polar opposite of her televisual alter ego Sister George, a lovable district nurse who goes about the place on her motorcycle dispensing goodwill.

In her television persona June is a softhearted soul, but in her private life she exhibits many unseemly character traits. She boozes, swears, and chomps on cigars. She's living with a young woman called Childie (Susannah York). York is Childie by name and by nature. She collects dolls as a hobby.

One night when she's drunk, June abuses two nuns in a taxi. "Hello, girls," she gushes, "out on a mission, are we?" She proceeds to harass them, to their bewilderment. Soon afterward, the incident comes to the attention of her boss at the television station, Mercy Croft (Coral Browne).

Croft warns June about her behavior but tells her there won't be any official sanctions against her on this occasion. Relieved to be out of the line of fire, June invites her to join her for a drink at a lesbian club she frequents.

Croft was once married but her husband died. She now expresses an interest in Childie. During one of their conversations, she tells her June is about to be written out of the show. This is the "killing" referred to in the film's title. Plans are afoot to have the chirpy nurse mowed down by a truck while she's out riding her scooter.

A farewell party is held for June at the studio. Here she's informed she's about to be offered the part of a cow on a children's show as a sop for losing her main role. It's a voiceover part, a humiliating comedown for the once successful actress. Rage descends on her. She gets drunk and proceeds to insult everyone in sight.

Croft brings Childie home from the party. Afterward she makes a sexual advance on her. Childie succumbs to it. When June arrives back, she finds Croft and Childie in a sexually compromising position together. Enraged, she starts roaring at Childie but Childie stands up to her. She tells her she's going to move in with Croft. It's the last straw for June. She's now a totally broken woman. Croft has destroyed both her personal and professional life.

June returns to the studio at the end of the film. She walks around the empty set of the axed TV show. She sees the coffin intended for the body of Sister George and opens the lid. When she sees it's made of cheap balsa, she exclaims, "Even the bloody coffin's a fake!" In a rage, she starts smashing lights and props all around her. She demolishes almost everything in sight. She then sits down on a bench and screams out, "Moo!" in a mock preparation for the animated role she's been offered. In this act, as Patricia White remarked, lies a certain blackly comic

Robert Aldrich (1918–83)

Aldrich isn't one of the first names that spring to mind when one considers LGBTQ cinema, but he featured themes tangential to it in much of his work during a highly versatile career.

Neither was *The Killing of Sister George* his first exposition lesbianism. In the original opening scene of *World for Ransom* (1954), for example, a female couple was seen embracing. (This was later dropped.) His revisionist Western *The Last Sunset* (1961) could also be queered. So, at least, Mark Rappaport thought when he mentioned it in his docu-essay, *Rock Hudson's Home Movies*. He quotes Rock Hudson saying to Kirk Douglas in the penultimate scene, "I'll come for you at sundown" and Douglas replying, "I'll be waiting for you." It needs to be mentioned that this is for a showdown rather than a romantic tryst, but many Westerns had coded references to being gay, as we've seen often before in this book.

Aldrich's most famous LGBTQ movie was *What Ever Happened to Baby Jane?* Bette Davis and Joan Crawford were gay icons. Their masculine status here, combined with the film's grisly overtones, saw it serenade Davis's renaissance as a demonic figure in the latter phase of her career. She was happy to exploit this, in contrast to her more glamour-conscious costar.

Crawford was so obsessed by her appearance she was rumored to have even applied makeup before putting out the garbage. "If you want to see the girl next door," she taunted, "go next door" (Jarski, 2000: 185). When she made *What Ever Happened to Baby Jane?* with her archenemy—she and Davis had a lengthy history of feuding—she despised having herself uglified by the makeup department. Such transmogrifications weren't practiced as much at Columbia (Crawford's studio) as they were at Warner Bros., where Davis mainly worked.

Aldrich featured a number of gay men in *The Choirboys* (1979) but more from the perspective of the homophobic protagonists in the film than from the inside. In 1981 he made a film about women wrestlers called *All the Marbles*. This continued his penchant for expanding one's preconceptions about expectable gender behavior. He enjoyed experimenting with intriguing themes, and if he didn't always hit the mark, that was the price any imaginative director paid for going out on a limb.

The only thing one could say for sure about this man's work was that there was no one thing one could say for sure about it.

Further Reading
Jarski, Rosemarie, ed. 2000. *Hollywood Wit: Classic Hollywood Quips and Quotes*. London: Prion.

triumph. Even as a cow she will still enter the homes of countless television viewers (Creekmur and Doty, 1995: 92).

Robert Aldrich directed this landmark film as a kind of corrective to the number of "hagsploitation" films that preceded it. At times he fails to reprise the sensitivity of the Frank Marcus play on which it's based, but he adroitly captures June's loneliness as she throws caution to the wind in her misery. The concluding installment of his Actress Trilogy—the other two were *What Ever Happened to Baby Jane?* (1962) and *The Legend of Lylah Clare* (1968)—isn't a very attractive movie by and large, but it's performed with admirable conviction by all concerned.

Lukas Heller's screenplay is also suitably wry, as when Childie says to June, "Not all girls are raving lesbians, you know." June replies with the Wildean, "That is a misfortune that I am perfectly aware of."

The seduction of Childie by Croft was handled poorly, however, especially when Croft kisses Childie's breast. One viewer described this as being similar to "an ichthyologist finding something that has drifted up on the beach" (White, 1999: 12).

The scene was shot with noirish lighting, and this gave it a somewhat creepy aura. When the film was submitted to John Trevelyan, the British film censor of the time, he found it too daring for public consumption. He regarded himself as a liberal, but this was a bridge too far in his book and he insisted on cuts.

Reid was heterosexual in real life, but after the film was released she became tagged with being a lesbian. One day a taxi driver said to her, "May I kiss you? I've never kissed a lesbian before." She replied, "You may if you like but you still haven't" (Braun, 2002: 213).

The film was shot mainly in America, but the scene in the lesbian bar took place in an actual gay bar in London called Gateways. Reid was shocked at the actions she saw there. Her mother, who'd accompanied her to London, was more laid-back about it. She looked at some of the masculine patrons and said to Beryl, "I'd say that's a collar-and-tie job, Beryl" (Bourne, 1996: 210).

The masculine-feminine dialectic Aldrich attempted to create with June and Childie was only partly successful. They're too diverse in their orientations to convince audiences that this is a relationship that could have come about in the first place, or could work now under any circumstances, even without Croft's intervention. June is far too rough for Childie's baby-doll sensibilities. (York was an even unlikelier lesbian in *X, Y and Zee* three years later.)

Reid's character owed more to the forties stereotype of the "ugly" lesbian than anything more progressive promulgated by the gay liberation movement. The fact that she rides a motorcycle—she describes it as "fifty cubic centimeters" between her legs—copper-fastened this image.

When the film was released, censorship laws were giving way to the ratings system, and this rendered it viewable under an X certificate. In some cities, however, it was banned. A Boston judge branded its treatment of being lesbian "unsightly and lewd," and the theater manager who distributed it was fined and jailed. In other cities, various segments of it were edited out to render it palatable to the masses (Weiss, 1992: 52–3).

Many newspapers refused to carry advertisements for X-rated films at this time (Lewis, 2000: 166–7). Aldrich placed an ad for it in the *Los Angeles Times*, but it was altered both visually and verbally to accommodate itself to what that newspaper deemed to be suitable for mass viewing. Aldrich sued the paper for misrepresenting his film but lost, the case setting a precedent that allowed editors to bowdlerize advertisements even when they were being paid to insert them.

The Killing of Sister George is an important film despite its flaws. It's difficult to believe the Reid role was first offered to Doris Day. How could anyone believe she would have accepted it? Bette Davis was the next choice. Even though Davis broke down many barriers in acting—and was a gay icon—she found the film's explicitness unsavory. Browne went on to play a lesbian role in *The Legend of Lylah Clare*, an Aldrich misfire that had Kim Novak and Peter Finch going through the motions of Tinseltown necromancy with varying degrees of contrivance.

Related Films
What Ever Happened to Baby Jane? (1962); *The Legend of Lylah Clare* (1968); *X, Y and Zee* (1971); *Late Flowering Love* (1981).

Further Reading
Bourne, Stephen. 1996. *Brief Encounters: Lesbians and Gays in British Cinema 1930–1971*. London: Cassell.
Creekmur, Corey K., and Alexander Doty, eds. 1995. *Out in Culture: Gay, Lesbian and Queer Essays on Popular Culture*. London: Cassell.
Gardiner, J. 2003. *From the Closet to the Screen: Women at the Gateways Club, 1945–85*. London: Pandora.
Lewis, Jon. 2000. *Hollywood V. Hard Core: How the Struggle over Censorship Saved the Modern Film Industry*. New York and London: New York University Press.
Marcus, Frank. 1967. *The Killing of Sister George: A Comedy*. New York: Random House.
Matthews, Tom Dewe. 1994. *Censored*. London: Chatto & Windus.
Sova, Dawn B. 2001. *Forbidden Films*. New York: Checkmark Books.
Weiss, Andrea, 1992. *Vampires and Violets: Lesbians in Film*. New York: Penguin.
White, Patricia. 1999. *Uninvited: Classical Hollywood Cinema and Lesbian Representability*. Bloomington and Indianapolis: Indiana University Press.

Kiss of the Spider Woman (1985)

This film is the story of an unlikely bonding that takes place between a transgender window dresser (William Hurt) and a political radical (Raul Julia) with whom he shares a cell in a grimy South American jail. Luis Molina (Hurt) has been arrested for molesting a minor. Valentin (Julia) is a journalist who's been jailed for writing left-wing articles and giving his passport to a revolutionary. Molina is obsessed with old movies and Valentin with political idealism.

The first time we see Molina, he's standing in a kimono with a towel wrapped turban-style around his head. When he talks to Valentin about the movies, he elicits little response from him.

Each day Molina acts out a scene from one of his favorite films featuring Sonia Braga. (Braga also appears as Valentin's lover, Marta.) Molina is naively unaware of the films' fascist elements. The Nazis incinerated gay prisoners, Valentine informs him sharply, annoyed at his ignorance in this regard. As the film goes on, however, the distinctions between them begin to blur. The fantasist is brought back to reality and the realist finds himself succumbing to the escapist allure of the cinema. On the surface, the two of them are poles apart. As they become warmer toward one another, we see the parallels between Molina's retreat into movieland and Valentin's political nous. Each of them, in their way, is seeking an impossible dream, one in the past and the other of the future.

The manner in which Valentin goes from revulsion toward Molina to an intimate relationship with him might appear far-fetched on paper, but because of Hector Babenco's dream-like direction and the powerful performances of both leads, the events develop credibility as they unfold. Both characters are doomed by the system, but before their mutual fates are sealed, they become physical with one another, having sex on the night before Molina's release.

Molina is released on parole on condition that he betrays Valentin. The police are convinced he'll do this. Valentin has given him the phone number of one of his colleagues. Molina rings this and sets up a meeting with him, but the police intercept it. A gun battle ensues in which Molina is wounded. He wanders around the streets and is subsequently picked up by the police. They demand the phone number from him, but he refuses to give it. Then he dies from his wounds. Valentin, who's now in the hospital recovering from the torture inflicted on him by the police in prison, has a fantasy about being with Marta on an idyllic island.

Babenco encountered fierce resistance when he first proposed the film to the studios. Who would want to see a story about a movie-mad gay man, they wondered (*Campaign*, February 1986).

On the first day of shooting, Hurt showed up in a ponytail. He also had heavy makeup and a beauty mark. Babenco was shocked. He asked him to tone his appearance down. He wanted Hurt to create the character from the inside out, not the other way around. He allowed him to wear lipstick, but he wanted him to concentrate more on his movements and gestures and less on his physical attributes.

Hurt did this. The change in his attitude contributed in large part toward him winning an Oscar for his performance. Moving like the titular spider and speaking in a voice as soft as velvet, he created a mesmeric aura around himself. He was perfect for the role with his sinewy build, his nasal tones, his lapidary air, his fey touch. The film was also nominated for Best Picture and Best Director, an incredible achievement for an "indie" undertaking.

The film had been completed for over a year before a distributor was found for it. It wasn't expected to be a hit in the United States because of its theme and downbeat style, but it was—its appeal no doubt aided by its Oscar benison. Before long, a film that seemed to have everything militating against it won the public over with the hypnotic spell it wove. Hurt's Best Actor Oscar was the icing on the cake. (Babenco lost out on Best Director to Sydney Pollack for the blander *Out of Africa*.) He was the first actor to convert a nomination for a gay role into a win. Peter Finch, Marcello Mastroianni, and Tom Courtenay had all fallen at the last fence in previous years.

The Kiss of the Spider Woman had many subsequent incarnations after its celluloid success. It was made into a play in Britain, an opera in Germany, and a musical in the United States.

Related Films
Midnight Express (1978); *Chained Heat* (1983); *Cinema Paradiso* (1988); *Strawberry and Chocolate* (1993); *Locked Up* (2004); *I Love You, Philip Morris* (2010); *Orange Is the New Black* (2013).

Further Reading
Campaign, February 1986.
Cruz, Barbara. 1998. *Raul Julia: Actor and Humanitarian*. Berkeley Heights, NJ: Enslow Books.

Manuel, Victor, and Amar Rodriguez. 1994. *Hector Babenco.* Madrid: Editorial Dykinson.

Puig, Manuel. 1984. *Kiss of the Spider Woman.* London: Vintage.

Stefoff, Rebecca. 1994. *Raul Julia.* Langhome, PA: Chelsea House Publishers.

Kissing

"It is difficult enough to be queer," wrote Derek Jarman, "but to be queer in the cinema is almost impossible." Heterosexuals had so monopolized the screen, he averred, "There's hardly room for us to kiss" (Murray, 1994: frontispiece).

One of the most famous girl-on-girl kisses in film history was that given by Marlene Dietrich to a woman she didn't even know in *Morocco* (1930). Dorothea Wieck and Hertha Thiele kissed more significantly in Leontine Sagan's groundbreaking German film *Mädchen in Uniform* (1931). In 1933, Greta Garbo gave a full-mouthed kiss to her lady-in-waiting in *Queen Christina.*

Strangely enough, none of these kisses caused any storm clouds to gather on the censorial horizon. The Production Code Association didn't have a problem with Garbo's kiss any more than it did with the other two. Was this because it was women who were involved in all three instances? Were women somehow more innocuous when it came to something like this? For some reason, the PCA seemed to take a stricter line with heterosexual kisses than same-sex ones, at least if the perpetrators were female.

The cross-dressing Katharine Hepburn of *Sylvia Scarlett* (1935) kisses her father's girlfriend in that film, making one writer question whether such a kiss could be classified as lesbian or heterosexual, considering she's in male garb when it takes place (Benshoff and Griffin, 2006: 54).

A vampiress kissed a woman in *Dracula's Daughter* (1936). Kissing in vampire films was generally regarded as more murderous than affectionate. Even so, it often had erotic undertones. Hollywood cleaned itself up in the forties, so there wasn't much same-sex kissing, not even in *Rope* (1948), where two gay men commit a murder together. In 1948, it seemed easier to get a gay murder past the censors than a gay kiss.

Tab Hunter's steamy kiss with Linda Darnell on a tropical locale in *Island of Desire* launched his career in 1951. He'd been arrested for attending a gay party the year before, but the story didn't reach the papers. The illusion of heterosexuality was preserved for the cameras, even if Darnell enjoyed the kiss more than he did.

Hunter was a friend of Rock Hudson, another closeted gay actor who was a fifties heartthrob. When we look at his films today, we're understandably tempted to examine his kissing scenes with women for signs of artifice. Douglas Sirk once told an interviewer that Hudson's leading ladies often complained that he didn't know how to kiss them properly (Cottingham, 2005: 26). Sirk didn't interfere even though he knew the reason for Hudson's laxity in this regard (Kashner and Macnair, 2002: 145).

There's a scene in Sidney Lumet's *A View from the Bridge* (1962) where the longshoreman played by Raf Vallone kisses the boyfriend of his niece, with whom he's infatuated, full on the lips as if to suggest he's gay. There's no evidence that he is in the script. Vallone kisses him to humiliate him. He has a gentle personality and is therefore open to the gay implication. Vallone's motivation is to break up his relationship with his niece. He himself has an incestuous fascination with the young girl. This was the first instance of male kissing on screen in a mainstream American film.

Andy Warhol's *Kiss* (1963) featured many close-ups of gay people kissing. Five years later, there was a plethora of kissing scenes in films like *The Fox, The Killing of Sister George, Les Biches*, and *Therese and Isabelle*. Censors and viewers, again, seemed to be less threatened by these films than ones where men kissed. It was reminiscent of the situation with Garbo and Dietrich in the thirties. One can only speculate as to the reason for this. Most censors were men, which may have been a factor. Heterosexual men seem to have been traditionally less offended by watching women kissing than they have been by watching men do so.

An important kiss between Joanne Woodward and Estelle Parsons took place in 1968 in *Rachel, Rachel*. The scene contained the film's first suggestion that Parsons was gay. She even blocked the fact from her own mind until then.

Perhaps the most repellent kiss in a film about a gay man occurs in *The Sergeant* (also 1968) where Rod Steiger obsesses about John Phillip Law for 107 minutes. When he finally works up the courage to kiss him, he becomes so disgusted by his action that he then commits suicide.

Peter Finch kissed Murray Head on the lips in John Schlesinger's *Sunday Bloody Sunday* (1971). The scene created much controversy because of Finch being a major league actor. There wasn't too much same-sex kissing on screen in subsequent years, though two Roman soldiers kissed in Derek Jarman's *Sebastiane* (1976). Helen Mirren kissed Teresa Ann Savoy in *Caligula* (1980).

Sidney Lumet's 1981 movie *Deathtrap* had Michael Caine and Christopher Reeve as two gay lovers attempting to become rich from literary fraud. When they kiss, it's the audience's first inkling that they're gay. To this extent it was essential to the plot. It was also the film's most surprising moment, but it drew a strongly negative reaction from audiences, Reeve claimed it cost the movie millions of dollars. Caine said the scene was a disaster because both he and Reeve drank brandy before it to work up the courage to do the scene and as a result forgot their dialogue (*Sunday Independent*, February 17, 2019).

Robert Towne featured some sexploitative kissing between two women in his "lipstick lesbian" offering, *Personal Best* (1982). This was a movie that angered LGBTQ viewers intensely. Rock Hudson also drew a lot of abuse from viewers when he kissed Linda Evans in the TV show *Dynasty* in 1984. It wasn't known that he was suffering from AIDS at the time. After he died from the disease, he was retrospectively castigated for exposing her to its dangers. At this time it was believed one could contract it from kissing. A similar paranoia was evident in *The Kiss* (1988) where a deadly African parasite is passed from woman to woman via openmouthed kissing.

The kissing scenes between Helen Shaver and Patricia Charbonneau in Donna Deitch's *Desert Hearts* (1985) were unusually intimate for the time. They were performed with explicitness but without prurience. The kisses exchanged between

Daniel Day-Lewis and his lover, Gordon Warnecke, in *My Beautiful Laundrette* (1985) were more affectionate than erotic. The opposite was the case in *Prick Up Your Ears* (1987) where the kissing scenes between Gary Oldman and Alfred Molina act as a prelude to murder.

There's an iconic kiss between Susan Sarandon and Geena Davis in *Thelma and Louise* (1991) that seals their relationship, spiriting them off to eternity in an automobile. Here again a kiss between two women was greeted warmly by audiences, but when it came to films like *An Early Frost* (1985) and *Philadelphia* (1993), two films dealing with male lovers, a "No kissing" rule applied. Admittedly AIDS was involved in both films, but there still seemed to be a double standard. When Gina Gershon and Jennifer Tilly engaged in passionate kissing in the lesbian chic thriller *Bound* (1996), audiences whooped in delight. One wonders what would have been the reaction if the two stars were male.

Three different kinds of kisses were involved in *The Hours* (2002), Stephen Daldry's eclectic adaptation of Virginia Woolf's novel *Mrs. Dalloway*. The film features women from different eras who have a lesbian connection. Woolf (Nicole Kidman) and her sister exchange two different kinds of kisses, one of affection and the other of defiance. For the suicidal Laura Brown (Julianne Moore), who tends to an ill neighbor, kissing acts as an example of compassion but also desire. The kiss between book editor Clarissa Vaughan (Meryl Streep) and her lover is meant to be one of mature love.

In Annie Proulx's short story *Brokeback Mountain*, which went on to become a megasuccessful movie, two male lovers reunite after being apart for a time, and their kisses actually draw blood. The film was almost as graphic, both Heath Ledger and Jake Gyllenhaal throwing one another against walls as they reignite their passion for one another. The scene is a powerful affirmation of the way they feel about one another as well as being heartbreaking for Ledger's wife, who spots them from an upstairs window. For her it's the first indication her husband is gay. As such, it's a seminal moment in the film.

Further Reading

Benshoff, Harry M., and Sean Griffin. *Queer Images: A History of Gay and Lesbian Film in America.* Lanham, MD: Rowman & Littlefield.

Cottingham, Laura. 2005. *Fear Eats the Soul.* London: British Film Institute.

Kashner, Sam, and Jennifer Macnair. 2002. *The Bad and the Beautiful: Hollywood in the Fifties.* London: Little Brown.

Murray, Raymond. 1994. *Images in the Dark: An Encyclopedia of Gay and Lesbian Film and Video.* Philadelphia: TLA Publications.

Sunday Independent, February 17, 2019.

L

Ladies or Gentlemen (2008)

Directed by Kevin Burns and narrated by Rupal, this is both an interesting and informative documentary about movie transvestism based on the book of the same name by Jean-Louis Ginibre. Ginibre's book is a beautifully illustrated 400-page tome that goes into more detail about the subject than any other volume on the shelves, combining mini-reviews of the films in question with thumbnail sketches of the stars who appeared in them. Burns's film is much less detailed but equally entertaining, going all the way from the Katharine Hepburn of *Christopher Strong* (1933) to the Cate Blanchett of *I'm Not There* (2007). It features clips from well-known cross-dressing films like *Tootsie* (1982) and *Mrs. Doubtfire* (1993) as well as ones such as *White Chicks* (2004), *She's the One* (1996), *Nuns on the Run* (1990), and a host of others. There are also interviews with writers, psychotherapists, and directors, all of whom enter into the spirit of the enterprise with good cheer. "If you ask what's it all about," John Landis maintains, "you're uncomfortable with your sexuality."

Cross-dressing, the film claims, goes all the way back to 550 BC when the ancient Greeks excluded women from theater, which meant men were playing female roles on stage from as long ago as that. The practice continued up to the time of Shakespeare, as was evidenced in the Gwyneth Paltrow film *Shakespeare in Love* in 1998.

The idea of women playing men has always evoked different reactions from viewers to men playing women. The latter phenomenon usually provokes guffaws of laughter whereas the former, the film alleges, suggests women are "moving up the power chain, stepping onto male privilege." Henry Gibson says straight men exaggerate both their dress and movements when they're in drag because they don't want to be thought of as gay. As a result, they lose any sense of realism in their performances. Apart from everything else, they make their lips "three times" the size of women's ones.

Camille Paglia talks about the "absurd version of women" given to audiences by Tony Curtis and Jack Lemmon in Billy Wilder's *Some Like It Hot* (1959). According to Tim Curry of *The Rocky Horror Picture Show* fame, Curtis looked pretty so he played it straight—or as straight as he could in the ridiculous getup Wilder made him wear—whereas Lemmon, who looked like a "wet weekend," chose to "guy" it instead. He entered more and more into the part as the film went on, Michael Musto asserts, so that by the end one knew he was going to marry Joe E. Brown and live "happily ever after" with him.

The film also studies people like Glenn Milstead—the "Divine" of so many John Waters movies—who didn't so much play drag as live it. Milstead wanted to be Elizabeth Taylor, *Ladies or Gentlemen* claims, from a young age. He became totally committed to the drag cosmos as his career developed, so much so that he even shaved the hair on the top of his head to give himself more forehead space for makeup. Milstead died after making *Hairspray* (1988), his most conservative film. Waters was heartened that audiences accepted him as a dowdy housewife here rather than his more usual demonstrative persona. The role was closer to the real Milstead than people realized, Waters states. For Milstead, less was more in the film. For all his outrageousness, Waters appreciated the artistic value of dressing down. If Dolly Parton took off all her makeup and played an alcoholic, he goes on to say, she would probably have won an Oscar.

One of the most fascinating cross-dressers in film history was Ed Wood, something the documentary is at pains to emphasize. It examines the hilarious director's most intriguing film, *Glen or Glenda?* (1953), and also a more recent biopic of him starring Johnny Depp, *Ed Wood* (1994). What made both of these films stand out for Waters was the fact that they didn't look over their shoulders. There were no cheap laughs or no nudge-wink condescensions. It's important to note that Wood didn't make *Glen or Glenda?* as a comedy. His apparent inability to see how funny it was made it funnier still. This sense of humor didn't extend to the Depp film for Rebecca Bell-Metereau, author of *Hollywood Androgyny*. *Ed Wood* wasn't a commercial success, she alleges, because audiences didn't know whether to laugh at Depp or feel sorry for him.

The last part of the documentary examines the darker elements of transvestism that were apparent in films like *Psycho* (1960) or Brian de Palma's *Dressed to Kill* (1980). Bell-Metereau believes *Psycho* "changed the landscape" for horror films in its fusion of voyeurism with incest, matricide, and necrophilia. Michael Musto claims Alfred Hitchcock directed it partly as a comedy. It's difficult to see it like this unless one considers some of its blackly comic lines. (In one scene, Anthony Perkins says to Janet Leigh that his mother "isn't quite herself today.")

The drag queen became a figure of fun more than fear in *The Rocky Horror Picture Show* (1975). Few would deny that Tim Curry gave the performance of his life as the transsexual from Transylvania. Paglia suggests he was influenced by people like Led Zeppelin and Jimi Hendrix in essaying the role. All of these people, for her, revived eighteenth-century dandyism in their various ways. They were rebels, she says, but comic rebels. Curry adds, "There are less rules in society now so it's more important to break the ones that are left."

Toward the end of *Ladies or Gentlemen* a question is posed: Why has transvestism always played such a major part in films? Waters provides the answer to that question. The reason, he says, is because it's such a major part of life. Nobody would know more about that than this man.

Related Films
Queen Christina (1930); *Christopher Strong* (1935); *Some Like It Hot* (1959); *The Rocky Horror Picture Show* (1975); *Annie Hall* (1977); *Tootsie* (1982); *Nuns on the Run* (1990).

Further Reading

Dickens, Homer. 1984. *What a Drag: Men as Women and Women as Men in the Movies.* New York: Quill.

Garber, Marjorie. 1992. *Vested Interests: Cross-Dressing and Cultural Anxiety.* London and New York: Routledge.

Ginibre, Jean-Louis. 2005. *Ladies or Gentlemen: A Pictorial History of Cross-Dressing in the Movies.* New York: Filipacchi.

Maddison, S. 2000. *Fags, Hags and Queer Sisters: Gender Dissent and Heterosexual Bonding in Gay Culture.* Basingstoke, UK: Palgrave Macmillan.

Newton, Esther. 1972. *Mother Camp: Female Impersonators in America.* Chicago: University of Chicago Press.

Charles Laughton (1899–1962)

"I have a face," Laughton once harrumphed, "like the behind of an elephant" (Jarman, 1991: 275). The remark was indicative of a poor self-image he carried with him right through his life. It flew in the face of the high esteem in which he was held by the film industry for his estimable talents. It didn't help that his wife, Elsa Lanchester, was dubbed "The Bride of Frankenstein," an allusion to her most famous role as well as her husband's lack of chocolate box good looks (Hadleigh, 1994: 110).

He was born in England and served in the army during World War I. He worked for five years in his father's hotel afterward. In 1925 he enrolled in the Royal Academy of Dramatic Arts. The following year he made his stage debut in Gogol's *The Government Inspector.*

He never came out of the closet, and it was only when police arrived at the door of his home in 1930 to report the fact that he'd been consorting with a boy in a local park that he opened up to Lanchester about his "other" life. "It was then that he broke down," she said, "and confessed his orientation. He cried and admitted he picked up boys from time to time. I told him it was perfectly all right, that I understood, that it didn't matter. But of course it did—particularly his deception. If he had only told be before our marriage" (McClelland, 1987: 159).

Her forbearance was incredible. To reassure him as she did, and to stay with him, is apt testament to the great love she had for him, and the equally formidable loyalty. They were, of course, great friends as well as frequent costars of one another. When Laughton's case finally came up in court, he gave the boy five shillings. A newspaper article reprimanded him for his "misguided generosity" but—mercifully—didn't say what his offence was. Lanchester was so affected by the incident she went deaf for a week afterward, "partly as a reaction to the news I hadn't wanted to hear." When she asked Laughton for the details of what happened, he confessed that he'd "had" a boy on their sofa. "Fine," she sniffed, "but get rid of the sofa." It was promptly disposed of (Lanchester, 1983: 97–8).

Her amazingly compliant attitude to her husband's indiscretions continued even after he told her he was only really comfortable with "his own kind." She accepted this with stoic resignation. She knew it was unusual not to show disapproval. Her failure to do so worsened Laughton's shameful feelings rather than ameliorated them. "He horrified himself," she said, "and needed to be reprimanded." To that extent, her tolerance was even a kind of cruelty (Lanchester, 200).

Laughton appeared on Broadway in 1931. Afterward he went to Hollywood. He made his film debut in a comedy horror film called *The Old Dark Horse*, directed by the gay James Whale, in 1932. That year also saw him in *Payment Deferred*, *If I Had a Million*, and *The Sign of the Cross*. In the last film, he was an effeminate Nero. This was probably the closest he came to giving a gay performance. He was outstanding as a gluttonous monarch in *The Private life of Henry VIII* the following year. Chewing the scenery as well as his favored chicken bones, he blew everyone else off the screen. In this and other roles he channeled his growing girth into his art. His screen presence earned him many kudos, but nothing could ease the pathological sense of self-loathing that continued to haunt him.

He was a villain in *White Woman* (1933) and a controlling patriarch in *The Barretts of Wimpole Street* (1934). In *Mutiny on the Bounty* (1935), he played the despotic Captain Bligh opposite Clark Gable. He adored Gable's looks as much as he despised his own. "You see Gable," he said, "and you say, 'I'll go out and have half a dozen dates'" (Callow, 1987: 98). Gable, however, was repulsed by Laughton. Their tension made for great drama on screen, and both of them were rewarded with Oscar nominations. So was Franchot Tone for the same film. The three nominations canceled each other out. Victor McLaglen stole in on the blind side to win for *The Informer*.

Laughton discovered the titian-haired Irish beauty Maureen O'Hara in 1939. With his colleague Erich Pommer, he was instrumental in her appearing in *Jamaica Inn*, an adaptation of Daphne du Maurier's gothic novel. It was directed by Alfred Hitchcock. Laughton argued with Hitchcock over how the film should be made. He also argued with Lanchester, who was envious of the excessive attention he was paying to O'Hara.

Lanchester's pain at his sexual infidelities made her firm in her resolve not to have children by him. O'Hara believed her childlessness had a different cause. She wrote in her autobiography that Laughton told her the reason Lanchester didn't have children was because she couldn't conceive as a result of a botched abortion she'd had in her burlesque days (O'Hara with Nicoletti, 2004: 31–2). Whatever the truth of the matter, in O'Hara Laughton found a kind of surrogate daughter. Other starlets filled this role for him afterward: Deanna Durbin, Margaret O'Brien, Maureen O'Sullivan. Lanchester, meanwhile, malingered in the wings and quietly smoldered. But she would always love her Charles.

O'Hara also appeared in Laughton's next film, *The Hunchback of Notre Dame* (1939), one of his greatest roles. His portrayal of the eponymous Quasimodo, who was hopelessly in love with the gypsy Esmeralda (O'Hara), could have drawn tears from a stone. O'Hara also appeared with Laughton in Jean Renoir's *This Land Is Mine* (1943), a poignant drama about the Nazi invasion of a French village.

There were many more standout performances in a prolific career: *The Paradine Case* (1948), *The Man on the Eiffel Tower* (1949), *Salomé* (1953), *Young Bess*

(1953). He was Henry VIII again here. In 1955, he even turned his hand to directing with *The Night of the Hunter* (1955), a strangely creepy portrayal of a deranged preacher (Robert Mitchum) that parlayed the techniques of German expressionism into a demonic tale of baroque sadism. Mitchum was rarely better, but there was no way Hollywood was ready for this kind of penumbral eeriness, especially from someone who'd never shown any signs of it before. Both Laughton and Mitchum were sailing into uncharted waters and each paid the price. The film sank without trace.

In 1956, bizarrely, Laughton deputized for Ed Sullivan on his TV show to introduce a singer by the name of Elvis Presley, then on the cusp of international fame. One can only imagine what longings he must have harbored for this Adonis, even if his brand of music would have meant nothing to him. He was back to more familiar territory the following year with *Witness for the Prosecution*, a Billy Wilder film where he excelled as an attorney having the wool pulled over his eyes by Tyrone Power as a charming murderer. Lanchester won a Best Supporting Actress Oscar for playing a nurse who's trying to stop Laughton ruining his health with his unhealthy eating and smoking. If one substitutes tobacco with young boys, it's possible to procure a picture of what their offscreen life together must have been like.

But whatever went on behind closed doors—or, more to the point, didn't—they kept up a good show of being physical together when people were around. Lanchester's friend Benita Armstrong observed: "I assumed they weren't very sexually involved from the way they never left each other alone in public. They were always *mauling* each other" (Callow, 1987: 282).

Laughton played a disastrous *King Lear* on stage in 1959. Its failure to interest audiences depressed him almost as much as the debacle of *The Night of the Hunter*. In his last two films, *Spartacus* (1960) and *Advise & Consent* (1962), he was a senator. On the set of the latter film, Henry Fonda called him a gay slur name, something he could never forgive (Lanchester, 1983: 235).

He died of cancer in 1962. On his deathbed he converted to Roman Catholicism, a move that may have been an attempt to salve the sins of his past. His manager, Paul Gregory, told the journalist Barry Norman that Laughton had a veritable ménage of male lovers during his marriage to Lanchester: "Some of them would end up in prison and you'd get calls from wardens and letters threatening him . . . They were the dregs . . . they'd come and go . . . I didn't have much to do except to write the checks for him and hide them from Elsa and his accountants" (Callow, 1987: 284). Because he despised the face that stared back at him from the mirror, his biographer Simon Callow surmised, he surrounded himself with young boys, "feeding off their beauty, hoping that by exposure to it in sufficient quantities he might catch it and suddenly find himself a member of that exclusive club, the beautiful of the earth" (Callow, 286).

Further Reading
Callow, Simon. 1987. *Charles Laughton: A Difficult Actor*. London: Methuen.
Hadleigh, Boze, ed. 1994. *Hollywood Babble On*. New York: Birch Lane.
Higham, Charles. 1976. *Charles Laughton: An Intimate Biography*. London: Coronet.

Jarman, Colin, ed. 1991. *The Guinness Dictionary of Poisonous Quotes.* London: Guinness Publishing.

Lanchester, Elsa. 1983. *Herself.* New York: St. Martin's Press.

McClelland, Doug, ed. 1987. *StarSpeak: Hollywood on Everything.* Boston and London: Faber & Faber.

O'Hara, Maureen, and John Nicoletti. 2005. *'Tis Herself: An Autobiography.* Dublin: TownHouse.

Liberace (1919–87)

As was the case with Elvis Presley, Liberace's twin brother died at birth. And, like Presley, he grew up in poverty. "I never had a chance to be a kid," he once said (Parish, 2004: 132).

After he became established as a singer, he was informed it wasn't advisable in show business to have a mother as a best friend, so he stopped referring to her in such terms, as was his practice heretofore. Instead he went the Rock Hudson route. He exaggerated the importance of a relationship he had with a woman he knew, Joanne Rio, to make it look like he was straight. They even became engaged to be married, or so at least he claimed, but parted before they went to the altar. By then Rio could be dispensed with: she'd served her purpose in giving him heterosexual street cred.

Liberace secured the lead in only one film, *Sincerely Yours* (1955). He played a blind pianist in it. He received his first and only screen kiss here from Dorothy Malone. He refused the role Rod Steiger took in *The Loved One* because, he said, it was an "effeminate mama's boy." Instead, with typical Liberace logic, he played a gay casket salesman in the film (Braun, 2002: 161).

Rumors of his being gay dogged him all his life. They refused to go away no matter how many women appeared on his arm. (Like Rio, the skating star Sonja Henie was another "date.") Such rumors weren't surprising considering his elaborate stage getups and general demeanor. In 1957, the scandal sheet *Confidential* published an article titled, "Why Liberace's Theme Song Should Be 'Mad about the Boy.'" It understandably enraged him. The article documented instances where he'd been in compromising situations with young men. Liberace ran to his lawyers and sued. He won the case, but the imbroglio didn't endear himself to other gay people. They felt this kind of subterfuge smacked of hypocrisy.

The *Daily Mirror* went into adjectival overload when it described him as a "deadly, winking, sniggering, snuggling, chromium-plated, scent-impregnated, luminous, quivering, giggling, fruit-flavored, mincing, ice-covered heap of mother love." He sued again, because of what he said was an "implication" of being gay (Summers, 2005: 200). Referring to this as an "implication" was surely an understatement.

Liberace had the unqualified support of his fans whenever his sexuality was challenged. The "blue rinse brigade" was always on hand to defend his masculinity to, as one writer put it, "the last hatpin"—despite his "feathered cloaks and bejeweled jumpsuits" (Braun, 2002: 161).

Asked once if he was gay, he replied, "I don't believe entertainers should publicly air their sexual tastes. I've always admitted my act borders on drag but I'm not a female impersonator. I have a general family audience appeal and I don't want to develop a gay following." He seemed to be cutting off his blood supply here. Perhaps this realization led him to add, "With a name like Liberace, I'm for anything that has L-I-B in it, and that includes gay lib" (Parish, 2004: 138).

As late as 1973, he was still vehemently denying his orientation, insisting the only reason he never married was there was so much divorce in his family history. He said he was tired of journalists writing stories about his double life that were "cancerous with innuendo" (Parish, 137).

In 1977 he met a man called Scott Thorson. He was fifty-seven at the time and Thorson a mere eighteen. He moved in with him and became his significant other for many years. As far as the public was concerned, Thorson was merely one of his staff, but they were practically inseparable from one another during these years. It was even thought Liberace sent Thorson to a plastic surgeon to have his face remodeled in his image. There were also stories about his adopting him as his son at one stage.

Their relationship fell apart in 1982 with Thorson being ejected from Liberace's plush Beverly Hills pad. He replaced him with the eighteen-year-old Cary James. This wasn't a situation Thorson was going to take lying down—to coin a phrase. Later that year, he filed a $113 million palimony suit against his ex-lover. Three years later the case was settled out of court, the singer digging into his pocket to the tune of $95,000 to see Thorson off. Considering the magnitude of the original claim, he got off relatively lightly.

By now he was suffering from AIDS, the disease that killed his friend Rock Hudson in 1985. But unlike Hudson, he refused to come clean about his sexuality. He continued such denials until the moment he drew his last breath in February 1987. An autopsy concluded he had indeed died of AIDS. James Brady understandably inquired, "What would candor have cost Liberace? Do you think the blue-haired ladies would have smashed their records and torn up their tickets to the music hall if, a few years ago, he'd talked openly? I doubt it. He wasn't selling macho up there" (Hadleigh, 2013: 129).

William Hale directed a sanitized version of his life in 1988. Simply called *Liberace*, it managed the unique feat of traversing his whole life without mentioning two significant words. One was "homosexual." The other was "AIDS."

Michael Douglas played him brilliantly in the 2013 film *Beyond the Candelabra*. It dealt mainly with this relationship with Thorson. Up until now, Douglas had been mainlining a hypermasculine persona in a plethora of unashamedly sexist films like *Fatal Attraction* (1987) and *Basic Instinct* (1992). In these a primarily sexist zeitgeist exhibited itself. In both films the women were murderous and one bisexual. Douglas was content to use them for sexual favors until the going got rough. A woman also came off badly in another Douglas venture, *Disclosure* (1994), pursing him like a predator on a bogus sexual harassment charge after he failed to reciprocate her interest in him. But in *Behind the Candelabra*, in one of the most amazing U-turns of any alpha male's career, he got in touch with his feminine side. He played Liberace with such conviction, one could be forgiven for thinking he'd spent his whole career finessing such androgyny instead of debunking it.

Related Films

Sincerely Yours (1955); *Liberace: Behind the Music* (1988); *Behind the Candelabra* (2013).

Further Reading

Braun, Eric. 2002. *Frightening the Horses: Gay Icons of the Cinema*. London: Reynolds & Hearn.

Faris, Jocelyn. 1995. *Liberace: A Bio-Bibliography*. Westport, CT: Greenwood Publishing.

Hadleigh, Boze. 2013. *Hollywood Gays*. New York: Magnus Books.

Parish, James Robert. 2004. *The Hollywood Book of Scandals*. New York: McGraw-Hill.

Summers, Claude J. 2005. *The Queer Encyclopedia of Film and Television*. San Francisco: Cleis Publishing.

Thorson, Scott. 2013. *Behind the Candelabra: My Life with Liberace*. London: Head of Zeus.

L.I.E. (2001)

"There are lanes going east, there are lanes going west, and there are lanes going straight to hell." That's the way Howie Blitzer (Paul Dano) introduces audiences to the Long Island Expressway (the *L.I.E.* of the title) in this strange, beguiling film. Sometimes he stands on a railing of the bridge crossing the expressway with his arms outstretched as if he's about to jump off it.

On the surface it's the story of a middle-aged pederast who preys on a fifteen-year-old boy, but it would be too easy to view it solely in these terms. Director/writer Michael Cuesta has a certain amount of sympathy for the predator, played brilliantly by Brian Cox. He presents his weakness as a morally gray area deserving of our sympathy as much as anything else.

As the film begins, Howie has recently lost his mother in a road accident on the expressway. His father (Bruce Altman) is a building contractor who spends more time with his new girlfriend than he does with Howie.

Howie is friends with a rootless bunch of teenagers who burglarize houses. Their ringleader is a boy called Gary (Billy Kay). In the course of one of these burglaries, they're interrupted by "Big John" Horrigan (Cox). He's a Vietnam veteran with a larger-than-life personality. A rent boy lives with him as his sexual partner.

When Howie's father is arrested for using unsafe building materials, Horrigan becomes a kind of substitute father to Howie. He invites him to his house and shows off his possessions to him, including a state-of-the-art car.

If Horrigan doesn't quite win audiences over with his personality, he doesn't appear as a threatening figure either. "You're just like James Bond," Howie tells him, "except James Bond doesn't go around blowing boys." He knows exactly what he's getting into with Horrigan, and to that extent he isn't afraid of him. Howie also displays some gay tendencies to complicate the situation further.

In an early scene, he recognizes a Chagall painting in Horrigan's house when he visits him to return a gun he's stolen from him. A bemused Horrigan chortles, "We're dealing with a higher class of criminal with you!" Howie is also clued in to films, picking up a reference to *Casablanca* in a later scene when Horrigan quotes from the movie.

The boy who lives with Horrigan is there for the visit where Howie returns the gun. He witnesses Horrigan showing Howie a pornographic film. One presumes this is his way of grooming him for sex. The implication is that he's about to become Horrigan's latest acquisition. "You should be ashamed of yourself," the boy says to Horrigan after Howie leaves the house. "I am," Horrigan says vaguely. "I always am." Here, as elsewhere, Cuesta adopts a nuanced approach to his pederasty.

Horrigan changes his attitude toward Howie after showing him the blue movie, becoming almost a cuddly figure for him. One is never quite sure what he wants from him or what he's going to do with him. He doesn't seem to know himself either. The pair of them become friends without benefits. One wonders if Horrigan has changed. Or does he simply feel sorry for Howie because of his father's problems with the law?

The film is open to the charge of fuzziness, but in such fuzziness lies its strength and depth. Cuesta refuses to simplify any of his characters or to judge them—not only Horrigan but all of the others too: the sexually confused Howie, his conniving father, his shiftless friends with their fake bravado and streetwise smart-aleckry.

"Big John" is a creepy figure at the beginning of the film, a dirty old man who sniffs a piece of Howie's trousers that have been ripped off in the burglary as he goes in search of him, but later on he becomes more like a genial patriarch to him—the patriarch Altman should be but isn't.

Horrigan isn't a standard pedophile. In the first half of the film he talks about bartering Howie's burglary debt to pay him for sex, but he doesn't carry through on this. In another scene he even accuses Howie (playfully, of course) of trying to seduce *him*. A complex man, he paces around his house like Hugh Hefner, dropping literary quotations such as, "Hail to thee, blithe spirit," or crooning the Irish song "Danny Boy" at his piano.

L.I.E. is a film about ambiguity—sexual, financial, geographical. There are lanes going east and lanes going west on the expressway, but there are also lanes in people's minds. Howie is between two motorways, two fathers, and his bisexuality. He says to his father when he visits him in prison, "Your whole life is a lie." This is another part of Cuesta's ambiguity. Most of the characters lead double lives of one sort or another.

Cox thought of the film as a rite-of-passage story rather than a tale of pederasty. "It's about sexual awakening," he said, "whether one is gay or straight." It was meant to unsettle audiences: "At its best it throws questions at you. It puts things into the ring for debate. That's why I'm very proud of this film" (Davies, 2008: 156).

It's also the story of a boy who's trying to come to terms with the loss of his mother. She's hardly referred to at all in the film, but at one stage Howie says, "I can still smell her perfume." In another scene he puts on her lipstick. Is this a sign of androgyny or a desperate search for any link with her? Cuesta lets the audience make its own mind up.

He used a lot of improvisation in the direction. In one scene he asked Altman to put more feeling into a scene. Altman overcompensated so much he ended up breaking a window in the car he was driving. It belonged to Cuesta, but he didn't mind. It was worth it to him to get what he wanted from the scene. In another scene, Altman's lawyer gets a heart attack in the middle of his lunch and dies. Altman thinks he's faking the attack. He starts to laugh at him before the horror of the situation dawns on him. At times like this, one is in the realm of black comedy.

L.I.E. is a film that teases one frequently without fulfilling its premises or threats. "Horrigan takes a pass on the boy," Cuesta said in an interview about it (*L.I.E.* DVD: Michael Cuesta Commentary). That doesn't mean he's reformed. Toward the end of the film, he goes back to a place where he's in the habit of picking up rent boys. Here he's shot dead by the one he's just abandoned. It might look like justice has been served, but this isn't Cuesta's intention. He's sympathetic to his plight.

Cox is wonderful in the film, mixing menace and erudition adeptly. He's manipulative but also humane. When he sings "Danny Boy," he becomes almost poignant. One of the lines is, "You must go and I must die"—a foreshadowing of his own fate after getting rid of the rent boy to make way for Howie. Dano is wonderful as Howie too. Cuesta tested over a hundred young boys for the part, but he always came back to him. "He has a way of not acting," he said (*L.I.E.* DVD: Michael Cuesta Commentary). A director can give no higher compliment to an actor than that.

Related Films
Death in Venice (1971); *My Own Private Idaho* (1991); *American Beauty* (1999); *Mysterious Skin* (2004).

Further Reading
Daniel, Lisa, and Claire Jackson. 2003. *The Bent Lens: A World Guide to Gay and Lesbian Film.* Los Angeles: Alyson Publications.
Davies, Steven Paul. 2008. *Out at the Movies: A History of Gay Cinema.* Herts, UK: Kamera Books.

The Living End (1991)

"We're victims of the sexual revolution," says AIDS-afflicted Luke (Mike Dytri) to his fellow victim Jon (Craig Gilmore) in this tragicomic road movie from Gregg Araki. "The generation before us had all the fun and we get to pick up the tab."

With that bitter attitude, this no-account pair hit the road hell-bent on having their last adventure before the Reaper calls. Along the way they meet homophobic killers and assorted weirdoes. Araki's Eliotesque wasteland of the mind and heart captures them in existential free-flow riding high on the road to hell.

Gregg Araki (1959–)

Born in Los Angeles to Japanese-American parents, Araki attended college in Santa Barbara and, after graduating, the University of Southern California's School of Cinematic Arts. His first film was *Three Bewildered People in the Night* (1987), a low-budget feature about the romance between a video artist, her boyfriend, and a gay male performance artist. He followed this with *The Long Weekend (O'Despair)* in 1989, another low-budget movie shot in black-and-white 16mm. It concerned three college couples getting together for some angst-ridden navel-gazing. *The Living End* brought him to a more general audience. He then made what he called his Teen Apocalypse Trilogy, comprising *Totally F***ed Up* (1993), *The Doom Generation* (1995), and *Nowhere* (1997). He made the trilogy to try to understand, if not stem, the tide of teen suicides he saw around him at this time.

*Totally F***ed Up* fuses the stories of six gay adolescents undergoing various forms of frustration about their orientations and their general lives. It exudes a Bret Easton Ellis vibe as they mate, relate, and separate to the backdrop of a cacophonous soundtrack that includes the works of the Jesus and Mary Chain., Pale Saints, Ride, The Wolfgang Press, Ministry, and His Name Is Alive. Four of them are gay men; the other two a lesbian couple. Araki mixes dysfunctionality with humor in a film that appears at times like a documentary. He zones in on the aimless lives of a confused sextet who see love lasting only as long as "a squirt in the dark."

The Doom Generation was a road movie about a heterosexual teenage couple and a bisexual male drifter who encourages them to push the boundaries of sexual experimentation after they unintentionally kill an LA convenience store owner, while *Nowhere* dealt with an eighteen-year-old boy, his girlfriend, her girlfriend, and a space alien wandering the streets. The film starred Kathleen Robinson, whom Araki now began dating. This led to rumors—which he subsequently confirmed—that he was bisexual. He later cast her in *Splendor* (1999), a postmodern reworking of Noel Coward's screwball comedy of the 1930s. Their relationship broke up shortly after the cameras stopped rolling. He was back to more familiar ground with *Mysterious Skin* (2004), another adaptation. This one dealt with a baseball coach who abuses two eight-year-old members of his team, one of whom responds to his advances.

In 2007 he won the Filmmaker on the Edge award at the Provincetown International Film Festival with *Smiley Face*. *Kaboom* (2010) was a sensation at Cannes, winning the inaugural Queer Palm award. A sci-fi comedy thriller about a bisexual college student and his friends, it had a dream-fueled, semisurreal style that bespoke quasi-apocalyptic notions of a bad moon rising. New York's Museum of Art and Design honored him with a retrospective, *God Help Me: Gregg Araki*, in 2013. Since then he's directed episodes of *American Crime* and *Red Oaks* (both 2016) as well as *13 Reasons Why* (2017–18) and *Riverdale* (2018).

The sociopathic Luke has killed a policeman offscreen. Jon—a film critic—is more subdued, but he's attracted to the aura of danger Luke exudes. Araki echoes Godard (the names Jon and Luke are probably a play on his hyphenated Christian name) in his savage indictment of a world that's happy to consign these lost souls to the dustbin of history without so much as a consolatory obituary in *Gay Times*. It's the ultimate "what the hell" trip, freedom being Kris Kristofferson's other word for nothing left to lose as they throw caution to the wind in their self-destructive odyssey.

In one scene a woman finds her husband in bed with a hustler. She hacks him to death with a kitchen knife, telling him, "It's not the seventies anymore, when being married to a bisexual was fashionable." Earlier on, a doctor tells Jon he's HIV-positive in the same tone of voice he might tell him he's got influenza. "No doubt AIDS is the epicenter of the film's rage," Roy Grundmann wrote, "but it's expressed mainly through a curious mix of *Dr. Strangelove* humor and the kind of campy horror of giant insect movies" (*Cineaste*, March 1993).

The fact that his characters are looking death in the face gives Araki the platform from which he can vent his wrath at those who've allowed AIDS to become so dangerous so soon. "Let's go to Washington," Luke suggests, "and inject our blood into the president. Wanna bet they'll find a cure in thirty seconds?" Araki dedicated his admittedly "irresponsible" movie to the hundreds of thousands who have died, and the hundreds of thousands more who *would* die, because of a White House full of Republican malfunctioners. (George Bush was presiding over them at the time.)

The acting in the film isn't all it might be, and some of the scenes overegg Araki's polemical omelet, but this was still a necessary antidote to the soft-pedaling road movies made at the time, and the soft-pedaling AIDS ones as well. Araki denied the accusation that it was intended to be a more aggressive version of *Thelma & Louise*, claiming it owed more to retro-noir films like *Bonnie and Clyde, Gun Crazy*, and *They Live by Night*. It was, he declared, first and foremost a love story where sex, desire, and passion became mixed up with violence. It's probably more applicable to talk about it in relation to a film like *Breathless* with its doomed lovers and multiple shifts in tone. Or even *Bringing Up Baby* with its repressed protagonist being simultaneously liberated and destroyed by a semi-deranged free spirit. It was the punk aspect of the film, Araki believed, that made it so threatening to the prevailing "vanilla" gay culture (Hayes, 2007: 38–9).

Peter Biskind praised it for being an exercise in agitprop that "mocked the positive role models so dear to the gay activists who made such a fuss over Sharon Stone's homicidal lesbian in *Basic Instinct*," substituting in her stead a pair of "proto-criminals who fantasized about infecting then-president George Bush with their diseased blood" (Biskind, 2007: 117). Araki liked it because it substituted the "positive gay imagery" of films like *Longtime Companion* with something more visceral (Summers, 2005: 31). For B. Ruby Rich, it was an existential film for a postporn age, a study of a stud and a john in "renegotiated terrain" (Rich, 2013: 27).

Araki is regarded as one of the central figures in New Queer Cinema, not only for his explosive subject matter but also the staccato style of direction he deploys to convey the fractured lives of his characters. In *The Living End*, as in so many of his music-soaked penetrations into the heart of darkness, he goes everywhere and nowhere. With a cast that includes the former Andy Warhol star Mary Woronov as a lesbian serial killer, it was derided for misogyny, but this was unfair. Araki's target is everyone. This is equal opportunity irresponsibility.

Jon tries to get away from Luke at the end, but Luke knocks him unconscious with the butt of his gun. He then licks the blood from his face and ties him up. When he regains consciousness, Luke rapes him while holding the barrel of the gun in his mouth. This is not, repeat not, *The Waltons*.

"What are you waiting for?" Jon screams at him. "Just do it." But the gun is out of bullets. The two men are condemned to live for whatever time remains to them.

In the final shot, they embrace on a deserted beach, locked together in a condemned love-hate pact. Some viewers would have preferred Armageddon, but Araki rarely serves up what's expected of him. This is literally the "living" end for two post-Kerouac bohemians slouching toward a dubious endgame in the only way they know how.

A love story for our time, in other words, framed against a silhouette of destruction birthed by the ripples of the "gay plague."

Related Films
Badlands (1973); *Swoon* (1992); *Natural Born Killers* (1994); *On the Road* (2012).

Further Reading
Aaron, Michele. 2004. *New Queer Cinema: A Critical Reader*. New Brunswick, NJ: Rutgers University Press.
Araki, Gregg. 1994. *The Living End: An Irresponsible Movie*. New York: William Morrow.
Biskind, Peter. 2007. *Down and Dirty Pictures: Miramax, Sundance and the Rise of Independent Film*. London: Bloomsbury.
Cineaste, March 1993.
Hart, Kylo-Patrick R. 2010. *Images from a Generation Doomed: The Films and Career of Gregg Araki*. Lanham, MD: Rowman & Littlefield.
Hayes, Matthew. 2007. *The View from Here: Conversations with Gay and Lesbian Filmmakers*. Vancouver: Arsenal Pulp Press.
Rich, B. Ruby. 2013. *New Queer Cinema: The Director's Cut*. Durham, NC, and London: Duke University Press.
Summers, Claude J. 2005. *The Queer Encyclopedia of Film and Television*. San Francisco: Cleis Publishing.
Tasker, Yvonne. 2010. *Fifty Contemporary Film Directors*. London: Routledge.

Longtime Companion (1990)

On a typically sunny morning on Fire Island, a group of friends wake up to a newspaper report of what's described as a "gay cancer" striking the United States. Director Norman René captures the "rabbit in the headlights" moment in his moving mosaic of a community in pain.

A film that combines forensic accuracy from a documentary-style standpoint with understated empathy for the suffering of a cross-section of sensitive souls, *Longtime Companion* hits all the right notes in its heartfelt inventory of gay people struck down with a disease that was as mysterious as it was frightening at the time in which the film is set.

The screenplay was written by Craig Lucas. Three couples constitute the main story. "Fuzzy" (Stephen Caffrey) is an attorney living with gym trainer Willy (Campbell Scott). Howard (Patrick Cassidy) is living with office worker Paul (John Dossett). Sean (Mark Lamos) is a writer of soap opera scripts living with David (Bruce Davison). David is a wealthy investor. The other members of the cast consist of John (Dermot Mulroney), an unattached friend, and Lisa (Mary Louise Parker), Willy's friend from childhood.

Some of the characters become more ill than others as the film goes on. Some become terminal. What they share in common is bewilderment at the sudden uprooting of their erstwhile comfortable lives. From now on, such lives will be characterized by hospital visits, fearful diagnoses, and emotional farewells.

The film has an interesting style of narration, showing one day per year from 1981 to 1989 as it documents the rising death toll. The emphasis is on solidarity rather than sensationalism, but René also highlights the negative reactions of the characters' employers to them, such as the TV station that cancels a role Howard had been promised. The film's title is the phrase newspapers of the era customarily used to refer to the survivor of a gay relationship in obituaries of the deceased. It gave a clue to the nature of the relationship rather than stating it explicitly.

Lucas made it his business to write about the day-to-day aspects of having the disease: "Who buys the groceries, who changes the diapers, who holds the dying man's hand, who calls the mortician." It pained him to reflect on the fact that the gay community didn't go to AIDS-themed movies as much as they might have. *Parting Glances* lost money, for instance, and so did *Buddies*: "It wasn't like you could assume the 25 to 30 million gay and lesbian Americans would go to see this movie. They go to *Batman*, like everyone else" (Hadleigh, 1993: 252).

Tragically, he went on to contract the disease himself. He documented the traumatic details of his experience to an interviewer in an evocative manner. "AIDS exploded into my life in the summer of 1981," he said. "There was no corner of my existence that wasn't completely threatened and fractured and in many cases, obliterated by it. Peace of mind, political naïveté, trust, hope, friendship, financial solidity—every single facet of my life was cast into a sudden and terrifying light. My lovers, friends and colleagues were getting sick and dying all around me. I was terrified for my life. It seemed like I lived every day and night in a cold sweat of panic and rage" (Hays, 2007: 199).

Without any special pleading, the film charts the change of René's dramatis personae from fun-loving innocents to fretful philosophers staring over their shoulders as time's winged chariot breathes down on them threateningly. Lucas wanted to display as much emotion as he could, saying, "Anyone who can formulate a stiff upper lip is to me already dead" (Lessard, 2008: 178).

Davison gave what was regarded as the film's best performance. The scene where he tells Lamos to "let go" after bringing him home from hospital to die at home was heart-scaldingly good. One knows how much it devastates him to lose his friend, which makes his words doubly emotional. The performance won him a New York Film Critics Award, a Golden Globe, and the National Society of Film Critics award for Best Supporting Actor. He was also nominated for an Academy Oscar, but he lost out to Joe Pesci for *Goodfellas*.

The film had a troubled history. When Lucas first floated it around the major studios, he was informed he'd never get backing unless he made Davison into a heterosexual woman. Americans hated gay men, he was told flatly. Thankfully, due to René's direction, they hated them a little less after viewing it.

In the final scene, three of the characters who survive stroll along a beach dreaming about the day when AIDS will be cured. A crowd suddenly surrounds them, including those they've lost to the disease. The mood is upbeat; everyone has suffered enough.

Longtime Companion was a roaring success with the critics and the public alike. It won the Audience Favorite Award at Sundance and was nominated for an Oscar by AMPAS. The profits went to AIDS organizations like Gay Men's Health Crisis, which increased respect for it. If it has a fault it's the fact that it locates itself too much in an upper-crust echelon. Also, it seems to sideline women. (Parker is the only significant female member of the cast.) Such caveats apart, it's a deeply felt exposé of a latter-day Black Plague during its decadelong reign of terror. If one doesn't learn enough about the characters as one should by the time the film reaches its visionary conclusion, it still achieves a lot in such a relatively short span of time.

Related Films
Parting Glances (1986); *Common Threads: Stories from the Quilt* (1989); *This Is Dedicated: Grieving When a Partner Dies* (1991).

Further Reading
Hadleigh, Boze. 1993. *The Lavender Screen.* New York: Citadel Press.
Hays, Matthew. 2007. *The View from Here: Conversations with Gay and Lesbian Filmmakers.* Vancouver, BC: Arsenal Pulp Press.
Lessard, John, ed. 2008. *To Quote a Queer.* Philadelphia: Quirk Books.
Pendergast, Tom, and Sara Pendergast, eds. 1998. *Gay and Lesbian Theatre; Volume 2.* Detroit: St. James Press.
Stewart, Steve. 1994. *Gay Hollywood Film and Video Guide: 75 Years of Gay and Lesbian Images in the Movies.* Laguna Hills, CA: Companion Publications.

Looking for Langston (1989)

Describing itself in the opening credits as "a meditation on Langston Hughes and the Harlem Renaissance," this monochrome mood piece dedicated to the memory of James Baldwin is much more than that. Along with Marlon Riggs's *Tongues Untied* (1989), it was one of the first independent productions to address the topic of being black and gay.

Opening with the original radio broadcast that transmitted the news of Hughes's death in 1967, it doesn't so much try to define the essence of the poet as etch in the world he inhabited. He's just one member of Isaac Julien's cast of characters who float around his stylized tableaus like friendly ghosts.

Some of them are elegantly dressed and some are nude. Tuxedoed couples dance and drink champagne in what looks like an up-market speakeasy. "Why should I be blue?" says the narrator. "I've been blue all night through." The voiceover is soporific, lulling one with its susurrating strains. The camerawork is smoky and atmospheric, making this a strictly art house piece with only a passing nod toward biography status.

It's only forty-two minutes long, but within that time frame it manages to capture both the pulse of the Renaissance and the jazz/blues ambience of the Cotton

Club clientele. It doesn't make any claims toward narrative exactitude, preferring to work in images that burn themselves into the subconscious. Men from high society disport themselves with arch abandon as archival footage of the era counterpoints the action. This was taken by Robert Mapplethorpe and collected by Julien's colleague Sunil Gupta.

The plot—if such it could be called—is wafer thin. Hughes (Ben Ellison) has a dream in which he seeks out Beauty (Matthew Baidoo). At first it seems to reject him, but when he awakes, it's sleeping beside him.

A funeral is taking place. Hughes's poetry acts as an accompaniment to it. Julien blends his words with those of writers like Bruce Nugent and Essex Hemphill. A patchwork quilt of soft-focus scenes build up a languorous collage of a world that seems to be receding even as one views it. Nina Kellgren's cinematography is majestic, underpinning Julien's ambition to tabulate black gay identity in a manner that's both explicit and coy.

A sense of formalized reverie permeates this homoerotic divertissement. In addition to the work of Hughes and the Beat poets, one is proffered quotations from people such as Kenneth Anger and Jean Cocteau, James Baldwin and Toni Morrison. The cumulative effect of the audiovisual smorgasbord is decadently intoxicating.

At the time the film was made, it was seen as heretical to even hint at the fact that Hughes might have been gay. He had a reverential status within the literary stratosphere, and the thinking was that this shouldn't be inveighed against. There was also a perception that to be black and gay was a double ignominy, "a sin against the tribe." From this point of view, Julien was playing with fire.

The film caused a furor at the New York Film Festival when it was first screened there (*Screen International*, August 25, 1990). Julien tried to soften the blow by dealing with Hughes's sexuality in a conceptual manner, parading his cast of characters as chimeras who drift dream-like across the screen to call up whatever reactions they will. It was a reasonable compromise, but the Hughes estate still tried to have his film pulled from circulation. Their stated reason, interestingly, wasn't obscenity or even the unwarranted invasion of a hallowed reputation. Instead they argued that Julien breached copyright restrictions in the relaying of Hughes's lyrics. The upshot was that the sound was turned down during some screenings of the film while such lyrics were being spoken. It was a move that placated the estate but didn't make the problem go away.

Julien always feared something like this would happen; hence the film's tentative title. The passage of time, thankfully, has meant that issues that were once inflammatory have now settled down. He deserves credit for tilting at a sacred windmill like Hughes and also opening debates about the possible orientations of other black icons of the time, such as Claude McKay and Alain Locke.

A hallmark of New Queer Cinema and a film that's popular for analysis on university courses, *Looking for Langston* is Julien's acknowledged *meisterwork*, a less-is-more offering that wasn't to everyone's liking because of its slightness. Repeated viewings will hopefully help it increase its fan base.

Despite its copyright problems, a tsunami of hosannas greeted it upon its release. It won the Teddy Award for Best Short Film at the 1989 Berlin Film

Festival and was also shown at that festival in 2016 to celebrate the thirtieth anniversary of the awards.

Related Films
Urinal (1988); *Tongues Untied* (1989); *James Baldwin: The Price of the Ticket* (1990); *Paris Is Burning* (1990); *B. D. Women* (1994).

Further Reading
Hawkeswood, William G. 2006. *One of the Children: Gay Black Men in Harlem*. Berkeley: University of California Press.
Hughes, Langston. 1990. *The Ways of White Folks*. London: Vintage.
Munoz, Jose Esteban. 1999. *Disidentifications: Queers of Color and the Performance of Politics*. Minneapolis: University of Minnesota Press.
Pavda, Gilad. 2014. *Queer Nostalgia in Cinema and Pop Culture*. London: Palgrave Macmillan.
Rutherford, Jonathan, ed. 1990. *Identity: Community, Culture, Difference*. London: Lawrence & Wishart.
Screen International, August 25, 1990.
Valentine, David. 2007. *Imagining Transgender: An Ethnography of a Category*. Durham, NC: Duke University Press.

Sidney Lumet (1924–2011)

In his riveting book *The Celluloid Closet*, Vito Russo praised Lumet for the affectionate manner with which he portrayed the character of Sonny Wortzik in *Dog Day Afternoon*. Sadly, he felt the film itself was an "ultimate freak show" that used a sensational story to titillate square audiences (Russo, 1987: 178–9). This was harsh. The story might have been sensational, but Lumet's treatment of it, even if it relegated Sonny's male wife to "also-ran" status, was both charming and ominous. Sonny's gayness was played down to give one a better insight into other aspects of his personality.

Sonny is married to both a man and a woman in the film. Russo's main problems were with Lumet's depiction of his male wife, Leon, played by Chris Sarandon. Sarandon is sidelined in the film, but this is as it should be; it's Sonny's film. He robs a bank to pay for a sex change operation Leon is hoping to have. This robbery happened for real in 1972. Lumet takes some liberties with the way events unfolded, but he still preserves their essence.

Lumet created another sexual milestone in 1966 with his screen adaptation of Mary McCarthy's novel *The Group*. This was the first time the word "lesbian" was spoken in a major Hollywood film. It's used by Larry Hagman to refer to his bisexual lover, Candice Bergen, in the scene where she returns from Europe with a masculine baroness in tow. "I never pegged you as a Sapphie," Hagman remarks, "or to put it crudely, a lesbo." The vocabulary was fruity, but this was as far as the film's pioneering spirit went. It was so restrained, United Artists dispensed with the ad campaign it'd planned to exploit it.

Russo also had problems with the gay jazz musician in Lumet's *The Pawnbroker* in 1967, and Martin Balsam's prissy antique dealer in *The Anderson Tapes* four years later. With his pompadour hairstyle and limp wrists, Balsam here plays the old maid who blithely asks Sean Connery, the film's main star, who's just been released from prison, "Meet anyone interesting in your cell?" This kind of trivial humor underscored his performance in general, causing *Variety* to note: "With the flashiest role and most of the laughs, Balsam swishes off with the honors, although gay activists will take umbrage at the general depiction of gay people as either aging queens with false eyelashes or willowy transvestites who live like Maria Montez" (Parish, 1993: 15).

Balsam himself saw the role differently. "It certainly didn't harm my career," he said. "I'm sort of an ugly, stocky guy and I had no romantic image to protect. My whole career was built on character parts and a flamboyant gay guy was just fine with me" (Porter and Prince, 2010: 458).

Lumet featured Michael Caine and Christopher Reeve as two gay men in *Deathtrap* in 1980, based on Ira Levin's long-running Broadway play. Caine is a failed playwright in desperate need of a hit while Reeve, his protégé, comes up with a script Caine tries to claim as his own. The pair of them conspire to kill Caine's wife, played by Dyan Cannon, and then one another.

The film had more red herrings than in a Leningrad fish market. Their gay bonding doesn't emerge until relatively late on in the proceedings. It was dismissed as a farce by many critics. Lumet saw it merely as a fun movie with some interesting twists. It was never meant to treat being gay seriously. For some people that was the general problem with Lumet when he featured gay people in his films. *Dog Day Afternoon* apart, they were usually peripheral figures, and sometimes caricatures.

A Warner Bros. spokesman thought *Deathtrap* would have worked better without the gay theme. If it hadn't had major stars in it, nor been helmed by a major director, he doubted it would have even reached the screen (Hadleigh, 1993: 198). When it went to TV, a kiss exchanged between Caine and Reeve was excised. Said Reeve, "I don't think America was ready to see Superman kiss another guy" (Stewart, 1993: 60). Caine was more convincing as a bisexual in *California Suite* a few years previously. Reeve would go on to play a gay pedophile in *A Bump in the Night* in 1991.

Lumet recovered some ground with gay audiences by featuring Harvey Fierstein—arguably the busiest gay actor of the 1980s—as a department store employee in the amiable *Garbo Talks* in 1984. Vito Russo's last salvo against Lumet concerned his rare Hollywood venture *The Morning After* in 1986. (Most of his films had been made in New York or thereabouts up to this.) This, Russo claimed, was a film in which the beleaguered director reduced gays to the level of minstrels who provided "comic relief from a murder mystery" (Russo, 1987: 254).

Lumet became controversial for a final time as a result of his 1990 movie, *Q&A*. This had Nick Nolte as a corrupt policeman who, in one scene, grabs a cross-dressing hooker in the crotch to intimidate him. Later on he abuses a gay character played by Paul Calderon, as well as a trans friend of Calderon's (Jose Malpica). It's a pity this fine director made LGBTQ characters into one-dimensional figures so often in his career. But he wasn't homophobic, as claimed by some of his detractors. He just seemed to have a blind spot in this area.

Further Reading

Boyer, Jay. 1993. *Sidney Lumet*. New York: Twayne Publishers.

Cunningham, Frank R. 1991. *Sidney Lumet: Film and Literary Vision*. Lexington: University Press of Kentucky.

Hadleigh, Boze, 1993. *The Lavender Screen*. New York: Citadel.

Lumet, Sidney. 1995. *Making Movies*. London: Bloomsbury.

Parish, James Robert. 1993. *Gays and Lesbians in Mainstream Cinema*. Jefferson, NC: McFarland.

Porter, Darwin, and Danforth Prince. 2010. *50 Years of Queer Cinema*. New York: Blood Moon Productions.

Rapf, Joanna E. 2006. *Sidney Lumet Interviews*. Jackson: University Press of Mississippi.

Russo, Vito. 1987. *The Celluloid Closet: Homosexuality in the Movies*. New York: Harper & Row.

Stewart, Steve. 1993. *Gay Hollywood Film and Video Guide*. Laguna Hills, CA: Companion Publications.

M

Midnight Cowboy (1969)

This film tells the story of would-be stud Joe Buck (Jon Voight) and the unlikely friendship he forms with a down-and-out tubercular hustler, Ratso Rizzo (Dustin Hoffman), during a hot summer in New York. It begins with Joe as a dishwasher in Texas. Bored with his life here, he heads for the Big Apple, where he hopes to make his fortune turning sexual tricks. He walks down Forty-Second Street in his silver-fringed jacket and cowboy hat, a transistor radio held close to his ear. Like an innocent abroad, he's fazed by everything he sees. A body lies on the street in front of him—asleep or dead. Nobody seems to mind too much. They walk by it.

In his innocence, Joe believes he's going to become rich by selling his body. This dream turns sour early on when a woman (Sylvia Miles) sticks him for a taxi fare instead of paying him for his "services." Other ungainly experiences follow as he comes to realize the city isn't the "bed" of opportunity he expected.

He meets Rizzo in a seedy bar. After some initial hustling, he tells him he wants to be his manager. He advises him to expand his operation to include men as well as women. Before long they're living together in a run-down apartment in a condemned building. This is a far cry from the five-star hotels he envisaged when he first hit the city. Director John Schlesinger hints at a gay element in their relationship. Schlesinger was gay himself, but not yet openly so.

Flashbacks to Joe's past reveal more about him than he himself is willing to. He's as defensive as Ratso when it comes to outlining any details about his character. One learns that he was raised by his mother and his grandmother. There's no sign of a father. Footage of the gang rape of a former girlfriend, and perhaps of himself, is intermixed with present events.

Ratso sets Joe up with a client (John McGiver) who turns out to be a religious extremist. Joe flees the room in terror. His dreams of becoming rich and successful seem more unlikely with each scene. Ratso tells him he has a dream of leaving the bricks and mortar of New York to go to Miami. Joe is willing to try to fund this trip.

After the two of them attend a psychedelic party, Ratso's TB starts to become worse. Winter is approaching and he shivers in the freezing cold of the apartment. When he sweats it's from his sickness, not the temperature. Joe now has to "go to work"—not so much to get rich as to earn enough money for them to be able to eat. The winter is coming on and all his dreams have turned to dust.

As Ratso's health weakens, Joe finds himself robbing an aging gay man (Barnard Hughes) to try to raise money for the trip to Miami. It would be an escape for both of them from the harshness of the city, but unfortunately it doesn't materialize. Ratso dies en route, to the backdrop of Harry Nilsson singing "Everybody's Talkin'," the song that became almost synonymous with the movie.

Both of their dreams have bitten the dust. One imagines Joe returning to his dishwashing job in the middle of nowhere having grown from boy to man in a way that's taken a huge toll on his self-esteem. Maybe, one imagines, he's been purified by suffering as he cradles his dead friend in his arms. As Nilsson sings "I'm goin' where the sun keeps shinin'," he underscores the optimism Joe has exhibited throughout the film. It seems to mock him now as his friend dies beside him. From now on the sun will shine only on Ratso's grave.

Midnight Cowboy was released just a month before the Stonewall riots. The timing was ideal. At the Oscar ceremonies it won Best Picture, Best Director, and Best Adapted Screenplay. Both Voight and Hoffman were nominated for Best Actor, but two stars nominated in the same category for the same film is usually a poisoned chalice, and so it proved here. John Wayne won instead for *True Grit*. It was really a Life Achievement Award in disguise for the aging cowpoke.

The film represents an unusual position in LGBTQ culture as it isn't ostensibly a gay work. In this sense it mirrors the position of its closeted director. One day it struck Hoffman that both he and Voight were meant to be gay. He asked Schlesinger why they weren't sleeping together. Schlesinger said, "Please! It was hard enough to get the financing!" He felt if it went down that road, such financing would have been withdrawn because of the conservatism of the time (*Vanity Fair*, March 2005).

Midnight Cowboy flirts with the notion that the pair are latently gay but leaves us (and them?) wondering. This adds to its curiosity if not its coyness. When Ratso's health deteriorates, the emotional connection between the two of them takes precedence over any sexual chemistry Schlesinger has suggested before this. At the end of the day, it's the story of two sheep in a city of wolves. They talk—and occasionally act—rough, but it's obvious they're just looking for a shoulder to cry on. This is the problem of the film, which purports to take us into the inner world of being gay in New York—like at the psychedelic party—but instead just presents us with perverse vignettes geared more to exhibit Joe's terrors than anything else. Whether he's running away from Jesus freaks like McGiver or self-loathing businessmen like Hughes, he's a small-town soul in a big-time suit, fooling nobody, not even Ratso, about his superstud ambitions.

The question of whether he can make it with women is a separate issue. Ratso helps him find himself, but he does so through the catharsis of his own suffering, the film ending on the age-old message of love being about giving rather than taking.

Midnight Cowboy offers us a two-tiered sexual world. On one side of it there's the pure and unconsummated relationship between Joe and Ratso; on the other the seedy demimonde where Joe hustles his wares to raise money for Ratso's trip to Florida. From that point of view, it isn't a gay-friendly film; only one that "permits" male-male relationships as long as they don't traverse boundaries, or involve backstreet assignations where men of questionable virtue relieve forbidden desires in tawdry fashion.

Schlesinger seems to be telling us that being gay is best when it's gentle rather than rough, an emotional rather than a primarily physical need. To that extent the film is almost prudish. This isn't to say one needed scenes of raunchy sex between Joe and Ratso to make it authentic; merely that its focus wasn't as wide as it might have been.

Ratso has to be "educated" into what constitutes machismo in the film. When he denounces Joe's cowboy outfit as something that's strictly for queers, Joe answers that this can't be true because John Wayne dressed like that and he was hardly queer. The irony is that Wayne was probably as intolerant as Ratso, as were many of the buckskin-clad heroes he played in his films. (A further irony, of course, is that this man "stole" an Oscar from under the noses of both stars that year, as mentioned, for *True Grit*.)

For all the film's surface modernity, *Midnight Cowboy* is basically an old-fashioned story about an innocent who comes from the sticks to the big city only to discover that the sidewalks weren't paved with gold. "I ain't a for-real cowboy," he tells us, "but I'm one hell of a stud." Well, at least half of that sentence is true.

Schlesinger's main achievement was probably the wonderful performance he drew from both leads, especially Hoffman. He worked incredibly hard at it, even going so far as to put stones in his shoes in one scene to accentuate his limp. In another one, in an effort to cough as realistically as he could, he threw up all over Voight's cowboy boots. Voight thought he did so on purpose and became annoyed (*Vanity Fair*, March 2005). The incident created an atmosphere of rivalry between them that lasted for most of the shoot. As Voight sighed at one point, "It was hard to upstage vomit" (Freedland, 1989: 68).

Related Films
Flesh (1968); *Lonesome Cowboys* (1968); *Scarecrow* (1973).

Further Reading
Bergen, Ronald. 1991. *Dustin Hoffman*. London: Virgin.
Buruma, Ian. 2006. *Conversations with John Schlesinger*. New York: Random House.
Freedland, Michael. 1989. *Dustin: A Biography of Dustin Hoffman*. London: Virgin.
Herlihy, James Leo. 1965. *Midnight Cowboy*. New York: Simon & Schuster.
Lang, Robert. 2002. *Masculine Interests*. New York: Columbia University.
Lewis, Jon. 2000. *Hollywood V. Hard Core: How the Struggle over Censorship Saved the Modern Film Industry*. New York and London: New York University Press.
Vanity Fair, March 2005.

Milk (2008)

Sean Penn won an Oscar for playing Harvey Milk in this biopic of the first openly gay man elected to public office. Tragically, Milk was assassinated within a year of that milestone achievement by a disgruntled former city supervisor named Dan White.

Written by Dustin Lance Black and directed by Gus Van Sant, the film combines real-life footage of events as they happened with juxtaposed images of Penn dictating his last will and testament into a tape recorder. (Milk left instructions that this be read publicly in the event of his being murdered, which he always felt was a possibility.) Penn shows great empathy with his character, capturing both his dignity and his sense of mischief as he morphs from a longhaired bohemian to a short-back-and-sides political canvasser.

Van Sant was one of three directors contemplating films based on Milk's life at this time. The other two were Oliver Stone and Bryan Singer, the gay director of the sleeper hit *The Usual Suspects*. Singer also had *The Usual Suspects*'s screenwriter, Christopher McQuarrie, on board for his film, but it was plagued with delays. He was going to base the film on Randy Shilts's book *The Mayor of Castro Street*. This was the area of San Francisco where Milk worked. Stone was working on the same script as Van Sant, intending to be his producer, but they differed in their vision of what each wanted to do so they went their separate ways. Matt Damon was originally scheduled to play White, but he dropped out due to scheduling difficulties. The part instead went to Josh Brolin.

Penn plays Milk as a human being with all the frailty that entailed rather than the crucified martyr some people expected. Because he died in the line of duty, Black wrote, he achieved a measure of sainthood in the gay world (Black, 2009: 117). Saints, however, don't generally make very interesting characters for films, and it's the last kind of approach Milk himself—a thoroughly self-deprecating man—would have wanted. He always resisted any attempt to sound solemn. A class clown in youth, he carried that persona into politics as well, though he never trivialized the issues for which he canvassed. He saw most of these as nothing more than common sense, all the way from gay rights to the necessity of people to scoop their dog's poop on public thoroughfares. Neither did he draw the line at camping himself up. "I'm sorry I left my high heels at home," he says during one of his speeches in the film.

The film opens with a collage of newsreel footage of police raids on gay bars and clubs from the 1950s. It then moves to 1969 when the Stonewall riots ended such intimidation, at least temporarily. In a poignant moment, one sees Dianne Feinstein, Milk's colleague on the San Francisco Board of Supervisors, tearfully announcing his death. Van Sant now flashes back to Milk on the occasion of his fortieth birthday. He's about to proposition Scott Smith (James Franco), the man who will soon become his partner. They kiss but do nothing more sexual. Soon afterward they head for San Francisco, having heard about the number of gay people who live happily in its Castro district. It's after Milk arrives here that he begins to think seriously about becoming a politician.

He sets up an office at the back of a shop called Castro Camera and begins his new career from there. Everything is slapdash—including the way he develops films. He recruits a man called Cleve Jones (Emile Hirsch) to his campaign, but it isn't long before their relationship breaks down. A new man now enters his life, the emotionally immature Jack Lira (Diego Luna). Lira resents the amount of time Milk spends away from him. Milk tries to explain to him that he's a very busy man, but Lira bridles at what he sees as neglect. Milk seems more amused by his volatile moods than anything else.

That all changes when Lira kills himself. Penn's grief at his death is heartfelt but all too brief. Soon afterward he's back politicking again. This is an important part of the film, and of Milk's life, but it's glossed over with the line, "I've loved four loves and three of them attempted suicide, and it's my fault because I made them stay in the closet." These are strong sentiments. Perhaps Penn—and Van Sant—needed to dwell more on them.

Milk's career now takes an upswing. He fails in his bid to become a city supervisor in 1973, 1975, and 1976, but he succeeds in 1977, winning a seat on the San Francisco Board. It's a cause for great euphoria, especially in view of the number of disappointments that preceded it.

Things start to go downhill for him after he meets Dan White, a Vietnam veteran and former police officer and fireman. He's light-years away from him with his antiliberal perspective on social and sexual matters.

They have an awkward relationship. Milk tries to paper over the cracks by doing things like attending the christening of White's child. He has his first serious clash with him when they differ on "Proposal 6," also known as the Briggs Initiative. This was a proposal that gave authorities the right to remove gay teachers from their posts in Californian schools and also to punish anyone who supported them. It was anathema to Milk. White's espousal of "family values" to the exclusion of other civil rights nauseated him in the same way as that of Anita Bryant, a singer with a well-known reputation for homophobic attitudes.

They locked horns repeatedly on "Prop 6." When this was defeated in November 1978, White was livid. It began his descent into depression and ultimately led him to murder Milk. On the same day he also shot San Francisco's, mayor George Moscone. Moscone refused White's request to be reappointed to the board of supervisors after he resigned from it. The two murders occurred within a half hour of one another.

Milk is a work of significant personal and political power. Van Sant chronicles his subject's failures and successes against a background of police harassment, gay bashing, and the bigoted utterances of Anita Bryant, a spokesperson for Florida's Save Our Children Organization. Many people in the cast play themselves, giving added authenticity to the film. The fact that it was shot mainly on location enhanced this sense. Its spirit and energy, Black believed, was the city of San Francisco itself; it was like a character in the story (Black, 131).

Van Sant refuses to dramatize Milk's murder, intent more on celebrating his life than his death. Neither does he demonize White even though he had every right to. Instead he gives us a very moving scene of the candlelight vigil that followed Milk's assassination. Over seventy thousand people made their way to the steps of City Hall that night to pay their respects to him. That was where his body was interred. A simple endnote informs us what happened to White at his trial and afterward. This is consistent with the muted nature of the film in general.

Milk received eight Oscar nominations and won two, Penn scooping the Best Actor gong and Black being awarded for Best Original Screenplay. It might have done with winning for Best Picture too. Neither hagiographic nor saccharine, it trod the kind of middle ground Milk himself would have wanted, ending with his favorite electoral phrase about his voters: "You've got to give them hope." This is a message that resonates even as the sound of the bullets that laid him low echoes in one's brain like a thunderbolt.

Related Films
The Times of Harvey Milk (1984); *See How They Run* (2001); *The Trip* (2004).

Harvey Milk (1930–78)

Milk wasn't your average politician. He was more the kind of man one would invite to a party rather than to be *in* one.

When he said something high-sounding, it didn't seem in character. When whoops of delight went up at his speeches, he seemed almost surprised. It wasn't that he didn't know how to work a crowd; he did. But he was usually too focused on what he was saying to be aware of how he was saying it.

Born into a retail clothing family on Long Island, he was anything but a snappy dresser, preferring to buy his clothes off the rack or even in secondhand stores. After he left school he joined the navy, serving as chief petty officer on a submarine rescue ship. He was discharged in 1955. Afterward he taught math and history in a high school. He then went to work in Wall Street as a research supervisor. He dabbled in off-Broadway theater productions there. Later on he moved to San Francisco with his then partner, Jack McKinley. McKinley was producing the musical *Hair* there. Milk worked in a finance company until he became bored with it. One day he burned his BankAmericard and was sacked.

He returned to New York in 1971. Here he met the actor Scott Smith in a subway station on his forty-first birthday. Almost immediately he began a serious relationship with him. Two years later he returned to San Francisco to enter politics.

He was always a man of the people. "Never take an elevator in City Hall," he advised (Black, 2009: 102). The staircase was more his style. Staircases were also places he was likely to meet voters. Every vote was crucial to him. He shaved off a mustache once for that reason: "I want no distractions. Fifty people might not like mustaches and I'm not going to lose by fifty votes" (Black, 59).

Milk received an avalanche of hate mail during his life. He received many abusive phone calls as well. Some of them carried threats of sexual dismemberment and murder (*Milk* DVD: Special Features). The fact that he managed to stay in office facing such venom was a minor miracle. He also had to face the contumely of people like Anita Bryant, who came out with statements like, "If homosexuality was the natural way, God would have made Adam and Bruce" (Black, 63). "Adam and Steve" would have sounded wittier; wit wasn't Bryant's forte.

He always had a premonition he would die young. "I'll never live to be a senior citizen," he predicted—presciently (Shilts, 2009: 241). He recorded a will in which he uttered perhaps his most famous line: "If a bullet should enter my brain, let that bullet destroy every closet door" (Lessard, 2008: 89). The one that killed him, from the gun of his political nemesis Dan White, didn't quite do that, but it certainly put dents in many of them.

The jury that adjudicated on White was composed mainly of people who shared his own homophobia. This was so virulent that jurors accepted what came to be known as his "Twinkie" defense, meaning he had diminished guilt as a result of having consumed too much junk food and thereby having his judgment impaired. He ended up being sentenced to a mere seven years for the double murder of Milk and George Moscone, the San Francisco mayor he shot on the same day as Milk.

Many people, it seemed, saw him as a hero who was trying to preserve a city from corruption. The ridiculously lenient sentence provoked the White Night

Riots, with over five thousand angry protestors storming City Hall to vent their rage. Cleve Jones, the founder of the Names Project AIDS Memorial Quilt, said: "My first reaction was to vomit" (Black, 106).

White was released from prison in January 1984 having served just five and a half years of his sentence. Fearing a backlash from disgruntled members of the public and descending further into the depression that had caused him to go off the rails, he took his own life in October 1985. It seemed like justice was served after all—in its way.

Milk went on to become hero-worshipped in the following years, culminating in the setting up of Harvey Milk Day in 2010. He wasn't, however, an angel. Shortly before his death, the U.S. attorney general authorized the FBI to investigate allegations that he had tried to direct funds from the Gay Pride Foundation into his own pocket (*Sunday Independent*, June 3, 2018). Neither was his love life all that it might have been, as one can deduce from the suicide of his partner Jack Lira, which was accompanied by an abusive letter to Milk about his relative neglect of him. This, however, was due to his political passion rather than anything else.

Further Reading

Black, Dustin Lance. 2009. *Milk: A Pictorial History of Harvey Milk*. New York: Newmarket Press.

Faderman, Lillian. 2018. *Harvey Milk: His Lives and Death*. London: Yale University Press.

Lessard, John. 2008. *To Quote a Queer*. Philadelphia: Quirk Books.

Shilts, Randy, 2009. *The Mayor of Castro Street: The Life and Times of Harvey Milk*. London: Atlantic.

Sunday Independent, June 3, 2018.

Sal Mineo (1939–76)

Mineo was of Sicilian origin, but he grew up in the Bronx. A troubled boy in his youth, he was expelled from school at the age of eight. A few years later he was arrested for attempted robbery. It was thought that he would be sent to an institution for delinquent children. As an alternative to this, he was offered entry to a professional stage school. He jumped at this; it proved to be the catalyst he needed to mend his ways.

He made his stage debut in Tennessee Williams's *The Rose Tattoo*. For two years he played Yul Brynner's son in *The King and I* on Broadway. He was only sixteen when he began his film career, making both *Six Bridges to Cross* and *Rebel without a Cause*, the movie that turned him into a star, in 1955. He was reputed to have slept with James Dean during the shoot, and also with the film's director, Nicholas Ray. He received an Oscar nomination for his performance. The film was a rallying call to youths everywhere to assert themselves against a repressive gerontocracy, but Mineo's turn as Dean's gay friend—he didn't get to express his love for him in any overtly sexual manner, this being 1955—received little succor. He died at the end, like many gay men of the time in films, either latent or otherwise, society putting a stamp on its sexual mores whatever about the perceived right of Dean and the film's other star, Natalie Wood, to bleat about their failure to be understood by their parents or society at large.

The following year he appeared in another James Dean film, *Giant*, directed by George Stevens. He played the Mexican son of Rock Hudson and Elizabeth Taylor, but he didn't share any scenes with Dean. After this watershed, perhaps due to his criminal past, Mineo became typecast as The Switchblade Kid in a number of tough guy roles that included *Crime in the Streets* (1956), *Somebody Up There Likes Me* (1956), *Dino* (1957), and *The Young Don't Cry* (1957). He broke out of the pigeonhole to play a jazz drummer in *The Gene Krupa Story* (1959), one of his few starring roles. He secured his second Oscar nomination for playing a terrorist in *Exodus* (1960), Otto Preminger's adaptation of Leon Uris's sprawling novel about the foundation of the Israeli state in 1948.

His career declined in the sixties. He was hoping to get the role of Sherif Kharish in *Lawrence of Arabia* (1962), but it went to Omar Sharif instead. (The Jordanian government refused to allow him into their country because of his pro-Israeli role in *Exodus*.) Afterward he became slotted into less ambitious roles in films like *The Longest Day* (1962), *Cheyenne Autumn* (1964), and *The Greatest Story Ever Told* (1965).

He frittered away his earnings and had to turn to television and the stage when money became a problem for him. He also liked to gamble and was a familiar figure at the slot machines in Las Vegas. In 1969, he made his debut as a director with *Fortune and Men's Eyes*, a play about sexuality in prison. Two years later it became a movie, directed by Harvey Hart.

By now his film career was at a standstill. Desperate to claw his way back to screen prominence, he took a role as a chimpanzee in *Escape from the Planet of the Apes* (1971). He hoped to make a film about drug trafficking, but the project ran into financial problems and was abandoned. Once again he retreated to the stage to keep body and soul together.

He had a refreshingly liberal attitude to his orientation, chirping "I like them all—men, I mean—and a few chicks now and then." When his mother said she couldn't understand how he turned out gay, he shot the question back at her, "Ma, how come my brothers *didn't*?" (Murray, 1994: 228).

He came out at a time when it wasn't the thing to do so. It could have ruined his career. Others weren't as brave. He saw people like Tab Hunter and Anthony Perkins living in terror of being outed and was amused by their fears. He liked to tell a story about the pair of them, who were friends. Apparently one day Hunter said to Perkins, "Some day you'll make a fine actor." Perkins replied, "I already have. Several of them!" (Hadleigh, 1999: 165).

Mineo was stabbed to death on February 13, 1976, after returning home from rehearsals for a play in which he was appearing. Nobody was sure if it was a bungled robbery or something more personal. When police entered his apartment and found nude photographs of men there, they thought the killer might have been a spurned lover, but afterward they found evidence against an ex-convict named Lionel Williams. He was arrested the following year and tried for the crime in 1979, the jury returning a guilty verdict. It was seen as a random act of violence rather than a personal grudge against Mineo, who was "into" neither leather nor S&M. Instead he was simply "a sweet and loving man" (Ruuth, 1991: 114). Williams was sentenced to life in prison for killing him.

Mineo had a strong presence on screen even if he failed to translate it into an adult context. People reacted to his death with fear, just as they had to the Charles Manson killings of 1969. Anthony Perkins adopted a more cynical attitude to his demise, saying, "His career was already over"—as if that was all his life represented (Hadleigh, 2005: 247).

His father was a coffin maker, which seemed grimly appropriate to the tragic train of events. The play he was rehearsing when he died was entitled—significantly—*P.S. Your Cat Is Dead.*

Related Films
Rebel without a Cause (1955); *The Gene Krupa Story* (1959); *Sal* (2011).

Further Reading
Byars, Jackie. 1991. *All That Heaven Allows: Re-Reading Gender in 1950s Melodrama.* London: Routledge.
Duncan, Amy. 2017. *The Murder of Sal Mineo.* CreateSpace.
Hadleigh, Boze, ed. 1999. *Hollywood Bitch.* London: Robson Books.
Hadleigh, Boze, ed. 2005. *Celebrity Diss and Tell.* Kansas City: Andrews McMeel.
Hollywood Reporter, July 16, 1991.
Michaud, Michael Gregg. 2011. *Sal Mineo: A Biography.* New York: Three Rivers Press.
Murray, Raymond. 1994. *Images in the Dark: An Encyclopedia of Gay and Lesbian Film and Video.* Philadelphia: TLA Publications.
Ruuth, Marianne. 1991. *Cruel City: The Dark Side of Hollywood's Rich and Famous.* Malibu, CA: Roundtable Publishing.

Monster (2003)

Charlize Theron knows all about violence. When she was just fifteen years of age, she watched her mother shooting her father dead in their Johannesburg home after he threatened them both in a drunken condition. To play the Florida killer Aileen Wuornos, however, she had to draw on different kinds of reserves because this was a woman who shot seven men in cold blood. Her mother killed in self-defense, but Wuornos had no such excuse, apart from the circumstances of the first murder, which remain hazy. How was Theron going to humanize her in a biopic about the highway prostitute's life and crimes?

The physical transformation she underwent to play the role in Patty Jenkins's directorial debut was nothing short of astounding. Her hair looked like it hadn't been washed in a year. She wore heavy dentures to weigh down the bottom half of her face and give her a semipermanent pout. Her eyes bulged with fury when she got worked up—which was most of the time. Her eyebrows were shaved and her teeth made crooked. She put on thirty pounds for the role, reminding one of Robert de Niro's Oscar-winning performance in *Raging Bull* where he basically ate his way around Italy to bulk up for the later years of the washed-up boxer Jake LaMotta. Theron also won an Oscar for *Monster*. De Niro put on most of his

Aileen Wuornos (1956–2002)

Wuornos's life was marked by travesty from birth. She never saw her father, as he was in jail for raping a child when she was born. When she was four, her mother abandoned both her and her brother, Keith, leaving them with her parents. Wuornos grew up believing these people were her parents rather than her grandparents. Her grandfather abused her sexually.

She traded sex for benefits as early as eleven and was also incestuous with Keith. In 1969 her father hanged himself in prison. A few months earlier she'd become pregnant after being raped by a friend of her father's. She gave birth to a boy at a home for unmarried mothers. He was put up for adoption after he was born. A few months later she dropped out of school. She took to prostitution to make ends meet, living rough in the woods near her home in Michigan.

When she was eighteen she was arrested for drunk driving and for firing a gun from a moving car. Two years later she hitchhiked to Florida. In March 1976 she met a wealthy sixty-nine-year-old man called Lewis Gratz Fell. She married him for his money but was violent with him. He soon had to get a restraining order against her. The marriage was annulled within months.

Keith died of cancer in July 1976. She inherited $10,000 from his life insurance. She spent part of the money on a car, which she soon totaled. In 1981 she was arrested for robbing a convenience store. She served a year in jail for the offense. She was arrested again in 1984, this time for passing forged checks at a bank in Key West. In 1986 she was charged with robbing a car. Later that year she was accused of pulling a gun on a man and demanding money from him.

She met Tyria Moore, the character upon whom Selby Wall was based in *Monster*, in a gay bar in Daytona in 1989. Soon afterward they started living together, Wuornos supporting the two of them by her prostitution. She started killing men for money, sometimes firing up to six bullets into them and leaving them either nude or partially clothed. She shot one of her victims nine times.

She was arrested in 1991 and charged with the murder of Richard Mallory. She claimed it was self-defense. When her other killings came to light, she claimed they were also committed in self-defense. She later admitted they were done for money, and in cold blood, but she kept changing her story. When she was diagnosed as being mentally unstable, she disputed this. Various court cases concerning her crimes dragged on over the years. She was eventually given six death sentences, but she wasn't executed until 2002. By now she'd spent twelve years on death row and made her peace with God.

Her last filmed words from Nick Broomfield's documentary on her were, "Thank you, society, for railroading my ass." Such words expressed both her acerbic humor and her bitterness at life. She died as she lived, her two fingers firmly thrust at that—to her—repellent life. Broomfield believed she was insane when she died. He also thought she had paranoid delusions, especially in her stated belief that the police knew she killed Mallory in cold blood but covered it up because they wanted her to kill again so she would be demonized even more in the public eye than she already was, which would eventually make her a more perverse—and lucrative—subject for books and movies, which they could profit from.

---

weight with pizzas eaten for breakfast, dinner, and tea. Theron did it with potato chips and Krispy Kremes. "I lived in sweatpants for five months," she said, "because they were the only things I could fit into" (*Telegraph*, February 3, 2012).

She felt too much was written about her weight gain. It wasn't only this that helped her get into Wuornos's character; not this or the brown contact lenses or the grubby clothes or any of the other appurtenances she used. Instead it was something more intangible: the experience of letting herself go, of giving up on life. Obesity was just one factor of such defeatism. Having said that, she knew how important it was to look—and move—like Wuornos. Actions like throwing her head back or walking with an arrogant strut were key to getting inside her skin. "This is a woman," she said, "who was five foot three but who looked like she was six foot four" (*Advocate*, February 17, 2004). In actual fact she was five foot six.

"She kind of blew herself up like a blowfish," Theron added. "Probably because of being homeless and living on the streets all those years, she didn't want to look vulnerable so she was constantly throwing her head back and trying to look bigger" (*Telegraph*, February 3, 2012). She replicated these mannerisms to perfection after watching hours on footage of Wuornos in court.

The film is mainly concerned with her relationship to Selby Wall, played equally convincingly by Christina Ricci. Wuornos meets Wall in a gay bar in 1989. The pair of them find an instant connection with one another, largely because of their shared outsider status. They live together until the full extent of Wuornos's violence comes to Wall's notice. Wuornos is initially straight but shows herself willing to become involved in a lesbian relationship. She meets Wall on a day when she's contemplating blowing her brains out from depression. Wall has been sent from her home in Ohio to Florida to stay with relatives after being disowned by her parents for her orientation.

Wall isn't much more than a child at this point of her life, but she's demanding. When Wuornos meets her, she has her arm in a cast. Wuornos wants to take care of her, but she finds it difficult to support her.

Wuornos's first killing takes place after she's sexually assaulted by one of her clients, Vincent Corey (Lee Tergesen). Afterward she decides she wants to give up prostitution. Work is hard to find, however, because of her lack of qualifications and a criminal record in her past, so she returns to it. From now on she kills her clients in a premeditated way rather than as a response to abuse. A beast has been unleashed and it won't be quelled.

Even so, she manages to delude herself into thinking that the men she kills have all been trying to rape her. She projects memories of sexual abuse she suffered in her childhood onto them, making them into something they're not. Each time she kills a "john," she tells herself she's saved another prostitute from being raped. She spares one man when he tells her he never had sex with a prostitute before. But her killing spree sees seven men dead before the law catches up with her.

Wuornos robs the men she kills. She initially only tells Well about the first victim, explaining that the killing was done in self-defense. Later on, when cars begin turning up at their nomadic abodes, Wall wonders what else might be going on behind the scenes, but she doesn't quiz Wuornos in any detail about such matters.

Their past, however, is about to catch up with them. One day a sketch is made of the two of them and televised. They're identified by a couple who witnessed their car going off the road onto their lawn.

When Wuornos is finally arrested, there's a suspicion Wall may have been complicit in some of the murders. Wall is anxious to knock this suspicion on the head. She betrays Wuornos by allowing the police to listen in on a phone call she places to her where Wuornos admits to having acted alone.

Wuornos is sentenced to death for her crimes. In the last scene of the film, she screams at the jury. She then goes out a door into a brilliant white light. It's as if she's headed for some sort of purification.

The film was made on a shoestring budget in just twenty-eight days. Jenkins's only indulgence was forking out $1,500 on Theron's set of false teeth. This was money well spent. "She carried all her tension in her mouth," Theron claimed (*Telegraph*, February 3, 2012).

Jenkins was castigated for trying to whitewash her, casting her in the role of victim rather than protagonist and thus turning the film into more of a lesbian love story than the "monster" of the film's title led one to expect. Such an impression was strengthened by the fact that some of the killings show Wuornos out of control, which softens them.

It's easy to see why people would hold these views but it's the job of art to understand rather than condemn, and this Jenkins—and Theron—did with commendable zeal. Theron said she saw the film as being about "the need and the willingness and the eagerness and the hunger and the survival of wanting to be loved by somebody, anybody" (*Advocate*, February 17, 2004). She played down its lesbian angle, claiming it wasn't about two women finding one another and falling in love as much as "two outcasts who wanted the same thing so desperately, to be accepted without being judged" (*Advocate*, February 17, 2004).

When she first read the script, Theron didn't know very much about Wuornos. The glamorous former model couldn't see herself in the role of a trailer park hooker who looked so ungainly and performed such horrific acts. She became more interested in Wuornos when she saw Nick Broomfield's two documentaries on her, *The Selling of a Serial Killer* (1993) and *Life and Death of a Serial Killer* (2003). She also started reading the letters Wuornos wrote from prison to her childhood friend Dawn Botkins. The more Theron learned, the more she felt Wuornos wasn't so much a bad person as someone who took a wrong direction in life as a result of being one of society's rejects.

For many viewers, this skewed the emphasis too far away from the gratuitous amount of blood Wuornos spilled, seeming to offer a green light to anyone who suffered abuse in their youth to go on a vengeful crusade to put it to rights. But if one reads *Dear Dawn*, a collection of Wuornos's letters to Botkins, one can see a woman of rich humor and warm energy in evidence.

There was no gainsaying Theron's commitment to the role, and few people quibbled about her Oscar win. Roger Ebert deemed her performance to be one of the greatest he'd ever seen in the history of cinema. It wasn't so much a performance, he said, as an "embodiment" (*Chicago Sun-Times*, January 1, 2004). He praised Ricci too. She created her performance, he said, from "bad movies, old songs and barroom romances" (*Chicago Sun-Times*, January 1, 2004).

Theron relished the opportunity *Monster* gave her to push herself further than she'd ever done before. "Usually in a film," she said, "you pick three moments in a script and you wait for these three days to come and really stretch your acting muscles. But in this case, *every* scene was that scene" (*Advocate*, February 17, 2004).

Broomfield's reaction to her performance put it best: "I thought I was watching Wuornos" (*Telegraph*, February 3, 2012).

Related Films
Overkill: The Aileen Wuornos Story (1992); *Aileen Wuornos: The Selling of a Serial Killer* (1993); *Aileen: Life and Death of a Serial Killer* (2003).

Further Reading
Advocate, February 17, 2004.
Chicago Sun-Times, January 1, 2004.
Faust, Nikki. 2016. *Aileen Wuornos: Serial Killer*. CreateSpace.
James, Rachel. 2016. *Hitch-Hiker from Hell: Aileen Wuornos*. Kindle.
Lindsay, David. 1991. *Mercy*. New York: Bantam Doubleday.
Russell, Sue. 2016. *Lethal Intent*. New York: Pinnacle Books.
Sanders, Lawrence. 2013. *The Third Deadly Sin*. Kindle: Open Road Mystery and Thriller.
Shipley, Stacey L., and Bruce A. Arrigo. 2003. *The Female Homicide Offender: Serial Murder and the Case of Aileen Wuornos*. London: Pearson Books.
Telegraph, February 3, 2012.
Wuornos, Aileen, and Christopher Berry Dee. 2006. *Monster: My True Story*. London: John Blake.
Wuornos, Aileen, and Lisa Kester. 2012. *Dear Dawn: Aileen Wuornos in Her Own Words*. Berkeley, CA: Soft Skull Press.

Moonlight (2016)

Most people remember this as the film that didn't win the Best Film Oscar in February 2017 . . . and then it did. What one really should remember it for is the fact that it's a masterpiece of understatement.

Cynics said it was unduly praised for the virtual airbrushing of black films out of the previous year's ceremonies, that after the famine came the feast. This is another shibboleth one needs to abandon.

A coming-of-age story about a sensitive African American boy called Chiron who grows up in the housing projects of Miami in the 1990s, it was based on Tarell Alvin McCraney's semiautobiographical drama, *In Moonlight Black Boys Look Blue*. It has three different actors playing Chiron at various stages of his life. Director Barry Jenkins didn't want them to meet prior to shooting for fear this might lead to unwanted influences on the performances. It proved to be a wise decision. They each capture different aspects of Chiron's personality and merge seamlessly into one other. If they'd met, such a transition might have been more labored.

Alex Hibbert plays him at age eleven. This is the quiet Chiron. It comes in a chapter of the film called "Little." (Scenes appear like chapters, as in a book.) His mother, Paula (Naomie Harris), is a crack addict with anger issues. His father has gone AWOL.

He's taken under the wing of local drug dealer Juan (Mahershala Ali), a kind man beneath a tough exterior. He becomes a surrogate father to Chiron as well as an enabler for Paula's drug habit. Only a director of Jenkins's empathy could weave such a skewed scenario into a balanced family structure. Ali received an Oscar for his performance. The achievement was rendered even more special by dint of the fact that he disappears a third of the way into the film. Like Chiron, he achieves most of his effects in a subdued but elegant manner. The scene where he teaches Chiron how to swim is almost like a baptism.

Even at this early stage of his life, Chiron senses he's different from other boys of his age. In one scene he asks Juan what being gay means, using a gay slur word he's been taunted with in school. There's a long pause after the question as Juan weighs it up. His girlfriend, Teresa (Janelle Monáe), is also present. She's as kind to him as Juan is. They provide an escape hatch for him from his dysfunctional mother and the school bullies who harass him.

Ashton Saunders is the second Chiron, playing him at age seventeen. By now the bullying has gotten worse and so has Paula's drug taking. Juan has died but Chiron still spends time with Teresa to get away from his mother.

He befriends a boy called Kevin (Jharrel Jerome) and even kisses him one day. Kevin is later delegated by the school bullies to beat Chiron. It's a test put to him to prove to them that he's part of their peer group and not in cahoots with Chiron. Chiron is shocked but he takes his beating. One wonders how deep the wounds of this will go. Will he see it as a betrayal? Will he be able to forgive it in future years?

Trevante Rhodes plays Chiron at twenty-five. He now calls himself "Black." This is the nickname that was given to him by Kevin when they were at school together. He's surer of himself now, or at least seems to be. But is the slick image a cover for someone who's still messed up inside? He's a drug dealer now, like Juan.

Kevin phones him one night and says he'd like to see him. The call gives Chiron a link to his past, where so many issues have been unresolved. They meet in a diner. Chiron sits facing the back door, as Juan once advised him to do, for protection. His guard is up. "Why did you call me?" he asks.

They go back to Kevin's apartment afterward and Kevin cooks him a meal. Chiron is wondering what's going on in his mind, in his life. Kevin's coolness contrasts with Chiron's apprehensiveness. He tells Chiron he's at a good place in his life, that he's settled down now and that he has a son he loves. "Who is you, Chiron?" he asks. "I'm me, man," Chiron replies. "I ain't tryin' to be nothin' else." But he is.

The film ends in midair. After all the things Chiron has been through, the scene seems almost like a nonevent. Does he blame Kevin for what happened all those years ago? Is he still attracted to him sexually? Is Kevin attracted to *him*?

One doesn't really need to know the answers to these questions. Jenkins isn't interested in providing them. Kevin teaches Chiron the importance of being himself, of developing a harmony inside himself that can conquer the demons of his past.

There haven't been many films made about black gay men searching for their identity, sexual or otherwise, so the ones that are there should be valued. *Moonlight* may end on a dying fall, but in another way it's cathartic. It backs its way into the limelight, completing Chiron's tripartite trajectory of self-knowledge. At the end, one feels, he's sloughed off his baggage. He can now move on to whatever future awaits him.

The best way to view the film is as a mood poem rather than a linear narrative. One writer said it's about "teaching a child to swim, about cooking a meal for an old friend, about the feeling of sand on skin and the sound of waves on a darkened beach" (*New York Times*, October 20, 2016). James Laxton's visual imagery tells the story just as much as the script or the plot or the actor's expressions. Or even as much as Nicholas Britell's evocative score, which mixes rap music with hip-hop and rock 'n' roll. The film is like a black version of Richard Linkletter's *Boyhood* (2014), but it's much more nuanced. McCraney described Miami as a "beautiful nightmare" for Chiron (*Moonlight* DVD: Bonus Features). The performances of the three actors who play him conjure up that dichotomy admirably.

The script is exemplary. Equally exemplary are the scenes where no words are spoken. Jenkins, said Ali, is "a master at explaining silence" (*Moonlight* DVD: Bonus Features). This is especially the case in the "Little" chapter where Hibbert has very few words to say as the eleven-year-old boy. He delivers these with a professionalism that belies his years. Said Jenkins, "He looks ten but feels like fifty-five" (*Moonlight* DVD: Bonus Features), He didn't direct his cast in a prescriptive manner, instead giving them the space to develop their own interpretations of the scenarios. The strategy bore fruit, freeing the actors up to go into areas they might have been too inhibited to with another director. When Monáe was nervous about a scene, he told her, "There's no such thing as a mistake" (*Moonlight* DVD: Bonus Features).

There are very few mistakes in *Moonlight*.

Related Films
A Different Kind of Black Man (2001); *Precious* (2009); *Boyhood* (2014).

Further Reading
Blount, Marcellus, and George P. Cunningham. 1996. *Representing Black Men*. New York: Routledge.
Harris, Keith. 2006. *Boys, Boyz, Bois: An Ethic of Black Masculinity in Film and Popular Media*. New York: Routledge.
Massood, Paula. 2003. *Black City Cinema: African American Urban Experiences in Cinema*. Philadelphia: Temple University Press.
Mercer, Kobena. 1994. *Welcome to the Jungle: New Positions in Black Cultural Studies*. New York: Routledge.
Munoz, Jose Esteban. 1999. *Disidentifications: Queers of Color and the Performance of Politics*. Minneapolis: University of Minnesota Press.
New York Times, October 20, 2016.

Mulholland Drive (2001)

A riddle wrapped in a mystery wrapped in an enigma. That's perhaps the most appropriate way to describe this film. But as its star Naomi Watts says, "Who wants to go to movies where everything is spelt out for you?" (*Mulholland Drive* DVD: Special Features).

David Lynch has made some obscure films in his time. This one, arguably his masterpiece, beats them all hands down for inscrutability. At what point in his shape-shifting universe does reality become dream? Or nightmare? Or nightmare flipping back on itself so that it becomes reality again? At what point does the wannabe actress Betty (Watts) turn into her alter ego? At what point does Rita (Laura Elena Harring), a character who's suffering from amnesia after the car crash that opens the film, become a person who only looks like Rita but acts like someone totally different, while Betty assumes her original role?

Lynch, the self-styled Samuel Beckett of celluloid, has spent his life either not answering questions about *Mulholland Drive* or appearing not to even acknowledge that they've been asked. Which means that one is better advised to take his film at face value, even if that face more resembles something from Picasso's blue period than anything close to representational art. As it moves from retro-noir horoscope to quasi-operatic psychodrama, one has to accept the fact that the film probably means just what Lynch wants it to mean, even if he's not quite sure himself. Asked who Godot was in *Waiting for Godot*, Beckett famously said, "If I knew, I would have said so in the play." So it is with Lynch here.

Originally conceived as a TV pilot, the idea for it came to him as a spin-off from *Twin Peaks*. In this version it was rejected by ABC as being too dark. The rejection did him a favor because it encouraged him to expand it into the engrossing behemoth it eventually became (Lim, 2015: 150).

It begins straightforwardly enough with the aforementioned accident on the LA freeway. Running away from the accident that has killed two gangsters who were about to liquidate her, "Rita"—the name is assumed—makes her way across waste ground. She eventually arrives at an apartment which she wanders into. It belongs to Betty's aunt. Betty, meanwhile, arrives in LA for a screen test. The first sign that this is going to be an unsettling movie is when a couple she's met on the flight grin deliriously in their car after leaving her.

When she reaches the apartment, Rita is in the shower. Betty assumes she knows her aunt. When she asks her what her name is, she replies, "Rita," choosing the name after spotting the actress Rita Hayworth on a movie poster on the wall. It later emerges that she doesn't know who she is—and that she doesn't know Betty's aunt either. The ever-obliging Betty assures her she'll do everything she can to help her discover her real identity.

Lynch now shifts his attention to a number of subplots, which makes the film even more confusing than it already is. Justin Theroux plays Adam Kesher, a put-upon filmmaker who's instructed by his bosses to put an actress called Camilla Rhodes into his latest film even though he doesn't want to. Robert Forster and Brent Briscoe play a pair of policemen who appear and then disappear—for reasons best known to Lynch. In Winkie's diner, two men have a heated conversation. When they go outside, they run into a monster.

A disheveled man shoots a friend of his in an office and then kills two other people for no apparent reason. Kesher returns home from work to find his wife in bed with his gardener (Billy Ray Cyrus). He expresses outrage, but when they struggle together it's the gardener who prevails. He throws Kesher out of his own house after beating him up.

Betty now attends an audition for a soap opera. It's a standard romantic scene she's asked to play but she turns it into something strongly erotic with a stunning performance. Everyone watching her seems entranced, as well they might be, but as soon as the scene is over she reverts to her bubbly, girl-next-door self. Nobody acts as if they've witnessed anything unusual.

Betty and Rita become lovers soon after this. The intimacy is initiated by Rita but enthusiastically responded to by Betty. Up to this point, neither of them has evinced a lesbian streak. The scene is handled in a tasteful manner. It doesn't seem out of place in a film in which everything, really, is out of place. Harring didn't think she or Watts were meant to be lesbians in the film. For her, sex was just Rita's way of thanking Betty for all she'd done for her. Because her character had amnesia, she couldn't say for sure if she'd been in bed with other women or not (*Salon*, October 12, 2001).

The two of them now go to a theater called Club Silencio. A Spanish singer, Rebekah Del Rio, comes on stage. She sings an a cappella rendition of Roy Orbison's "Crying." She collapses in the middle of it, but one still hears her voice singing as she's carried away in an unconscious state.

The film undergoes a tonal shift now. It's as if Del Rio's collapse signals the end of the "pure" relationship that existed between Betty and Rita to make way for the "doppelganger" one that follows it. Back at the apartment, Betty finds a box in her purse that matches Rita's key. Rita doesn't witness this. When she comes into the room, Betty has gone out. Rita unlocks the box but finds it empty.

Rita now decides her identity might be linked with a woman called Diane Selwyn. With Betty in tow she goes to an apartment where she believes Selwyn lives. They break into it but find her dead. Later on, Rita cuts Betty's hair. She then dons a blond wig. This makes her look uncannily like Betty. Selwyn now resurrects in the apartment where Betty and Rita have been. She looks like Betty but her personality is much pricklier. It turns out she's a failed actress who's suffering from depression over a botched love affair.

Camilla Rhodes now appears. She looks just like Rita. She invites Selwyn to a party on Mulholland Drive. Kesher's mother is in attendance. She's played by Ann Miller, who was a friend of Betty's aunt earlier in the film. Like Betty and Rita, she's also changed her identity. In the course of the party, Selwyn talks about how she came to Hollywood, her aunt having died and left her some money. She meets one of the men who was in Winkie's diner earlier. She tells him she wants him to kill Rhodes. Afterward she starts hallucinating. Finally, she shoots herself. The film ends with a woman from the theater Betty and Rita attended intoning just one word, "Silencio."

What's it all about? Rain forests of print have been expended trying to find out, most of them leading into blind alleys. One theory is that the first part of the film is a dream by Selwyn and the second part the real story. Another theory is that Rita is a figment of Betty's imagination. In a third one, Betty and Selwyn aren't the same person, just two people who look alike. Either way, Lynch isn't throwing any light on the subject. Not for nothing has he been called "Jimmy Stewart from Mars."

The film boasts wonderful performances from both Watts and Herring. They engage in a kind of role reversal that's reminiscent of Ingmar Bergman's *Persona* (1966) as they survey LA's grimy underbelly—before becoming an endemic part of it.

Watts thought her character was too one-dimensional at the beginning of the film before all her different layers opened up. "She doesn't belong in a story," she chafed. "She belongs on the side of a cereal box!" (Lim, 2015: 147). Little did she know then what plans Lynch had for her. The more complicated Betty became, the more intrigued she became by her, but Lynch remained poker-faced whenever she asked him to explain her character to her. He just sat there transfixed, taking a puff of his cigarette and a drink of coffee without offering any explanations of the film's abstruse motifs.

Is it a black comedy? A surreal fantasy? A poisonous valentine to Hollywood? It's all these things and more, but anyone looking for an "explanation" of it might as well expect to see the answers to a crossword puzzle materializing in front of them when they don't even understand the clues.

Perhaps it's best just to sit back and enjoy it. Or be terrified by it. Or both.

Related Films
Sunset Boulevard (1950); *Persona* (1966); *Three Women* (1977); *Blue Velvet* (1986); *Twin Peaks* (1990–1); *Lost Highway* (1997); *Being John Malkovich* (1999).

Further Reading
Bourriaud, Nicolas. 2017. *Return to Mulholland Drive: Fantastic Minimalism*. Balsamo, Italy: Silvana Editoriale.
Giannopoulou, Zina, ed. 2013. *Mulholland Drive: Philosophers in Film*. New York: Routledge.
Lim, Dennis. 2015. *David Lynch: The Man from Another Place*. New York: Amazon Publishing.
Lynch, David, and Christine McKenna. 2018. *Room to Dream*. Edinburgh: Canongate Publishing.
Odell, Colin, and Michelle Le Blanc. 2007. *David Lynch*. Herts, UK: Kamera Books.
Rodley, Chris, ed. 1997. *Lynch on Lynch*. London: Faber & Faber.
Salon, October 12, 2001.
Woods, Paul A. 2000. *Weirdsville USA: The Obsessive Universe of David Lynch*. London: Plexus.

Murder

The number of gay people who murder and/or are murdered in films is phenomenal. Both events don't only hint at screen homophobia—they scream it.

Lesbian killers first made their appearance in *Dracula's Daughter* (1936), the sequel to Bela Lugosi's *Dracula* from five years previously. The vampiress played by Gloria Holden added something more sensual than bloodsucking to her attack on Nan Grey before spiriting her off to eternity.

Other types of gay murders occurred over the next decade in films such as *Golden Boy* (1939), *Gilda* (1944), *The Big Sleep* (1946), and *Brute Force* (1947). *Rope* (1948) had two gay murderers (Farley Granger and John Dall) concealing a dead body in a trunk from the top of which they served drink to James Stewart and some relatives of the dead man in a posh New York apartment. The film was loosely based on the child killers Leopold and Loeb. It suggested Alfred

Hitchcock, the film's director, might have been homophobic. Granger also turned up in Hitchcock's *Strangers on a Train* three years later, playing a tennis player who's asked to "swap" murders with Robert Walker. Here the gay subtext was more subtle.

Other gay murders took place in films like *Caged* (1950) and *The Maltese Falcon* (1951). The unidentified actor who played the character of Sebastian in *Suddenly, Last Summer* (1959) was cannibalized by an angry horde of young men in one of the most melodramatic scenes in film history. One might have been watching a tribe of primitive savages in an African jungle. Apparently Sebastian had "serviced" most of them at one time or another in what must have been a very busy life. At this time in films, gay people had to suffer more than straight ones for their sins.

Gay murders were fairly prevalent in films of the sixties, with stars like Lotte Lenya in *From Russia with Love* (1963) meeting grisly ends. Capucine had to die in *Walk on the Wild Side* the previous year to protect her from the lesbian clutches of brothel madam Barbara Stanwyck. Ray Walston was pushed from a balcony in *Caprice* (1967). The latently gay major played by Marlon Brando kills the man he's been lusting after—and who's been lusting after Brando's wife—at the end of *Reflections in a Golden Eye* (1967), John Huston's adaptation of Carson McCuller's gothic novel.

In the Frank Sinatra film *The Detective* (1968), one of the most homophobic films ever made, Sinatra is assigned to track down the killer of a gay antiques dealer who's been castrated. Most of the gay men in the film are either pathetic or disgusting. The killer turns out to be a man who's gay himself, William Windom. Fearing his sexuality, he tries to eradicate it by killing gay people. His murders are a kind of sexual suicide induced by internalized homophobia. This is hand-me-down Freud with a very nasty aftertaste.

When a killer goes on the rampage in *The Boston Strangler* (1968), the police immediately suspect the culprit to be Hurd Hatfield, a gay man. In the end it turns out to be the married heterosexual played by Tony Curtis. One of the disguises used by Rod Steiger's serial killer in *No Way to Treat a Lady* (also 1968) is that of a gay hairdresser. Posing as a barfly in one scene, he sets Kim August in his sights. The film's in-joke is that August is actually a man in disguise.

The gay man played by Cliff Gorman was murdered in *Justine* (1969). There was a mass murder of gay people in Luchino Visconti's *The Damned* in the same year. The lesbian designer played by Erica Gavin was murdered in *Beyond the Valley of the Dolls* (1970). Two gay men were drowned in *Diamonds Are Forever* (1971).

There was a plethora of gay murders in 1973: Shelley Winters in *Cleopatra Jones*, Robert Morley in *Theatre of Blood*, James Coburn in *The Last of Sheila*, a gay man in a steam bath in *The Day of the Jackal*, a gay murderer terrorizing San Francisco in *The Laughing Policeman*. In 1974, Christopher Morley was murdered in *Freebie and the Bean*. So was Jack Cassidy in *The Eiger Sanction* in 1975, and the lesbian brothel madam in *Farewell, My Lovely* the same year.

Sal Mineo was the token gay guy who had to die in Nicholas Ray's *Rebel without a Cause* in 1955. He was stabbed to death in real life in 1976. The same year in movies, a gay accountant was thrown out of a window in *The Man Who Fell to Earth*, an ironic title in the circumstances. Another gay man was crushed under barbells in that movie. Peter Boyle was also murdered in a film that year, *The Swashbuckler*. John Calicos was castrated and then killed in *Drum*.

Michael Wills was shot in *The Choirboys* in 1977. The following year saw two gay models murdered in *Eyes of Laura Mars*. Paul Freeman was murdered in *The Long Good Friday* (1979). A number of gay people were murdered in *Cruising* (1980), a film that was so virulent in its homophobia that it caused rioting in the streets. It was one of the few movies despised by gay people before it even reached the screen.

The sad strain continued throughout the eighties. Jimmy Brown was murdered in *The Road Warrior* (1981). So was Mitchell Lichtenstein in *Streamers* (1983) and Richard C. Dancer in *The Boys Next Door* (1985). The upsurge of AIDS seemed to give gay people a breather, Hollywood apparently taking the line that if gay people were going to die of natural causes offscreen there was no need to kill as many of them on it. The stay of execution stopped in 1987 when Alfred Molina brutally murdered Gary Oldman in *Prick Up Your Ears*—before committing suicide. Matters became even more grisly in *The Silence of the Lambs* (1991) when a gay character going by the name of Buffalo Bill expressed an urge to make coats from the skins of his victims. The following year, Sharon Stone became the ice-pick-wielding serial killer Catherine Tramell in Paul Verhoeven's gratuitous ode to lesbophobia, *Basic Instinct*.

Single White Female (1992) seemed to take up where *Basic Instinct* left off with its killer lesbian theme. It had Jennifer Jason Leigh becoming so fascinated by her roommate, Bridget Fonda, that she all but took on her identity. The theme was interesting in theory, but the film degenerated into a slasher film in the last reel.

The TV movie *Overkill* (1992) starred Jean Smart as the rampaging Aileen Wuornos, who lived with a woman during a killing spree that saw her murder seven men between 1989 and 1990. A documentary on her life, *The Selling of a Serial Killer*, followed this in 1993. *Girlfriends* —a Mark Bosko/Wayne Harold film that dealt with two lesbian killers who pick up men, kill them, and then steal their wallets—was made the same year. It billed itself as a comedy.

Butterfly Kiss (1994) was a strange British film about a lesbian serial killer played by Amanda Plummer. She picks up Saskia Reeves at a service station before unleashing her mayhem. This was like *Overkill* for slow learners, an ill-thought-out road movie that merely scratched the surface of mental illness while purporting to be an analysis of two women discarded by the harsh economic policies of Margaret Thatcher's Britain. By some oblique osmosis, this seems to be the cause of so much blood being shed.

Todd Verow's *Frisk* (1995) was a narrative about a gay serial killer's slide into insanity. *Who Killed Pasolini?* was made the same year. It concerned the murder of the renowned film director Pier Paolo Pasolini. *Perverted Justice* (1996) was a documentary that asked the question: Do lesbians kill more often than straight people? It made the point that statistically they didn't, but added that 40 percent of the women on death row were lesbian at the time the film was made. There was also, it pointed out, an inordinate number of poor people and people of color on death row, in contrast to other demographics.

One of the most brutal murders of an LGBTQ character occurred in *Boys Don't Cry* (1999), Kimberly Peirce's grueling account of the life and death of Brandon Teena, a transgender character played by Hilary Swank. The fact that it was based on a true story doubled its horror. It was followed in 2000 by the German film *No One Sleeps.* This dealt with the murder of AIDS victims in San Francisco.

Patty Jenkins's *Monster* (2003) tried to rehabilitate the reputation of Aileen Wuornos. It made significant strides in doing so thanks to a pulsating performance by Charlize Theron in the lead role, but the random nature of Wuornos's murders, as well as their brutality, made it difficult for people to sympathize with her as much as Theron and Jenkins did. Wuornos had a horrifying youth, to be sure, but using this to mitigate, if not condone, her multiple murders seemed to be a case of attempting to defend the indefensible. Wuornos didn't start killing until her lesbian partner caused her to explore her own lesbian nature. What does that say to us about being gay? Or Hollywood? Once again there was an alliance drawn between gay sex and psychosis.

Monster was a well-intentioned film. The same could hardly be said for *The Roommate* (2011), a trashy spin-off of *Single White Female*, with the psycho played by Leighton Meester. She immerses herself so much in the life of Minka Kelly that she even gets a tattoo of her dead sister on her chest so she can "become" her.

In more recent years, the violent deaths of gay people in films has shifted from murder to suicide, which suggests a softening in tone from directors, but unfortunately one is still dealing with death instead of life here, which is far from an ideal situation.

Further Reading

Bataille, George. 1986. *Erotism: Death and Sensuality.* San Francisco: City Lights.
Duggan, Lisa. 2000. *Sapphic Slashers: Sex, Violence and American Modernity.* Durham, NC: Duke University Press.
Edelman, Lee. 2004. *No Future: Queer Theory and the Death Drive.* Durham, NC: Duke University Press.
Hart, Lynda. 1994. *Fatal Women: Lesbian Sexuality and the Mark of Aggression.* Princeton, NJ: Princeton University Press.
Howes, Keith. 1993. *Broadcasting It.* London: Cassell.
Renzetti, Claire M., and Charles H. Miley. 1996. *Violence in Gay and Lesbian Domestic Partnerships.* New York: Routledge.

My Own Private Idaho (1991)

Gus Van Sant excelled himself with this poignant trendsetter starring River Phoenix as Mike Waters, a narcoleptic rent boy searching for his mother and in the process engaging the affections of fellow street hustler Scott Favor (Keanu Reeves), a mayor's son. Scott has forsaken his life of comfort to live on the streets. Mike is attracted to him but too inhibited to express his true feelings for him.

His narcolepsy means he's often picked up by strangers and sexually exploited by them. Such is his character that he seems unfazed by this, as if anything that happens without his being aware of it doesn't reflect on him, even subconsciously. Mike is determinedly gay, but Scott has sex with men purely (or rather impurely) for mercenary reasons. This is also a rebellious gesture against his privileged background.

Mike and Scott live in a derelict building for a time but are then forced out by the police. Afterward they travel to Italy. Here Scott falls in love with Carmelia (Chiara Caselli). When his father dies, he inherits the family fortune. He then deserts Mike and a small-time crook, Bob (William Richert), who'd hoped to be brought in on it.

Van Sant resists few opportunities to display all the beauties of his art house direction on us as the shiftless trio go on the road together. The film is a visual symphony that draws one hypnotically into its web in almost every scene. Strongly inspired by German expressionism in his style, Van Sant weaves his tapestry of desire and rejection in mesmeric fashion, drawing performances from his two leads that belie their pretty-boy status. Reeves especially rebuts charges that he could never amount to more than eye candy. The film is like an extended dream, a tone poem about the outsider's need to belong.

There's a subplot based on Shakespeare's *Henry IV.* Van Sant telegraphs it to us by dint of some juicy Elizabethan verbiage. The film goes its own way so innovatively, one feels it would be nitpicking to carp about its detours. Asked why he featured Shakespeare in the film, Van Sant replied that it was his way of showing how life on the street hadn't changed since the days of the Stratford bard (Hays, 2007: 334).

The poetic script adds to the dreamy atmosphere. At one point, Scott says to Mike, "You wouldn't even look at a clock unless hours were lines of coke, or dials looked like the signs of gay bars, or time itself was a fair hustler in black leather." "I'm a connoisseur of roads," Mike explains. "I've been tasting them my whole life. This road will never end. It probably goes all around the world." That may be so, but it also travels cyclically back to himself. He ends as he began, rootless and love hungry.

Mike finally gets up the courage to tell Scott he loves him. "I only have sex for money," Scott declares. "Two guys can't love each other."

Van Sant eroticizes the relationship between them with some highly charged imagery. During a scene of fellatio, he counterpoints Mike's face with the spectacle of a barn falling from the sky and crashing into pieces. It's just one of the inspired symbols in the film.

Both Reeves and Phoenix researched their roles by hanging out with actual street hustlers, stopping just short of getting into cars with their clients (*BoxOffice*, October 1991). There's an obvious male and female dynamic at work in their relationship, Mike is clearly the more vulnerable of the two. In an interview about the film, Reeves stated that he liked working with Phoenix so much he'd like to do a Shakespeare play with him. Phoenix countered that he'd be happy to play Juliet to Reeves's Romeo (Hart, 2013: 27).

Phoenix was seen as the James Dean of his generation before he died, a sensitive icon who may have been either straight or gay—or even bisexual—while almost not being aware of this. Such ambiguity seemed to increase his desirability for both sexes. Women wanted to bed him and men wanted to be him—and maybe bed him too.

The fact that neither Reeves nor Phoenix was gay in real life opened the film to a wider audience than it might otherwise have had. This was a coup for Van Sant. Not all A-list stars feel comfortable playing characters of different sexual persuasions. Both Reeves and Phoenix were comfortable doing so and it showed.

The film wasn't liked in all quarters. Paul Roen thought Reeves's performance was at odds with his "skuzzy, neo-realist surroundings" (Roen, 1997: 134). Others felt it was too self-indulgent. But most people regarded it as a revelation. It wasn't shown at the Los Angeles Gay and Lesbian Film and Video Festival because the distributors didn't want it marketed as a gay film. They felt such a tag would frighten straight people away. Such an attitude was disappointing. It seemed to hark back to a much earlier era (*Los Angeles Times*, July 9, 1991).

My Own Private Idaho is the film most people remember River Phoenix for today. "He was beautiful," Michael Ferguson wrote. "He carried with him the baggage of a one-time teen star whose extraordinary natural talent insisted he had more to give than just another face on a magazine cover." His performance gave "cultural empowerment" to gay men, Ferguson contended. "He has inner beauty as Mike. He yearns for us to reach out to the screen and take him in our arms" (Ferguson, 2003: 247).

Related Films
Midnight Cowboy (1969); *Mala Noche* (1985); *Drugstore Cowboy* (1989); *Hustler White* (1995); *Johns* (1995); *French Dressing* (1997).

Further Reading
BoxOffice, October 1991.
Ferguson, Michael. 2003. *Idol Worship: A Shameless Celebration of Male Beauty in the Movies*. Sarasota, FL: STARbooks.
Glatt, John. 1995. *Lost in Hollywood: The Fast Times and Short Life of River Phoenix*. New York: Primus.
Hart, Kylo-Patrick R. 2013. *Queer Males in Contemporary Cinema*. Lanham, MD: Scarecrow Press.
Hays, Matthew. 2007. *The View from Here: Conversations with Gay and Lesbian Filmmakers*. Vancouver, BC: Arsenal Pulp Press.
Lang, Robert. 2002. *Masculine Interests*. New York: Columbia University Press.
Los Angeles Times, July 9, 1991.
Parish, James Robert. 2001. *Gus: An Unauthorized Biography of Gus Van Sant*. New York: Thunder's Mouth Press.
Roen, Paul. 1997. *High Camp: A Gay Guide to Camp and Cult Films*. San Francisco: Leyland Publications.
Stempel, Penny. 2000. *River Phoenix: They Died Too Young*. Philadelphia: Chelsea House.

Myra Breckinridge (1970)

Sex reassignment surgery doesn't always go well. But Myron, a gay film critic played by Rex Reed, can have few gripes when surgery turns her into one of the most desirable women on the planet in this trashy adaptation of Gore Vidal's satire from writer/director Michael Sarne.

After Myron transitions to be the delectable Myra (Raquel Welch), she heads for Hollywood to claim her share of an Acting Academy founded by her uncle Buck (John Huston).

She tells Uncle Buck she's Myron's widow and demands her inheritance from him. He's reluctant to give this to her. Instead he offers her a teaching job in the academy. But Myra isn't very interested in acting. A bigger ambition she nurtures is to emasculate any virile men she sees. Thus it isn't long before the handsome stud Rusty (Roger Herren) is raped by the transsexual. He runs to the beach home of talent agent Leticia van Allen (Mae West) for succor. Rusty's bewildered girlfriend, Mary Ann (Farrah Fawcett), tells Myra how terrible she feels. She expects empathy from her, but instead of consoling her, Myra tries to seduce her.

Myra is knocked down by a car toward the end of the film. As she lies in the hospital, she turns back into Myron. Myron looks for his breasts but can't find them. He realizes all the events he thought happened to him were just a dream. The film in essence has been a hoax, a very elaborate one. Myron now goes out onto the street and starts dancing. Myra appears beside him. Together they take a cab into the sunset.

Love it or hate it, the film has something weirdly different about it from most others. Myron sees life in terms of a Hollywood fantasy. Sarne used film clips to punctuate his thoughts, even during the rape scene where he had Shirley Temple milking a goat. As she did so, the milk squirted up into her face. The orgasmic symbolism was hardly subtle. It was like something one might see in a Russ Meyers movie, or a John Waters one.

This footage was later excised. It was replaced by clips from a Laurel and Hardy film. These weren't nearly as funny. It was Richard Nixon, of all people, who objected. He'd heard about the sequence and he felt Temple, who was a dedicated Republican, would hardly have been amused. He was probably right, but the film suffered as a result. The sexual charge went out of it.

Myra Breckinridge is probably more famous—or rather infamous—today for the circumstances surrounding the making of it than anything endemic in the film itself. So many people fought on the set, the exceptions were the ones who didn't. Almost before the ink was dry on their contracts, most of the cast seemed to realize they'd made a terrible mistake in signing up for it. Elizabeth Taylor, who'd been offered the Welch role, breathed a large sigh of relief as she heard about the squabbling.

Most of the friction emanated from the film's two sex symbols. "I've admired you for so long," Welch told West. This was a left-handed compliment hinting at her age. When they got talking about how much sex they might be able to get away with in the film, West remarked, "Honey, I used to have censor trouble when a man even sat on my lap" (Cashin, 1982: 170). She secured top billing over Welch, which was some achievement for a seventy-eight-year-old.

She also got most of the film's raunchiest lines. When she asks a man how tall he is, he replies, "Six feet seven inches." West says, "Never mind the six feet. Let's discuss the seven inches!" This was amusing but vulgar, unlike her one-liners of yore. The famous innuendoes of yesteryear were gone. Had she sold out to the current penchant for crudity? The fact that she was threatened by Welch, who was to hot-blooded men what West had been almost a half century before, made her

Mae West (1892–1980)

West was once defined as "a plumber's idea of Cleopatra" (Jarman, 1991: 144). She had sex appeal to be sure, but she masculinized it by her leers, by the way she stood, by the way she put her hands on her hips as she spoke. Her husky voice was also androgynous, as it was for actresses like Marlene Dietrich and Lauren Bacall, and even Lizabeth Scott. Vincent Canby described her in *Sextette*, one of her later films, as "a disorienting freak show . . . a plump sheet that's been stood on its hind legs, dressed in a drag queen's idea of chic, bewigged and then seared with pink plaster" (*New York Times*, June 8, 1979).

Her 1926 play, *Sex*, dealt with being gay. It was regarded as before its time, but it was closed down for obscenity. The cast spent ten days in jail as a result. Not to be deterred, West wrote another one the following year (*The Drag*) on a similar theme.

She sometimes referred to gay people as her "sisters" (Braun, 2002: 51). Her attitude to them was sympathetic but somewhat quaint. Many men suspected of being in the closet (Cary Grant, Randolph Scott, etc.) starred opposite her in her films.

Pamela Robertson thought she was grotesque, "a man in drag, a joke on women but not a woman" (Robertson, 1996: 29). "So complete was her androgyny," wrote Molly Haskell, "that one hardly knows to which sex she belongs. By any ideological standards of film criticism she's an anomaly—too masculine to be a female impersonator, too gay in her taste to be a woman." Paul Roen likened her to a gay man trapped in a woman's body (Roen, 1994: 14).

Further Reading

Braun, Eric. 2002. *Frightening the Horses: Gay Icons of the Cinema*. London: Reynolds & Hearn.
Haskell, Molly. 1987. *From Reverence to Rape: The Treatment of Women in the Movies*. Chicago and London: University of Chicago Press.
Jarman, Colin, ed. 1991. *The Guinness Dictionary of Poisonous Quotes*. London: Guinness Publishing.
New York Times, June 8, 1979.
Robertson, Pamela. 1996. *Guilty Pleasures: Feminist Camp from Mae West to Madonna*. Durham, NC, and London: Duke University Press.
Roen, Paul. 1994. *High Camp*. San Francisco: Leyland Publications.

---

look for her effects too quickly. Such a tendency seemed to emanate from a sense of frustration that her time in the sun had long gone.

The film was based on a Gore Vidal novel. Vidal saw his work sabotaged by three things: West's desperation, Welch's parading of her vital statistics, and Sarne's desire to make a fast buck. Huston tried to preserve his dignity in the midst of it all, comparing himself to "a piano player in a whorehouse" (Porter and Prince, 2010: 435). He was just one of a number of lovably kitschy freaks on Sarne's overheated set.

The film was booed when it premiered, its outrageous sense hardly appreciated by a world still reeling from the recent deaths of Sharon Tate and so many of her friends at the hands of the demonic Charles Manson "family." The manner in which it embraced excess was untimely, but it enjoyed something of a cult following. Crowds started to attend it when it went on general release, many doing so more out of curiosity than anything else. Vidal referred to it as "a hearse" rather than a "vehicle." He claimed that "for the first time in the history of paperback publishing, the film of a book proved to be so bad that sales of the book stopped" (Leonard, 1991: 365).

Reviewers dipped their pens in acid to find the most vituperative phrases they could to debunk it. "The most literally immortal Mae West," one of them sniped, "heaves through the film like an ancient Cunarder, still pulsating to the churning of her turbines" (Cashin, 172).

The horse was dead but it continued to be flogged. After the rape scene, Vincent Canby wrote in the *New York Times*, the film collapsed "like a tired, smirking elephant." He had a point. After running out of ideas, it tried to fill the gaps with ever more outlandish scenarios that only served to fortify its artistic bankruptcy (Parish, 1993: 264).

The *Hollywood Reporter* was even more vicious than the *New York Times*. Steven Daly wrote of a photographic advertisement for the film: "There was Welch, pneumatic and Stepford serene; Mae West looking more and more like a Madame Tussauds exhibit than a working actress, and game old John Huston in cowboy drag. Then there was Sarne, bearded and beatific, resembling a superannuated beach bum" (*Vanity Fair*, April 2001). *Time* thought it was about as funny as a child molester (*Time*, July 6, 1970).

As the executives at Twentieth Century Fox fought to have its X rating removed, West remained unperturbed. "I would be insulted if a film of mine didn't get an X rating," she assured them (Cashin, 172).

Because of the rape, and other elements of the plot, the film sailed dangerously close to pornography. Another scene had Welch engaged in a lesbian clinch with Farrah Fawcett. Middle America was outraged. Many viewers thought it was representative of everything that was wrong with the country. It was a flop at the box office, but its cult following continued for years after its release. In a sense this is still going on.

Daring for its time, today it looks more like a tame divertissement. From Welch's point of view, it reassured her about the fact that she was able to stretch her sex appeal in a kind of avant-garde direction, which brought her from beyond the pages of men's magazines and one-dimensional T&A ventures where she appeared to do little but parade her estimable mammaries at salivating costars.

Most people hated the film, but such hatred was so passionate it adversely conferred a kind of iconoclastic status on it. Today it's widely regarded as one of the worst films ever made. So why are we still talking about it? This is probably its greatest mystery of all.

Related Films
Bedazzled (1967); *Beyond the Valley of the Dolls* (1970); *Sextette* (1978).

Further Reading
Cashin, Fergus. 1982. *Mae West: A Biography*. London: W. H. Allen.

Dyer, Richard, ed. 1984. *Gays and Film*. London: Zoetrope.

Leonard, Maurice. 1991. *Mae West: Empress of Sex*. London: HarperCollins.

Parish, James Robert. 1993. *Gays and Lesbians in Mainstream Cinema*. Jefferson, NC: McFarland.

Porter, Darwin, and Danforth Prince. 2010. *50 Years of Queer Cinema*. New York: Blood Moon Productions.

Time, July 6, 1970.

Vanity Fair, April 2001.

Vidal, Gore. 1993. *Myra Breckinridge and Myron*. London: Abacus.

The Oscars

When *Midnight Cowboy* won a Best Picture Oscar in 1969, it was a breakthrough not so much for LGBTQ films as X-rated ones, because the relationship between Jon Voight and Dustin Hoffman wasn't strictly gay. No X-rated film had won an Academy Award for Best Picture before this. It created a precedent in that it won an Oscar for its gay director, John Schlesinger, though he was in the closet in those days.

Two years later Schlesinger was nominated for Best Director again, this time for *Sunday Bloody Sunday*, which had an overtly gay theme. Peter Finch and Glenda Jackson were also nominated for Best Actor and Best Actress for their performances, and Penelope Gilliatt for Best Adapted Screenplay. Finch played a gay man in the film. All three went home empty-handed, unfortunately, *The French Connection* scooping most of the awards on offer that year.

Bob Fosse won Best Director for *Cabaret* in 1972. Liza Minnelli was adjudged to be Best Actress for playing the androgynous Sally Bowles in the film. Joel Grey scooped the Best Supporting Actor award as the gloriously decadent MC of the Kit Kat Club. Geoffrey Unsworth also received an Oscar for his cinematography.

Valerie Perrine won a Best Actress Oscar for playing the stripper wife of Lenny Bruce in *Lenny* in 1974. The film included a scene of her making love to another woman. Al Pacino was nominated for his scintillating turn as a gay bank robber with a heart of gold in Sidney Lumet's *Dog Day Afternoon* the following year. So was Lumet, but neither of them won. The Academy often showered its benison on a single film, as it did with *The French Connection* in 1971. In 1974 it was the turn of Milos Forman's *One Flew Over the Cuckoo's Nest* to sweep the boards.

LGBTQ films did very well at the 1982 ceremonies. *Victor/Victoria* received seven nominations and *Tootsie* received ten. John Lithgow was nominated for his endearing portrayal of a transsexual in *The World According to Garp*. In 1983, Linda Hunt won Best Supporting Actress for playing a male photographer in *The Year of Living Dangerously*. In 1984, *The Times of Harvey Milk* won Best Documentary, another LGBTQ first. In front of a million people watching the ceremonies worldwide, producer Robert Epstein thanked his partner, John Wright, and his coproducer, Richard Schmiechen. He said he was proud to be gay and looked forward to a time when there would be mutual respect between gay and heterosexual communities. Vanessa Redgrave was the first actress to be nominated for a leading role as a gay person in *The Bostonians* when that honor was conferred on her that year. Two years later, William Hurt became the first actor to win an Oscar for playing a transgender man. This was in Hector Babenco's *The Kiss of the Spider Woman*, which was also nominated for Best Picture.

Common Threads: Stories from the Quilt followed on the success of *The Times of Harvey Milk* by winning Best Documentary in 1989. Another boost for the fight against AIDS came when Bruce Davison was nominated for Best Actor for a very dignified performance in Norman René's *Longtime Companion* the following year. Sadly, the damagingly homophobic Jonathan Demme feature, *The Silence of the Lambs*, took everything before it in 1991, winning all four of the "upstairs" awards—Best Picture, Best Director, Best Actor, and Best Actress. It was the first time this had been achieved since Milos Forman's *One Flew over the Cuckoo's Nest* in 1975 Jodie Foster's Best Actress award for the film angered people who knew she was a closet lesbian at this time.

Ireland's Neil Jordan won an Oscar for Best Original Screenplay in 1992 for *The Crying Game*, a film with one of the biggest sexual surprises in film history when Jaye Davison, playing a character believed to be a woman up until this point, suddenly displays a penis.

Tom Hanks won an Oscar for *Philadelphia* in 1993. The film drew much attention both to AIDS and LGBTQ issues, though many people had problems with its sexual coyness. Neither did it help that Hanks—like William Hurt—was straight in real life. Gay people wondered if the day would ever come when a gay actor would win an Oscar for playing a gay man or woman.

The Adventures of Priscilla, Queen of the Desert won an Oscar for Costume Design the following year. Kevin Spacey won an Oscar for playing a man who fantasizes about an underage girl in Sam Mendez's *American Beauty* (1999). The film focused primarily on Spacey's Lolita-like obsession with Mena Suvari, but a subtheme—disappointingly sidelined—was the repressed marine played so hysterically by Chris Cooper, and the contrasting tranquility of the openly gay couple who lived next door to Spacey, Scott Bakula and Sam Robards.

Todd Haynes is a director who's been knocking on the door for an Oscar for many years now. He was nominated for *Far from Heaven* in 2002 to no avail. The film's other nominations—for Best Actress, Cinematography, Score, and Writing Directly for the Screen—also came up short. Charlize Theron won Best Actress for a powerhouse performance as the serial killer Aileen Wuornos in Patty Jenkins's *Monster* in 2003. The film gave rise to a debate about whether Wuornos was lesbian or just someone who lived with a woman because she hated men so much.

Brokeback Mountain, a film based on an Annie Proulx short story about two men who fall in love in Wyoming in the 1960s, created a sensation when A-list actors Heath Ledger and Jake Gyllenhaal took the two lead roles. People such as Leonardo DiCaprio, Brad Pitt, Matt Damon, and Ryan Philippe all passed on it before Ledger and Gyllenhaal decided to take the plunge (*Irish Independent*, July 28, 2018).

Ang Lee won Best Director for it. It picked up many other nominations as well, but the Oscar for Best Film eluded it, going instead to *Crash*, a film about smoldering racial tension in LA. Both Lee and Proulx made their dissatisfaction manifest about this. Should the Best Film award not go to the Best Director almost as a matter of course? It seemed so. *Crash* won Best Film. Paul Haggis, who helmed it, had been nominated for Best Director but he was beaten by Lee. There was a lot of tension in the air in the days following the distribution of the awards, most of it coming from the *Brokeback* camp. Lee's award was seen as a kind of Trojan horse designed to lull people into thinking intolerance on screen was at an end instead of being merely in abeyance.

Brokeback Mountain won Best Adapted Screenplay and Best Original Score. It was the favorite to win Best Film in the run-up to the ceremonies but crashed and burned in the final stretch (Piazza, 200: 331). One writer felt the reason for this was the rawness of its first sex scene—"what gay men do to each other." This, he felt, made straight America "squirm" and enticed voters to go for the "safe, feel-good film about racism" (Handley, 2011: 113).

Ledger was nominated for Best Actor but not Gyllenhaal. He was beaten by Philip Seymour Hoffman for *Capote*. It was the first time two actors playing gay men had gone head-to-head in an Oscar race. As if that wasn't enough, Felicity Huffman was nominated for Best Actress for her role as a transgender character in *Transamerica* that year too. Unfortunately, she lost to Reese Witherspoon. Witherspoon played Johnny Cash's wife, June, in *Walk the Line*. Once again, the Academy had gone for the safe option.

Alicia Vikander won Best Supporting Actress for *The Danish Girl* in 2015. This was another cause for concern in LGBTQ circles. Who was the real "Danish" girl of the film, the straight Vikander or her husband, played by Eddie Redmayne? Redmayne took on the role of a character based on Lily Elbe. Elbe pioneered sex reassignment surgery in the 1920s. Redmayne was captivating in the film, but he couldn't convert his Oscar nomination into a win. He had, of course, already won an Oscar for playing Stephen Hawking in *The Theory of Everything* in 2014. This was possibly a factor in the Academy's decision.

Todd Haynes's *Carol* earned a string of nominations that year. There were citations for Cinematography, Costume Design, Original Music Score, and Adapted Screenplay, but all the nominees were bypassed in the end. Haynes himself hadn't been nominated, which seemed anomalous in the circumstances.

Moonlight won Best Film in 2017 for telling the story of the young life of a black gay man in a very elegiac manner—but only after Faye Dunaway announced that the award was being given to *La La Land* instead. This was one of the most embarrassing mistakes in Oscar history. The right decision was made in the end but heads rolled in PricewaterhouseCoopers in the aftermath of the ceremonies, which seemed to launch a double broadside against both gay people and African Americans by its momentous gaffe.

Further Reading

Bona, Damien. 2002. *Inside Oscar 2*. New York: Ballantine Books.

Handley, William R., ed. 2011. *The Brokeback Book: From Story to Cultural Phenomenon*. Lincoln and London: University of Nebraska Press.

Irish Independent, July 28, 2018.

Levy, Emanuel. 2003. *All about Oscar: The History and Politics of the Academy Awards*. New York and London: Abbeville Press.

Osborne, Robert. 2008. *80 Years of the Oscar: The Official History of the Academy Awards*. New York and London: Abbeville Press.

Piazza, Jim, and Gail Kinn. 2008. *The Academy Awards: The Complete Unofficial History*. New York: Black Dog & Leventhal.

P

Paris Is Burning (1990)

Drag balls were the most visible manifestation of queer culture in Harlem in the early years of the twentieth century. At a time when it was illegal to cross-dress in public, they provided a forum for people of a certain persuasion to transport themselves as they pleased in whatever getups they liked without fear of censure or police harassment. They were called "spectacles of color" by the Harlem Renaissance poet Langston Hughes and were attended by both black and white audiences (Hilderbrand, 2013: 45).

Jennie Livingston, a white lesbian, celebrates this appetizing tapestry in *Paris Is Burning*, a documentary on the balls as experienced by African American and Latino people of different gender identities. They were sanctuaries for such people, places of refuge as well as temporary releases from their often poverty-stricken lives.

Legendary queens like Dorian Corey and Pepper LaBeija take center stage in the film. Willi Ninja also struts his stuff in an effort to win some silverware. There's also Venus Extravaganza, Freddie Pendavis, and Octavia Saint Laurent. They organize themselves in "houses" that are named after French haute couture, taking on the roles of parents, children, and businessmen on imaginary runways. The characters have to immerse themselves in a fictitious role. One of the roles featured involves going back into the closet. Wearing conventional dress isn't enough. To win a prize one has to act the part as well. Other parts are Femme Queen Realness, Butch Queen Realness, Military Realness, and Butch Queen First Time in Drag Realness.

The general expression used for such role-playing was "vogueing." This was a term that was new to most straight people, and indeed many gay ones, in 1990. After the film was released, however, it entered the mainstream. It was first coined by *Vogue* magazine to denote a form of moving that was halfway between dancing and striking the kinds of poses supermodels used on catwalks. One of its great advantages is that any form of music can be used as an accompaniment to it.

Livingston's film is a paean both to interpretive dancing and joie de vivre. She presents us with a truly diverse crew of gay people who dress up (and sometimes down) to make their moves. Everyone from roughneck street thugs to sharp-suited Wall Street executives appear. The contestants mimic both the grime they've come from and the opulence they can never aspire to. AIDS may be decimating the outside world, but here in this haven of goodwill they act out their fantasies. "A lot of these kids," says LaBeija, "they don't have two of nothing. Some of them don't even eat. They come to the balls starving and they sleep on the pier. They don't have a home to go to."

Livingston draws their life histories from them in a series of interviews that are both uplifting and heartbreaking. They talk about everything from racism to transphobia to being evicted from their homes. Some of them have resorted to prostitution to keep a roof over their heads.

Venus expresses a wish to be a "rich spoiled white girl." Being poor and black are two disadvantages for her in life. Perhaps being a "girl" is a third in a male-dominated universe. Tragically, she died during the making of the film. She was found dead under a bed in the Duchess Hotel in New York on Valentine's Day 1988. It's believed she was murdered by an enraged "john" who discovered she was TG. Her killer was never found.

Livingston was castigated by some viewers of the film for exploiting the lives of disenfranchised black people for the edification of white art house audiences. This was a preposterous charge. She spent five years living among New York's black and Hispanic cross-dressing community to make her film. Hardly a day went by that she didn't fret about the danger of it failing to reach fruition. She felt the plug could be pulled by her backers at any moment. She was turned down a number of times for funding, even once by the Resource Center that put up the money for *The Times of Harvey Milk* in 1984. It didn't fit their agenda, she lamented, because the gay mainstream, "which is essentially white and middle-class, doesn't want to be shown drag queens" (*Village Voice*, March 26, 1991).

If one feels in form for some wickedly inventive fantasy-play, it might be an idea to dive into the diverse delights on display here as an underprivileged but never bitter set of jivers get their collective mojos working. It isn't only Paris that's burning in this heady brew but New York too. Its ethnic mix and funky music score makes for an irresistible cocktail.

Related Films
The Salt Mines (1990); *Adventures in the Gender Trade* (1993); *Octavia St. Laurent: Queen of the Underground* (1993); *Neptune's Rocking Horse* (1996); *Lavender Limelight* (1997); *The Cockettes* (2002); *How Do I Look?* (2006).

Further Reading
Butler, J. 1999. *Feminist Film Theory: A Reader.* Edinburgh: Edinburgh University Press.

Dubois, W. E. B. 1969. *The Souls of Black People.* New York: New American Library.

Hilderbrand, Lucas. 2013. *Paris Is Burning: A Queer Film Classic.* Vancouver, BC: Arsenal Pulp Press.

Kipnis, Laura. 1999. *Bound and Gagged: Pornography and the Politics of Fantasy in America.* Durham, NC: Duke University Press.

Marangoly George, Rosemary. 1998. *Burning Down the House: Recycling Domesticity.* Boulder, CO: Westview Press.

Noriega, Chon A., and Ana M. Lopez, eds. 1992. *In the Ethnic Eye.* Latino Media Arts, Minneapolis: University of Minnesota Press.

Village Voice, March 26, 1991.

Parting Glances (1986)

This emotional tale of love lost and won takes place within a twenty-four-hour period in Manhattan. Centering on the problems in a relationship between a man whose job in a health organization is about to take him to Africa and the lover he's going to be leaving behind, it's refreshingly free from sensationalism and refuses to wear its (large) heart on its sleeve. Bill Sherwood directs.

Robert (John Bolger) plays the character about to depart for Africa. Michael (Richard Ganoung) is the partner he's leaving behind. The parting would be more traumatic if their relationship was stronger, but it's started to become stale of late. The film largely comprises Robert's series of farewells, not only to Michael but also to Michael's ex-lover Nick (Steve Buscemi), an eccentric rock musician who's contracted the AIDS virus. It was directed and written by Bill Sherwood, who would himself die of an AIDS-related illness four years after it was made. Sherwood downplays his tableaus, but he's never downbeat. It's a mainly laid-back film full of kooky characters.

The plot kicks off when Robert and Michael attend a farewell dinner for Robert hosted by his boss, Cecil (Patrick Tull), and his wife, Betty (Yolande Bava). Later on they attend a party thrown by their mutual friend Joan (Kathy Kinney). Here Michael overhears Robert trivializing his relationship with Nick. Later on he confronts him about his cynical attitude to people. In the course of their conversation it emerges that it was Robert himself who asked for the move overseas because of his discomfort at being around Nick. He can't cope with the prospect of his impending demise. He's also aware that his relationship with Michael is problematic. He tells Michael to spend more time with Nick. He himself is starting to feel "in the way."

The turning point of the film comes when Michael realizes he cares more for Nick more than he does for Robert. As Nick's depression about his illness increases, Robert decides not to go away after all. By the end, it looks as if Michael and Robert are going to stay together, despite Michael's strong emotional link to Nick. The interplay between the three men is continually thrown into flux, but Sherwood weaves them together in a manner that's both credible and low-key as the film winds toward its (literally) dying fall. Of the three of them, Nick's story lingers longest in the memory thanks to Buscemi's bravura performance. This never solicits our sympathy but gains it for that precise reason.

The "day in the life" format of the film works very well, giving it an urgency lacking in many films dealing with terminal illness and/or pivotal moments in people's lives. It also has moments of humor. These soften its plaintive edge, as in the scene where one of Nick's friends reveals to him how he realized he was gay during puberty. There were other interesting peripheral characters too, like the secretly bisexual Cecil.

The script is succinct. When a friend of Michael's asks him what he's going to do when Nick is gone, he says simply, "Miss him." In another scene Nick says to Michael, "You know the difference between straight guys and gay guys?" When Michael tells him he forgets, Nick says, "There's none. This is a scary and seldom understood fact. Straight guys are jerks. Gay guys are jerks." It's this determination not to try to be profound, either about death or the differences between sexual orientations, that makes the film unique. By refusing to become saccharine it wins us over on the double.

It was both Sherwood's maiden voyage and his swan song. He would undoubtedly have had a prolific career had he lived. Instead we have only this to remember him by. He had the good sense to employ Christine Vachon as his assistant editor, however, and she went on to produce the kind of work he could have had if fortune smiled on him, with films like *Go Fish* (1994) and *Boys Don't Cry* (1999) on her CV.

Parting Glances was well received. Janet Maslin thought it was superficial in parts but conceded that it portrayed the anguish of AIDS intelligently, "as part of a larger fabric, understood in context, and never in a maudlin light" (*New York Times*, February 19, 1986). It was one of the first films to deal with the disease in a sensitive way at a time when the Reagan administration was being deafeningly silent about it.

Related Films
Buddies (1985); *An Early Frost* (1985); *Longtime Companion* (1990); *The Dinner Guest* (1995); *It's My Party* (1996).

Further Reading
Davies, Steven Paul. 2008. *Out at the Movies: A History of Gay Cinema.* Herts, UK: Kamera Books.
Duralde, Alonso. 2005. *101 Must-See Movies for Gay Men.* New York: Advocate Books.
New York Times, February 19, 1986.
Stewart, Steve. 1994. *Gay Hollywood Film and Video Guide.* Laguna Hills, CA: Companion Publications.
Wade, Chris. 2017. *Steve Buscemi: Top Ten Movies.* www.lulu.com.

Anthony Perkins (1932–92)

Perkins's father, Osgood, who was also an actor, died when Anthony was five. This possibly explains his extrastrong relationship to his mother, which would bleed into his most famous film role, *Psycho.*

He played a man suspected of being gay in *Tea and Sympathy* on Broadway in 1953, taking over the role from John Kerr, but Kerr was preferred for the film version opposite Deborah Kerr (no relation). He got his first film break from George Cukor, who was also gay. He cast him as Jean Simmons's boyfriend in *The Actress* in the same year.

Perkins received a Best Supporting Actor nomination for playing Gary Cooper's son in *Friendly Persuasion* in 1956. He followed this with *The Lonely Man* (1957), a film in which he played a character with an excessive devotion to his mother. Already the connections between art and life were making themselves felt.

Fear Strikes Out (also 1957) was his first starring role. He was a sheriff in *The Tin Star*, his third 1957 outing. The following year he dressed up as a woman for a scene in *The Matchmaker,* a kind of nonmusical version of *Hello, Dolly.* He played

Sophia Loren's stepson in the film version of Eugene O'Neill's *Desire Under the Elms* that year too, and also appeared in *This Angry Age*.

Perkins stayed in the closet during these years, as did his friend Tab Hunter, with whom he had a long-standing relationship. "I was crazy about Tony," said Hunter, "but our careers pulled us every which way. We lived moment to moment" (Hunter with Muller, 2005: 139). When *Confidential* magazine tried to out them, Perkins became nervous about being seen in public with Hunter, fearing it might "foul up" his contract with Paramount. He even started wearing disguises to fool fans. Hunter found "the whole cloak and dagger thing" ridiculous (Hunter with Muller, 139–40).

He made two films in 1959 (*Green Mansions* and *On the Beach*), and in 1960 appeared in a comedy with Jane Fonda called *Tall Story*. It was her acting debut. Rumors had it that she tried to seduce him on set without success. One scene had them in a shower together.

A much more ominous shower scene occurred with Janet Leigh in his next film, *Psycho*, which changed his life. The role of the psychologically tortured Norman Bates made him famous but also became a monkey on his back. Everything he did afterward was an attempt to break out of its straitjacket, to stop using the mannerisms he'd deployed to such advantage as the schizophrenic Bates.

Made at a time when audiences didn't know too much about Oedipus complexes or gender confusion, Alfred Hitchcock pushed the boat out there, unleashing a mild-mannered motel proprietor who turns into a psychotic killer when his maternal half disapproves of his sexual attraction to Leigh and forces him to slash her to bits. The film took Perkins from boy-next-door status to someone who could do psychosis with terrifying conviction. Few people wanted to talk to him about any of his other films after he made it, which depressed him. Leigh suffered the same fate (Leigh, 1984: 263).

There were many uncanny resemblances between the lives of Bates and Perkins, both of them being the children of overpossessive mothers and absent fathers. Both of their fathers died when they were five years old, both were isolationists, both were pathologically shy with women, and both had confused sexual drives and unnaturally strong ties to their mothers. Perkins admitted to his analyst, in language reminiscent of Bates, "I loved my father but I also wanted him dead so I could have my mother to myself" (Bergan, 1995: 5).

His mother seemed to have had an erotic attraction to him as a child, often fondling him in a sexual manner. "She clearly channeled all the feelings she had had for my father onto me," he believed. "Sometimes I think we were more like lovers than mother and son" (Bergan, 6).

Perkins blocked such memories from his mind for many years. They all came flooding out when he went into therapy, as did his bisexual nature. His main attraction was to men. Though he eventually married and had children, the idea of having sex with a woman appalled him until he was in his forties. "Before then I saw women only as beautiful predators," he explained (Bergan, 7).

His career really stopped with *Psycho*. It became his *Portrait of Dorian Gray*. Wherever he went after the film, people used to come up to him on the street and ask him about it. Some men claimed their wives and girlfriends were afraid to take showers because of him. He grew so frustrated with these revelations he eventually lost his patience with such people and started to make sarcastic comments to them like, "Tell them to get dry-cleaned!" A friend of Perkins's son Osgood even said to him one day in school, "Are you not afraid to take a shower when your father is in the house?" (Bergan, 157).

He made *The Ravishing Idiot* with sex bomb Brigitte Bardot in 1965, but her charms were lost on him. Asked how they got on together, he replied crisply, "We didn't" (Braun, 2002: 180). Many of his films exploited his manic edge. In *The Fool Killer*, also made that year, he played an amnesiac war veteran suspected of being a killer. He appeared with Tuesday Weld in *Pretty Poison* in 1968. The surprise here is that it's Weld who's crazy, not him. He teamed up with her again for *Play It as It Lays* (1972). This time he was a gay film producer who's suicidal.

Offscreen his orientation bothered him so much he had electroshock therapy to try to effect a "cure." He was so much in denial about it he had an affair with Victoria Principal, his costar in *The Life and Times of Judge Roy Bean* (1971), to try to convince himself he was straight (Hunter with Muller, 287).

He had an affair with Joan Hackett in 1973 for the same reason. Afterward he married Berinthia Berenson to complete the "recovery." Sidney Lumet put him into *Lovin' Molly* the following year. He had some love scenes to play with Blythe Danner. Vincent Canby of the *New York Times* felt he showed more feelings for his male costar in the film, Beau Bridges, than he did for Danner (Winecoff, 1997: 343). Lumet used him again for *Murder on the Orient Express* (1974), an Agatha Christie venture where he played a hysterical gay murderer. In *Mahogany* (1975), there was a suggestion his character was bisexual. By the end of the seventies, he was appearing in dross like the sci-fi clunker *The Black Hole* (1979). It was followed by a fifth-rate terrorist film, *ffolkes* (1980).

George Cukor, the director who "discovered" him, said he was attracted to him by his boyishness but that after *Psycho* "Norman Bates began catching up with him." The actor who played all those "lunatics and kooks," he maintained, was not the man he chose for *The Actress* all those years ago (Hadleigh, 2013: 61). Cukor found the facial changes he'd undergone since then deeply upsetting. Boze Hadleigh described him as a "haunted Peter Pan" (Hadleigh, 61).

Perkins was well aware of the fact that his career fell into a time warp after *Psycho*. He told Alan Arkin he was sitting in the back of a taxi one day when the driver said to him, "Excuse me, but didn't you used to be Anthony Perkins?" (Arkin, 2011: 65).

By now he was sufficiently chastened to go back to the film that made him a household name. It was like a murderer returning to the scene of the crime—literally. He made a ham-fisted *Psycho II* in 1983, telling Tab Hunter creepily, "I *am* Norman Bates" (Hunter with Muller, 321). At the time the film takes place, Bates has been released from the asylum in which he was incarcerated at the end of the original film. He's ready for more blood-spattering, but unfortunately there was no Alfred Hitchcock to make this version of the franchise work. The phrase "a sequel never equals" sprang to mind.

Perkins played a preacher in Ken Russell's camp comedy, *Crimes of Passion*, in 1984, going into drag for one scene. He followed this with *Twice a Woman* (1985), a film where he gets lines like the cringe-inducing, "They say you're a lesbian. Is that why you can't have children?" Afterward it was back to basics again with *Psycho III* (1986). This time he went behind the camera as well as appearing in it, but it didn't help matters. Maybe it even made them worse.

He contracted AIDS in the late eighties, having continued to make love to men during his marriage to Berenson. He learned about it in the cruelest manner possible, when he spotted a *National Inquirer* headline as he was standing in line at the checkout of his local supermarket. He'd gone to a doctor some time before with facial palsy. The doctor, knowing he was gay, secretly tested his blood. After discovering it to be infected, he broke all trace of medical ethics by leaking the story to *The Inquirer* (Hunter with Muller, 347).

Perkins's last film was *Psycho IV* (1990), a TV prequel that went back to Bates's youth to try to explain his derangement. He wanted to play Hannibal Lecter in *The Silence of the Lambs* (1991), but he wasn't considered for this. Instead he was offered the smaller role of the gay cross-dressing killer in the film, but that didn't appeal to him.

If he'd lived he would probably have made *Psycho V* and maybe even *Psycho VI*, but he died from AIDS in 1992. He declined to take part in fund-raisers for the disease but said from his deathbed, "I've learned more about love and understanding from the people I've met in this great adventure of AIDS than I ever did in the cutthroat competitive world in which I've spent my life" (Hunter with Muller, 347). It was a sad end to a career that promised so much but was so repeatedly derailed by the film most people remember him for today. "With *Psycho*," he lamented, "suddenly I abandoned being the leading man and became the slightly quirky, slightly nervous, tic-ridden juvenile" (Winecoff, 201). The film was synonymous with him right up to the end, with newspaper headlines around the world proclaiming the fact that Norman Bates, not Anthony Perkins, had gone up to that big studio in the sky.

Further Reading
Arkin, Alan. 2011. *An improvised Life: A Memoir*. Cambridge, MA: Da Capo Press.
Bergan, Ronald. 1995. *Anthony Perkins: A Haunted Life*. London: Little Brown.
Braun, Eric. 2002. *Frightening the Horses: Gay Icons of the Cinema*. London: Reynolds & Hearn.
Hadleigh, Boze. 2013. *Hollywood Gays*. Bronx, NY: Magnus Books.
Hunter, Tab, with Eddie Muller. 2005. *Tab Hunter Confidential: The Making of a Movie Star*. Chapel Hill, NC: Algonquin Books.
Leigh, Janet. 1984. *There Really Was a Hollywood*. New York: Jove Books.
Winecoff, Charles. 1997. *Split Image: The Life of Anthony Perkins*. New York: Plume.

Personal Best (1982)

Robert Towne directed this tale of two female athletes whose friendship turns to love during tryouts for the Olympics. Their relationship collapses when a man arrives on the scene.

Chris (Mariel Hemingway) is a hurdler who's being coached by her father when the film begins. Afterward she falls in love with a famous pentathlete, Tory

(Patrice Donnelly). Tory helps her get a spot on the Olympic team and they practice together.

Towne wrote the script as well, but it doesn't ring true to the way lesbians actually relate to one another, either verbally or physically. For him, being lesbian is a temporary diversion from the main highway of life, a side order to the main course. Chris has a "fling" with Tory the way a man from a previous era, in a break from his relationship with his steady girlfriend, might have a fling with a woman. If one thinks of Tory as a man, the film becomes a conventional tale of two athletes becoming physical with one another like a man and a woman under soft lights like in any other sports movie.

The film deals with four years in the two athletes' lives but only in a cursory fashion. One doesn't get to know much about them as people. Neither are the sexual scenes between them realistic. Towne specializes in lush camerawork that explores various areas of their anatomies voyeuristically.

The sexuality on view in *Personal Best* is gratuitous and exploitative. One senses the leering presence of Towne in the scenes where he shows the two women in training for their athletic endeavors on the track, as if this is his way of preparing his heterosexual male viewers up for the "money shots" to come in the boudoir. His slow-mo scenes of Chris and Tori running on beaches also look staged. For an arm-wrestling scene between the two girls, he told them he wanted them naked from the waist down (Biskind, 1998: 396).

Towne said of his two stars, "I like looking at their thighs. I adore them" (*SoHo News*, February 16, 1982). He had an affair with Donnelly on set, but she tired of him and ended their relationship. He then took up with Hemingway.

He also snorted cocaine during the shooting of the film. Bud Smith, who cut it, recalled: "He wasn't paying as much attention to what he was shooting because he was chasing the girls. He was basically a playboy. He loved women, he loved drink and he loved drugs. That, to him, would be a full life" (Biskind, 394–6).

Towne defined being lesbian like this: "It's like a metaphor for losing yourself in someone because you're of the same sex. It's like, I'm not going to be able to tell where I end and someone else begins" (Hadleigh, 1993: 145). It isn't clear what this is a definition of (onanism?) but it's certainly not being gay. Maybe it's Towne's way of saying his focus is going to be on bodies, not minds.

On the other hand, as everyone knows, no director ever went bankrupt showing beautiful women making love, either with one another or with a man. The film turned a handsome profit despite its prominence of prurience over emotional truth. Everybody went home happy except the people to whom it pretended to be made for, LGBTQ audiences. As for the rationale behind it all, Norma McLain Stoop put it best when she said that, for Towne, being gay was like acne, "an inconvenient adolescent affliction one will prayerfully grow out of" (Hadleigh, 145).

Personal Best gave one a "Bounty Bar" version of being lesbian. Both women could have been pictured on the cover of *Vogue* magazine. They didn't represent real emotion any more than *Romeo & Juliet* represents real heterosexual love. It's a sanitized version of it. Audiences may have escaped the "ugly lesbian" scenario, but what Towne has replaced it with is even more tasteless.

When Chris meets Denny (Kenny Moore), he straightens her out by turning her back to her "better" heterosexual self. He says he doesn't care about the rumors floating about that she and Tory did more than push-ups when they were together. She's meant to feel grateful for his "understanding."

The fact that Chris eventually goes straight will evoke groans of "Here we go again" from a generation schooled on films like *The Fox* where being lesbian was seen as a momentary aberration. What makes it even more irksome in this instance is that Towne inserts a nasty rumor about Tory into the plot. At one point Chris suspects she intends to scupper her chances of winning an event by trying to injure her in training. Not only would this be out of character for Tory, it would also be uncharacteristic of Chris to imagine it. The detail shows up the fundamental untrustworthiness of the film. From this point on, one's fears that it will go the way of all former homo-hatred ventures come chillingly to pass.

"I never thought of it as a lesbian relationship when I read the script," Hemingway said, somewhat astoundingly. "That word sounds so perverse, so wrong. What I saw were two people, both innocent. The relationship between them seemed natural. It didn't seem morbid or sordid" (Howes, 1993: 615). Towne had a relatively easy time convincing her the cop-out at the end was valid. Her grandfather Ernest, who wrote an interesting gender-bending book called *The Garden of Eden*—it was unfinished at the time of his death and was published posthumously—would have been disappointed in her simplistic evaluation of the storyline. At least Donnelly didn't throw herself off a cliff at the end, as would probably have happened a decade earlier. This time her punishment was merely "narrative banishment" (Brunsdon, 1987: 152).

Hemingway did a *Playboy* spread after making the film. If *Personal Best* is an exercise in soft porn, which it basically is, she went from there to the nadir of the genre with the Hugh Hefner hookup.

Related Films
The Fox (1968); *A Different Story* (1978); *Women of Gold* (1990); *Personal Best* (Documentary, 1991); *Spikes and Heels* (1994); *The Sex Monster* (1999).

Further Reading
Biskind, Peter. 1998. *Easy Riders, Raging Bulls.* London: Bloomsbury.
Brunsdon, Charlotte, ed. 1987. *Films for Women.* London: British Film Institute.
Hadleigh, Boze. 1993. *The Lavender Screen.* New York: Citadel.
Howes, Keith. 1993. *Broadcasting It.* London: Cassell.
SoHo News, February 16, 1982.
Weiss, Andrea. 1992. *Vampires and Violets.* London: Penguin.

Philadelphia (1993)

Tom Hanks played an AIDS-afflicted lawyer, Andrew Beckett, in this big-budget feature from Jonathan Demme. When he's informed he's going to be sacked from his job, he takes his firm to court for unfair dismissal. The reason given is poor productivity, but he knows it's his health that's behind the decision. He can't get a top lawyer to take his case, so he settles for a down-market homophobic one instead. This is Joe Miller, played by Denzel Washington.

Hanks's partner in the film, Miguel, is played by Antonio Banderas. It was the first major Hollywood production to tackle AIDS, but for much of the time it seems to be more about human rights than the disease itself. Neither does it tackle being gay in any depth. It also has a saccharine element to it.

Hanks said his motive in taking on the role wasn't because he was on a social crusade. Rather it was because "It's a great part with a great director" (Trakin, 1995: 173). But is it? Demme more or less admitted it was a film about gays for heterosexuals when he said his template for it was *Terms of Endearment*. It's a feel-good film about feeling bad, delivered with all the Capra-corn one can pack inside a politically correct tearjerker.

One doesn't get to see anything about the kind of life Beckett led with Miguel before he's stricken down with his condition. The film isn't about their relationship but rather its ending. Neither does one get to see their friends. The only social scene in the film is a Halloween party full of clichés about gay people's perceived penchant for dressing up. It's attended by that icon of sartorial splendor, Quentin Crisp.

Hanks won an Oscar for his performance against a strong field that included Liam Neeson for *Schindler's List* and Daniel Day-Lewis (Demme's original choice to play Beckett) for *In the Name of the Father*. He gave a rousing acceptance speech that toasted the memory of all the people who'd died of AIDS. Larry Kramer, however, said, "*Philadelphia* doesn't have anything to do with the AIDS I know or with the gay world I know" (Piazza and Kinn, 2008: 279). The fact that Hanks received warm support from his family also ran contrary to the experiences of many people with AIDS (Miller, 1994: 252).

The film arguably Grishamized the disease, turning it into a legal potboiler. It could also be seen as a judicial *Rocky*, a David and Goliath story where one always felt the small guy was going to beat the big bad wolf of Wall Street—in this case Beckett's bigoted boss, Charles Wheeler (Jason Robards).

The conversion of Miller to the gay cause also rankled. It hardly looked likely from one's initial impression of him. When he first meets Beckett, he's even afraid to shake hands with him for fear of contracting the disease. One's mind went back to the Ben Gazzara of *An Early Frost* (1985) when Aidan Quinn—who was also a lawyer—tells him he has AIDS. *Philadelphia* represents the "education" of Miller about the pandemic, largely at the behest of his more empathetic wife, Lisa (Lisa Summerour). When Miller goes to his doctor and expresses the fear that he may have contracted the disease from a handshake, the doctor reassures him that it can be transmitted only through the exchange of bodily fluids like blood and semen. *Philadelphia* shares the didacticism of *An Early Frost* in scenes like this.

It cost $30 million to make and went on to gross over four times that amount. The bankability of Hanks was a large factor in this. So was the film's middle-of-the-road approach to its subject. The closest Hanks and Banderas come to having sex is a slow dance they do together. The fact that they were both straight in real life also helped it at the box office, as did the fact that Neil Young and Bruce Springsteen had been recruited to write songs for it. (Springsteen's won an Oscar.)

Hanks didn't evince any gay streaks in the film. Hollywood played it safe in casting one of its most loved actors in the role. He was the ideal vehicle to make being gay look respectable, if not an ideal for those who previously shunned movies on this theme. As Tri-Star president Marc Platt remarked, "This is a guy you like whether he's gay or straight, sick or healthy" (Trakin, 175).

The promotional campaign for the film highlighted the "Unfair Dismissal" aspect of the plot rather than the fact that Hackett has AIDS. "No one would take on his case," it proclaims, "until one man was willing to take on the system." This appeared to market it as a kind of *Mr. Deeds Goes to Town* rather than a groundbreaking sexual story. This was apparently what Demme intended, or what he felt was expected from his studio. Whatever his motive, it prepared audiences for its tame tone. Hanks is presented as a too-good-to-be-true character and Banderas as his almost invisible lover. If the film concerned the romance between a man and a woman, it would have found much favor with the Legion of Decency in the forties, so chaste was it in its presentation. Banderas is allowed to kiss Hanks's hands but nothing more, either above or below the waist. Their relationship could almost have been conducted in a monastery without censure.

Demme and his screenwriter, Ron Nyswaner, had been working on the project for four years before it reached the screen, spending much of that time talking with friends of theirs who had AIDS. Hanks lost thirty pounds to play the role and did extensive research on how it affected its victims. The high point of his performance is the scene where he dances to Maria Callas singing "La Mama Morta" (The Dance of Death) from the opera *Andrea Chénier*.

Praise for the film was limited among LGBTQ viewers. While it was admired for highlighting the scourge of AIDS, its more general effect, for one gay man, was no more than "persuading homophobes to hate us all a little less, or at least those of us who wear smart suits and avoid kissing our boyfriends in public" (Burston, 1995: 168).

This is harsh. The film didn't go as far as many gay people wanted it to, but if it had it might have been killed by the studio at birth. Breakthrough films often have some degree of conservatism about them. This can be necessary to get themselves made. *Philadelphia* soft-pedaled some of its issues, but it had its heart in the right place. If it didn't convert the doggedly homophobic, it at least made them think. And it widened awareness not only of the prevalence of HIV-related illnesses but also the abuse its sufferers had to undergo while being treated for them.

Related Films
An Early Frost (1985); *Parting Glances* (1986); *Longtime Companion* (1990); *Savage Nights* (1992); *Silverlake Life* (1993).

Further Reading
Burston, Paul. 1995. *What Are You Looking At? Queer Sex, Style and Cinema*. London: Cassell.
Edwards, Gavin. 2018. *The World According to Tom Hanks: The Life, the Obsessions, The Good Deeds of America's Most Decent Guy*. New York: Grand Central Publishing.
Kepsis, Robert E. 2008. *Jonathan Demme Interviews*. Jackson: University Press of Mississippi.

Miller, Frank. 1994. *Censored Hollywood: Sex, Sin and Violence on Screen*. Atlanta: Turner Publishing.

Piazza, Jim, and Gail Kinn. 2008. *The Academy Awards: The Complete Unofficial History*. New York: Black Dog & Leventhal.

Trakin, Roy. 1995. *Tom Hanks: Journey to Stardom*. London: Virgin.

Prick Up Your Ears (1987)

This film is the tragicomic story of the anarchic British playwright Joe Orton and his partner, Kenneth Halliwell, who brutally murdered him. Directed by Stephen Frears, it's narrated through flashbacks, diary entries, and interviews that had been conducted by John Lahr (Wallace Shawn) with Orton's agent, Peggy Ramsay (Vanessa Redgrave), and others for his 1987 biography of Orton. Gary Oldman gives a suitably irreverent performance as the roguish Orton. He also bears an uncanny physical resemblance to him. Alfred Molina was an unusual choice for Halliwell with his Spanish-Italian background. Ian McKellen had been the original choice, but he passed.

Frears, coming off the back of another LGBTQ movie, *My Beautiful Laundrette*, chronicles the sea changes in their relationship over the many years they lived together. During these years they indulged in all sorts of mischief, including defacing library books, for which they served some time in prison. At this time, being gay was also a practice punishable by prison. The center of power in their relationship—initially held by Halliwell—changed dramatically when he gave up his writing career to act as Orton's Svengali. Kenneth MacKinnon wrote: "Kenneth is the wife, Joe the husband" (Griffiths, 2006: 129) As Orton cruised public toilets for rough sex, Halliwell was like the put-upon wife he was getting ready to leave.

In a staccato movie that captures the electrifying pulse of the sixties as well as the cabin fever of a disintegrating couple, Frears breezily documents Halliwell's psychological meltdown. "I caught up on a big backlog of dusting," he tells Orton in one scene, "then I slipped down the road to replenish our stock of cornflakes. When I returned I rinsed through a selection of your soiled underclothes, by which time it was four o'clock, the hour of your scheduled return." The sardonic formalism of the phrasing captures Halliwell's personality to perfection. Resentment isn't far away as he sees his dignity crumble. Halliwell once wrote a letter to Ramsay and signed it, "Kenneth Halliwell, secretary to Joe Orton" (Lahr, 2002: 13).

Orton and Halliwell first met at the Royal Academy of Dramatic Art. Halliwell was the more confident party then. As time went on, Orton leapfrogged him, and he found it difficult to deal with that. As he puts it in one scene, "You do everything better than me. You even sleep better than me."

After Orton's meteoric success on the West End, Halliwell becomes increasingly depressed about the changing nature of their relationship. He begins to feel more like his gofer than an equal, and that ramps up his hostility toward him. The pressure cooker is brewing. It reaches boiling point in the most horrific manner possible in Frears's cataclysmic finale.

As their bickering becomes worse, they begin to resemble, in the words of one writer, "a pair of precocious mushrooms in a dim cold-water flat in an unfashionable part of London" (*Washington Post*, May 16, 1987). "I was programmed to be a novelist or a playwright," Halliwell sniffs, as if there are divine rights for such professions, "but I'm not. And you are." He bludgeons him in a fit of rage. The iconoclastic clown of the West End is no more.

Orton was going by the Christian name of John when Halliwell met him first. After he kills him, he calls out, "Joe? John?" as if his victim has suddenly reverted back to the person he fell in love with, before Dame Fame stepped in. Maybe this is wish fulfillment on his part. If so, it makes the murder achingly sad, a pathetic stab at an idyllic past.

Prick Up Your Ears isn't easy viewing, even for strong stomachs. The material is inflammatory, and the treatment reflects that. It's also a more mature examination of a gay relationship than one has been vouchsafed heretofore. As *American Film* noted, previous films of this type treated gay people like problems. This one treated them *with* problems (Hadleigh, 1993: 242).

Orton was a man who believed in grasping at every experience. He'd sooner murder an infant in its cradle than nurse an unacted desire. Indulgence was his god. He said of Kenneth Williams, "Williams is the stereotype of the comedian who's laughing on the outside and crying on the inside. All he'd have to do to be happy is to get laid but he can't bring himself to do that. He'd rather be celibate than be disapproved of" (Hadleigh, 1994: 168).

Such epicureanism eventually cost Orton his life. The man who attacked so many sacred cows in such cavalier fashion was dead at thirty-four. London's theatrical ambience would never be quite so raucous again. A kind of low-rent Oscar Wilde, he cocked a snook at anything smacking of convention with his dizzying array of queens and male prostitutes feasting on pleasure. His laser wit was directed at everything—including himself—but the more devastating it became, the more Halliwell brooded about his own literary stasis. He could write well, but never as well as the man who was behind *Entertaining Mr. Sloane, Loot*, and *What the Butler Saw*. It was this knowledge, combined with a growing isolation from the world and a resounding fear that Orton was going to leave him, that tipped him over the edge on August 9, 1967, on 25 Noel Road, Islington. His breakdown resulted in a murder not even he could properly understand. Suicide followed with an overdose of Nembutals.

He left a note that said, "If you read his diary, all will be explained" (Lahr, 1991: 266). But there could really be no explanation for an act of such ferocity. He delivered nine hammer blows to Orton's head. They were so deep, his skull bore the imprint of the hammer head. Parts of his brain even ended up on the ceiling.

Maybe he should have seen it coming. It was clear to many people that Halliwell was psychologically unhinged. His troubled childhood had a lot to do with this. When he was eleven, his mother was stung in the mouth by a wasp and within minutes choked to death before his eyes. When he was twenty-three, he came down to breakfast one day to see his father with his head in the oven, dead from asphyxiation. He exorcised some of his demons in his writing, but he did this in a morose way. Orton was better able to transform pain into comedy.

Halliwell may have killed Orton, but he couldn't kill his plays. What was left after the murder was a brilliant, if uneven, body of work. Orton's legacy to posterity was his "evergreen laughter, the last testament of the fierce, sad kingdom of self from which it came: his diaries" (Lahr, 31). Reading them, one feels the steam rising from the pages. Frears successfully transfers that steam to celluloid in his quirky threnody to two mismatched rebels.

Molina played a much more sympathetic gay man in a more recent film called *Love Is Strange*. Here he was a Catholic school music teacher married to John Lithgow. He loses his job when news of his marriage comes to the attention of the archdiocese. The two of them have to sell their apartment and live separate lives at the homes of friends afterward, leading to much distress on both their parts.

Related Films
Entertaining Mr. Sloane (1970); *Loot* (1970); *Star 80* (1983); *Love Is Strange* (2014).

Further Reading
Aaron, Michele. 1999. *The Body's Perilous Pleasures: Dangerous Desires and Contemporary Culture*. Edinburgh: Edinburgh University Press.
Doty, Alexander. 1993. *Making Things Perfectly Queer: Interpreting Mass Culture*. Minneapolis: University of Minnesota Press.
Griffiths, Robin, ed. 2006. *British Queer Cinema*. London and New York: Routledge.
Hadleigh, Boze. 1993. *The Lavender Screen*. New York: Citadel.
Hadleigh, Boze, ed. 1994. *Hollywood Babble On*. New York: Birch Lane.
Keough, Peter, ed. 1995. *Flesh and Blood: The National Society of Film Critics on Sex, Violence and Censorship*. San Francisco: Mercury House.
Lahr, John, ed. 1991. *The Orton Diaries*. London: Minerva.
Lahr, John. 2002. *A Biography of Joe Orton*. London: Bloomsbury.
Washington Post, May 16, 1987.

Queen Christina (1933)

The German film *Mädchen in Uniform* (1931) was a seminal release that documented the lesbian infatuation of a schoolgirl for her teacher in a boarding school for the daughters of German army officers prior to World War I. It was a European precursor of this Rouben Mamoulian offering starring Greta Garbo and John Gilbert.

Telling the story of Christina Vasa, a monarch who ruled Sweden from 1626 to 1654, when she abdicated the throne, it had Garbo in the kind of male attire she was reputed to wear offscreen but hadn't, until now, donned before the camera. There had been lesbian cameos in big-budget Hollywood films before this, but *Queen Christina* was the first time a lesbian moved to center stage.

Photoplay magazine speculated that she was taking a gamble with her image by appearing in the film (*Photoplay*, July 1933). The trousers-versus-skirts debate that was frequently aired in articles about Marlene Dietrich at the time now had a new object of scrutiny. Was Garbo jealous of all the attention Dietrich was receiving? Was she trying to outdo her by this bold gambit?

Queen Christina was reputed to have been born with the external sex organs of a man and the internal reproductive ones of a woman, so Garbo's interpretation wasn't without historical import. When she was born, her father expressed dissatisfaction that she wasn't a boy. He persuaded her to wear knickerbockers to correct the fetal error, as he saw it.

Christina has a valet (C. Aubrey Smith) rather than a chambermaid. She takes her oath of allegiance as a king rather than as a queen. Her relationship to her lady-in-waiting, Ebba (Elizabeth Young), is so warm she kisses her on the lips in one scene. In another scene, Ebba complains, "You're surrounded by musty old men and I can't get near you." When the two of them fall out, Ebba laments, "Since I've lost your favor I've not slept."

The queen resists marrying for a long time. When she's informed she can't be allowed to die an old maid, she shoots back, "I have no intention to. I shall die a *bachelor*." For LGBTQ audiences this was a resounding declaration of intent. It still resonates almost a century on.

In an early scene in the film, Ebba runs into the queen's chamber and curtsies, kissing her hand. When she stands up, Christina takes her head in her hands and kisses her firmly on the lips.

Later on, Christina proposes that she and Ebba spend some nights together at an inn. Ebba demurs because she's now engaged to be married to a guardsman. Christina is shocked when she learns this and breaks off her friendship with her.

The script was written by Salka Viertel, a woman with whom Garbo was alleged to be having an affair at the time. This hasn't been corroborated, but during the making of the film Viertel had a conversation with studio head Irving Thalberg. He asked her if she'd seen *Mädchen in Uniform.* He went on to say, "Does not Christina's affection for her lady-in-waiting indicate something like that?" He asked her to "keep it in mind" as she wrote her script. If this relationship were handled with taste, he speculated, "It would give us some very interesting scenes" (Viertel, 1969: 175).

"What a pity I was not born a man," Christina says to Ebba in a sequence of dialogue that was taken out of the final print of the movie because of censorial objections. "I would have made you queen. There would have been no trouble then about the succession." It was one thing to feature a kiss; quite another to speculate about gay marriage (Barrios, 2003: 120).

The film heterosexualizes the monarch by introducing a male character, Don Antonio (Gilbert), to take the attention away from Ebba. While disguised as a man, Christina meets him at a village inn. They fall into conversation and he suggests they go upstairs to a bedroom, though without any sexual intent. When he discovers she's a woman he remains friends with her. They then embark on a love affair.

Ebba's romance with her guardsman and Christina's with Don Antonio thematically "correct" their lesbian interlude, but their full-mouthed kiss is what people remember from the film rather than the cosmetic carpentry of the plot threads that follow it. Crucially, Christina is asked to Don Antonio's bedroom when he thinks she's a man. They don't kiss in the film. When they share the bedroom, she seems more interested in admiring herself in a mirror than she does at him, thereby underlining the lesbian code with a homoerotic one.

The film had to water down the queen's sexuality, but it did so in a qualified way. Christina abdicates the throne to marry Don Antonio, but then he's killed in a duel. Mamoulian has honored his duty to Hollywood to "save" Christina sexually without having to follow through on the heterosexual face-saving of the proposed nuptials. In the last scene, the woman who always said she wanted to be alone is exactly like that as she sails away from Sweden.

The final image of her standing at the ship's helm is iconic. Her expression is as enigmatic as that of the Mona Lisa. She's lost the man she loved. And the woman she loved? One can only wonder.

Hollywood didn't want films like *Queen Christina* to become a habit. This was made blindingly clear by Jack Warner's edict in the *Los Angeles Times*, which stated bluntly, "We believe the current trend toward mannish attire for women is a freakish fad and our fashion experts agree with us. We have refrained all along from showing any woman dressed as a man in our pictures and we will continue to do it. The order becomes effective immediately. Our feminine stars have been warned that they must stay feminine" (*Los Angeles Times*, February 17, 1933).

Queen Christina opened in theaters at the end of the year to the chagrin of the prudish Joseph Breen, who had the power to release or refuse to release anything from his perch in the Production Code Association. Films without codes usually died at the box office. In January 1934, however, a jury of studio executives voted unanimously to approve the film over Breen's head. This was surprising considering the suggestive nature of the dialogue, especially Garbo's line "I shall die a bachelor" and the rumors about her bisexuality that were circulating around Hollywood at the time.

The Code had been introduced under pressure from the Catholic Church and the Legion of Decency. Films were "cleaned up" to suit the tastes of those who believed in binary sexuality and formulaic lives. From now on, even married couples had to sleep in separate beds. People couldn't be shown using the bathroom or kissing longer than a few seconds without interruption. Breen would have edited *Queen Christina* with a meat cleaver if he could, leaving only the bare bones remaining, if even those. By the end, one would have been left in little doubt that it was Gilbert the ill-fated queen was thinking of as she stood on the prow of her ship rather than her lady-in-waiting.

Garbo wanted to play Christina as she looked historically, with a large nose and masculine eyebrows, but the studio ruled against this (White and Averson, 1968: 99). She starts to wear dresses as the film goes on, turning from a feminine male, as one writer put it, to a masculine female (Bell-Metereau, 1993: 75). Her hands were tied at every turn by the dictates of the time. A scene in which the sluttish servant girl Elsa (Barbara Barondess) ran her hands up and down Garbo's legs also ended up on the cutting room floor (Porter and Prince, 2007: 203).

Related Films
Mädchen in Uniform (1931); *The Abdication* (1974); *Edward II* (1992).

Further Reading
Barrios, Richard. 2003. *Screened Out: Playing Gay in Hollywood from Edison to Stonewall*. New York and London: Routledge.
Bell-Metereau, Rebecca. 1993. *Hollywood Androgyny*. New York: Columbia University Press.
Los Angeles Times, February 17, 1933.
Photoplay, July 1933.
Porter, Darwin, and Danforth Prince. 2007. *Guide to Gay and Lesbian Film: Second Edition*. New York: Blood Moon Productions.
Vieira, Mark A. 1999. *Sin in Soft Focus: Pre-Code Hollywood*. New York: Harry N. Abrams.
Viertel, Salka. 1969. *The Kindness of Strangers*. New York: Holt, Rinehart and Winston.
White, David, and Richard Averson. 1968. *Sight, Sound and Society*. Boston: Beacon Press.
Wingate, James. 1933. *Queen Christina File: Motion Picture Association of America*. Production Code Administration Records.

R

Rebecca (1940)

Alfred Hitchcock's first Hollywood film was a gothic adaptation of Daphne du Maurier's multilayered novel about a woman (played by Joan Fontaine) who struggles to replace the memory of the first wife of her husband, Maxim de Winter (Laurence Olivier). This is the Rebecca of the title. She died in mysterious circumstances; there's even a rumor Olivier killed her. (In the book he did.) Fontaine's tensions are exacerbated by the hostility she experiences from Rebecca's housekeeper, Mrs. Danvers (Judith Anderson).

Though Fontaine is the main star, Hitchcock doesn't name her. Rebecca doesn't appear even in flashback. But she dominates the film nonetheless, her spirit hovering over every frame like an all-consuming presence.

The fact that Mrs. Danvers is inconsolable about her death, and Fontaine is unable to take her place, threatens her. Her devotion to Maxime put Danvers out of her range. The first Mrs. de Winter had no such devotion to him. That made it easier for Danvers to engage her affections. In her frustration at this state of affairs, Danvers tries to make Fontaine as uncomfortable as possible, shredding her self-confidence. "I'm not the sort of person men marry," she even says at one point.

Fontaine is restless throughout the film, all too well aware that Maxime's dead wife haunts her new home, if not him. Rebecca vicariously usurps her authority as his new bride. For most of the time Maxime denies this, but Fontaine believes it to be true. She also *knows* Danvers usurps her authority. A whiff of cordite surrounds her; she's the symbolic "whore" to Fontaine's "virgin."

The film purports to be about the relationship between Maxime and Fontaine, but from relatively early on one finds oneself not caring too much about this, or even whether Maxime has murdered his previous spouse. What holds our attention is Anderson's unnatural devotion to her former mistress. Were they lovers? Hitchcock leaves that up to our imagination. She seems to go into a trance whenever she talks about her. These are the only times she seems capable of warmth. In du Maurier's novel, Danvers exhibits both cruelty and obsequiousness as she exhibits her clothes and underclothes to the second Mrs. de Winter. "Her manner was fawning," du Maurier writes, "intimate and unpleasant. The smile on her face was a false, unnatural thing" (du Maurier, 2015: 194).

Sartorially, Danvers is very masculine. She wears a long black skirt and keeps her hair pulled back in a bun. In a seminal scene in the film, she takes a fur coat from Rebecca's closet. (The term "closet" is relevant here.) She caresses her face with the sleeve and then rubs the coat along Fontaine's cheek. Hitchcock suggests the possibility that the bond between Rebecca and Danvers might be continued with the second Mrs. De Winter, but only for these few moments. In another reading of the scene, she's taunting Fontaine with the knowledge that she can never live up to Rebecca.

There were rumors that Anderson was a lesbian in real life, but she refused to confirm or deny them. When asked directly if she was by Boze Hadleigh, she glared at him and clenched her fists, telling him she wouldn't come out in a million years: "Why should I? I don't owe anyone any explanations and I won't join up with anything. Ever. They never gave me anything and I certainly don't need them. I live my own life, and good luck to them, but leave me alone. Everybody, just leave me alone!" (Hadleigh, 1994: 176). There's a lot of anger here, some of which she channeled into her performance. (Presumably by "them" she means gay groups.)

There was also a question mark around du Maurier. Though married with three children, she once described herself as "a half breed, someone internally male and externally female" (Braun, 2002: 24).

Surprisingly, Anderson didn't see Danvers as gay in the film, merely "sexless" (Hadleigh, 1994: 169). She didn't like Fontaine, believing her to be "phony" (Hadleigh, 168). Their offscreen tensions added to the film's power. Joseph Breen, who was vetting it for the Production Code Association, warned its producer, David O. Selznick, that no insinuation of perversion between Danvers and Rebecca was to be conveyed at any cost (Corber, 1999: 76). Breen was unhappy with some lines in the final script, and these had to be deleted. They included innocuous, if suggestive, lines like, "She was incapable of love," "She wasn't even normal," and "She told me things I could never repeat to a living soul" (Bryant, 1997: 54).

The original script had more extensive dialogue hinting at a definite lesbian relationship between the two women, but the Hays Office insisted these be removed. Hitchcock had to compensate by inserting some of his own—like the one where she tells Fontaine her former employer's underwear was handmade by cloistered nuns. This detail seemed to take the harm out of the eroticism of the scene for the censors. Hitchcock was clever at sneaking such nuances into his films to keep as much footage as he could. It was usually violence he wanted to preserve, but here it was sex.

The lesbian relationship in *Rebecca* is unusual for two reasons: it's fetishized more than realized and the main protagonist of it is dead. We learn about it secondhand from Danvers. Her involvement in it therefore becomes posthumous, without any guarantee that it might repeat itself with Fontaine. Fontaine has to try to vanquish the power of her predecessor in order to take up her new role as her replacement, but it becomes clear early on that this is going to be practically impossible (Modleski, 1988: 51).

For all its erotic charge, *Rebecca* still had to abide by the taboos of the time. Thus Danvers has to die—she's burned to death—to atone for her sins. This allows the "new" Rebecca to conduct her life within the nuclear family fold, far away from Danvers's innuendoes and eeriness. The evil has been exorcised and the traditional marital felicities can be ushered in, albeit somewhat later than expected for audiences weaned on a diet of instant domestic bliss following a trip down the aisle.

Related Films
The Uninvited (1944); *The Dream of Olwen* (1946); *The Second Woman* (1951).

Further Reading
Braun, Eric. 2002. *Frightening the Horses: Gay Icons of the Cinema.* London: Reynolds & Hearn.
Bryant, Wayne M. 1997. *Bisexual Characters in Film from Anais to Zee.* New York and London: Harrington Park Press.
Corber, Robert J. 1999. *Cold War Femme: Lesbianism, National Identity and Hollywood Cinema.* Durham, NC, and London: Duke University Press.
Creekmur, Corey K., and Alexander Doty. 1995. *Out in the Culture: Gay, Lesbian and Queer Essays on Popular Culture.* London: Cassell.
du Maurier, Daphne. 2015. *Rebecca.* London: Virago.
Hadleigh, Boze. 1994. *Hollywood Lesbians.* New York: Barricade Books.
Modleski, Tania. 1988. *The Women Who Knew Too Much: Hitchcock and Feminist Theory.* New York: Methuen.

Rebel without a Cause (1955)

Nicholas Ray tapped into the frenzied "youthquake" of 1950s America with this teenage parable of three vulnerable teenagers band together in a kind of soulful alliance against a life-denying status quo.

James Dean is Jim and Natalie Wood is Judy. Rounding off the trio is Sal Mineo as Plato. They all attend the same high school.

The film begins with the three of them at a police station. Jim has been arrested for being drunk and disorderly. Judy is there because she's been wandering the streets after midnight. Plato has shot a bunch of pups.

Plato is a poor little rich kid. His father has left home and his mother seems to be permanently out. It's left to the family maid to take care of him. Jim fares little better, being misunderstood by both parents. It's the classic generation gap scenario. The stage is set for a new "family" to develop between the three neglected children. In the absence of a traditional family unit they form their own one. Jim and Judy are like surrogate parents to Plato. Plato is also sexually attracted to Jim. Mineo claimed to be the first gay teenager in films (*Vanity Fair*, March 2005). One of the indicators of this is the fact that he wears odd socks.

"Hey," Plato says to Jim in one scene. "Want to come home with me? We could talk, and in the morning we could have breakfast." In 1955, nothing more lascivious was allowed to be suggested.

Plato's orientation is transmitted to us by the fact that he has a poster of Alan Ladd in his locker. Jim may be latently gay, but his bond to Plato seems to be based more on a protective sense than anything else. He's Plato's only friend. Off-screen things were different. There was sexual chemistry between them. Mineo said they didn't have an affair, "but we could have—like that!" (Hadleigh, 2000: 251).

Jim's gender confusion is apparent in a symbolic scene that occurs early on. He goes into the girls' room by mistake on his first day in school while looking

Johnny Guitar (1954)

Nicholas Ray (1911–79) also made *Johnny Guitar*, a Western that was neglected at the time of its release but that has now—deservedly—come to be regarded as a camp classic. Sterling Hayden is the nominal lead, but the real chemistry takes place between Joan Crawford and Mercedes McCambridge. They turn it into a kind of sagebrush precursor of *What Ever Happened to Baby Jane?* They gun for one another in a thinly disguised love-hate relationship, a duel to the death carried out under Ray's revisionist lens.

Crawford was Vienna, the aggressive operator of a gambling saloon. McCambridge was Emma, the sexually frustrated lead of the cattle drive. From the start, they vied with one another to be the better actress in the film. Ray fed into their rivalry by complimenting each of them in front of the other one.

"I wouldn't trust her as far as I could throw a battleship," Crawford said of the younger star (Thomas, 1978: 190). McCambridge tried to wave an olive branch, but Crawford wasn't interested. Hayden felt her wrath too. After filming finished, he said, "There isn't enough money in Hollywood to lure me into making another picture with Joan Crawford. And I like money" (Thomas, 192).

The dialogue was crisp and whip-smart. "How many men have you forgotten?" he asks her at one point. "As many women as you've remembered," she replies tartly.

When Hayden kisses Crawford, McCambridge fumes, not because she wants him but rather her. She kills him in the end to make way for her standoff with Crawford.

Offscreen the two stars continued to fight nonstop. Ray said he threw up on his way to work every morning in terror of what lay ahead of him from the two of them. One night he even claimed Crawford vandalized McCambridge's room in a fit of pique after McCambridge had received an ovation from the crew for how well she'd done a scene.

Further Reading

Thomas, Bob. 1978. *Joan Crawford*. London: Weidenfeld & Nicolson.

---

for the bathroom. When he befriends Plato, it triangulates his relationship with Judy. Plato's awe of him is undisguised, establishing the homoerotic subtext of the film that can't be consummated, merely indicated by lingering looks on Plato's part.

Judy is the former girlfriend of Buzz (Corey Allen), the leader of the school gang, but she's more interested in Jim. She tells Jim she's waiting on a man who is "gentle and sweet, like you are." She notices how kind he is to Plato. This elevates him further in her eyes.

When she becomes Jim's girlfriend, it creates tension with Buzz. A conflict develops between them. They seek to resolve this by a "chicken run," a car race that takes place close to the edge of a cliff. The idea is that they race their cars toward the cliff. The "chicken" is the first to jump out before the car careens over. This is the macho credo, the ethos of the alpha male prominent in many schools of the time, and indeed of our own time. Jim doesn't like it, but he goes along with it to win Judy. As things work out, Buzz gets the cuff of his jacket caught in the door handle of his car when he tries to jump out of it. The car plunges over the cliff and he dies.

The other members of his gang now threaten to kill Jim, blaming him for the tragedy even though the contest was Buzz's idea. Plato gets his father's gun and runs to meet Jim so he can protect him. In the planetarium, he shoots one of Buzz's gang. Jim pleads with him to give the gun to him but he refuses. Afterward Jim takes the bullets out of the gun without telling him he's done so.

The shots have been heard by police. They surround the planetarium. Plato raises his gun at them in fright. They tell him to come out, assuring him he'll come to no harm if he does. He's reluctant to do this. Jim gets around him eventually, but as Plato goes out he panics and brandishes his gun at the police. When he does so, they shoot him. Like him, they're unaware it's empty. Jim cries out, "I've got the bullets!" but it's too late. Plato has been mortally wounded.

Jim goes over to his body and sees he's dead. He's distraught. He zips up his jacket. "Poor kid," he says. "He was always cold." There's a suggestion of impotence in the coldness—and in the empty gun.

The gay teenager is dead. Respectable America can breathe easily once again; the world can move on in a better direction. Jim can devote his attention to Judy without the temptation of an alien sexual invasion to his body. The queer part of the love triangle has been removed. The rebel's cause is no more.

Now that Plato has been removed from the equation, Jim can also reconcile with his parents. (They're at the scene.) He can walk into the sunset with Judy now that there are just two of them now, not three. Plato's name has been written on a bullet from the moment he combed his hair in front of that locker photo of Alan Ladd.

Mineo also died young in real life, being stabbed to death in an alleyway in 1976. Dean may have escaped tragedy in the chicken run, but life itself wasn't so kind. Before the film was released, he broke his neck in a car crash just days after his last film (*Giant*) was released. Different tragedies befell other members of the cast in years to come. Wood died in a freak drowning accident that still poses questions today. Nick Adams, who had a smaller part in the film, died from a drug overdose in 1968 at the age of thirty-seven. There seemed to be a curse on the film. Its vision of a new society of cool youths certainly wasn't carried through in real life, unless one adopted the maxim of "live fast, die young, and make a good looking corpse."

Dean was immortalized after his death, freeze-framed forever as the vulnerable youth of *East of Eden, Giant*, and this film. His face adorned key rings, coffee mugs, fridge magnets. He became a brand, an industry, a way of looking at life. For LGBTQ viewers he was the classic bisexual, a man totally in touch with his feminine side.

Rebel without a Cause also became a brand, a record of a trio of lonely souls breaking out of a familial cocoon for a brief time before the mothering arms of the world they tried to disown enclosed them like a vise.

Related Films
The Blackboard Jungle (1955); *East of Eden* (1955); *West Side Story* (1961).

Further Reading
Byars, Jackie. 1991. *All That Heaven Allows: Re-Reading Gender in 1950s Melodrama.* London: Routledge.
Doherty, Thomas. 1988. *Teenagers and Teenpics: The Juvenilization of American Movies in the 1950s.* Boston: Unwin and Hyman.

Eisenschitz, Bernard. 1993. *Nicholas Ray: An American Journey.* London and Boston: Faber & Faber.

Hadleigh, Boze. 2000. *In or Out: Gay and Straight Celebrities Talk about Themselves and Each Other.* New York: Barricade.

Morella, Joe, and Edward Z. Epstein. 1971. *Rebels: The Rebel Hero in Films.* New York: Citadel.

Parish, James Robert. 2001. *The Hollywood Book of Death.* New York: McGraw-Hill.

Vanity Fair, March 2005.

Reflections in a Golden Eye (1967)

"There is a fort in the South where a few years ago a murder was committed." These words from Carson McCullers's novel begin John Huston's incandescent exploration of sexual tension, psychosis, and tortured violence.

Elizabeth Taylor is Leonora, a highly sexed army wife married to the gay Major Penderton (Marlon Brando). She's having an affair with Penderton's fellow officer Morris Langdon (Brian Keith) on the side while Langdon's psychologically disturbed wife, Alison (Julie Harris)—she recently tried to cut off her nipples with a garden shears—malingers in the background as she flirts with the camp Filipino houseboy, Anacleto (Zorro David).

Huston's film treads a delicate path between passion and farce, occasionally oscillating from one to the other. It leaves one with a strong feeling of desperation at the end, not only because of the quality of the director and his cast but also the power of McCullers's writing, which has been transmuted into a slightly less potent screenplay by Chapman Mortimer and Gladys Hill.

Brando's Major Penderton is a pathetic figure who spends a lot of time admiring himself in the mirror, smiling coquettishly and even talking to himself. At other times he ogles postcards of Greek statues featuring naked men. Not surprisingly, his marriage to Leonora is on the rocks. His primary sexual focus is a young private, Williams (Robert Forester), whom he follows around the army camp at night.

He salutes himself in the mirror like a little boy playing at being a soldier. In a way this is what his life is—pretense. His orientation is just one part of that. His body language signifies the fact that he's a congenitally repressed individual: the erect posture, the staccato movements, the tightly buttoned uniform enclosing all that yearning inside it. He pats his head in preparation for a visit from Williams that will never come, reminding one of a teenage girl awaiting a gentleman caller.

In an early scene, Leonora has a laugh with Anacleto about "two little queers." This is a red flag to Penderton. It infuses him with a rage that's as latent as his being gay. This will erupt before the film ends.

In a central scene in the film, Penderton is thrown from a horse, Firebird, that's owned by Leonora. Brando immersed himself so much in the part that he developed a fear of horses on the set to match Penderton's. He'd been raised on a ranch and was relaxed with horses, so the fear was "created" by the Method actor in him. After he's thrown, he shows such a range of emotions—anger, guilt, fear, a strange kind of elation—that one isn't sure how to react. It's a master class in acting. He laughs and cries almost simultaneously as he thrashes Firebird with his riding crop in temper for being thrown by him.

Firebird is a metaphor for Leonora's sexual domination of Penderton. His thrashing of him attempts to diminish that domination. Williams passes by him as he lies on the ground, totally ignoring him. Leonora is in the habit of ignoring him too. Even though she doesn't know about Williams's obsession with her, the two of them treat Penderton with the same disdain. "Firebird is a stallion!" she crows at him, with the unspoken addition, "And you aren't." He appears to ignore the comment, but her taunts bite deep into his tormented heart.

Ground down to basics, this is a story of unfulfilled desire. Williams lusts after Leonora while Penderton lusts after Williams. The fact that both of them are fetishists—Williams demonstrates this in the final scene where he seems content to linger by Leonora's bed rather than climb into it—adds a certain frisson to this.

Richard Schickel cited *Reflections* as Brando's single great performance of the sixties. He mobilized his sexuality implosively rather than explosively here, he claimed, "menacing only himself with it" (Schickel, 1991: 167). Watching him putting Leonora's cold cream on his face, or picking up a candy wrapper Williams drops and keeping it as a man might keep a lock of a woman's hair, are all totally in character. The only time he smiles in the film is at himself, an exemplification of the autoeroticism that's eating away at his insides.

The way he tilts his head or contorts his facial muscles is telling. He's so tightened up that he's like an elastic band waiting to snap. This is a man who's uncomfortable in his skin, giving himself pep talks to try to make him feel better about himself as he juggles between infantilism and a myopic arrogance. He appears to enjoy these little face-offs he gives to himself, admiring himself in the mirror in a manner that prefigures his Method godchild Robert De Niro as he says, "You talkin' to me?" in *Taxi Driver*.

Brando looked heavy in the film, but this suited his character. Weight would eventually make him seem like a parody of the way he looked in films like *A Streetcar Named Desire*. "He flounders porpoise-like in his uniform," one writer observed, "his head and legs and arms like flapping extensions of a body that doesn't know its purpose. He walks with rigid care, as if the ground might open suddenly and swallow him whole" (Mizruchi, 2014: 202).

Montgomery Clift was originally supposed to play Penderton. It would have been an unprecedented move for him as he always shied away from anything smacking of being gay. (He stayed in the closet all his life.) Unfortunately, he died before filming began, which devastated Taylor. They'd been friends since 1951 when they starred together in George Stevens's *A Place in the Sun*. By now Clift's poor health—and alcoholism—had made him virtually uninsurable, but Taylor had somehow covered for him.

Richard Barrios thought it was a blessed release for him to have died before filming began: "The pressures on one unstable closeted man playing another," he said, "would have been horrendous, and possibly fatal" (Barrios, 2003: 333n).

Clift might have captured the vulnerability of Penderton with his slim build, but Brando's bulk, if not his history of playing brutish characters like the Stanley Kowalski of *Streetcar*, made his effeminate undercurrents more powerful. One of

Brando's biographers went so far as to say his performance here paved the way for films like *The Boys in the Band*. One might view it today and regard it as dated, but in 1966 it was brave of him to push himself into these areas (Offen, 1973: 176).

The public saw Penderton as a pathetic character, but he also has noble streaks. These are particularly evident in the lecture he gives to his soldiers about the life of enlisted men in an early scene. Here he shows his reverence for leadership qualities. His punctiliousness in correcting the time of a clock in one scene perfectly conveys the military nature of a man who's never given vent to his feelings, a man whose idea of war is intellectual, something far removed from experience.

In another scene he discovers Leonora in a drunken sleep. He carries her to bed and undresses her in a totally unsensuous manner. It's just another routine chore he has to perform, like lifting his barbells or polishing his spoons. All these details show Brando at the top of his powers. Harris said of him, "His work was so beautiful and so pure, there was no explaining where it came from" (Thomson, 2003: 122).

He camps Penderton up throughout the film, preening and pruning himself in a manner that effectively makes him into a drag queen in uniform. Huston contrasts such self-indulgence with moments of genuine pathos where his unfulfilled desires seem stretched to the breaking point. "It is morally honorable," Penderton tells his students, "for the square peg to keep scraping around in the round hole rather than discover the orthodox one that would fit." But this square peg never does, which leads to the film's dramatic climax.

Brando took second billing to Taylor in the film, which seemed symbolic of his character's inferiority to her. It was almost unprecedented for him to do this. The ghost of Clift hovered over the production to that extent. Not since *Streetcar* did an actress have her name above his. (That was Vivien Leigh.) Taylor castigated the actor she called "Mr. Mumbles" for speaking some of his lines indistinctly—and kept reminding him he was merely deputizing for the dead Clift.

Brando talked in a clipped manner in the film. This gave his Southern accent a soft edge. He worked extra hard on his performance because he respected Huston so much. (If he didn't like a director, he tended to "walk" through a film.) He also respected Taylor greatly, and he knew Harris from his stage days. Everyone gave of their best, but the material was too baroque for audiences and the film died at the box office.

It was given a seal despite Huston's refusal to make a series of cuts demanded both by the MPAA and the Catholic Office for Motion Pictures. This was a sign of the times. In spite of a "C" (for Condemned) rating by the COMP, it was distributed in all of the first-run cinemas, a clear indication that this body had all but lost its teeth.

Related Films
The Strange One (1957); *The Sergeant* (1968); *Sergeant Matlovich vs. the U.S. Air Force* (1978); *Biloxi Blues* (1988); *Sis: The Perry Watkins Story* (1994).

Further Reading
Barrios, Richard. 2003. *Screened Out: Playing Gay in Hollywood from Edison to Stonewall*. New York and London: Routledge.

Colombani, Florence. 2013. *Marlon Brando: Anatomy of an Actor.* Paris: Cahiers du Cinema.
Higham, Charles. 1989. *Brando: The Unauthorized Biography.* London: Grafton Books.
Huston, John. 1994. *An Open Book.* New York: Da Capo.
McCullers, Carson. 1941. *Reflections in a Golden Eye.* New York: Penguin.
Mizruchi, Susan L. 2014. *Brando's Smile.* New York and London: W. W. Norton.
Offen, Ron. 1973. *Brando.* Chicago: Henry Regnery.
Russo, William, and Jan Merlin. 2012. *Troubles in a Golden Eye.* Marston Gate, UK: Long Time Ago Books.
Schickel, Richard. 1991. *Brando: A Life in Our Times.* New York: Atheneum.
Shipman, David. 1989. *Marlon Brando.* London: Sphere.
Thomas, Bob. 1992. *The Films of Marlon Brando.* New York: Citadel.
Thomson, David. 2003. *Marlon Brando.* New York: Dorling Kindersley.

The Rocky Horror Picture Show (1975)

Nobody has ever really been able to explain the supersonic appeal of this sci-fi classic, so perhaps it would be advisable to stop trying. Featuring the frenetic fortunes of Dr. Frank N. Furter (Tim Curry) when he's visited at his castle by the straitlaced Brad (Barry Bostwick) and his beloved Janet (Susan Sarandon), the diverse cast also included Richard O'Brien as a hunchbacked Riff Raff, Patricia Quinn as Magenta, Nell Campbell as Columbia, Peter Hinwood as Rocky, Charles Gray as a criminologist narrator, and Meatloaf as Eddie, an adrenalized rock star. They all go for broke in a song and dance extravaganza that, like a Duracell battery, seems to intrigue each generation endlessly with its endearing blend of genre clichés and their jollified subversion.

The crossover between LGBTQ themes and horror movies reached its apogee here, confirming a connection that had long existed, even if it wasn't recognized by the casual filmgoer.

So what of the plot? (As if it matters.)

Brad and Janet have just tied the knot. On a very wet night their car breaks down in the middle of nowhere. Brad remembers having passed a castle, so they decide to return to it for help. When they get there, the ominous–looking Riff Raff admits them. Soon afterward they witness the show of the title in all its depraved glory.

Dr. Frank—a "transsexual transvestite from Transylvania"—appears. He looks like a cross between Mick Jagger and Freddie Mercury, with a soupçon of Joan Crawford thrown in for good measure. He offers them a "satanic mechanic" for their car. "Come to the lab," he trills, "and see what's on the slab." Janet nervously intones, "It's not the Junior Chamber of Commerce."

He then unveils his new creation to them, a kind of blond Charles Atlas whom he calls Rocky. He throws a party to celebrate. His last creation, Eddie, failed. Eddie now interrupts the party by driving in on a motorbike and singing like Elvis Presley on helium. Frank isn't pleased with this and hacks him to death. Dinner consists of his remains.

The doctor now defiles both Brad and Janet. Then everyone dresses up in red and black satin. They head for the swimming pool. Here the mother and father of all orgies take place. Afterward Frank calcifies some of the party guests. When he unfreezes them it's time for a cabaret show.

Our diverse band of party animals kiss and fondle one another. They sing, "Don't dream it, do it." Even Brad joins in. He sings, "Help me, Mommy, I feel sexy." Riff Raff and Magenta gate-crash the party, creating mayhem. Frank and Columbia die in the bloodbath. Rocky plunges to his death in the swimming pool. Afterward Riff Raff and Magenta take off into outer space.

It was Curry's debut and it's his film. His bra and garters, added to a suggestive bulge between his legs, confer epitomic she-male status on him. It's copper-fastened by his in-your-face exhibitionism. Wayne Bryant said of his manic—and talismanic—performance, "Every head toss, nostril flare and arched eyebrow is a tribute to the legendary camp screen actresses who preceded him" (Bryant, 1997: 100).

Based on a 1970s stage show, *Rocky Horror* was a flop on its initial run, finding its real niche only afterward as word of mouth caused it to go viral. It became a sensation at film festivals and later began to be performed in places other than cinemas—village halls, outdoor plazas, gyms. Then the video explosion of the 1980s arrived. Prints of the film were rented or bought as if they were rare Caravaggios. Midnight showings of it were originally targeted toward LGBTQ audiences but later became sought out by the general public. This was because of the number of boundaries it challenged. And the number of genres it blended so deliciously.

As famous for the cult following it established as for itself, it's been referenced in films as different as *Fame* and *Willie and Phil* (both 1980). It should also be credited with giving birth to interactive cinema because of the feedback it continues to engender in its groupies. For decades people have been attending it dressed as its characters and roaring out its dialogue at the screen along with—or even before—the actors. Some fans host fancy dress parties in its honor. Some even name their children after its daffy cast members, all of whom seem blissfully unaware they're creating a phenomenon of pre-Pythonesque lunacy.

Time has increased its appeal rather than diluted it. Audiences still get excited about it. They still throw rice at the screen during the wedding scene. They dance in the aisles. They run up to the screen and touch it when Janet sings, "T-T-T-T-T-Touch me."

Its tongue is so deeply embedded in its cheek it creates a bulge almost as great as the one in Dr. Frank N. Furter's bondage gear. Like *Myra Breckinridge* or *Glen or Glenda?*, it's one of the best worst films ever made, a monument to kitsch whose appeal shows no sign of abating in our quote unquote "sophisticated" era of retro-punk rockumentaries.

Related Films
Barbarella (1968); *Young Frankenstein* (1974); *Tommy* (1975); *Scream, Teen, Scream* (1996).

Further Reading

Benshoff, Harry M. 1997. *Monsters in the Closet: Homosexuality and the Horror Film.* Manchester and New York: Manchester University Press.

Bryant, Wayne. 1997. *Bisexual Characters in Film from Anais to Zee.* New York and London: Harrington Park Press.

Halberstam, Judith. 1995. *Skin Shows: Gothic Horror and the Technology of Monsters.* Durham, NC: Duke University Press.

Jancovich, Mark, Antonio Lazaro Reboll, Julian Stringer, and Andy Willis, eds. 2003. *Defining Cult Movies: The Cultural Politics of Oppositional Taste.* Manchester and New York: University of Manchester Press.

Smith, Justin. 2010. *Withnail and US: Cult Films and Film Cults in British Cinema.* London: I. B. Tauris.

Straayer, Chris. 1996. *Deviant Eyes, Deviant Bodies: Sexual Re-Orientation in Film and Video.* New York: Columbia University Press.

Transamerica DVD, Special Features, 2006.

Rope (1943)

This film was Alfred Hitchcock's first film in color. It was also the only film he made where he departed from his usual storyboarding style of direction, opting instead for a series of lengthy takes that reminded one more of the European auteurs—someone like Cristian Mungiu, perhaps—than the Master of the Macabre.

That said, the material was macabre indeed. Basing the film loosely on the gay child killers Nathan Leopold and Richard Loeb, Hitchcock adapted their circumstances to fit the neo-noir ambience within which he crafted the film.

Directing lead actors Farley Granger (Philip) and John Dall (Brandon)—both were gay offscreen as well—Hitchcock pulled off a major coup by sneaking this kind of material past the censors. Their sexuality plays second fiddle to the nonchalance with which they commit murder, and the even more casual manner in which they keep the body of the dead boy in their apartment. They then throw a party there. It's attended not only by the victim's father (Cedric Hardwicke) but also his fiancée (Joan Chandler) and the rest of his family. The murderers' college tutor, Rupert (James Stewart), is there as well. Arthur Laurents, who was living with Granger at the time, wrote the screenplay in collaboration with Hume Cronyn and Ben Hecht.

Rupert eventually rumbles them. Hitchcock keeps things tense as the net closes in on them and the sick parlor room game they've been playing reaches its grisly conclusion. Some viewers felt the film lacked drama, but that was only because they'd been spoiled too much in previous years by Hitchcock's more elaborate plot twists. This was connoisseur material, a game of cheeky subterfuge played by two shiftless bohemians whose cocking a snook at society's conventions eventually got the better of them.

The sense of invincibility with which they committed the crime is underlined by the same cockiness they display in throwing the party with the body in the

Leopold and Loeb

Nathan Leopold (1904–71) and Richard Loeb (1905–36) killed a fourteen-year-old boy called Robert Franks in 1929 after offering him a lift in their car. The crime had been planned for months beforehand. It was motiveless unless one regarded a feeling of superiority over everyone else as a motive. It was masterminded by Loeb. Leopold acceded to it as a way to ensure Loeb would stay with him. He was emotionally dependent on him.

After they killed the boy, they poured hydrochloric acid on his face and body. This was to try to make him unidentifiable, but when Leopold's glasses were discovered at the scene, he became an immediate suspect. The pair of them were arrested and after a high-profile trial found guilty.

Clarence Darrow, who disapproved of capital punishment, saved them from death with his eloquent defense, claiming they were insane when they killed Franks. They were sentenced to life imprisonment instead. Loeb was murdered twelve years later by an inmate who claimed he propositioned him. Leopold was released in 1958. He moved to Puerto Rico, where he married. Interviewed about Loeb, he spoke of him as a great friend but a dangerous influence.

Both of them were brilliant college students, graduating in their teens. Arrogant as well as academic, they espoused atheism, sociopathy, and ideas about love that were ahead of their time. United by the outsider status conferred upon them by their Jewishness and orientations, their murder of Franks seemed to be a statement to society that, in the absence of a belief in God, they could become gods themselves by deciding who should live and who should die. In this perverted scenario, Bobby Franks drew the short straw.

Leopold and Loeb were the first American gay couple to become celebrities. The fact that they were murderers to boot was the price LGBTQ people had to pay for the privilege.

Further Reading

Baatz, Simon. 2008. *For the Thrill of It: Leopold, Loeb and the Murder That Shocked Chicago.* New York: HarperCollins.

---

room. But pride comes before a fall. The "perfect" crime is rarely that in films, whatever about in life.

Both Brandon and Philip feel untouchable after committing their crime. They also feel amoral about it. They think they have an entitlement to kill those whom they wish out of the way. It's as if life is a negligible commodity to be dispensed with in the interests of expediency.

The circumstances of the film raise a number of questions for LGBTQ viewers anxious to decipher their sexuality. Why do they not have women in their lives? Do they live together? They seem to be joined at the hip and rarely out of one another's presence. A bedroom is mentioned in the film but not the fact that they share it. This subject couldn't even be broached in 1948. As one writer explained, "It's not simply that *Rope* cannot tell us that the two men sleep together; it also cannot tell us that they don't, since that would imply that they might" (Wood, 1989: 351).

Rope draws a direct link between being gay and psychosis. This was par for the course at the time it was made. Even so, the sexuality had to be conveyed subtly in order to ensure it made its way past the Production Code Administration. Lest one suspect that Brandon and Philip have eyes only for one another, care is taken to mention that Brandon had a girlfriend in the past. This unqueers him, at least to an extent.

"Homosexuality" was an unmentionable word in Hollywood at this time. It was usually referred to as "it" in films. Nonetheless, Hitchcock wanted "it" in *Rope*. As Laurents remarked, "He was innuendoing to the converted. I knew it had to be self-evident, but not so self-evident that the censors or the Legion [of Decency] would scream. You have to look but it's there all right. Without it, motives and relationships would have been altered" (Laurents, 2000: 127).

Beginning with a shocking strangulation, *Rope* afterward settles down to seventy-six minutes of dialogue. Hitchcock works his audience up and then brings it down again, all the while knowing that the main focus is going to be on when, not if, the perpetrators are caught. The plot of the film is skeletal and thus open to the charge of tedium. It crawls toward the climax, shocking and all as it is. Patient viewers were rewarded, but those who expected instant bloodcurdling of the more familiar Hitchcock variety went home disappointed.

His long takes made *Rope* look more like a play than a film. Since the technology of the time permitted only ten sequential minutes maximum, he had to use trick photography to achieve a trompe l'oeil effect. He achieved this by putting his camera on a character's back at the end of a reel and starting another one with the same image. It passed for continuity. Many people felt the film dragged, but nobody could create tension like Hitchcock. One waits for the body to be found with bated breath. In the end it is. After the party finishes, Rupert makes a surprise return to the apartment and catches the two killers in a compromising position.

The script is straight out of film noir. "You strangled the life out of a human being," Rupert accuses, "that could live and love like you never could." Brandon replies nonchalantly, "Pity we couldn't have done it with the curtains open."

Brandon is cool throughout whereas Philip seems always about to crack. At one point Brandon slaps him in the face. He's the man in the relationship and Philip the woman. Such one-dimensional polarities worked fine in 1948.

Everything about the film hints at what it hides—the body in the trunk, the Leopold/Loeb connection, the sexuality that dares not speak its name. "In Hollywood it's okay to be subtle." Hitchcock joked, "as long as you make it obvious" (Hadleigh, 1999: 30).

Why did they do it? Because they could. The adjective most ascribed to them is "Nietzschean." They could also be called Dostoevskian. Their motive in killing was nothing more that the thrill. "How did you feel during it?" Brandon asks Philip. Philip replies that when the body went limp he felt "tremendously exhilarated."

Is Rupert gay too? Hitchcock leaves the possibility open. He seems to resent Philip's involvement with Brandon, which suggests he may have had a physical involvement with him at some stage, possibly when he was in college. Laurents intended this to be inferred from his script (Laurents, 130). He said he created Rupert from some "silver and china queens" he'd known from his time in New

York but that Stewart played him straight (Clum, 2002: 118). This hardly comes as a surprise. He was from the era where "it" wasn't discussed.

Stewart, as John Clum remarked, "strolls through the picture with the air of a suspicious teacher on hall duty. When he apprehends the miscreants and lectures them on the value of all mankind he's back in *Mr. Smith Goes to Washington*" (Clum, 119). His apprehending of them represents a victory for good over evil. This time he isn't fighting City Hall but an even greater threat to solid values: being gay.

Hitchcock knew Laurents was living with Granger when the film was being shot. Laurents said it "tickled" him to know Granger was playing a gay man in a movie written by another gay man: "We were lovers; we had a secret that he knew, that I knew he knew—the permutations were titillating to him. They added a kinky touch to the proceedings" (McGilligan, 2003: 404).

Hitchcock originally wanted Montgomery Clift and Cary Grant as the two killers. Said Laurents, "Since Grant was bisexual and Monty was gay, they were scared to death and they wouldn't do it" (McGilligan, 406). Clift once told Hitchcock he would never do any role that would "raise eyebrows" (Chandler, 2005: 170).

Brandon and Philip became poster boys for the "thrill kill" culture in the film's aftermath. This was the type of image gay people could have done without in 1948 as a brave new world of sexual translucency was opening up. The timing, as a result, was terrible. But even worse was to come. Three years later, Hitchcock would present another psychotic gay man to audiences in *Strangers on a Train*.

We were a long way from Stonewall yet.

Related Films
Strangers on a Train (1951); *Compulsion* (1959); *Swoon* (1992).

Further Reading
Chandler, Charlotte. 2005. *It's Only a Movie: A Personal Biography of Alfred Hitchcock.* London: Simon & Schuster.

Clum, John M. 2002. *Learning Masculinity, Gayness and Love from American Movies.* New York: Palgrave.

Corber, Robert J. 1993. *In the Name of National Security: Hitchcock, Homophobia and the Political Construction of Gender in Postwar America.* Durham, NC: Duke University Press.

Hadleigh, Boze. 1999. *Hollywood Bitch.* London: Robson.

Laurents, Arthur. 2000. *Original Story By.* New York and London: Applause Books.

McGilligan, Patrick. 2003. *Alfred Hitchcock: A Life in Darkness and Light.* West Sussex: John Wiley & Sons.

Price, Theodore. 1992. *Hitchcock and Homosexuality.* Metuchen, NJ: Scarecrow Press.

Pullen, Christopher. 2017. *Straight Girls and Queer Guys.* Edinburgh: Edinburgh University Press.

Taylor, John Russell. 1981. *Hitchcock: The Authorized Biography of Alfred Hitchcock.* London: Abacus.

Wood, Robin. 1989. *Hitchcock's Films Revisited.* New York: Columbia University Press.

S

The Servant (1963)

This chilling tale of role reversal from Joseph Losey unpicked the British class system with forensic skill and also put paid to Dirk Bogarde's boy-next-door credentials. Telling the story of a manservant who goes to work for a foppish aristocrat in his Chelsea house, it has him gradually turning the tables on him so that he, in effect, becomes the master and the master becomes the slave.

James Fox played the upper-crust weakling opposite Bogarde's ruthless valet. Based on a short story by the gay novelist Robin Maugham, its sexual elements are implied rather than stated but more potent because of that.

Bogarde is Hugo Barrett. Fox is simply "Tony." Caught in the middle of their sadomasochistic behavior is Tony's fiancée, Susan (Wendy Craig). Sarah Miles is Barrett's supposed sister Vera. (Later on it emerges that she's his lover.) The screenplay was written by Harold Pinter. It was his first and one of his most memorable. Nobody could create impish ominousness like this man. The fact that it's tinged with a gay underlay added to its charge.

There's little doubt that Barrett is meant to be gay. The way he walks, the way he talks, the way he cooks and arranges flowers all underscore this impression. Its subtext is indicated from the moment he undertakes his tasks of cooking and interior decoration, tasks that would usually be undertaken by women. When he starts playing games of hide-and-seek with Tony, such a subtext is amplified.

Bogarde sloughed off the heartthrob image imposed on him by his studio to play Barrett. The famous "raised eyebrow" was never more effective than here. He draws Tony into his game of cat and mouse almost without his being aware of it.

The main problem with the film from an LGBTQ point of view is that in Barrett it creates yet another gay stereotype. Gay people on screen in the past had usually been either effeminate or sadistic; Barrett is both. His unattractive nature is underlined by a similar unattractiveness in Tony. The fact that there's nobody to like in the film (including the women) gives it a spikiness that focuses one's attention more on Losey's auteurism—and Pinter's layered script—than anything else.

Sylvia Sims, who'd been so good with Bogarde in *Victim*, was the original choice for Susan, but she became pregnant before shooting began. She would have exerted a stronger charge than Craig in the role.

The film was released just a few months after Christine Keeler brought down the Tory government in Britain after having an affair with John Profumo, the Secretary of State for War Sex was in the air and people were beginning to realize it had a price. Nobody paid a higher one than Fox here.

> **Joseph Losey (1909–84)**
>
> Losey wasn't gay but many of his films contain LGBTQ elements, either overtly or covertly. They're most obvious in *The Servant*. He gained international acclaim for that film, but it didn't really translate into work. A drinking problem and a Stalinist conscience were enough to put him out of the running for major Hollywood contracts. Later on in life he reneged on his communist leanings, but by then it was too late.
>
> If his output didn't result in the kind of fame—and fortune—he deserved, it's still there to be admired and enjoyed. Some of his best work he did with Dirk Bogarde, and vice versa. Apart for *The Servant* there was *Modesty Blaise* (1965), a spy spoof also scripted by Harold Pinter. In one scene in this fetishized pop art outing, Bogarde is almost strangled by the legs of a lesbian. He also turned up in *Accident* (1967), another Pinter/Losey collaboration with sexual yearning at its core.
>
> *Boom!* (1968) was an adaptation of a Tennessee Williams play that was praised by Williams himself, a rarity for this man when it came to films of his plays. Losey drew offbeat performances from Elizabeth Taylor and Richard Burton. Noel Coward appeared in a role originally intended for a woman.
>
> That year Losey also directed *Secret Ceremony*, a kinky film starring Taylor again. This time her costar was Mia Farrow. Taylor becomes a kind of surrogate daughter to her after her birth daughter dies. She goes to live at Farrow's mansion at one point and they canoodle like lovers. Robert Mitchum is the wicked stepfather. He takes a backseat when Farrow and Taylor bath together, and when Farrow erotically combs Taylor's hair.
>
> Losey continued to make oddly fascinating films right through to the end of his career. One of his last ones was *La Truite* (1982), the story of a country girl who moves to Paris with her gay husband to see if she can make it in the world of business.

Bogarde won the British Film Academy Award for his performance. He might have won an Oscar if it took off in Hollywood, but it didn't have enough international appeal. It was too dark for American audiences (Morley, 1996, 110). Bogarde shocked everyone when he said the character of Barrett was more like himself than people realized (Coldstream, 2009: 86).

The film came about under unusual circumstances as three of its main participants were all suffering from displacement in some shape or form when it was made. Losey had just been exiled from the United States to England because of his left-wing political views. Pinter had moved from the East End of London, where he grew up, to the West End, where fame found him, and Bogarde was making an art house film and thereby waving good-bye to the soft-centered fan base of all his lightweight "Doctor" outings (Morley, 1999: 111).

Though it won him the BFA award, awards didn't pay the rent. He told Losey he loved working with him but that he couldn't afford to keep doing so (Morley, 111). A tight script laden with Pinter pauses and a summary shredding of the class system was all very well for intellectuals, but such iconoclasm, no matter how well it was presented, rarely found favor with High Street filmgoers.

The film caught British society at a time when it was just about ready to call a halt on class discrimination. What the country didn't expect was the gleefully malevolent manner in which it would be dismantled by Bogarde, Fox, Losey, and

Pinter with their eroticized infantilism. *The Servant* posed a headache for the censors in Britain, but it was passed in France for an unusual reason: two members of the Censorship Commission fell asleep during the showing! (Mathews, 1994: 160).

Related Films
The Caretaker (1964); *Accident* (1967); *The Hireling* (1973); *The Night Porter* (1974).

Further Reading
Biressi, A., and H. Nunn. 2016. *Class and Contemporary British Culture.* London: Palgrave Macmillan.
Caute, David. 1996. *Joseph Losey: A Revenge on Life.* London: British Film Institute.
Coldstream, John, ed. 2009. *Ever, Dirk: The Bogarde Letters.* London: Phoenix.
Gardiner, Colin. 2004. *Joseph Losey.* Manchester: Manchester University Press.
Mathews, Tom Dewe. 1994. *Censored.* London: Chatto & Windus.
Morley, Sheridan. 1996. *Dirk Bogarde: Rank Outsider.* London: Bloomsbury.
Walker, Alexander. 1968. *Sex in the Movies: The Celluloid Sacrifice.* London: Pelican.
Welshman, John. 2007. *Underclass: A History of the Excluded, 1880–2000.* London: Continuum.

Silkwood (1983)

This film was the story of Karen Silkwood, a nuclear plant worker who died in a mysterious car accident in 1974 while in the process of investigating her employers for dangerous working conditions. The film explores her various efforts to take the executives at the plant to task for their laxity. She died when she was on the way to a meeting with the press to discuss her fears on this score. Foul play has always been suspected but never proven.

Meryl Streep gives one of the most resounding performances of her career in the title role. The script was written by Nora Ephron and Alice Arlen. It won an Academy Award nomination. Kurt Russell play's Silkwood's boyfriend, Drew. Cher is her lesbian roommate, Dolly. Mike Nichols directed the film with great conviction, though some people felt he overemphasized Silkwood's private life at the expense of her nuclear concerns (Francke, 1994: 107). This was hardly a legitimate grievance. At the end of the day it's a film rather than a documentary. The human interest factor is what interests audiences primarily. Here it's that of Silkwood. The emotional fragility of Dolly, who can't find a steady partner, is equally moving.

Nichols dovetails his sociopolitical massage neatly with the personal story at the film's core. As it begins, Silkwood is having a troubled time in her relationship with Drew. She's also fighting for custody of children she had from a previous marriage. Her relationship with Dolly is close but not sexual. Ephron said she didn't write Dolly as a lesbian character but rather one who's sexuality didn't overtake everything she did. "How do we write about Oklahoma people who work in a plutonium plant?" she asked. It was a rhetorical question. Her belief was that when the factory workers were having their coffee in the morning, what they talked about wasn't their sexuality but "Who was on *Johnny Carson* last night?" (Russo, 1987: 292).

Cher's mother worried that she might appear too masculine in the film. She allayed her fears on that score, telling her, "I didn't want to play Dolly with a pack of Marlboros rolled up in my T-Shirt sleeve" (Murray, 1994: 366).

She was willing to cut her hair tight, but Nichols didn't want that, encouraging her to work on her role from the inside. The ploy paid off, which wasn't to say the actress—or the director—advocated such an approach for every screen lesbian. Here the emphasis was on her loneliness, so they felt a softer approach was called for.

Cher's secret was to play the role as dreamy rather than in-your-face. She wins one over by her vulnerability, by her refusal to engage in self-pity about the multiple rejections she's received from lovers in the past. When she finds one here, it turns out to be a mortuary beautician, hardly an attractive job title. Angela (Diana Scarwid) is taking a break from her husband—but then she goes back to him.

Dolly is one of the most endearing characters in the film, but Nichols gives her short shrift. It's a shame that Cher, who can be so attractive when she wants, "dressed down" for the part. Was this to look suitably grim to befit the serially rejected lesbian? Whatever way one slices it, it was a thankless role. The film proved to be an excellent statement about the victimization of a woman who crusades on behalf of nuclear improprieties but not much in the way of a statement for sexual diversity. It was a pity that Cher didn't fight Nichols to make her role more central to the storyline.

Dolly's being lesbian was a subplot but not a particularly good one. She might equally have been having an affair with a man as far as Ephron was concerned. Her prime motive was to take attention away from the agitprop nature of the film, to make the characters more human. The family unit was Drew, Karen, and Dolly. In some ways she was like their daughter. Therein lay the problem.

Karen has been denied access to her children. This makes her involvement with Dolly more important to her. It changes the contours of their relationship from romantic to maternal. Dolly is a kind of surrogate child to her, a waif to whom she sings lullabies on the porch to soothe her. Dolly's involvement with Angela becomes a vague threat to this cozy setup. There's a suggestion Angela could replace Karen as her Significant Other. When Dolly moves in with Angela, both Karen and Drew are shocked. Her lesbian involvements aren't supposed to be permanent or even semipermanent. She can't be allowed to engage in the domestic activities in which "normal" people like Karen and Drew indulge. These are only the practices of heterosexual men and women, not people "afflicted" with being lesbian.

In contrast to previous lesbians on screen, Dolly is at least allowed to express her same-sex desire. What she shares in common with them is her inability to realize it. When Angela goes back to her husband, thus leaving Dolly bereft, it places her in the tradition of the lost lesbian, the heritage of so many of her screen ilk up to now. Nichols should have known better. He didn't have to wrap the story up in pink ribbons, but neither should he have consigned her to the love Dumpster.

She's the gooseberry to Karen and Drew, the reject of someone who works in a mortuary. Can Nichols heap any more humiliation on her than this? Not only does the living world not want her; those who preside over the dead don't either.

Nichols strains credulity when Drew leaves Karen at one point of the film. Dolly tells her she misses him even more than Karen herself does. This doesn't make sense, a lesbian missing her girlfriend's boyfriend more than his girlfriend does.

Silkwood was bisexual in real life, but Nichols is having none of this. In the film her primary love focus is Drew. She puts up with Dolly's sexual advances because she likes her as a person, not because she's a possible replacement for Drew. Silkwood is being poisoned by radiation in the film. God forbid that the American public should be contaminated by something even more toxic—Dolly's sexuality.

Related Films
Chastity (1969); *The China Syndrome* (1978); *Erin Brockovich* (2000).

Further Reading
Ephron, Nora. 2016. *Nora Ephron: The Last Interview and Other Conversations*. New York: Melville House Publishing.
Francke, Lizzie. 1994. *Script Girls: Women Screenwriters in Hollywood*. London: British Film Institute.
Hadleigh, Boze. 2000. *In or Out: Gay and Straight Celebrities Talk about Themselves and Each Other*. New York: Barricade.
Kohn, Howard. 1994. *Who Killed Karen Silkwood?* London: Hodder & Stoughton.
Murray, Raymond. 1994. *Images in the Dark: An Encyclopedia of Gay and Lesbian Film and Video*. Philadelphia: TLA Publications.
Quirk, Lawrence J. 1992. *Cher: Her Life and Wild Times*. London: Sphere.
Rashke, Richard. 2016. *The Whistleblower's Dilemma: Snowden, Silkwood and Their Quest for Truth*. New York: HarperCollins.
Russo, Vito. 1987. *The Celluloid Closet: Homosexuality in the Movies*. New York: Harper & Row.

Smoking

Truman Capote once said, "I've never written a word without a cigarette in my hand" (Lessard, 2008: 402). Marlene Dietrich looked sexier when she had a cigarette in her mouth than when she was kissing someone. She was said to have had some of her back teeth extracted to give her a sunken-jaw look. When she inhaled, the smoke seemed to go down to her toes. And who can forget the scene in *Now, Voyager* (1942) when Paul Henreid lights two cigarettes at the same time, one for himself and one for that quintessential gay icon, Bette Davis. Davis looked well when she was smoking too, especially if she was insulting someone as she exhaled. She could turn the air blue with her language at times like this.

Maybe the person Fred MacMurray really loved in *Double Indemnity* (1944) wasn't Barbara Stanwyck at all, but Edward G. Robinson. "You were just across the room from me all these years," MacMurray croaks to his insurance boss as he gasps his last at the end of the film. Robinson replies, "Closer than that, Walter, closer than that." MacMurray has been lighting Robinson's cigarettes for him all through the film but now he's too weak to even light his own one, so Robinson obliges. Parker Tyler described this as "one of the great love scenes in the history of the movies" (Howes, 1993: 120).

Tony Curtis lit Burt Lancaster's cigarettes throughout Alexander Mackendrick's corrosive satire of the media, *Sweet Smell of Success* (1957). He played the fawning press agent Sidney Falco to Lancaster's corrosive columnist. Women were negligible items in this film, mere ciphers who came second to careers. Falco's only lust was to make it to the top. The catalyst for that was Lancaster as J. J. Hunsecker. Hunsecker begins many of his diatribes by putting a cigar into his mouth and giving the waspish injunction to his partner in crime, "Match me, Sidney!"

John Dall has to take a drag of a cigarette to cool himself down in *Rope* (1948) after he commits a murder. His conversation with fellow killer Farley Granger bears all the hallmarks of a postcoital light-up. In *Strangers on a Train* (1951), Hitchcock's "MacGuffin"—the plot device he wove into his films like motifs—is a cigarette lighter left behind him by a passenger—Granger again—that the villain of the piece (Robert Walker) uses to entice him into a murder conspiracy with him. Walker threatens to plant the cigarette lighter at the scene of a murder he commits to implicate Granger in it. He dies with it in his hand. In another scene he pops a child's balloon with a lit cigarette.

In Ed Wood's *Glen or Glenda?* (1953), the much-practiced gay ritual of "seeking a light" from a potential love partner is acted out by an older man on a younger one. It calls to mind the number of scenes in LGBTQ films where cigarettes are symbols of seduction.

One of the most disquieting scenes in *The Killing of Sister George* (1968) occurs when Beryl Reid forces Susannah York to "eat" a cigar, an obvious symbol of oral sex. It's made even more disquieting by York's pretense of enjoying the activity. This annoys Reid because it deprives her of the feeling of having "punished" York in their semierotic S&M charade. An infinitely more erotic acting out of a fellatio theme occurred in Jean Genet's short film *Un Chant D'Amour* (1950). This was set in a prison. It concerned the sexual misery of men serving life sentences for murder. A famous scene features two of them blowing smoke at one another through a straw.

Michael York conveys his attraction to Helmut Griem in *Cabaret* (1972) by lighting a cigarette for him. Griem holds York's hand tightly as he does so and then the two men stare at one another. The second their eyes meet, one knows they're going to have a sexual relationship.

An interesting smoking scene occurs in the Blake Edwards's sex inversion comedy *Victor/Victoria* (1982) when the character played by James Garner discovers Julie Andrews is really a woman in disguise. He doesn't tell her he knows this, offering her a cigar instead. She has to smoke it to preserve, as she sees it, the illusion of being a man. Rebecca Bell-Metereau remarked, "The cigar is so frequently used in genre-based comedies, it's practically a trope, one that surely would have delighted Freud" (Bell-Metereau, 1993: 225).

In Tiona Nekkia McClodden's short film *Bumming Cigarettes* (2012), a young black lesbian woman shares her hopes and fears about her health with a middle-aged black gay man who's HIV-positive. She's waiting for the results of an AIDS test she's had. In ten minutes they get to know more about one another than some people do in ten years—over a cigarette.

Further Reading

Bell-Metereau, Rebecca. 1993. *Hollywood Androgyny.* New York: Columbia University Press.

Howes, Keith. 1993. *Broadcasting It.* London: Cassell.

Lessard, John, ed. 2008. *To Quote a Queer.* Philadelphia: Quirk Books.

Some Like It Hot (1959)

When Jack Lemmon (Jerry) and Tony Curtis (Joe) took on the guises of two women in this evergreen Billy Wilder comedy to hide from a gang of hoods, little did they know what was in store for them. This wasn't just a case of dressing up in women's clothes as far as Wilder was concerned. He wanted them to be so like women that they would be mistaken for them, even by fellow cast members.

In the famous last scene of the film, Joe E. Brown says he wants to marry Lemmon, whom he's been canoodling with for some time. When Lemmon pulls off his wig and tells Brown he can't marry him because he's a man, Brown gives a broad grin and trills, "Nobody's perfect!"

This film turns up in a phenomenal number of polls as people's favorite one of all time, and that includes polls from all sections of the sexual divide. Though not manifestly gay, it's become a camp classic and has grown in stature over the years for its gender-bending zaniness. Brown may not think anyone is perfect, but Wilder came close to perfection with his impeccable valentine to the screwball comedies of the forties, and he also gave Lemmon, Curtis, and Marilyn Monroe the film for which they would be most remembered.

Monroe was leery about taking it on when Wilder informed her she wouldn't see through the men's disguises. She thought only dumb blondes would be fooled by them, and she was trying to rid herself of her dumb blonde image at the time. Her then husband, Arthur Miller, persuaded her to say yes. His decision proved wise.

The first time Curtis and Lemmon tried out their new apparel as Josephine and Daphne, they went into a ladies' room to see if they could pass themselves off as women. Lemmon couldn't wait to try out his disguise, but Curtis was terrified. He had to be coaxed out by Wilder. When he faced the women, he was amazed to discover none of them showed any interest in either himself or Lemmon. "They thought we were extras or bit players doing a period piece," he said, "but they thought we were women" (Chandler, 2002: 211).

Lemmon was satisfied at this, but Curtis looked deeper. He imagined they were ignored because they were ugly. He insisted on going back to makeup for more mascara and higher heels. He also had his breasts enhanced. Lemmon, meanwhile, had his rump "reupholstered." The result this time was disastrous. No sooner had they reentered the ladies' room than one of the girls in there said, "Hi, Tony" (Chandler, 211–2).

Lemmon decided to exaggerate his role from the get-go, camping up his walk and flashing a banana-shaped grin. Curtis was more reserved. He tried to model Josephine on women he knew—his mother, Grace Kelly, anyone he could think of. Janet Leigh was also on his mind (*Saturday Evening Post*, July 25, 1959).

Leigh was amused that her husband was finally realizing that being a woman wasn't all peaches and cream: "Those high heels were uncomfortable and it was difficult to keep on balance. The wigs were hot and itchy, and they had a heck of a time with the makeup and the five o'clock shadow" (Leigh, 1984: 251).

Lemmon and Curtis suffered "the tortures of the damned" with muscle cramps. Such tortures were mitigated only when Wilder called "Cut!" and they were able to douse their feet in ice-cold buckets of water. Afterward they poured lotion on them to make them ready for the next take. Curtis found it helpful to let go of his muscles to get into the part. Otherwise they became too defined. He wanted to look "slinky, supple" (*The Telegraph*, September 30, 2010).

Wilder recruited the famous Texan cross-dresser Barbette as a consultant to the two cross-dressers. Barbette had been born Vander Clyde. He was now in retirement. He'd had a glittering circus career before it ended prematurely because of poor health. Curtis took his advice as regards how to walk like a woman and so on, but Lemmon was more intractable. After three days, Barbette blew up at Wilder. "Curtis can be magnificent," he fumed, "but Lemmon is hopeless" (Freedland, 2003: 77).

Curtis explained what happened: "Jack told Barbette he didn't want anything to do with him. He said he didn't want to walk like a woman. He wanted to walk like a man trying to walk like a woman. He was so right. We should have been hamming it up as much as we could. And of course Jack did that. The reason I didn't was because I wanted to give him something to bounce off. I played a straight man—or should I say straight woman—to him. We were going screwball" (*The Telegraph*, September 30, 2010).

Curtis really played three roles in the film. As well as Joe and Josephine, in the last third he becomes a Cary Grant soundalike suffering from impotence. "I don't know how to put it," he tells Monroe, "but I've got this thing about girls." "What thing?" she inquires. "They just sort of leave me cold," he tells her. Such a remark has added overtones today considering the number of column inches that have been expended on Grant's possible bisexuality. Monroe excites him and he seems to enjoy it, but after the film wrapped he was quoted as saying that kissing her was "like kissing Hitler" (Munn, 2011: 156). Despite this, Curtis claimed to have had sex with her on the set and that afterward she became pregnant with his child, which she later aborted (Munn, 157).

Related Films
Fanfare of Love (1935); *Fanfaren der Liebe* (1951); *Nuns on the Run* (1990); *Connie and Carla* (2004); *White Chicks* (2004).

Further Reading

Chandler, Charlotte. 2002. *Nobody's Perfect: A Biography of Billy Wilder.* New York: Simon & Schuster.

Crowe, Cameron. 2001. *Conversations with Wilder.* New York: Alfred A. Knopf.

Curtis, Tony, and Mark A. Vieira. 2009. *Me, Marilyn and the Movie.* London: Virgin.

Freedland, Michael, 2003. *The Charmed Life of Jack Lemmon.* London: Robson.

Hunter, Allan. 1985. *Tony Curtis: The Man and His Movies.* Edinburgh: Paul Harris Publishing.

Leigh, Janet. 1984. *There Really Was a Hollywood.* New York: Jove Books.

Maslon, Laurence. 2009. *Some Like It Hot: The Official 50th Anniversary Companion.* London: Pavilion.

Munn, Michael. 2011. *Tony Curtis: Nobody's Perfect.* London: JR Books.

Saturday Evening Post, July 25, 1959.

Sikov, Ed. 1998. *On Sunset Boulevard: The Life and Times of Billy Wilder.* New York: Hyperion Books.

Spoto, Donald. 2001. *Marilyn Monroe.* Lanham, MD: Cooper Square Press.

The Telegraph, September 30, 2010.

Zolotow, Maurice. 1996. *Billy Wilder in Hollywood.* New York: Limelight Editions.

Staircase (1969)

This film was adapted by Stanley Donen from a play about a pair of gay barbers who've been living together for years. It had some curiosity value from the point of view that it featured two A-list stars (Richard Burton and Rex Harrison) in the main roles, but the critical consensus was that they would have been better advised not to bother. Their performances don't range far beyond the kind of one might see in a *"Carry On"* film. Did they do it to prove they weren't homophobic? To show that they were "liberal"? That they didn't want to turn down a challenge?

Staircase is like a gay version of *Who's Afraid of Virginia Woolf?* without the good writing. In the limp-wristed posturing of its irritating barbers, Harry (Burton) and Charlie (Harrison), one witnesses a crude attempt on both of their parts to "do" a gay role in the same way as one might "do" a murderer or an autistic savant. The staid dutifulness of the enterprise was toe-curlingly banal.

The plot is negligible. Charlie is arrested for appearing in drag in a gay bar. As the hearing approaches, he tries to act straight. As if to apprise us of his heterosexual chops, he reminds us that he was once married and that he even bore a child. Harry wasn't so privileged, much as he would like to have been. The pair of them are stuck with one another now like a desiccated pair of old shoes, condemned to live out their lives with as much dry wit as they can muster up from what's left of their brains.

Harrison didn't seem to be interested in giving any kind of a credible performance in the film. It was as if he did it simply to have it on his CV that he once played a gay character. This was evident from the one-dimensional approach he took to the role, parodying gay people in a series of queenie mannerisms like the ones myopic straight people deploy when they wish to make fun of gay people.

Villain (1971)

Burton here plays a gay London sadist called Vic Dakin who's obsessed with his mother (Cathleen Nesbitt). The conflation of "sadistic," "gay," and "mother-obsessed" brings one back to the bad old days of *Rope* (1948) and *Psycho* (1960).

Director Michael Tuchner plays fast and loose with James Barlow's novel *The Burden of Proof* to exhibit a Ronnie Kray style ne'er-do-well. Burton plays him seedily. Dakin rules the East End with an iron fist, liquidating anyone who gets in his way but still finding time to bring his mum on day trips to Brighton when she's up to it, driving home at a moderate thirty miles per hour "so she doesn't get the hiccups."

His toyboy lover in the film is small-time crook Wolfie Lissner (Ian McShane). Lissner blackmails politicians. Vic likes rough sex so Wolfie is never sure if he's going to get punched or kissed under the feathers. It could well be both.

But Scotland Yard is closing in on Vic's empire, and he's getting increasingly nervous he's going to be ratted on by one of his colleagues. Such nervousness makes him even more violent than usual—if that's possible.

The film flopped both in the United Kingdom and the United States. It has a look of "straight to video" about it. Most of the sex scenes were edited out when it eventually hit the small screen.

The fact that Burton followed *Staircase* with *Villain* is interesting. If one film was too fey, the other erred on the side of coarseness. The antidote to gentleness shouldn't have been cruelty; it should have been strength. Meeting his friend Peter O'Toole shortly after it wrapped, O'Toole smirked, "It looks as though you've cornered the limp wrist market, duckie" (Bourne, 1996: 234). The comment was fairly typical of the thinking of the time. Maybe Burton deserved O'Toole's sarcastic gibe. He'd played two gay stereotypes in a row. One could have been forgiven. The second underlined his intolerant mind-set.

When Burton was making *Villain*, his wife, Elizabeth Taylor, was having a bath with Susannah York in *Zee & Co.*, a film based on a Tennessee Williams screenplay. It wasn't one of Williams's better works, but it was a masterpiece in comparison with *Villain*. The attempt to humanize Dakin by having him minister to his mother while carving up his enemies didn't work quite so well for Burton as it did for James Cagney in *White Heat* (1949). The missing ingredients were emotion and empathy.

Further Reading

Bourne, Stephen. 1996. *Brief Encounters: Lesbians and Gays in British Cinema: 1930–1971*. London: Cassell.

Burton wasn't much better, but at least he tried to flesh out his character, showing different sides to him like worrying about his weight and alopecia—he wears a turban to hide his baldness—and showing concern about his bedridden mother.

What one is really looking at here is two music hall stereotypes. Both of them seem nervous of playing the roles too well in case people might have suspected they were latently gay in real life. One writer rightly observed that they were more believable as the heterosexual camp characters they played in *My Fair Lady* (1964) and *Boom!* (1968) (Tyler, 1973: 351).

"I didn't see it as a story of homosexuals," Burton derided, "but about two neurotic individuals who needed each other desperately." "The film was a risk," said Harrison, "but I felt I was old enough and rich enough to take it on and Richard did too. We discussed it. It was a case of, 'If you do it, I'll do it.' So we did it. It was a mistake, a dreadful mistake, but that's what risks are all about" (Munn, 2008: 173).

Burton was careful to point out that he wasn't gay in real life. He hardly needed to with his reputation for satyriasis. He tried to seduce Joan Collins on the set of their 1956 movie *The Sea Wife*. She said, "Richard, I believe you'd screw a snake if you had the chance." He replied, "Only if it was wearing a skirt, darling. It would have to be a female snake" (Downing, 1990: 49).

Paul Scofield, Burton's old nemesis, had played Harry on stage. Donen wanted him for the film version, but he demurred. Burton was glad to occupy the vacant throne. Scofield had denied him an Oscar three years previously when they were both conominated, Burton for *Anne of the Thousand Days* and Scofield for *A Man for All Seasons*. Scofield won and the defeat rankled with Burton. He thought *Staircase* might be sweet revenge, but it wasn't. By the end of the shoot, he must have known why Scofield rejected the idea. Once again he'd been bested by his theatrical rival—this time by default.

Considering both Burton and Harrison were intelligent men, it's surprising that they had such antediluvian attitudes to being gay. Harrison said he took the role purely for the opportunity to work with Burton as he hadn't had any scenes with him in *Cleopatra*, a previous film in which they'd costarred (Harrison, 1990: 201). Burton had a frivolous attitude to being gay, claiming to have done a queer version of *Hamlet* once but "nobody noticed" (Downing, 1990: 29). He also believed that an actor had to establish his credentials as a straight man before he could "risk" playing a gay one. He added more revealingly, "Perhaps most actors are latent homosexuals and we cover it with drink. I was once homosexual but it didn't work" (Hadleigh, 2000: 188).

Burton mistakenly imagined the film would work with audiences, but his radar was on the blink. They saw through its fraudulence. It wasn't only gay people who realized it was trying to manipulate people's emotions in an attempt to be trendy; everyone did. "What the hell," he harrumphed when the sneak previews proved disastrous, "I'll just grow another callus. I'll end up with a mind like a miner's hands" (Bragg, 1988: 302).

The self-piteous characters of *Staircase* rankle even today, replete as they are with all the tired mannerisms of those who perform drag acts at workingmen's clubs for the titillation of those who like to watch mincing movements associated with third-rate impressionists. By the end, one is left in little doubt that both of them would prefer to be with women if their orientation permitted this. They're probably the only two gay homophobes on film. For that alone, the film deserves attention.

These "poofs," to quote Burton, are hardly adverts for being gay. They're like bad habits of one another, like one of those formulaic heterosexual marriages with which Hollywood's back lot is littered. They're together from need rather than desire, and a rather tenuous need at that.

Many gay men in films made around this time tried to pretend to themselves that they were straight. The two characters in *Staircase* are like two straights trying to pretend they're gay. Unfortunately, they don't succeed.

Related Films
The Boys in the Band (1970); *The Choirboys* (1977); *Partners* (1982).

Further Reading
Bragg, Melvyn. 1988. *Rich: The Life of Richard Burton.* London: Hodder & Stoughton.
Downing, Christopher, ed. 1990. *Burton Stories.* London: Futura.
Dyer, Charles. 2011. *Staircase.* London: Samuel French.
Hadleigh, Boze. 2000. *In or Out: Gay and Straight Celebrities Talk about Themselves and Each Other.* New York: Barricade.
Harrison, Rex. 1990. *A Damned Serious Business: My Life in Comedy.* London: Bantam.
Munn, Michael. 2008. *Richard Burton: Prince of Players.* London: JR Books.
Tyler, Parker. 1973. *Screening the Sexes: Homosexuality in the Movies.* Garden City, NY: Anchor Press.
Walker, Alexander. 2002. *Fatal Charm: The Life of Rex Harrison.* London: Gollancz.

Strangers on a Train (1951)

On a train going from Washington, DC, to New York, a sociopath called Bruno Antony (Robert Walker) spots tennis ace Guy Haines (Farley Granger) and starts talking to him in what Peter Bogdanovich described as a "cute meet" (*Strangers on a Train* DVD: Special Features, Warner Bros. Entertainment Inc.). As the conversation develops, it turns out that he's much more familiar with his circumstances than Haines expected. He knows that he's anxious to divorce his wife, Miriam (Laura Elliott), and also that he wants to marry another woman, Anne (Ruth Roman).

Bruno tells Guy that he loves his mother but hates his father. He suggests semi-playfully that they could do one another a favor by removing the unwanted person in their lives. In other words, Bruno could murder Miriam and Guy could kill Bruno's father in a "crisscross" arrangement. Neither murder would be traced to the perpetrator because they wouldn't have a discernible motive. Guy listens to this with a mixture of amusement and incredulity. Is the conversation really taking place? Is it being conducted in jest or is there an ominous undertow to it?

Guy is flummoxed by Bruno's suggestion, but he tries to keep cool. "I may be old-fashioned," he says, "but I thought murder was against the law." He departs the train carriage after sharing a reluctant drink with Bruno.

Without further ado, Bruno now goes to Guy's home town and strangles Miriam at a funfair. He informs the shocked Guy about what he's done. He tells him it's now time for him to honor his part of the "bargain." The stage is set for an intriguing battle of wits between the psychopath and his unwilling dupe.

A dozen writers turned down the offer to turn the murder swap story of the then unknown Patricia Highsmith into a film before Raymond Chandler saw its potential and said yes. It sounded far too outlandish to be believed, but in director Alfred Hitchcock's hands it bears all the hallmarks of a gripping film noir, with the added bonus of the sexual electricity that passes between Bruno and Guy. Sex and death had been combined in films before, of course—most notably in *Double*

Indemnity—but apart from *Rope* (1948), another Hitchcock film, it was usually between a man and a woman rather than two men.

Hitchcock originally wanted William Holden for Haines. If he played the role, he thought, Bruno's attraction to him would really make him—and audiences—squirm. Granger was a little too fey for him, which gave the dapper Bruno less to bounce off. Both of them could be classified as being effeminate in their ways, which detracted from the homoerotic charge of Highsmith's book.

Highsmith loved the "elegance and humor" Walker brought to Bruno. She was also impressed by his devotion to his mother. She does his nails; he kisses her hand. He giggles with her like a little boy. His combination of childishness and the need to control made for a potent mix (*Sight and Sound*, Autumn 1988).

Bruno intrigues even as he repulses. His charismatic devilry is served up in sharp contrast to the boring hesitancy of his somewhat droll foil. He plays Guy like a violin with chat-up lines like, "We speak the same language, don't we?" The fact that Guy doesn't agree is irrelevant. He's about to become his conspirator whether he likes it or not. Bruno may be mother-dominated, but there his lack of control in life ends. He dominates Guy just as his mother dominates him, such domination resulting in his near-ubiquitous presence in Guy's life. Peter Bogdanovich referred to him as cinema's "first stalker" (*Strangers on a Train* DVD: Special Features).

The sexual charge between the two men wasn't in the script. It was Walker's idea to play Bruno as a gay man trying to seduce Bruno vicariously. Granger went along with it and so did Hitchcock. It's evident in touches like when their shoes brush off one another when they first meet on the train. Trains were classic pickup venues for gay characters in films. Here the "seductive" events are transmitted in details like Bruno's "flirty eye contact" with Guy (*Strangers on a Train* DVD: Special Features).

Bruno represents the kind of arch character first seen in *Rope*. Murder makes him feel good. He thinks he's entitled to kill without being called to account for it.

The film created a strong link between queerness and mental illness, as had *Rope*, leading to beliefs in many circles that Hitchcock was homophobic. Jonathan Goldberg wrote, "Comparison to *Rope* underscores the confluence of a murder plot and a homosexual one, indeed the virtual transposition of one upon the other" (Goldberg, 2012: 48). Granger played the more timorous member of the duo in both films.

Bruno was the stereotypical screen gay man on of the time: a psychopath with a mother complex. He also shared something else with screen gay men of the fifties: Hollywood keeps him in the closet. According to Darwin Porter, Walker told talk show host Merv Griffin that both he and Granger knew they were "playing it homo," but the hip ones in the audience will get it (Porter, 2009: 100).

In Highsmith's novel, Guy kills Bruno's father. Then Bruno kills himself by throwing himself off a boat. Hitchcock changed almost everything Highsmith wrote into his own concept after the opening scene, which was basically the same as hers.

Walker died a year after making the film, distraught after his then wife, Jennifer Jones, divorced him to marry David O. Selznick. Depressed beyond reason, he went on a spiral of drink and drugs that led to respiratory failure at the age of thirty-seven. It was almost as if Bruno Antony was being punished by whatever gods presided over celluloid morality.

Related Films
Rope (1948); *Psycho* (1960); *Once You Kiss a Stranger* (1969); *Remaining Strangers* (1986); *Throw Momma from the Train* (1987).

Further Reading
Allen, Richard. 2007. *Hitchcock's Romantic Irony.* New York: Columbia University Press.
Goldberg, Jonathan. 2012. *Strangers on a Train: A Queer Film Classic.* Vancouver, BC: Arsenal Pulp Press.
Gottlieb, Sidney, ed. 2003. *Alfred Hitchcock Interviews.* Jackson: University of Mississippi Press.
Granger, Farley, and Robert Calhoun. 2008. *Include Me Out: My Life from Goldwyn to Broadway.* New York: St. Martin's Press.
Highsmith, Patricia. 1999. *Strangers on a Train.* London: Vintage.
Krohn, Bill. 2008. *Hitchcock at Work.* New York: Phaidon.
Linet, Beverly. 1986. *Star-Crossed: The Story of Robert Walker and Jennifer Jones.* New York: G. P. Putnam & Sons.
Porter, Darwin. 2009. *Merv Griffin: A Life in the Closet.* New York: Blood Moon Productions.
Sight and Sound, Autumn, 1988.
Walker, Michael. 2005. *Hitchcock's Motifs.* Amsterdam: Amsterdam University Press.

Suddenly, Last Summer (1959)

The character of Sebastian in this adaptation of Tennessee Williams's play of the same name was one of the first gay men to appear in a mainstream American film. He isn't identified, but his violent death on a Caribbean island forms the film's crucial backstory.

His cousin Catherine Holly (Elizabeth Taylor) witnessed it and has become traumatized as a result. Her mother, Violet (Katharine Hepburn), wants a lobotomy performed on her. Catherine's trauma is the ostensible reason for this, but the real one is that Violet wants to cover up a secret: Sebastian used both Cathy and Violet to procure men for him for sexual purposes. "He used us for bait!" Cathy blurts out at one point. Violet wants this fact hidden to protect the family's reputation.

Montgomery Clift plays Dr. Cukrowicz, the man Violet wants to perform the lobotomy. If he does so, she says she'll pay for a new wing he wishes to add to his hospital. As the film goes on and he becomes friendly with Catherine, he shows less and less interest in Violet's offer.

Under his gentle urgings, Catherine starts to remember how Sebastian was killed. He was, in fact, cannibalized by a gang of impoverished youths who chased him to his death. These were presumably victims of previous liaisons with him. There are so many of them, it seems as if Sebastian sodomized half the island.

A series of flashback sequences brings this back to Catherine. When she finally sees it all in her mind's eye, it's obvious to everyone that, far from needing a lobotomy, she's one of the sanest people in the film. She emits a kind of primal scream when the full horror of Sebastian's fate comes back to her.

This was an incredible performance from Taylor. Many people felt she should have won an Oscar for it. She was nominated but didn't win.

Her enlightenment coincides with Violet's slide into madness. This is a more mannered performance from Hepburn. She was conominated with Taylor. Neither of them took home the gold. (Simone Signoret won instead for *Room at the Top*.)

Violet's denial of Sebastian's acts was reprised by a similar denial of Hepburn offscreen. She wasn't happy with Williams's dialogue. "If you knew what it means to me when I say these things!" she complained to the film's director, Joseph L. Mankiewicz. "That's the play," he replied, "and that's what we have to do." Their relationship was fraught with tension right through the shoot. On the last day she spat in his face with the words, "You're just a pig in a silk suit" (Leaming, 1995: 481).

The film remains unique in that it had a gay screenwriter (Gore Vidal) adapting a play by a gay playwright (Williams) and still came across as homophobic. This was some kind of achievement. "I never thought about homosexuality or cannibalism while I was directing it," Mankiewicz pronounced, "only its basic humanity" (Barrios, 2003: 262). If this was the case, he was in a minority of one.

Williams didn't show much interest in the film. He'd had his fingers burned too often by Hollywood. Blanche DuBois's marriage to a gay man had been airbrushed out of *A Streetcar Named Desire*, as had Brick's gay college liaison with a dead lover from *Cat on a Hot Tin Roof*. He expected the same sanitization to apply here.

He purportedly wrote it to try to come to terms with the lobotomy that had been performed on his beloved sister, Rose, but it only exacerbated his depression over this. The catharsis experienced by Catherine in the film wasn't shared by him—or by audiences. There were too many excavations of the dark corners of the psyche for comfort. Hollywood wasn't ready for it and neither was Geoffrey Shurlock at the Production Code Association. Sam Spiegel, the producer, offered to delete the references to cannibalism. This pacified Shurlock somewhat. Spiegel argued that Sebastian paid for his sexual orientation with his life, which again placated Shurlock.

Suddenly, Last Summer was the first studio-produced film featuring a gay relationship to be granted a special dispensation from the Motion Picture Production Code Office. Lest one become enthused by its forward-looking attitude, it should be remembered that the reason for this was Sebastian's horrific death. Once again, as was the case with so many LGBTQ films in the past, the gay character often has to pay the ultimate price for his or her "crime"—death.

This was a baroque film that was overacted and overdirected, though the material was sufficiently melodramatic to justify some of the carpet chewing, especially on Hepburn's part. It was the only film based on a Williams play that referred directly to being gay, but he still didn't like it. Spiegel gave him $50,000 up front and a 20 percent share of any residuals. Unfortunately, there weren't many of these. "The profits were as good," Williams snorted, "as the movie was bad" (Williams, 1977: 176).

There were many inconsistencies in the plot. Boze Hadleigh found it difficult to believe Catherine would have been oblivious to Violet's manipulation of her for Sebastian's sexual favors. "It stretched credulity," he sniffed, "to believe that such a hip doll as Liz wouldn't know she was being used for evil. Liz would have dragged Sebastian home by his ears and saved them both from considerable embarrassment that summer" (Hadleigh, 1993: 28). Another writer noted that her high eligibility as a sex object "italicized the hideous perversity" of the disgusting Sebastian (Tyler, 1973: 307).

From a more pragmatic point of view, the grotesque elements of the story were hardly the stuff of Saturday night at the drive-in. The appropriation of an A-league cast only served to emphasize the "underground" nature of the material. Everyone did their best to look suitably intense, but inside themselves they must have been wondering why they signed up for such an ill-advised project.

Taylor and Clift had earlier appeared together in George Stevens's *A Place in the Sun* (1951). Albert Dekker played a doctor in the film. His son was shot to death in 1967, and he never got over it. The following year he was found dead in the bathroom of his apartment, bound and gagged and hanging from the shower rod. He was dressed in silk lingerie. On his body he'd smeared some of the unkind things that had been said about his performances over the years—in lipstick (Underwood, 1992: 183). Maybe this would have made a better story.

Related Films
A Place in the Sun (1951); *A Streetcar Named Desire* (1951); *Cat on a Hot Tin Roof* (1958).

Further Reading
Barrios, Richard, 2003. *Screened Out: Playing Gay in Hollywood from Edison to Stonewall.* New York and London: Routledge.
Farmer, Brett. 2000. *Spectacular Passions: Cinema, Fantasy, Gay Male Partnerships.* Durham, NC, and London: Duke University Press.
Hadleigh, Boze. 1993. *The Lavender Screen.* New York: Citadel Press.
Leaming, Barbara. 1995. *Katharine Hepburn.* London: Weidenfeld & Nicolson.
Spoto, Donald. 1986. *The Kindness of Strangers: The Life of Tennessee Williams.* Boston: Little Brown & Company.
Tyler, Parker. 1973. *Screening the Sexes: Homosexuality in the Movies.* Garden City, NY: Anchor Press.
Underwood, Peter. 1992. *Death in Hollywood.* London: Piatkus.
Williams, Tennessee. 1977. *Memoirs.* London: W. H. Allen.

Suicide

King George V is alleged to have remarked about gay men once, "I thought men like that shot themselves." As far as Hollywood was concerned in its "golden" years, he was often right.

In the early years of the film about LGBTQ characters, suicide was one of the most common "solutions" to their predicament. It was almost endorsed by the time, a termination of the condition that prevented something worse—its practice.

The first screen suicide of a gay character was Paul Komer in *Anders als die Andern* in 1919. A decade or so later, Hertha Thiele leaped to her death in *Mädchen in Uniform* (1931). In the following decades, gay characters either cut their wrists, jumped off cliffs, overdosed, or shot themselves in the head. Of thirty-two films with major gay or lesbian characters made between 1961 and 1976, thirteen of them featured suicides (Howes, 1993: 118).

Sometimes the suicide wasn't in the film but in its backstory, as was the case in *Cat on a Hot Tin Roof* (1958) where Paul Newman's gay friend kills himself in grief over Newman's leaving him. This was deemed to be too much of a hot potato in the film version of Tennessee Williams's play. Anyone who wasn't *au fait* with the original text could have been forgiven for wondering why Newman was so traumatized, or why he seemed to be immune to the estimable sexual charms of Elizabeth Taylor.

In *Victim* (1961), an offscreen suicide occurs as a result of a gay character being bribed by people threatening to out him. A similar scenario unfolded in *Advise & Consent* (1962). In *The Children's Hour* (1961), Shirley MacLaine hangs herself because she can't face the fact that she has feelings for her fellow teacher Audrey Hepburn. In those days, same-sex "feelings" were loathsome things to be whispered about in alleyways or woodlands under cover of night.

In the French film *This Special Friendship* (1964), a boy falls in love with another pupil in a Catholic school. When a priest interferes, causing one of the boys to leave the school, the other kills himself. Gay killer William Windom killed himself in *The Detective* (1968) after leaving a trail of bodies in his wake. These were gay too. One may interpret his killing of them as a kind of vicarious murder of himself. In the same year, Rod Steiger killed himself in *The Sergeant* after kissing John Phillip Law, whom he's spent most of the film lusting after. The treatment of Steiger's orientation here is so over the top as to make it almost into a psychopathic disease. He carries it, in the words of one writer, "as if it were a sore thumb in a flesh-toned Band-Aid" (Tyler, 1973: 257). It's difficult to sympathize with him. When he kills himself, one almost feels he's done himself a favor. There's been too much self-disgust, too much willful angst. At times it appears almost masochistic.

Zooey Hall commits suicide in *Fortune and Men's Eyes* (1971) by slitting his throat. Anthony Perkins takes an overdose of pills in *Play It as It Lays* (1972). *The Tenant* (1976) is all tied up with identity confusion as Roman Polanski takes on the guise of a woman who tried to kill herself by throwing herself from a tall building. When a teenager experiences problems with his girlfriend in *Ode to Billy Joe* (1976), he has a gay experience that eventually leads to his jumping off a bridge. Paul Rudd poisons himself in *The Betsy* (1978).

The eighties brought some diminution in the number of people who felt they had to go to their grave for having urges that didn't ally with those of the common run of humanity. *Desert Hearts* (1985) was one of the first films to portray a gay relationship that didn't end in heartache and/or suicide. The goalposts were shifting. This decade had many films featuring happy gay and lesbian relationships, like *Making Love* (1981), *Personal Best* (1982), and *Lianna* (1983). They weren't all masterpieces but neither did they end tragically with deaths, as seemed to be the norm in previous decades. *Thelma and Louise* (1991) ended in a suicidal act, but it was a happy one, the final seal of a relationship.

Christopher O'Hare made an interesting documentary in 1995 called *Better Dead Than Gay*. It concerned a twenty-six-year-old British boy who commits suicide in his car as the song "To God and Glory" plays on his radio. He's unable to reconcile his sexuality with his Christian upbringing. His father says at one point, "To discover my son was gay was as bad as losing him," a shocking revelation. On a similar theme, the gay son of Sigourney Weaver kills himself in *Prayers for Bobby* (2009) when she tells him being gay is a sin and that he needs to pray to God for a cure. Weaver's character was based on the Christian crusader Mary Griffith. She experiences remorse after he dies. The film is as much about her softening her attitude as his death.

In the same year, Isild Le Besco attempts suicide in *Highly Strung* when her friend Judith Davis leaves her for a male lover. This was an unusual French film, thematically like a cross between *The Page Turner* (2006) and *Single White Female* (1992). Le Besco is obsessed with Davis, an aspiring pianist, and becomes highly distressed when she expresses any interest in men. Davis succumbs to her lesbian advances early on in the film, but it's Le Besco who makes most of the running; Davis is primarily heterosexual. When she moves her boyfriend into Le Besco's apartment, she's playing with fire. If this were an American film it would probably have ended violently, but director Sophie Laloy opted for a more subdued finale by having Le Besco turn her violence on herself rather than the object of her love. Laloy is nuanced. She gives us a tender story of obsession and the manner in which Davis's mixed signals to a fragile sensibility prove tragic.

Further Reading
Cover, R. 2012. *Queer Youth Suicide, Culture and Identity: Unbearable Lives?* Farnham, UK: Ashgate Publishing.
Dorais, Michael. 2004. *Dead Boys Can't Dance: Sexual Orientation, Masculinity and Suicide*. Montreal: McGill-Queens University Press.
Howes, Keith. 1993. *Broadcasting It*. London: Cassell.
Tyler, Parker. 1973. *Screening the Sexes: Homosexuality in the Movies*. Garden City, NY: Anchor Press.
Underwood, Peter. 1992. *Death in Hollywood*. London: Piatkus.

Sunday Bloody Sunday (1971)

This John Schlesinger film is mainly remembered today for a kiss exchanged between the Jewish doctor Daniel Hirsch (Peter Finch) and his sculptor boyfriend, Bob (Murray Head). Heterosexual personnel executive Alex Greville (Glenda Jackson) is, like, Hirsch, in love with Bob. She's a divorcee working in an employment agency. She shares an answering service with Hirsch as well as a boyfriend. Bob doesn't care as much about either of them as they do about him.

The fact that Hirsch is Jewish as well as gay increased the drama of his situation for audiences of the film considering the emphasis Judaism places on family life—and the fact that it's rooted in the Old Testament's pronounced antigay stance.

Bob doesn't hide his male and female lovers from one another. They're more grudging about the situation than they admit. It's London during the swinging sixties; they don't want to be thought untrendy. But it's Bob who's calling the shots.

The problem with the film is that the actor who's the common thread between the lovers, Head, is its weakest link. Finch and Jackson have only one scene together. One wonders what they see in Bob besides his youth. Their own characters are infinitely more interesting than his.

Head was aware of his place in the pecking order. "My two older lovers," he admitted, "knew what they wanted but my character was too wishy-washy, stuck in a sexual twilight zone" (Porter and Prince, 2010: 454).

Finch took the part reluctantly. He didn't want to play a gay role initially, but Schlesinger won him over. In the end he saw the sexuality of his character as a relatively minor part of what he wanted to convey when he played him. "He might just as easily be a girl," he concluded. "This is the first script I've seen in which homosexuality is just a fact about a character rather than an issue. There are no revelations, no confrontations, no dramatic turns of fate." The characters in the film "go on living while life and circumstance" settle things for them (Howes, 1993: 259).

The kiss scene was by far the most dramatic one in the film. There was huge tension on the set for it. It was referred to simply as "The Scene" by the crew. There was no dialogue in it. They got through it unfussily, but the tension returned when they viewed the rushes. According to Head, "Everybody was smoking four cigarettes at a time, crossing and re-crossing their legs, coughing and spluttering." He was asked if he was shocked by it. He said he wasn't. He thought older people might have been: "The war generation, where the roles had to be clearly defined. The men fought, the women stayed home or worked in munitions factories. For these people, after the war there was a continuation of this role-playing." Boys were boys and girls were girls at that time and they got together and raised families: "Then came my generation in the sixties with our emotional explosion. There were young people with long hair and—to them—effeminate views and gestures." Head thought the previous generation repressed their feelings too much. They couldn't understand how he could do something like kiss another man with such ease (Dundy, 1980: 311).

Bob jets off to greener pastures at the end. His two lovers are left gazing wryly at one another as they wonder what just happened. They're desolate and there's nothing they can do about it, not even gravitate toward one another.

The film leaves one with a sense of flatness. It's as if a further scene conveying their frustration with Bob—or one another—is missing. This was both its artistic strength and its commercial weakness. It was true to life, but people don't always go to films for truth. They want escapism, exaggerated realism. They don't always want the kitchen sink. They often prefer quick emotional fixes.

Schlesinger resisted the temptation to have Hirsh licking his wounds in the last scene where, interestingly, he speaks to camera. "People say to me, 'He never made you happy.'" He sighs. "And I say, 'But I *am* happy.' Apart from missing him." His emotions are muddled. This is representative of the film in general. It doesn't give us pat answers. It may not be Schlesinger's most resounding work, but as an offbeat chronicle of the vagaries of triangulated affection, it strikes a chord. It also captures the liberal atmosphere of the sixties in the scenes of family life—and at a bar mitzvah—where the sophistication is very chic and natural to the characters.

Finch slotted himself into the role like a hand into a glove. He also played a man who loved foolishly in another Schlesinger film, *Far from the Madding Crowd*—and a gay man in *The Trials of Oscar Wilde*.

American audiences avoided the film like the plague, put off by "that kiss" more than anything else. In England, Finch's friend Shirley Bassey was so disgusted she walked out of the cinema. Bassey was a gay icon so her reaction was surprising.

Head was out of work for a year and a half after the film wrapped. The only scripts he was sent were gay ones, as if that was all he could do. He referred to the kiss with Finch as "The Kiss of Death." John Hurt told him he went through the same kind of career crisis after playing Quentin Crisp on TV (Dundy, 314).

Schlesinger said the film wasn't so much about sexuality as loneliness. Rod Steiger said the same thing about *The Sergeant* in 1968 and so did Rex Harrison about *Staircase* in 1971. The fact is that it was all about all these things. Schlesinger's remark was easier to appreciate than those of Steiger and Harrison. They could have been accused of downplaying the LGBTQ content of what they did, not being gay themselves. Regarding the Jewish aspect of the film he had this to say: "I know somebody who is Jewish and homosexual. His parents told him, 'We know . . . but you must marry.' I consider this the most awful piece of family advice I've ever heard" (Hadleigh, 1999: 27).

Finch once said, "Some of the most constructive and loving relationships I've seen are between men or women but because most gays hide their true nature, even from relatives, the world doesn't realize this" (Hadleigh, 1993: 16). The world has changed, thankfully, since he spoke these words, but they probably meant *Sunday Bloody Sunday* did less business in 1971 than it would have done today.

It's an excellent film with an at times almost documentary-style approach to its subject. Schlesinger was deservedly nominated for Best Director but lost out to William Friedkin for *The French Connection*. Both Finch and Jackson were nominated for Best Actor and Best Actress, but they didn't win either. Somehow this seemed appropriate to the roles they played on screen. They were unlucky both in love and life.

Related Films
The Trials of Oscar Wilde (1960); *Darling* (1965); *Midnight Cowboy* (1969); *The Next Best Thing* (2000).

Further Reading
Cook, M. 2014. *Queer Domesticities: Homosexuality and Home Life in Twentieth-Century London*. London: Palgrave Macmillan.

David, Hugh. 1998. *On Queer Street: A Social History of British Homosexuality, 1895–1995*. London: HarperCollins.

Dundy, Elaine. 1980. *Finch, Bloody Finch*. New York: Holt, Rinehart and Winston.
Hadleigh, Boze, 1993. *The Lavender Screen*. New York: Citadel.
Hadleigh, Boze, ed. 1999. *Hollywood Bitch*. London: Robson.
Howes, Keith. 1993. *Broadcasting It*. London: Cassell.
Philips, Gene. 1981. *John Schlesinger*. Boston: Twayne.
Porter, Darwin, and Danforth Prince. 2010. *50 Years of Queer Cinema*. New York: Blood Moon Productions.

Swoon (1992)

Tom Kalin used some very moody camerawork in this monochrome reworking of the infamous Leopold-Loeb murder of the 1920s. These had already been covered in *Compulsion* (1959) and in coded form in Alfred Hitchcock's *Rope* (1948). Here for the first time the killers are mentioned by name. Kalin skews the emphasis away from the murder to launch a full-frontal attack on a homophobic, anti-Semitic society.

Richard Leopold (Daniel Schlachet) and Nathan Loeb (Craig Chester) kill Bobby Franks, a fourteen-year-old-boy who's Loeb's second cousin. They want to commit the perfect crime, and they arrogantly believe they have the intelligence to do that. This is their only motive.

Loeb is more obsessed with killing than Leopold, but Leopold is more obsessed with sex than Loeb. Loeb is sexually immature but more lethal with regard to violence. The trade-off is death for sex. Loeb promises this to Leopold if he goes along with the murder.

This isn't just amorality; it's perversion beyond the so-called Nietzschean imperative that was alleged to have motivated the two men. One is close to Camus's Meursault from *The Outsider* here. It's a meaningless, existential act.

The murder itself is gruesome. Acid is poured over the boy's face and genitals to try to make him unrecognizable and thus decrease their chances of being caught. When the police find the body, however, a pair of reading glasses is discovered nearby. This leads them to the perpetrators.

Both of them deny killing Franks at first. They say they were with two girls on the night it occurred. But this alibi falls apart. Afterward they turn on one another.

The prosecuting attorney seems more interested in the sexuality of the pair than their derangement—or perhaps a connection between the two facets of the case is seen. This leads Kalin into his perception of the prejudices that are his main target. When a judge says in one scene that the killers wanted to satisfy "unnatural lusts," one isn't sure if he's referring to sex or murder. Whatever about that, they're found guilty and sentenced to life imprisonment. Loeb is killed in jail in the course of serving his sentence.

There was undoubtedly homophobia in America at this time in history, and anti-Semitism too. Both prejudices are still in existence today. But was a gratuitous killing a suitable vehicle for Kalin to make these points? *Swoon* is an excellently made film with an authentic feel for the period, but his slant leaves him open

Compulsion (1959)

In 1956, Meyer Levin published a novel based on the Leopold-Loeb case called *Compulsion*. It became a play in 1957 and was made into a film two years later by Richard Fleischer. Levin's main thesis was that Loeb committed the murder to destroy the feminine side of himself. Leopold was shocked at this depiction of him and sued Levin for invasion of privacy. He lost the case.

Loeb is called Artie Straus in the film. He's played by Bradford Dillman. Dean Stockwell plays the character based on Leopold, Judd Steiner. Loeb is the superior personality, as was the case in real life. "You said you wanted me to command you," he says to Steiner at one stage. Steiner replies, "I do, as long as you keep your part of the agreement." The unspoken condition is that Straus goes to bed with him.

The film is interesting in that, unlike *Rope* or *Swoon*, it introduces a woman into the cast. Diane Varsi plays Ruth, a woman Steiner tries to rape to prove his masculinity. But he even fails at this. Says Ruth: "He couldn't go through with it. He was like a child, a sick, frightened child." Ruth's courtroom testimony about Steiner's fragile state of mind helps him avoid the death penalty, but his being gay is seen as pitiable. Because society was able to look down on this rather than become threatened by it, it allowed the "weak" gay man to live. By proxy, Straus fell into this barrow too.

Compulsion busied itself with the killing and the trial that followed it rather than the relationship between the two killers. Orson Welles dominated most films in which he appeared (physically as well as in every other way), and this was no exception. He played Clarence Darrow, the lawyer who defended them brilliantly by his persuasive arguments against capital punishment, which he saw as barbaric.

to the charge of appearing to condone, if not glorify, the crime he explores in such forensic detail. Hollywood has a woeful history of demonizing innocent gay people in years gone by, but the antidote to this isn't to romanticize guilty ones.

As Michele Aaron pointed out, Kalin doesn't seem to be as interested in the horrific act the killers performed as he is in the fact that a 1920s society "could unite discrete communities of outsiders (Jews, queers, blacks, murderers) into a commonality of perversion" (Aaron, 2004: 21).

Kalin fetishizes the men's relationship in a series of rituals. Their delicacy makes the gore of the murder more shocking. At the beginning of the film they exchange rings in a mock-wedding ceremony. When Loeb dies, Leopold takes the ring he's given him and puts it into his mouth. This gesture references a tradition in Greek mythology where coins are placed in a dead person's mouth to pay the ferryman for their journey to the hereafter. Leopold, therefore, is effectively sending Loeb on his way with the promise of eternal devotion. The murder has bonded them forever.

Kalin grew up in Chicago, where the murder took place. His father worked for the National Council on crime and delinquency. His grandmother kept a scrapbook of newspaper cuttings about the case. "Even as a kid I was obsessed with them," he recalled. "I'd see the photographs of these two beautiful boys from the 1920s. There was something in them that told me they were homosexual" (Burston, 1995: 134).

The atmospheric chiaroscuros of *Swoon* lock one into a very seductive embrace, perhaps the kind of embrace that caused two sophisticated loners to commit a murder people are still talking about today almost a century after it happened.

Related Films
Rope (1948); *Compulsion* (1959); *Murder by Numbers* (2002).

Further Reading
Aaron, Michele, ed. 2004. *New Queer Cinema.* New Brunswick, NJ: Rutgers University Press.
Burston, Paul. 1995. *What Are You Looking At? Queer Sex, Style and Cinema.* London: Cassell.
Higdon, Hal. 1975. *Leopold and Loeb: The Crime of the Century.* Urbana: University of Illinois Press.
Leopold, Nathan, Jr. 1958. *Life Plus 99 Years.* Garden City, NY: Doubleday & Co.

T

Tea and Sympathy (1956)

Based on Robert Anderson's long-running Broadway play, this was directed by Vincente Minnelli. All three of the main leads reprised their roles from the theatrical production. John Kerr is Tom Lee, a shy seventeen-year-old student who's taunted by his classmates for his effeminacy. (They call him "Sister Boy.") He's attracted to the house mistress, Laura (Deborah Kerr). Leif Erickson plays Laura's husband, Bill, the housemaster.

Laura's main chore as Bill's wife is to provide "tea and sympathy" to the boys. For one of them, she provides something more than that.

Tom is regarded as gay because he doesn't hang out with the cool gang. He prefers to play the guitar than football. When his father—a jock—visits him in university, he looks around his excessively tidy room and asks, "Do you spend all your allowance money on curtains?" Tom replies tamely, "I wanted to make it look like home."

After a botched attempt to bed the local hooker, Ellie (Norma Crane), Tom tries to kill himself. At this point of the proceedings Laura rides over the horizon and goes to bed with "Sister Boy" to convince him that in no way is he gay, despite the deluded taunts of the school bullies. It's "pity sex," to use the contemporary parlance. It costs Laura her marriage and her good name.

The central conceit of the film—that sex with a woman can "cure" a gay man of his errant proclivities—was fairly standard for the time. It isn't established that Tom is gay, but his bookish nature, his ineptitude at sports, and his problems with women lead one to suspect he's headed in that unfortunate direction.

It's the accusation of being gay rather than its confirmation that causes most of Tom's problems. His attraction to Laura should suggest that he's straight. Sometimes the love of a young man for an older woman is a film code for being gay, but that isn't the case here.

The actual gay person in the cast is Bill. He married Laura to try to prove to himself that he wasn't. In some ways his story is more interesting than Tom's. Laura says to him, "You persecute in Tom the thing you fear in yourself." She's to be pitied. She helps two sexually tortured men in the boudoir to try to make them feel good about themselves.

Tom is presumed to be gay in Anderson's play because he's been seen sunbathing in the nude with one of his male teachers. In the film he's more sissy. He doesn't sunbathe nude here; he merely sews with a group of faculty wives. (Not very macho, you'll agree.)

Anderson said his ambition in writing the play was to widen the definition of masculinity, "to attack the often fostered notion that a man is only a man if he can carry Vivien Leigh up a winding staircase." This was a reference to the marital rape scene from *Gone with the Wind* (Levy, 2009: 280). In the play, which doubled as a political allegory, being gay was equated with communism. In this reading it became an allegory against McCarthyism.

Minnelli had to airbrush Tom's orientation out of the script to get the film made. One is expected to believe he would wish to commit suicide merely because he was shy, a preposterous notion. "It's really a play about persecution," Kerr maintained (Howes, 1993: 816). That's Deborah, not John.

Tom writes poetry. He likes gardening. He walks like a girl. He dresses in drag for a school play. Everything about him indicates his orientation, but he isn't gay. He proves this when he sleeps with Laura. In doing so, she saves him from the self-loathing he experienced, but she commits career suicide by this action. Hollywood could see no other way out of this plotline. Good deeds for boys who fear they're gay didn't qualify for light celluloid sentencing if they involved extramarital sex in the fifties.

The final scene of the film occurs ten years after its main events. Tom is now married—to the relief of the Hays Office—and comes back to his alma mater for a class reunion. Bill is still there. Laura isn't with him anymore, but he gives Tom a letter she's written to him. In it she writes that she had to leave Bill in disgrace as a result of her infidelity. The church wanted Minnelli to insert the word "sin" into the letter, but he refused, putting the softer "wrong" there instead. This was grudgingly accepted. The author of the letter, one commentator observed, wasn't really Laura but the Production Code Administration (Tropiano, 2009: 73).

One may smile at incidents like this that appear tame today, but in 1956 they were hot potatoes. Minnelli had to watch what he was doing every step of the way for fear of further action from the PCA. He filmed the seduction scene so reverentially that Anderson was amused. "With the birds twittering and the special lighting," he chuckled, "it looked more like the second coming of Christ than the first coming of Tom Lee" (Russo, 1987: 114).

The Breen Office, which oversaw the PCA, insisted the film include a prologue and an epilogue. At one point it was suggested that Laura pay for her adultery by taking her life. Again Minnelli resisted. Laura was allowed to live, but only as a shamed and lonely woman.

In solving one censorial problem (implied being gay), the film created another one (marital infidelity). If gay men were usually punished in films of this time by suicide or unfulfillment, for cheating wives the punishment was a lifetime of pain. This is what Laura has to endure in the aftermath of her tryst with Tom. After setting him up for a life of marital bliss, her own marriage falls apart. She isn't even seen in the latter part of the film, her misery transmitted simply by the letter handed to Tom by Bill.

A point needs to be made here about the way Hollywood saw things: it wasn't Laura's sleeping with Tom that ruined her marriage. It was dead anyway. The studio had to strangle the plot like this to get it past the PCA.

The film states that even if a person is merely effeminate rather than gay, he's still likely to be persecuted by homophobes. Tom needs Laura to "blood" him, to usher his patch into the world of virility where sex with a woman—of whatever age—acts as the cachet. She brings the man out in him but substitutes his shame with her own. So nobody really wins. Hurray for Hollywood.

On the credit side, this was another career-changing performance for Kerr, who'd been the chaste rose for so many years. Now, thanks to this and *From Here to Eternity* (1953), where she played another unhappy wife going between the sheets with someone who wasn't her husband—in this case Burt Lancaster—she opened up new screen vistas for herself. In 1958 she appeared with Lancaster again in *Separate Tables* and was nominated for a Best Actress Oscar. In the same year as *Tea and Sympathy*, she was nominated for *The King and I*. The times they were a-changing, as Bob Dylan might have put it.

Related Films
From Here to Eternity (1953); *The King and I* (1956); *Separate Tables* (1958); *Take a Giant Step* (1959).

Further Reading
Anderson, Robert. 1955. *Tea and Sympathy*. New York: Samuel French.
Capua, Michelangelo. 2010. *Deborah Kerr: A Biography*. Jefferson, NC: McFarland.
Harvey, Stephen. 1989. *Directed by Vincente Minnelli*. New York: Harper & Row.
Howes, Keith. 1993. *Broadcasting It*. London: Cassell.
Levy, Emanuel. 2009. *Vincente Minnelli: Hollywood's Dark Dreamer*. New York: St. Martin's Press.
Lewis, Jon. 2000. *Hollywood V. Hard Core: How the Struggle over Censorship Saved the Modern Film Industry*. New York and London: New York University Press.
Naremore, James. 1988. *The Films of Vincente Minnelli*. New York: Cambridge University Press.
Russo, Vito, 1987. *The Celluloid Closet: Homosexuality in the Movies*. New York: Harper & Row.
Street, Sarah. 2018. *Deborah Kerr*. London: British Film Institute.
Tropiano, Stephen. 2009. *Obscene, Indecent, Immoral and Offensive: 100 Years of Censored, Banned and Controversial Films*. New York: Limelight Editions.

Thelma and Louise (1991)

If Paul Newman and Robert Redford took male bonding to a new level as the tragic antiheroes on the run in George Roy Hill's *Butch Cassidy and the Sundance Kid* in 1969, Ridley Scott did likewise on the distaff side in this spirited parable.

Thelma (Geena Davis) and Louise (Susan Sarandon) are two women disenchanted with the male of the species and, more generally, with their humdrum small-town lives. They go on the road looking for some fun, but when Louise shoots a man who's trying to rape Thelma, it becomes much more than that. Their picaresque endeavors now have a separate agenda: they know they can never go back to their former lives. Their connection with one another increases, as does their distance from the world they've departed, which now includes the forces of law and order. The relationship doesn't become overtly sexual, but it's stronger in some ways because of that. Attraction is conveyed by looks and gestures.

Louse is the stronger woman at the beginning of the film. This is evident even sartorially by her waitress uniform. It situates her in the world of work as opposed to the stay-at-home sundress Thelma wears. This hollers "subdued housewife" at us.

Louise, in contrast, wears a bandanna around her neck. She also drives. As the film goes on, however, Thelma becomes more streetwise. Her confidence increases. This is reflected in her change of attire. The sundress makes way for a work shirt. She wears torn jeans and cowboy (cowgirl) boots.

It's also reflected in the enthusiastic manner in which she learns how to steal from a man who comes into their lives. He's played by the then unknown Brad Pitt (JD). JD's pretty-boy status is nicely counterpointed with Thelma's incipient "male" qualities. JD's androgyny replaces the brute masculinity of her husband, Darryl, whom she's deserted for her new life. It's a man's world so she might as well be a man in it. Louise—who throws away her lipstick in a seminal scene—is her tutor in such a transmogrification. She masculinizes her.

The two ne'er-do-wells eventually reach the end of the road. Their adventure is over. The only other business that needs to be completed now is a quick kiss on the lips and a plunge to their death in the Grand Canyon. They still have to die in the grand tradition of old-school screen lesbians, but at least it's a lovers' leap this time, a double act. In that moment, as Gloria Steinem wrote, they go "into our imaginations and into mythology" (Bell-Metereau, 1993: 251).

The fact that this film's release coincided with the trial of Clarence Thomas for sexual harassment of Anita Hill caused some people to see it as a footnote to that high-profile case. Many critics also thought it depicted men in a degrading light, featuring a number of pathetic stereotypes of testosterone-crazed behavior.

Its scriptwriter, Callie Khouri, begged to disagree with such viewpoints. She claimed she'd written a screenplay not so much about feminists as outlaws. "We see plenty of movies of this genre with men," she railed, "I don't see why it shakes everyone up to see it with women." The fact that Thelma and Louise's aggressors were male wasn't meant to be seen in any antimen light, but neither was she going to contrive "some monstrous female" to be the villain. "Even if this were the most man-bashing movie ever made," she argued, "it wouldn't even begin to make up for the 99% of movies where the women are there to be caricatured as bimbos, or to be skinned and decapitated." She said of the dramatic ending where the two heroines drive off the cliff: "I just kept seeing this image of Thelma at the kitchen sink at the beginning and knowing she was never, never going to be there again" (Francke, 1994: 129–31).

It became a cult film, a long-overdue corollary to *Bonnie and Clyde*. The two women at its core had the kind of fun previously available only to men. By this time, "women's pictures" had been rechristened "chick flicks." Though neither Susan Sarandon nor Geena Davis were sweet sixteen, they were allowed to act like that here, and also suggest a lesbian underpinning to their friendship. The freeze-frame at the end was, as stated, reminiscent of *Butch Cassidy and the Sundance Kid*, as were some of the seriocomic exchanges between the pair up to this point. But this was still a welcome addition to the rite-of-passage genre that had been the preserve of men up to now.

The Academy of Motion Picture Arts and Sciences designated 1991 "The Year of the Woman," so it was appropriate that *Thelma & Louise* became one of its showpieces. It was nominated for Best Picture. Also nominated were Sarandon and Davis for Best Actress, Khouri for Best Screenplay, and Scott for Best Director.

The film uttered a cautionary note to any man who might think about catcalling a wife or a waitress in the future. As Margaret Carlson wrote: "The next time a woman passes an 18-wheeler and points her finger like a pistol at the tires, the driver might just put his tongue back in his mouth where it belongs" (Howes, 1993: 837).

Did the film really empower women or did it merely empower them in the way men defined empowerment–by the use of cars, guns, explosions and that suicidal finale? That was the $64 dollar question. Perhaps films need to show women being better than men not by aping them but by transcending them. Otherwise one ends up with *Bonnie and Bonnie*.

Related Films
Bonnie and Clyde (1967); *Butch Cassidy and the Sundance Kid* (1969); *Leaving Normal* (1992); *The Living End* (1992).

Further Reading
Bell-Metereau, Rebecca. 1993. *Hollywood Androgyny*. New York: Columbia University Press.
Francke, Lizzie. 1994. *Script Girls: Women Screenwriters in Hollywood*. London: British Film Institute.
Howes, Keith. 1993. *Broadcasting It*. London: Cassell.
Sturken, Marita. 2000. *Thelma & Louise*. London: British Film Institute.

The Times of Harvey Milk (1984)

This coproduced documentary from Robert Epstein and Richard Schmiechen—the first film made about the slain politician—won an Oscar. It was extensively researched and sensitively made, etching in the events leading up to and including his assassination, and the insulting seven-year sentence given to his killer, Dan White, by a bigoted jury. Was life regarded so cheaply by the legislative system? Few tears were shed by Milk's mourners when White committed suicide shortly after his release. Many of Milk's friends and colleagues were interviewed for the film. Their reminiscences capture his charisma with some resonance.

Epstein had been preparing a documentary about Milk when he was shot, so he was an obvious choice to produce it. Schmiechen was working with him at the time. They originally intended to have more interviews but decided to whittle them down to a half dozen or so to give them more focus.

The film begins with Dianne Feinstein, the then president of the San Francisco Board of Supervisors, announcing that Milk and Mayor George Moscone have been shot dead and that the suspect is White, another supervisor. Epstein freezes her face as she finishes the statement to allow the full effect of her declaration to sink in. Archival footage of the time follows, after which we get the interviews.

The first one is with Anne Kronenberg, one of Milk's main aides in the camera shop he ran on Castro Street. She talks about her first impressions of him. At that time she saw him throwing a tantrum about something trivial. This led her to deduce that he had the emotional maturity of a young child. Then comes Tom Ammiano, a gay schoolteacher who says he would have lost his job had Proposition 6—a directive that sought to remove gay teachers from their posts in California—been passed. Milk was instrumental in its removal from the San Francisco Constitution.

A man called Jim Elliot appears now. He's a car mechanic and union leader. He says he was nervous about Milk running for election considering he was a "fruit" who worked in a crummy camera store and didn't even know how to dress. As time went on, however, he warmed to him. Another person interviewed is Tory Hartman, a charming lady who shows both her humor and her big heart in various clips slotted intermittently throughout the film. In the first one she talks about miscarrying a baby and how Milk was so kind to her after her ordeal. He arrived at her door one day with a dozen roses and then offered to do her shopping for her. This threw her for a loop as she hardly even knew him at the time. In later interviews she fights tears back talking about him.

Further interviews are conducted with people like Jeannine Yeomans, a TV reporter, and other colleagues and friends. All of them testify to the great commitment of "the little kid with the big ears" who became the most unlikely politician of his time and who devoted himself not only to gay people but also to the elderly and the poor. He fought hard on issues like rent control and also on something one might see as trivial: dog poop on the streets. "If someone solves the dog problem in this city," he told a colleague, "they'll be elected mayor." One never knew if he was being serious or not when he made comments like this.

The film documents the three defeats he endured before finally being elected as a city supervisor. His elation at the victory was something to behold. He wasn't a drinker, but that night he poured a whole bottle of champagne over himself to show his exuberance.

The Times of Harvey Milk came out in 1984, the year of Ronald Reagan's reelection, so it went against the grain of the political climate of the time. Reagan had virtually airbrushed gay issues like the AIDS epidemic out of public discourse and was virulently intolerant. That was one reason many people were surprised when the film won Best Documentary at the Oscar ceremonies. It did so because of its passion and authenticity.

The final third documents the aftermath of the assassination, including the arrest and trial of White. An extract from his confession is played in which he insists that the two murders weren't premeditated. The jury, which mainly comprised people who thought like he did—some of them even coming from the area in which he lived—"bought" this, ridiculous and all as it sounded, considering he sneaked into City Hall that morning through a basement window to avoid setting off any alarms that would have been triggered by the gun he carried. He also reloaded it between shooting Milk and Moscone. His defense team's tortured logic, and its belief by the jury, meant White was convicted of manslaughter rather than murder. The film was completed after he was released from prison, having served just five and a half years of the seven he was handed down for the double homicide.

Most clear-thinking people in the city were enraged at such a miscarriage of justice. Such anger is palpable in the documentary, but Epstein doesn't dramatize it. He coolly points out how a generation of people who thought all their dreams had come true when Milk was elected saw such dreams come tumbling down around their ears when he was killed, and when his killer treated with kid gloves in his court case, thereby adding insult to injury. Ammiano says, "We turned the case over to a system that had been responsible for the crimes." It didn't so much punish what White did as corroborate it. Elliot notes that if White had only killed Moscone, who was straight, he might well have got "the chair." Many people saw him doing a service to society by adding Milk to his hit list.

The film ends with the torchlight vigil in which thousands of people marched in silence to honor their dead hero before his ashes were scattered into the Pacific Ocean. It then segues into the White Night Riots that took place as a protest against White's sentence. Over sixty people ended up in hospital as a result of these. They were absent from Gus Van Sant's biopic of *Milk*. Van Sant also excluded many of the women who were so important to Milk's life and work, like Sally Gearhart, another person interviewed by Epstein and Schmiechen in this engrossing documentary. Perhaps it's unfair to compare it with Van Sant's film as they're both excellent in their way, but this probably shades it in verisimilitude. It's a poignant paean to an unlikely martyr, and it richly deserved its accolade at the Dorothy Chandler Pavilion.

It also won the Special Jury Prize at the first Sundance Film Festival, and Best Documentary at the San Francisco Lesbian and Gay Film Festival.

Related Films
Rights and Reactions (1987); *The Trip* (2004); *Milk* (2008).

Further Reading
Faderman, Lillian. 2018. *The Lives of Harvey Milk*. London: Yale University Press.
Hays, Matthew. 2007. *The View from Here: Conversations with Gay and Lesbian Film-makers*. Vancouver, BC: Arsenal Pulp Press.
Shilts, Randy. 2009. *The Mayor of Castro Street: The Life and Times of Harvey Milk*. London: Atlantic Books.

Torch Song Trilogy (1988)

This film was an adaptation of a hit Broadway play written by the openly gay Harvey Fierstein that merged three one-act plays of his: *The International Stud* (1978), *Fugue in a Nursery* (1981), and *Widows and Children First* (1981). It concerns the life and loves of a wisecracking but emotionally vulnerable New York drag queen,

Arnold Beckhoff, played by Fierstein himself with an affecting blend of humor and pathos. It was the first gay-themed play to win a Tony award. It ran for nearly four hours. The film version was trimmed down to 117 minutes by director Paul Bogart.

Set mainly in the 1970s and 1980s, the opening scene is a flashback to 1952, showing Arnold's mother, Ma—Anne Bancroft in one of her familiar ethnic roles—opening the door of her bedroom closet to discover Arnold dressed in drag and putting makeup on himself. It then leaps forward to 1971, which provides the first part of the trilogy. Arnold is performing a drag act in a gay club where he sings the eponymous torch songs in a Tom Waits–style growl using the stage name Virginia Hamm. One night he's picked up by bisexual schoolteacher Ed (Brian Kerwin) and falls for him. The relationship appears to be going well until Ed starts dating a girl, Laurel (Karen Young), which spells the end of his involvement with Arnold.

The second part of the trilogy begins with a night in 1973 when Arnold, still performing in drag at the gay bar—he'd done this in real life too—is being heckled by some drinkers. One of them, a handsome model called Alan (Matthew Broderick), is threatened with a knife because of this, which causes him to pass out with fright. Arnold brings him to his apartment to revive him, his kindness impressing Alan.

Even though Alan is fifteen years younger than Arnold, he pursues him. Arnold at first resists his advances, but eventually he succumbs. It turns out that Alan has spent some time hustling in the past but is now ready to settle into a stable relationship.

He moves in with Arnold, and the pair of them are happy together for four years. The relationship hits a stumbling block when Ed and Lauren invite them to visit them at their country home. Ed is still struggling with his sexuality. In the course of the visit, he makes a pass at Alan, and Alan responds.

Arnold forgives him for this when he learns about it. Back in New York, the pair of them decide to adopt a teenage boy, David (Eddie Castrodad), but life is about to deal Arnold another cruel blow. On the night before the adoption process is finalized, they decide to celebrate with a bottle of champagne. Alan goes out to buy it but runs into a gang of violent homophobes in the act of throttling an elderly man. He tries to stop them, but in the process receives a blow from a baseball bat that proves fatal. Arnold is inconsolable.

The third segment of the trilogy takes place in 1980. Ed has just come back to Arnold, having decided he loves him more than Lauren, whom he's married. The marriage was a sham, he realizes. He's now ready to embrace his orientation, something he's been in denial about all his life. Arnold tries to come to terms with having him back in his life as well as being a good father to David. Matters are further complicated when Ma, who's now a widow, says she wants to visit him from Florida. She knows nothing about David or Ed, so she's shocked at his unconventional living arrangements when she arrives.

The pair of them spar off one another, matters reaching a head during a visit to the family cemetery where both Alan and Ma's husband are buried in adjoining plots. Arnold has his work cut out trying to convince Ma that he's been equally distraught losing Alan as she has losing her husband. He may have been with him for only four years, as opposed to Ma's thirty-five with Arnold's father, but that hasn't made his grief any less traumatic than hers.

Arnold is devastated when Ma tells him she would have preferred not to have given birth to him if she knew he was going to turn out to be gay. She apologizes, but the damage has been done. Arnold is furious with her and tries to drown his sorrows with drink. Ed comforts him and assures him of his love for him. Consoled by this after so many losses and rejections, Arnold is now in the right frame of mind to make up with Ma. He tells her he still wants her to leave the apartment, but they part on good terms, the future looking as bright for Arnold as is possible in his chaotic life.

Torch Song Trilogy has a lot to say about need, belonging, bereavement, survival, and being true to oneself. It's also interesting in its portrayal of a gay man—especially an effeminate gay man, like Arnold—who wants the things heterosexual people have (a husband, a child, stability in domestic circumstances) within a gay context. Unfortunately, it didn't tap into the public consciousness as much as might have been expected.

This was partly due to the difficulty experienced by Bogart, whose history was in television rather than cinema, in distilling three separate plays into one unified film. The attraction of Alan to Arnold is also difficult to accept, as is Alan's hustling past. He looks too timid for this. (Broderick was more appropriately cast as David in the stage version). The film also has a tendency toward bathos. And Fierstein is never too far from parody with his relentless bouts of self-denigration.

There was also a chronological problem. Between the time of its Broadway and Hollywood manifestations, AIDS had decimated much of the gay population of America. Bogart chose to soften some aspects of the text so that the material wouldn't be too depressing to audiences. This results in a sometimes uneasy mix of comedy and pathos in the script.

Fierstein's foghorn voice—"Is that natural or have you a cold?" Ed asks upon first meeting him—is somewhat draining too. Bancroft could almost have phoned in her performance, so familiar is she with this kind of "Jewish Mama" role, which unfortunately carries many stereotyped mannerisms with it—the same kind of mannerisms she used in *Garbo Talks* (which also costarred Fierstein). But this is still a touching depiction of a man struggling for respect in a world that continually deals him cards from the bottom of the deck.

The script is laced with witty one-liners ("I'm aging about as well as a beach party") and clever exchanges ("I told my mother I was gay when I was thirteen." "At thirteen you knew that?" "At thirteen I knew everything!").

The film gave Fierstein a bigger profile than any of his other films, but it wasn't a commercial success, retrieving only $3 million of its $7 million budget upon its release into theaters. By then, patrons seemed more interested spending their money watching the likes of Arnold Schwarzenegger flexing his muscles than his namesake soul-searching about a need to belong.

Related Films
Garbo Talks (1984); *Longtime Companion* (1989); *Tidy Endings* (1989).

Further Reading
De Jongh, Nicholas. 1992. *Not in Front of the Audience: Homosexuality on Stage.* London: Routledge.
Fierstein, Harvey. 1988. *Harvey Fierstein's Safe Sex.* New York: Atheneum.
Fierstein, Harvey. 2018. *Torch Song Trilogy.* Quezon City, Manila: Pisces Books.

Transamerica (2005)

The year 2005 was interesting for LGBTQ films. Not only were *Capote* and *Brokeback Mountain* shortlisted for Best Picture at the Oscar ceremonies; Felicity Huffman was also nominated for Best Actress as Bree, a transsexual person in this touching road movie from Duncan Tucker. She gives a beautiful performance as a sensitive but stubborn character who captures the confusion and pain of her situation with great charm and not a little eccentricity. It's a road movie but, like many road movies, a journey of the heart as well. Tucker allegorizes Bree's predicament.

When we first meet Bree, she's already had hormonal treatment. She's awaiting the sex reassignment surgery that will complete her transition. As she's saving up the money for her surgery in Los Angeles, where she lives, she receives a phone call telling her that she has a sixteen-year-old son, Toby (Kevin Zegers), whom she didn't know about. He's the product of a one-night stand in her past. His mother committed suicide some years ago. His estranged stepfather is now living in Tennessee with his wife and daughter. Before Bree's therapist will allow her to undergo her surgery, she insists she deal with Toby's problems. At present he's in jail in New York for hustling drugs.

Bree has to fly to New York to bail him out. She's understandably nervous about telling him who she is, so she pretends she's a Christian missionary whose vocation is to reform him. The film is the story of how they bond against all the odds. The fact that Toby is gay adds an extra dimension to the plot.

At first he's grateful to her for her concern for him, and for her financial generosity, but when he learns she has a penis, he becomes aggressive and disrespectful. Bree's challenge now is to win him over. Before she does that, she brings him to the family of his stepfather. These scenes have a comic element touched with pathos. Bree has to suffer the scorn of her mother, Elizabeth (Fionnula Flanagan), as well as the shock of her father (Burt Young) and that of her alcoholic sister, Sydney (Carrie Preston), before emerging from the film with the dignity she deserves to form a relationship with Toby, who starts a career in pornography films.

Tucker took on a broad range of plot themes here, but he negotiates the varying threads of his assignment with a quirkiness that endears. Bree's twittery personality, which veers from laughter to tears, is a delight. Huffman captures her with just the right degree of transgender diversity. One could be forgiven for imagining it's a man playing the part. Testosterone is raging on certain occasions, but it's mainly her tenderness that's in evidence, tinged with an assertiveness that won't be swayed no matter how much resistance she receives from transphobic people regarding her imminent transition.

There are some challenges to be negotiated before that, like when Toby comes on to her at one stage. This scene, like the one where he holds her nightgown up to himself as he admires himself in a mirror, strains credibility. As Bob Gonsalves remarked, the film seems to be saying that Toby shares Bree's genes so he must be confused too (Hart, 2013: 125). Elizabeth's myopia ("This wouldn't have happened if you'd gone to church when you were little!") is contrasted with the easygoing nature of the rest of her family. When Sydney offers her a fluffy dress to try on, she puts her in her place with a firm, "I'm a transsexual, not a transvestite." She's equally sure of herself when, in answer to Elizabeth's distressed, "I miss you, son," she shoots back, "You never had a son." Her stance throughout is that she isn't gender-challenged, rather gender-gifted. "My body may be a work in progress," she asserts, "but there's nothing wrong with my soul."

Few people could fail to be won over by this landmark movie that never strives after effect and becomes much more effective on account of that. The manner in which Bree accepts Toby for his dysfunctuality paves the way for his own burgeoning acceptance of her as she becomes much more of a mother to him than his "real" one on their odyssey across the country.

As they make their way to LA, they encounter all sorts of adventures en route, including an American Indian, Calvin Manygates (Graham Greene), who's attracted to Bree. They also pick up a hippie (Grant Monohan) who steals their car.

Tucker permits himself some levity in the relationship between Calvin and Bree. "There's things about her she's not tellin' you," Toby says to Calvin, to which Calvin replies, "Every woman has a right to a little mystery." (He never gets to see just how much mystery this "woman" possesses.)

Neither Tucker nor Huffman saw *Transamerica* as a movie about transexuality. For them it was an old-fashioned coming-of-age film that didn't beat one over the head with issues or causes. "Bree is like your uptight spinster aunt," said Tucker (*Transamerica* DVD, Special Features, 2006). Huffman lowered her voice many octaves to get Bree sounding like she wanted. She did exercises religiously each day to keep the tone right. She walked with the same erectness as a man but developed feminine mannerisms that caught the ambivalent balance of someone in transition, but they were subservient to the heart of the character. Huffman always prioritized that.

Writer/director Tucker tempers the emotional traumas Bree has to undergo with humor, even in the scene where Toby discovers her secret as he sees her penis while she's urinating. For Huffman, having to wear a prosthetic penis was an experience she would never forget. "Having it in your pants," she observed, "puts all your focus there. No wonder it's all men think about." "This wasn't a movie about a downtrodden person who makes it," Tucker insisted. "It was more a wacky movie using humor as a weapon" (*Transamerica* DVD, Special Features, 2006). For Huffman it was the role of a lifetime, the story of two people trying to find themselves in very difficult circumstances. Bree had to learn to love herself to become the parent whom Toby needed, and he had his own journey to make alongside hers. For both of them it was a kind of catharsis.

Everyone in the cast worked tirelessly to make themselves as good as they could be. At first Tucker thought Zegers was too handsome. Handsome actors, he felt, didn't work as hard as those who weren't, due to a sense of pamperedness or "entitlement." Thankfully, Zegers didn't suffer from that, investing himself in the essence of Toby to mirror Bree's troubled journey toward self-acceptance. Flanagan was also a huge help to Huffman, offering almost as many suggestions about how to play the role as Tucker did. Greene was a dear too. "I'm sorry Bree didn't stay with him," she pined in an interview. Tucker chipped in, "Maybe in the sequel" (*Transamerica* DVD, Special Features, 2006).

This was a film in which everything came together after initial Hollywood resistance to what it saw as yet another standard-issue "tyranny" movie. A positive review in *Variety* changed that perception. Afterward it started to pick up good word of mouth. When Dolly Parton came in with a brilliant theme song, "Travelin' Thru"—this was also nominated for an Oscar—everything seemed to harmonize like a perfectly made soufflé.

Related Films
The Adventures of Priscilla, Queen of the Desert (1994); *To Wong Foo, Thanks for Everything, Julie Newmar* (1995).

Further Reading
Burston, Paul, and Colin Richardson, eds. 1995. *A Queer Romance: Lesbians, Gay Men and Popular Culture*. London and New York: Routledge.
Hart, Kylo-Patrick. 2013. *Queer Males in Contemporary Cinema Becoming Visible*. Plymouth, UK: Scarecrow Press.
Salin-Pascual, Rafael J. 2009. *Cinema and Sexual Diversity*. www.lulu.com
Straayer, Chris. 1996. *Deviant Eyes, Deviant Bodies: Sexual Re-Orientation in Film and Video*. New York: Columbia University Press.
Transamerica DVD, Special Features, 2006.

Gus Van Sant (1953–)

Van Sant made his first film on a Super-8 camera at the age of twelve. After completing high school, he became an art student at the Rhode Island School of Design. He then cut his celluloid teeth with a string of shorts before venturing into the world of TV commercials.

His first feature film was *Mala Noche* (1985), the story of a doomed love affair between a young man, Walt (Tim Streeter), who sells liquor to vagrants for a living, and an illegal sixteen-year-old Mexican immigrant, Johnny (Doug Cooeyate). Walt is gay. Johnny is straight and refuses to have sex with him, but his friend Roberto (Ray Monge) agrees to do so for money. Shot in black and white on a shoestring budget, the film won the Los Angeles Film Critics Award as the best independent film of the year.

Four years later Van Sant made *Drugstore Cowboy*. It dealt with four junkies who rob drugstores to feed their habit. He developed the screenplay from an unpublished novel by James Fogle. Matt Dillon played the lead so well he silenced those critics who saw him as little more than a pin-up. There were also fine performances from Kelly Lynch, James Le Gros, and Heather Graham. William S. Burroughs appeared in a cameo as a drug-addicted priest.

My Own Private Idaho (1991) was the third part of Van Sant's "trilogy of the streets." It starred River Phoenix as a narcoleptic rent boy and Keanu Reeves as a mayor's son to whom Phoenix is attracted. Van Sant hit the jackpot here, shooting the film in a semisurrealist manner that struck a chord with alienated teenagers of the nineties just as Nicholas Ray's *Rebel without a Cause* had for an earlier generation. Phoenix was near angelic in the role. Reeves matched him scene for scene, proving to Van Sant that given the right role he could break out of his "handsome hunk" pigeonhole, just as Dillon had with *Drugstore Cowboy*. The film documented Phoenix's search for his mother against the backdrop of his seesaw relationship with Reeves. The Shakespearean dialect threaded through it gave it a theatrical feel, moving it onto another level. It showed Van Sant at the height of his powers and remains his most emblematic film.

The fact that Phoenix and Reeves were both straight in real life was seen as a weakness by some but not by Van Sant. He didn't care what proclivities his actors had as long as they produced the goods when he called "Action!" Phoenix died not long after making the film, which gave it an extra connection to *Rebel without a Cause*—and Phoenix an extra connection to James Dean. He had the same finely chiseled features, the same childlike vulnerability. He wrote himself into film history as a result of the fireside scene where he expresses his devotion to Reeves with the words, "I love you and you don't have to pay me."

Van Sant now intended to make a film about Harvey Milk, the assassinated San Francisco politician, with Robin Williams in the role, but the project collapsed amid creative differences with Oliver Stone, its putative producer. Instead he directed *Even Cowgirls Get the Blues* (1994), a disappointing adaptation of Tom Robbins's 1976 novel. Uma Thurman played a hitchhiker with an unusually large thumb who finds herself at a ranch inhabited by a number of lesbian cowgirls. She falls in love with one of them, Bonanza Jellybean, played by Rain Phoenix. Van Sant assembled a gilt-edged cast that included Keanu Reeves, Lorraine Bracco, Angie Dickinson, and John Hurt, but the project was a case of "Too many cooks spoil the broth." It couldn't seem to make up its mind if it was a comedy, a drama, or a satire. Once again, William Burroughs made a cameo appearance. This time he had just one word to say: "Ominous." It was Van Sant's first flop.

He picked himself up off the ground to make the searing black comedy *To Die For* (1995), a send-up of the American Dream with Nicole Kidman as a deranged woman who dreams of being a TV celebrity. Her husband (Matt Dillon) thwarts that ambition, so she persuades her teenage lover (Joaquin Phoenix) to see him off. Van Sant continued his run of good form with *Good Will Hunting* (1997), the story of a shy janitor (Matt Damon) with a genius for mathematics. Robin Williams won an Oscar for playing a kindly therapist who helps him with his emotional problems. Damon cowrote the screenplay with his friend Ben Affleck, and this also won an Oscar. The film represented a converted move toward the center by Van Sant.

He reaped the financial rewards of this, but it was followed by the most disastrous film of his career, a totally unnecessary retread of Hitchcock's *Psycho* that replicated it frame by frame. To remake a film that could hardly have been improved on was a ludicrous activity. To unashamedly copy it to the letter made the exercise seem even more ludicrous still. Vince Vaughn lacked Anthony Perkins's nerviness as Norman Bates, and neither had Anne Heche anything new to add to the role Janet Leigh immortalized in the original. The critics justifiably savaged it.

Having his hands burned in this manner propelled Van Sant toward another "safe" project in the *Good Will Hunting* mold. In 2000 he made *Finding Forrester*. It had Sean Connery as a reclusive writer who's drawn out of his academic bunker by a talented young scribe played by Rob Brown. It was a moderate success.

He cowrote his next film, *Gerry* (2002), with Casey Affleck (Ben's brother) and Matt Damon. It featured two friends, both called Gerry, who become lost in the wilderness during a hiking expedition. It had the same languid direction as *My Own Private Idaho*, as well as some of its evocative landscapes, but lacked its inspiration.

Elephant (2003) was another offbeat experiment for Van Sant, but his urge for experimentation sometimes blurred his judgment. A treatise on high school violence, it came off like a poor man's *Bowling for Columbine*. He then made *Last Days* (2005), a rock 'n' roll drama in the Kurt Cobain mode. In 2008 he finally got around to bringing his Harvey Milk movie to fruition. Called simply *Milk*, it was everything one hoped it would be and won Sean Penn an Oscar in the title role.

Restless—which described its director's personality—was a typically quirky Van Sant offering in 2011. It told the story of a terminally ill teenage girl who falls for a boy who likes to attend funerals with the ghost of a World War II Japanese Kamikaze pilot. *Promised Land* (2012) was a more mainstream offering boasting a fine performance from Van Sant stalwart Matt Damon as a corporate salesman trying to persuade the population of a small town to accept a fee to drill through their properties. The film hinged on Damon developing a conscience before carrying through on his company's ruthless excavations for natural gas.

The Sea of Trees (2015) was a meditation on the value of life and the problem of suicide as experienced by Matthew McConaughey at the base of Japan's Mount Fuji. Yet another example of Van Sant the experimenter, it was followed by *Don't Worry, He Won't Get Far on Foot* (2018). This had Joaquin Phoenix as alcoholic cartoonist Bill Callahan, a man who used irreverent newspaper animation as therapy for himself after suffering a near-fatal car accident that has paralyzed him from the waist down.

From his CV, one can see the depth and breadth of Van Sant's work, which resolutely refuses to limit itself to LGBTQ themes. Having said that, he claims his work has brought him out of the closet (Parish, 2001: 44). "I don't think of a gay culture as separate from a mass culture," he maintains. "I just look at it as human culture. It's obvious there's all kinds of stuff oriented toward heterosexual culture because that's the majority but it's also oriented toward white culture because that's also the majority" (Levy, 2015: 205). What he's saying is that gay people, like black people, have to suffer exclusion, but if he were black it wouldn't stop him going to see films oriented toward white people. Likewise, he doesn't want to be heterophobic.

He doesn't like being referred to as a gay director. He prefers to see himself as a director who happens to be gay. "You never hear anyone referred to as hetero," he notes. "That doesn't really say anything and that's why people don't say it. If you're gay, that also isn't saying anything. It's too broad. There's something more to sexual identity than a label" (*Village Voice*, October 1, 1991).

Further Reading
Ehrenstein, David. 2000. *Open Secret: Gay Hollywood 1928–2000*. New York: HarperCollins.
Lang, Robert. 2002. *Masculine Interests*. New York: Columbia University Press.
Levy, Emanuel. 2015. *Gay Directors, Gay Films*. New York: Columbia University Press.
Parish, James Robert. 2001. *Gus Van Sant: An Unauthorized Biography*. New York: Thunder's Mouth Press.

Victim (1961)

The idea that a married man could be gay was something people found it difficult to accept in 1961, but the main character in this Basil Dearden film was. Dirk Bogarde plays Melville Farr, a nonpracticing barrister. "I may share your instincts," he says to a gay man in one scene, "but I've resisted them." This hasn't always been the way for him. Two of his previous lovers have died, one he knew from his university days and the other, "Boy" Barrett (Peter McEnery), when he sacrifices his life for him. Barrett is being blackmailed and the blackmailers threaten to "out" both him and Farr.

Farr is now respectably married. His wife, Laura (Sylvia Sims), knows nothing about his past. He faces a dilemma. He can either pay the blackmailers off to save his name—and marriage—or confront them.

Laura is devastated when she learns of his past. "I thought you loved me," she says. "What did you feel for him?"—meaning Barrett. He doesn't try to paper over the cracks, saying bluntly to her, "I stopped seeing him because I wanted him. Do you understand? I wanted him! Now what good has that done you?" He's being brutally frank here, fully acknowledging the depth of his feelings for the man who's gone to his grave on his behalf.

"I wanted him!" was an incredible line for a man to speak on screen in 1961, especially a man like Bogarde who was hardwired into the public psyche at the time as a kind of pre–George Clooney figure, his *ER* being all those fluffy *Doctor* films that were cuddly and inoffensive. (In a late decade he might have said "I had him!" but this was enough to be going on with.)

When Farr delves deeper into what's happening, he realizes he's just one of a large number of gay men being targeted by the blackmailers. Once he infiltrates their ring, it becomes a case of them or him. There's no hiding place. He can choose to go back into the closet and let them win or take them on. He decides on the latter option with the line, "Fear is the oxygen of blackmail." Later on it turns out that one of the blackmailers (Derren Nesbitt) is himself gay. It's the ultimate betrayal, the ultimate irony.

From now on, Bogarde becomes the hunter as well as the hunted. He's found his courage, but Laura is worried about his "other" side. "The rot's still there," she derides. "You haven't changed, in spite of our marriage."

Victim was before its time. As well as being a strong drama, it's a cultural landmark. Its depiction of a bleak England where sexuality threatened careers—and lives—was devastating.

There's a gay bar in it too. Most people believe the first gay bar shown on screen was in Otto Preminger's *Advise & Consent*, which was made the following year, but that's not the case. Preminger's film featured the first *American* gay bar. Here the mild-mannered owner expresses his hatred of gay people even as he pockets their money.

The dialogue in the film pulls no punches about society's attitude to gay people in the sixties. A bookstore clerk screams out at one point, "They're everywhere! Someone's got to make them pay for their filthy blasphemy!" Elsewhere a friend of Barrett's offers this would-be consolation to Farr, "Well, it used to be witches. At least they don't burn you."

The fact that being gay was a crime in Britain at this time made gay people particularly susceptible to blackmailers, especially people in high-ranking jobs like Farr's. Somebody once called this law "the blackmailer's charter," a phrase that's quoted in the film. Most people caved in to their demands. Barrett's refusal to do so gives Farr the courage to take them on. He's determined to make sure his death hasn't been in vain.

Victim was a seismic breakthrough for the depiction of being gay on film. Bogarde had a lot to lose if it went wrong for him. The film could have spelled career suicide for him just as his character's sexuality could have been for Farr. A frisson of excitement ran through London when it opened in theaters. There were long lines of filmgoers winding around corners, many of them people who weren't even sure if they were gay or not until now. The film was their "coming out."

It was X-rated, which gave the distributors some cause for concern. "I knew the X cert would cut off a large slice of my young public," Bogarde said, "but I decided it was a risk worth taking. Better one film like *Victim* than a dozen of those full of dashing chaps wearing sporty cravats and driving pretty popsies around in Bentleys. You can't leave *all* the intelligent films to the French, Italians and Swedes" (Bourne, 1996: 155).

It was denied a seal for its American release, the Production Code Association finding problems both with its acceptance of being gay and also its plea for an acceptance of it. Pathe-American appealed the ruling without success, which meant it was condemned to the art house circuit. Its viewers there, as Richard Barrios remarked, wore black turtlenecks, sipped complimentary coffee, and made sure they said "film" instead of "movie" when discussing it (Barrios, 2003: 304).

Some critics castigated it for being morbid, which was a valid accusation, but it had to be. There wasn't much to laugh about in the story. Those who pointed out that it didn't show any physical contact between gay men made a better point, but if it went down this road it would probably have been blocked by the censors.

It was primarily important for the manner in which it led to the decriminalization of being gay between consenting adults in England and Wales, and also for the way it set Bogarde off on a career that freed him from the straitjacket of mindless twaddle. It lifted him into an orbit where he was working with the likes of Joseph Losey and Luchino Visconti in films like *The Servant* and *Death in Venice*. Dearden gave his subject the consideration it deserved, refusing to patronize either his characters or his audience. It signaled a shift in the way the gay world saw itself—as something with good and bad people in it rather than the vanilla perspective of yesteryear. England led the way in this transmogrification, and America was happy to carry the baton in future years.

The change, however, didn't happen overnight. In 1963 a twenty-two-year-old laborer and a twenty-four-year-old airman were sentenced to three years imprisonment in Britain for buggery. E. M. Forster wrote in the Afterword to his semiautobiographical novel *Maurice*, which dealt with the theme of queer love at Cambridge University: "What the public really loathes about homosexuality is not the thing itself but having to think about it" (Lahr, 2002: 157). His book wasn't published until 1970 and didn't reach the screen until 1987. By that stage most of the floodgates had opened.

Related Films
Advise & Consent (1962); *The Best Man* (1962); *The Servant* (1963).

Further Reading
Barrios, Richard. 2003. *Screened Out: Playing Out: Playing Gay in Hollywood from Edison to Stonewall*. New York and London: Routledge.

Bourne, Stephen. 1996. *Brief Encounters: Lesbians and Gays in British Cinema 1930–1971.* London: Cassell.

Burton, Alan, and Tim O'Sullivan. 2009. *The Cinema of Basil Dearden and Michael Relph.* Edinburgh: Edinburgh University Press.

Griffiths, Robin, ed. 2006. *British Queer Cinema.* London and New York: Routledge.

Hyde, Montgomery. 1970. *The Other Love.* London: Heinemann.

Jivani, Alkarim. 1997. *It's Not Unusual: The History of Lesbian and Gay Britain in the Twentieth Century.* London: Michael O'Mara.

Lahr, John. 2002. *Prick Up Your Ears: The Biography of Joe Orton.* London: Bloomsbury.

Lewis, Brian. 2016. *Wolfenden's Witnesses: Homosexuality in Postwar Britain.* London: Palgrave Macmillan.

Menninger, K. 1963. *The Wolfenden Report: Report on the Committee of Homosexual Offenses and Prostitution.* New York: Stein and Day.

Morley, Sheridan. 1999. *Dirk Bogarde: Rank Outsider.* London: Bloomsbury.

Village Voice, October, 1991.

Weeks, Jeffrey. 2016. *Coming Out: The Emergence of LGBT Identities in Great Britain from the Nineteenth Century to the Present.* London: Quartet.

Victor/Victoria (1982)

This film was derived from a 1933 German musical comedy, *Viktor and Viktoria*. It was remade in Britain as *First a Girl* three years later. This was the third screen version of the story.

In Jazz Age Paris, Julie Andrews (Victoria) is seeking work. Gay cabaret entertainer Toddy (Robert Preston) gets her a job as a female "impersonator." So a woman pretends to be a man pretending to be a woman.

As well as promoting her drag act, where she becomes Victor, Toddy pretends to be her lover. The scam works until she meets King Marchan (James Garner), a Chicago mobster, and he takes a shine to her. But is she really a "her"? He's confused. He's worried about making a pass at her in case he's thought to be gay. Then one day he discovers she's female. That emboldens him to kiss her. The relationship takes off from there.

Marchan's bodyguard, Squash (Alex Karras), is gay. One day he finds King and "Victor" in bed together. Thinking this means his boss is also gay, he admits his own leanings in that regard. Squash and Toddy later end up in bed together.

The film is homophobic in the sense that it has Garner fighting his attraction toward Andrews until he finds out she's really a woman. Toward the end, Toddy takes over Victoria's act, which seems ludicrous as he's an effeminate gay man while she's a masculine-looking woman. There's no connection between them at all. As for Marchan and Victoria, they both give up their careers for one another. This is about as feminist as a Blake Edwards film is ever going to get. Victoria dumps her tuxedo and sails off into the sunset with Marchan. After her little camp foray, she's back in a dull heterosexual cosmos. And they all live happily ever after—presumably.

Preston gives the film's most endearing performance, especially when he's delivering killer lines like, "There's nothing more inconvenient than an old queen with a head cold." He was nominated for an Oscar. One of his rivals was John Lithgow. Lithgow had been equally charming as a transsexual in *The World According to Garp*. Maybe they canceled each other out. That year the Academy went for machismo over gentleness, giving the award to Louis Gosset Jr. instead. He'd been the routine "tough sergeant" in *An Officer and a Gentleman*. Preston took the defeat philosophically. "Actors never win in gay roles," he declared. "The Academy pats you on the back with a nomination as if they're saying things like, 'How brave of you,' and 'Quite a stretch.' But there's also an innuendo to their comments. They can't help wondering if you played the role too well" (Hadleigh, 1994: 30). He clearly relished the experience, though, telling a journalist, "I've been making films since June 30, 1938 and no one cared about me until I wore Blake Edwards's wife's clothes in *Victor/Victoria*" (*Daily Variety*, November 21, 1983).

Paul Roen made a good point when he said the film's message was that being gay was no worse than being a mobster. It was, he observed, more concerned with women's lib than gay lib. It's Andrews's film, in other words, her friendship with Preston simply being one of the chic things trendy women do. Of course she's rescued from too deep an immersion in the gay world by Garner, who's meant to thrill us by "donating" his bodyguard to Preston (Roen, 1994: 233).

Vito Russo saw the relationship between Andrews and Preston as a throwback to the pre-Code era. Here gay and straight characters could be friends without benefits—and "a musical number made everything rosy" (Russo, 1987: 280).

Russo also had problems with the relationship between Preston and Karras, especially in the scene where they share a bed fully clothed, "propped up primly like two maiden aunties." A chance to eroticize the asexual effeminate characters of the 1930s was lost here, he thought, in a scene that served little purpose save to underline stereotypes (Russo, 280–2).

Roen thought the best scene in the film was the one where Andrews made her debut as a drag queen: "With eerie solemnity she takes off her wig, revealing her apparent 'manhood' (short hair) while the camera treats us to a panoply of reaction shots." Earlier, at rehearsal, a covey of gay chorus boys give her some "provocatively appraising glances." Roen also liked the scene where Garner seems to be turned on by the male Andrews, as he sees it, making love to Preston, which fires him up with what seems to be gay lust. Roen notes that when Garner afterward tries to make love with his previous girlfriend (Leslie Ann Warren), he finds he's impotent (Roen, 1994: 233).

Whether Andrews succeeded in breaking out of her "Mother Teresa" image or not, one still had to commend Edwards for his brave efforts to try to bring this about. Anyone who began their career with *Mary Poppins* (1964) and *The Sound of Music* (1965) was always going to struggle to be seen as an actress with an edge, but she never stopped trying, either here or when she bared her breasts in *S.O.B.* (1981).

Despite Edwards's best efforts to give his good lady some ballast, however, she always seemed to look more Victoria than Victor, even in her tuxedo.

The Marlene Dietrich throne was still holding firm.

Related Films
Viktor and Viktoria (1933); *George et Georgette* (1934); *First a Girl* (1936); *Cabaret* (1972).

Further Reading
Daily Variety, November 21, 1983.
Ginibre, Jean-Louis. 2005. *Ladies or Gentlemen: A Pictorial History of Male Cross-Dressing in the Movies.* New York: Filipacchi Publishing.
Hadleigh, Boze, ed. 1994. *Hollywood Babble On.* New York: Birch Lane.
Roen, Paul. 1994. *High Camp: A Gay Guide to Camp and Cult Films.* San Francisco: Leyland Publications.
Russo, Vito. 1987. *The Celluloid Closet: Homosexuality in the Movies.* New York: Harper & Row.
Straayer, Chris. 1996. *Deviant Eyes, Deviant Bodies: Sexual Reorientation in Film and Video.* New York: Columbia University Press.

Gore Vidal (1925–2012)

Vidal wrote his first book, *Williwaw*, when he was just nineteen. Two years later he published *The City and the Pillar*, the first American novel to deal with being gay in a humane and open way. He began writing for television in the fifties. This led to a screenwriting career. It began in 1956 with the Paddy Chayefsky work *The Catered Affair*, an early Bette Davis vehicle. Two years later he scripted the revisionist Western *The Left Handed Gun* for Arthur Penn. It was one of Paul Newman's most interesting movies but was too introspective to be a commercial hit. The story of Billy the Kid and his eventual death at the hands of Pat Garrett, Vidal wrote him as repressed but felt this element of the screenplay was lost under Penn's direction.

Suddenly, Last Summer, based on one of Tennessee Williams's strangest plays, was his next assignment. Being gay was present here too but again only as a subtext. Under Joseph L. Mankiewicz's direction, it became even more confused as a film than it was as a play. Williams collaborated with Vidal on the screenplay. When it flopped, each blamed the other for its failure.

Katharine Hepburn played a character tormented by the death of her predatory gay cousin. Elizabeth Taylor was the niece she does her best to have lobotomized. Montgomery Clift rounded off the cast as a neurosurgeon drafted in to decide whether Taylor needs the lobotomy or not. There was too much psychosis for comfort. The film collapsed under the weight of it all.

Vidal contributed to the screenplay of *Ben-Hur* in 1959, telling Stephen Boyd, who played Ben-Hur's childhood friend Messala, he wanted to inject a gay subtext into his relationship with the title character. "But don't tell Chuck," he said, referring to Charlton Heston, the actor playing him. He knew Heston would have a seizure at such a suggestion. So did the film's director, William Wyler. He replaced Vidal with Karl Tunberg shortly afterward. Vidal's idea was that the two had been adolescent lovers. As the film begins, he wants to revive the relationship but Ben-Hur doesn't. This causes Messala to send him into slavery.

Caligula (1980)

It's sometimes said that the more screenwriters a film has, the more mediocre it becomes. This had three. It also had three producers and three directors. On such a mathematical premise, one could multiply its mediocrity by nine.

Documenting the career of probably the most repulsive Roman ruler in history, the first screenplay was written by Gore Vidal (Eugene Louis Vidal). The original director was Tinto Brass. Bob Guccione, he of *Penthouse* fame, or rather infamy, was funding it so he overruled the decisions of Brass and Vidal as regards to its focus. This shocked them so much they decided they wanted to have nothing to do with the finished product. Vidal actually went so far as to sue for this to come about. Some of the actors in it—including Peter O'Toole, Malcolm McDowell, and Sir John Gielgud—also asked to be dissociated from it when they saw the final cut. Guccione didn't honor these requests. McDowell played Caligula himself.

The film has overtones of pornography, which makes the sight of mainstream stars in the leading roles appear incongruous. Have they wandered in from another set inadvertently? One wonders. Guccione didn't advise them of his full intent, inserting the more grotesque aspects of the film into it after they'd departed the set. This was an underhanded move. It's no surprise they feared for their careers after it—though Gielgud appeared to enjoy the notoriety it afforded him.

In one scene, Caligula deflowers both a virgin and her fiancé before their marriage. This was Guccione's doing rather than something Vidal or Brass wanted. It was one in a series of sexual excesses in the film.

Penthouse becomes 3D in this hymn to debauchery. Outrageous for its time, it still raises eyebrows today. Murder, decapitation, disembowelment—these were routine occurrences for the insane emperor. He even gave his horse political office at one point.

He had an incestuous relationship with his sister, Drusilla. He killed his stepfather and his half brother. He married a prostitute to have a child but preferred sex with Drusilla. He made orgies into almost daily events, forcing the wives of many of his senators to work in brothels he set up. He declared himself a god. He licked his dead sister's naked corpse. He slept with his horse.

He was also a pedophile. When O'Toole says to him, "I hear you have a taste for little boys," he replies, "No, big boys."

Vidal wanted the chariot race to represent the way both of them expressed their sexual energy vicariously, with Ben-Hur symbolically conquering his orientation in killing off his old friend. His idea was that sex separated the two men rather than the original plotline. That had Messala selling Ben-Hur into slavery because he failed to give him the names of various enemies of Rome. Ben-Hur, in his version, "had turned straight as a die under the fierce Palestinian sun" while Messala, "the decadent gentile," wanted to resume their affair where it left off all those years before (Malone, 2010: 27).

Wyler wanted it to play itself out as a run-of-the mill affair climaxing in the race rather than in Messala's boudoir. So did Heston. Once Heston learned of Vidal's intentions, they were rapidly removed from the equation (Vidal, 1995: 305).

Vidal's version would have made a much meatier film than Wyler's, which had all of Heston's square-jawed integrity but not too much in the way of passion. Haya Harareet, Ben-Hur's heterosexual replacement for Messala, was a bland alternative. If they cut her out, Vidal always insisted, and concentrated on the two men, everything would have been more credible. Maybe so, but the film would hardly have been the success it was. Neither would it have won Heston an Oscar. Wyler caved in to studio pressure to make a conventional biblical epic. (Perhaps he felt a conscience about this, which could have motivated him to bring being lesbian to the screen for the first time two years later with *The Children's Hour*.)

Vidal wrote the screenplay for *The Best Man* in 1964, adapting his play about two politicians campaigning for the presidency, Henry Fonda and Cliff Robertson. Robertson has to contend with allegations that he had gay experiences in the past.

When Hollywood optioned his transsexual novel, *Myra Breckinridge*, in 1970, he was excited about the prospect initially, but when he saw what rookie director Michael Sarne was doing with it he disowned it. He did the same with *Caligula* (also 1970), a film about the decadent Roman emperor. He also scripted this.

He was living in Rome at this time. The same year saw a documentary on him, *Gore Vidal: Portrait of a Writer*. Made by a German director, Hans-Jorg Weyhmuller, it showed him discoursing on the city's ruins as well as other parts of Italy. He used the opportunity to settle some scores with people he'd fallen out with, like Truman Capote and Norman Mailer. These were two writers with whom he conducted long-standing feuds. Mailer famously head-butted him on one occasion. He was resentful of his rivals, but confessedly so. "Every time a friend succeeds," he admitted, "a little something in me dies" (Howard, 2006: 652). This was the case with Capote, whom he described as "a Republican housewife from Kansas, with all the prejudices" (Hadleigh, 2005: 267).

He scripted the gay murder mystery *Dress Gray* in 1987. Set in a military academy during the Vietnam War, this TV movie starred Alec Baldwin as a cadet who becomes involved in the cover-up of the circumstances surrounding the death of another cadet who was raped and murdered. Apparently he'd been in love with Baldwin, who also dated his sister. Vidal adapted another TV movie, *Lincoln*, from his own novel the following year. At 191 minutes, however, it was dull and leaden-footed. One wit remarked that it seemed longer than the Civil War itself.

Vidal revisited the terrain of *The Left Handed Gun* for *Billy the Kid* in 1989. Val Kilmer played the gunfighter this time. Again the film focuses on his relationship to Pat Garrett, but this time there's no gay subtext. It was believed he wrote it to make up for Penn's lapse in the 1958 feature. But if he wasn't going to add anything new, why go back to the well a second time?

Vidal was a talented writer who didn't receive the recognition he deserved. He was also very witty. Asked once if his first sexual partner was male or female he replied, "I was too polite to ask" (Jarski, 2004: 171). He traversed both worlds with imagination and flair, but it's a pity his body of work both on the page and stage alike is so uneven. It's as if either his discipline or his inspiration let him down whenever he was on the verge of doing something that would have made his reputation more secure than it is.

Further Reading

Hadleigh, Boze, ed. 2005. *Celebrity Diss and Tell*. Kansas City: Andrews McMeel.
Howard, Philip, ed. 2006. *The Times Quotations: From Homer to Homer Simpson*. London: HarperCollins.

Jarski, Rosemarie, ed. 2004. *The Funniest Things You Never Said.* London: Ebury Books.

Kaplan, Fred. 1999. *Gore Vidal: A Biography.* New York: Doubleday.

Malone, Aubrey. 2010. *Sacred Profanity: Spirituality at the Movies.* Santa Barbara, CA: Praeger.

Parini, Jay. *2015. Every Time a Friend Succeeds, Something in Me Dies: The Life of Gore Vidal.* London: Little Brown.

Vidal, Gore. 1995. *Palimpsest: A Memoir.* London: Andre Deutsch.

Waugh, Thomas, ed. 2000. *The Fruit Machine: Twenty Years of Writings on Queer Cinema.* Durham, NC, and London: Duke University Press.

Andy Warhol (1928–87)

Born in Pittsburgh to Slovakian parents, Warhol began his career as a commercial illustrator before setting up shop in his New York aerie The Factory. This became a magnet for bohemians and writers. It allowed him to hone his precocious talents and indulge his eccentricities.

His films, like his art, were often stark and tacky. Their essence was captured in the titles. *Sleep* (1963) was fifteen minutes of someone sleeping. *Kiss* (1963) involved little more than that activity. *Blow Job* (1963) was forty minutes of a man's face as he receives oral sex. For some people this was false advertising as the main action was three feet below the camera. Warhol defended himself by saying his ambition was to show the "demystification of love" (Ultra Violet, 1988: 32).

Empire, made the following year, exhibited the unchanging face of the Empire State Building for no less than eight hours and five minutes. Warhol said the effect he was looking for here was *stasis* (Bourdon, 1989: 188). He certainly achieved that. "I like boring things," he said. "I like things to be exactly the same over and over again" (Wrenn, 1991: 16). He described the film as "an eight hour hard-on. It's like Flash Gordon riding into space" (Wrenn, 34).

Even by his own standards, his 1964 release *Taylor Mead's A*s* was a disappointment. It was a seventy-minute silent black-and-white film focusing on that man's derriere. Was he trying to annoy people or entertain them? One never knew for sure.

Warhol also made stag movies. *Haircut* (1963) was a homoerotic film that had many seminude men getting (and giving) haircuts. *Couch* (1964) featured scenes of explicit sex on—what else?—a couch.

Not content to stop there, he queered vampire movies with *Batman Dracula* (1964). *Camp* (1965) starred Mario Montez. It parodied adventure movies. Warhol liked Montez and used him frequently afterward. He became a gay icon after appearing in over a dozen of Warhol's films.

He never liked being referred to as an underground artist. On his own estimation, he would have gone to the opening of an envelope. Underground figures were usually recluses. How could the originator of "pop" art describe himself as anything like that?

He made the camp Western film, *Lonesome Cowboys*, in 1968. The plot mirrored *Romeo & Juliet* and prefigured *Brokeback Mountain*. Even though the sex is heterosexual, the cowboys practice ballet moves and discuss hair perms. When they ride off into the sunset at the end—to a life of surfing in California—it's obvious that Warhol is sending up the cowboy genre.

> **Paul Morrissey (1938–)**
>
> Morrissey was the man behind so many Warhol films he almost qualifies for being called his doppelganger. He was engaged in experimental work from the early sixties. He met Warhol in 1963 at a screening of *Sleep*. The first Warhol film he lent his name to was *The Chelsea Girls* (1966). When Joe Dallesandro came on board, he directed him in films like *Bike Boy* (1967), *The Loves of Ondine* (1967), and *Lonesome Cowboys* (1968).
>
> He got his first big break when Warhol was shot by Valerie Solanas. As Warhol was recovering in the hospital, Morrissey took over the direction of *Flesh*. He was also heavily involved in *Trash* and *Heat*. Each film gave him added responsibilities and duties. He wrote the screenplay for *Trash* and also did the cinematography.
>
> In the seventies he found his voice, creeping out from under Warhol's shadow. His film *Women in Revolt* (1971) purported to be about women's liberation, but it wasn't. The casting of drag queens like Candy Darling and Holly Woodlawn as feminists, and naming their organization PIGS (an acronym for Politically Involved Girls), telegraphed a more mischievous intent.
>
> Morrissey expanded his range to include lesbian vampirism in *Blood for Dracula* in 1974. Like Warhol he brought the underground overground, taking countercultural subjects into the mainstream with confidence and calmness.
>
> His work trailed off in the late seventies. His eighties films—*Madame Wong's* (1981), *Forty Deuces* (1982), and *Beethoven's Nephew* (1985)—failed to garner much interest. When Warhol died, one might have imagined him to flourish now that his Svengali wasn't looking over his shoulder, but the opposite happened. Warhol's passing seemed to rob him of his spirit. In retrospect, maybe it was appropriate that they both folded their tents in unison.
>
> **Further Reading**
>
> Yacowar, Maurice. 1993. *The Films of Paul Morrissey*. New York: Cambridge University Press.

The film had a mixed reception. "Warhol's best movie to date," *Variety* rasped, "which is like saying a three-year-old has graduated from smearing mud on a wall to occasional use of finger paints" (*Variety*, November 6, 1968).

The notorious pop artist-cum-filmmaker was shot in 1968 by a woman called Valerie Solanas, the founder (and solitary member) of a society called SCUM, an acronym for The Society for Cutting Up Men. Males were biologically obsolete, Solanas believed.

She was also an artist. After she got to know Warhol, she developed the fear that he would steal her work. Hence the attempted assassination. She fired four bullets at him. He was, needless to say, traumatized by it all.

It changed his attitude to what he did. "Being famous isn't that important," he sniffed. "If I wasn't famous I wouldn't have been shot" (Lessard, 2008: 132). Later on he changed tack, dismissing it as mere happenstance: "I was in the wrong place at the wrong time" (Ultra Violet, 178). As he lay in the hospital recovering from his wounds, he kept seeing TV footage of Robert Kennedy. He mistook him for his dead brother, John, in his semiconscious state. Why, he wondered, was JFK on the television? It was only days later he learned that the younger brother had been assassinated two days after the Solanas incident. "If only Kennedy were shot at a different time," he grumbled, "I would have gotten all that publicity" (Ultra Violet, 180).

Paul Morrissey started working with Warhol around now, either directing or codirecting many films ascribed to him. He lent his hand to *Flesh for Frankenstein* and *Blood for Dracula*, two 1974 horror spoofs, and Warhol's trilogy of *Flesh* (1968), *Trash* (1970), and *Heat* (1972). These were all improvised works made on small budgets. They all starred Joe Dallesandro.

Dallesandro was visiting friends in an apartment in Greenwich Village when he saw Warhol and Morrissey shooting a film in a room with the door half-open. He was curious to know what was happening so he wandered in. Ever the opportunist, Warhol looked admiringly at his torso. He asked him if he wanted to be in the film. Dallesandro said he did.

He had the body of a Greek god. Warhol exploited it to the full when he started working with him in earnest, shooting him in long, lingering takes. In *Flesh* he was a gay hustler sent out onto the streets by his wife (Geraldine Smith) to earn money for an abortion for her lesbian lover. He was the drug-addicted lover of drag queen Holly Woodlawn in *Trash*, a film in which Woodlawn masturbates with a beer bottle in one scene and then pretends she's pregnant. In *Heat*, a satire of Billy Wilder's *Sunset Boulevard* (1950), he was involved in a ménage à quatre with Sylvia Miles, her lesbian daughter, and the boyfriend of her former husband. Dallesandro also appeared in *Flesh for Frankenstein* and *Blood for Dracula*. In the latter he was the stud who sees to it that the vampire's victims aren't virgins when he drains their blood. It's a task he undertakes with some relish.

Warhol took his foot off the gas in the seventies. The Solanas shooting had a lot to do with this. His colleague Ultra Violet wrote, "Only one bullet punctured Andy's body but all four penetrated the creative spirit inside him, killing the artist" (Ultra Violet, 181). From now on he spent much of his time doing portraits purely—or rather impurely—for money. His subjects certainly had it: Mick Jagger, Liza Minnelli, the Shah of Iran, Diana Ross, John Lennon. He also spent a lot of his time socializing. If one reads his diaries, he's somewhere glitzy almost every night. The pattern continued into the eighties. If art was what sold, as he believed, it helped to socialize with as many rich patrons as he could.

Warhol claimed to be asexual, but his array of lovers knocked that notion on the head. He said he was engaged to Truman Capote for ten years. The relationship, he explained, was mainly conducted over the phone. It ended when Warhol decided to marry his tape recorder instead (Ultra Violet, 157–9).

He said he was twenty-three when he first had sex with a man. He liked the mechanical nature of it. His favorite film was *Barbarella* (1968), especially the scene where Jane Fonda has sex with a machine. "Sex is an illusion," he declared. "The most exciting thing is not making it." When it happened it was usually gross: "Only in telephone sex, robot sex and computer sex is there escape from ugliness and cruelty. Machine sex is the only kind left that his uncomplicated, antiseptic, clean, even a little mysterious. Let's not think about affection and tenderness—they are entirely beyond expectation" (Ultra Violet, 165).

Warhol died in 1987 after failing to recover from a gallbladder operation. His family sued the hospital for malpractice and received an undisclosed sum in recompense. His art continues to sell and his films to be shown at festivals. In 1996 Mary Harron made a film about Valerie Solanas called *I Shot Andy Warhol*. Here one learns that she slept with men for money and women for enjoyment. Lili Taylor played her with a neat blend of genius and madness. The film captures the period evocatively as Warhol and his motley crew of Factory friends all seek their fifteen minutes of fame in the BoHo wildness of the sixties.

In 2013 Juha Lilja remade *Sleep*. It was its fiftieth anniversary. The remake seemed some kind of endorsement of a film people had sneered at half a century before.

In the end, though, Warhol is probably more notable as a cultural phenomenon than an artist in his own right. His greatest creation was himself.

Related Films
Andy Warhol and His Work (1973); *Superstar: The Life and Times of Andy Warhol* (1990); *I Shot Andy Warhol* (1995); *Absolute Warhola* (2001); *Beautiful Darling* (2010); *Sleep* (2013).

Further Reading
Bourdon, David. 1989. *Warhol*. New York: Abrams & Co.
Colacello, Bob. 1990. *Holy Terror: Andy Warhol Close Up*. New York: Harper Perennial.
Doyle, Jennifer, and Jonathan Flatley. 1996. *Pop Out: Queer Warhol*. Durham, NC: Duke University Press.
Dyer, Richard. 1990. *Now You See It: Studies on Gay and Lesbian Film*. London and New York: Routledge.
Glick, Eliza. 2009. *Materializing Queer Desire: Oscar Wilde to Andy Warhol*. New York: State University of New York Press.
Hackett, Pat, ed. 1992. *The Andy Warhol Diaries*. London: Pan.
Lessard, John, ed. 2008. *To Quote a Queer*. Philadelphia: Quirk Books.
Suarez, Juan A. 1996. *Bike Boys, Drag Queens and Superstars: Avant-Garde, Mass Culture and Gay Identities in the 1960s Underground Cinema*. Indianapolis: Indiana University Press.
Tinkcom, Matthew. 2002. *Working Like a Homosexual: Camp, Capital, Cinema*. Durham, NC, and London: Duke University Press.
Ultra Violet. 1988. *Famous for Fifteen Minutes: My Years with Andy Warhol*. Orlando, FL: Harcourt Brace.
Variety, November 6, 1968.
Wrenn, Mike, ed. 1991. *Andy Warhol in His Own Words*. London: Omnibus.

John Waters (1946–)

The self-styled Pope of Trash looks on it as a compliment if someone throws up after seeing one of his films. "To me," he gloats, "bad taste is what entertainment is all about" (Winokur, 1992: 216).

Waters demonstrated the seamy side of suburbia in a subversive manner in his adolescent comedies. His LGBTQ figures are often ridiculously cartoonish, his satirical melodramas disconcertingly toxic.

The man who once described himself as "Walt Disney for strange children" began his career with *Eat Your Makeup* in 1968. The film mocked the assassination of John F. Kennedy. Two years later he was similarly tasteless in trivializing

Hairspray (1988)

John Waters was in rare form with this uncharacteristic feel-good flick. It was an amiable homage to teen movies with Ricki Lake as Tracy Turnblad, queen of Baltimore's number one dance party. She irritates the snobbish characters played by Debbie Harry and Sonny Bono, who want their daughter to win a dancing competition. Divine also warms his hands at the fire. Waters even finds time to deliver an antiracism message as Tracy's black friends are refused entry to the show.

It's a valentine to the bobby socks era with the dance competition giving him ample opportunity to rope together his diverse cast. Divine is Tracy's mother, Edna. She has a "hairdon't" instead of a hairdo, but her heart is in the right place. Divine also plays Arvin Hodgepile.

The cast members seem blithely unaware of their cartoon-like status, but this only increases the fun. Waters (who appears in a cameo) parodies the teen queen theme in a series of wacky vignettes.

The dance moves are laugh-out-loud funny. The backing vocals transport one back to the days of Sandra Dee and Ricky Nelson. Apart from some brief touches, like Tracy kicking a mouse off her foot as she says to the boys she's kissing, "This is so romantic," *Hairspray* doesn't have the look of a John Waters film.

Tracy's dreams come true when she gets to appear on the coolest show in Baltimore, the *Corny Collins Show*. But has she bitten off more than she can chew by going head-to-head with reigning teen queen Amber von Tussle? And who's going to win the heart of the local Lothario, Link?

Abolish racism, Tracy, and rid the world of pampered people like Amber. In the meantime, shake that booty.

---

the suicide of a troubled teenager in *The Diane Linkletter Story*. Even this early he was stretching the boundaries of where a satirist was entitled to go to make a point.

The Diane Linkletter Story starred 300-pound drag queen Divine, who was born Glenn Milstead. He lived in Baltimore like Waters himself. Divine also turned up in *Mondo Trasho* to create more havoc in the same year. In *Multiple Maniacs* (1971), s/he commits mass murder and is afterward raped by a giant lobster. It's just another day in her life. The film is replete with typical Waters outrageousness. Other scenes show Jesus feeding the masses with hot dogs and cans of tuna instead of loaves and fishes. Mink Stole, a religious extremist, penetrates Divine anally with rosary beads. Waters isn't "watering down" his sacrilege here.

Pink Flamingos (1972) continued where *Multiple Maniacs* left off. With various characters vying to be the Filthiest Person Alive, one witnesses cannibalism, fellatio, murder, ingestion of dog turds, and babies being sold to lesbian couples. The money raised from this activity goes toward a heroin ring for elementary schoolchildren. In other words it's business as usual for Waters.

Most of his films are parodies of genres or subgenres. *Female Trouble* (1974) sends up the "bad girl" one. Divine runs the gamut from teenage rage all the way to the electric chair. The film also thumps the tub for being gay as Ida Nelson (Edith Massey) advises Gator (Michael Potter) to become gay. "Queers are just better," she states. "I'd be so proud if you had a nice beautician boyfriend. I'd never have to worry. The world of heterosexuals is a sick and disgusting life."

In 1977 he made *Desperate Living*. This had Mink Stole as a woman who kills her husband and then runs off with her maid. They find safety in a kingdom ruled by the porcine tyrant Queen Carlotta (Edith Massey). Afterward matters become slightly barmy even by Waters's standards.

More satires followed in the eighties. In *Polyester* (1981) he sent up romance movies. Who better to do this but Tab Hunter, the pinup of yesteryear, cozying up with Divine to comfort her when her husband has an affair? It took Hunter's career (which was wilting at the time) into a whole new direction and gave Divine something old-fashioned to bounce off. Then came *Hairspray* (1988), a film with a "Big Is Beautiful" theme. Divine played a double role and was irresistible to everyone, including Ricki Lake, in the world of beauty pageants. Alas, Divine died soon after filming was completed.

Waters landed an even bigger coup than Hunter when he persuaded the hotter-than-hot Johnny Depp to appear in his next film, *Cry-Baby* (1989). This parodied musicals in the same way *Hairspray* parodied teen movies. Depp was "Cry-Baby" Walker, a leather-clad hotrod chasing the more up-market Amy Locane (Allison Vernon-Williams) and dragging her down to his level. One can see *Grease—The Antidote* writ large in the scenario. There are also echoes of Elvis Presley and the young Marlon Brando. Iggy Pop and Troy Donahue also appear, which isn't too surprising. But so does Patty Hearst, which is. And porn queen Traci Lords.

Serial Mom (1994) was like an encapsulation of all Waters's previous burlesques, creating in Kathleen Turner a Stepford Wife–style mother who goes into meltdown when her apple pie/white picket fence/Middle American cosmos is derailed. A satire of our celebrity criminal culture, it seemed to predate the media circus that surrounded the O.J. Simpson imbroglio. It serves as a hilarious corrective to everything he epitomized. It had Waters in supreme form as he unpicked most of the sacred cows of his native land in the process of having the kind of fun Freddie Krueger might have had if let loose in Disneyland on a weekend pass. The standout scene has Turner, who rises to the occasion with some élan, killing one of her victims with a leg of lamb to the background of the soundtrack from the movie *Annie*.

Serial Mom has Waters deliciously deconstructing the idea of women's labor and its phallocentric social arrangements. In referencing films like *Mildred Pierce* and exaggerating the impulses Joan Crawford showed in that movie with her urge to "clean the world and make it over in the image of domestic orderliness"—no mean achievement considering Crawford's penchant for overacting—he upended not only a genre but a culture. He was trying to make audiences root for his deranged antiheroine, he said, "to find people's limits, how far you can go, and make them a little bit nervous that they're enjoying something they've been taught not to enjoy. Nobody likes serial killers but this one, not only did she do it, she got off. And you're glad" (Tinkcom, 2002: 158–9). If Milstead was alive, Waters would have wanted him for the title role, but he wasn't. Neither would the studios have allowed it (Hays, 2007: 358).

Waters has been quiet since the turn of the century. He made *Cecil B Demented*, a spoof on the film business, in 2000, but it lacked his usual spirit and didn't do well at the box office. Its failure gave him pause. He took a sabbatical from directing, busying himself with TV appearances and occasional cameo roles in films.

This Filthy World, a documentary about his life and work, was made by Jeff Garlin in 2006. It tells people everything they might wish to know about the maverick director, including this overall view of himself: "When I was young I wanted to be Visconti, but now I realize my career is becoming similar to Paul Lynde's."

Neil Genzlinger wrote of it in the *New York Times*, "Those who think of Waters only as a sicko, a wacko, a pervert, a psycho, a multi-fetishist, a deviant, a menace and/or a nut job will be surprised to discover that he would also make an excellent dinner guest." Genzlinger added, however, that they would have to tolerate stories about singing rectums if they invited him to their house (Porter, 2007: 391).

People like Tab Hunter, Debbie Harry, and Pia Zadora, etc., were content to work for scale in Waters's films. They did so out of respect for the manner in which he brought an underground conscience to his films, though often with a slight fear that they might never work again because of their association with him. On the other hand, if something worked, it could take their career onto another level and extend their street cred. One always walked this tightrope with him even as he walked it himself.

He used his camera like a scalpel, digging into society's murky underbelly for his scalding parables. Suburbia could be turned into dystopia in a heartbeat under Waters's scabrously sadistic gaze. He explores the insanity at the core of society in general but specialized in that aspect of it that threatened the status quo.

He isn't embarrassed by his sobriquet The Pope of Trash because it was a description of him by William Burroughs: "To me that's divine intervention. That's like the Pope giving you a title" (Hays, 2007: 361). Other descriptions of him include the Anal Ambassador, the Marquis de Sade, the Duke of Dirt. Despite his reputation for obscenity, Waters insists he's not a fan of hardcore pornography. "It always looks like open heart surgery to me," he remarks (Samuels, 120).

Asked if he would do anything differently if he had his life to live over, he said, "In *Mondo Trasho* we chopped off chickens' heads. I regret that. It was a joke no one ever understood" (Hays, 2007: 360). Art for him is the practice of a luxuriant escapism. "I pride myself," he states, "on the fact that my work has no redeeming social value" (Winokur, 1992: 36). "I'd love to sell out completely," he says. "It's just that nobody has been willing to buy" (Winokur, 35). When they didn't, the latter-day Mephistopheles busied himself cranking out gloriously decadent pastiches that sent grossness into a whole new direction.

Elsewhere he made outrageous comments like, "I don't dislike animals but I don't have a problem if they test medicines or even cosmetics on them. Eyeliner has been important in my life. If ten chickens have to die to make one drag queen happy, so be it" (Hadleigh, 1999: 59).

He has few ambitions, having pushed the envelope so far there's really nowhere else to go. Some years ago he expressed an interest in filming the Grace Metalious story: "She wrote *Peyton Place*, became rich, bought Cadillacs and killed herself" (Winokur, 34). It sounds like Waters material all right.

Behind all the grotesqueries, maybe there's a romantic in him trying to get out. "I've tried everything but coprophagia and necrophilia," he claims, "but I still like kissing best" (Jarski, 2000: 266).

Further Reading
Hadleigh, Boze, ed. 1999. *Hollywood Bitch*. London: Robson.
Hays, Matthew. 2007. *The View from Here: Conversations with Gay and Lesbian Filmmakers*. Vancouver, BC: Arsenal Pulp Press.
Ives, John G. 1992. *John Waters*. New York: Thunder's Mouth Press.
Jarski, Rosemarie, ed. 2000. *Hollywood Wit*. London: Prion.
Maier, Robert G. 2011. *Low Budget Hell: Making Underground Movies with John Waters*. Davidson, NC: Full Page Publishing.
Porter, Darwin, and Danforth Prince. 2007. *Blood Moon's Guide to Gay and Lesbian Film: Second Edition*. New York: Blood Moon Productions.
Samuels, Stuart. 1983. *Midnight Movies*. New York: Macmillan.
Stevenson, Jack. 1996. *Desperate Visions 1, Camp America: The Films of John Waters and the Kuchar Brothers, Interviews and Essays*. London: Creation Books.
Tinkcom, Matthew. 2002. *Working Like a Homosexual: Camp, Capital, Cinema*. Durham, NC, and London: Duke University Press.
Waters, John. 1981. *Shock Value: A Tasteful Book about Bad Taste*. New York: Delta.
Winokur, Jon, ed. 1992. *True Confessions: The World's Most Famous People Reveal Their Intimate Secrets*. London: Victor Gollancz.

Oscar Wilde (1854–1900)

Oscar Wilde was the classic "double life" queer, living in denial of his primary orientation as he settled down to married life in the late 1880s. It wasn't until he met the dashing young Oxford student Lord Alfred Douglas and became infatuated with him that he gave full vent to being gay. Their relationship ultimately led to his downfall, and to the collapse of his marriage to Constance Lloyd, by whom he had two sons.

Wilde was brought down as much by his arrogance as his sexuality. It should be remembered that it was he who first sued the Marquis of Queensbury for his allegation of buggery. If he let this go unchallenged, the whole train of events that caused his eventual shaming and subsequent incarceration could have been avoided. But Wilde, as he often said, could resist anything but temptation. Letting this go would have been too much for him. In the end, the accusation proved to be the Marquis of Queensbury's Trojan horse, a trap set to draw the witty wordsmith out of the closet.

Robert Morley played Wilde in the black-and-white film *Oscar Wilde* in 1960. This was a rather lugubrious affair. The Irish actor Micheál MacLiammóir, himself gay, was much more interesting in *On Trial: Oscar Wilde*, a Granada television film also made in 1960. MacLiammóir did many one-man shows as Wilde during his career and caught his personality perfectly. Peter Finch was also impressive in *The Trials of Oscar Wilde*, the third film made about him in 1960, surely an unprecedented phenomenon for any writer. The Morley and Finch biopics appeared in theaters in the very same week. Finch was less camp than MacLiammóir, but he brought a charm to his performance that still resonates.

Morley admitted he hadn't given a good performance in the film. He'd played the role on stage in both London and New York in the thirties and was unhappy with these performances too. "When I did the play I was ten years too young," he said in 1977, "and when the play was filmed I was ten years too old" (*Gay News*, May 1977). This was refreshingly frank. Finch's interpretation of Wilde was much deeper. John Fraser was also very effective as Bosie, the man who brings Wilde down. Finch essayed the role fatalistically as if he knew what was in store for him but could do nothing about it. His infatuation with the younger man is a poisoned chalice that destroys his marriage, his career, and ultimately his life. Lionel Jeffries played the Marquis of Queensbury, Bosie's father. He brings the action against Wilde. James Mason was lethal as the prosecuting counsel.

Quentin Crisp upbraided Wilde for suing Bosie's father. "He could have feigned to be above confession and denial. Of his friends, some would have known he was queer; some would not" (Kettlehack, 1984: 51). In either case a dignified silence would have sufficed.

Wilde sometimes seemed like a character from one of his plays. When he said he put his genius into his life and his mere talent into his plays he wasn't joking. He had wit at will, and sometimes it worked against him. Asked if he'd kissed one of the young men mentioned by the prosecution, he replied that he hadn't because the boy wasn't pretty enough (Kettlehack, 51). The remark may have gotten a titter from the gallery but its effect was damning. In denying the allegation he was confirming a more pernicious one: he liked kissing pretty boys.

Stephen Fry played him in *Wilde* (1997), a spirited retelling of his rise and fall directed by Brian Gilbert. The most recent film to cover his life was a fascinating one starring Rupert Everett called *The Happy Prince* (2018).

Everett has been fascinated by Wilde for most of his life. He acted in many of his plays on Broadway and played his alter ego in films like *The Importance of Being Earnest* and *An Ideal Husband*. He also played Wilde himself in David Hare's *The Judas Kiss* on the West End.

In this, his directorial debut, he explored the posttrial Oscar, something other biopics hadn't done. Why did prison crush his spirits so much? Many people completed longer sentences and went on to have fulfilling lives, but Wilde was never the same after Reading Gaol.

Undoubtedly his spell there was arduous. The fall was greater because he lived such a high life before his incarceration. There's "easy time" and "hard time." Considering his demeanor, it was always going to be the latter for the erstwhile *bon viveur*.

From this point of view, the title of Everett's film—which he also scripted—is a misnomer. It's based on a children's story Wilde wrote of the same name, but "The *Unhappy* Prince" would have been more appropriate.

Such gripes apart, this was a fine piece of filmmaking. It documented the alcohol-soaked destitution of the once-flamboyant playwright with elegiac accuracy. This wit is gone, whatever slivers of it that remain only accentuating his misery. In its place is a man who's fallible, real, tarnished.

Stephen Fry was more physically similar to him than Everett, but Everett buried himself under layers of prostheses to evince a more nuanced character living off the scraps of former glory. He cut a forlorn figure in cinematographer John Conroy's grimly lush mise-en-scenes.

The broken-down Wilde looks back at his halcyon years from Paris, Naples, Normandy, Rouen. "Like dear Saint Francis of Assisi," he sighs, "I'm wedded to poverty. But in my case the marriage is not a happy one." He waits for death in a dilapidated hotel room with bad wallpaper.

Emily Watson plays Constance, the wife who puts up the money for him to keep body and soul together until she becomes frustrated about the fact that he's still seeing Bosie. Edwin Thomas is Robbie Ross, his literary executor and former lover. A mustached Colin Firth—Everett's costar in *Another Country*—is his friend Reggie Turner. Colin Morgan is Bosie.

This was a heartrending threnody to a heart grown brutal from the fare. "Why should a perfectly divine leopard change his spots?" Wilde asks at one point. But he does.

Today Wilde is championed as much for his suffering as his literary legacy. Wilfrid Hyde-White remarked, "They sent Oscar Wilde, that poor man, to Reading Gaol for doing what all other actors (*sic*) get knighted for" (McClelland, 1987: 158).

Related Films
Oscar Wilde (1960); *The Trials of Oscar Wilde* (1960); *Forbidden Passion: Oscar Wilde* (1986); *The Ballad of Reading Gaol* (1988); *Salome's Last Dance* (1988); *Indecent Acts* (1994); *Wilde* (1997); *The Happy Prince* (2018).

Further Reading
Frankel, Nicholas. 1997. *Oscar Wilde: The Unrepentant Years*. Cambridge, MA: Harvard University Press.

Gay News, May 1977.

Howes, Keith. 1995. *Outspoken: Keith Howes' Gay News Interviews 1976–83*. London: Cassell.

Janes, Dominic. 2016. *Oscar Wilde Prefigured: Queer Fashioning and British Caricature 1750–1900*. Chicago: University of Chicago Press.

Kettlehack, Guy, ed. 1984. *The Wit and Wisdom of Quentin Crisp*. New York: Harper & Row.

McClelland, Doug, ed. 1987. *StarSpeak: Hollywood on Everything*. Boston and London: Faber & Faber.

McKenna, Neil. 2004. *The Secret Life of Oscar Wilde*. London: Arrow.

Mendelssohn, Michele. 2018. *Making Oscar Wilde*. Oxford: Oxford University Press.

Sinfield, Alan. 1994. *The Wilde Century: Oscar Wilde, Effeminacy and the Queer Moment*. London: Cassell.

Tennessee Williams (1911–83)

If George Cukor is the film world's most feted "women's director," one could dub Tennessee Williams the quintessential "woman's writer." Many of his plays feature women who are broken down physically and/or mentally. The template for these is probably his beloved sister, Rose, with whom he had an almost umbilical connection. When Rose was admitted to an asylum, he was devastated. Some people would say he never recovered. But her plights bequeathed him many rich literary creations, including the crippled young woman played by Jane Wyman in *The Glass Menagerie* (1950), Irving Rapper's moving version of one of Williams's most admired plays. Gertrude Lawrence plays her mother and Arthur Kennedy is her son. Kirk Douglas is the "gentleman caller" upon whom Wyman and Lawrence pin their romantic hopes. But Williams always played better with unrequited love. Such is the case here too. It was remade for television in 1973 with Katharine Hepburn. Another screen version followed in 1987 with Paul Newman directing his wife, Joanne Woodward.

Williams was attracted to the young Marlon Brando when he came to read the part of Stanley Kowalski for his play *A Streetcar Named Desire* in the late 1940s, but Brando had a woman with him at the time. He ended up doing some electrical and plumbing work for Williams instead of sharing his bed. Williams was entranced with the way he read. Brando went on to become a sensation on Broadway playing the sweat-stained Polack. He said he'd never go to Hollywood, but the lure of the almighty dollar proved too great and he played the film role to euphoric reviews in 1951. Vivien Leigh was equally impressive as the woman he destroys, Blanche DuBois.

Williams became disenchanted with Hollywood when it refused to carry the subtext of DuBois's attraction toward young boys in the film. In the play she talks about her dead husband, Allan Gray, telling the audience there was something "different" about him, "a softness and tenderness which wasn't like a man's." She goes on to talk about "that thing," meaning being gay, and how one night she came home to find him with an older man "who had been his friend for years" (Williams, 1947: 70). Her revulsion at what she saw drove her husband to suicide. Blanche subsequently developed an affection for young boys as a kind of tribute to his memory. Gray's gentleness acts as a contrast to the brutish Kowalski, whom Brando played so brilliantly, but the Production Code Administration refused Elia Kazan, directing, to suggest such gentleness came from a gay root. His "different" nature became simply his inability to function as a breadwinner. Kazan capitulated to the PCA just as he did to the McCarthy witch hunt when he "named names."

"I wouldn't put the homosexuality back in the picture if the Code had been revised last night," he said tamely, "and it was now permissible. I don't want it. I prefer the delicately suggested impotence theme. I prefer debility and weakness over any suggestion of perversion" (Schumach, 1975: 74). It's sad to see such homophobia in such a gifted director. Kazan put his head in the sand, ostrich style, simply because the PCA had a fatwa on anything smacking even vaguely of "sex perversion" (Walsh, 1996: 244).

Anna Magnani refused to appear in Williams's play *The Rose Tattoo*, which he wrote for her, when it was first staged, but she won an Oscar for the movie version in 1955. She gave a searing portrayal of a woman obsessed with the memory of her late husband, stealing everything but the cameras. Not many actresses could make Burt Lancaster look insignificant, but she did here. Williams wrote the screenplay for *Baby Doll* the following year. It scandalized America at the time with its pre-Lolita depiction of child bride Carroll Baker gravitating between Eli Wallach and her husband, Karl Malden.

Being gay was an endemic part of the play version of *Cat on a Hot Tin Roof*, but when it was filmed in 1958 this disappeared under the aegis of the Hollywood moguls. Paul Newman played Brick. He had a relationship with a gay boy called Skipper when he was in college. Skipper killed himself when Brick left him. In the film, Brick can't perform sexually with his wife, Maggie (Elizabeth Taylor). One isn't informed why. Impotence is the most likely reason. He's given a pair of crutches to walk around in after suffering an accident. Exactly how lameness could cause impotence beggars the imagination. Richard Brooks, the film's director, caved in to pressure from the PCA to find something to replace Brick's orientation (Phillips, 1980: 144). A ridiculous plot tag had Newman thinking Maggie seduced Skipper, which caused him to take his life (Black, 1997: 185). The play was revived for TV in 1984 with Rip Torn and Jessica Lange. His being gay was given center stage here, where it should have been all along.

Williams was similarly underwhelmed by Joseph L. Mankiewicz's film of *Suddenly, Last Summer* (1959), though in fairness there was very little that could have been done with this by any director. How could one make cannibalism wholesome? Or the prospect of a perfectly healthy woman being threatened with a lobotomy?

Quentin Crisp saw all of Williams's early plays as being about women brought "deliciously low" by their sexual appetites: "His heroines are really men in drag and therefore their lovers are brutes" (Kettlehack, 1984: 86). The reverence he had for Rose was deemed to be the inspiration for *Suddenly, Last Summer*. It continued his frequent depiction of wounded animals, these gentle doves forced to suffer under the rapacious intent of so many Stanley Kowalskis.

Williams linked up with Magnani again for *The Fugitive Kind*. Marlon Brando played the lead. He knew his character was no Stanley Kowalski. He was too passive for him. This was a troubled production. Brando didn't get on with Magnani, who made advances on him that were rebuffed. He fought with Joanne Woodward as well. He even argued with his old Actors Studio colleague, Maureen Stapleton. His only friend on the set seemed to be the film's director, Sidney Lumet, who had him on a pedestal.

The tense atmosphere should have made for good drama, but it didn't. The reworking of Williams's hell-themed play, *Orpheus Descending*, became hellish itself, an aimless descent into a hothouse Hades in the Deep South with its characters ill-conceived and ill-developed. Williams told everyone he knew to stay away from it after it was released. A 1990 TV film that returned it to its original title fared somewhat better. Here Vanessa Redgrave played the Magnani role of Lady Torrance. She loves not wisely but too well and suffers the consequences. Kevin Anderson took the Brando role of the drifter who meets a tragic fate.

When a young stud romances an older woman in films, it's often a code for the fact that he's gay. Such would seem to be the case in *The Roman Spring of Mrs. Stone* (1961), based on Williams's only novel. It starred Warren Beatty in just his second film and Vivien Leigh in her second-to-last one. It became turgid fare under Jose Quintero's plodding direction. It's interesting today more as a curiosity piece than anything else.

Geraldine Page played the repressed daughter of a minister in *Summer and Smoke* (1961). Laurence Harvey is the doctor she falls madly in love with, but Harvey is more drawn to the dancer played by Rita Moreno. Page was entrancing but the film itself, like so many Williams adaptations, failed to reach liftoff. *Period of Adjustment* (1962), an uncharacteristic light piece, fared surprisingly better. It dealt with two troublesome marriages, one between confused Southern belle Jane Fonda and her battle-scarred husband, Jim Hutton, and the other between Hutton's wartime friend Tony Franciosa and Lois Nettleton. Nettleton stole the film with her comic timing.

If Geraldine Page was impressive in *Summer and Smoke*, she excelled in *Sweet Bird of Youth*, Williams's poignant tale of a faded movie diva who takes to the bottle in a small Southern town. Paul Newman costarred.

Williams's adaptations continued to be intermittently successful on screen. Richard Burton was excellent as a defrocked cleric in *The Night of the Iguana* (1964). He was ably supported by Ava Gardner as a hotelier and Deborah Kerr as the third part of a love triangle explored with the consummate skill one had come to expect from director John Huston.

Francis Ford Coppola, then relatively unknown, was one of three writers who adapted Williams's play *This Property Is Condemned* for the screen in 1966. It had Natalie Wood being used by her mother to attract customers to her boardinghouse during the Depression. Wood falls for Robert Redford in the course of it, hoping he'll release her from her stultifying life.

Williams wasn't in a good place during these years. His partner, Frank Merlo, died of cancer in 1963, which made him feel as low as he was when he lost Rose. He continued to write, but Hollywood seemed to have turned its back on him. Sidney Lumet filmed one of his lesser-known plays, *The Seven Descents of Myrtle*, in 1970. The film version was called *The Last of the Mobile Hot Shots*, but it was a disaster. It's a collector's item today.

There are very few overtly gay characters in Williams's work. He claimed to have sought a broader church. It might be beneficial to see his female characters as his gay side. His reticence could have been the result of bashfulness. "I was a virgin with either sex until the age of 26," he said once (Spoto, 1985: 65). In general he regarded his libido as a "powerful burden" (Spoto, 109).

His health failed him during his later years. He had high blood pressure, his head feeling like a smoking volcano as he tried to keep his energy levels up with alcohol, or anything else that was ready to hand. Insomnia also plagued him. He took pills to sleep and black coffee to adrenalize him when he woke. He had an irregular heartbeat; his mind was prey to the fusillade of nervous traumas that found their way into his work.

By the time *Cat on a Hot Tin Roof* was revived on TV, Williams had died from a freakish cause, choking on the cap of the bottle he used for his eyedrops. This had somehow got into his mouth. Perhaps he was groggy or drugged at the time. He'd been prey to substance abuse all his life.

He left behind him a legacy of some of the most explosive plays ever written. If they didn't always make great films, one shouldn't necessarily blame the people involved. Film and theatre are two diametrically opposed disciplines. Often they mix about as well as oil and water.

Related Films
A Streetcar Names Desire (1951); *Cat on a Hot Tin Roof* (1958); *Suddenly, Last Summer* (1959); *The Tennessee Williams South* (1973); *Cat on a Hot Tin Roof* (1984); *You Taste American* (1986); *Talk to Me Like the Rain* (1989); *The Tennessee Williams Film Collection* (2006); *The Sons of Tennessee Williams* (2010).

Further Reading
Black, Gregory D. 1997. *The Catholic Crusade against the Movies: 1940–1975*. Cambridge: Cambridge University Press.

Hayman, R. 1993. *Tennessee Williams: Everybody Else in an Audience*. New Haven, CT: Yale University Press.

Kettlehack, Guy, ed. 1984. *The Wit and Wisdom of Quentin Crisp*. New York: Harper & Row.

Phillips, Gene D. 1980. *The Films of Tennessee Williams*. Philadelphia: Arts Alliance Press.

Schumach, Murray. 1975. *The Face on the Cutting Room Floor: The Story of Movie and Television Censorship*. New York: Da Capo.

Spoto, Donald. 1985. *The Kindness of Strangers: The Life of Tennessee Williams*. New York: Ballantine Books.

Walsh, Frank. 1996. *Sin and Censorship: The Catholic Church and the Motion Picture Industry*. New Haven, CT, and London: Yale University Press.

Williams, Tennessee. 1947. *A Streetcar Named Desire*. New York: Modern Library.

Yacowar, Maurice. 1977. *Tennessee Williams and Film*. New York: Frederick Ungar Publishing.

Glossary

ACT UP
AIDS Coalition to Unleash Power.

AMPAS
American Motion Picture Academy of Arts and Sciences.

BDD
Body Dysmorphic Disorder; the feeling that some aspect of one's body or appearance is severely flawed and warrants exceptional measures to fix or hide it.

Beits Society
The first lesbian civil and political rights organization in the United States.

BFI
British Film Institute.

CRA
Code and Ratings Administration.

FDA
Food and Drug Administration.

GLAAD
Gay and Lesbian Alliance Against Defamation.

Gran Fury
AIDS activist collective.

Homophobia
Dislike of or prejudice toward gay people.

HUAC
House Un-American Activities Committee.

MPAA
Motion Picture Association of America.

MPPDA
Motion Picture Producers and Distributors of America.

NCOMP
National Catholic Office for Motion Pictures.

New Queer Cinema
Term coined by B. Ruby Rich in the late 1980s to describe a style of LGBTQ filmmaking that evinced a politicized attitude toward queer culture.

OutRage
British LGBTQ rights group that was in existence from 1990 to 2011.

PCA
Production Code Administration.

PFLAG
Parents, Families, and Friends of Lesbians and Gays, the first and largest organization in the United States devoted to uniting LGBTQ families.

Pre-Code
Denoting a time in films that predated the PCA directive of 1934 to rid films of "moral turpitude."

SAG
Screen Actors Guild.

Sex Reassignment Surgery (SRS)
Surgical procedure by which a transgender person's physical appearance and/or their sexual characteristics are altered to resemble those associated with their identified gender.

SRC
Studio Relations Committee.

TAG
Treatment Action Group.

Transgender
A person whose sense of identity fails to correspond with their birth sex.

Transphobia
Dislike of or prejudice against transsexual and/or transgender people.

Select Bibliography

Aaron, Michele. 1999. *The Body's Perilous Pleasures: Dangerous Desires and Contemporary Culture.* Edinburgh: Edinburgh University Press.
Aitken, Will. 2011. *Death in Venice: A Queer Film Classic.* Vancouver, BC: Arsenal Pulp Press.
Angelides, Steven. 2001. *A History of Bisexuality.* Chicago: University of Chicago Press.
Anger, Kenneth. 1986. *Hollywood Babylon.* London: Arrow.
Aquino, Eloisa. 2009. *The Life and Times of Bitch Dykes: Gladys Bentley.* Montreal: B&D Press.
Barson, Michael. 1995. *The Illustrated Who's Who of Hollywood Directors.* New York: Farrar, Straus and Giroux.
Bataille, George. 1986. *Erotism: Death and Sensuality.* San Francisco: City Lights.
Benshoff, Harry. 2004. *Queer Cinema: The Film Reader.* New York: Routledge.
Berenstein, Rhona. 1996. *Attack of the Leading Ladies: Gender, Sexuality and Spectatorship in Classic Horror Cinema.* New York: Columbia University Press.
Bronski, Michael. 1984. *The Making of Gay Sensibility.* Boston: South End Press.
Brown, Shane. 2016. *Queer Sexualities in Early Film: Cinema with Male-Male Intimacy.* London: I. B. Tauris.
Brunow, Dagmar, and Simon Dickel, eds. 2018. *Queer Cinema.* Mainz, Germany: Ventil Verlag.
Butler, J. 1999. *Feminist Film Theory: A Reader.* Edinburgh: Edinburgh University Press.
Byars, Jackie. 1991. *All That Heaven Allows: Re-reading Gender in 1950s Melodrama.* London: Routledge.
Castle, Terry. 1993. *The Apparitional Lesbian: Female Homosexuality and the Modern Culture.* New York: Columbia University Press.
Chauncey, George. 1994. *Gay New York: Gender, Urban Culture and the Making of the Gay Male World 1890–1940.* New York: Basic.
Cleto, Fabio, ed. 1999. *Queer Aesthetics and the Performing Subject: A Reader.* Edinburgh: Edinburgh University Press.
Clover, Carol J. 1992. *Men, Women and Chainsaws: Gender in the Modern Horror Film.* Princeton, NJ: Princeton University Press.

Coon, David R. 2018. *Turning the Page: Storytelling as Activism in Queer Film and Media*. New Brunswick, NJ: Rutgers University Press.
Crisp, Quentin. 2008. *How to Become a Virgin*. New York: Flamingo.
De Lauretis, Teresa, ed. 1994. *The Practice of Love: Lesbian Sexuality and Perverse Desire*. Bloomington: Indiana University Press.
Devor, Holly. 1989. *Gender Bending: Confronting the Limits of Duality*. Bloomington: Indiana University Press.
Doty, Alexander. 1993. *Making Things Perfectly Queer: Interpreting Mass Culture*. Minneapolis: University of Minnesota Press.
Duberman, Martin Baum. 1994. *Stonewall*. New York: Penguin.
Dyer, Richard, ed. 1984. *Gays and Film*. London: Zoetrope.
Elliott-Smith, Darren. 2016. *Queer Horror Film and Television*. London: I. B. Tauris.
Epstein, Julia, and Kristina Straub. 1991. *Body Guards: The Cultural Politics of Gender Ambiguity*. New York: Routledge.
Farmer, Brett. 2000. *Spectacular Passions: Cinema, Fantasy, Gay Male Partnerships*. Durham, NC, and London: Duke University Press.
Franzen, Trisha. 1996. *Spinsters and Lesbians*. New York: New York University Press.
Fuss, Diana, ed. 1992. *Inside/Out: Lesbian Theories, Gay Theories*. New York: Routledge.
Gamman, L., and M. Makinen. 1994. *Female Fetishism*. New York: New York University Press.
Gamman, Lorraine, and Margaret Marshment, ed. 1988. *The Female Gaze*. London: The Women's Press.
Geraghty, C. 2005. *My Beautiful Laundrette*. London: I. B. Tauris.
Gill, John. 1995. *Queer Noises: Male and Female Sexuality in Twentieth-Century Music*. London: Cassell.
Gilman, Sander. 1985. *Difference and Pathology: Stereotypes of Sexuality, Race, and Madness*. Ithaca, NY: Cornell University Press.
Greven, David. 2017. *Intimate Violence: Hitchcock, Sex and Queer Theory*. London and New York: Oxford University Press.
Griffiths, Robin. 2009. *Queer Cinema in Europe*. Chicago: University of Chicago Press.
Hanson, Ellis. 1999. *Out Takes: Essays on Queer Theory and Film*. Durham, NC: Duke University Press.
Hart, Kylo-Patrick. 2000. *The AIDS Movie: Representing a Pandemic in Film and Television*. New York: Haworth Press.
Higham, Charles, and Roy Moseley. 1989. *Cary Grant: The Hungry Heart*. New York: Avon Books.
Higham, Charles. 2009. *In and Out of Hollywood: A Biographer's Memoir*. London: Terrace Books.
Holmlund, Christine. 2017. *Female Trouble: A Queer Film Classic*. Vancouver, BC: Arsenal Pulp Press.
Hoskyns, Barney. 1992. *Montgomery Clift: Beautiful Loser*. New York: Grove Atlantic.

Jancovich, Mark, Antonio Lazaro Reboll, Julian Stringer, and Andy Willis, eds. 2003. *Defining Cult Movies: The Cultural Politics of Oppositional Taste.* Manchester and New York: University of Manchester Press.

Jay, Karla, ed. 1995. *Lesbian Erotics.* New York: New York University Press.

Jivani, Alkarim. 1997. *It's Not Unusual: The History of Lesbian and Gay Britain in the Twentieth Century.* London: Michael O'Mara.

Jones, Dan. 2017. *50 Queers Who Changed the World: A Celebration of LGBTQ Icons.* Melbourne: Hardie Grant Books.

Katz, Jonathan Ned. 1992. *Gay American History: Lesbians and Gay Men in the U.S.A.* New York: Penguin.

Kuznier, Alice A. 2000. *The Queer German Cinema.* Palo Alto, CA: Stanford University Press.

Lewes, Kenneth. 1995. *Psychoanalysis and Male Homosexuality.* Northvale, NJ: Jason Aranson Inc.

Lindner, Katharine. 2017. *Film Bodies: Queer Feminist Encounters with Gender and Sexuality in Cinema.* London: I. B. Tauris.

Loughery, John. 1998. *The Other Side of Silence: Men's Lives and Gay Identities.* New York: Henry Holt.

Loughlin, Gerard. 2004. *Alien Sex: The Body and Desire in Cinema and Theology.* Oxford: Blackwell Publishing.

Maddison, S. 2000. *Fags, Hags and Queer Sisters: Gender Dissent and Heterosocial Bonding in Gay Culture.* Basingstoke, UK: Palgrave Macmillan.

Malone, Michael. 1979. *Heroes of Eros: Male Sexuality in the Movies.* New York: Dutton.

Mann, William J. 1998. *Wisecracker: The Life and Times of William Haines, Hollywood's First Openly Gay Star.* New York: Viking.

Marmor, Judd. 1985. *Sexual Inversion: Multiple Roots of Homosexuality.* New York: Basic Books.

Mennel, M. 2007. *The Representation of Masochism and Queer Desire in Film and Literature.* New York: Palgrave.

Mercer, Kobena. 1994. *Welcome to the Jungle: New Positions in Black Cultural Studies.* New York: Routledge.

Money, John. 1988. *Gay, Straight and In-Between: The Sexology of Erotic Orientation.* New York: Oxford University Press.

Munn, Michael. 1997. *The Sharon Stone Story.* London: Robson.

Namaste, Viviane K. 2000. *Invisible Lives: The Erasure of Transsexual and Transgender People.* Chicago: University of Chicago Press.

Pavda, Gilad. 2014. *Queer Nostalgia in Cinema and Pop Culture.* London: Palgrave Macmillan.

Peele, T., ed. 2011. *Queer Popular Culture: Literature, Media, Film and Television.* New York: Palgrave Macmillan.

Pramaggiore, Maria T. 2008. *Neil Jordan.* Champaign: University of Illinois Press.

Price, Theodore. 1992. *Hitchcock and Homosexuality.* Metuchen, NJ: Scarecrow Press.

Prono, Luca. 2008. *Encyclopedia of Gay and Lesbian Popular Culture*. London and Westport, CT: Greenwood Press.
Reading, Mario. 2006. *The Movie Companion*. London: Constable & Robinson.
Rees-Roberts, Nick. 2008. *French Queer Cinema*. Edinburgh: Edinburgh University Press.
Richards, Stuart James. 2016. *The Queer Festival: Popcorn and Politics*. New York: Palgrave Macmillan.
Rodowick, David N. 1991. *The Difficulty of Difference: Psychoanalysis, Sexual Difference and Film Theory*. New York: Routledge.
Rogin, Michael Paul. 1987. *Ronald Reagan: The Movies and Other Episodes in Political Demonology*. Berkeley: University of California Press.
Rutherford, Jonathan, ed. 1990. *Identity: Community, Culture, Difference*. London: Lawrence & Wishart.
Samuels, Stuart. 1983. *Midnight Movies*. New York: Macmillan.
Schoonover, Karl, and Rosalind Galt. 2016. *Queer Cinema in the World*. Durham, NC: Duke University Press.
Sedgwick, Eve Kosofsky. 1990. *Epistemology of the Closet*. Berkeley: University of California Press.
Signorile, Michelangelo. 1993. *Queer in America: Sex, Media and the Closets of Power*. New York: Random House.
Smith, Justin. 2010. *Withnail and Us: Cult Films and Film Cults in British Cinema*. London: I. B. Tauris.
Smith, Paul Julian. 1994. *Desire Unlimited: The Cinema of Pedro Almodovar*. New York: Verso.
St. Michael, Mick. 1989. *James Dean in His Own Words*. London: Omnibus Press.
Stacey, Jackie, and Sarah Street. 2007. *Queer Screen: A Screen Reader*. New York: Routledge.
Stempel, Penny. 2000. *River Phoenix: They Died Too Young*. New York: Parragon Books.
Tasker, Yvonne. 2010. *Fifty Contemporary Film Directors*. London: Routledge.
Thomas, Bob. 1992. *The Films of Marlon Brando*. New York: Citadel.
Troy, Michael, and Darren G. Davis. 2017. *The Stonewall Riots*. Vancouver, WA: TidalWave.
Valentine, David. 2007. *Imagining Transgender: An Ethnography of a Category*. Durham, NC: Duke University Press.
Vieira, Mark A. 1999. *Sin in Soft Focus: Pre-Code Hollywood*. New York: Harry N. Abrams.
Viertel, Salka. 1969. *The Kindness of Strangers*. New York: Holt, Rinehart and Winston.
Walker, Alexander. 1968. *Sex in the Movies: The Celluloid Sacrifice*. London: Pelican.
Walters, Margaret. 1978. *The Nude Male: A New Perspective*. London: Penguin.
Warner, Michael, ed. 1993. *Fear of a Queer Planet*. Minneapolis: University of Minnesota Press.
Watney, Simon. 1989. *Policing Desire: Pornography, AIDS and the Media*. Minneapolis: University of Minnesota Press.

Waugh, Thomas. 1996. *Hard to Imagine: Gay Male Eroticism in Photography and Film from Their Beginnings to Stonewall.* New York: Columbia University.
Weeks, Jeffrey. 1985. *Sexuality and Its Discontents: Meanings, Myths and Modern Sexualities.* London: Routledge & Kegan Paul.
Weeks, Jeffrey. 2016. *Coming Out: The Emergence of LGBT Identities in Great Britain from the Nineteenth Century to the Present.* London: Quartet.
Williams, C. 1996. *Cinema: The Beginnings and the Future.* London: University of Westminster Press.
Wilson, Andrew. 2010. *Beautiful Shade: A Life of Patricia Highsmith.* London: Bloomsbury.
Wingate, James. 1933. *Queen Christina File: Motion Picture Association of America.* Production Code Administration Records.
Woodlawn, Holly, and Jeff Copeland. 1991. *A Low Life in High Heels: The Holly Woodlawn Story.* New York: St. Martin's Press.

Index

Page references to main entries are indicated by **bold type**.

Aaron, Michele, 257
Abba, 1
About a Boy, 113
Abrupt Decision, xxv
Absolute Beginners, 26
Academy Awards. *See* Oscars
Accident, 237
ACT UP, xxvi, 7, 109
Actor's Studio, The, 32
Actress, The, 208, 210
Adams, Margie, 119
Adams, Nick, 87, 226
Adam's Rib, 72
Adventures of Huckleberry Finn, The, 61
Adventures of Priscilla, Queen of the Desert, The, **1–2**, 65, 75, 203
Advise & Consent, xvi, **3–4**, 161, 252, 274. *See also* Blackmail; Gay bars on screen; Suicide
Affleck, Ben, 272
Affleck, Casey, 272
Agitprop, 7, 108–109, 168, 239
Aherne, Brian, 61
AIDS, xix, xxiii, xxvi, **5–7**, 87, 107, 109, 112, 128, 155, 195, 196, 203, 205, 242. *See also Dallas Buyers Club*; *Early Frost, An*; Hudson, Rock; Jarman, Derek; Liberace; *Living End, The*; *Longtime Companion*; *Parting Glances*; Perkins, Anthony; *Philadelphia*
AIDS: Words from One to Another, 7
Airbrushing of gay/lesbian elements from films. *See Bonnie and Clyde*; *Cat on a Hot Tin Roof*; *Children's Hour, The*; *Fox, The*; *Fried Green Tomatoes at the Whistle Stop Café*; *Queen Christina*; *Streetcar Named Desire, A*; *Tea and Sympathy*
Albert Nobbs, 65
Alda, Alan, 6
Alderman, Naomi, 98
Aldrich, Robert, 11–12, 63, 150, 151
Alexander the Great, 146
Algie the Miner, 48
Ali, Mahershala, 188–189, 190
All about Eve, xiv, **8–10**
All about My Mother, 7
All That Heaven Allows, 114, 115
All the Marbles, 150
All the Queen's Men, 65
Allen, Corey, 225
Allen, Jay Presson, 50, 89
Allen, Karen, 66, 67
Allen, Peter, 87
Allen, Woody, xviii
Almodovar, Pedro, 7
Altman, Bruce, 164, 166
Altman, Robert, xvii, 87, 88
American Beauty, 203
American Crime, 167
American Film, 217
American Gigolo, xviii
American Motion Picture Academy of Arts and Sciences (AMPAS), 171, 263
Ammiano, Tom, 265
And the Band Played On, 6, 264
Anders als die Andern, 252
Anderson, John, 1
Anderson, Judith, xiv, 222–223
Anderson, Robert, 259–260
Anderson Tapes, The, 173–174
Andrea Chénier, 7, 215

Andresen, Bjorn, 22
Andress, Ursula, xviii–xix
Andrews, Julie, 64, 241, 276, 277
Androgyny, 41, 58, 71, 87, 128, 131, 164, 200, 202. *See also* Bankhead, Tallulah; Bowie, David; Brando, Marlon; Clift, Montgomery; Cross-dressing; Dietrich, Marlene; Garbo, Greta; Hepburn, Katharine; *Ladies or Gentlemen*; *Rocky Horror Picture Show, The*
Angeli, Pier, 86, 87
Angelic Conversation, The, 146
Anger, Kenneth, 172
Angus, David, 133
Anna Karenina, 120
Anne of the Thousand Days, 246
Annie, 287
Annie Hall, 64
Another Country, 111, 291
Another Gay Movie, xxiii
Anti-semitism, 256–257
Any Day Now, xxvi
Araki, Gregg, xx, 6, 166–168
Arbuckle, Fatty, 60, 75
Arkin, Alan, 210
Arlen, Alice, 238
Armstrong, Benita, 161
Arnette, Jeanetta, 27
Aron, Ernie, 103
Aronofsky, Darren, xxiv
Arquette, Patricia, 112
Art house, xx, 69, 146, 171, 197, 206, 237
Arzner, Dorothy, **10–12**
(A)Sexual, xxv
Ashley, xxvii
Assassins, 127
August, xxv, 26
August, Kim, 194
Avnet, Jon, xx

Babenco, Hector, 152, 153, 202
Baby Doll, 292–293
Bacall, Lauren, xiv, 200
Backbeat, 134
Backstage Passes, 26
Baideo, Matthew, 172
Baker, Carroll, 293
Baker, Roy Ward, 21
Bakula, Scott, 203
Balcony, The, 53

Baldwin, Alec, 280
Baldwin, James, 172
Baldwin, William, xx
Bale, Christian, 128, 129
Ball, Lucille, 11, 118
Ballad of Little Joe, 64
Balsam, Martin, 173–174
Bambi, xxvii
Bancroft, Anne, 138, 266
Banderas, Antonio, xxi, 7, 214–215
Bankhead, Tallulah, 8, 9, **13–14**
Barbarella, 284
Barbette, 243
Bardot, Brigitte, 210
Barlow, James, 245
Barnett, Angela. *See* Bowie, Angie
Barondess, Barbara, 221
Barretts of Wimpole Street, The, 160
Barrios, Richard, xxviii–xxix
Bartel, Paul, 144
Basic Instinct, **15–17**, 163–164, 168, 195
Basic Instinct 2, 16, 113
Basquiat, 26
Bassey, Shirley, 255
Bast, William, 63, 87
Bates, Alan, 125
Bates, Barbara, 8, 9
Batman, 170
Batman Dracula, 282
Battle Cry, 141
Battle of the Sexes, xxviii
Baxter, Anne, xiv, 8, 54
Be Like Others, xxiii
Beach Rats, xxviii
Bean, Sean, 147
BearCity, xxiv
"Beards." *See* Heterosexual relationships of gay/lesbian characters in films; Heterosexual relationships of gay/lesbian people in real life; Marriage as gay/lesbian cover
Beatles, The, 82, 84, 131–132, 133, 134
Beaton, Cecil, 119
Beatty, Ned, xvii
Beatty, Warren, xvi
Beautiful Darling, xxiv
Beckett, Samuel, 191
Becoming Chaz, xxv
Beethoven's Nephew, 283
Before Stonewall, **18–20**
Beginners, xxiv
Behind the Candelabra, 163–164

Index

Behind the Screen, 48
Bell-Metereau, Rebecca, 61, 88, 158, 241
Belmondo, Jean-Paul, 62
Benevides, Robert, 38–39
Ben-Hur, 50, 278–280
Benshoff, Harry, 139
Bentley, Gladys, 18
Berenson, Berintha, 210, 211
Berg, A. Scott, xviii
Bergen, Candice, 53, 72, 173
Berger, Helmut, 62, 96
Bergman, Ingmar, 33, 192
Berkeley, Xander, 128
Berkowitz, Richard, xxiii
Berlin Film Festival, xx, 172–173
Berlin Stories, The, 41
Bernhardt, Sandra, 99
Bernstein, Elmer, 114
Bernstein, Leonard, 32
Bertolucci, Bernardo, 33
Bessie, xxvii
Best, Pete, 132
Best Man, The, 4, 280
Betsy, The, 252
Better Dead Than Gay, 253
Beymer, Richard, 144
Beyond the Valley of the Dolls, 194
Bi the Way, xxiii
Big Mamma's House, 65
Big Sleep, The, 193
Bike Boy, 283
Bill of Divorcement, A, 71
Billy the Kid (film), 280
Billy the Kid (person), 278
Binarism, xiv, xxiii, xxvi, 35, 221
Biopics. *See Dallas Buyers Club*; *Danish Girl, The*; *Dog Day Afternoon*; *Milk*; *Queen Christina*; *Silkwood*
Birdcage, The, xviii–xxix, 65
Birds Do It, 144
Bisexuality, xvii, 12, 30, 33, 58, 74–75, 167, 174, 207, 210, 243. *See also Basic Instinct*; Bowie, David; Brando, Marlon; *Cabaret*; *Carol*; Dean, James; *Desert Hearts*; Dietrich, Marlene; Everett, Rupert; *Fox, The*; *Hours and Times, The*; Mineo, Sal; *Silkwood*; *Spartacus*; *Staircase*; *Sunday Bloody Sunday*; Vidal, Gore; Warhol, Andy
Biskind, Peter, xx, 168
Bisset, Jacqueline, 72

Bissinger, Karl, 44
Black, Dustin Lance, xxiii, 178
Black, Karen, xvii, 88
Black Comedy, 6, 23, 100, 149–150, 158, 166, 272
Black Hole, The, 210
Black Mama, White Mama, 75
Black Sheep of Whitehall, The, 62
Black Swan, xxiv
Blackmail, 133–134. *See also Advise & Consent*; *Victim*
Blackstar, 26
Blanchett, Cate, xxvii, 46, 129, 157
Blinders, xxv
Blonde Venus, 61, 93
Blood for Dracula, 283, 284
Blood Money, 61
Bloomington, xxiv
Blow Job, 282
Blue, 147
Blue Angel, The, 93
Blue Is the Warmest Color, xxvii
Bogarde, Dirk, xv, 4, **21–23**, 55, 97, 136, 236–238
Bogart, Paul, 266, 267
Bogdanovich, Peter, 247, 248
Bolger, John, 207
Bonnie and Clyde, xvi, 168, 262
Bono, Sonny, 286
Boom!, 237, 245
Boorman, John, xvii, 84–85
Bosko, Mark, 195
Boston Strangler, The, 75, 194
Bostonians, The, 202
Bostwick, Barry, 230
Bosworth, Patricia, 54
Botkins, Dawn, 187
Bound, **23–24**, 156
Bourdet, Edouard, 18
Bourne, Stephen, xv, 21
Bow, Clara, 11
Bowie, Angie, 26
Bowie, David, **25–26**, 130, 138, 139–140
Bowie, Duncan, 25
Bowling for Columbine, 272
BoxOffice, 109
Boy Erased, xxviii
Boy George, xxii, 69
Boy Meets Girl, xxvii
Boyd, Stephen, 278
Boyhood, 190
Boyle, Peter, 195

Boys Don't Cry, xxii, **27–29**, 196, 208. *See also* Teena, Brandon; Homophobia; Murder; *Rope*
Boys in the Band, The, xvii, xxix, **29–31**, 50, 65, 228–229
Boys Next Door, The, 195
Bracco, Lorraine, 272
Brady, James, 163
Braga, Sonia, 152
Brambell, Wilfred, 83
Brando, Marlon, xiv, **31–34**, 86, 87, 194, 287
    cross-dresses in *The Missouri Breaks*, 64
    Fugitive Kind, The, 293
    interview ambush by Truman Capote, 44–45
    Reflections in a Golden Eye, 227–229
    Streetcar Named Desire, A, 292
Brando Unzipped, 31–32
Brandon, Michael, 88
Brandon, Teena. *See* Teena, Brandon
Brandon Teena Story, The, xxiv, 29
Brass, Tinto, 279
Bratt, Benjamin, 112
Braveheart, 109
Break My Fall, xxv
Breaking the Rules, xxvii
Breathless, 168
Breen, Joseph, 3, 14, 49–50, 220–221, 223
Brian, Denis, 14
Bridegroom, xxvii
Bridges, Beau, 210
Bridges, Jeff, 63
Brief Encounter, 47, 84, 99
Briggs, John, 53
Briggs Initiative. *See* Proposal 6
Bright, Susie, 24, 49
Bringing Up Baby, 61, 168
Briscoe, Brent, 191
Britell, Nicholas, 190
British Film Institute, 48
Broadway Melody, 48
Broderick, Matthew, 266, 267
Brodie, V. S., 123
Brokeback Mountain, xxii, xxix, **34–36**, 125–126, 156, 203–204
Brolin, Josh, 179
Brook, Kelly, xx
Brooks, Louise, 119
Brooks, Richard, 293
Broomfield, Nick, 185, 187

Browbeat, 134
Brown, Jimmy, 195
Brown, Joe E., 61, 70, 157, 242
Brown, Rita Mae, 18
Brown, Rob, 272
Browne, Coral, 149–150, 151
Browning, Tod, 100
Bruce, Lenny, 202
Brute Force, 193
Bryant, Anita, 180, 181
Bryant, Wayne, 231
Brynner, Yul, 182
Buchanan, Pat, xx
Buddies, 5
"Buddy" films. *See Brokeback Mountain*; *Kiss of the Spider Woman*; *Living End, The*; *Midnight Cowboy*
Bullock, Sandra, 16
Bumming Cigarettes, 242
Bump in the Night, A, 174
Burden of Proof, The, 245
Burning Hills, The, 141–142
Burns, Kevin, 157
Burr, Geraldine, 39
Burr, Raymond, xv, **37–39**, 142. *See also* Heterosexual relationships of gay/lesbian characters in films; Heterosexual relationships of gay/lesbian people in real life; Marriage as gay/lesbian cover; Transvestism
Burroughs, William S., 271, 272, 288
Burston, Paul, 69
Burton, Mary, 54
Burton, Richard, 237, 244–246, 294
Burton, Tim, 122
Burwell, Carter, 47
Buscemi, Steve, 207
Bush, George, xx, 168
Butch Cassidy and the Sundance Kid, 35, 50, 261, 262–263
Butch Jamie, xxiii
Butler, Ken, 109
Butler, Robert, 87–88
Butterfly Kiss, 195

Cabaret, **41–43**, 95, 202, 241
Caffrey, Stephen, 169
Cage aux Folles, La, xviii, 64, 65
Caged, xiv, 50, 194
Cagney, James, 61
Cain, James M., 129

Index

Caine, Michael, xviii, 64, 89–91, 155, 174
Calamity Jane, 62
Calderon, Paul, 174
Calhoun, Rory, xiv, 141
Calicos, John, 195
California Suite, 174
Caligula, 155, 279, 280
Call Me Kuchu, xxvi
Callas, Maria, 7
Callow, Simon, xxi, xxii, 161
Camille, 72, 120
Camp (film), 282
Camp (style), xxi, 26, 61–62, 75, 121, 122, 231, 242–243. *See also Adventures of Priscilla, Queen of the Desert, The*; Bowie, David; *Boys in the Band, The*; *Cabaret*; *Capote*; *Celluloid Closet, The*; Crisp, Quentin; Cross-dressing; *Crying Game, The*; *Dallas Buyers Club*; Divine; *Edward II*; *Glen or Glenda?*; *Hedwig and the Angry Inch*; *Ladies or Gentlemen*; Laughton, Charles; Liberace; *Looking for Langston*; *Myra Breckinridge*; *Paris Is Burning*; *Rocky Horror Picture Show, The*; *Staircase*; *Torch Song Trilogy*; *Victor/Victoria*; Waters, John; Wilde, Oscar
Campbell, Nell, 230
Campbell, Sandy, 32–33
Camus, Albert, 256
Canby, Vincent, 200, 201
Cannes Film Festival, The, 83
Cannon, Dyan, 89, 90, 174
Cantor, Eddie, 60–61
Capote, **43–45**, 204
Capote, Truman, xxii, 32–33, 43–45, 56, 94, 240, 284
Capra, Frank, xxi
Caprice, xvi
Captive, The, 18
Capucine, 50, 194
Caravaggio, 146–147
Caravaggio, Michelangelo Merisi de, 146
Carell, Steve, xxviii
Carlson, Margaret, 263
Carol, xix, xxvii, **46–48**, 129, 204
Caron, Leslie, xv–xvi, 135
Carpenter, Karen, 127
Carpenter, Richard, 127
Carson, Johnny, 45

Casablanca, 165
Casanova and Co., 75
Case Against 8, The, xxvii
Caselli, Chiara, 197
Cash, Johnny, 204
Cash, June, 204
Cassidy, Jack, 194
Cassidy, Patrick, 169
Castrodad, Eddie, 266
Cat on a Hot Tin Roof, xvi, 250, 252, 293, 294
Catered Affair, The, 278
Catholic League of Decency, xiii, 49, 72, 74, 75, 215, 221, 234, 278
Catholic Office for Motion Pictures, 229
Caton-Jones, Michael, 16
Cavalcade of Perversions, A, 100
Cavani, Liliana, 23
Cazale, John, 103
Cecil B. Demented, 288
Celebrity Big Brother, 26
Celluloid Closet, The (book), 11, 173
Celluloid Closet, The (film), xviii, **48–51**, 59
Certificates, xvi, xxiv, 121–122, 151, 174, 201, 202
Chamberlain, Richard, xvii
Chandler, Joan, 232
Chandler, Kyle, 46
Chandler, Raymond, 247
Chaplin, Charlie, 48, 60, 62
Charbonneau, Patricia, 91, 92, 155
Chayefsky, Paddy, 278
Cheever, John, 115
Chelsea Girls, The, 283
Cher, 112, 238, 239
Chester, Craig, 256
Chevalier, Maurice, 119
Cheyenne Autumn, 183
Children, 83
Children's Hour, The, xvi, 50, **51–53**, 117–118, 252, 280
Choirboys, The, 150, 195
Chopin, Frederic, 62
Choreau, Etchika, 143
Chorus Line, A, xxiii
Christian, Marc, 135, 137
Christie, Agatha, 210
Christopher Strong, 11, 61, 157
Cimino, Michael, 63
Circumstance, xxv
City and the Pillar, The, 278

Claire of the Moon, xx
Clark, Gerald, 43, 44, 45
Clarkson, Patricia, 115
Cleopatra, 200, 246
Cleopatra Jones, xvii, xviii, 194
Clift, Montgomery, xiv, 32, **54–57**, 86, 229, 278
    fear of playing sexually ambiguous roles, 235
    original cast choice for *Reflections in a Golden Eye*, 228
    Suddenly, Last Summer, 249–251
Cline, Patsy, 92
Clooney, George, 274
Close, Glenn, 65
Closeted gay and lesbian characters. *See Advise & Consent*; *Bound*; *Desert Hearts*; *Early Frost, An*; *Far from Heaven*; *Parting Glances*; *Victim*
Closeted gay and lesbian directors. *See* Arzner, Dorothy; Cukor, George; Schlesinger, John
Closeted gay and lesbian stars. *See* Bogarde, Dirk; Burr, Raymond; Clift, Montgomery; Everett, Rupert; Foster, Jodie; Hudson, Rock; Hunter, Tab; Laughton, Charles; Liberace; Perkins, Anthony
Clothing as gay/lesbian clue. *See Brokeback Mountain*; Cross-dressing; *Ladies or Gentlemen*; *Rebecca*; *Thelma and Louise*
Cloudburst, xxv
Clum, John, 235
Clyde, Vander. *See* Barbette
Cobain, Kurt, 272
Coburn, James, 194
Cocteau, Jean, 172
Coded gay/lesbian messages. *See All about Eve*; *Children's Hour, The*; Davies, Terence; Gay codes; Hudson, Rock; *Queen Christina*; *Rebecca*; *Rebel without a Cause*; *Rock Hudson's Home Movies*; *Roman Spring of Mrs. Stone, The*; Smoking; *Spartacus*; Vidal, Gore; Williams, Tennessee
Coen Brothers, The, 23
Coffee Date, xxiii
Cohan, Steve, 55
Cole, Nat King, 83
Collette, Toni, 128

Collins, Joan, 246
Collins, Kevin, 110
Collymore, Stan, 16
Combs, Frederick, 30
Come Back to the Five and Dime, Jimmy Dean, Jimmy Dean, 88
Comfort of Strangers, The, 112
Common Threads: Stories from the Quilt, 5–6, 48, 203
Communist Connection with Gay Life, 19, 141
Compulsion, 256, 257
Concussion, xxvii
Confederacy of Dunces, 84
Confidential, xiv–xv, 135, 137, 141, 209
    closure of magazine due to plethora of legal actions, 142–143
    plans to out Marlene Dietrich, 95
    protection of sexuality of Raymond Burr, 38
    sued by Liberace, 162
Conn, Nicole, xx
Connery, Sean, 174, 272
Connolly, Ray, 87
Connotative Homosexuality. *See* Coded gay/lesbian messages
Conroy, John, 291
Continuing Adventures of Reptile Man and His Faithful Sidekick Tadpole, 75
Cooeyate, Doug, 271
Cooper, Chris, 203
Cooper, Gary, xxi, 35, 49, 94, 208
Corber, Robert, 9
Corey, Dorian, 205
Cornelius, Henry, 41
Cotton Club, The, 171–172
Couch, 282
Court, Margaret, xxviii
Courtenay, Tom, 153
Courtneidge, Cicely, xv–xvi
Coward, Noel, 167
Cowgirl roles, 62, 91, 225, 262
Cox, Brian, 164–166
Cox, Richard, 66, 67
Cox, Wally, 32
Craig, Wendy, 236
Crane, Norma, 259
Crash, 203
Crawford, Joan, 13, 61, 62, 72, 120, 129, 150, 225, 230, 287
Crime in the Streets, 183
Crimes of Passion, 210

Crisp, Quentin, xvii, 4, **57–60**, 255
   appears in *Philadelphia*, 214
   on Oscar Wilde, 290
   on Tennessee Williams, 293
   review of *The Hunger*, 139, 140
Cromwell, Vaughn, xx
Cronyn, Hume, 232
Crosby, Bing, 62
Cross-dressing, **60–65**, 144, 208, 211, 277. See also Burr, Raymond; Camp; *Celluloid Closet, The*; Crisp, Quentin; Dekker, Albert; Divine; Drag; *Ladies or Gentlemen*; Wood, D. Edward, Jr.
Crowley, Mart, 29–31
Cruise, Tom, xxi
Cruising, xxvi–xxvii, **65–68**
   homophobic allegations against William Friedkin, 31
   rioting caused by film, 195
Cruz, Penelope, 7
Cry-Baby, 287
"Crying," 192
Crying Game, The, xxix, **68–70**, 203
Cuesta, Michael, xxii, 164–166
Cukor, George, xiii, xv, 61, **71–72**, 208, 210, 291
Cult films. See *Glen or Glenda?*; *Go Fish*; *Hedwig and the Angry Inch*; *Johnny Guitar*; *Killing of Sister George, The*; *Myra Breckinridge*; *Rebel without a Cause*; *Rocky Horror Picture Show, The*; Waters, John
Cumming, Alan, xxvi
Curry, Tim, 63, 157, 158, 230, 231
Curtis, Jill, 75
Curtis, Tony, 48, 60–61, **73–75**, 87, 157, 194, 241, 242–243
Curtiz, Michael, 129
Cyrus, Billy Ray, 191

Daily Mirror, 162
Daldry, Stephen, 156
Dall, John, 193, 232, 241
Dallas Buyers Club, xxvi, xxvii–xxviii, 7, **77–79**, 82. See also AIDS; Oscars; Weight changes for roles
Dallesandro, Joe, 283, 284
Daly, Stephen, 201
Damned, The, 62, 96, 194
Damon, Matt, 17, 179, 203, 272, 273
Damone, Vic, 87

Dance, Girl, Dance, 11
Dance with a Stranger, 112
Dancer, Richard C., 195
Daniels, Jeff, 106
Danish Girl, The, xxvii–xxviii, **79–82**, 204
Danner, Blythe, 210
Dano, Paul, 164–166
Dark Victory, 9
Darling, Candy, xxiv, 283
Darnell, Linda, 154
Darren, Alison, 139
Darrow, Clarence, 233, 257
Daughters of Bilitis Society, 20
David, Zorro, 227
Davidson, Jaye, 68–69, 70, 203
Davies, Terence, **82–85**
Davis, Bette, 7–9, 61, 73, 150, 151, 240, 278
Davis, Brad, 6
Davis, Daniel, 121
Davis, Geena, 156, 261, 262, 263
Davis, Judith, 253
Davis, Viola, 115
Davison, Bruce, 169–170, 203
Day, Doris, xiv, 62, 83, 135, 136–137, 151
Day of the Jackal, The, 194
Day-Lewis, Daniel, 156, 214
De Acosta, Mercedes, 93–94, 119
De Havilland, Olivia, 54, 72
De Mille, Cecil B., 62. See also Cecil B. Demented
De Niro, Robert, 78, 184–185, 228
De Palma, Brian, 64, 158
De Rossi, Portia, xxii
Dean, James, 32, **85–88**, 142, 182–183
   Rebel without a Cause, 224, 226
   River Phoenix comparison, 197–198
   See also Bisexuality; Heterosexual relationships of gay/lesbian characters in films; Heterosexual relationships of gay/lesbian people in real life
Dear Dawn, 187
Deardon, Basil, 273, 275
Death and Transfiguration, 83
Death in Venice, 21, 22, 275
Death of gay/lesbian characters on screen. See *Advise & Consent*; *And the Band Played On*; *Brokeback Mountain*; *Children's Hour, The*; *Cruising*; *Dallas Buyers Club*; *Danish Girl,*

Death of gay/lesbian characters on screen (*cont.*)
    The; *Edward II*; *Fox, The*; *Hunger, The*; *L.I.E.*; *Living End, The*; *Midnight Cowboy*; *Milk*; *Monster*; *Murder*; *Parting Glances*; *Philadelphia*; *Prick Up Your Ears*; *Rebecca*; *Rebel without a Cause*; *Rocky Horror Picture Show, The*; *Strangers on a Train*; *Suddenly, Last Summer*; *Suicide*; *Swoon*; *Thelma and Louise*; *Times of Harvey Milk, The*; *Torch Song Trilogy*; *Victim*
Deathtrap, **89–91**, 155, 174
Decriminalization of homosexuality, 275
Dee, Sandra, 286
Deep Blue Sea, The, 84
Defiant Ones, The, 75
"De-gaying." *See Boy Erased*; *Far from Heaven*; Gay "cures"; *Miseducation of Cameron Post, The*
DeGeneres, Ellen, xxii
Deitch, Donna, xix, 91, 92, 93, 155
Dekker, Albert, 251
Del Rio, Rebekah, 192
Deliverance, xvii
Demme, Jonathan, xxi, 7, 203, 213–215
Dench, Dame Judi, 31
Deneuve, Catherine, 26, 138, 139, 140
Denial of Gay Orientation. *See* Heterosexual relationships of gay/lesbian characters in films; Heterosexual relationships of gay/lesbian people in real life; Marriage as gay/lesbian cover
Dennis, Sandy, xvi, 88, 117–118
Depp, Johnny, 88, 122, 158, 287
Derivative films, 2, 45, 64, 65, 93, 125–126, 168. *See also Far from Heaven*; *Thelma and Louise*
Desert Hearts, xix, **91–93**, 155, 252
Desert of the Heart, 91, 196
Desire, 95
Desire Under the Elms, 143, 208–209
Desperate, 38
Desperate Living, 287
Destry Rides Again, 95
Detective, The, xvi, 50, 67, 194, 252
Devils, The, 146
DeVine, Phillip, 28, 29
DeYoung, Cliff, 138
Diamonds Are Forever, 194
Diane Linkletter Story, The, 99–100, 285–286

Diaz, Cameron, 112
DiCaprio, Leonardo, xxv, 88, 203
Dick, Kirby, xxiv
Dickinson, Angie, 64, 272
Dickinson, Emily, 84
Dietrich, Marlene, 25, 42, 62, **93–96**, 119, 154, 155, 277
    androgynous quality compared to Mae West, 200
    church censure of same sex kiss in *Morocco*, 49
    male attire penchant shared by Greta Garbo, 219
    sex appeal of smoking, 240
    See also Bisexuality; Cross-dressing; Garbo, Greta
Dillman, Bradford, 257
Dillon, Matt, 271, 272
Dino, 183
Dirty Girl, xxiv
Dirty Laundry, xxiii
Disclosure, 163
Disobedience, xi, **96–99**
Distant Voices, Still Lives, 83
Divine, xxvii, **99–102**, 144–145
    collaborations with John Waters, 286–287
    complex nature, 158
    outrageousness, 63
Documentaries. *See Before Stonewall*; *Ladies or Gentlemen*; *Rock Hudson's Home Movies*; *Times of Harvey Milk, The*
Dog Day Afternoon, xvii, 66, **103–104**, 173, 174, 202
Donahue, Troy, 287
Donen, Stanley, 244, 246
Donnelly, Patrice, 211–212
Don't Worry, He Won't Get Far on Foot, 273
Doom Generation, The, 167
Dorian Blues, xxii
D'Orsay, Fifi, 119
Dossett, John, 169
Dottie Gets Spanked, 127
Double Indemnity, 240–241, 247–248
Double Life, A, 72
Dough Boys, The, 60
Douglas, Kirk, xiv, 150, 292
Douglas, Lord Alfred, 289
Douglas, Melvyn, 72
Douglas, Michael, xix, 15, 16, 17, 163–164
Down and Out in Beverly Hills, 5

Index

Dr. Strangelove, 168
Dracula, 193
Dracula's Daughter, xv, 49–50, 154, 193
Drag, 18, 30, 38, 42, 58, 59, 63, 64, 134, 144–145, 163, 200, 206, 210, 229, 265–266, 277. *See also* Camp; Cross-dressing; *Ladies or Gentlemen*
Drag, The, 200
Drag Balls, xxiv, 205–206
Dresden Municipal Women's Clinic, 81
Dress Gray, 280
Dressed to Kill, 64, 158
Dru, Joanne, 55
Drugstore Cowboy, 271
Drum, 195
Drury, Allan, 3
Du Maurier, Daphne, 9, 160
Duchess of Windsor, The, 94
Dukakis, Olympia, xxv
Duke of Burgundy, The, xxvii
Dullea, Keir, 117–118
Dunaway, Faye, xxix, 204
Dunne, Griffin, 77
Dunye, Cheryl, xx
Duralde, Alonso, 66
Durbin, Deanna, 160
Dwan, Allan, 62
Dylan, Bob, 32, 46, 112, 129
Dynasty, 155
Dytri, Mike, 166

Early Frost, An, 5, **106–108**, 156, 214
East of Eden, 85, 88, 226
Eastwood, Clint, xviii, xxv, 63
Eat Your Makeup, 99, 285
Eating Raoul, 144
Ebershoff, David, 80–82
Ebert, Roger, 187
Ed Wood, 122, 158
Eden, Liz, 103
Edie and Thea, xxiv
Edison, Thomas, 48
Edward II (film), xx, **108–111**, 146, 147
Edward II (person), 146
Edwards, Blake, 241, 276, 277
Ehlers, Beth, 138
Eiger Sanction, The, xvii, xviii, 67, 194
Eisenhower, Dwight, xiv, xxvi
Elbe, Lili, xxvii–xxviii, 80–81, 204. *See also Danish Girl, The*
Elephant, 272
Eliot, T. S., 128
Elliot, J. M., 264, 265

Elliott, Laura, 247
Elliott, Stephen, 1, 2
Ellis, Bret Easton, 167
Ellis, Ruth, 112
Ellison, Ben, 172
Emerson, Hope, xiv
Empire, 282
Eno, Brian, 147
Entertaining Mr. Sloane, 217
Ephron, Nora, 238, 239
Epstein, Brian, 131–134
Epstein, Robert, 5–6, 48, 202, 263, 264, 265, 274
ER, 274
Erickson, Leif, 259
Erman, John, 106–107
Escape from the Planet of the Apes, 183
Eszterhas, Joe, 15
Eurythmics, The, 109
Evans, Linda, 155
Even Cowgirls Get the Blues, 272
Evening with Quentin Crisp, An, 59, 60
Everett, Rupert, xxviii, **111–113**, 290–291
Every Act of Life, xxviii
Everybody Loves Sunshine, 26
"Everybody's Talkin'," 177
Exodus, 183
Experimental Films. *See* Haynes, Todd; Jarman, Derek; Troche, Rose; Van Sant, Gus; Warhol, Andy; Waters, John
Extravaganza, Venus, 205, 206
Eyes of Laura Mars, 195

Fairbanks, Douglas, Jr., 13
"Falling in Love Again," 93
Fame, 231
Fanaka, Jamaa, xx
Fantastic Woman, A, 98
Far from Heaven, xxii, xxvii, **114–116**
 compared to *Carol*, 47
 contrasted to *Carol*, 48
 Douglas Sirk influence, 128–129
 Oscar frustration for Todd Haynes, 203
Far from the Madding Crowd, 255
Farewell My Lovely, 194
Farewell to Arms, A, 135
Farrell, Timothy, 121
Farrow, Mia, 237
Fashions for Women, 10–11
Fassbinder, Rainer Maria, 6

Fatal Attraction, 17, 163
Fawcett, Farrah, 199–201
Fear Strikes Out, 142, 208
Feinstein, Dianne, 179, 264
Fell, Lewis Gratz, 185
Female Gothic. See *Hunger, The*; *Rebecca*; Vampirism
Female Trouble, 101, 286–287
Fenn, Sherilyn, xx
Ferguson, Michael, 73
Ferrer, Mel, 95
Fetishism, 222–223, 228, 237, 257
Ffolkes, 210
Fickle Finger of Fate, The, 144
Fields, W. C., 62
Fierstein, Harvey, 48–49, 174, 265–266, 267
Fifth of July, 106
52 Tuesdays, xxvii
Finch, Peter, 90, 151, 153, 155, 202, 253–255, 289–290
Finding Forrester, 272
First a Girl, 272, 276
Firth, Colin, xxiii, 111, 291
Five Easy Pieces, xvii
Flagg, Fannie, xx
Flanagan, Fionnuala, 268, 270
Fleischer, Richard, 257
Fleming, Victor, 71–72
Flesh, 283, 284
Flesh for Frankenstein, 284
Flynn, Errol, 38
Fogle, James, 271
Fonda, Bridget, 195
Fonda, Henry, 2, 4, 161, 280
Fonda, Jane, 54, 209, 284, 294
Fontaine, Joan, 72, 222, 223
Fool Killer, The, 210
For the Bible Tells Me So, xxiii
Forbes, Bryan, xv–xvi
Ford, Harrison, xix
Ford, Tom, xxiii, xxiv
Forman, Milos, 203
Forster, E. M., 275
Forster, Robert, 203
Fortune and Men's Eyes, 183, 252
Forty Deuces, 283
Forwood, Tony, 21
Fosse, Bob, 41–43, 202
Foster, Jodie, 203
Foster, Robert, 191
Four Weddings and a Funeral, xxii

Fox, James, 236, 237–238
Fox, The, xvi, xviii, 50, 53, 63, **116–118**, 155, 213
Franciosa, Tony, 294
Franco, James, xxv, xxvii, 88, 179
Franklin, Marcus Carl, 129
Franks, Robert, 233, 256
Fraser, John, 290
Freaks, 100
Frears, Stephen, 23, 216
Freebie and the Bean, xvii, 50, 63, 67, 194
Freeman, Paul, 195
French Connection, The, 202, 255
Freud, 54, 56–57
Freud, Sigmund, 135
Frey, Leonard, 30
Fricker, Brenda, xxv
Friday the 13th, 144
Fried Green Tomatoes at the Whistle Stop Café, xx
Friedberg, Mark, 116
Friedkin, William, xxvi–xxvii, 29–31, 65–68, 255
Friedman, Jeffrey, 5–6
Friendly Persuasion, 208
Frisk, 195
From Here to Eternity, 56, 261
From Reverence to Rape, 49
From Russia with Love, 194
Fry, Stephen, 7, 290, 291
Fugitive Kind, The, 293
Fugue in a Nursery, 265
Fuller, Dolores, 121
Further off the Straight and Narrow, xxiii

Gable, Christopher, xvii
Gable, Clark, xvii
Gallagher, Maureen, xxiv
Ganoung, Richard, 207
Garbo, Greta, 13, 61, 72, 94, 95, 99, **119–120**, 154, 155, 219–222. See also De Acosta, Mercedes; Dietrich, Marlene; *Queen Christina*
Garbo Talks, 174, 267
Garden, The, 147
Garden of Eden, The, 213
Gardner, Ava, 294
Garland, Judy, 20, 42, 83
Garlin, Jeff, 288
Garner, James, 52, 53, 118, 241, 276, 277
Garner, Jennifer, 77, 78
Garrett, Pat, 278, 280

Index

Gaslight, 72
Gates, Phyllis, 135–136. *See also* Hudson, Rock; Marriage as gay/lesbian cover
Gateways, 151
Gavin, Erica, 194
Gay and Lesbian Alliance Against Defamation (GLAAD), xxv, xxvii, 15–17, 27, 48, 87
Gay bars on screen, 46, 63, 88, 133, 186. *See also Advise & Consent*; *Killing of Sister George, The*; Stonewall Inn; *Victim*
Gay Brothers, The, 48
Gay codes, 10, 21, 53, 55, 71, 74, 135, 136–137, 150
Gay covers, xiv, 121. *See also* "Beards"; Marriage as gay/lesbian cover
Gay "cures," xvii, xxiii, 26, 114–116, 117, 210, 220, 259. *See also Far from Heaven*; *Fox, The*; *Perkins, Anthony*; *Personal Best*; *Tea and Sympathy*
Gay Deceivers, The, xvi
Gay directors. *See* Araki, Gregg; Davies, Terence; Haynes, Todd; Jarman, Derek; Kalin, Tom; Laughton, Charles; Van Sant, Gus; Waters, John
"Gay disease." *See* AIDS
Gay Divorcee, The, 48
Gay employment bigotry, 6, 7, 20, 113, 118, 255
Gay films for straight audiences. *See Brokeback Mountain*; *Fox, The*; *Making Love*; *Personal Best*; *Philadelphia*; *Silkwood*; *To Wong Foo, Thanks for Everything, Julie Newmar*
Gay/lesbian icons, xiv, 8, 24, 144, 150, 151, 172, 197–198, 220, 240, 255, 282
Gay/lesbian identification with evil, xiv, 8, 15–17, 66–67, 121
Gay/lesbian identification with mental illness, 33, 81, 196, 233, 248, 252. *See also Basic Instinct*; *Cruising*; *Living End, The*; *Rope*; *Servant, The*; *Swoon*
Gay/lesbian rumors surrounding stars. *See* Anderson, Judith; Capucine; Davis, Brad; Dietrich, Marlene; Garbo, Greta; Grant, Cary; Hughes, Langston; Kaye, Danny; Power, Tyrone; Scott, Randolph; Stanwyck, Barbara; Webb, Clifton

Gay/lesbian stereotypes, xviii–xix, 48–49, 64, 113, 137, 236, 244–246, 248, 277
Gay liberation, xxv
Gay Men's Health Crisis (GMHC), 171
Gay people in the military, xvi, 19. *See also Gay Deceivers, The*; *Reflections in a Golden Eye*; *Sergeant, The*
Gay Pride Foundation, 182
Gay Times, 110, 167
Gay Zombie, xxiii
Gayby, xxvi
Gaynor, Gloria, 1
"Gayola" scandal, 20
"Gaysploitation," 117. *See also* Homophobia; Lesbophobia
Gazzara, Ben, 107, 214
Gearhart, Sally, 265
Gender disguise films. *See* Cross-dressing; Drag; *Ladies or Gentlemen*
Gene Krupa Story, The, 183
Genet, Jean, 241
Gentlemen Prefer Blondes, 50
Genzlinger, Neil, 288
Gere, Richard, xviii, xix
Gerry, 272
Gershon, Gina, 23, 24, 156
Get 'Em Young, 63
Giant, 86, 87, 183
Gibson, Henry, 157, 226
Gibson, Mel, 109
Gielgud, Sir John, 32, 279
Gilbert, Brian, 290
Gilbert, John, 119, 219, 220, 221
Gilbert, Paul, 62
Gilda, 193
Gilliatt, Penelope, 202
Gilmore, Craig, 166
Gilmore, John, 87
Ginibre, Jean Louis, 157
Ginsberg, Allen, xxiv
Girl He Left Behind, The, 142
Girl Like Me, A: The Gwen Araujo Story, xxii
Girlfriends, 195
Girls about Town, 71
Girls Will Be Boys, 61
Glam Rock, 131. *See also* Bowie, David; *Hedwig and the Angry Inch*; *Velvet Goldmine*
Glaser, Allan, 144, 145
Glaser/Hunter Productions, 145

Index

Glass Menagerie, The, 292
Glen or Glenda?, 62, 63, **120–122**, 158, 231, 241
Gless, Sharon, xxiv
Glitterbug, 147
Gloria, 98
Glover, John, 107
Go Fish, **122–124**, 208
God Help Me, Gregg Araki, 167
Godard, Jean-Luc, 167
Goddard, Paulette, 72
Godfather, The, 43
God's Own Country, **125–126**
Godzilla, King of the Monsters, 38
Gogol, Nikolai, 159
Going Down in La La Land, xxv
Goldberg, Jonathan, 248
Golden Arrow, The, 144
Golden Boy, 193
Goldman, Albert, 133
Gone with the Wind, 71, 260
Gonsalves, Bob, 269
Good Machine, 124
Good Will Hunting, 272
Goodfellas, 23, 170
Gore Vidal: Portrait of a Writer, 280
Gorenson, Alicia, 27
Gorman, Cliff, 30, 194
Gossett, Louis, Jr., 277
Gotham Independent Film Festival, xxv
Government Inspector, The, 159
Graduate, The, 138
Graham, Heather, 271
Graham, Sheilah, 136
Grahame, Gloria, 86
Grand Hotel, 120
Grandma, xxvii
Granger, Farley, 193–194, 232, 235, 241, 247–248
Granger, John, 3
Grant, Cary, 32, 61, 87, 200, 235, 243
Gray, Charles, 230
Grease 2, 144
Great Expectations, 84
Great Imposter, The, 75
Greatest Story Ever Told, The, 183
Green, The, xxv
Green Mansions, 209
Greene, Graham, 269, 270
Greene, Reuben, 30
Greenstreet, Sydney, 102
Gregory, Paul, 161

Grey, Joel, 41–43, 202
Grey, Nan, 193
Griem, Helmut, 41, 241
Griffin, Merv, 248
Griffith, Mary, 253
Griffith, Melanie, 99
Group, The, 53, 173
Grundmann, Roy, 168
Guccione, Bob, 279
Gun Crazy, 168
Gun Hill Road, xxv
Gupta, Sunil, 172
Guthmann, Edward, 30
Gyllenhaal, Jake, 34, 156, 203, 204
Gymnast, The, xxii

Haas, Dolly, 61
Hackett, Joan, 210
Hadleigh, Boze, 223, 251
Haggis, Paul, 203
Hagman, Larry, 173
"Hagsploitation," 150
Haines, William, xiii, 71
Hair, 181
Haircut, 282
Hairdressers of St. Tropez, The, 113
Hairspray, 102, 158, 286, 287
Halberstam, Judith, 17
Hale, William, 163
Hall, Zooey, 252
Halliwell, Kenneth, 216–218
Halston, Julie, 127
Hamlet, 246
Hamlin, Harry, xviii–xix, xxi
Hanks, Tom, xviii, 7, 48, 124
  "everyman" appeal, xxi
  Philadelphia, 213–215
  problem of straight actors playing queer roles, 203
Hannah Free, xxiv
Hanson, Curtis, 144
Happy Prince, The, xxviii, 113, 290–291
Harareet, Haya, 279–280
Hardwicke, Cecil, 232
Hare, David, 290
Harlem Renaissance, The, 171
Harold, Wayne, 195
Harring, Laura Elena, 191, 192
Harris, Julie, 227, 229
Harris, Naomie, 188
Harrison, Rex, 244–246, 255
Harrison, Robert, 135, 141

Index

Harron, Mary, 284
Harry, Debbie, 286, 288
Hart, Harvey, 183
Hart, Ian, 125, 133, 134
Hartman, Tory, 264
Harvey, Laurence, 294
Harvey Milk Day, 182. *See also Milk*; Milk, Harvey; *Times of Harvey Milk, The*
Haskell, Molly, 49, 200
Hatfield, Hurd, 194
Hathaway, Anne, 34, 36
Hawking, Stephen, 81, 204
Hawks, Howard, 55, 61
Hawn, Goldie, 64
Hay, Harry, 18
Hayden, Sterling, 225
Haynes, Todd, xix, xx, xxii, xxvii, **127–130**, 203, 204
   Carol, 46–48
   Far from Heaven, 114–116
Hays, Will, 49–50, 52, 62
Hays Office, The, 52, 223, 260
Haysbert, Dennis, 114
Hayworth, Rita, xxiii, 191
He or She. See Glen or Glenda?
Head, Murray, 155, 253–255
Heard, Amber, 79
Hearst, Patty, 287
Heart Breaks Open, xxv
Hearts of Fire, 112
Heat, 283, 284
Heche, Anne, xxii, 272
Hedwig and the Angry Inch, xxii, **130–131**
Hefner, Hugh, 165, 213
Heiress, The, 54
Heller, Lucas, 150
Hellmann, Lillian, 51
Hello, Darling, Are You Working?, 113
Hello, Dolly, 208
Hemingway, Ernest, 213
Hemingway, Mariel, 211–213
Hemmings, David, 25
Hemphill, Essex, 172
Hendrix, Jimi, 158
Henie, Sonja, 162
Henreid, Paul, 240
Henry IV, 197
Hepburn, Audrey, 52, 53, 118, 252
Hepburn, Katharine, 11, 17, 61, 71, 95, 154, 157, 249–250, 278, 292
Hero, 127

Herren, Roger, 199
Heston, Charlton, 278–279
Heteronormativity. *See* Binarism
Heterophobia, 109, 123, 273
Heterosexual relationships of gay/lesbian characters in films. *See Crying Game, The*; *Fox, The*; Marriage as gay/lesbian cover; *Personal Best*; *Queen Christina*
Heterosexual relationships of gay/lesbian people in real life. *See* Burr, Raymond; Hudson, Rock; Hunter, Tab; Liberace; Marriage as gay/lesbian cover; Perkins, Anthony
Heywood, Anne, 63, 117–118
Hibbert, Alex, 188, 190
Hickock, Richard, 43, 44, 45
Highlights, 147
Highly Strung, 253
Highsmith, Patricia, 46, 129, 247–248
Hill, Anita, 262
Hill, George Roy, 261
Hill, Gladys, 227
Hiller, Arthur, xviii, xxii
Hinwood, Peter, 230
Hirsch, Emile, 179
Hirschfeld, Magnus, 18–19
His Name Is Alive, 167
Hit So Hard, xxv
Hitchcock, Alfred, 13, 38, 46, 62, 64, 160, 232, 234, 235, 241, 247–248, 256
   accusations of homophobia, 193–194
   Anthony Perkins straitjacketing by *Psycho*, 209, 210
   conflation of evil with gay undercurrent in *Rope*, 232–235
   lesbian motif in *Rebecca*, 222
   Psycho seen as black comedy, 158
HIV. *See* AIDS
Hocking, Anthony, 75
Hoffman, Dustin, 64, 138, 176–178, 202
Hoffman, Philip Seymour, xxii, 44–45, 204
Holden, Gloria, 193
Holden, William, 248
Holding the Man, xxviii
Hollywood Androgyny, 158
Hollywood from Vietnam to Reagan, 104
Hollywood Reporter, 201
Holm, Celeste, 9
Home at the End of the World, A, xxii

Homophobia, xiv, xvi, xviii, xxi, 4, 5, 7, 9, 77–78, 115, 150, 181, 203, 244, 246, 248, 250, 256, 266. *See also Basic Instinct*; *Boys Don't Cry*; *Boys in the Band, The*; *Children's Hour, The*; *Cruising*; Everett, Rupert; *Far from Heaven*; *Fox, The*; *Living End, The*; *Longtime Companion*; *Milk*; *Monster*; *Personal Best*; *Rope*; *Silkwood*; *Staircase*; *Strangers on a Train*; *Swoon*
Hoodlum, The, 60
Hooper, Robin, 83
Hooper, Tom, 80, 81, 82
Hoover, J. Edgar, xxv, xxvi
Hope, Bob, 62
Hope, Leslie, 47
Hope, Ted, 124
Hopkins, Miriam, 51, 52
Hopper, Dennis, 87
Hopper, Edward, 115
Hopper, Hedda, 38, 136
Horne, Lena, 1
Horror, 127
Horror movies, 100, 284. *See also Hunger, The*; *Psycho*; *Rocky Horror Picture Show, The*; Vampirism
Hot Chick, The, 65
Hours, The, xxii, xxvii, 156
Hours and Times, The, **131–134**
House of Mirth, The, 84
House Un-American Activities Committee, The (HUAC), xiv, 19, 141
Houston, Whitney, 131
How to Survive a Plague, xxvi
Howard, Leslie, 37
Howes, Keith, 21
Howl, xxiv
Hoyer, Niels, 80
Hudson, Rock, xiv–xv, xix, 21, 61, 73, 74, 115, **135–137**, 154, 155, 162, 163, 183
  Confidential magazine's plans to "out" him, 141
  conflict with James Dean on the set of *Giant*, 86, 87
  contracts AIDS, 5
  discomfort in love scenes with women, 154
  See also Heterosexual relationships of gay/lesbian characters in films; Heterosexual relationships of gay/lesbian people in real life; Marriage as gay/lesbian cover
Huffman, Felicity, 204, 268, 269
Hughes, Barnard, 176, 177
Hughes, Langston, 171–172, 205
Hunchback of Notre Dame, The, 160
Hunger, The, 26, **138–140**
Hunt, Linda, 202
Hunter, Tab, xv, 101–102, **140–145**, 210, 288
  closeted lifestyle, 183
  creates illusion of heterosexuality, 154
  Polyester revives career, 287
  problematic relationship with Anthony Perkins, 209
Hurt, John, 59, 255, 272
Hurt, William, 124, 152, 153, 202, 203
Hush Hush, 141
Huston, Anjelica, 6
Huston, John, 33, 54, 56–57, 63, 144, 194, 199–200, 227, 229, 294
Hutton, Jim, 294
Hyde-White, Wilfrid, 291
Hysteria, 113

I Am a Camera, 41, 42
I Am Divine, xxvii
I Am Michael, xxviii
I Changed My Life, 120
I Confess, 54
I Do, xxvi
I Led Two Lives, 120
I Now Pronounce You Chuck and Larry, xxiii
I Shot Andy Warhol, 284–285
I Want to Get Married, xxv
I Want What I Want, 63
I Want Your Love, xxvi
I Was a Male War Bride, 61
Ibsen, Henrik, 22
Ideal Husband, An, 113
Identity confusion, 28, 62, 63–64, 86, 99, 129, 191–192, 196, 210, 252
If I Had a Million, 160
Iggy Pop, 287
I'm Not There, 46, 129, 157
Iman, 26
Imitation of Life, 115
Importance of Being Ernest, The, 113, 290
In Cold Blood, 43
In Moonlight Black Boys Look Blue, 188

In the Name of the Father, 214
Infamous, 45
Informer, The, 160
Inside Monkey Zetterland, 112
Institute for Sex Research, The, 19
Interior, Leather Bar, xxvi–xxvii
International Stud, The, 265
Interview with the Vampire, xxi
Into the Night, 26
Ireland, John, 55
Ironside, 37
Isherwood, Christopher, 41, 42
Island of Desire, 154
It's My Party, 7
Izzard, Eddie, 65

J. Edgar, xxv
Jack and Diane, xxvi
Jackson, Glenda, xvii, 202, 253–255
Jackson, Kate, xviii
Jagger, Bianca, 112
Jagger, Mick, 26, 230, 284
Jamaica Inn, 160
James, Cary, 163
James Dean, 87–88
James Dean: The First American Teenager, 87
James Dean Story, The, 87
Jamie and Jessie Are Not Together, xxvi
Jannings, Emil, 93
Jarman, Derek, 69, 108–111, **146–147**, 154, 155
Jeffries, Lionel, 290
Jenkins, Berry, 188, 189
Jenkins, Patty, 184, 187, 196, 203
Jenner, Bruce, 82
Jenner, Caitlin, 82
Jennings, Rich, 15–16
Jeremy, 25
Jerome, Jharrel, 189
Jesus and Mary Chain, The, 167
Jobriath, A.D., xxvi
Johnny Carson, 239
Johnny Guitar, 50, 62, 225
Jones, Cleve, 182
Jones, David, 25
Jones, Gemma, 125
Jones, Jennifer, 135, 248
Jones, Lorenzo, 57
Jones, Toby, 45
Jordan, Neil, xxi, 68–69, 203

Jorgensen, Christina, 80
Joyce, James, 62
Jubilee, 146
Judas Kiss, The, 290
Judgment at Nuremburg, 55, 95–96
Juke Box Jury, 142
Julia, Raul, 152
Julien, Isaac, 171, 172
Just a Gigolo, 25
Justin and the Knights of Valor, 113
Justine, 194

Kaboom, xxiv, 167
Kael, Pauline, 117–118
Kalin, Tom, xx, 124, 256–257
Kanfer, Stefan, 32
Karras, Alex, 276
Kashfi, Anna, 32
Katie: Portrait of a Centerfold, 144
Kato, David, xxvi
Kay, Billy, 164
Kaye, Danny, 62
Kazan, Elia, 32, 33, 85
Keaton, Buster, 60
Keaton, Diane, 64
Keeler, Christine, 236
Keener, Christine, 44, 45
Keep the Lights On, xxvi
Keith, Brian, 227
Kellgren, Nina, 172
Kelly, Gene, 83
Kelly, Grace, 243
Kelly, Minka, 196
Kelly, Patsy, 13
Kelm, Arthur. *See* Hunter, Tab
Kennedy, Arthur, 87, 292
Kennedy, John F., 283, 285
Kennedy, Robert, 283
Kerr, Deborah, 56, 208, 259–261, 294
Kerr, John, 208, 259–260
Kervin, Brian, 266
Khouri, Callie, 262, 263
Kid Like Jake, A, xxviii
Kidman, Nicole, 156, 272
Kidron, Beeban, 2
Kids Are All Right, The, xxiv
Kill Bill, xxiv
Killing of Sister George, The, 63, **149–151**, 155, 241. *See also* Gay bars; "Hagsploitation"
Kilmer, Val, 280

King, Billy Jean, xxviii
King, Martin Luther, 20
King, Stephen, 67
King and I, The, 182, 261
King George V, 251
King Lear, 161
Kinney, Kathy, 207
Kinsey, Alfred, 19
Kiss, 155, 282
Kiss, The, 155
Kiss of the Spider Woman, **152–153**, 202
Kissing, 50, 58, 90, 91, 123, 133, **154–156**, 174, 215, 225, 262, 290. *See also* AIDS; *Bound*; *Brokeback Mountain*; *Deathtrap*; *Early Frost, An*; *Go Fish*; *Hunger, The*; *Moonlight*; *Morocco*; *Queen Christina*; Smoking; *Some Like It Hot*; *Sunday Bloody Sunday*; *View from the Bridge, A*
Klein, Andy, xix
Komer, Paul, 252
Kramer, Larry, 214
Kray, Ronnie, 245
Kremlin Letter, The, 63
Krim, Arthur, 52
Kristofferson, Kris, 167
Kruschen, Jack, 63
Kubrick, Stanley, 74–75

La La Land, 204
La Tourneaux, Robert, 30
LaBeija, Pepper, 205–206
Labyrinth, 26
Lachman, Ed, 47, 48
Ladd, Alan, 224, 226
Ladder, The, 20
Ladies or Gentlemen, **157–158**. *See also* Cross-dressing; Mannish women; "Sissies"
Lafayette Escadrille, 143
Lahr, John, 216
Lake, Ricki, 286
Laloy, Sophie, 253
Lambert, Lisa, 28, 29
Lamos, Mark, 169
LaMotta, Jake, 184
Lancaster, Burt, 32, 241, 261, 292
Lanchester, Elsa, 159–160, 161
Landau, Martin, 87, 122
Landis, John, 157
Lange, Jessica, 64, 293
Larkin, Philip, 85

Last Days, 272
Last Married Couple in America, The, xviii
Last of England, The, 147
Last of Sheila, The, 194
Last of the Mobile Hot Shots, The, 294
Last Sunset, The, 150
Last Tango in Paris, 33
Last Temptation of Christ, The, 26
Latent homosexuality/lesbianism. *See Bound*; *Brokeback Mountain*; *Crying Game, The*; *Desert Hearts*; *Disobedience*; *Far from Heaven*; *Midnight Cowboy*; *Mulholland Drive*; *Thelma and Louise*
Laughing Policeman, The, 194
Laughton, Charles, 104, **159–161**
Laurel and Hardy, 63
Laurents, Arthur, 50, 232, 234–235
Laurie, Piper, 73
Law, John Phillip, 155, 252
Lawrence, D. H., 116, 117
Lawrence, Gertrude, 292
Lawrence, Martin, 65
Lawrence of Arabia, 183
Laxton, James, 190
Lazarus, 26
Le Besco, Isild, 253
Le Blanc, Matt, 65
Le Gros, James, 271
Leading Ladies, xxiv
Lean, David, 84, 99
Led Zeppelin, 158
Ledger, Heath, xxii, 34, 36, 129, 156, 203, 204
Lee, Ang, 125–126
  Brokeback Mountain, 34–36
  Oscar success, 203–204
Lee, Francis, 125–126
Lee, Harper, 44, 45
Lee, Sondra, 33
Left-Handed Gun, The, 278, 280
Legend of Lylah Clare, The, 150, 151, 158
Leguizamo, John, 2
Leigh, Janet, 209, 243, 272
Leigh, Jennifer Jason, 195
Leigh, Malcolm, 146
Leigh, Mike, 84–85
Leigh, Vivien, 32, 71–72, 229, 260
Lelio, Sebastian, 98, 99
Lemmon, Jack, 60–61, 74, 157, 242–243
Lemon Drop Kid, The, 62

Lenkiewicz, Rebecca, 98
Lennon, John, 132–134, 284
Lennox, Annie, 109
Lenny, 202
Lenya, Lotte, 194
Leopold, Nathan, 232–233, 256–257
Leopold and Loeb, 193, 232–233, 234, 256–257
Les Biches, 155
Lesbians and Gay Men of Color. *See Far from Heaven*; *Go Fish*; *Looking for Langston*; *Moonlight*; *Paris is Burning*; Racism; *Tongues Untied*; *Watermelon Woman, The*
Lesbophobia. *See Basic Instinct*; *Fox, The*; *Killing of Sister George, The*; *Personal Best*; *Silkwood*
Leto, Jared, xxvi, 77, 78
Letter from an Unknown Woman, 84
Levin, Ira, 89, 174
Levin, Meyer, 257
Lewis, Robert, 32
Lianna, xix, xx–xxi, 163, 253
Liberace, 163
Liberace, 5, **162–164**
Lichtenstein, Mitchell, 195
L.I.E., xxii, **164–166**
Life, 103
Life and Death of a Serial Killer, 187
Life and Times of Judge Roy Bean, The, 144, 210
Life Support, 7
Lifeboat, 13
Lilith, 53
Lilja, Juha, 285
Lincoln, 280
Lindley, Audra, 91
Linkletter, Art, 100
Linkletter, Diane, 100, 190, 285–286
Linkletter, Richard, 190
"Lipstick lesbianism," 154
    Bound, 24
    Desert Hearts, 92
    See also *Basic Instinct*; *Hunger, The*; *Personal Best*
Lira, Jack, 179, 182
Literary Adaptations. *See All about Eve*; *Brokeback Mountain*; *Cabaret*; *Children's Hour, The*; *Danish Girl, The*; *Death in Venice*; *Desert Hearts*; *Disobedience*; *Edward II*; *Fox, The*; *Midnight Cowboy*; *Moonlight*; *Myra Breckinridge*; *Prick Up Your Ears*; *Rebecca*; *Reflections in a Golden Eye*; *Servant, The*
Lithgow, John, 202, 218
Litigation. *See Confidential*; Hudson, Rock; Liberace; *Philadelphia*
Little Foxes, The, 9
Little Women, 71
Living End, The, 6, **166–169**
Livingston, Jennie, xxiv, 64, 205–206
Lloyd, Constance, 289
Lochary, David, 100, 101
Locke, Alain, 192
Loeb, Richard, 232–233
Logan, Joshua, 32
Lonely Man, The, 208
Lonesome Cowboys, 282–283
Long Day Closes, The, 83–84
Long Good Friday, The, 195
Long Weekend (O'Despair), The, 167
Longest Day, The, 183
Longtime Companion, xxix, 168, **169–171**, 203
Looking for Langston, **171–173**
Loos, Anita, 72
Loot, 217
Lord Beaverbrook, 13
Lorde, Audre, 20
Lords, Traci, 287
Loren, Sophia, 143, 208–209
Lorre, Peter, 50
Los Angeles Gay and Lesbian Film Festival, 198
Los Angeles Times, 151, 220
Losey, Joseph, 236–238, 275
Lotter, John, 28
Love, Courtney, xxv
Love and Death, xviii
Love Happy, 38
Love Is Strange, 218
Loved One, The, 162
Lover Come Back, 136–137
Loves of Ondine, The, 283
Lovett, Lyle, 69
Lovin' Molly, 210
Lowdown, 141
Lowe, Edmund, 119
L-Shaped Room, The, xv–xvi
Lubitsch, Ernst, 72, 95
Lucas, Craig, 169–170
Luce, Clare Boothe, 72
Luckinbill, Lawrence, 30

Lugosi, Bela, 121, 122, 193
Lumet, Sidney, 99, **173–174**, 179, 202, 210
   adapts works by Tennessee Williams, 293, 294
   Deathtrap, 89–90, 155
   Dog Day Afternoon, 103–104
   That Kind of Woman, 143
   View from a Bridge, A, 154–155
Luna, Diego, 179
Lust in the Dust, 102, 144
Lynch, David, 190–193
Lynch, Kelly, 271
Lynde, Paul, 136, 288

MacDonald, Jeanette, 119
"Macguffins," 241
Mackendrick, Alexander, 241
Mackinney, Kenneth, 216
MacLaine, Shirley, 48, 52, 53, 252
MacLiammóir, Mícheál, 289–290
MacMurray, Fred, 240–241
Madame Wong's, 283
Madchen in Uniform, 252
   groundbreaking kiss, 154
   influence on *Queen Christina*, 220
   as pioneering LGBTQ work, 219
Madonna, 112
Madonna and Child, 83
Madsen, Axel, 119
Magnani, Anna, 292, 293
Magnificent Ambersons, The, 84
Mahlsdorf, Charlotte, von, 64
Mahogany, 210
Mailer, Norman, 280
Making Love, xxi, xxix, 50, 253
   negative impact on Harry Hamlin's career, xviii–xix
   sexual softness, xxii
Mala Noche, 271
Malden, Karl, 293
Mallory, Richard, 185
Malone, Dorothy, 142, 162
Maloney, Frank, 82
Malpica, Jose, 174
Maltese Falcon, The, xxiii, 50, 194
Mamoulian, Rouben, 219, 220
Man for all Seasons, A, 246
Man in the Eiffel Tower, The, 160
Man into Woman, 80
Man Who Fell to Earth, The, 25, 194–195
Man Who Sold the World, The, 25

Manhandled, 62
Mankiewicz, Joseph L., 8, 9, 71, 250, 278, 293
Mann, Thomas, 11, 22
Mannish women, 49, 61–62, 94–95, 220. *See also* Cross-dressing; *Ladies or Gentlemen*
Man's Favorite Sport, 135
Manso, Peter, 32
Manson, Charles, 184, 200
Mapplethorpe, Robert, 172
Mara, Rooney, xxvii, 46, 129
Marchak, Alice, 34
Marcus, Frank, 150
Mariani-Berenger, Josanne, 32
Marine Story, A, xxiv
Marlene, 95–96
Marlowe, Christopher, 108, 109
Marquand, Christian, 32
Marquis of Queensbury, The, 289
Marriage as gay/lesbian cover. *See Brokeback Mountain*; Burr, Raymond; *Disobedience*; *Dog Day Afternoon*; *Far from Heaven*; Hudson, Rock; Hunter, Tab; Laughton, Charles; Liberace; Perkins, Anthony; *Reflections in a Golden Eye*; *Victim*; Wilde, Oscar
Martin, Steve, 6
MaruMaru, 38
Marx Brothers, The, 119
Mary Poppins, 64, 277
*M*A*S*H*, xvii
Maslin, Janet, 208
Mason, James, 290
Massey, Edith, 101, 286, 287
Masterson, Mary Stuart, xx
Mastroianni, Marcello, 153
Matchmaker, The, 208
Mathews, Travis, xxvii
Matrix, The, 81
Mattachine Society, xiv, 18, 20
Maugham, Robin, 236
Maupin, Amistad, 50
Maurice, 275
Mawdsley, Philip, 83
Maxwell, Larry, 127
Mayer, Louis B., 71
Mayne, Judith, 11, 12
Mayor, John, 108

Mayor of Castro Street, The, 179
McAdams, Rachel, 96
McCambridge, Mercedes, 62, 225
McCarthy, Mary, 173
McCarthy, Senator Joseph, xiv, 19, 260, 292
McClements, Catherine, 112
McClodden, Tiona Nekkia, 242
McConaughey, Matthew, xxvi, 7, 77–79, 273
McCormack, Leigh, 83
McCraney, Tarell Alvin, 188, 190
McCrea, Joel, 51
McCullers, Carson, 33, 56–57, 194, 227
McDonald, Robin, 133
McDowell, Malcolm, 279
McEnery, Peter, 273–274
McGiver, John, 176, 177
McGoohan, Patrick, 109
McGrath, Douglas, 45
McGrath, Matt, 27
McGregor, Ewan, 128
McHattie, Stephen, 88
McKay, Claude, 172
McKellen, Sir Ian, xxii
McKinley, Jack, 181
McLaglen, Victor, 160
McLuhan, Marshall, 103
McMullen, T. Wendy, 123
McMurtry, Larry, 36
McNally, Terrence, xxviii
McQuarrie, Christopher, 179
McShane, Ian, 245
Meatloaf, 230
Meester, Leighton, 196
Meet Me in St. Louis, 83
Meet the Browns, 65
Melendez, Migdalia, 123
Mendez, Sam, 203
Merck, Mandy, 92
Mercury, Freddie, 230
Merlo, Frank, 294
Merrily We Go to Hell, 11
Metalious, Grace, 288
Meyers, Russ, 199
Midler, Bette, 5, 99
Midnight Cowboy, 144, **176–178**, 202
Midnight Express, 6
Midsummer Night's Dream, A, 61
Mildred Pierce, 101, 129, 287
Miles, Sarah, 236

Miles, Sylvia, 176, 284
Milk, xxiii, **178–180**, 272
Milk, Harvey, xii, xxiii, xxvi, 67, 178–180, **181–182**, 263, 272
Miller, Ann, 192
Miller, Arthur, 242
Miller, Bennett, 43, 44, 45
Miller, Mark, xv
Mills, Danny, 101
Mills, John, 21
Milstead, Glenn. *See* Divine
Mimetic Desire. *See Highly Strung*; Identity confusion; *Persona*; *Psycho*; *Roommate, The*; *Single White Female*; *Tenant, The*
Mineo, Sal, xv, 87, **182–184**
  biopic made of his life, xxv
  Rebel without a Cause, 224–226
  stabbed to death, 194
Ministry, 167
Minnelli, Liza, 41–43, 87, 95, 202, 284
Minnelli, Vincente, xv, 51, 259–260
Mirimax, 69
Mirren, Helen, 155
Miseducation of Cameron Post, The, xxviii
Misfits, The, 56, 57, 93
Miss Peregrine's House for Peculiar Children, 113
Missouri Breaks, The, 33, 64
Mitchell, John Cameron, 130–131
Mitchell, Julien, 111
Mitchum, Robert, 161, 237
"Mockumentaries." *See Diane Linkletter Story, The*; *Glen or Glenda?*
Modesty Blaise, 23, 237
Moffett, D. W., 106
Molina, Alfred, 156, 195, 216, 218
Monae, Janelle, 189, 190
Monaghan, Josephine, 64
Mondo Trasho, 99–100, 286, 288
Monge, Ray, 271
Monkees, The, 25
Monohan, Grant, 269
Monroe, Marilyn, 9, 54, 56, 57, 74, 85, 132, 242–243
Monster, **184–187**, 196, 203. *See also* Weight changes for roles
Montez, Mario, 174, 282
Moon Is Blue, The, 3

324　Index

Moonlight, xxix, **188–190**, 204
Moore, Bob, xvii
Moore, Julianne, 114–116, 127–128, 128–129, 130, 156
Moore, Kenny, 213
Moore, Tyria, 185
Moreno, Rita, 294
Moreno, Sergio, 133
Morgan, Claire, 46
Morgan, Colin, 291
Morgan, Laura Andrina, 37
Morgan, Marion, 12
Moriarty, Michael, 88
Morley, Christopher, 63, 194
Morley, Robert, 194, 289–290
Morning After, The, 174
Morocco, 49, 61, 93, 94, 154
Morrison, Toni, 172
Morrissey, David, 16
Morrissey, Paul, 283, 284
Mortimer, Chapman, 227
Moscone, George, 181, 264–265
Moss, Kate, 112
Mother fixations, 87, 130, 162, 165–166, 208–209
Motion Picture Association of America, The, 3, 49, 121, 229
Motion Picture Production Code Association, 55, 74
Motion Picture Production Code Office, 250
Mr. Deeds Goes to Town, 215
Mr. Smith Goes to Washington, 235
Mrs. Dalloway, 156
Mrs. Doubtfire, 60, 157
Mulholland Drive, xxii, **190–193**
Mulligan, Robert, 142
Mulroney, Dermot, 112, 169
Multiple Maniacs, 100, 286
Munch, Christopher, 132–134
Mungiu, Cristian, 232
Murder, xxii, 50, 68, **193–196**, 256–257. See also *Brokeback Mountain*; *Cruising*; *Living End, The*; *Milk*; Mineo, Sal; *Prick Up Your Ears*; *Silkwood*; *Suddenly, Last Summer*; *Times of Harvey Milk, The*; *Torch Song Trilogy*
Murder on the Orient Express, 210
Murfin, Jane, 72
Muriel's Wedding, 1
Murphy, Tommy, xxviii

Murray, Don, 3
Murray, Melvin, xv
Music in LGBTQ films. See Bowie, David; *Cabaret*; Davies, Terence; *Hedwig and the Angry Inch*; Liberace; *Rocky Horror Picture Show, The*
Music Lovers, The, xvii
Muska, Susan, xxiv, 29
Musto, Michael, 157, 158
Mutiny on the Bounty, 160
My Beautiful Laundrette, 23, 156, 216
My Best Friend's Wedding, 112
"My Bonnie," 132
My Fair Lady, 72, 245
My Little Chickadee, 62
My Own Private Idaho, xx, **196–198**, 271, 272. See also Van Sant, Gus
My Summer of Love, xxii, 126
Myra Breckinridge, xvii, 63, **198–201**
    disowned by Gore Vidal, 280
    seen as "good/bad" film, 231
Myrt and Marge, 48
Mysterious Skin, 167

Nader, George, xiv–xv, 135
Naked Boys Singing, xxiii
Naked Civil Servant, The, xvii, 58, 59. See also Crisp, Quentin
National Gay Task Force, 66
National Inquirer, 211
National Organization for Women, 17
Nazimova, Alla, 10
Nazism, 19, 64, 96, 155
Neeson, Liam, 214
Nelson, Kenneth, 30
Nelson, Lori, 142
Nelson, Ricky, 55, 286
Neon Bible, The, 84
Nesbitt, Cathleen, 245
Nesbitt, Derren, 274
Nettleton, Lois, 294
New Queer Cinema, xx, 127, 146, 168, 172. See also Araki, Gregg; Haynes, Todd; Jarman, Derek; Kalin, Tom; Van Sant, Gus
New York Film Festival, 172
New York Times, 43–44, 201, 210
Newman, Paul, xvi, 50, 106, 252, 261, 292–294
Next Best Thing, The, 112
Nichols, Mike, 238, 239, 240

Nicholson, Jack, xvii
Nicolella, John, 135
Night of the Hunter, The, 161
Night of the Iguana, The, 294
Night Porter, The, 23
Nilsson, Harry, 177
Ninja, Willi, 205
Nissen, Tom, 28
Nivola, Alessandro, 96
Nixon, Richard, 100, 199
No One Sleeps, 196
No Way to Treat a Lady, 62, 194
Nolte, Nick, 174
Normal Heart, The, 7
Norman, Barry, xviii, 161
Notes on a Scandal, 31
Nouvelle vague, xx
Novak, Kim, 25, 151
Now, Voyager, 84, 240
Nowhere, 167
Nugent, Bruce, 172
Nuns on the Run, 157
Nyswaner, Ron, 215

Oberon, Merle, 51, 62
O'Brien, Conan, xxii
O'Brien, Geoffrey, 115
O'Brien, Margaret, 160
O'Brien, Richard, 230
Observer, 113
O'Connor, Josh, 125
Ode to Billy Joe, 252
Odets, Clifford, 32
Odorama, 101
Of Time and the City, 84
Officer and a Gentleman, An, 277
O'Hara, Maureen, 11, 143, 160
O'Hare, Christopher, 253
O'Hare, Denis, 77
Olafsdottir, Greta, xxiv, 29
Old Dark House, The, 160
Oldman, Gary, 156, 195, 216
Olivier, Laurence, 32, 74–75, 147, 222
On the Beach, 209
On the QT, 101
On the Waterfront, 33
On Trial: Oscar Wilde, 289
One, 20
One, The, xxvi
One Flew Over the Cuckoo's Nest, 202, 203
120 Beats Per Minute, 7

O'Neill, Eugene, 208–209
Ontkean, Michael, xvii
Operation Bikini, 144
Orbison, Roy, 192
Orlando, xxvi, 58
Orpheus Descending, 293
Orton, Joe, 216–218
Oscar Wilde, 289
Oscars, xxix, xxii, 2, 7, 29, 43, 45, 48, 63, 69, 71, 72, 78, 81, 101, 103, 118, 122, 124, 129, 158, 160–161, 170, 177, 178, 180, 182, 183, 184–185, 187, 188, **202–204**, 214, 246, 250, 255, 261, 264, 268, 270, 272, 276–277, 292
O'Shea, Milo, 62
Ossana, Diana, 36
O'Sullivan, Maureen, 160
O'Sullivan, Terry, 83
O'Toole, Peter, 245, 279
Our Sons, 107
Out of Africa, 153
Outrage, xxiv
Outsider, The, 256
Overkill, 195
Owen, Wilfred, 147
Oxenbay, Jay, 51

Pacino, Al, xvii, 66–67, 103–104, 202
Pack, Stephanie, 133
Page, Geraldine, 294
Page, Patti, 1
Page Turner, The, 253
Paglia, Camille, 157, 158
Pale Saints, 167
Palmy Days, 60–61
Pandemonium, 144
Pantoliano, Joe, 24
Paradine Case, The, 160
Pariah, xxiv
Paris Is Burning, xxiv, 64, **205–206**
Paris When It Sizzles, 95
Parish, James Robert, 11
Park, Oliver, 113
Parker, Alan, 6
Parker, Mary Louise, 169, 171
Parsons, Estelle, 155
Parsons, Louella, 136, 143
Parting Glances, xx, 170, **207–208**
Parton, Dolly, 158, 270
Pasolini, Pier Paolo, 195
Pass, The, xxvii
Pawlikowski, Pawel, 126

Pawnbroker, The, 173–174
Payment Deferred, 160
Pearce, Guy, 1
Pearce, Mary Vivian, 99–100, 101
Peck, Gregory, 106–107
Pedophilia, 22, 159, 174, 279
Pedro, xxiii
Peirce, Kimberley, 196
Pendavis, Freddie, 205
Penn, Arthur, 64, 278, 280
Penn, Sean, xxiii, 178–179, 180, 272
Penthouse, 279
Peretz, Susan, 103
Perfect Family, A, xxvi
Period films. *See Caligula*; *Danish Girl, The*; *Death in Venice*; *Edward II*; *Orlando*; *Queen Christina*
Period of Adjustment, 294
Periods of Rain, xxiv
Perkins, Anthony, xv, 141, 158, **208–211**, 252, 272
   attitude to Sophia Loren, 143
   debunks Sal Mineo, 184
   fear of being outed, 183
   reaction to contracting AIDS, 5
   relationship to Tab Hunter, 142
Perkins, Osgood (father), 208
Perkins, Osgood (son), 210
Perrine, Valerie, 202
Perry, Tyler, 65
Perry Mason, 37, 39
Persona, 64, 99, 192
Personal Best, xviii, 155, **211–213**, 253. *See also* Gay films for straight audiences; Triangulation of gay/lesbian relationships
Perverted Justice, 195–196
Pesci, Joe, 170
Pet Shop Boys, The, 147
Peter Potter's Platter Parade, 142
Peter's Friends, 6–7
Peyton Place, 288
Philadelphia, xxi, xxii, xxviii–xxix, 51, 59, **213–215**
   absence of kissing scenes, 137
   characters' lack of physical intimacy, 156
   first major movie to be made about AIDS, 7
   Oscar success, 203
   See also AIDS; Gay employment bigotry; Gay films for straight audiences

Philadelphia Story, The, 72
Phoenix, Joaquin, 272, 273
Phoenix, Rain, 272
Phoenix, River, 196–198, 271
Picerni, Paul, 38
Pickford, Mary, 60
Pierce, Richard, 6
Pierson, John, 124
Pillow Talk, 136, 137
Pink Flamingos, xvii, xxiv, 63, 100–101, 102, 286
Pitfall, 38
Pitt, Brad, xxi, 88, 203, 262
Pitt, Michael, 130
Place in the Sun, A, 38, 54, 228, 251
Plagiarism. *See* Derivative films
Plan 9 from Outer Space, 122
Platt, Mark, 215
Play It as It Lays, xvii, xviii, 210, 252
Playboy, 213, 219
Pleasure of His Company, The, 144
Plimpton, George, 45
Plummer, Amanda, 195
Plunkett, Walter, 72
Poison, xx, 127
Polanski, Roman, 63, 64, 252
Political themes in films. *See Advise & Consent*; *Crying Game, The*; *Edward II*; *Kiss of the Spider Woman*; *Milk*; *Times of Harvey Milk, The*
Pollack, Sydney, 153
Polyester, 101–102, 144–145, 287
Pommer, Eric, 160
Pornography, 69, 145, 201, 279
Pors, Nikolaj, 80
Porter, Cole, 109
Porter, Darwin, 31–32, 120, 248
Portman, Natalie, xxiv
Portrait of Dorian Gray, 209
Potter, Michael, 286
Potter, Sally, 58
Power, Tyrone, 32, 54, 95, 161
Pratt, Dennis Charles. *See* Crisp, Quentin
Prayers for Bobby, 253
Preminger, Otto, 3, 4, 183, 274
Prentice, Keith, 30
Presley, Elvis, 73, 85, 92, 142, 161, 162, 287
Prestige, The, 26
Preston, Carrie, 268
Preston, Robert, 64, 276–277
Pretty Poison, 210
Price, Tammy, 17

Index

Price of Salt, The, 46, 129
Prick Up Your Ears, 23, 156, 195, **216–218**
Prince of Wales, The, 13
Prince Who Was a Thief, The, 73
Princess and the Pirate, The, 62
Principal, Victoria, 210
Private Benjamin, 64
"Private Dirk Bogarde, The," 21
Private Life of Henry VIII, The, 160
Private Lives, 141
Private Romeo, xxvi
Prodigal Sons, xxiii
Production Code, xiii, 24, 220–221
Production Code Association (PCA), xiii, 260, 293
    airbrushes gay theme from *A Streetcar Named Desire*, 292
    The Children's Hour, 51, 52
    denies seal to *Victim*, 275
    and *Queen Christina*, 220–221
    and *Rebecca*, 223
    sexuality in *Rope*, 233–234
    and *Spartacus*, 74
    strictness with male kissing, 154
    and *Suddenly, Last Summer*, 25
Profumo, John, 236
Promised Land, 273
Proposal 6, 180, 264
Proulx, Annie, 34, 36, 156, 203
Provincetown International Film Festival, 167
Pruvot, Marie-Pierre, xxvii
P.S. Your Cat Is Dead, 184
Psycho (directed by Alfred Hitchcock), xv, 62, 64, 114, 158, 208, 209, 210, 211, 245, 272
Psycho (directed by Gus Van Sant), 114, 272
Psycho II, 210
Psycho III, 211
Psycho IV, 211

Q&A, 174
Quaid, Dennis, xxvii, 114, 129
Quaid, Randy, 34
Queen Christina, **219–221**
    cross-dressing by Greta Garbo, 95
    full mouthed kiss to her lady-in-waiting, 154, 219
    "Mannish lesbian" cult, 61
Queen Elizabeth I, 58
Queen Latifah, xxvii, 7

Queer Film Award, 167
Queering mainstream films. *See* Coded gay/lesbian messages; Symbolism
Quentin, John, 147
Querelle, 6
Question of Love, A, 47
Question One, xxv–xxvi
Quiet Passion, A, 84
Quinn, Aidan, 5, 106
Quinn, Patricia, 230
Quintero, Jose, 293–294

Rachel, Rachel, 155
Racism, 114–116, 206
Raft, George, 61
Raging Bull, 78, 184–185
Ralston, Esther, 10–11
Rampling, Charlotte, 23
Rancho Notorious, 95
Randall, Tony, 137
Raphael, Sally Jesse, 59
Rappaport, Mark, 135, 150
Rapper, Irving, 292
Ratings. *See* Certificates
Rattigan, Terence, 84
Ravishing Idiot, The, 210
Raw Deal, 38
Ray, Johnnie, 92
Ray, Nicholas, 62, 142, 182, 194, 224–225, 271
Rea, Stephen, 68
Reagan, Ronald, 92, 208
    denial of extent of AIDs pandemic, xix
    refusal to use the term "AIDS," 137
    and *The Times of Harvey Milk*, 264
Rear Window, 38
Rebecca, xiv, **222–223**
Rebel without a Cause, xxv, 50, 85, 87, 88, 142, 194, **224–226**, 271
Red Carpets and Other Banana Skins, 113
Red Hot & Blue, 109
Red Oaks, 167
Red River, 35, 50, 55
Red without Blue, xxiii
Redford, Robert, 50, 261, 294
Redgrave, Vanessa, xv, 202, 216
Redmayne, Eddie, xxvii–xxviii, 79–81, 204
Redwoods, xxiv
Reed, Oliver, 125
Reed, Rex, xix, 198

Reeve, Christopher, 89–90, 155, 174
Reeves, Jim, 92
Reeves, Keanu, 16, 196–198, 271, 272
Reeves, Saska, 195
Reflections in a Golden Eye, 33, 56–57, 194, **227–229**. *See also* Gay people in the military
Reid, Beryl, 63, 149, 151, 241
Religious elements in LGBTQ films, xxiii, xxviii, 21, 83–85, 96–98, 142, 146, 176, 253, 254–255, 268. *See also Disobedience; Sunday Bloody Sunday*
Remembrance of Things Past, 112
Remick, Lee, 54
René, Norman, 169–170, 203
Rent, 7
Repulsion, 64
Resident Alien, 59
Restless, 273
Reynolds, Alexandra, 81
Reynolds, Debbie, 83, 142
Reynolds, Ray ("Libby"), 38
Rhodes, Trevante, 189
Rhys Meyers, Jonathan, 128
Ricci, Christina, 186
Rice, Anne, xxi
Rich, B. Ruby, xii
   on *Brokeback Mountain*, 36
   on *The Crying Game*, 69
   defends *Basic Instinct*, 17
   on *The Living End*, 168
Rich and Famous, 72
Richards, James, 126
Richardson, Miranda, 69, 112
Richardson, Tony, xv
Richert, William, 197
Ride, 167
Ride the Wild Surf, 144
Riese, Randall, 87
Riggs, Bobby, xxviii
Riggs, Marlon, xix, 171
Right Hand Man, The, 112
Rimbaud, Arthur, 127
Rio, Joanne, 162
Rio Bravo, 55
Riseborough, Andrea, xxviii
Rite of passage films. *See Brokeback Mountain; Carol; Dallas Buyers Club; Danish Girl, The; Go Fish; L.I.E.; Midnight Cowboy; Moonlight; Thelma and Louise; Torch Song Trilogy; Transamerica*
Ritter, Thelma, 9
Riverdale, 167
Road movies. *See Adventures of Priscilla, Queen of the Desert, The; Hedwig and the Angry Inch; Living End, The; My Own Private Idaho; Thelma and Louise; Transamerica*
Road to Morocco, The, 62
Road Warrior, The, 195
Robards, Jason, 214
Robards, Sam, 203
Robbins, Tom, 272
Roberts, Julia, 112
Robertson, Cliff, 280
Robertson, Pamela, 200
Robertson, Ronnie, 142
Robinson, Edward G., 240–241
Robinson, Kathleen, 167
Rock Hudson, 135
Rock Hudson's Home Movies, 135, 150
Rocky, 214
Rocky Horror Picture Show, The, 25, 101, 131, 157, **230–231**
   defies definition, 63
   influences on Tim Curry's performance, 158
   redefines horror genre, xv
Roen, Paul, 198, 200, 277
Rogers, Ginger, 13
Role models. *See* Gay/lesbian icons
Role/Play, xxiv
Roman, Ruth, 38, 99, 247
Roman Candles, 99
Roman Spring of Mrs. Stone, The, 293–294
Romance, 120
Romeo and Juliet, xxiv, 61, 212, 282
Romero, Eddie, 75
Room at the Top, 250
Roommate, The, 196
Rooney, Mickey, 61
Rope, 193, **232–235**, 245, 247–248, 256, 257
   same sex kissing deemed more reprehensible than murder, 154
   smoking motif, 241
   theatrical style of direction, 234
Rose Tattoo, The, 182, 292
Rosenberg, Robert, 18

Rosenberg, Tom, 112
Ross, Diana, 284
Rowlands, Gena, 47, 107
Royal Army Service Corps, 132
Royal Night Out, A, 113
Rudd, Paul, 252
Rule, Jane, 91, 92
Rules of Attraction, xxii
Rupal, 157
Russell, Jane, 50
Russell, Ken, xvii, 125, 146, 210, 238
Russell, Kurt, 238
Russell, Rosalind, 72
Russo, Vito, xviii
   biopic made of his life, xxv
   on dangers of "coming out," 11
   defends *The Boys in the Band*, 31
   denounces *The Morning After*, 174
   on *Dog Day Afternoon*, 173
   film made of his landmark book *The Celluloid Closet*, 48–51
   on *Victor/Victoria*, 277
Rydell, Mark, 63, 116–117

Sackville-West, Vita, 58
Sadomasochism, 23, 66, 67, 146, 183–184, 241
Safe, 127–128, 128–129
Sagan, Leontine, 154
Saint, Eva Marie, 33
Saint Francis of Assisi, 291
Saint-Laurent, Octavia, 205
Sal, xxv
Salomé, 18, 160
Same sex marriage, xxii, xxv–xxvi, xxvii, 18, 144
San Quentin, 38
Sand, George, 62
Sanders, George, 9, 10, 63, 143
Sanitization of gay/lesbian elements in films. See Airbrushing of gay/lesbian elements from films
Sarafian, Richard, xviii
Sarandon, Chris, 103
Sarandon, Susan, 26, 48, 50, 138, 139, 140, 156, 230, 261, 262, 263
Sarelle, Leilani, 15
Sarne, Michael, 63, 198–201, 280
Sarsgaard, Peter, 27
Saunders, Ashton, 189
Save Me, xxiii

Savoy, Teresa Ann, 155
Sayles, John, xix
Scarwid, Diane, 239
Scenes from a Gay Marriage, xxvi
Schell, Maximillian, 96, 228
Schemel, Patty, xxv
Schickel, Richard, 228
Schiller, Greta, 18
Schindler's List, 214
Schlachet, Daniel, 256
Schlesinger, John, 90, 112, 144, 155, 176–178, 202, 253–255, 263–265
Schmiechen, Richard, 202
Schneider, Maria, 33
Schneider, Rob, 65
Schumach, Murray, 74
Schumacher, Joel, 6
Schwarzenegger, Arnold, 267
Scofield, Paul, 246
Scorsese, Martin, 26
Scott, Campbell, 169
Scott, Lizbeth, xiv, 200
Scott, Randolph, 61, 87, 200
Scott, Ridley, 139, 261, 263
Scott, Tony, 139
SCUM (Society for Cutting Up Men), 283
Sea God Nurseries, 39
Sea of Trees, 273
Sea Wife, The, 246
Sebastiane, 146, 155
Seberg, Jean, 53
Secareanu, Alec, 125
Secret Ceremony, 237
Section 28, 110
Segal, George, xviii
Self-loathing, 56, 57–58, 123, 177. *See also* Boys in the Band, The; Detective, The; Far from Heaven; Gay "cures"; Laughton, Charles; Staircase
Selling of a Serial Killer, The, 187, 195
Seltaeb, 132
Selznick, David O., 71, 223, 248
Send Me No Flowers, 137
Separate Tables, 261
Sergeant, The, 155, 252, 255
Serial Mom, 287
Servant, The, 21, **236–238**, 275
Seven Descents of Myrtle, The, 294
Sevigny, Chloe, 27, 28, 29
Sex, 200
Sex Positive, xxiii

Sex reasssignment therapy, xxiii, xxvi–xxvii, 27, 28, 63, 78–79, 80, 81, 82, 130, 198–199, 268
Sexing the Transmen, xxv
Sextette, 200
Sexton, Brandon, III, 27
Sexual Behavior in the Human Female, 19
Sexual Behavior in the Human Male, 19
Shah of Iran, The, 284
Shakespeare, William, 61, 146, 157, 197
Shakespeare in Love, 157
Sharif, Omar, 183
Sharman, Jim, xv
Sharp, Anastasia, 123
Shaver, Helen, 91, 155
Shaw, George Bernard, 13, 22
Shaw, Sandra, 61
Shawn, Wallace, 216
Sheridan, Ann, 61
Sherwood, Bill, 207
She's the One, 157
Shilts, Randy, 6, 179
Shor, Miriam, 130–131
Shotton, Pete, 133
Showgirls, 15, 24
Shrek the Third, 113
Shriek of Araby, The, 60
Shurlock, Geoffrey, 74, 250
Shut My Big Mouth, 61
Sidewalks of New York, 60
Sign of the Cross, The, 160
Signoret, Simone, 250
Silence of the Lambs, The, 195, 203, 211
Silkwood, **238–240**
Silkwood, Karen, 238–240
Simmons, Jean, 208
Simpson, O. J., 287
Sims, Sylvia, 236, 274
Sinatra, Frank, 3, 56
Sincerely Yours, 162
Singer, Bryan, 179
Singer, Isaac Bashevis, 64
Singer Not the Song, The, 21, 55
Single Man, A, xxiii–xxiv
Single White Female, 99, 195, 196, 253
Sirk, Douglas, 48, 114–116, 129, 154
"Sissies," 48–49, 60, 202
Six Bridges to Cross, 182
Skinny, The, xxvi
Sleep, 282, 283, 285
Sleuth, 90
Smart, Jean, 195

Smiley Face, 167
Smith, Bessie, xxvii, 167
Smith, Bud, 213
Smith, C. Aubrey, 219
Smith, Geraldine, 284
Smith, Perry, 43, 44, 45
Smith, Scott, 181
Smoking, **240–242**
Snipes, Wesley, 2
S.O.B., 277
Solanas, Valerie, 283, 284–285
Some Like It Hot, 60–62, 70, 74, **242–243**
Somebody, 32
Somebody Up There Likes Me, 183
Song of Songs, 95
Song to Remember, A, 62
Sons of Tennessee Williams, The, xxiv
Sound of Music, The, 64, 277
Spacey, Kevin, 203
Spanier, Ginette, 93
Spartacus, 74–75, 161
Speed, 16
Spellman, Cardinal, 94
Spiegel, Sam, 250
Spillane, Mickey, 67
Splendor, 167
Spoilers, The, 95
Spottiswoode, Roger, 6
Springsteen, Bruce, 214
Stage Door Canteen, 13
Staggs, Sam, 9
Staircase, 50, **244–246**, 255
Stamp, Terence, 1, 75
"Stand by Your Man," 69
Stanwyck, Barbara, xvi, 13, 50, 194, 240
Stapleton, Maureen, 293
Star Is Born, A, 72
Stardust, Ziggy. *See* Bowie, David
Starr, Michael Seth, 38
Starr, Ringo, 132
Steiger, Rod, 62, 155, 162, 194, 252, 255
Stein, Gertrude, 94
Steinem, Gloria, 262
Stevens, George, 38, 86, 183, 228, 251
Stewart, James, xxi, 35, 95, 192, 193, 232, 234–235
Stockwell, Dean, 257
Stole, Mink, 101, 287
Stone, Emma, xxviii
Stone, Oliver, 179, 272
Stone, Sharon, 15–17, 168, 195
Stonewall Inn, xxxiii, 18

Index

Stonewall Riots, xii, xvi–xvii, xxiv, 18–19, 30, 177, 179
Stonewall Uprising, xxiv
Stoop Norm McLain, 212
Stranger Among Us, A, 99
Strangers on a Train, 46, 194, 235, 241, **247–249**
Streamers, 195
Streep, Meryl, 156, 238
Street Wars, xx
Streetcar Named Desire, A, 1, 32, 228, 229, 250, 292
Streeter, Tim, 271
Streisand, Barbra, 64
Strick, Joseph, 62
Suddenly, Last Summer, 194, **249–251**, 278, 293. See also Clift, Montgomery; Vidal, Gore; Williams, Tennessee
Suicide, xvi, 60, 87, 100, 179, 182, 210, **251–253**, 263, 292. See also *Advise & Consent*; *Children's Hour, The*; Epstein, Brian; *Glen or Glenda?*; *Prick Up Your Ears*; *Tea and Sympathy*; *Thelma and Louise*; *Victim*; *Suddenly, Last Summer*
Suicide, The, 127
Sullivan, Ed, 161
Summer and Smoke, 294
Summerour, Lisa, 214
Sundance Film Festival, The, 122, 124, 134, 171, 265
Sunday Bloody Sunday, 90, 155, 202, **253–255**
Sunset Boulevard, 8, 62, 284
Sunset Song, 84
Superman, 90
Superstar: The Karen Carpenter Story, 127, 128
Susan Lenox, 120
Sutherland, Annette, 37
Suvari, Mena, 203
Swank, Hilary, 27–29, 196
Swanson, Gloria, 62
Swashbuckler, The, 195
Swayze, Patrick, 2
Sweet Bird of Youth, 294
Sweet Kill, 144
Sweet Smell of Success, 75, 241
Swinton, Tilda, 58, 108, 110, 147
Swoon, xx, **256–258**
Sydney, Sylvia, 107
Sylvia, 62

Sylvia Scarlett, 53, 61, 71, 95, 154
Symbolism, 23, 53, 93, 117–118, 128, 131, 165, 199, 222, 224–225, 241, 257

Tab Hunter Show, The, 144
TAG, xxvi
Talbot, Lyle, 121
Tall Story, 209
Tammy, 83
Tarantino, Quentin, xxiv, 24
Tashman, Lilyan, 119
Taste of Honey, A, xv
Tate, Sharon, 200
Taxi Driver, 228
Taylor, Elizabeth, xviii, 38, 54, 56, 106–107, 183, 237, 245, 252, 278, 293
  Divine's wish to be her, 158
  outs James Dean, 87
  Reflections in a Golden Eye, 227–229
  refuses *Myra Breckinridge*, 199
  saves Montgomery Clift's life, 55
  Suddenly, Last Summer, 249–251
Taylor, Lili, 285
Taylor Mead's A*s, 282
Tchaikovsky, PyotrIlyich, xvii, 110
Tea and Sympathy (film), 50, 51, 208, **259–261**
Tea and Sympathy (play), 208
Teena, Brandon, 27, 28, 29, 196
Tell Me That You Love Me, Junie Moon, xvii
Tempest, The, 146
Temple, Shirley, 63, 199
Tenant, The, 63, 252
Tennessee Queer, xxvi
Terence Davies Trilogy, The, 82–83
Tergeson, Lee, 186
Terms of Endearment, 214
Terry, Nigel, 108
Test, xxvii
Thalberg, Irving, 220
That Kind of Woman, 143
That Minstrel Man, 60
Theatre of Blood, xvii, 194
Theatrical adaptations. See *Boys in the Band, The*; *Children's Hour, The*; *Deathtrap*; *Edward II*; *Hedwig and the Angry Inch*; *Killing of Sister George, The*; *Moonlight*; *My Own Private Idaho*; *Rocky Horror Picture Show, The*; *Staircase*; *Tea and Sympathy*; *Torch Song Trilogy*

Thelma and Louise, 139, 168, **261–263**
    empowerment of women, 50
    final kiss of title characters, 156
    upbeat suicide, 253
Theory of Everything, The, 81, 204
Therese and Isabelle, 155
Theron, Charlize, 184–187, 196, 203
Theroux, Justin, 191
These Three, 51, 52, 53
Thewlis, David, 16
They Live by Night, 168
Thiele, Hertha, 154, 252
13 Reasons Why, 167
This Angry Age, 208–209
This Film Is Not Yet Rated, xxiv
This Filthy World, 288
This Land Is Mine, 160
This Property Is Condemned, 294
This Special Friendship, 252
Thomas, Clarence, 262
Thomas, Edwin, 291
Thomas, Richard, 106
Thorson, Scott, 163
Three Bewildered People in the Night, 167
3 Needles, 7
Three of Hearts, xx–xxi
Thunderbolt and Lightfoot, 63
Thurman, Uma, 272
Ticked Off Trannies with Knives, xxiv
Tiernan, Andrew, 108, 110
Tilly, Jennifer, 23, 156
Time, 41, 61, 90, 143
Time to Kill, A, 78
Times of Harvey Milk, The, 48, 202, 203, 206, **263–265**
Tin Star, The, 208
Tisdel, Lana, 28
To Die For, 272
To Kill a Mockingbird, 44
To Wong Foo, Thanks for Everything, Julie Newmar, 2, 59, 65
Toback, James, 72
Tomboy, xxv
Tomlin, Lily, 6, 48
Tone, Franchot, 160
Tongues Untied, xix–xx, 171
Toole, John Kennedy, 84
Tootsie, xxiii, 60, 64, 157, 202
Top Secret, 141
Torch Song Trilogy, xxix, **265–267**
Torn, Rip, 293
Toronto Film Festival, The, 79, 83, 98

*Totally F***ed Up*, 167
Touch of Evil, 95
Towne, Robert, 155, 211–213
Tracy, Spencer, 55
Tragedy as norm for gay/lesbian characters, xvii, 46, 50–51, 53, 182–183, 194, 213, 223, 262. *See also* Murder; Suicide
Transamerica, xxii, 204, **268–270**
Transparent, 82
Transphobia, 206
Transvestism, 157, 158
Trash, 23, 283, 284
Trash cinema. *See* Warhol, Andy; Waters, John
Trevelyan, John, 151
Trials of Oscar Wilde, The, 255, 289
Triangulation of gay/lesbian relationships. *See Brokeback Mountain*; *Fox, The*; Heterosexual relationships of gay/lesbian characters in films; Heterosexual relationships of gay/lesbian people in real life; Marriage as gay/lesbian cover; *Queen Christina*; *Rebel without a Cause*; *Sunday Bloody Sunday*
Trimble, Lonnie, 133
Troche, Rose, 122–124
Trouble in Mind, 102
True Grit, 177, 178
Truite, La, 237
Truth, xxvii
Tuchner, Michael, 245
Tucker, Duncan, 268, 269, 270
Tull, Patrick, 207
Turnberg, Karl, 278
Turner, Guinevere, 123–124
Turner, Kathleen, xxvi, 287
Turpin, Ben, 60
Tushingham, Rita, xv
Twice a Woman, 210–211
Twice Two, 63
Twin Peaks, 191
Two-Faced Woman, The, 72
Two Minutes Later, xxiii
Tyler, Parker, 3
Tynan, Kenneth, 96, 119
Typecasting. *See* Bogarde, Dirk; Curtis, Tony; Everett, Rupert; Garbo, Greta; Hudson, Rock; Mineo, Sal; Perkins, Anthony

Index

Ultra Violet, 284
Ulysses, 62
Un Chant d'Amour, 241
Uncensored, 141
Uncommercial nature of queer films, xxviii–xxix, 170, 237, 267
Unconditional Love, 113
Underground cinema, 139, 202, 251, 282, 283, 288
Unexpected Love, An, 47
United in Anger, xxvi
Unsworth, Geoffrey, 202
Up to His Ears, 62
Updike, John, 115
Uris, Leon, 141, 183
Usual Suspects, The, 179

Vachon, Christine, 124
Valandray, Charlotte, 58
Valentino, Rudolph, xiii
Vallee, Jean Marc, 78
Vallone, Raf, 154–155
Vampirism, xxi, 49–50, 284. *See also Hunger, The*; *Rocky Horror Picture Show, The*
Van Druten, John, 41
Van Sant, Gus, xx, xxiii, 265, **271–273**
  Milk, 178–180
  My Own Private Idaho, 196–198
  Psycho remake, 114
Vanishing Point, The, xviii, 50
Vanity Fair, 94, 95
Variety, 109, 174, 270
Varsi, Diane, 257
Vasa, Christina, 219
Vaughn, Vince, 272
Vega, Daniela, 98
Velvet Goldmine, 128
Verhoeven, Paul, 15–17, 195
Verlaine, Paul, 127
Vernon-Williams, Allison, 287
Verow, Todd, 195
Very Special Favor, A, 135, 136–137
Victim, 21, 97, 252, **273–275**
  career changing role for Dirk Bogarde, 22–23
  first use of word "homosexual" on screen, xv
  See also Advise & Consent; *Blackmail*; Bogarde, Dirk
Victor/Victoria, xxviii–xxix, 64, 202, 241, **276–277**

Vidal, Gore, 32, 198, 200–201, 250, **278–280**
Vidor, Charles, 62
Viertel, Salka, 119, 220
View from the Bridge, A, 154–155
Vikander, Alicia, xxviii, 79–81, 204
Viktor and Viktoria, 276
Village People, 1
Village Voice, 16
Villain, 245
Violence against gay people. *See Before Stonewall*; *Boys Don't Cry*; *Brokeback Mountain*; Crisp, Quentin; *Cruising*; *Edward II*; *Midnight Cowboy*; *Moonlight*; Murder
Visconti, Luchino, 22, 62, 96, 194, 275, 288
Vita and Virginia, xxvii
Vito, xxv
Vogue, 82, 205, 212
"Vogueing," 64, 205–206
Voight, Jon, 176–178, 202
Von Praunheim, Rosa, 64
Von Sternberg, Josef, 93, 94, 95

Wachowski, Lana, 81
Wachowskis, The, 23, 24
Waddington, Steven, 108
Wagner, Robert, 37, 142
Waiting for Godot, 191
Waits, Tom, 266
Waldoff, Claire, 93
Walk a Mile in My Pradas, xxv
Walk on the Wild Side, xvi
Walk the Line, 204
Walken, Christopher, 112
Walker, Gerald, 65
Walker, Robert, 194, 241, 247–249
Wallach, Eli, 293
Walsh, Sydney, 107
Walston, Ray, xvi, 194
Walters, Charles, xv
Waltons, The, 168
War Gods of the Deep, 144
War Requiem, 147
Ward, Isabella, 37
Warhol, Andy, xxiv, 23, 26, 64, 104, 155, 168, **282–285**
Warlock, 35
Warnecke, Gordon, 156
Warner, Jack, 9, 220
Warren, Lesley Ann, 277

Washington, Denzel, 7
Watermelon Woman, The, xx
Waters, John, xvii, xxiv, xxvii, 63, 99, 100, 101–102, 144, 145, 158, 199, **285–289**
Watson, Emily, 291
Watts, Naomi, 190–193
Wayne, John, 35, 36, 54, 55, 95, 177, 178
We Are Animals, xxvii
We Once Were Wide, xxv
We Were Here, 7
Weaver, Sigourney, 253
Weaving, Hugo, 1
Webb, Clifton, 10, 87
Wedding Most Strange, A, xxv
Weekend, xxv
Wehymuller, Hans-Jorg, 280
Weight changes for roles, 7, 78–79, 184–185, 215
Weinstein, Harvey, 69, 70
Weiss, Andrea, 139
Weissmuller, Johnny, 119
Weisz, Rachel, 84, 96, 98
Welch, Elizabeth, 146
Welch, Raquel, 199–201
Weld, Tuesday, 210
Well of Loneliness, The, 18
Welles, Orson, xxiii, 84, 95, 257
West, Mae, xiii–xiv, 95, 199–201
West, Vita-Sackville, xxvii
West Side Story, 144
Whale, James, xv, 11–12
Wharton, Edith, 84
What Ever Happened to Baby Jane?, 8, 150, 225
What the Butler Saw, 217
What You Looking At?, xxv
Wheeler, Julie, 69
Whisper, 141
Whitaker, Forest, 68
White, Dan, 67, 178
  conflict with Harvey Milk, 180
  featured in *The Times of Harvey Milk*, 263–265
  trial for murder of Milk, 180–181
White, Patricia, 119, 149–150
White, Peter, 30
White Chicks, 157
White Christmas, 62
White Heat, 245
White Night Riots, 67, 181–182, 265
White Woman, 160
Who Killed Pasolini?, 195

Widows and Children First, 265
Wieck, Dorothea, 154
Wild Party, The, 11
Wild River, 54
Wild Target, 113
Wilde, 290
Wilde, Oscar, xxviii, 9, 13, 18, 113, 128, 217, **289–291**. *See also Happy Prince, The*; Marriage as gay/lesbian cover
Wilder, Billy, 62, 74, 95, 157, 161, 242–243, 284
Williams, Kenneth, 217
Williams, Lionel, 183–184
Williams, Michelle, 34, 36
Williams, Robin, 65, 272
Williams, Rose, 250, 291–292, 293, 294
Williams, Tennessee, xvi, 55, 182, 237, 245, 252, **291–295**
  infatuation with Marlon Brando, 32
  sanitization of *Cat on a Hot Tin Roof*, 278
  and *Suddenly, Last Summer*, 249–251
Willie and Phil, 231
Williwaw, 278
Wills, Michael, 195
Willson, Henry, 136, 141
Wilroy, Channing, 101
Wilson, Lanford, 106
Windom, William, xvi, 194, 252
Windsor, Edie, xxiv
Winslet, Kate, 129
Wint, Maurice Dean, 130
Winters, Shelley, 38, 53, 54, 194
Wish Me Away, xxiv–xxv
Witherspoon, Reese, 204
Witness for the Prosecution, 95, 161
Wittgenstein, 147
Wizard of Oz, The, 42, 100
Wojtowicz, John, 104
Wolfgang Press, The, 167
Woman, A, 60
Women, The, 72
Women in Love, 125
Women in Revolt, 283
Won Ton Ton, the Dog Who Saved Hollywood, 144
Wonderstruck, 129–130
Wood, D. Edward, Jr., xxv, 62, 121, 158, 241
Wood, Natalie, xviii, 37, 87, 141–142, 182–183, 224, 226, 294

Wood, Robin, 104
Woodlawn, Holly, 59, 104, 283, 284
Woodruff, 77–79
Woodward, Joanne, 155, 292, 293
Woolf, Virginia, xxvii, 58, 156
Wordsworth, William, 85
World According to Garp, The, 202, 277
World for Ransom, 150
Worth, Irene, 89
Wright, Chely, xxiv–xxv
Wright, John, 202
Written on the Wind, 137
Wuornos, Aileen, 184–187, 195, 196, 203
Wuornos, Keith, 185
Wyler, William, 51–53, 118
Wyman, Jane, 115, 292

X, Y and Zee, xviii, 151

Yates, Paula, 112
Year of Living Dangerously, The, 202
Yentl, 64

Yeomans, Jeannine, 264
Yoko One, 134
York, Michael, 41, 42, 241
York, Susannah, xviii, 63, 149, 151, 241, 245
You and I, xxv
You Should Meet My Son, xxiv
Young, Burt, 268
Young, Elizabeth, 219
Young, Karen, 266
Young, Loretta, 21, 63
Young, Neil, 134, 214
Young Bess, 160
Young Don't Cry, The, 183
Young Love, 142
Young Man with a Horn, xiv

Zadora, Pia, 288
Zamora, Pedro, *xxiii*
Zee & Co., 245
Zegers, Kevin, 268, 269–270
Zoolander, 26

About the Author

Aubrey Malone was born in the west of Ireland. He was educated at University College, Dublin, graduating with a BA in English and philosophy. He went on to do an MA in English, majoring on the literary style of Ernest Hemingway. He wrote a biography of Hemingway for Robson Books in 1999. Malone was a teacher for ten years before becoming a freelance journalist with various newspapers and magazines. He has written over one hundred books, including two novels, four books of short stories, and three collections of poetry. He has been writing professionally about the cinema since 1973. His first book, *Hollyweird* (Michael O'Mara, 1994), focused on the eccentricities of film stars. He followed that up with two books on movies made in Ireland, *Michael Collins* and *Ryan's Daughter* (GLI, both 1996). In 1997 he wrote *The Rise and Fall and Rise of Elvis Presley* (Leopold Publishing). Three years later he wrote *I Was a Fugitive from a Hollywood Film Factory*, subsequently reissued as *Hollywood Trivia* (Prion, 2004). In 2011 he wrote *Censoring Hollywood* (McFarland), a book about the history of film censorship. *The Defiant One*, a biography of Tony Curtis (also McFarland) followed in 2013. In the same year he wrote *Maureen O'Hara: A Biography* for the University of Kentucky Press. McFarland also published *Hollywood's Second Sex*, his history of the mistreatment of women in movies from 1900 to 1999 in 2016, and *Writing under the Influence,* a study of the relationship between alcohol and literature for thirteen American authors. In 2018 he published a book about people who unfairly failed to win Oscars, *And the Loser Is* (Vernon Press). That year he also published *The Elvis Diaries* (One Media), a work of creative fiction based on fact. He has published one previous book with ABC-CLIO, *Sacred Profanity*, a study of spirituality in films. He is currently working on a biography of Marlon Brando for Propertius Press.

Printed in the USA
CPSIA information can be obtained
at www.ICGtesting.com
LVHW081026171024
794074LV00007B/47